Marketing Classics
A Selection of Influential Articles

Marketing Classics

A Selection of Influential Articles

FIFTH EDITION

Ben M. Enis
University of Southern California

Keith K. Cox
University of Houston

ALLYN AND BACON, INC.
Boston • London • Sydney • Toronto

Library of Congress Cataloging in Publication Data
Main entry under title:

Marketing classics.

Includes bibliographies and index.
1. Marketing–Addresses, essays, lectures.
I. Enis, Ben M. II. Cox, Keith Kohn.
HF5415.M29748 1985 658.8 84-18417
ISBN 0-205-08341-2

Production Administrator: Jane Schulman
Production Services: Wordsworth Associates
Designer: Patricia T. Torelli
Cover Designer: Virginia J. Mason

Printed in the United States of America.

10 9 8 7 6 5 4 3 2 1 90 89 88 87 86 85

Contributors

Derek F. Abell
William J. Abernathy
Russell L. Ackoff
Wroe Alderson
Richard P. Bagozzi
Russell W. Belk
Neil H. Borden
Louis P. Bucklin
Robert D. Buzzell
Gilbert A. Churchill, Jr.
George S. Day
Peter F. Drucker
James R. Emshoff
Neil M. Ford
Bradley T. Gale
William Gregor
Joseph P. Guiltinan
Mason Haire
Russell I. Haley
Robert H. Hayes
Stanley C. Hollander
John A. Howard
Shelby D. Hunt
George Katona
Robert J. Keith
Philip Kotler
Robert J. Lavidge
Sidney J. Levy
Theodore Levitt
David B. Montgomery
Torger Reve
Al Ries
Everett M. Rogers
William Rogers
Jagdish N. Sheth
G. Lynn Shostack
John E. Smallwood
Wendell R. Smith
Gary Steiner
Louis W. Stern
Ralph G. M. Sultan
Jack Trout
Orville C. Walker, Jr.
Scott Ward
Frederick E. Webster, Jr.
Charles B. Weinberg
William Wells
Yoram Wind

Contents

Preface

When *Marketing Classics* was conceived, we commented in the Preface:

> Marketing is that phase of human activity that produces economic want-satisfaction by matching consumers' needs and the resources of business firms. From the firm's point of view, consumer-satisfaction is the result of its marketing strategy. Strategy is based on marketing philosophy and is derived from the analysis of consumers and their functional interrelationships with such market forces as economic conditions, competitors' actions, institutional change, and other environmental factors. This volume is a compilation of articles that provide broad insight into the field of marketing.
>
> The authors consider these works to be among the classics of marketing literature. These articles are generally recognized by marketing scholars as being of enduring significance to marketing thought. They are widely quoted, have led to new directions in marketing research, and reflect the views of influential scholars. Consequently, these are works with which serious marketing students should be familiar and to which they should have ready access. We believe the book will be a useful supplement to advanced undergraduate courses in marketing management and marketing strategy and to graduate courses in marketing fundamentals and marketing theory. The practitioner might also enjoy having these familiar works in his library.
>
> The articles in this volume were chosen on the basis of extensive research in marketing literature, and the authors were fortunate to obtain the suggestions of a number of colleagues. Nevertheless, it would be presumptuous to imply that we have compiled *the* classic works of marketing. Marketing is too rich, too complex, too diverse a discipline to be subsumed in one volume. Our selections reflect our own perceptions of and biases about marketing. . . .

This fifth edition of *Marketing Classics* reflects our continuing attempt to match this concept to the needs of marketing students. Responses to questionnaires sent to some adopters of the fourth edition revealed that this anthology is used in a variety of courses, ranging from introductory marketing to doctoral-level seminars, in the United States, Canada, Europe, South America, Africa, and the Pacific Rim.

Marketing Classics, fifth edition, includes several new articles that have stood the test of time and deletes a few genuine classics that our research indicates for various reasons are no longer frequently assigned to students. We also continue to offer several types of comprehension aids, described in the following section, "To the Reader."

Again, we are grateful to the authors and publishers who granted permission to reprint their work. This literally is their book. We appreciate comments and criticism on our selections. Many readers have returned questionnaires or sent letters to us over the years. For the fifth edition, we particularly thank Professor Gene R. Laczniak, Marquette University, who sent us a detailed, thoughtful critique of the fourth edition; some of our decisions were directly influenced by his suggestions. The people at Allyn and Bacon, Jack Peters and Wendy Ritger, and everyone we've dealt with, have been cooperative and helpful through the years.

Our thanks also to Grace Sheldrick, Wordsworth Associates, for her editorial/production assistance on the third, fourth, and fifth editions of *Marketing Classics.*

In spite of all this assistance, errors of omission and commission are possible, and differences of opinion about the nature of marketing classics are inevitable. We are, of course, responsible and would appreciate feedback.

K. K. C.
B. M. E.

To The Reader

The purpose of a readings book is to present the work of various authorities in the field in convenient form. *Marketing Classics* represents, in our judgment, the best that the marketing discipline has to offer. To aid you in efficiently comprehending these articles, we have added the following material:

1. A suggested procedure for systematically evaluating an article
2. A key relating the articles to standard textbooks in marketing
3. Short introductions to each part of the book
4. Brief biographical sketches of each author
5. An index

Please make whatever use of the comprehensive aids that you deem appropriate.

Critical Evaluation of an Article: A Suggested Procedure

1. *Who is the author?* (What are his qualifications for writing on this topic?)
   Scholarly achievements
   Business or administrative experience
   Other published work
2. *What is the author's message?*
   Major theme (in one sentence, if possible)
   Purpose of the message
   Author's viewpoint
3. *What evidence is offered to support this theme?*
   Three or four key points supported by references, facts, quotes, etc.
4. *How well is the argument presented?*
   Logical consistency
   Limitations and/or assumptions
   Completeness
5. *How does this article relate to other work in this area of marketing?*
   Other authorities (articles, books, etc.)
   Personal experience
6. *What is the significance of this article for marketing management?*
   Managerial usefulness of ideas presented
   Future direction of work in this area

Principles and Marketing Textbooks Correlated with *Marketing Classics,* 5th ed.

	Text Chapter Number(s)						
Marketing Classics Article Number	Kinnear & Bernhardt[1]	Kotler, *Principles*[2]	Murphy & Enis[3]	Schoell & Ivy[4]	Buell[5]	Kotler, *Management*[6]	Lovelock & Weinberg[7]
1	1, 2	1, 2	1, 3	1, 3	1, 2, 8	1, 2	1, 2
2	1, 3	1, 2, 4	1, 2	1, 2	1, 2, 3	1, 2	1, 2
3	1, 3, 7, 21	1, 4, 21	1, 5, 23	1, 22	1, 3	1, 3	1
4	1, 2	1, 2	1, 2	1, 3	1, 2	1, 2	1, 3
5	1, 20	1, 2, 22	1, 3, 11	1, 3	1, 2	1, 2	1, 3
6	1, 2, 20	1, 2	1, 2, 3	1, 2, 3	1, 2, 8	1, 2	1, 2, 3
7	1, 2, 6	1, 2, 6	1, 2, 3, 24	1, 4	1, 5	1, 2	1, 3
8	1, 22	1, 23	1, 24	1	1, 2	1, 2	1, 3
9	5, 6	6, 7	4, 6, 7, 8	4, 7	3, 6	4, 6	4, 6
10	5, 6	3, 6	4, 7	4, 7	5, 6	4, 6	4, 6
11	5, 6	3, 7	4, 8	6	5, 6	5, 6	4, 6
12	5, 6	6, 7	4, 7, 8, 9	6	5, 6	4, 6	4, 6
13	5, 6	6, 7	4, 7, 9	6	5, 6	4, 6	4, 6
14	5, 9	6, 11	4, 7, 8, 10	6, 11	5, 7, 17	4, 10	4, 11
15	5, 6	3, 6	4, 6	4, 7	5, 6	4, 6	4, 6
16	5, 6	3, 6	4, 6, 9	4, 7	5, 6	4, 6	4, 6
17	1, 2, 18	1, 2, 23	1, 3, 21	1, 3	1, 2, 8	2, 9	2, 8, 10
18	1, 2, 18	1, 2, 23	1, 3, 21	1, 2, 3	1, 2, 8	2, 9	2, 8, 10
19	4, 6	2, 8	3, 9	8, 9	2, 8, 9	7, 9	7, 8, 10

20	4, 6	3, 8	3, 4	7	6, 7, 8, 9	6, 7, 9	6, 7, 8
21	6, 22	20	3, 19	3, 7	10, 12	24	8, 9
22	4	8, 9	9	8, 9	3, 4	8	5
23	4	8, 9	9	8, 9	4, 5	8	5
24	9, 13	10, 16	10, 12, 18	10, 17	17, 21	12, 19	8, 14
25	2, 22	2, 19, 20	3, 21, 22	3	8, 10, 12	9, 24	8, 10
26	2, 22	2, 19, 20	3, 21, 22	3	8, 10, 12	9, 24	8, 10
27	2, 8–17	2, 10–18	2, 10–19	3, 10–21	2, 16–21	2, 10–22	1, 11–15
28	8, 9	11	10, 11, 12	11	17	10, 11	11
29	19	22	10, 11	11	17	10, 15	3, 11
30	11, 21	15	6, 17, 23	14	19	17, 18	12
31	10–12	15	10, 17	14	19	17, 18	12
32	10–12	14, 15	15, 16, 17	13, 14, 15, 16	19	17, 18	12
33	16, 17	12, 13	13, 14	20, 21	18	16	13
34	13, 14	16, 17	18, 20	17, 18	21	19, 20	14
35	6, 14	3, 17	4, 18, 20	7, 17	6, 21	8, 20	14
36	15	18	19	19	21	22	14

[1] Kinnear, Thomas C. and Kenneth L. Bernhardt, *Principles of Marketing* (Scott, Foresman, 1983).
[2] Kotler, Philip, *Principles of Marketing,* 2nd ed. (Prentice-Hall, 1983).
[3] Murphy, Patrick E. and Ben M. Enis, *Marketing: Principles and Practice* (Scott, Foresman, 1985).
[4] Schoell, William F. and Thomas T. Ivy, *Marketing,* 2nd ed. (Allyn & Bacon, 1985).
[5] Buell, Victor P., *Marketing Management: A Strategic Planning Approach* (McGraw-Hill, 1984).
[6] Kotler, Philip *Marketing Management: Analysis, Planning and Control,* 5th ed. (Prentice-Hall, 1984).
[7] Lovelock, Christopher C. and Charles B. Weinberg, *Marketing for Public and Nonprofit Managers* (John Wiley & Sons, 1984).

Marketing Classics
A Selection of Influential Articles

I

Marketing Philosophy

Any discipline or area of human inquiry is based on a philosophy, a set of principles that provide the rationale for the existence of the discipline. The articles in Part I present a cross-section of the philosophy of marketing.

Theodore Levitt's article sets the stage. Perhaps the discipline's most quoted and reprinted paper vividly demonstrates the need for a broad interpretation of the marketing function; it is the discipline's single best definitive statement. Levitt's thoughts on the continuing relevance of the paper are also included. Wroe Alderson, in his trenchent style, provides an overview of marketing. He envisions the discipline based on the economics of imperfect competition, composed of the problem-solving activities of consumers and firms, and illuminated by concepts from the social sciences. Peter Drucker illustrates Levitt's viewpoint and Alderson's framework as they energize economic development. Robert Keith's paper complements Drucker's; it emphasizes marketing's micro or managerial role in the operation of a business firm.

The major marketing philosopher of the 1970s was unquestionably Philip Kotler. Two of his papers are essential to articulating marketing's rise to managerial and social prominence during this decade. Kotler and Sidney Levy began the decade with the provocative statement that marketing activities were not confined to business firms but had broader applicability to all organizations. Marketing management, they therefore maintain, is a pervasive social activity. Kotler subsequently delineated this thinking more precisely. In "The Generic Concept of Marketing," he outlined the nature of the tasks and responsibilities of marketing managers.

The thinking of Kotler and Levy, illustrated in the above papers as well as in several others written singly and together, had a major impact on the marketing discipline. Their work was deepened by the rigorous work of their student Richard Bagozzi, who carefully set forth the condition for exchange. In addition, Shelby Hunt focused the tools of the philosophy of science on the discipline, devising the three-dichotomies taxonomy of the domain of marketing.

1 Theodore Levitt

Marketing Myopia

Every major industry was once a growth industry. But some that are now riding a wave of growth enthusiasm are very much in the shadow of decline. Others which are thought of as seasoned growth industries have actually stopped growing. In every case the reason growth is threatened, slowed, or stopped is *not* because the market is saturated. It is because there has been a failure of management.

FATEFUL PURPOSES

The failure is at the top. The executives responsible for it, in the last analysis, are those who deal with broad aims and policies. Thus:

> The railroads did not stop growing because the need for passenger and freight transportation declined. That grew. The railroads are in trouble today not because the need was filled by others (cars, trucks, airplanes, even telephones), but because it was *not* filled by the railroads themselves. They let others take customers away from them because they assumed themselves to be in the railroad business rather than in the transportation business. The reason they defined their industry wrong was because they were railroad-oriented instead of transportation-oriented; they were product-oriented instead of customer-oriented.
>
> Hollywood barely escaped being totally ravished by television. Actually, all the established film companies went through drastic reorganizations. Some simply disappeared. All of them got into trouble not because of TV's inroads but because of their own myopia. As with the railroads, Hollywood defined its business incorrectly. It thought it was in the movie business when it was actually in the entertainment business. "Movies" implied a specific, limited product. This produced a fatuous contentment which from the beginning led producers to view TV as

Reprinted by permission of the Harvard Business Review. "Marketing Myopia" by Theodore Levitt (July–August 1960). This article won the 1960 McKinsey Award as best article of the year. The retrospective commentary was published in the *Harvard Business Review*, Vol. 53 (September–October, 1975),

Theodore Levitt, a professor in the Harvard Business School, is the author of many widely read publications, including Innovation in Marketing *and numerous articles. He received his B.A. from Antioch College and the Ph.D. in economics from Ohio State University. His best known book is* Marketing for Business Growth.

> a threat. Hollywood scorned and rejected TV when it should have welcomed it as an opportunity – an opportunity to expand the entertainment business.
>
> Today TV is a bigger business than the old narrowly defined movie business ever was. Had Hollywood been customer-oriented (providing entertainment), rather than product-oriented (making movies), would it have gone through the fiscal purgatory that it did? I doubt it. What ultimately saved Hollywood and accounted for its recent resurgence was the wave of new young writers, producers, and directors whose previous success in television had decimated the old movie companies and toppled the big movie moguls.

There are other less obvious examples of industries that have been and are now endangering their futures by improperly defining their purposes. I shall discuss some in detail later and analyze the kind of policies that lead to trouble. Right now it may help to show what a thoroughly customer-oriented management *can* do to keep a growth industry growing, even after the obvious opportunities have been exhausted; and here there are two examples that have been around for a long time. They are nylon and glass – specifically, E.I. duPont de Nemours & Company and Corning Glass Works:

> Both companies have great technical competence. Their product orientation is unquestioned. But this alone does not explain their success. After all, who was more pridefully product-oriented and product-conscious than the erstwhile New England Textile companies that have been so thoroughly massacred? The duPonts and the Cornings have succeeded not primarily because of their product or research orientation but because they have been thoroughly customer-oriented also. It is constant watchfulness for opportunities to apply their technical know-how to the creation of customer-satisfying uses which accounts for their prodigious output of successful new products. Without a very sophisticated eye on the customer, most of their new products might have been wrong, their sales methods useless.

Aluminum has also continued to be a growth industry, thanks to the efforts of two wartime-created companies which deliberately set about creating new customer-satisfying uses. Without Kaiser Aluminum & Chemical Corporation and Reynolds Metals Company, the total demand for aluminum today would be vastly less than it is.

Error of Analysis

Some may argue that it is foolish to set the railroads off against aluminum or the movies off against glass. Are not aluminum and glass naturally so versatile that the industries are bound to have more growth opportunities than the railroads and movies? This view commits precisely the error I have been talking about. It defines an industry, or a product, or a cluster of know-how so narrowly as to guarantee its premature senescence. When we mention "railroads," we should make sure we mean "transportation." As transporters, the railroads still have a good chance for very considerable growth. They are not limited to the railroad business as such (though in my opinion rail transportation is potentially a much stronger transportation medium than is generally believed).

What the railroads lack is not opportunity, but some of the same managerial imaginativeness and audacity that made them great. Even an amateur like Jacques Barzun can see what is lacking when he says:

> I grieve to see the most advanced physical and social organization of the last century go down in shabby disgrace for lack of the same comprehensive imagination that built it up. What is lacking is the will of the companies to survive and to satisfy the public by inventiveness and skill.[1]

SHADOW OF OBSOLESCENCE

It is impossible to mention a single major industry that did not at one time qualify for the magic appellation of "growth industry." In each case its assumed strength lay in the apparently unchallenged superiority of its product. There appeared to be no effective substitute for it. It was itself a runaway substitute for the product it so triumphantly replaced. Yet one after another of these celebrated industries has come under a shadow. Let us look briefly at a few more of them, this time taking examples that have so far received a little less attention:

Dry cleaning. This was once a growth industry with lavish prospects. In an age of wool garments, imagine being finally able to get them safely and easily clean. The boom was on.

Yet here we are 30 years after the boom started and the industry is in trouble. Where has the competition come from? From a better way of cleaning? No. It has come from synthetic fibers and chemical additives that have cut the need for dry cleaning. But this is only the beginning. Lurking in the wings and ready to make chemical dry cleaning totally obsolescent is that powerful magician, ultrasonics.

Electric utilities. This is another one of those supposedly "no-substitute" products that has been enthroned on a pedestal of invincible growth. When the incandescent lamp came along, kerosene lights were finished. Later the water wheel and the steam engine were cut to ribbons by the flexibility, reliability, simplicity, and just plain easy availability of electric motors. The prosperity of electric utilities continues to wax extravagant as the home is converted into a museum of electric gadgetry. How can anybody miss by investing in utilities, with no competition, nothing but growth ahead?

But a second look is not quite so comforting. A score of nonutility companies are well advanced toward developing a powerful chemical fuel cell which could sit in some hidden closet of every home silently ticking off electric power. The electric lines that vulgarize so many neighborhoods will be eliminated. So will the endless demolition of streets and service interruptions during storms. Also on the horizon is solar energy, again pioneered by nonutility companies.

Who says that the utilities have no competition? They may be natural monopolies now, but tomorrow they may be natural deaths. To avoid this prospect, they too will have to develop fuel cells, solar energy, and other power sources. To survive, they themselves will have to plot the obsolescence of what now produces their livelihood.

Grocery stores. Many people find it hard to realize that there ever was a thriving establishment known as the "corner grocery store." The supermarket has taken over with a powerful effectiveness. Yet the big food chains of the 1930's narrowly escaped being completely wiped out by the aggressive expansion of independent supermarkets. The first genuine supermarket was opened in 1930, in Jamaica, Long Island. By 1933 supermarkets were thriving in California, Ohio, Pennsylvania, and elsewhere. Yet the established chains pompously ignored them. When they chose to notice them, it was with such derisive descriptions as "cheapy," "horse-and-buggy," "cracker-barrel store-keeping," and "unethical opportunities."

The executive of one big chain announced at the time that he found it "hard to believe that people will drive for miles to shop for foods and sacrifice the personal service chains have perfected and to which Mrs. Consumer is accustomed."[2] As late as 1936, the National Wholesale Grocers convention and the New Jersey Retail Grocers Association said there was nothing to fear. They said that the supers' narrow appeal to the price buyer limited the size of their market. They had to draw from miles around. When imitators came, there would be wholesale liquidations as volume fell. The current high sales of the supers was said to be partly due to their novelty. Basically people wanted convenient neighborhood grocers. If the neighborhood stores "cooperate with their suppliers, pay attention to their costs, and improve their services," they would be able to weather the competition until it blew over.[3]

It never blew over. The chains discovered that survival required going into the supermarket business. This meant the wholesale destruction of their huge investments in corner store sites and in established distribution and merchandising methods. The companies with "the courage of their convictions" resolutely stuck to the corner store philosophy. They kept their pride but lost their shirts.

Self-Deceiving Cycle

But memories are short. For example, it is hard for people who today confidently hail the twin messiahs of electronics and chemicals to see how things could possibly go wrong with these galloping industries. They probably also cannot see how a reasonably sensible businessman could have been as myopic as the famous Boston millionaire who 50 years ago unintentionally sentenced his heirs to poverty by stipulating that his entire estate be forever invested exclusively in electric streetcar securities. His posthumous declaration, "There will always be a big demand for efficient urban transportation," is no consolation to his heirs who sustain life by pumping gasoline at automobile filling stations.

Yet, in a casual survey I recently took among a group of intelligent business executives, nearly half agreed that it would be hard to hurt their heirs by tying their estates forever to the electronics industry. When I then confronted them with the Boston street car example, they chorused unanimously, "That's different!" But is it? Is not the basic situation identical?

In truth, *there is no such thing* as a growth industry, I believe. There are only companies organized and operated to create and capitalize on growth opportunities. Industries that assume themselves to be riding some automatic growth escalator invariably descend into stagnation. The history of every dead and dying "growth" industry shows a self-deceiving cycle of bountiful expansion and undetected decay. There are four conditions which usually guarantee this cycle:

1. The belief that growth is assured by an expanding and more affluent population.
2. The belief that there is no competitive substitution for the industry's major product.
3. Too much faith in mass production and in the advantages of rapidly declining unit costs as output rises.
4. Preoccupation with a product that lends itself to carefully controlled scientific experimentation, improvement, and manufacturing cost reduction.

I should like now to begin examining each of these conditions in some detail. To build my case as boldly as possible, I shall illustrate the points with reference to three industries—petroleum, automobiles, and electronics—particularly petroleum, because it spans more years and more vicissitudes. Not only do these three have excellent reputations with the general public and also enjoy the confidence of sophisticated investors, but their managements have become known for progressive thinking in areas like financial control, product research, and management training. If obsolescence can cripple even these industries, it can happen anywhere.

POPULATION MYTH

The belief that profits are assured by an expanding and more affluent population is dear to the heart of every industry. It takes the edge off the apprehensions everybody understandably feels about the future. If consumers are multiplying and also buying more of your product or service, you can face the future with considerably more comfort than if the market is shrinking. An expanding market keeps the manufacturer from having to think very hard or imaginatively. If thinking is an intellectual response to a problem, then the absence of a problem leads to the absence of thinking. If your product has an automatically expanding market, then you will not give much thought to how to expand it.

One of the most interesting examples of this is provided by the petroleum industry. Probably our oldest growth industry, it has an enviable record. While there are some current apprehensions about its growth rate, the industry itself tends to be optimistic. But I believe it can be demonstrated that it is undergoing a fundamental yet typical change. It is not only ceasing to be a growth industry, but may actually be a declining one, relative to other business. Although there is widespread awareness of it, I believe that within 25 years the oil industry may find itself in much the same position of retrospective glory that the railroads are now in. Despite its pioneering work in developing and applying the present-value method of investment evaluation, in employee relations, and in working with backward countries, the petroleum business is a distressing example of how complacency and wrongheadedness can stubbornly convert opportunity into near disaster.

One of the characteristics of this and other industries that have believed very strongly in the beneficial consequences of an expanding population, while at the same time being industries with a generic product for which there has appeared to be no competitive substitute, is that the individual companies have sought to outdo their competitors by improving on what they are already doing. This makes sense, of course, if one assumes that sales are tied to the country's population strings, because the customer can compare products only on a feature-by-feature basis. I believe it is significant, for example, that not since John D. Rockefeller sent free kerosene lamps to China has the oil industry done anything really outstanding to create a demand for its product. Not even in product improvement has it showered itself with eminence. The greatest single improvement, namely, the development of tetraethyl lead, came from outside the industry, specifically from General Motors and duPont. The big contributions made by the industry itself are confined to the technology of oil exploration, production, and refining.

Asking for Trouble

In other words, the industry's efforts have focused on improving the *efficiency* of getting and making its product, not really on improving the generic product or its marketing. Moreover, its chief product has continuously been defined in the narrowest possible terms, namely, gasoline, not energy, fuel, or transportation. This attitude has helped assure that:

> Major improvements in gasoline quality tend not to originate in the oil industry. Also, the development of superior alternative fuels comes from outside the oil industry, as will be shown later.
>
> Major innovations in automobile fuel marketing are originated by small new oil companies that are not primarily preoccupied with production or refining. These are the companies that have been responsible for the rapidly expanding multipump gasoline stations, with their successful emphasis on large and clean layouts, rapid and efficient driveway service, and quality gasoline at low prices.

Thus, the oil industry is asking for trouble from outsiders. Sooner or later, in this land of hungry inventors and entrepreneurs, a threat is sure to come. The possibilities of this will become more apparent when we turn to the next dangerous belief of many managements. For the sake of continuity, because this second belief is tied closely to the first, I shall continue with the same example.

Idea of Indispensability

The petroleum industry is pretty much persuaded that there is no competitive substitute for its major product, gasoline – or if there is, that it will continue to be a derivative of crude oil, such as diesel fuel or kerosene jet fuel.

There is a lot of automatic wishful thinking in this assumption. The trouble is that most refining companies own huge amounts of crude oil reserves. These have value only if there is a market for products into which oil can be converted – hence the tenacious belief in the continuing competitive superiority of automobile fuels made from crude oil.

This idea persists despite all historic evidence against it. The evidence not only shows that oil has never been a superior product for any purpose for very long, but it also shows that the oil industry has never really been a growth industry. It has been a succession of different businesses that have gone through the usual historic cycles of growth, maturity, and decay. Its over-all survival is owed to a series of miraculous escapes from total obsolescence, of last minute and unexpected reprieves from total disaster reminiscent of the Perils of Pauline.

Perils of Petroleum

I shall sketch in only the main episodes:

> First, crude oil was largely a patent medicine. But even before that fad ran out, demand was greatly expanded by the use of oil in kerosene lamps. The prospect of lighting the world's lamps gave rise to an extravagant promise of growth. The prospects were similar to those the industry now holds for gasoline in other parts of the world. It can hardly wait for the underdeveloped nations to get a car in every garage.
>
> In the days of the kerosene lamp, the oil companies competed with each other and against gaslight by trying to improve the illuminating characteristics of kerosene. Then suddenly the impossible happened. Edison invented a light which was totally nondependent on crude oil. Had it not been for the growing use of kerosene in space heaters, the incandescent lamp would have completely finished oil as a growth industry at that time. Oil would have been good for little else than axle grease.
>
> Then disaster and reprieve struck again. Two great innovations occurred, neither originating in the oil industry. The successful development of coal-burning domestic central-heating systems made the space heater obsolescent. While the industry reeled along came its most magnificent boost yet – the internal combustion engine, also invented by outsiders. Then when the prodigious expansion for gasoline finally began to level off in the 1920's, along came the miraculous escape of a central oil heater. Once again, the escape was provided by an outsider's invention and development. And when that market weakened, wartime demand for aviation fuel came to the rescue. After the war the expansion of civilian aviation, the deiselization of railroads, and the explosive demand for cars and trucks kept the industry's growth in high gear.

Meanwhile centralized oil heating – whose boom potential had only recently been proclaimed – ran into severe competition from natural gas. While the oil companies themselves owned the gas that now competed with their oil, the industry did not originate the natural gas revolution, nor has it to this day greatly profited from its gas ownership. The gas revolution was made by newly formed transmission companies that marketed the product with an aggressive ardor. They started a magnificent new industry, first against the advice and then against the resistance of the oil companies.

By all the logic of the situation, the oil companies themselves should have made the gas revolution. They not only owned the gas; they also were the only people experienced in handling, scrubbing, and using it, the only people experienced in pipeline technology and transmission, and they understood heating problems. But, partly because they knew that natural gas would compete with their own sale of heating oil, the oil companies pooh-poohed the potentials of gas.

The revolution was finally started by oil pipeline executives who, unable to persuade their own companies to go into gas, quit and organized the spectacularly successful gas transmission companies. Even after their success became painfully evident to the oil companies, the latter did not go into gas transmission. The multibillion dollar business which should have been theirs went to others. As in the past, the industry was blinded by its narrow preoccupation with a specific product and the value of its reserves. It paid little or no attention to its customers' basic needs and preferences.

The postwar years have not witnessed any change. Immediately after World War II the oil industry was greatly encouraged about its future by the rapid expansion of demand for its traditional line of products. In 1950 most companies projected annual rates of domestic expansion around 6% through at least 1975. Though the ratio of crude oil reserves to demand in the Free World was about 20 to 1, with 10 to 1 being usually considered a reasonable working ratio in the United States, booming demand sent oil men searching for more without sufficient regard to what the future really promised. In 1952 they "hit" in the Middle East; the ratio skyrocketed to 42 to 1. If gross additions to reserves continue at the average rate of the past five years (37 billion barrels annually), then by 1970 the reserve ratio will be up to 45 to 1. This abundance of oil has weakened crude and product prices all over the world.

Uncertain Future

Management cannot find much consolation today in the rapidly expanding petrochemical industry, another oil-using idea that did not originate in the leading firms. The total United States production of petrochemicals is equivalent to about 2% (by volume) of the demand for all petroleum products. Although the petrochemical industry is now expected to grow by about 10% per year, this will not offset other drains on the growth of crude oil consumption. Furthermore, while petrochemical products are many and growing, it is well to remember that there are nonpetroleum sources of the basic raw material, such as coal. Besides, a lot of plastics can be produced with relatively little oil. A 50,000-barrel-per-day oil refinery is not considered the absolute minimum size for efficiency. But a 50,000-barrel-per-day chemical plant is a giant operation.

Oil has never been a continuously strong growth industry. It has grown by fits and starts, always miraculously saved by innovations and developments not of its own making. The reason it has not grown in a smooth progression is that each time it thought it had a superior product safe from the possibility of competitive substitutes, the product turned out to be inferior and notoriously subject to obsolescence. Until now, gasoline (for motor fuel, anyhow) has escaped this fate. But, as we shall see later, it too may be on its last legs.

The point of all this is that there is no guarantee against product obsolescence. If a company's own research does not make it obsolete, another's will. Unless an industry is especially lucky, as oil has been until now, it can easily go down in a sea of red figures – just as the railroads have, as the buggy whip manufacturers have, as the corner grocery chains have, as most of the big movie companies have, and indeed as many other industries have.

The best way for a firm to be lucky is to make its own luck. That requires knowing what makes a business successful. One of the greatest enemies of this knowledge is mass production.

PRODUCTION PRESSURES

Mass-production industries are impelled by a great drive to produce all they can. The prospect of steeply declining unit costs as output rises is more than most companies can usually resist. The profit possibilities look spectacular. All effort focuses on production. The result is that marketing gets neglected.

John Kenneth Galbraith contends that just the opposite occurs.[4] Output is so prodigious that all effort concentrates on trying to get rid of it. He says this accounts for singing commercials, desecration of the countryside with advertising signs, and other wasteful and vulgar practices. Galbraith has a finger on something real, but he misses the strategic point. Mass production does indeed generate great pressure to "move" the product. But what usually gets emphasized is selling, not marketing. Marketing, being a more sophisticated and complex process, gets ignored.

The difference between marketing and selling is more than semantic. Selling focuses on the needs of the seller, marketing on the needs of the buyer. Selling is preoccupied with the seller's need to convert his product into cash; marketing with the idea of satisfying the needs of the customer by means of the product and the whole cluster of things associated with creating, delivering, and finally consuming it.

In some industries the enticements of full mass production have been so powerful that for many years top management in effect has told the sales departments, "You get rid of it; we'll worry about profits." By contrast, a truly marketing-minded firm tries to create value-satisfying goods and services that consumers will want to buy. What it offers for sale includes not only the generic product or service, but also how it is made available to the customer, in what form, when, under what conditions, and at what terms of trade. Most important, what it offers for sale is determined not by the seller but by the buyer. The seller takes his cues from the buyer in such a way that the product becomes a consequence of the marketing effort, not vice versa.

Lag in Detroit

This may sound like an elementary rule of business, but that does not keep it from being violated wholesale. It is certainly more violated than honored. Take the automobile industry:

> Here mass production is most famous, most honored, and has the greatest impact on the entire society. The industry has hitched its fortune to the relentless requirements of the annual model change, a policy that makes customer orientation an especially urgent necessity. Consequently the auto companies annually spend millions of dollars on consumer research. But the fact that the new compact cars are selling so well in their first year indicates that Detroit's vast researchers have for a long time failed to reveal what the customer really wanted. Detroit was not persuaded that he wanted anything different from what he had been getting until it lost millions of customers to other small car manufacturers.
>
> How could this unbelievable lag behind consumer wants have been perpetuated so long? Why did not research reveal consumer preferences before consumers' buying decisions themselves revealed the facts? Is that not what consumer research is for – to find out before the fact what is going to happen? The answer is that Detroit never really researched the customer's wants. It only researched his preferences between the kinds of things which it had already decided to offer him. For Detroit is mainly product-oriented, not customer-oriented. To the extent that the customer is recognized as having needs that the manufacturer should try to satisfy, Detroit usually acts as if the job can be done entirely by product changes. Occasionally attention gets paid to financing, too, but that is done more in order to sell than to enable the customer to buy.
>
> As for taking care of other customer needs, there is not enough being done to write about. The areas of the greatest unsatisfied needs are ignored, or at best get stepchild attention. These are at the point of sale and on the matter of automotive repair and maintenance. Detroit views these problem areas as being of secondary importance. That is underscored by the fact that the retailing and servicing ends of this industry are neither owned and operated nor controlled by the manufacturers. Once the car is produced, things are pretty much in the dealer's inadequate hands. Illustrative of Detroit's arm's-length attitude is the fact that, while servicing holds enormous sales-stimulating, profit-building opportunities, only 57 of Chevrolet's 7,000 dealers provide night maintenance service.
>
> Motorists repeatedly express their dissatisfaction with servicing and their apprehensions about buying cars under the present selling setup. The anxieties and problems they encounter during the auto buying and maintenance processes are probably more intense and widespread today than 30 years ago. Yet the automobile companies do not *seem* to listen to or take their cues from the anguished consumer. If they do listen, it must be through the filter of their own preoccupation with production. The marketing effort is still viewed as a necessary consequence of the product, not vice versa, as it should be. That is the legacy of mass production, with its parochial view that profit resides essentially in low-cost full production.

What Ford Put First

The profit lure of mass production obviously has a place in the plans and strategy of business management, but it must always follow hard thinking about the customer. This is one of the most important lessons that we can learn from the contradictory behavior of Henry Ford. In a sense Ford was both the most brilliant and the most senseless marketer in American history. He was senseless because he refused to give the customer anything but a black car. He was brilliant because he fashioned a production system designed to fit market needs. We habitually celebrate him for the wrong reason, his production genius. His real genius was marketing. We think he was able to cut his selling price and therefore sell millions of $500 cars because his invention of the assembly line had reduced the costs. Actually he invented the assembly line because he had concluded that at $500 he could sell millions of cars. Mass production was the *result* not the cause of his low prices.

Ford repeatedly emphasized this point, but a nation of production-oriented business managers refuses to hear the great lesson he taught. Here is his operating philosophy as he expressed it succinctly:

> Our policy is to reduce the price, extend the operations, and improve the article. You will notice that the reduction of price comes first. We have never considered any costs as fixed. Therefore we first reduce the price to the point where we believe more sales will result. Then we go ahead and try to make the prices. We do not bother about the costs. The new price forces the costs down. The more usual way is to take the costs and then determine the price, and although that method may be scientific in the narrow sense; it is not scientific in the broad sense, because what earthly use is it to know the cost if it tells you that you cannot manufacture at a price at which the article can be sold? But more to the point is the fact that, although one may calculate what a cost is, and of course all of our costs are carefully calculated, no one knows what a cost ought to be. One of the ways of discovering . . . is to name a price so low as to force everybody in the place to the highest point of efficiency. The low price makes everybody dig for profits. We make more discoveries concerning manufacturing and selling under this forced method than by any method of leisurely investigation.[5]

Product Provincialism

The tantalizing profit possibilities of low unit production costs may be the most seriously self-deceiving attitude that can afflict a company, particularly a "growth" company where an apparently assured expansion of demand al ready tends to undermine a proper concern for the importance of marketing and the customer.

The usual result of this narrow preoccupation with so-called concrete matters is that instead of growing, the industry declines. It usually means that the product fails to adapt to the constantly changing patterns of consumer needs and tastes, to new and modified marketing institutions and practices, or to product developments in competing or complementary industries. The industry has its eyes so firmly on its own specific product that it does not see how it is being made obsolete.

The classical example of this is the buggy whip industry. No amount of product improvement could stave off its death sentence. But had the industry defined itself as being in the transportation business rather than the buggy whip business, it might have survived. It would have done what survival always entails, that is, changing. Even if it had only defined its business as providing a stimulant or catalyst to an energy source, it might have survived by becoming a manufacturer of, say, fanbelts or air cleaners.

What may some day be a still more classical example is again, the oil industry. Having let others steal marvelous opportunities from it (e.g., natural gas, as already mentioned, missile fuels, and jet engine lubricants), one would expect it to have taken steps never to let that happen again. But this is not the case. We are now getting extraordinary new developments in fuel systems specifically designed to power automobiles. Not only are these developments concentrated in firms outside the petroleum industry, but petroleum is almost systematically ignoring them, securely content in its wedded bliss to oil. It is the story of the kerosene lamp versus the incandescent lamp all over again. Oil is trying to improve hydrocarbon fuels rather than to develop *any* fuels best suited to the needs of their users, whether or not made in different ways and with different raw materials from oil.

Here are some of the things which non-petroleum companies are working on:

> Over a dozen such firms now have advanced working models of energy systems which, when perfected, will replace the internal combustion engine and eliminate the demand for gasoline. The superior merit of each of these systems is their elimination of frequent, time-consuming, and irritating refueling stops. Most of these systems are fuel cells designed to create electrical energy directly from chemicals without combustion. Most of them use chemicals that are not derived from oil, generally hydrogen and oxygen.
>
> Several other companies have advanced models of electric storage batteries designed to power automobiles. One of these is an aircraft producer that is working jointly with several electric utility companies. The latter hope to use off-peak generating capacity to supply overnight plug-in battery regeneration. Another company, also using the battery approach, is a medium-size electronics firm with extensive small-battery experience that it developed in connection with its work on hearing aids. It is collaborating with an automobile manufacturer. Recent improvements arising from the need for high-powered miniature power storage plants in rockets have put us within reach of a relatively small battery capable of withstanding great overloads or surges of power. Germanium diode applications and batteries using sintered-plate and nickel-cadmium techniques promise to make a revolution in our energy sources.
>
> Solar energy conversion systems are also getting increasing attention. One usually cautious Detroit auto executive recently ventured that solar-powered cars might be common by 1980.

As for the oil companies, they are more or less "watching developments," as one research director put it to me. A few are doing a bit of research on fuel cells, but almost always confined to developing cells powered by hydrocarbon chemicals. None of them are enthusiastically researching fuel cells, batteries, or solar power plants. None of them are spending a fraction as much on research in these profoundly important areas as they are on the usual run-of-the-mill things like reducing combustion chamber deposit in gasoline engines. One major integrated petroleum company recently took a tentative look at the fuel cell and concluded that although "the companies actively working on it indicate a belief in ultimate success . . . the timing and magnitude of its impact are too remote to warrant recognition in our forecasts."

One might, of course, ask: Why should the oil companies do anything different? Would not chemical fuel cells, batteries, or solar energy kill the present product lines? The answer is that they would indeed, and that is precisely the reason for the oil firms having to develop these power units before their competitors, so they will not be companies without an industry.

Management might be more likely to do what is needed for its own preservation if it thought of itself as being in the energy business. But even that would not be enough if it persists in imprisoning itself in the narrow grip of its tight product orientation. It has to think of itself as taking care of customer needs, not findings, refining, or even selling oil. Once it genuinely thinks of its business as taking care of people's transportation needs, nothing can stop it from creating its own extravagantly profitable growth.

Creative Destruction

Since words are cheap and deeds are dear, it may be appropriate to indicate what this kind of thinking involves and leads to. Let us start at the beginning – the customer. It can be shown that motorists strongly dislike the bother, delay, and experience of buying gasoline. People actually do not buy gasoline. They cannot see it, taste it, feel it, appreciate it, or really test it. What they buy is the right to continue driving their cars. The gas station is like a tax collector to whom people are compelled to pay a periodic toll as the price of using their cars. This makes the gas station a basically unpopular institution. It can never be made popular or pleasant, only less unpopular, less unpleasant.

To reduce its unpopularity completely means eliminating it. Nobody likes a tax collector, not even a pleasantly cheerful one. Nobody likes to interrupt a trip to buy a phantom product, not even from a handsome Adonis or a seductive Venus. Hence, companies that are working on exotic fuel substitutes which will eliminate the need for frequent refueling are heading directly into the outstretched arms of the irritated motorists. They are riding a wave of inevitability, not because they are creating something which is technologically superior or more sophisticated, but because they are satisfying a powerful customer need. They are also eliminating noxious odors and air pollution.

Once the petroleum companies recognize the customer-satisfying logic of what another power system can do, they will see that they have no more choice about working on an efficient, long-lasting fuel (or some way of delivering present fuels without bothering the motorist) than the big food chains had a choice about going into the supermarket business, or the vacuum tube companies had a choice about making semiconductors. For their own good the oil firms will have to destroy their own highly profitable assets. No amount of wishful thinking can save them from the necessity of engaging in this form of "creative destruction."

I phrase the need as strongly as this because I think management must make quite an effort to break itself loose from conventional ways. It is all too easy in this day and age for a company or industry to let its sense of purpose become dominated by the economies of full production and to develop a dangerously lopsided product orientation. In short, if management lets itself drift, it invariably drifts in the direction of thinking of itself as producing goods and services, not customer satisfactions. While it probably will not descend to the depths of telling its salesmen, "You get rid of it; we'll worry about profits," it can, without knowing it, be practicing precisely that formula for withering decay. The historic fate of one growth industry after another has been its suicidal product provincialism.

DANGERS OF R & D

Another big danger to a firm's continued growth arises when top management is wholly transfixed by the profit possibilities of technical research and development. To illustrate I shall turn first to a new industry – electronics – and then return once more to the oil companies. By comparing a fresh example with a familiar one, I hope to emphasize the prevalence and insidiousness of a hazardous way of thinking.

Marketing Shortchanged

In this case of electronics, the greatest danger which faces the glamorous new companies in this field is not that they do not pay enough attention to research and development, but that they pay *too much* attention to it. And the fact that the fastest growing electronics firms owe their eminence to their heavy emphasis on technical research is completely beside the point. They have vaulted to affluence on a sudden crest of unusually strong general receptiveness to new technical ideas. Also, their success has been shaped in the virtually guaranteed market of military subsidies and by military orders that in many cases actually preceded the existence of facilities to make the products. Their expansion has, in other words, been almost totally devoid of marketing effort.

Thus, they are growing up under conditions that come dangerously close to creating the illusion that a superior product will sell itself. Having created a successful company by making a superior product, it is not surprising that managment continues to be oriented toward the product rather than the people who consume it. It develops the philosophy that continued growth is a matter of continued product innovation and improvement.

A number of other factors tend to strengthen and sustain this belief:

1. Because electronic products are highly complex and sophisticated, managements become top-heavy with engineers and scientists. This creates a selective bias in favor of research and production at the expense of marketing. The organization tends to view itself as making things rather than satisfying customer needs. Marketing gets treated as a residual activity, "something else" that must be done once the vital job of product creation and production is completed.
2. To this bias in favor of product research, development, and production is added the bias in favor of dealing with controllable variables. Engineers and scientists are at home in the world of concrete things like machines, test tubes, production lines, and even balance sheets. The abstractions to which they feel kindly are those which are testable or manipulatable in the laboratory, or, if not testable, then functional, such as Euclid's axioms. In short, the managements of the new glamour-growth companies tend to favor those business activities which lend themselves to careful study, experimentation, and control—the hard, practical, realities of the lab, the shop, the books.

What gets shortchanged are the realities of the *market*. Consumers are unpredictable, varied, fickle, stupid, shortsighted, stubborn, and generally bothersome. This is not what the engineer-managers say, but deep down in their consciousness it is what they believe. And this accounts for their concentrating on what they know and what they can control, namely, product research, engineering, and production. The emphasis on production becomes particularly attractive when the product can be made at declining unit costs. There is no more inviting way of making money than by running the plant full blast.

Today the top-heavy science-engineering-production orientation of so many electronics companies works reasonably well because they are pushing into new frontiers in which the armed services have pioneered virtually assured markets. The companies are in the felicitous position of having to fill, not find markets; of not having to discover what the customer needs and wants, but of having the customer voluntarily come forward with specific new product demands. If a team of consultants had been assigned specifically to design a business situation calculated to prevent the emergence and development of a customer-oriented marketing viewpoint, it could not have produced anything better than the conditions just described.

Stepchild Treatment

The oil industry is a stunning example of how science, technology, and mass production can divert an entire group of companies from their main task. To the extent the consumer is studied at all (which is not much), the focus is forever on getting information which is designed to help the oil companies improve what they are now doing. They try to discover more convincing advertising themes, more effective sales promotional drives, what the market shares of the various companies are, what people like or dislike about service station dealers and oil companies, and so forth. Nobody seems as interested in probing deeply into the basic human needs that the industry might be trying to satisfy as in probing into the basic properties of the raw material that the companies work with in trying to deliver customer satisfaction.

Basic questions about customers and markets seldom get asked. The latter occupy a stepchild status. They are recognized as existing, as having to be taken care of, but not worth very much real thought or dedicated attention. Nobody gets as excited about the customers in his own backyard as about the oil in the Sahara Desert. Nothing illustrates better the neglect of marketing than its treatment in the industry press:

> The centennial issue of the *American Petroleum Institute Quarterly*, published in 1959 to celebrate the discovery of oil in Titusville, Pennsylvania, contained 21 feature articles proclaiming the industry's greatness. Only one of these talked about its achievements in marketing, and that was only a pictorial record of how service station architecture has changed. The issue also contained a special section on "New Horizons," which was devoted to showing the magnificent role oil would play in America's future. Every reference was ebulliently optimistic, never implying once that oil might have some hard competition. Even the reference to atomic energy was a cheerful catalogue of how oil would help make atomic energy a success. There was not a single apprehension that the oil industry's affluence might be threatened or a suggestion that one "new horizon" might include new and better ways of serving oil's present customers.
>
> But the most revealing example of the stepchild treatment that marketing gets was still another special series of short articles on "The Revolutionary Potential of Electronics." Under that heading this list of articles appeared in the table of contents:
>
> "In the Search for Oil"
> "In Production Operations"
> "In Refinery Processes"
> "In Pipeline Operations"
>
> Significantly, every one of the industry's major functional areas is listed, *except* marketing. Why? Either it is believed that electronics holds no revolutionary potential for petroleum marketing (which is palpably wrong), or the editors forgot to discuss marketing (which is more likely, and illustrates its stepchild status).
>
> The order in which the four functional areas are listed also betrays the alienation of the oil industry from the consumer. The industry is implicitly defined as beginning with the search for oil and ending with its distribution from the refinery. But the truth is, it seems to me, that the industry begins with the needs of the customer for its products. From that primal position its definition moves steadily backstream to areas of progressively lesser importance, until it finally comes to rest at the "search for oil."

Beginning & End

The view that an industry is a customer-satisfying process, not a goods-producing process, is vital for all businessmen to understand. An industry begins with the customer and his needs, not with a patent, a raw material, or a selling skill. Given the customer's needs, the industry develops backwards, first concerning itself with the physical *delivery* of customer satisfactions. Then it moves back further to *creating* the things by which these satisfactions are in part achieved. How these materials are created is a matter of indifference to the customer, hence the particular form of manufacturing, processing, or what-have-you cannot be considered as a vital aspect of the industry. Finally, the industry moves back still further to *finding* the raw materials necessary for making its products.

The irony of some industries oriented toward technical research and development is that the scientists who occupy the high executive positions are totally unscientific when it comes to defining their companies' over-all needs and purposes. They violate the first two rules of the scientific method – being aware of and defining their companies' problems, and then developing testable hypotheses about solving them. They are scientific only about the convenient things, such as laboratory and product experiments. The reason that the customer (and the satisfaction of his deepest needs) is not considered as being "the problem" is not because there is any certain belief that no such problem exists, but because an organizational lifetime has conditioned management to look in the opposite direction. Marketing is a stepchild.

I do not mean that selling is ignored. Far from it. But selling, again, is not marketing. As already pointed out, selling concerns itself with the tricks and techniques of getting people to exchange their cash for your product. It is not concerned with the values that the exchange is all about. And it does not, as marketing invariably does, view the entire business process as consisting of a tightly integrated effort to discover, create, arouse, and satisfy customer needs. The customer is somebody "out there" who, with proper cunning, can be separated from his loose change.

Actually, not even selling gets much attention in some technologically minded firms. Because there is a virtually guaranteed market for the abundant flow of their new products, they do not actually know what a real market is. It is as if they lived in a planned economy, moving their products routinely from factory to retail outlet. Their successful concentration on products tends to convince them of the soundness of what they have been doing, and they fail to see the gathering clouds over the market.

CONCLUSION

Less than 75 years ago American railroads enjoyed a fierce loyalty among astute Wall Streeters. European monarchs invested in them heavily. Eternal wealth was thought to be the benediction for anybody who could scrape a few thousand dollars together to put into rail stocks. No other form of transportation could compete with the railroads in speed, flexibility, durability, economy, and growth potentials. As Jacques Barzun put it, "By the turn of the century it was an institution, an image of man, a tradition, a code of honor, a source of poetry, a nursery of boyhood desires, a sublimest of toys, and the most solemn machine – next to the funeral hearse – that marks the epochs in man's life."[6]

Even after the advent of automobiles, trucks, and airplanes, the railroad tycoons remained imperturbably self-confident. If you had told them 60 years ago that in 30 years they would be flat on their backs, broke, and pleading for government subsidies, they would have thought you totally demented. Such a future was simply not considered possible. It was not even a discussable subject, or an askable question, or a matter which any sane person would consider worth speculating about. The very thought was insane. Yet a lot of insane notions now have matter-of-fact acceptance – for example, the idea of 100-ton tubes of metal moving smoothly through the air 20,000 feet above the earth, loaded with 100 sane and solid citizens casually drinking martinis – and they have dealt cruel blows to the railroads.

What specifically must other companies do to avoid this fate? What does customer orientation involve? These questions have in part been answered by the preceding examples and analysis. It would take another article to show in detail what is required for specific industries. In any case, it should be obvious that building an effective customer-oriented company involves far more than good intentions or promotional tricks; it involves profound matters of human organization and leadership. For the present, let me merely suggest what appear to be some general requirements.

Visceral Feel of Greatness

Obviously the company has to do what survival demands. It has to adapt to the requirements of the market, and it has to do it sooner rather than later. But mere survival is a so-so aspiration. Anybody can survive in some way or other, even the skid-row bum. The trick is to survive gallantly, to feel the surging impulse of commercial mastery; not just to experience the sweet smell of success, but to have the visceral feel of entrepreneurial greatness.

No organization can achieve greatness without a vigorous leader who is driven onward by his own pulsating *will to succeed.* He has to have a vision of grandeur, a vision that can produce eager followers in vast numbers. In business, the followers are the customers. To produce these customers, the entire corporation must be viewed as a customer-creating and customer-satisfying organism. Management must think of itself not as producing products but as providing customer-creating value satisfactions. It must push this idea (and everything it means and requires) into every nook and cranny of the organization. It has to do this continuously and with the kind of flair that excites and stimulates the people in it. Otherwise, the company will be merely a series of pigeonholed parts, with no consolidating sense of purpose or direction.

In short, the organization must learn to think of itself not as producing goods or services but as *buying customers,* as doing the things that will make people *want* to do business with it. And the chief executive himself has the inescapable responsibility for creating this environment, this viewpoint, this attitude, this aspiration. He himself must set the company's style, its direction, and its goals. This means he has to know precisely where he himself wants to go, and to make sure the whole organization is enthusiastically aware of where that is. This is a first requisite of leadership, for *unless he knows where he is going, any road will take him there.*

If any road is okay, the chief executive might as well pack his attaché case and go fishing. If an organization does not know or care where it is going, it does not need to advertise that fact with a ceremonial figurehead. Everybody will notice it soon enough.

1975: RETROSPECTIVE COMMENTARY

Amazed, finally, by his literary success, Isaac Bashevis Singer reconciled an attendant problem: "I think the moment you have published a book, it's not any more your private property. . . . If it has value, everybody can find in it what he finds, and I cannot tell the man I did not intend it to be so." Over the past 15 years, "Marketing Myopia" has become a case in point. Remarkably, the article spawned a legion of loyal partisans – not to mention a host of unlikely bedfellows.

Its most common and, I believe, most influential consequences is the way certain companies for the first time gave serious thought to the question of what business they are really in.

The strategic consequences of this have in many cases been dramatic. The best-known case, of course, is the shift in thinking of oneself as being in the "oil business" to being in the "energy business." In some instances the payoff has been spectacular (getting into coal, for example) and in others dreadful (in terms of the time and money spent so far on fuel cell research). Another successful example is a company with a large chain of retail shoe stores that redefined itself as a retailer of moderately priced, frequently purchased, widely assorted consumer specialty products. The result was a dramatic growth in volume, earnings, and return on assets.

Some companies, again for the first time, asked themselves whether they wished to be masters of certain technologies for which they would seek markets, or be masters of markets for which they would seek customer-satisfying products and services.

Choosing the former, one company has declared, in effect, "We are experts in glass technology. We intend to improve and expand that expertise with the object of creating products that will attract customers." This decision has forced the company into a much more systematic and customer-sensitive look at possible markets and users, even though its stated strategic object has been to capitalize on glass technology.

Deciding to concentrate on markets, another company has determined that "we want to help people (primarily women) enhance their beauty and sense of youthfulness." This company has expanded its line of cosmetic products, but has also entered the fields of proprietary drugs and vitamin supplements.

All these examples illustrate the "policy" results of "Marketing Myopia." On the operating level, there has been, I think, an extraordinary heightening of sensitivity to customers and consumers. R&D departments have cultivated a greater "external" orientation toward uses, users, and markets – balancing thereby the previously one-sided "internal" focus on materials and methods; upper management has realized that marketing and sales departments should be somewhat more willingly accommodated than before; finance departments have become more receptive to the legitimacy of budgets for market research and experimentation in marketing; and salesmen have been better trained to listen to and understand customer needs and problems, rather than merely to "push" the product.

A Mirror, Not a Window

My impression is that the article has had more impact in industrial-products companies than in consumer-products companies – perhaps because the former had lagged most in customer orientation. There are at least two reasons for this lag: (1) industrial-products companies tend to be more capital intensive, and (2) in the past, at least, they have had to rely heavily on communicating face-to-face the technical character of what they made and sold. These points are worth explaining.

Capital-intensive businesses are understandably preoccupied with magnitudes, especially where the capital, once invested, cannot be easily moved, manipulated, or modified for the production of a variety of products – e.g., chemical plants, steel mills, airlines, and railroads. Understandably, they seek big volumes and operating efficiencies to pay off the equipment and meet the carrying costs.

At least one problem results: corporate power becomes disproportionately lodged with operating or financial executives. If you read the charter of one of the nation's largest companies, you will see that the chairman of the finance committee, not the chief executive officer, is the "chief." Executives with such backgrounds have an almost trained incapacity to see that getting "volume" may require understanding and serving many discrete and sometimes small market segments, rather than going after a perhaps mythical batch of big or homogeneous customers.

These executives also often fail to appreciate the competitive changes going on around them. They observe the changes, all right, but devalue their significance or underestimate their ability to nibble away at the company's markets.

Once dramatically alerted to the concept of segments, sectors, and customers, though, managers of capital-intensive businesses have become more responsive to the necessity of balancing their inescapable preoccupation with "paying the bills" or breaking even with the fact that the best way to accomplish this may be to pay more attention to segments, or sectors, and customers.

The second reason industrial-products companies have probably been more influenced by the article is that, in the case of the more technical industrial products or services, the necessity of clearly communicating product and service characteristics to prospects results in a lot of face-to-face "selling" effort. But precisely because the product is so complex, the situation produces salesmen who know the product more than they know the customer, who are more adept at explaining what they have and what it can do than learning what the customer's needs and problems are. The result has been a narrow product orientation rather than a liberating customer orientation, and "service" often suffered. To be sure, sellers said, "We have to provide service," but they tended to define service by looking into the mirror rather than out the window. They *thought* they were looking out the window at the customer, but it was actually a mirror – a reflection of their own product-oriented biases rather than a reflection of their customers' situations.

A Manifesto, Not a Prescription

Not everything has been rosy. A lot of bizarre things have happened as a result of the article:

- Some companies have developed what I call "marketing mania" – they've become obsessively responsive to every fleeting whim of the customer. Mass production operations have been converted to approximations of job shops, with cost and price consequences far exceeding the willingness of customers to buy the product.

- Management has expanded product lines and added new lines of business without first establishing adequate control systems to run more complex operations.
- Marketing staffs have suddenly and rapidly expanded themselves and their research budgets without either getting sufficient prior organizational support or, thereafter, producing sufficient results.
- Companies that are functionally organized have converted to product, brand, or market-based organizations with the expectation of instant and miraculous results. The outcome has been ambiguity, frustration, confusion, corporate infighting, losses, and finally a reversion to functional arrangements that only worsened the situation.
- Companies have attempted to "serve" customers by creating complex and beautifully efficient products or services that buyers are either too risk-averse to adopt or incapable of learning how to employ – in effect, there are now steam shovels for people who haven't yet learned to use spades. This problem has happened repeatedly in the so-called service industries (financial services, insurance, computer-based services) and with American companies selling in less-developed economies.

"Marketing Myopia" was not intended as analysis or even prescription; it was intended as manifesto. It did not pretend to take a balanced position. Nor was it a new idea – Peter F. Drucker, J. B. McKitterick, Wroe Alderson, John Howard, and Neil Borden had each done more original and balanced work on "the marketing concept." My scheme, however, tied marketing more closely to the inner orbit of business policy. Drucker – especially in *The Concept of the Corporation* and *The Practice of Management* – originally provided me with a great deal of insight.

My contribution, therefore, appears merely to have been a simple, brief, and useful way of communicating an existing way of thinking. I tried to do it in a very direct, but responsible, fashion, knowing that few readers (customers), especially managers and leaders, could stand much equivocation or hesitation. I also knew that the colorful and lightly documented affirmation works better than the tortuously reasoned explanation.

But why the enormous popularity of what was actually such a simple preexisting idea? Why its appeal throughout the world to resolutely restrained scholars, implacably temperate managers, and high government officials, all accustomed to balanced and thoughtful calculation? Is it that concrete examples, joined to illustrate a simple idea and presented with some attention to literacy, communicate better than massive analytical reasoning that reads as though it were translated from the German? Is it that provocative assertions are more memorable and persuasive than restrained and balanced explanations, no matter who the audience? Is it that the character of the message is as much the message as its content? Or was mine not simply a different tune, but a new symphony? I don't know.

Of course, I'd do it again and in the same way, given my purposes, even with what more I now know – the good and the bad, the power of facts and the limits of rhetoric. If your mission is the moon, you don't use a car. Don Marquis's cockroach, Archy, provides some final consolation: "an idea is not responsible for who believes in it."

NOTES

1. Jacques Barzun, "Trains and the Mind of Man," *Holiday* February 1960, p. 21.
2. For more details see M. M. Zimmerman, *The Super Market: A Revolution in Distribution* (New York, McGraw-Hill Book Company, Inc. 1955), p. 48.
3. Ibid., pp. 45–47.
4. *The Affluent Society* (Boston, Houghton-Mifflin Company, 1958), pp. 152–160.
5. Henry Ford, *My Life and Work* (New York, Doubleday, Page & Company, 1923), pp. 146–147.
6. Op. cit., p. 20.

2 Wroe Alderson

The Analytical Framework for Marketing

My assignment is to discuss the analytical framework for marketing. Since our general purpose here is to consider the improvement of the marketing curriculum, I assume that the paper I have been asked to present might serve two functions. The first is to present a perspective of marketing which might be the basis of a marketing course at either elementary or advanced levels. The other is to provide some clue as to the foundations in the social sciences upon which an analytical framework for marketing may be built.

Economics has some legitimate claim to being the original science of markets. Received economic theory provides a framework for the analysis of marketing functions which certainly merits the attention of marketing teachers and practitioners. It is of little importance whether the point of view I am about to present is a version of economics, a hybrid of economics and sociology, or the application of a new emergent general science of human behavior to marketing problems. The analytical framework which I find congenial at least reflects some general knowledge of the social sciences as well as long experience in marketing analysis. In the time available I can do no more than present this view in outline or skeleton form and leave you to determine how to classify it or whether you can use it.

An advantageous place to start for the analytical treatment of marketing is with the radical heterogeneity of markets. Heterogeneity is inherent on both the demand and the supply sides. The homogeneity which the economist assumes for certain purposes is not an antecedent condition for marketing. Insofar as it is ever realized, it emerges out of the marketing process itself.

The materials which are useful to man occur in nature in heterogeneous mixtures which

Reprinted from Delbert Duncan (ed.), *Proceedings: Conference of Marketing Teachers from Far Western States* (Berkeley: University of California, 1958), pp. 15–28.

Wroe Alderson was, until his death, professor at the Wharton School of Finance and Commerce at the University of Pennsylvania and director of that school's Management Science Center. He also founded a management consulting firm and served as president of the American Marketing Association. He studied at the George Washington University, the University of Pennsylvania, and the Massachusetts Institute of Technology and was author or editor of several books on marketing. His Marketing Behavior and Executive Action *is hailed as a landmark in marketing thought.*

might be called conglomerations since these mixtures have only a random relationship to human needs and activities. The collection of goods in the possessions of a household or an individual also constitutes a heterogeneous supply, but it might be called an assortment since it is related to anticipated patterns of future behavior. The whole economic process may be described as a series of transformations from meaningless to meaningful heterogeneity. Marketing produces as much homogeneity as may be needed to facilitate some of the intermediate economic processes but homogeneity has limited significance or utility for consumer behavior or expectations.

The marketing process matches materials found in nature or goods fabricated from these materials against the needs of households or individuals. Since the consuming unit has a complex pattern of needs, the matching of these needs creates an assortment of goods in the hands of the ultimate consumer. Actually the marketing process builds up assortments at many stages along the way, each appropriate to the activities taking place at that point. Materials or goods are associated in one way for manufacturing, in another way for wholesale distribution, and in still another for retail display and selling. In between the various types of heterogeneous collections relatively homogeneous supplies are accumulated through the process of grading, refining, chemical reduction and fabrication.

Marketing brings about the necessary transformations in heterogeneous supplies through a multiphase process of sorting. Matching of every individual need would be impossible if the consumer had to search out each item required or the producer had to find the users of a product one by one. It is only the ingenious use of intermediate sorts which make it possible for a vast array of diversified products to enter into the ultimate consumer assortments as needed. Marketing makes mass production possible first by providing the assortment of supplies needed in manufacturing and then taking over the successive transformations which ultimately produce the assortment in the hands of consuming units.

To some who have heard this doctrine expounded, the concept of sorting seems empty, lacking in specific behavioral content, and hence unsatisfactory as a root idea for marketing. One answer is that sorting is a more general and embracing concept than allocation, which many economists regard as the root idea of their science. Allocation is only one of the four basic types of sorting, all of which are involved in marketing. Among these four, allocation is certainly no more significant than assorting, one being the breaking down of a homogeneous supply and the other the building up of a heterogeneous supply. Assorting, in fact, gives more direct expression to the final aim of marketing but allocation performs a major function along the way.

There are several basic advantages in taking sorting as a central concept. It leads directly to a fundamental explanation of the contribution of marketing to the overall economy of human effort in producing and distributing goods. It provides a key to the unending search for efficiency in the marketing function itself. Finally, sorting as the root idea of marketing is consistent with the assumption that heterogeneity is radically and inherently present on both sides of the market and that the aim of marketing is to cope with the heterogeneity of both needs and resources.

At this stage of the discussion it is the relative emphasis on assorting as contrasted with allocation which distinguishes marketing theory from at least some versions of economic theory. This emphasis arises naturally from the preoccupation of the market analyst with consumer behavior. One of the most fruitful approaches to understanding what the consumer is doing is the idea that she is engaged in building an assortment, in replenishing or extending an inventory of goods for use by herself and her family. As evidence that this paper is not an attempt to set up a theory in opposition to economics it is acknowledged that the germ of this conception of consumer behavior was first presented some eighty years ago by the Austrian economist Böhm-Bawerk.

The present view is distinguished from that of Böhm-Bawerk in its greater emphasis on the probabilistic approach to the study of market behavior. In considering items for inclusion in her assortment the consumer must make judgments concerning the relative probabilities of future occasions for use. A product in the assortment is intended to provide for some aspect of future behavior. Each such occasion for use carries a rating which is a product of two factors, one a judgment as to the probability of its incidence and the other a measure of the urgency of the need in case it should arise. Consumer goods vary with respect to both measures. One extreme might be illustrated by cigarettes with a probability of use approaching certainty but with relatively small urgency or penalty for deprivation on the particular occasion for use. At the other end of the scale would be a home fire extinguisher with low probability but high urgency attaching to the expected occasion of use.

All of this means that the consumer buyer enters the market as a problem-solver. Solving a problem, either on behalf of a household or on behalf of a marketing organization means reaching a decision in the face of uncertainty. The consumer buyer and the marketing executive are opposite numbers in the double search which pervades marketing; one looking for the goods required to complete an assortment, the other looking for the buyers who are uniquely qualified to use his goods. This is not to say that the behavior of either consumers or executives can be completely characterized as rational problem-solvers. The intention rather is to assert that problem-solving on either side of the market involves a probabilistic approach to heterogeneity on the other side. In order to solve his own problems arising from the heterogeneous demand, the marketing executive should understand the processes of consumer decisions in coping with heterogeneous supplies.

The viewpoint adopted here with respect to the competition among sellers is essentially that which is associated in economics with such names as Schumpeter, Chamberlin, and J. M. Clark and with the emphasis on innovative competition, product differentiation and differential advantage. The basic assumption is that every firm occupies a position which is in some respects unique, being differentiated from all others by characteristics of its products, its services, its geographic location or its specific combination of these features. The survival of a firm requires that for some group of buyers it should enjoy a differential advantage over all other suppliers. The sales of any active marketing organization come from a core market made up of buyers with a preference for this source and a fringe market which finds the source acceptable, at least for occasional purchases.

In the case of the supplier of relatively undifferentiated products or services such as the wheat farmer, differential advantage may pertain more to the producing region than to the individual producer. This more diffused type of differential advantage often becomes effective in the market through such agencies as the marketing cooperative. Even the individual producer of raw materials, however, occupies a position in the sense that one market or buyer provides the customary outlet for his product rather than another. The essential point for the present argument is that buyer and seller are not paired at random even in the marketing of relatively homogeneous products but are related to some scale of preference or priority.

Competition for differential advantage implies goals of survival and growth for the marketing organization. The firm is perenially seeking a favorable place to stand and not merely immediate profits from its operations. Differential advantage is subject to change and neutralization by competitors. In dynamic markets differential advantage can only be preserved through continuous innovation. Thus competition presents an analogy to a succession of military campaigns rather than to the pressures and attrition of a single battle. A competitor may gain ground through a successful campaign based on new product features or merchandising ideas. It may lose ground or be forced to fall back on its core position because of the successful campaigns of others. The existence of the core position helps to explain the paradox of survival in the face of the destructive onslaughts of innovative competition.

Buyers and sellers meet in market transactions, each side having tentatively identified the other as an answer to its problem. The market transaction consumes much of the time and effort of all buyers and sellers. The market which operates through a network of costless transactions is only a convenient fiction which economists adopt for certain analytical purposes. Potentially the cost of transactions is so high that controlling or reducing this cost is a major objective in market analysis and executive action. Among economists John R. Commons has given the greatest attention to the transaction as the unit of collective action. He drew a basic distinction between strategic and routine transactions which for present purposes may best be paraphrased as fully negotiated and routine transactions.

The fully negotiated transaction is the prototype of all exchange transactions. It represents a matching of supply and demand after canvassing all of the factors which might affect the decision on either side. The routine transaction proceeds under a set of rules and assumptions established by previous negotiation or as a result of techniques of pre-selling which take the place of negotiation. Transactions on commodity and stock exchanges are carried out at high speed and low cost but only because of carefully established rules governing all aspects of trading. The economical routines of self-service in a supermarket are possible because the individual items on display have been presold. The routine transaction is the end-result of previous marketing effort and ingenious organization of institutions and processes. Negotiation is implicit in all routine transactions. Good routines induce both parties to save time and cost by foregoing explicit negotiations.

The negotiated transaction is the indicated point of departure for the study of exchange values in heterogeneous markets. Many considerations enter into the decision to trade or not to trade on either side of the market. Price is the final balancing or integrating factor which permits the deal to be made. The seller may accept a lower price if relieved from onerous requirements. The buyer may pay a higher price if provided with specified services. The integrating price is one that assures an orderly flow of goods so long as the balance of other considerations remains essentially unchanged. Some economists are uneasy about the role of the negotiated transaction in value determination since bargaining power may be controlling within wide bargaining limits. These limits as analyzed by Commons are set by reference to the best alternatives available to either partner rather than by the automatic control of atomistic competition. This analysis overlooks a major constraint on bargaining in modern markets. Each side has a major stake in a deal that the other side can live with. Only in this way can a stable supply relationship be established so as to achieve the economics of transactional routines. Negotiation is not a zero sum game since the effort to get the best of the other party transaction by transaction may result in a loss to both sides in terms of mounting transactional cost.

In heterogeneous markets price plays an important role in matching a segment of supply with the appropriate segment of demand. The seller frequently has the option of producing a stream-lined product at a low price, a deluxe product at a high price or selecting a price-quality combination somewhere in between. There are considerations which exert a strong influence on the seller toward choosing the price line or lines which will yield the greatest dollar volume of sales. Assuming that various classes of consumers have conflicting claims on the productive capacity of the supplier, it might be argued that the price-quality combination which maximized gross revenue represented the most constructive compromise among these claims. There are parallel considerations with respect to the claims of various participants in the firm's activities on its operating revenue. These claimants include labor, management, suppliers of raw materials and stockholders. Assuming a perfectly fluid situation with respect to bargaining among these claimants, the best chance for a satisfactory solution is at the level of maximum gross revenue. The argument becomes more complicated when the claims of stockholders are given priority, but the goal would still be maximum gross revenue as suggested in a recent paper by William J. Baumol. My own intuition and experience lead me to believe that the maximization of gross revenue is a valid goal of marketing management in heterogeneous markets and adherence to this norm appears to be widely prevalent in actual practice.

What has been said so far is doubtless within the scope of economics or perhaps constitutes a sketch of how some aspects of economic theory might be reconstructed on the assumption of heterogeneity rather than homogeneity as the normal and prevailing condition of the market. But there are issues raised by such notions as enterprise survival, expectations, and consumer behavior, which in my opinion cannot be resolved within the present boundaries of economic science. Here marketing must not hesitate to draw upon the concepts and techniques of the social sciences for the enrichment of its perspectives and for the advancement of marketing as an empirical science.

The general economist has his own justifications for regarding the exchange process as a smoothly functioning mechanism which operates in actual markets or which should be taken as the norm and standard to be enforced by government regulation. For the marketing man, whether teacher or practioner, this Olympian view is untenable. Marketing is concerned with those who are obliged to enter the market to solve their problems, imperfect as the market may be. The persistent and rational action of these participants is the main hope for eliminating or moderating some of these imperfections so that the operation of the market mechanism may approximate that of the theoretical model.

To understand market behavior the marketing man takes a closer look at the nature of the participants. Thus he is obliged, in my opinion, to come to grips with the organized behavior system. Market behavior is primarily group behavior. Individual action in the market is most characteristically action on behalf of some group in which the individual holds membership. The organized behavior system is related to the going concern of John R. Commons but with a deeper interest in what keeps it going. The organized behavior system is also a much broader concept including the more tightly organized groups acting in the market such as business firms and households and loosely connected systems such as the trade center and the marketing channel.

The marketing man needs some rationale for group behavior, some general explanation for the formation and persistence of organized behavior systems. He finds this explanation in the concept of expectations. Insofar as conscious choice is involved, individuals operate in groups because of their expectations of incremental satisfactions as compared to what they could obtain operating alone. The expected satisfactions are of many kinds, direct and indirect. In a group that is productive activity is held together because of an expected surplus over individual output. Other groups such as households and purely social organizations expect direct satisfactions from group association and activities. They also expect satisfactions from future activities facilitated by the assortment of goods held in common. Whatever the character of the system, its vitality arises from the expectations of the individual members and the vigor of their efforts to achieve them through group action. While the existence of the group is entirely derivative, it is capable of operating as if it had a life of its own and was pursuing goals of survival and growth.

Every organized behavior system exhibits a structure related to the functions it performs. Even in the simplest behavior system there must be some mechanism for decision and coordination of effort if the system is to provide incremental satisfaction. Leadership emerges at an early stage to perform such functions as directing the defense of the group. Also quite early is the recognition of the rationing function by which the leader allocates the available goods or satisfactions among the members of the group.

As groups grow in size and their functions become more complex functional specialization increases. The collection of individuals forming a group with their diversified skills and capabilities is a meaningful heterogeneous ensemble vaguely analogous to the assortment of goods which facilitates the activities of the group. The group, however, is held together directly by the generalized expectations of its members. The assortment is held together by a relatively weak or derivative bond. An item "belongs" to the assortment only so long as it has some probability of satisfying the expectations of those who possess it.

This outline began with an attempt to live within the framework of economics or at least within an economic framework amplified to give fuller recognition to heterogeneity on both sides of the market. We have now plunged into sociology in order to deal more effectively with the organized behavior system. Meanwhile we attempt to preserve the line of communication to our origins by basing the explanations of group behavior on the quasi-economic concept of expectations.

The initial plunge into sociology is only the beginning since the marketing man must go considerably further in examining the functions and structure of organized behavior systems. An operating group has a power structure, a communication structure and an operating structure. At each stage an effort should be made to employ the intellectual strategy which has already been suggested. That is, to relate sociological notions to the groundwork of marketing economics through the medium of such concepts as expectations and the processes of matching and sorting.

All members of an organized behavior system occupy some position or status within its power structure. There is a valid analogy between the status of an individual or operating unit within the system and the market position of the firm as an entity. The individual struggles for status within the system having first attained the goal of membership. For most individuals in an industrial society, status in some operating system is a prerequisite for satisfying his expectations. Given the minimal share in the power of the organization inherent in membership, vigorous individuals may aspire to the more ample share of power enjoyed by leadership. Power in the generalized sense referred to here is an underlying objective on which the attainment of all other objectives depends. This aspect of organized behavior has been formulated as the power principle, namely, "The rational individual will act in such a way to promote the power to act." The word *promote* deliberately glosses over an ambivalent attitude toward power, some individuals striving for enhancement and others being content to preserve the power they have.

Any discussion which embraces power as a fundamental concept creates uneasiness for some students on both analytical and ethical ground. My own answer to the analytical problem is to define it as control over expectations. In these terms it is theoretically possible to measure and evaluate power, perhaps even to set a price on it. Certainly it enters into the network of imputations in a business enterprise. Management allocates or rations status and recognition as well as or in lieu of material rewards. As for the ethical problem, it does not arise unless the power principle is substituted for ethics as with Machiavelli. Admitting that the power principle is the essence of expediency, the ethical choice of values and objectives is a different issue. Whatever his specific objectives, the rational individual will wish to serve them expediently.

If any of this discussion of power seems remote from marketing let it be remembered that the major preoccupation of the marketing executive, as pointed out by Oswald Knauth, is with the creation or the activation of organized behavior systems such as marketing channels and sales organizations. No one can be effective in building or using such systems if he ignores the fundamental nature of the power structure.

The communication structure serves the group in various ways. It promotes the survival of the system by reinforcing the individual's sense of belonging. It transmits instructions and operating commands or signals to facilitate coordinated effort. It is related to expectations through the communication of explicit or implied commitments. Negotiations between suppliers and customers and much that goes on in the internal management of a marketing organization can best be understood as a two-way exchange of commitments. A division sales manager, for example, may commit himself to produce a specified volume of sales. His superior in turn may commit certain company resources to support his efforts and make further commitments as to added rewards as an incentive to outstanding performance.

For some purposes it is useful to regard marketing processes as a flow of goods and a parallel flow of informative and persuasive messages. In these terms the design of communication facilities and channels becomes a major aspect of the creation of marketing systems. Marketing has yet to digest and apply the insights of the rapidly developing field of communication theory which in turn has drawn freely from both engineering and biological and social sciences. One stimulating idea expounded by Norbert Wiener and others is that of the feedback of information in a control system. Marketing and advertising research are only well started on the task of installing adequate feedback circuits for controlling the deployment of marketing effort.

Social psychology is concerned with some problems of communication which are often encountered in marketing systems. For example, there are the characteristic difficulties of vertical communication which might be compared to the transmission of telephone messages along a power line. Subordinates often hesitate to report bad news to their superiors fearing to take the brunt of emotional reactions. Superiors learn to be cautious in any discussion of the subordinate's status for fear that casual comment will be interpreted as a commitment. There is often a question as to when a subordinate should act and report and when he should refer a matter for decision upstream. Progress in efficiency, which is a major goal in marketing, depends in substantial part on technological improvement in communication facilities and organizational skill in using them.

The third aspect of structure involved in the study of marketing systems is operating structure. Effective specialization within an organization requires that activities which are functionally similar be placed together but properly coordinated with other activities. Billing by wholesaler grocers, for example, has long been routinized in a separate billing department. In more recent years the advances in mechanical equipment have made it possible to coordinate inventory control with billing, using the same set of punch cards for both functions. Designing an operating structure is a special application of sorting. As in the sorting of goods to facilitate handling, there are generally several alternative schemes for classifying activities presenting problems of choice to the market planner.

Functional specialization and the design of appropriate operating structures is a constant problem in the effective use of marketing channels. Some functions can be performed at either of two or more stages. One stage may be the best choice in terms of economy or effectiveness. Decisions on the placement of a function may have to be reviewed periodically since channels do not remain static. Similar considerations arise in the choice of channels. Some types of distributors or dealers may be equipped to perform a desired service while others may not. Often two or more channels with somewhat specialized roles are required to move a product to the consumer. The product's sponsor can maintain perspective in balancing out these various facilities by thinking in terms of a total operating system including his own sales organization and the marketing channels employed.

The dynamics of market organization pose basic problems for the marketing student and the marketing executive in a free enterprise economy. Reference has already been made to the competitive pursuit of differential advantage. One way in which a firm can gain differential advantage is by organizing the market in a way that is favorable to its own operations. This is something else than the attainment of a monopolistic position in relation to current or potential competitors. It means creating a pattern for dealing with customers or suppliers which persists because there are advantages on both sides. Offering guarantees against price declines on floor stocks is one example of market organization by the seller. Attempts to systematize the flow of orders may range from various services offered to customers or suppliers all the way to complete vertical integration. Another dynamic factor affecting the structure of markets may be generalized under the term "closure." It frequently happens that some marketing system is incomplete or out of balance in some direction. The act of supplying the missing element constitutes closure, enabling the system to handle a greater output or to operate at a new level of efficiency. The incomplete system in effect cries out for closure. To observe this need is to recognize a form of market opportunity. This is one of the primary ways in which new enterprises develop, since there may be good reasons why the missing service cannot be performed by the existing organizations which need the service. A food broker, for example, can cover a market for several accounts of moderate size in a way that the individual manufacturer would not be able to cover it for himself.

There is a certain compensating effect between closure as performed by new or supplementary marketing enterprises and changes in market organization brought about by the initiative of existing firms in the pursuit of differential advantage. The pursuit of a given form of advantage, in fact, may carry the total marketing economy out of balance in a given direction creating the need and opportunity for closure. Such an economy could never be expected to reach a state of equilibrium, although the tendency toward structural balance is one of the factors in its dynamics. Trade regulation may be embraced within this dynamic pattern as an attempt of certain groups to organize the market to their own advantage through political means. Entering into this political struggle to determine the structure of markets are some political leaders and some administrative officials who regard themselves as representing the consumer's interests. It seems reasonable to believe that the increasing sophistication and buying skill of consumers is one of the primary forces offsetting the tendency of the free market economy to turn into something else through the working out of its inherent dynamic forces. This was the destiny foreseen for the capitalistic system by Schumpeter, even though he was one of its staunchest advocates.

The household as an organized behavior system must be given special attention in creating an analytical framework for marketing. The household is an operating entity with an assortment of goods and assets and with economic functions to perform. Once a primary production unit, the household has lost a large part of these activities to manufacturing and service enterprises. Today its economic operations are chiefly expressed through earning and spending. In the typical household there is some specialization between the husband as primary earner and the wife as chief purchasing agent for the household. It may be assumed that she becomes increasingly competent in buying as she surenders her production activities such as canning, baking and dressmaking, and devotes more of her time and attention to shopping. She is a rational problem solver as she samples what the market has to offer in her effort to maintain a balanced inventory or assortment of goods to meet expected occasions of use. This is not an attempt to substitute Economic Woman for the discredited fiction of Economic Man. It is only intended to assert that the decision structure of consumer buying is similar to that for industrial buying. Both business executive and housewife enter the market as rational problem solvers, even though there are other aspects of personality in either case.

An adequate perspective on the household for marketing purposes must recognize several facets of its activities. It is an organized behavior system with its aspects of power, communication, and operating structure. It is the locus of forms of behavior other than instrumental or goal-seeking activities. A convenient three-way division, derived from the social sciences, recognizes instrumental, congenial, and symptomatic behavior. Congenial behavior is that kind of activity engaged in for its own sake and presumably yielding direct satisfactions. It is exemplified by the act of consumption as compared to all of the instrumental activities which prepare the way for consumption. Symptomatic behavior reflects maladjustment and is neither pleasure-giving in itself nor an efficient pursuit of goals. Symptomatic behavior is functional only to the extent that it serves as a signal to others that the individual needs help.

Some studies of consumer motivation have given increasing attention to symptomatic behavior or to the projection of symptoms of personality adjustment which might affect consumer buying. The present view is that the effort to classify individuals by personality types is less urgent for marketing than the classification of families. Four family types with characteristically different buying behavior have been suggested growing out of the distinction between the instrumental and congenial aspects of normal behavior. Even individuals who are fairly well adjusted in themselves will form a less than perfect family if not fully adapted to each other.

On the instrumental side of household behavior it would seem to be desirable that the members be well coordinated as in any other operating system. If not, they will not deliver the maximum impact in pursuit of family goals. On the congenial side it would appear desirable for the members of a household to be compatible. That means enjoying the same things, cherishing the same goals, preferring joint activities to solitary pursuits or the company of others. These two distinctions yield an obvious four-way classification. The ideal is the family that is coordinated in its instrumental activities and compatible in its congenial activities. A rather joyless household which might nevertheless be well managed and prosperous in material terms is the coordinated but incompatible household. The compatible but uncoordinated family would tend to be happy-go-lucky and irresponsible with obvious consequences for buying behavior. The household which was both uncoordinated and incompatible would usually be tottering on the brink of dissolution. It might be held together formally by scruples against divorce, by concern for children, or by the dominant power of one member over the others. This symptomology of families does not exclude an interest in the readjustment of individuals exhibiting symptomatic behavior. Such remedial action lies in the sphere of the psychiatrist and the social worker, whereas the marketer is chiefly engaged in supplying goods to families which are still functioning as operating units.

All of the discussion of consumers so far limits itself to the activities of the household purchasing agent. Actually the term *consumption* as it appears in marketing and economic literature nearly always means consumer buying. Some day marketing may need to look beyond the act of purchasing to a study of consumption proper. The occasion for such studies will arise out of the problems of inducing consumers to accept innovations or the further proliferation of products to be included in the household assortment. Marketing studies at this depth will not only borrow from the social sciences but move into the realm of esthetic and ethical values. What is the use of a plethora of goods unless the buyer derives genuine satisfaction from them? What is the justification of surfeit if the acquisition of goods serves as a distraction from activities which are essential to the preservation of our culture and of the integrity of our personalities?

It has been suggested that a study of consumption might begin with the problem of choice in the presence of abundance. The scarce element then is the time or capacity for enjoyment. The bookworm confronted with the thousands of volumes available in a great library must choose in the face of this type of limitation.

The name *hedonomics* would appear to be appropriate for this field of study suggesting the management of the capacity to enjoy. Among the problems for hedonomics is the pleasure derived from the repetition of a familiar experience as compared with the enjoyment of a novel experience or an old experience with some novel element. Another is the problem of direct experience versus symbolic experience, with the advantages of intensity on the one hand and on the other the possibility of embracing a greater range of possible ideas and sensations by relying on symbolic representations. Extensive basic research will probably be necessary before hedonomics can be put to work in marketing or for the enrichment of human life through other channels.

This paper barely suffices to sketch the analytical framework for marketing. It leaves out much of the area of executive decision-making in marketing on such matters as the weighing of uncertainties and the acceptance of risk in the commitment of resources. It leaves out market planning which is rapidly becoming a systematic discipline centering in the possibilities for economizing time and space as well as resources. It leaves out all but the most casual references to advertising and demand formation. Advertising is certainly one of the most difficult of marketing functions to embrace within a single analytical framework. It largely ignores the developing technology of physical distribution. Hopefully what it does accomplish is to show how the essentially economic problems of marketing may yield to a more comprehensive approach drawing on the basic social sciences for techniques and enriched perspective.

3

Peter F. Drucker

Marketing and Economic Development

MARKETING AS A BUSINESS DISCIPLINE

The distinguished pioneer of marketing, whose memory we honor today, was largely instrumental in developing marketing as a systematic business discipline – in teaching us how to go about, in an orderly, purposeful and planned way to find and create customers; to identify and define markets; to create new ones and promote them; to integrate customers' needs, wants, and preferences, and the intellectual and creative capacity and skills of an industrial society, toward the design of new and better products and of new distributive concepts and processes.

On this contribution and similar ones of other Founding Fathers of marketing during the last half century rests the rapid emergence of marketing as perhaps the most advanced, certainly the most "scientific" of all functional business disciplines.

But Charles Coolidge Parlin also contributed as a Founding Father toward the development of marketing as a *social discipline.* He helped give us the awareness, the concepts, and the tools that make us understand marketing as a dynamic process of society through which business enterprise is integrated productively with society's purposes and human values. It is in marketing, as we now understand it, that we satisfy individual and social values, needs, and wants – be it through producing goods, supplying services, fostering innovation, or creating satisfaction. Marketing, as we have come to understand it, has its focus on the cus-

Reprinted from the *Journal of Marketing*, published by the American Marketing Association (January, 1958), pp. 252–259. This article is based on the Charles Coolidge Parlin Memorial Lecture sponsored by the Philadelphia Chapter of the American Marketing Association in 1957.

Peter F. Drucker, an internationally recognized management consultant and professor at Claremont Graduate School, is perhaps best known for his widely read management books, including Managing for Results *and* Management: Tasks, Responsibilities, Practices. *A native of Vienna, he holds an LL.D. degree from the University of Frankfurt and honorary degrees from two American universities and from one in Japan.*

tomer, that is, on the individual making decisions within a social structure and within a personal and social value system. Marketing is thus the process through which economy is integrated into society to serve human needs.

I am not competent to speak about marketing in the first sense, marketing as a functional discipline of business. I am indeed greatly concerned with marketing in this meaning. One could not be concerned, as I am, with the basic institutions of industrial society in general and with the management of business enterprise in particular, without a deep and direct concern with marketing. But in this field I am a consumer of marketing alone – albeit a heavy one. I am not capable of making a contribution. I would indeed be able to talk about the wants and needs I have which I, as a consumer of marketing, hope that you, the men of marketing, will soon supply: – a theory of pricing, for instance, that can serve, as true theories should, as the foundation for actual pricing decisions and for an understanding of price behavior; or a consumer-focused concept and theory of competition. But I could not produce any of these "new products" of marketing which we want. I cannot contribute myself. To use marketing language, I am not even "effective demand," in these fields as yet.

THE ROLE OF MARKETING

I shall today in my remarks confine myself to the second meaning in which marketing has become a discipline: The role of marketing in economy and society. And I shall single out as my focus the role of marketing in the economic development, especially of underdeveloped "growth" countries.

My thesis is very briefly as follows. Marketing occupies a critical role in respect to the development of such "growth" areas. Indeed marketing is the most important "multiplier" of such development. It is in itself in every one of these areas the least developed, the most backward part of the economic system. Its development, above all others, makes possible economic integration and the fullest utilization of whatever assets and productive capacity an economy already possesses. It mobilizes latent economic energy. It contributes to the greatest needs: that for the rapid development of entrepreneurs and managers, and at the same time it may be the easiest area of managerial work to get going. The reason is that, thanks to men like Charles Coolidge Parlin, it is the most systematized and, therefore, the most learnable and the most teachable of all areas of business management and entrepreneurship.

INTERNATIONAL AND INTERRACIAL INEQUALITY

Looking at this world of ours, we see some essentially new facts.

For the first time in man's history the whole world is united and unified. This may seem a strange statement in view of the conflicts and threats of suicidal wars that scream at us from every headline. But conflict has always been with us. What is new is that today all of mankind shares the same vision, the same objective, the same goal, the same hope, and believes in the same tools. This vision might, in gross over-simplification, be called "industrialization."

It is the belief that it is possible for man to improve his economic lot through systematic, purposeful, and directed effort – individually as well as for an entire society. It is the belief that we have the tools at our disposal – the technological, the conceptual, and the social tools – to enable man to raise himself, through his own efforts, at least to a level that we in this country would consider poverty, but which for most of our world would be almost unbelievable luxury.

And this is an irreversible new fact. It has

been made so by these true agents of revolution in our times: the new tools of communication – the dirt road, the truck, and the radio, which have penetrated even the furthest, most isolated and most primitive community.

This is new, and cannot be emphasized too much and too often. It is both a tremendous vision and a tremendous danger in that catastrophe must result if it cannot be satisfied, at least to a modest degree.

But at the same time we have a new, unprecedented danger, that of international and interracial inequality. We on the North American continent are a mere tenth of the world population, including our Canadian friends and neighbors. But we have at least 75 per cent of the world income. And the 75 per cent of the world population whose income is below $100 per capita a year receive together perhaps no more than 10 per cent of the world's income. This is inequality of income, as great as anything the world has ever seen. It is accompanied by very high equality of income in the developed countries, especially in ours where we are in the process of proving that an industrial society does not have to live in extreme tension between the few very rich and the many very poor as lived all earlier societies of man. But what used to be national inequality and economic tension is now rapidly becoming international (and unfortunately also interracial) inequality and tension.

This is also brand new. In the past there were tremendous differences between societies and cultures: in their beliefs, their concepts, their ways of life, and their knowledge. The Frankish knight who went on Crusade was an ignorant and illiterate boor according to the standards of the polished courtiers of Constantinople or of his Moslem enemies. But economically his society and theirs were exactly alike. They had the same sources of income, the same productivity of labor, the same forms and channels of investment, the same economic institutions, and the same distribution of income and wealth. Economically the Frankish knight, however much a barbarian he appeared, was at home in the societies of the East; and so was his serf. Both fitted in immediately and without any difficulty.

And this has been the case of all societies that went above the level of purely primitive tribe.

The inequality in our world today, however, between nations and races, is therefore a new – and a tremendously dangerous – phenomenon.

What we are engaged in today is essentially a race between the promise of economic development and the threat of international worldwide class war. The economic development is the opportunity of this age. The class war is the danger. Both are new. Both are indeed so new that most of us do not even see them as yet. But they are the essential economic realities of this industrial age of ours. And whether we shall realize the opportunity or succumb to danger will largely decide not only the economic future of this world – it may largely decide its spiritual, its intellectual, its political, and its social future.

SIGNIFICANCE OF MARKETING

Marketing is central in this new situation. For marketing is one of our most potent levers to convert the danger into the opportunity.

To understand this we must ask: What do we mean by "under-developed"?

The first answer is, of course, that we mean areas of very low income. But income is, after all, a result. It is a result first of extreme agricultural over-population in which the great bulk of the people have to find a living on the land which, as a result, cannot even produce enough food to feed them, let alone produce a surplus. It is certainly a result of low productivity. And both, in a vicious circle, mean that there is not enough capital for investment and very low productivity of what is being invested – owing largely to misdirection of investment into unessential and unproductive channels.

All this we know today and understand. Indeed we have learned during the last few years a very great deal both about the structure of an under-developed economy and about the theory and dynamics of economic development.

What we tend to forget, however, is that the essential aspect of an "under-developed" economy and the factor of absence which keeps it "under-developed," is the inability to organize economic efforts and energies, to bring together resources, wants, and capacities, and so to convert a self-limiting static system into creative, self-generating organic growth.

And this is where marketing comes in.

Lack of Development in "Under-developed" Countries

First, in every "under-developed" country I know of, marketing is the most under-developed – or the least developed – part of the economy, if only because of the strong, pervasive prejudice against the middle-man.

As a result, these countries are stunted by inability to make effective use of the little they have. Marketing might by itself go far toward changing the entire economic tone of the existing system – without any change in methods of production, distribution of population, or of income.

It would make the producers capable of producing marketable products by providing them with standards, with quality demands, and with specifications for their product. It would make the product capable of being brought to markets instead of perishing on the way. And it would make the consumer capable of discrimination, that is, of obtaining the greatest value for his very limited purchasing power.

In every one of these countries, marketing profits are characteristically low. Indeed, the people engaged in marketing barely eke out a subsistence living. And "mark-ups" are minute by our standards. But marketing costs are outrageously high. The waste in distribution and marketing, if only from spoilage or from the accumulation of unsalable inventories that clog the shelves for years, has to be seen to be believed. And marketing service is by and large all but non-existent.

What is needed in any "growth" country to make economic development realistic, and at the same time produce a vivid demonstration of what economic development can produce, is a marketing system: – a system of physical distribution, a financial system to make possible the distribution of goods, and finally actual marketing, that is, an actual system of integrating wants, needs, and purchasing power of the consumer with capacity and resources of production.

This need is largely masked today because marketing is so often confused with the traditional "trader and merchant" of which every one of these countries has more than enough. It would be one of our most important contributions to the development of "under-developed" countries to get across the fact that marketing is something quite different.

It would be basic to get across the triple function of marketing – the function of crystallizing and directing demand for maximum productive effectiveness and efficiency; the function of guiding production purposefully toward maximum consumer satisfaction and consumer value; the function of creating discrimination that then gives rewards to those who really contribute excellence, and that then also penalizes the monopolist, the slothful, or those who only want to take but do not want to contribute or to risk.

Utilization by the Entrepreneur

Marketing is also the most easily accessible "multiplier" of managers and entrepreneurs in an "under-developed" growth area. And managers and entrepreneurs are the foremost need of these countries. In the first place, "economic development" is not a force of nature. It is the result of the action, the purposeful, responsible, risk-taking action, of men as entrepreneurs and managers.

Certainly it is the entrepreneur and manager who alone can convey to the people of these countries an understanding of what economic development means and how it can be achieved.

Marketing can convert latent demand into effective demand. It cannot, by itself, create purchasing power. But it can uncover and channel all purchasing power that exists. It can, therefore, create rapidly the conditions for a much higher level of economic activity than existed before, can create the opportunities for the entrepreneur.

It then can create the stimulus for the development of modern, responsible, professional management by creating opportunity for the producer who knows how to plan, how to organize, how to lead people, how to innovate.

In most of these countries markets are of necessity very small. They are too small to make it possible to organize distribution for a single-product line in any effective manner. As a result, without a marketing organization, many products for which there is an adequate demand at a reasonable price cannot be distributed; or worse, they can be produced and distributed only under monopoly conditions. A marketing system is needed which serves as the joint and common channel for many producers if any of them is to be able to come into existence and to stay in existence.

This means in effect that a marketing system in the "under-developed" countries is the *creator of small business*, is the only way in which a man of vision and daring can become a businessman and an entrepreneur himself. This is thereby also the only way in which a true middle class can develop in the countries in which the habit of investment in productive enterprise has still to be created.

Developer of Standards

Marketing in an "under-developed" country is the developer of standards—of standards for product and service as well as of standards of conduct, of integrity, of reliability, of foresight, and of concern for the basic long-range impact of decisions on the customer, the supplier, the economy, and the society.

Rather than go on making theoretical statements let me point to one illustration: The impact Sears Roebuck has had on several countries of Latin America. To be sure, the countries of Latin America in which Sears operates—Mexico, Brazil, Cuba, Venezuela, Colombia, and Peru—are not "under-developed" in the same sense in which Indonesia or the Congo are "under-developed." Their average income, although very low by our standards, is at least two times, perhaps as much as four or five times, that of the truly "under-developed" countries in which the bulk of mankind still live. Still in every respect except income level these Latin American countries are at best "developing." And they have all the problems of economic development—perhaps even in more acute form than the countries of Asia and Africa, precisely because their development has been so fast during the last ten years.

It is also true that Sears in these countries is not a "low-price" merchandiser. It caters to the middle class in the richer of these countries, and to the upper middle class in the poorest of these countries. Incidentally, the income level of these groups is still lower than that of the worker in the industrial sector of our economy.

Still Sears is a mass-marketer even in Colombia or Peru. What is perhaps even more important, it is applying in these "under-developed" countries exactly the same policies and principles it applies in this country, carries substantially the same merchandise (although most of it produced in the countries themselves), and applies the same concepts of marketing it uses in Indianapolis or Philadelphia. Its impact and experience are, therefore, a fair test of what marketing principles, marketing knowledge, and marketing techniques can achieve.

The impact of this one American business which does not have more than a mere handful of stores in these countries and handles no more than a small fraction of the total retail business of these countries is truly amazing. In the first place, Sears' latent purchasing power has fast become actual purchasing power. Or to put it less theoretically, people have begun to organize their buying and to go out for value in what they do buy.

Secondly, by the very fact that it builds one store in one city, Sears forces a revolution in retailing throughout the whole surrounding area. It forces store modernization. It forces consumer credit. It forces a different attitude toward the customer, toward the store clerk, toward the supplier, and toward the merchandise itself. It forces other retailers to adopt modern methods of pricing, of inventory control, of training, of window display, and what have you.

The greatest impact Sears has had, however, is the multiplication of new industrial business for which Sears creates a marketing channel. Because it has had to sell goods manufactured in these countries rather than import them (if only because of the foreign exchange restrictions), Sears has been instrumental in getting established literally hundreds of new manufacturers making goods which, a few years ago, could not be made in the country, let alone be sold in adequate quantity. Simply to satisfy its own marketing needs, Sears has had to insist on standards of workmanship, quality, and delivery – that is, on standards of production management, of technical management, and above all of the management of people – which, in a few short years, have advanced the art and science of management in these countries by at least a generation.

I hardly need to add that Sears is not in Latin America for reasons of philanthropy, but because it is good and profitable business with extraordinary growth potential. In other words, Sears is in Latin America because marketing is the major opportunity in a "growth economy" – precisely because its absence is a major economic gap and the greatest need.

The Discipline of Marketing

Finally, marketing is critical in economic development because marketing has become so largely systematized, so largely both learnable and teachable. It is the discipline among all our business disciplines that has advanced the furthest.

I do not forget for a moment how much we still have to learn in marketing. But we should also not forget that most of what we have learned so far we have learned in a form in which we can express it in general concepts, in valid principles and, to a substantial degree, in quantifiable measurements. This, above all others, was the achievement of that generation to whom Charles Coolidge Parlin was leader and inspiration.

A critical factor in this world of ours is the learnability and teachability of what it means to be an entrepreneur and manager. For it is the entrepreneur and the manager who alone can cause economic development to happen. The world needs them, therefore, in very large numbers; and it needs them fast.

Obviously this need cannot be supplied by our supplying entrepreneurs and managers, quite apart from the fact that we hardly have the surplus. Money we can supply. Technical assistance we can supply, and should supply more. But the supply of men we can offer to the people in the "under-developed" countries is of necessity a very small one.

The demand is also much too urgent for it

to be supplied by slow evolution through experience, or through dependence on the emergence of "naturals." The danger that lies in the inequality today between the few countries that have and the great many countries that have not is much too great to permit a wait of centuries. Yet it can take centuries if we depend on experience and slow evolution for the supply of entrepreneurs and managers adequate to the needs of a modern society.

There is only one way in which man has ever been able to short-cut experience, to telescope development, in other words, to *learn something*. That way is to have available the distillate of experience and skill in the form of knowledge, of concepts, of generalization, of measurement–in the form of *discipline*, in other words.

THE DISCIPLINE OF ENTREPRENEURSHIP

Many of us today are working on the fashioning of such a discipline of entrepreneurship and management. Maybe we are further along than most of us realize.

Certainly in what has come to be called "Operation Research and Synthesis" we have the first beginnings of a systematic approach to the entrepreneurial task of purposeful risk-taking and innovation–so far only an approach, but a most promising one, unless indeed we become so enamored with the gadgets and techniques as to forget purpose and aim.

We are at the beginning perhaps also of an understanding of the basic problems of organizing people of diversified and highly advanced skill and judgment together in one effective organization, although again no one so far would, I am convinced, claim more for us than that we have begun at last to ask intelligent questions.

But marketing, although it only covers one functional area in the field, has something that can be called a discipline. It has developed general concepts, that is, theories that explain a multitude of phenomena in simple statements. It even has measurements that record "facts" rather than opinions. In marketing, therefore, we already possess a learnable and teachable approach to this basic and central problem not only of the "under-developed" countries but of all countries. All of us have today the same survival stake in economic development. The risk and danger of international and interracial inequality are simply too great.

Marketing is obviously not a cure-all, not a panacea. It is only one thing we need. But it answers a critical need. At the same time marketing is most highly developed.

Indeed without marketing as the hinge on which to turn, economic development will almost have to take the totalitarian form. A totalitarian system can be defined economically as one in which economic development is being attempted without marketing, indeed as one in which marketing is suppressed. Precisely because it first looks at the values and wants of the individual, and because it then develops people to act purposefully and responsibly–that is, because of its effectiveness in developing a free economy–marketing is suppressed in a totalitarian system. If we want economic development in freedom and responsibility, we have to build it on the development of marketing.

In the new and unprecedented world we live in, a world which knows both a new unity of vision and growth and a new and most dangerous cleavage, marketing has a special and central role to play. This role goes beyond "getting the stuff out the back door," beyond "getting the most sales with the least cost," beyond "the optimal integration of our values and wants as customers, citizens, and persons, with our productive resources and intellectual achievements"–the role marketing plays in a developed society.

In a developing economy, marketing is, of course, all of this. But in addition, in an economy that is striving to break the age-old bondage of man to misery, want, and destitution, marketing is also the catalyst for the transmutation of latent resources into actual resources, of desires into accomplishments, and the development of responsible economic leaders and informed economic citizens.

4 Robert J. Keith

The Marketing Revolution

The consumer, not the company, is in the middle.

In today's economy the consumer, the man or woman who buys the product, is at the absolute dead center of the business universe. Companies revolve around the customer, not the other way around.

Growing acceptance of this consumer concept has had, and will have, far-reaching implications for business, achieving a virtual revolution in economic thinking. As the concept gains ever greater acceptance, marketing is emerging as the most important single function in business.

A REVOLUTION IN SCIENCE

A very apt analogy can be drawn with another revolution, one that goes back to the sixteenth century. At that time astronomers had great difficulty predicting the movements of the heavenly bodies. Their charts and computations and celestial calendars enabled them to estimate the approximate positions of the planets on any given date. But their calculations were never exact—there was always a variance.

Then a Polish scientist named Nicolaus Copernicus proposed a very simple answer to the problem. If, he proposed, we assume that the sun, and not the earth, is at the center of our system, and that the earth moves around the sun instead of the sun moving around the earth, all our calculations will prove correct.

The Pole's idea raised a storm of controversy. The earth, everyone knew, was at the center of the universe. But another scientist named Galileo put the theory to test—and it worked. The result was a complete upheaval in scientific and philosophic thought. The effects of Copernicus's revolutionary idea are still being felt today.

Reprinted from the *Journal of Marketing*, published by the American Marketing Association (January, 1960), pp. 35-38.

The late Robert J. Keith was president of The Pillsbury Company and a director of Pillsbury and other national companies. During his 25 years with Pillsbury, his responsibility centered around the grocery products division and the refrigerated-products division.

A REVOLUTION IN MARKETING

In much the same way American business in general – and Pillsbury in particular – is undergoing a revolution of its own today: a marketing revolution.

This revolution stems from the same idea stated in the opening sentence of this article. No longer is the company at the center of the business universe. Today the customer is at the center.

Our attention has shifted from problems of production to problems of marketing, from the product we *can* make to the product the consumer *wants* us to make, from the company itself to the market place.

The marketing revolution has only begun. It is reasonable to expect that its implications will grow in the years to come, and that lingering effects will be felt a century, or more than one century, from today.

So far the theory has only been advanced, tested, and generally proved correct. As more and more businessmen grasp the concept, and put it to work, our economy will become more truly marketing oriented.

PILLSBURY'S PATTERN: FOUR ERAS

Here is the way the marketing revolution came about at Pillsbury. The experience of this company has followed a typical pattern. There has been nothing unique, and each step in the evolution of the marketing concept has been taken in a way that is more meaningful because the steps are, in fact, typical.

Today in our company the marketing concept finds expression in the simple statement, "Nothing happens at Pillsbury until a sale is made." This statement represents basic reorientation on the part of our management. For, not too many years ago, the ordering of functions in our business placed finances first, production second, and sales last.

How did we arrive at our present point of view? Pillsbury's progress in the marketing revolution divides neatly into four separate eras – eras which parallel rather closely the classic pattern of development in the marketing revolution.

1st ERA – PRODUCTION ORIENTED

First came the era of manufacturing. It began with the formation of the company in 1869 and continued into the 1930s. It is significant that the *idea* for the formation of our company came from the *availability* of high-quality wheat and the *proximity* of water power – and not from the availability and proximity of growing major market areas, or the demand for better, less expensive, more convenient flour products.

Of course, these elements were potentially present. But the two major elements which fused in the mind of Charles A. Pillsbury and prompted him to invest his modest capital in a flour mill were, on the one hand, wheat, and, on the other hand, water power. His principal concern was with production, not marketing.

His thought and judgment were typical of the business thinking of his day, and such thinking was adequate and proper for the times.

Our company philosophy in this era might have been stated this way: "We are professional flour millers. Blessed with a supply of the finest North American wheat, plenty of water power, and excellent milling machinery, we produce flour of the highest quality. Our basic function is to mill high-quality flour, and of course (and almost incidentally) we must hire salesmen to sell it, just as we hire accountants to keep our books."

The young company's first new product reveals an interesting example of the thinking of this era. The product was middlings, the bran left over after milling. Millfeed, as the product came to be known, proved a valuable product because it was an excellent nutrient for cattle. But the impetus to launch the new product came not from a consideration of the nutritional needs of cattle or a marketing analysis. It came primarily from the desire to dispose of a by-product! The new product division was production oriented, not marketing oriented.

2nd ERA – SALES ORIENTED

In the 1930s Pillsbury moved into its second era of development as a marketing company. This was the era of sales. For the first time we began to be highly conscious of the consumer, her wants, and her prejudices, as a key factor in the business equation. We established a commercial research department to provide us with facts about the market.

We also became more aware of the importance of our dealers, the wholesale and retail grocers who provided a vital link in our chain of distribution from the mill to the home. Knowing that consumers and dealers as well were vital to the company's success, we could no longer simply mark them down as unknowns in our figuring. With this realization, we took the first step along the road to becoming a marketing company.

Pillsbury's thinking in this second era could be summed up like this: "We are a flour-milling company, manufacturing a number of products for the consumer market. We must have a first-rate sales organization which can dispose of all the products we can make at a favorable price. We must back up this sales force with consumer advertising and market intelligence. We want our salesmen and our dealers to have all the tools they need for moving the output of our plants to the consumer."

Still not a marketing philosophy, but we were getting closer.

3rd ERA – MARKETING ORIENTED

It was at the start of the present decade that Pillsbury entered the marketing era. The amazing growth of our consumer business as the result of introducing baking mixes provided the immediate impetus. But the groundwork had been laid by key men who developed our sales concepts in the middle forties.

With the new cake mixes, products of our research program, ringing up sales on the cash register, and with the realization that research and production could produce literally hundreds of new and different products, we faced for the first time the necessity for selecting the best new products. We needed a set of criteria for selecting the kind of products we would manufacture. We needed an organization to establish and maintain these criteria, and for attaining maximum sale of the products we did select.

We needed, in fact, to build into our company a new management function which would direct and control all the other corporate functions from procurement to production to advertising to sales. This function was marketing. Our solution was to establish the present marketing department.

This department developed the criteria which we would use in determining which products to market. *And these criteria were, and are, nothing more nor less than those of the consumer herself.* We moved the mountain out to find out what Mahomet, and Mrs. Mahomet, wanted. The company's purpose was no longer to mill flour, nor to manufacture a wide variety of products, but to satisfy the needs and desires, both actual and potential, of our customers.

If we were to restate our philosophy during the past decade as simply as possible, it would read: "We make and sell products for consumers."

The business universe, we realized, did not have room at the center for Pillsbury or any other company or groups of companies. It was already occupied by the customers.

This is the concept at the core of the marketing revolution. How did we put it to work for Pillsbury?

The Brand-manager Concept

The first move was to transform our small advertising department into a marketing department. The move involved far more than changing the name on organizational charts. It required the introduction of a new, and vitally important, organizational concept – the brand-manager concept.

The brand-manager idea is the very backbone of marketing at Pillsbury. The man who bears the title, brand manager, has total accountability for results. He directs the marketing of his product as if it was his own business. Production does its job, and finance keeps the profit figures. Otherwise, the brand manager has total responsibility for marketing his product. This responsibility encompasses pricing, commercial research, competitive activity, home service and publicity coordination, legal details, budgets, advertising plans, sales promotion, and execution of plans. The brand manager must think first, last, and always of his sales target, the consumer.

Marketing permeates the entire organization. Marketing plans and executes the sale – all the way from the inception of the product idea, through its development and distribution, to the customer purchase. Marketing begins and ends with the consumer. New product ideas are conceived after careful study of her wants and needs, her likes and dislikes. Then marketing takes the idea and marshals all the forces of the corporation to translate the idea into product and the product into sales.

In the early days of the company, consumer orientation did not seem so important. The company made flour, and flour was a staple – no one would question the availability of a market. Today we must determine whether the American housewife will buy lemon pudding cake in preference to orange angel food. The variables in the equation have multiplied just as the number of products on the grocers' shelves have multiplied from a hundred or so into many thousands.

When we first began operating under this new marketing concept, we encountered the problems which always accompany any major reorientation. Our people were young and frankly immature in some areas of business; but they were men possessed of an idea and they fought for it. The idea was almost too powerful. The marketing concept proved its worth in sales, but it upset many of the internal balances of the corporation. Marketing-oriented decisions resulted in peaks and valleys in production, schedules, labor, and inventories. But the system worked. It worked better and better as maverick marketing men became motivated toward tonnage and profit.

4th ERA – MARKETING CONTROL

Today marketing is coming into its own. Pillsbury stands on the brink of its fourth major era in the marketing revolution.

Basically, the philosophy of this fourth era can be summarized this way: "We are moving from a company which has the marketing concept to a marketing company."

Marketing today sets company operating policy short-term. It will come to influence long-range policy more and more. Where today consumer research, technical research, procurement, production, advertising, and sales swing into action under the broad canopy established by marketing, tomorrow capital and financial planning, ten-year volume and profit goals will also come under the aegis of marketing. More than any other function, marketing must be tied to top management.

Today our marketing people know more about inventories than anyone in top management. Tomorrow's marketing man must know capital financing and the implications of marketing planning on long-range profit forecasting.

Today technical research receives almost all of its guidance and direction from marketing. Tomorrow marketing will assume a more creative function in the advertising area, both in terms of ideas and media selection.

Changes in the Future

The marketing revolution has only begun. There are still those who resist its basic idea, just as there are always those who will resist change in business, government, or any other form of human institution.

As the marketing revolution gains momentum, there will be more changes. The concept of the customer at the center will remain valid; but business must adjust to the shifting tastes and likes and desires and needs which have always characterized the American consumer.

For many years the geographical center of the United States lay in a small Kansas town. Then a new state, Alaska, came along, and the center shifted to the north and west. Hawaii was admitted to the Union and the geographical midpoint took another jump to the west. In very much the same way, modern business must anticipate the restless shifting of buying attitudes, as customer preferences move north, south, east, or west from a liquid center. There is nothing static about the marketing revolution, and that is part of its fascination. The old order has changed, yielding place to the new – but the new order will have its quota of changes, too.

At Pillsbury, as our fourth era progresses, marketing will become the basic motivating force for the entire corporation. Soon it will be true that every activity of the corporation – from finance to sales to production – is aimed at satisfying the needs and desires of the consumer. When that stage of development is reached, the marketing revolution will be complete.

Philip Kotler
Sidney J. Levy

5

Broadening the Concept of Marketing

The term *marketing* connotes to most people a function peculiar to business firms. Marketing is seen as the task of finding and stimulating buyers for the firm's output. It involves product development, pricing, distribution, and communication; and in the more progressive firms, continuous attention to the changing needs of customers and the development of new products, with product modifications and services to meet these needs. But whether marketing is viewed in the old sense of "pushing" products or in the new sense of "customer satisfaction engineering," it is almost always viewed and discussed as a business activity.

It is the authors' contention that marketing is a pervasive societal activity that goes considerably beyond the selling of toothpaste, soap, and steel. Political contests remind us that candidates are marketed as well as soap; student recruitment by colleges reminds us that higher education is marketed; and fund raising reminds us that "causes" are marketed. Yet these areas of marketing are typically ignored by the student of marketing. Or they are treated cursorily as public relations or publicity activities. No attempt is made to incorporate these phenomena in the body proper of marketing thought and theory. No attempt is made to redefine the meaning of product develop-

"Broadening the Concept of Marketing," by Philip Kotler and Sidney J. Levy. Reprinted from the *Journal of Marketing* (January 1969), pp. 10–15, published by the American Marketing Association. This article received the 1969 Alpha Kappa Psi award as outstanding article of the year.
Philip Kotler, Harold T. Martin professor of marketing at Northwestern University, received his Ph.D. in economics from Massachusetts Institute of Technology. He did post doctoral work in mathematics and behavioral sciences at Harvard and the University of Chicago respectively. His articles have appeared in numerous scholarly journals; several have won best article awards. His Marketing Management: Analysis, Planning and Control, *now in its fifth edition, is widely used.*
Sidney J. Levy is professor of marketing at Northwestern University and vice president of Social Research, Inc. He earned his Ph.D. in psychology at the University of Chicago. He is the author of Promotion: A Behavioral View *and many articles. His latest book is* Marketplace Behavior – Its Meaning for Management.

ment, pricing, distribution, and communication in these newer contexts to see if they have a useful meaning. No attempt is made to examine whether the principles of "good" marketing in traditional product areas are transferable to the marketing of services, persons and ideas.

The authors see a great opportunity for marketing people to expand their thinking and to apply their skills to an increasingly interesting range of social activity. The challenge depends on the attention given to it; marketing will either take on a broader social meaning or remain a narrowly defined business activity.

THE RISE OF ORGANIZATIONAL MARKETING

One of the most striking trends in the United States is the increasing amount of society's work being performed by organizations other than business firms. As a society moves beyond the stage where shortages of food, clothing, and shelter are the major problems, it begins to organize to meet other social needs that formerly had been put aside. Business enterprises remain a dominant type of organization, but other types of organizations gain in conspicuousness and in influence. Many of these organizations become enormous and require the same rarefied management skills as traditional business organizations. Managing the United Auto Workers, Defense Department, Ford Foundation, World Bank, Catholic Church, and University of California has become every bit as challenging as managing Proctor and Gamble, General Motors, and General Electric. These non-business organizations have an increasing range of influence, affect as many livelihoods, and occupy as much media prominence as major business firms.

All of these organizations perform the classic business functions. Every organization must perform a financial function insofar as money must be raised, managed, and budgeted according to sound business principles. Every organization must perform a production function in that it must conceive of the best way of arranging inputs to produce the outputs of the organization. Every organization must perform a personnel function in that people must be hired, trained, assigned, and promoted in the course of the organization's work. Every organization must perform a purchasing function in that it must acquire materials in an efficient way through comparing and selecting sources of supply.

When we come to the marketing function, it is also clear that every organization performs marketing-like activities whether or not they are recognized as such. Several examples can be given.

The police department of a major U.S. city, concerned with the poor image it has among an important segment of its population, developed a campaign to "win friends and influence people." One highlight of this campaign is a "visit your police station" day in which tours are conducted to show citizens the daily operations of the police department, including the crime laboratories, police lineups, and cells. The police department also sends officers to speak at public schools and carries out a number of other activities to improve its community relations.

Most museum directors interpret their primary responsibility as "the proper preservation of an artistic heritage for posterity."[1] As a result, for many people museums are cold marble mausoleums that house miles of relics that soon give way to yawns and tired feet. Although museum attendance in the United States advances each year, a large number of citizens are uninterested in museums. Is this indifference due to failure in the manner of presenting what museums have to offer? This nagging question led the new director of the Metropolitan Museum of Art to broaden the museum's appeal through sponsoring contemporary art shows and "happenings." His marketing philosophy of museum management led to substantial increases in the Met's attendance.

The public school system in Oklahoma City sorely needed more public support and funds to prevent a deterioration of facilities and exodus of teachers. It recently resorted to television programming to dramatize the work the public schools were doing to fight the high school dropout problem, to develop new teaching techniques, and to enrich the children. Although an expensive medium, television quickly reached large numbers of parents whose response and interest were tremendous.

Nations also resort to international marketing campaigns to get across important points about themselves to the citizens of other countries. The junta of Greek colonels who seized power in Greece in 1967 found the international publicity surrounding their cause to be extremely unfavorable and potentially disruptive of international recognition. They hired a major New York public relations firm and soon full-page newspaper ads appeared carrying the headline "Greece Was Saved From Communism," detailing in small print why the takeover was necessary for the stability of Greece and the world.[2]

An anti-cigarette group in Canada is trying to press the Canadian legislature to ban cigarettes on the grounds that they are harmful to health. There is widespread support for this cause but the organization's funds are limited, particularly measured against the huge advertising resources of the cigarette industry. The group's problem is to find effective ways to make a little money go a long way in persuading influential legislators of the need for discouraging cigarette consumption. This group has come up with several ideas for marketing anti-smoking to Canadians, including television spots, a paperback book featuring pictures of cancer and heart disease patients, and legal research on company liability for the smoker's loss of health.

What concepts are common to these and many other possible illustrations of organizational marketing? All of these organizations are concerned about their "product" in the eyes of certain "consumers" and are seeking to find "tools" for furthering their acceptance. Let us consider each of these concepts in general organizational terms.

Products

Every organization produces a "product" of at least one of the following types:

Physical products. "Product" first brings to mind everyday items like soap, clothes, and food, and extends to cover millions of *tangible* items that have a market value and are available for purchase.

Services. Services are *intangible* goods that are subject to market transaction such as tours, insurance, consultation, hairdos, and banking.

Persons. Personal marketing is an endemic *human* activity, from the employee trying to impress his boss to the statesman trying to win the support of the public. With the advent of mass communications, the marketing of persons has been turned over to professionals. Hollywood stars have their press agents, political candidates their advertising agencies, and so on.

Organizations. Many organizations spend a great deal of time marketing themselves. The Republican Party has invested considerable thought and resources in trying to develop a modern look. The American Medical Association decided recently that it needed to launch a campaign to improve the image of the American doctor.[3] Many charitable organizations and universities see selling their *organization* as their primary responsibility.

Ideas. Many organizations are mainly in the business of selling *ideas* to the larger society. Population organizations are trying to sell the idea of birth control, and the Women's Christian Temperance Union is still trying to sell the idea of prohibition.

Thus the "product" can take many forms, and this is the first crucial point in the case for broadening the concept of marketing.

Consumers

The second crucial point is that organizations must deal with many groups that are interested in their products and can make a difference in its success. It is vitally important to the organization's success that it be sensitive to, serve, and satisfy these groups. One set of groups can be called the *suppliers. Suppliers* are those who provide the management group with the inputs necessary to perform its work and develop its product effectively. Suppliers include employees, vendors of the materials, banks, advertising agencies, and consultants.

The other set of groups are the *consumers* of the organization's product, of which four subgroups can be distinguished. The *clients* are those who are the immediate consumers of the organization's product. The clients of a business firm are its buyers and potential buyers; of a service organization those receiving the services, such as the needy (from the Salvation Army) or the sick (from County Hospital); and of a protective or a primary organization, the members themselves. The second group is the *trustees* or *directors*, those who are vested with the legal authority and responsibility for the organization, oversee the management, and enjoy a variety of benefits from the "product." The third group is the active *publics* that take a specific interest in the organization. For a business firm, the active publics include consumer rating groups, governmental agencies, and pressure groups of various kinds. For a university, the active publics include alumni and friends of the university, foundations, and city fathers. Finally, the fourth consumer group is the *general public*. These are all the people who might develop attitudes toward the organization that might affect its conduct in some way. Organizational marketing concerns the programs designed by management to create satisfactions and favorable attitudes in the organization's four consuming groups: clients, trustees, active publics, and general public.

Marketing Tools

Students of business firms spend much time studying the various tools under the firm's control that affect product acceptance: product improvement, pricing, distribution, and communication. All of these tools have counterpart applications to nonbusiness organizational activity.

Nonbusiness organizations to various degrees engage in product improvement, especially when they recognize the competition they face from other organizations. Thus, over the years churches have added a host of nonreligious activities to their basic religious activities to satisfy members seeking other bases of human fellowship. Universities keep updating their curricula and adding new student services in an attempt to make the educational experience relevant to the students. Where they have failed to do this, students have sometimes organized their own courses and publications, or have expressed their dissatisfaction in organized protest. Government agencies such as license bureaus, police forces, and taxing bodies are often not responsive to the public because of monopoly status; but even here citizens have shown an increasing readiness to protest mediocre services, and more alert bureaucracies have shown a growing interest in reading a user's needs and developing the required product services.

All organizations face the problem of pricing their products and services so that they cover costs. Churches charge dues, Universities charge tuition, governmental agencies charge fees, fund-raising organizations send out bills. Very often specific product charges are not sufficient to meet the organization's budget, and it must rely on gifts and surcharges to make up the difference. Opinions vary as to how much the users should be charged for the individual services and how much should be made up through general collection. If the university increases its tuition, it will have to face losing some students and putting more students on scholarship. If the hospital raises its charges to cover rising costs and additional services, it may provoke a reaction from the community. All organizations face complex pricing issues although not all of them understand good pricing practice.

Distribution is a central concern to the manufacturer seeking to make his goods conveniently accessible to buyers. Distribution also can be an important marketing decision area for nonbusiness organizations. A city's public library has to consider the best means of making its books available to the public. Should it establish one large library with an extensive collection of books, or several neighborhood branch libraries with duplication of books? Should it use bookmobiles that bring the books to the customers instead of relying exclusively on the customers coming to the books? Should it distribute through school libraries? Similarly the police department of a city must think through the problem of distributing its protective services efficiently through the community. It has to determine how much protective service to allocate to different neighborhoods; the respective merits of squad cars, motorcycles, and foot patrolmen; and the positioning of emergency phones.

Customer communication is an essential activity of all organizations although many nonmarketing organizations often fail to accord it the importance it deserves. Managements of many organizations think they have fully met their communication responsibilities by setting up advertising and/or public relations departments. They fail to realize that *everything about an organization talks.* Customers form impressions of an organization from its physical facilities, employees, officers, stationery, and a hundred other company surrogates. Only when this is appreciated do the members of the organization recognize that they all are in marketing, whatever else they do. With this understanding they can assess realistically the impact of their activities on the consumers.

CONCEPTS FOR EFFECTIVE MARKETING MANAGEMENT IN NONBUSINESS ORGANIZATIONS

Although all organizations have products, markets, and marketing tools, the art and science of effective marketing management have reached their highest state of development in the business type of organization. Business organizations depend on customer goodwill for survival and have generally learned how to sense and cater to their needs effectively. As other types of organizations recognize their marketing roles, they will turn increasingly to the body of marketing principles worked out by business organizations and adapt them to their own situations.

What are the main principles of effective marketing management as they appear in most forward-looking business organizations? Nine concepts stand out as crucial in guiding the marketing effort of a business organization.

Generic Product Definition

Business organizations have increasingly recognized the value of placing a broad definition on their products, one that emphasizes the basic customer need(s) being served. A modern soap company recognizes that its basic product is cleaning, not soap; a cosmetics company sees its basic product as beauty or hope, not lipsticks and makeup; a publishing company sees its basic product as information, not books.

The same need for a broader definition of its business is incumbent upon nonbusiness organizations if they are to survive and grow. Churches at one time tended to define their product narrowly as that of producing religious services for members. Recently, most churchmen have decided that their basic product is human fellowship. There was a time when educators said that their product was the three R's. Now most of them define their product as education for the whole man. They try to serve the social, emotional, and political needs of young people in addition to intellectual needs.

Target Groups Definition

A generic product definition usually results in defining a very wide market, and it is then necessary for the organization, because of limited resources, to limit its product offering to certain clearly defined groups within the market. Although the generic product of an automobile company is transportation, the company typically sticks to cars, trucks, and buses, and stays away from bicycles, airplanes, and steamships. Furthermore, the manufacturer does not produce every size and shape of car but concentrates on producing a few major types to satisfy certain substantial and specific parts of the market.

In the same way, nonbusiness organizations have to define their target groups carefully. For example, in Chicago the YMCA defines its target groups as men, women and children who want recreational opportunities and are willing to pay $20 or more a year for them. The Chicago Boys Club, on the other hand, defines its target group as poorer boys within the city boundaries who are in want of recreational facilities and can pay $1 a year.

Differentiated Marketing

When a business organization sets out to serve more than one target group, it will be maximally effective by differentiating its product offerings and communications. This is also true for nonbusiness organizations. Fund-raising organizations have recognized the advantage of treating clients, trustees, and various publics in different ways. These groups require differentiated appeals and frequency of solicitation. Labor unions find that they must address different messages to different parties rather than one message to all parties. To the company they may seem unyielding, to the conciliator they may appear willing to compromise, and to the public they seek to appear economically exploited.

Customer Behavior Analysis

Business organizations are increasingly recognizing that customer needs and behavior are not obvious without formal research and analysis; they cannot rely on impressionistic evidence. Soap companies spend hundreds of thousands of dollars each year researching how Mrs. Housewife feels about her laundry, how, when, and where she does her laundry, and what she desires of a detergent.

Fund raising illustrates how an industry has benefited by replacing stereotypes of donors with studies of why people contribute to causes. Fund raisers have learned that people give because they are getting something. Many give to community chests to relieve a sense of guilt because of their elevated state compared to the needy. Many give to medical charities to relieve a sense of fear that they may be struck by a disease whose cure has not yet been found. Some give to feel pride. Fund raisers have stressed the importance of identifying the motives operating in the marketplace of givers as a basis for planning drives.

Differential Advantages

In considering different ways of reaching target groups, an organization is advised to think in terms of seeking a differential advantage. It should consider what elements in its reputation or resources can be exploited to create a special value in the minds of its potential customers. In the same way Zenith has built a reputation for quality and International Harvester a reputation for service, a nonbusiness organization should base its case on some dramatic value that competitive organizations lack. The small island of Nassau can compete against Miami for the tourist trade by advertising the greater dependability of its weather; the Heart Association can compete for funds against the Cancer Society by advertising the amazing strides made in heart research.

Multiple Marketing Tools

The modern business firm relies on a multitude of tools to sell its product, including product improvement, consumer and dealer advertising, salesmen incentive programs, sales promotions, contests, multiple-size offerings, and so forth. Likewise nonbusiness organizations also can reach their audiences in a variety of ways. A church can sustain the interest of its members through discussion groups, newsletters, news releases, campaign drives, annual reports, and retreats. Its "salesmen" include the religious head, the board members, and the present members in terms of attracting potential members. Its advertising includes announcements of weddings, births and deaths, religious pronouncements, and newsworthy developments.

Integrated Marketing Planning

The multiplicity of available marketing tools suggests the desirability of overall coordination so that these tools do not work at cross purposes. Over time, the business firms have placed under a marketing vice-president activities that were previously managed in a semiautonomous fashion, such as sales, advertising, and marketing research. Nonbusiness organizations typically have not integrated their marketing activities. Thus, no single officer in the typical university is given total responsibility for studying the needs and attitudes of clients, trustees, and publics, and undertaking the necessary product development and communication programs to serve these groups. The university administration instead includes a variety of "marketing" positions such as dean of students, director of alumni affairs, director of public relations, and director of development; coordination is often poor.

Continuous Marketing Feedback

Business organizations gather continuous information about changes in the environment and about their own performance. They use their salesmen, research department, specialized research services, and other means to check on the movement of goods, actions of competitors, and feelings of customers to make sure they are progressing along satisfactory lines. Nonbusiness organizations typically are more casual about collecting vital information on how they are doing and what is happening in the marketplace. Universities have been caught off guard by underestimating the magnitude of student grievance and unrest, and so have major cities underestimated the degree to which they were failing to meet the needs of important minority constituencies.

Marketing Audit

Change is a fact of life, although it may proceed almost invisibly on a day-to-day basis. Over a long stretch of time, it might be so fundamental as to threaten organizations that have not provided for periodic reexaminations of their purposes. Organizations can grow set in their ways and unresponsive to new opportunities or problems. Some great American companies are no longer with us because they did not change definitions of their businesses, and their products lost relevance in a changing world. Political parties become unresponsive after they enjoy power for a while and every so often experience a major upset. Many union leaders grow insensitive to new needs and problems until one day they find themselves out of office. For an organization to remain viable, its management must provide for periodic audits of its objectives, resouces, and opportunities. It must reexamine its basic business, target groups, differential advantage, communication channels, and messages in the light of current trends and needs. It might recognize when change is needed and make it before it is too late.

IS ORGANIZATIONAL MARKETING A SOCIALLY USEFUL ACTIVITY?

Modern marketing has two different meanings in the minds of people who use the term. One meaning of marketing conjures up the terms selling, influencing, persuading. Marketing is seen as a huge and increasingly dangerous technology, making it possible to sell persons on buying things, propositions, and causes they either do not want or which are bad for them. This was the indictment in Vance Packard's *Hidden Persuaders* and numerous other social criticisms, with the net effect that a large number of persons think of marketing as immoral or entirely self-seeking in its fundamental premises. They can be counted on to resist the idea of organizational marketing as so much "Madison Avenue."

The other meaning of marketing unfortunately is weaker in the public mind; it is the concept of sensitively *serving and satisfying human needs.* This was the great contribution of the marketing concept that was promulgated in the 1950s, and that concept now counts many business firms as its practitioners. The marketing concept holds that the problem of all business firms in an age of abundance is to develop customer loyalties and satisfaction, and the key to this problem is to focus on the customer's needs.[4] Perhaps the short-run problem of business firms is to sell people on buying the existing products, but the long-run problem is clearly to create the products that people need. By this recognition that effective marketing requires a consumer orientation instead of a product orientation, marketing has taken a new lease on life and tied its economic activity to a higher social purpose.

It is this second side of marketing that provides a useful concept for all organizations. All organizations are formed to serve the interest of particular groups: hospitals serve the sick, schools serve the students, governments serve the citizens, and labor unions serve the members. In the course of evolving, many organizations lose sight of their original mandate, grow hard, and become self-serving. The bureaucratic mentality begins to dominate the original service mentality. Hospitals may become perfunctory in their handling of patients, schools treat their students as nuisances, city bureaucrats behave like petty tyrants toward the citizens, and labor unions try to run instead of serve their members. All of these actions tend to build frustration in the consuming groups. As a result some withdraw meekly from these organizations, accept frustration as part of their condition, and find their satisfactions elsewhere. This used to be the common reaction of ghetto Negroes and college students in the face of indifferent city and university bureaucracies. But new possibilities have arisen, and now the same consumers refuse to withdraw so readily. Organized dissent and protest are seen to be an answer, and many organizations thinking of themselves as responsible have been stunned into recognizing that they have lost touch with their constituencies. They had grown unresponsive.

Where does marketing fit into this picture? Marketing is that function of the organization that can keep in constant touch with the organization's consumers, read their needs, develop "products" that meet these needs, and build a program of communications to express the organization's purposes. Certainly selling and influencing will be large parts of organizational marketing; but, properly seen, selling follows rather than precedes the organization's drive to create products to satisfy its consumers.

CONCLUSION

It has been argued here that the modern marketing concept serves very naturally to describe an important facet of all organizational activity. All organizations must develop appropriate products to serve their sundry consuming groups and must use modern tools of communication to reach their consuming publics. The business heritage of marketing provides a useful set of concepts for guiding all organizations.

The choice facing those who manage nonbusiness organizations is not whether to market or not to market, for no organization can avoid marketing. The choice is whether to do it well or poorly, and on this necessity the case for organizational marketing is basically founded.

NOTES

1. This is the view of Sherman Lee, Director of the Cleveland Museum, quoted in *Newsweek,* Vol. 71 (April 1, 1968), p. 55.
2. "PR for Colonels," *Newsweek,* Vol. 71 (March 18, 1968), p. 70.
3. "Doctors Try an Image Transplant," *Business Week,* No. 2025 (June 22, 1968), p. 64.
4. Theodore Levitt, "Marketing Myopia," *Harvard Business Review,* Vol. 38 (July–August, 1960), pp. 45–56.

6

Philip Kotler

A Generic Concept of Marketing

One of the signs of the health of a discipline is its willingness to reexamine its focus, techniques, and goals as the surrounding society changes and new problems require attention. Marketing has shown this aptitude in the past. It was originally founded as a branch of *applied economics* devoted to the study of distribution channels. Later marketing became a *management discipline* devoted to engineering increases in sales. More recently, it has taken on the character of an *applied behavioral science* that is concerned with understanding buyer and seller systems involved in the marketing of goods and services.

The focus of marketing has correspondingly shifted over the years. Marketing evolved through a *commodity focus* (farm products, minerals, manufactured goods, services); an *institutional focus* (producers, wholesalers, retailers, agents); a *functional focus* (buying, selling, promoting, transporting, storing, pricing); a *managerial focus* (analysis, planning, organization, control); and a *social focus* (market efficiency, product quality, and social impact). Each new focus had its advocates and its critics. Marketing emerged each time with a refreshed and expanded self-concept.

Today marketing is facing a new challenge concerning whether its concepts apply in the nonbusiness as well as the business area. In 1969, this author and Professor Levy advanced the view that *marketing is a relevant discipline for all organizations insofar as all organizations can be said to have customers and products.*[1] This "broadening of the concept of marketing" proposal received much attention, and the 1970 Fall Conference of the American Marketing Association was devoted to this theme.

"A Generic Concept of Marketing," Philip Kotler, Vol. 36 (April 1972), pp. 46–54. Reprinted from the *Journal of Marketing*, published by the American Marketing Association. This article won the Alpha Kappa Psi Award as best article of the year.

Philip Kotler, Harold T. Martin professor of Marketing at Northwestern University, received his Ph.D. in Economics from the Massachusetts Institute of Technology. He did post doctoral work in the Mathematics and behavioral sciences at Harvard and the University of Chicago respectively. His textbook Marketing Management: Analysis, Planning, and Control, *now in its fifth edition, is widely used.*

Critics soon appeared who warned that the broadening concept could divert marketing from its true purposes and dilute its content. One critic did not deny that marketing concepts and tools could be useful in fund raising, museum membership drives, and presidential campaigns, but he felt that these were extracurricular applications of an intrinsical business technology.[2]

Several articles have been published which describe applications of marketing ideas to nonbusiness areas such as health services, population control, recycling of solid wastes, and fund raising.[3] Therefore, the underlying issues should be reexamined to see whether a more generic concept of marketing can be established.

This author concludes that the traditional conception of marketing would relegate this discipline to an increasingly narrow and pedestrian role in a society that is growing increasingly postindustrial. In fact, this article will argue that the broadening proposal's main weakness was not that it went too far but that it did not go far enough.

This article is organized into five parts. The first distinguishes three stages of consciousness regarding the scope of marketing. The second presents an axiomatic treatment of the generic concept of marketing. The third suggests three useful marketing typologies that are implied by the generic concept of marketing. The fourth describes the basic analytical, planning, organization, and control tasks that make up the logic of marketing management. The fifth discusses some interesting questions raised about the generic concept of marketing.

THREE STAGES OF MARKETING CONSCIOUSNESS

Three different levels of consciousness can be distinguished regarding the boundaries of marketing. The present framework utilizes Reich's consciousness categories without his specific meanings.[4] The traditional consciousness, that marketing is essentially a business subject, will be called *consciousness one.* Consciousness one is the most widely held view in the mind of practitioners and the public. In the last few years, a marketing *consciousness two* has appeared among some marketers holding that marketing is appropriate for all organizations that have customers. This is the thrust of the original broadening proposal and seems to be gaining adherents. Now it can be argued that even consciousness two expresses a limited concept of marketing. One can propose *consciousness three* that holds that marketing is a relevant subject for all organizations in their relations with all their publics, not only customers. The future character of marketing will depend on the particular consciousness that most marketers adopt regarding the nature of their field.

Consciousness One

Consciousness one is the conception that marketing is essentially a business subject. It maintains that marketing is concerned with *sellers, buyers,* and *"economic" products and services.* The sellers offer goods and services, the buyers have purchasing power and other resources, and the objective is an exchange of goods for money or other resources.

The core concept defining marketing consciousness one is that of *market transactions.* A market transaction involves the transfer of ownership or use of an economic good or service from one party to another in return for a payment of some kind. For market transactions to occur in a society, six conditions are necessary:

1. Two or more parties
2. A scarcity of goods
3. Concept of private property
4. One party must want a good held by another

5. The "wanting" party must be able to offer some kind of payment for it
6. The "owning" party must be willing to forego the good for the payment.

These conditions underlie the notion of a market transaction, or more loosely, economic exchange.

Market transactions can be contrasted with nonmarket transactions. Nonmarket transactions also involve a transfer of resources from one party to another, *but without clear payment by the other.* Giving gifts, paying taxes, receiving free services are all examples of nonmarket transactions. If a housekeeper is paid for domestic services, this is a market transaction; if she is one's wife, this is a nonmarket transaction. Consciousness one marketers pay little or no attention to nonmarket transactions because they lack the element of explicit payment.

Consciousness Two

Consciousness two marketers do not see *payment* as a necessary condition to define the domain of marketing phenomena. Marketing analysis and planning are relevant in all organizations producing products and services for an intended consuming group, whether or not payment is required.

Table 6-1 lists several nonbusiness organizations and their "products" and "customer groups." All of these products, in principle, can be priced and sold. A price can be charged for museum attendance, safe driving lessons, birth control information, and education. The fact that many of these services are offered "free" should not detract from their character as products. A product is something that has value to someone. Whether a charge is made for its consumption is an incidental rather than essential feature defining value. In fact, most of these social goods are "priced," although often not in the normal fashion. Police services are paid for by taxes, and religious services are paid for by donations.

Each of these organizations faces marketing problems with respect to its product and customer group. They must study the size and composition of their market and consumer wants, attitudes, and habits. They must design their products to appeal to their target markets. They must develop distribution and communication programs that facilitate "purchase" and satisfaction. They must develop customer feedback systems to ascertain market satisfaction and needs.

Thus consciousness two replaces the core concept of *market transactions* with the broader concept of *organization-client transactions.* Marketing is no longer restricted only to transactions involving parties in a two-way exchange of economic resources. Marketing is a useful perspective for any organization producing

TABLE 6-1 *Some Organizations and Their Products and Customer Groups*

Organization	Product	Customer Group
Museum	Cultural appreciation	General public
National Safety Council	Safer driving	Driving public
Political candidate	Honest government	Voting public
Family Planning Foundation	Birth control	Fertile public
Police department	Safety	General public
Church	Religious experience	Church members
University	Education	Students

products for intended consumption by others. *Marketing consciousness two states that marketing is relevant in all situations where one can identify an organization, a client group, and products broadly defined.*

Consciousness Three

The emergence of a marketing consciousness three is barely visible. Consciousness three marketers do not see why marketing technology should be confined only to an organization's transactions with its client group. An organization—or more properly its management—may engage in marketing activity not only with its customers but also with all other publics in its environment. A management group has to market to the organization's supporters, suppliers, employees, government, the general public, agents and other key publics. *Marketing consciousness three states that marketing applies to an organization's attempts to relate to all of its publics, not just its consuming public.* Marketing can be used in multiple institutional contexts to effect transactions with multiple targets.

Marketing consciousness three is often expressed in real situations. One often hears a marketer say that his real problem is not *outside marketing* but *inside marketing;* for example, getting others in his organization to accept his ideas. Companies seeking a preferred position with suppliers or dealers see this as a problem of marketing themselves. In addition, companies try to market their viewpoint to congressmen in Washington. These and many other examples suggest that marketers see the marketing problem as extending far beyond customer groups.

The concept of defining marketing in terms of *function* rather than *structure* underlies consciousness three. To define a field in terms of function is to see it as a process or set of activities. To define a field in terms of structure is to identify it with some phenomena such as a set of institutions. Bliss pointed out that many sciences are facing this choice.[5] In the field of political science, for example, there are those who adopt a structural view and define political science in terms of political institutions such as legislatures, government agencies, judicial courts, and political parties. There are others who adopt a functional view and define political science as the study of *power* wherever it is found. The latter political scientists study power in the family, in labor-management relations, and in corporate organizations.

Similarly, marketing can be defined in terms of functional rather than structural considerations. Marketing takes place in a great number of situations, including executive recruiting, political campaigning, church membership drives, and lobbying. Examining the marketing aspects of these situations can yield new insights into the generic nature of marketing. The payoff may be higher than from continued concentration in one type of structural setting, that of business.

It is generally a mistake to equate a science with a certain phenomenon. For example, the subject of *matter* does not belong exclusively to physics, chemistry, or biology. Rather physics, chemistry and biology are logical systems that pose different questions about matter. Nor does *human nature* belong exclusively to psychology, sociology, social psychology, or anthropology. These sciences simply raise different questions about the same phenomena. Similarly, traditional business subjects should not be defined by institutional characteristics. This would mean that finance deals with banks, production with factories, and marketing with distribution channels. Yet each of these subjects has a set of core ideas that are applicable in multiple institutional contexts. An important means of achieving progress in a science is to try to increase the generality of its concepts.

Consider the case of a hospital as an institution. A production-minded person will want to know about the locations of the various facilities, the jobs of the various personnel, and in general the arrangement of the elements to produce the product known as health care. A financial-minded person will want to know the hospital's sources and applications of funds and its income and expenses. A marketing-minded person will want to know where the patients come from, why they appeared at this particular hospital, and how they feel about the hospital care and services. Thus the phenomena do not create the questions to be asked; rather the questions are suggested by the disciplined view brought to the phenomena.

What then is the disciplinary focus of marketing? The core concept of marketing is the *transaction. A transaction is the exchange of values between two parties.* The things-of-values need not be limited to goods, services, and money; they include other resources such as time, energy, and feelings. Transactions occur not only between buyers and sellers, and organizations and clients, but also between any two parties. A transaction takes place, for example, when a person decides to watch a television program; he is exchanging his time for entertainment. A transaction takes place when a person votes for a particular candidate; he is exchanging his time and support for expectations of better government. A transaction takes place when a person gives money to a charity; he is exchanging money for a good conscience. *Marketing is specifically concerned with how transactions are created, stimulated, facilitated, and valued.* This is the generic concept of marketing.

THE AXIOMS OF MARKETING

The generic concept of marketing will now be more rigorously developed. Marketing can be viewed as a *category of human action* distinguishable from other categories of human action such as voting, loving, consuming, or fighting. As a category of human action, it has certain characteristics which can be stated in the form of axioms. A sufficient set of axioms about marketing would provide unambiguous criteria about what marketing is, and what it is not. Four axioms, along with corollaries, are proposed in the following section.

Axiom 1. Marketing involves two or more social units, each consisting of one or more human actors.

Corollary 1.1. The social units may be individuals, groups, organizations, communities, or nations.

Two important things follow from this axiom. First, marketing is not an activity found outside of the human species. Animals, for example, engage in production and consumption, but do not engage in marketing. They do not exchange goods, set up distribution systems, and engage in persuasive activity. Marketing is a peculiarly human activity.

Second, the referent of marketing activity is another social unit. Marketing does not apply when a person is engaged in an activity in reference to a *thing* or *himself*. Eating, driving, and manufacturing are not marketing activities, as they involve the person in an interactive relationship primarily with things. Jogging, sleeping, and daydreaming are not marketing activities, as they involve the person in an interactive relationship primarily with himself. An interesting question does arise as to whether a person can be conceived of marketing something to himself, as when he undertakes effort to change his own behavior. Normally, however, marketing involves actions by a person directed toward one or more other persons.

Axiom 2. At least one of the social units is seeking a specific response from one or more other units concerning some social object.

Corollary 2.1. The social unit seeking the

response is called the *marketer,* and the social unit whose response is sought is called the *market.*

Corollary 2.2. The social object may be a product, service, organization, person, place, or idea.

Corollary 2.3. The response sought from the market is some behavior toward the social object, usually acceptance but conceivably avoidance. (More specific descriptions of responses sought are purchase, adoption, usage, consumption, or their negatives. Those who do or may respond are called buyers, adopters, users, consumers, clients, or supporters.)

Corollary 2.4. The marketer is normally aware that he is seeking the specific response.

Corollary 2.5. The response sought may be expected in the short or long run.

Corollary 2.6. The response has value to the marketer.

Corollary 2.7. Mutual marketing describes the case where two social units simultaneously seek a response from each other. Mutual marketing is the core situation underlying bargaining relationships.

Marketing consists of actions undertaken by persons to bring about a response in other persons concerning some specific social object. A social object is any entity or artifact found in society, such as a product, service, organization, person, place, or idea. The marketer normally seeks to influence the market to accept this social object. The notion of marketing also covers attempts to influence persons to avoid the object, as in a business effort to discourage excess demand or in a social campaign designed to influence people to stop smoking or overeating.[6] *The marketer is basically trying to shape the level and composition of demand for his product.* The marketer undertakes these influence actions because he values their consequences. The market may also value the consequences, but this is not a necessary condition for defining the occurrence of marketing activity. The marketer is normally conscious that he is attempting to influence a market, but it is also possible to interpret as marketing activity cases where the marketer is not fully conscious of his ends and means.

Axiom 2 implies that "selling" activity rather than "buying" activity is closer to the core meaning of marketing. The merchant who assembles goods for the purpose of selling them is engaging in marketing, insofar as he is seeking a purchase response from others. The buyer who comes into his store and pays the quoted price is engaging in buying, not marketing, in that he does not seek to produce a specific response in the seller, who has already put the goods up for sale. If the buyer decides to bargain with the seller over the terms, he too is involved in marketing, or if the seller had been reluctant to sell, the buyer has to market himself as an attractive buyer. The terms "buyer" and "seller" are not perfectly indicative of whether one, or both, of the parties are engaged in marketing activity.

Axiom 3. The market's response probability is not fixed.

Corollary 3.1. The probability that the market will produce the desired response is called the *market's response probability.*

Corollary 3.2. The market's response probability is greater than zero; that is, the market is capable of producing the desired response.

Corollary 3.3. The market's response probability is less than one; that is, the market is not internally compelled to produce the desired response.

Corollary 3.4. The market's response probability can be altered by marketer actions.

Marketing activity makes sense in the context of a market that is free and capable of yielding the desired response. If the target social unit *cannot respond* to the social object, as in the case of no interest or no resources, it is not a market. If the target social unit *must respond* to the social object, as in the case of addiction or perfect brand loyalty, that unit is a market but there is little need for marketing activity. In cases where the market's response probability is fixed in the short run but variable in the long run, the marketer may undertake marketing activity to prevent or reduce the erosion in the response probability. Normally, marketing activity is most relevant where the market's response probability is less than one and highly influenced by marketer actions.

Axiom 4. Marketing is the attempt to produce the desired response by creating and offering values to the market.

Corollary 4.1. The marketer assumes that the market's response will be voluntary.

Corollary 4.2. The essential activity of marketing is the creation and offering of value. Value is defined subjectively from the market's point of view.

Corollary 4.3. The marketer creates and offers value mainly through configuration, valuation, symbolization, and facilitation. (Configuration is the act of designing the social object. Valuation is concerned with placing terms of exchange on the object. Symbolization is the association of meanings with the object. Facilitation consists of altering the accessibility of the object.)

Corollary 4.4. Effective marketing means the choice of marketer actions that are calculated to produce the desired response in the market. *Efficient marketing* means the choice of *least cost* marketer actions that will produce the desired response.

Marketing is an approach to producing desired responses in another party that lies midway between *coercion* on the one hand and *brainwashing* on the other.

Coercion involves the attempt to produce a response in another by forcing or threatening him with agent-inflicted pain. Agent-inflicted pain should be distinguished from object-inflicted pain in that the latter may be used by a marketer as when he symbolizes something such as cigarettes as potentially harmful to the smoker. The use of agent-inflicted pain is normally not a marketing solution to a response problem. That is not to deny that marketers occasionally resort to arranging a "package of threats" to get or keep a customer. For example, a company may threaten to discontinue purchasing from another company if the latter failed to behave in a certain way. But normally, marketing consists of noncoercive actions to induce a response in another.

Brainwashing lies at the other extreme and involves the attempt to produce a response in another by profoundly altering his basic beliefs and values. Instead of trying to persuade a person to see the social object as serving his existing values and interests, the agent tries to shift the subject's values in the direction of the social object. Brainwashing, fortunately, is a very difficult feat to accomplish. It requires a monopoly of communication channels, operant conditioning, and much patience. Short of pure brainwashing efforts are attempts by various agents to change people's basic values in connection with such issues as racial prejudice, birth control, and private property. Marketing has some useful insights to offer to agents seeking to produce basic changes in people, although its main focus is on creating products and messages attuned to existing attitudes and values. It places more emphasis on preference engineering than attitude conditioning, although the latter is not excluded.

The core concern of marketing is that of producing desired responses in free individuals by the judicious creation and offering of values. The marketer is attempting to get value from the market through offering value to it. The marketer's problem is to create attractive values. Value is completely subjective and exists in the eyes of the beholding market. Marketers must understand the market in order to be effective in creating value. This is the essential meaning of the marketing concept.

The marketer seeks to create value in four ways. He can try to design the social object more attractively (configuration); he can put an attractive term on the social object (valuation); he can add symbolic significance in the social object (symbolization); and he can make it easier for the market to obtain the social object (facilitation). He may use these activities in reverse if he wants the social object to be avoided. These four activities have a rough correspondence to more conventional statements of marketing purpose, such as the use of product, price, promotion, and place to stimulate exchange.

The layman who thinks about marketing often overidentifies it with one or two major component activities, such as facilitation or symbolization. In *scarcity economies,* marketing is often identified with the facilitation function. Marketing is the problem of getting scarce goods to a marketplace. There is little concern with configuration and symbolization. In *affluent economies*, marketing is often identified with the symbolization function. In the popular mind, marketing is seen as the task of encoding persuasive messages to get people to buy more goods. Since most people resent persuasion attempts, marketing has picked up a negative image in the minds of many people. They forget or overlook the marketing work involved in creating values through configuration, valuation, and facilitation. In the future postindustrial society concern over the quality of life becomes paramount, and the public understanding of marketing is likely to undergo further change, hopefully toward an appreciation of all of its functions to create and offer value.

TYPOLOGIES OF MARKETING

The new levels of marketing consciousness make it desirable to reexamine traditional classifications of marketing activity. Marketing practitioners normally describe their type of marketing according to the *target market or product.* A *target-market classification* of marketing activity consists of consumer marketing, industrial marketing, governmental marketing, and international marketing.

A *product* classification consists of durable goods marketing, nondurable goods marketing, and service marketing.

With the broadening of marketing, the preceding classifications no longer express the full range of marketing application. They pertain to business marketing, which is only one type of marketing. More comprehensive classifications of marketing activity can be formulated according to the *target market, product,* or *marketer.*

Target Market Typology

A *target-market classification* of marketing activity distinguishes the various *publics* toward which an organization can direct its marketing activity. *A public is any group with potential interest and impact on an organization.* Every organization has up to nine distinguishable publics (Figure 6-1). There are three *input publics* (supporters, employees, suppliers), two *output publics* (agents, consumers), and four *sanctioning publics* (government, competitors, special publics, and general public). The organization is viewed as a resource conversion machine which takes the resources of supporters (e.g., stockholders, directors), employees, and suppliers and converts these into products that go directly to consumers or through agents. The

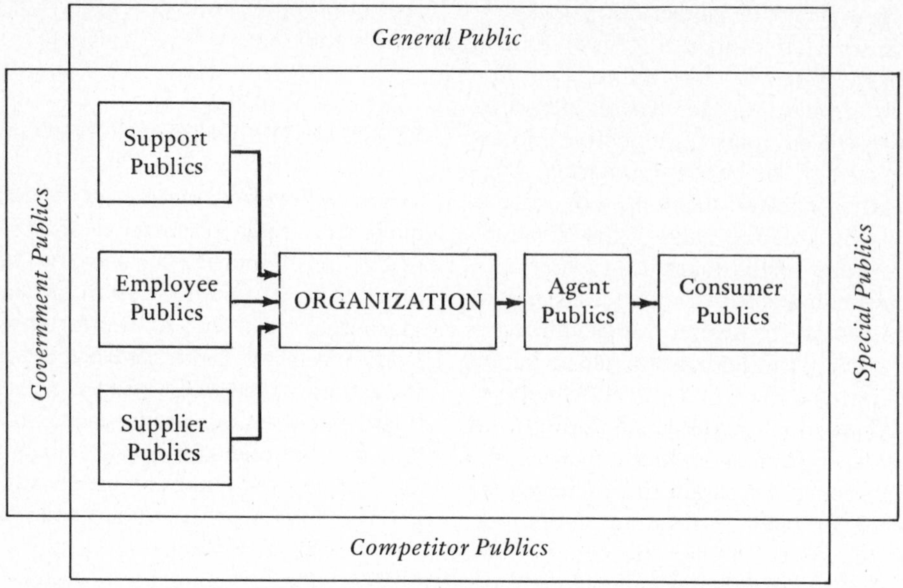

FIGURE 6-1 *An Organization's Publics*

organization's basic input-output activities are subject to the watchful eye of sanctioning publics such as government, competitors, special publics, and the general public. All of these publics are targets for organizational marketing activity because of their potential impact on the resource converting efficiency of the organization. Therefore, a *target-market classification* of marketing activity consists of supporter-directed marketing, employee-directed marketing, supplier-directed marketing, agent-directed marketing, consumer-directed marketing, general-public-directed marketing, special-public-directed marketing, government-directed marketing, and competitor-directed marketing.

Product Typology

A typology of marketing activity can also be constructed on the basis of the *product* marketed. Under the broadened concept of marketing, the product is no longer restricted to commercial goods and services. An organization can try to market to a public up to six types of products or social objects. A product classification of marketing consists of goods marketing, service marketing, organization marketing, person marketing, place marketing, and idea marketing.

Goods and service marketing, which made up the whole of traditional marketing, reappear in this classification. In addition, marketers can specialize in the marketing of organizations (e.g., governments, corporations, or universities), persons (e.g., political candidates, celebrities), places (e.g., real estate developments, resort areas, states, cities), and ideas (e.g., family planning, Medicare, antismoking, safe driving).

Marketer Typology

A typology can also be constructed on the basis of the *marketer*, that is, the organization that is carrying on the marketing. A first approximation would call for distinguishing between business and nonbusiness organization marketing. Since there are several types of nonbusiness organizations with quite different products and marketing tasks, it would be desirable to build a marketer classification that recognizes the different types of organizations. This leads to the following classifications: Business organization marketing, political organization marketing, social organization marketing, religious organization marketing, cultural organization marketing, and knowledge organization marketing.

Organizations are classified according to their primary or formal character. Political organizations would include political parties, government agencies, trade unions, and cause groups. Social organizations would include service clubs, fraternal organizations, and private welfare agencies. Religious organizations would include churches and evangelical movements. Cultural organizations would include museums, symphonies, and art leagues. Knowledge organizations would include public schools, universities, and research organizations. Some organizations are not easy to classify. Is a nonprofit hospital a business or a social organization? Is an employee credit union a political or social organization? The purpose of the classification is primarily to guide students of marketing to look for regularities that might characterize the activities of certain basic types of organizations.

In general, the purpose of the three classifications of marketing activity is to facilitate the accumulation of marketing knowledge and its transfer from one marketing domain to another. Thus political and social organizations often engage in marketing ideas, and it is desirable to build up a generic knowledge about idea marketing. Similarly, many organizations try to communicate a program to government authorities, and they could benefit from the accumulation of knowledge concerning idea marketing and government-directed marketing.

BASIC TASKS OF MARKETING MANAGEMENT

Virtually all persons and organizations engage in marketing activity at various times. They do not all engage in marketing, however, with equal skill. A distinction can be drawn between *marketing* and *marketing management*. *Marketing* is a descriptive science involving the study of how transactions are created, stimulated, facilitated, and valued. *Marketing management* is a normative science involving the efficient creation and offering of values to stimulate desired transactions. Marketing management is essentially a disciplined view of the task of achieving specific responses in others through the creation and offering of values.

Marketing management is not a set of answers so much as an orderly set of questions by which the marketer determines what is best to do in each situation. Effective marketing consists of intelligently analyzing, planning, organizing, and controlling marketing effort.

The marketer must be skilled at two basic analytical tasks. The first is *marketing analysis*. He must be able to identify the market, its size and location, needs and wants, perceptions and values. The second analytical skill is *product analysis*. The marketer must determine what products are currently available to the target, and how the target feels about each of them.

Effective marketing also calls for four major planning skills. The first is *product development*, i.e., configuration. The marketer should know where to look for appropriate ideas, how to choose and refine the product concept, how to stylize and package the product, and how to test it. The second is *pricing*, i.e., valuation. He must develop an attractive set of terms for the product. The third is *distribution*, i.e., facilitation. The marketer should determine how to get the product into circulation and make it accessible to its target market. The fourth is *promotion*, i.e., symoblization. The marketer must be capable of stimulating market interest in the product.

Effective marketing also requires three organizational skills. The first is *organizational design.* The marketer should understand the advantages and disadvantages of organizing market activity along functional, product, and market lines. The second is *organizational staffing.* He should know how to find, train, and assign effective comarketers. The third is *organizational motivation.* He must determine how to stimulate the best marketing effort by his staff.

Finally, effective marketing also calls for two control skills. The first is *market results measurement,* whereby the marketer keeps informed of the attitudinal and behavioral responses he is achieving in the marketplace. The second is *marketing cost measurement,* whereby the marketer keeps informed of his costs and efficiency in carrying out his marketing plans.

SOME QUESTIONS ABOUT GENERIC MARKETING

The robustness of the particular conception of marketing advocated in this article will be known in time through testing the ideas in various situations. The question is whether the logic called marketing really helps individuals such as educational administrators, public officials, museum directors, or church leaders to better interpret their problems and construct their strategies. If these ideas are validated in the marketplace, they will be accepted and adopted.

However, academic debate does contribute substantially to the sharpening of the issues and conceptions. Several interesting questions have arisen in the course of efforts by this author to expound the generic concept of marketing. Three of these questions are raised and discussed below.

1. Isn't generic marketing really using influence as the core concept rather than exchange? It is tempting to think that the three levels of consciousness of marketing move from *market transactions* to *exchange* to *influence* as the succeeding core concepts. The concept of influence undeniably plays an important role in marketing thought. Personal selling and advertising are essentially influence efforts. Product design, pricing, packaging, and distribution planning make extensive use of influence considerations. It would be too general to say, however, that marketing is synonymous with interpersonal, intergroup, or interorganizational influence processes.

Marketing is a particular way of looking at the problem of achieving a valued response from a target market. It essentially holds that exchange values must be identified, and the marketing program must be based on these exchange values. Thus the anticigarette marketer analyzes what the market is being asked to give up and what inducements might be offered. The marketer recognizes that every action by a person has an opportunity cost. The marketer attempts to find ways to increase the person's perceived rate of exchange between what he would receive and what he would give up in *freely* adopting that behavior. The marketer is a specialist at understanding human wants and values and knows what it takes for someone to act.

2. How would one distinguish between marketing and a host of related activities such as lobbying, propagandizing, publicizing, and negotiating? Marketing and other influence activities and tools share some common characteristics as well as exhibit some unique features. Each influence activity has to be examined separately in relation to marketing. *Lobbying,* for example, is one aspect of government-directed marketing. The lobbyist attempts to evoke support from a legislator through offering values to the legislator (e.g., information, votes, friendship, and favors). A lobbyist thinks through the problem of marketing his legislation as carefully as the business marketer thinks through the problem of marketing his product or service. *Propagandizing* is the marketing of a political or social idea to a mass audience. The propagandist attempts to package the ideas in such a way as to constitute values to the target audience in exchange for support. *Publicizing* is the effort to create attention and interest in a target audience. As such it is a tool of marketing. *Negotiation* is a face-to-face mutual marketing process. In general, the broadened concept of marketing underscores the kinship of marketing with a large number of other activities and suggests that marketing is a more endemic process in society than business marketing alone suggests.

3. Doesn't generic marketing imply that a marketer would be more capable of managing political or charitable campaigns than professionals in these businesses? A distinction should be drawn between marketing as a *logic* and marketing as a *competence*. Anyone who is seeking a response in another would benefit from applying marketing logic to the problem. Thus a company treasurer seeking a loan, a company recruiter seeking a talented executive, a conservationist seeking an antipollution law, would all benefit in conceptualizing their problem in marketing terms. In these instances, they would be donning a marketer's hat although they would not be performing as professional marketers. A professional marketer is someone who (1) regularly works with marketing problems in a specific area and (2) has a specialized knowledge of this area. The political strategist, to the extent he is effective, is a professional marketer. He has learned how to effectively design, package, price, advertise, and distribute his type of product in his type of market. A professional marketer who suddenly decides to handle political candidates would need to develop competence and knowledge in this area just as he would if he suddenly decided to handle soap or steel. Being a marketer only means that a person has mastered the logic of marketing. To master the particular market requires additional learning and experience.

SUMMARY AND CONCLUSION

This article has examined the current debate in marketing concerning whether its substance belongs in the business area, or whether it is applicable to all areas in which organizations attempt to relate to customers and other publics. Specifically, *consciousness one marketing* holds that marketing's core idea is *market transactions,* and therefore marketing applies to buyers, sellers, and commercial products and services. *Consciousness two marketing* holds that marketing's core idea is *organization-client transactions,* and therefore marketing applies in any organization that can recognize a group called customers. *Consciousness three marketing* holds that marketing's core area is *transactions,* and therefore marketing applies to any social unit seeking to exchange values with other social units.

This broadest conception of marketing can be called *generic marketing.* Generic marketing takes a functional rather than a structural view of marketing. Four axioms define generic marketing.

> *Axiom 1. Marketing involves two or more social units.*
>
> *Axiom 2. At least one of the social units is seeking a specific response from one or more other units concerning some social object.*
>
> *Axiom 3. The market's response probability is not fixed.*
>
> *Axiom 4. Marketing is the attempt to produce the desired response by creating and offering values to the market.*

These four axioms and their corollaries are intended to provide unambiguous criteria for determining what constitutes a marketing process.

Generic marketing further implies that marketing activity can be classed according to the *target market* (marketing directed to supporters, employees, suppliers, agents, consumers, general public, special publics, government, and competitors); the *product* (goods, services, organizations, persons, places, and ideas); and the *marketer* (business, political, social, religious, cultural, and knowledge organizations).

Marketers face the same tasks in all types of marketing. Their major analytical tasks are *market analysis* and *product analysis.* Their major planning tasks are *product development, pricing, distribution,* and *promotion.* Their major organizational tasks are *design, staffing,* and *motivation.* Their major control tasks are *marketing results measurement* and *marketing cost measurement.*

Generic marketing is a logic available to all organizations facing problems of market response. A distinction should be drawn between applying a marketing point of view to a specific problem and being a marketing professional. Marketing logic alone does not make a marketing professional. The professional also acquires competence, which along with the logic, allows him to interpret his problems and construct his marketing strategies in an effective way.

NOTES

1. Philip Kotler and Sidney J. Levy, "Broadening the Concept of Marketing," *Journal of Marketing,* Vol. 33 (January, 1969), pp. 10-15.
2. David Luck, "Broadening the Concept of Marketing—Too Far," *Journal of Marketing,* Vol. 33 (July, 1969), pp. 53-54.
3. *Journal of Marketing,* Vol. 35 (July, 1971).
4. Charles A. Reich, *The Greening of America* (New York: Random House, 1970).
5. Perry Bliss, *Marketing Management and the Behavioral Environment* (Englewood Cliffs, N.J.: Prentice-Hall, Inc., 1970), pp. 106-108, 119-120.
6. See Philip Kotler and Sidney J. Levy, "Demarketing, Yes, Demarketing," *Harvard Business Review,* Vol. 49 (November-December, 1971), pp. 71-80.

7

Richard P. Bagozzi

Marketing As Exchange

The exchange paradigm has emerged as a framework useful for conceptualizing marketing behavior. Indeed, most contemporary definitions of marketing explicitly include exchange in their formulations.[1] Moreover, the current debate on "broadening" centers on the very notion of exchange: on its nature, scope, and efficacy in marketing.

This article analyzes a number of dimensions of the exchange paradigm that have not been dealt with in the marketing literature. First, it attempts to show that what marketers have considered as exchange is a special case of exchange theory that focuses primarily on direct transfers of tangible entities between two parties. In reality, marketing exchanges often are indirect, they may involve intangible and symbolic aspects, and more than two parties may participate. Second, the media and meaning of exchange are discussed in order to provide a foundation for specifying underlying mechanisms in marketing exchanges. Finally, social marketing is analyzed in light of the broadened concept of exchange.

The following discussion proceeds from the assumptions embodied in the generic concept of marketing as formulated by Kotler, Levy, and others.[2] In particular, it is assumed that marketing theory is concerned with two questions: (1) Why do people and organizations engage in exchange relationships? and (2) How are exchanges created, resolved, or avoided? The domain for the subject matter of marketing is assumed to be quite broad, encompassing all activities involving "exchange" and the cause and effect of phenomena associated with it. As in the social and natural sciences, marketing owes its definition to the outcome of debate and competition between divergent views in an evolutionary process that Kuhn terms a "scientific revolution."[3] Although the debate is far from settled, there appears to be a growing consensus that exchange forms the core phenomenon for study in marketing. Whether

"Marketing as Exchange," Richard P. Bagozzi, Vol. 39 (October 1975), pp. 32–39. Reprinted from the *Journal of Marketing,* published by the American Marketing Association.
Richard Bagozzi is a professor of marketing at The Massachusetts Institute of Technology. He received his Ph.D. from Northwestern University and has taught at the University of California at Berkeley. His latest book is Causal Models in Marketing.

the specific instances of exchange are to be limited to economic institutions and consumers in the traditional sense or expanded to all organizations in the broadened sense deserves further attention by marketing scholars and practitioners. Significantly, the following principles apply to exchanges in both senses.

THE TYPES OF EXCHANGE

In general, there are three types of exchange: restricted, generalized, and complex.[4] Each of these is described below.

Restricted Exchange

Restricted exchange refers to two-party reciprocal relationships which may be represented diagrammatically as A ↔ B, where "↔" signifies "gives to and receives from" and A and B represent social actors such as consumers, retailers, salesmen, organizations, or collectivities.[5] Most treatments of, and references to, exchanges in the marketing literature have implicitly dealt with restricted exchanges; that is, they have dealt with customer-salesman, wholesaler-retailer, or other such dyadic exchanges.

Restricted exchanges exhibit two characteristics:

> First, there is a great deal of attempt to maintain equality. This is especially the case with repeatable social exchange acts. Attempts to gain advantage at the expense of the other is [*sic*] minimized. Negatively, the breach of the rule of equality quickly leads to emotional reactions. . . . Secondly, there is a *quid pro quo* mentality in restricted exchange activities. Time intervals in mutual reciprocities are cut short and there is an attempt to balance activities and exchange items as part of the mutual reciprocal relations.[6]

The "attempt to maintain equality" is quite evident in restricted marketing exchanges. Retailers, for example, know that they will not obtain repeat purchases if the consumer is taken advantage of and deceived. The "breach" in this rule of equality – which is a central tenet of the marketing concept – has led to picketing, boycotts, and even rioting. Finally, the fact that restricted marketing exchanges must involve a *quid pro quo* notion (something of value in exchange for something of value) has been at the heart of Luck's criticism of broadening the concept of marketing.[7] However, as will be developed below, there are important exceptions to the *quid pro quo* requirement in many marketing exchanges.

Generalized Exchange

Generalized exchange denotes univocal, reciprocal relationships among at least three actors in the exchange situation. Univocal reciprocity occurs "if the reciprocations involve at least three actors and if the actors do not benefit each other directly but only indirectly."[8] Given three social actors, for instance, generalized exchange may be represented as A → B → C → A, where "→" signifies "gives to." In generalized exchange, the social actors form a system in which each actor gives to another but receives from someone other than to whom he gave. For example, suppose a public bus company (B) asks a local department store chain (A) to donate or give a number of benches to the bus company. Suppose further that, after the department store chain (A) gives the benches to the bus company (B), the company (B) then places the benches at bus stops for the convenience of its riders (C). Finally, suppose that a number of the riders (C) see the advertisements placed on the benches by the department store chain (A) and later patronize the store as a result of this exposure. This sequence of exchange, A→B→C→A, is known as generalized exchange; while it fails to conform to the usual notions of *quid pro quo,* it certainly constitutes a marketing exchange of interest.

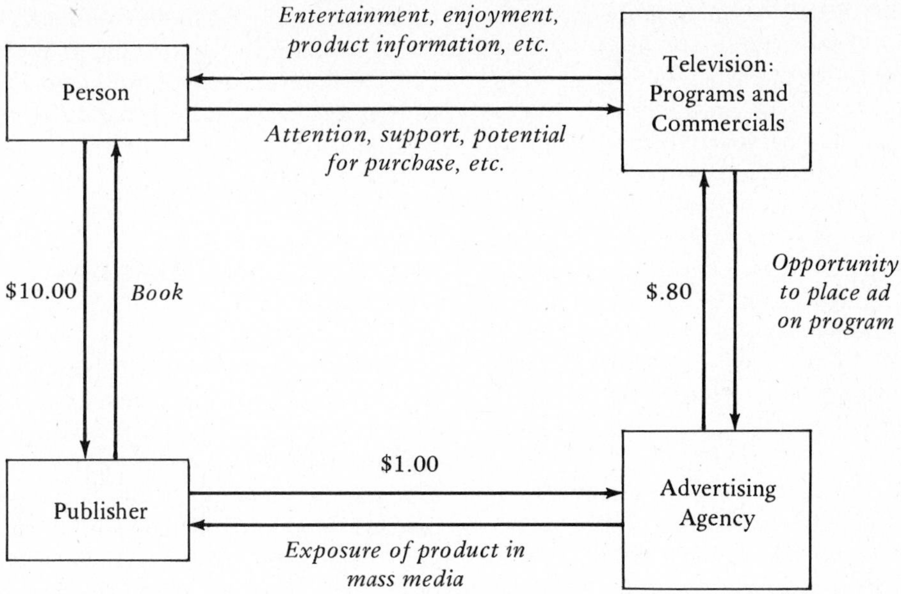

FIGURE 7-1 *An Example of Complex Circular Exchange*

Complex Exchange

Complex exchange refers to a system of mutual relationships between at least three parties. Each social actor is involved in at least one direct exchange, while the entire system is organized by an interconnecting web of relationships.

Perhaps the best example of complex exchange in marketing is the channel of distribution. Letting A represent a manufacturer, B a retailer, and C a consumer, it is possible to depict the channel as A↔B↔C. Such open-ended sequences of direct exchanges may be designated *complex chain exchanges.*

But many marketing exchanges involve relatively closed sequences of relationships. For example, consider the claim made by Kotler that a "transaction takes place . . . when a person decides to watch a television program."[9] Recently, Carman and Luck have criticized this assertion, maintaining that it may not exhibit an exchange.[10] The differences stem from: (1) a disagreement on whether exchange must consist of transfers of tangible (as opposed to intangible) things of value, and (2) a neglect of the possibility of systems of exchange. Figure 7-1 illustrates the exchange between a person and a television program and how it may be viewed as a link in a system termed *complex circular exchange.*[11] In this system of exchange, the person experiences a direct transfer of intangibles between himself and the program. That is, he gives his attention, support (for example, as measured by the Nielsen ratings), potential for purchase, and so on, and receives entertainment, enjoyment, product information, and other intangible entities. The person also experiences an indirect exchange with the television program via a sequence of direct, tangible exchanges. Thus, after being informed of the availability of a book through an exchange with the television program and its advertising, a person may purchase it for, say, $10.00. The book's publisher, in turn, may purchase the services of an advertiser, paying what amounts to a percentage of each sale, say, $1.00. Finally, the advertiser receives the opportunity to place a commercial on the air from the television network in exchange for what amounts to a percentage of each sale, say, $.80. In this particular example, the occurrence of the direct intangible exchange was a necessary prerequisite for the development of the series of indirect tangible exchanges. Thus, an exchange *can* occur between a person and a television program.

Complex chain and complex circular exchanges involve predominantly conscious systems of social and economic relationships. In this sense, there is an overt coordination of activities and expectations, which Alderson called an organized behavioral system and which he reserved for the household, the firm, and the channel of distribution.[12] However, it should be evident that the designation "organized" is a relative one and that other exchange systems, such as the one shown in Figure 7-1, also evidence aspects of overt coordination in an economic, social, and symbolic sense.

Generalized and complex exchanges are also present in relatively unconscious systems of social and economic relationships. Thus, a modern economy may experience a covert coordination of activities through exchanges that occur when many individuals, groups, and firms pursue their own self-interest. This is what Adam Smith meant by his reference to an "invisible hand."[13] Similarly, in his analysis of primitive societies and marketing systems, Frazer has shown that exchange and the pursuit of self-interest can be the foundation for the web of kinship, economic, and social institutions.[14] The recent exchange theories of Homans and Blau are also based on this individualistic assumption of self-interest.[15] It should be stressed, however, that the exchange tradition developed by Levi-Strauss is not an individualistic one but rather is built on social, collectivistic assumptions associated with generalized exchange.[16] These differences will become more apparent when social marketing is analyzed below.

THE MEDIA AND MEANING OF EXCHANGE

In order to satisfy human needs, people and organizations are compelled to engage in social and economic exchanges with other people and organizations. This is true for primitive as well as highly developed societies. Social actors obtain satisfaction of their needs by complying with, or influencing, the behavior of other actors. They do this by communicating and controlling the media of exchange which, in turn, comprise the links between one individual and another, between one organization and another. Significantly, marketing exchanges harbor meanings for individuals that go beyond the mere use of media for obtaining results in interactions.

The Media of Exchange

The media of exchange are the vehicles with which people communicate to, and influence, others in the satisfaction of their needs. These vehicles include money, persuasion, punishment, power (authority), inducement, and activation of normative or ethical commitments.[17] Products and services are also media of exchange. In consumer behavior research, marketers have extensively studied the effects of these vehicles on behavior. Moreover, it has been suggested that a number of these vehicles be used in conjunction with sociopsychological processes to explain the customer-salesman relationship.[18] It should be noted, however, that marketing is not solely concerned with influence processes, whether these involve manufacturers influencing consumers or consumers influencing manufacturers. Marketing is also concerned with meeting existing needs and anticipating future needs, and these activities do not necessarily entail attempts to influence or persuade.

To illustrate the multivariate nature of media in marketing exchanges, consider the example of the channel of distribution, a complex chain exchange. The firms in a channel of distribution are engaged in an intricate social system of behavioral relationships that go well beyond the visible exchange of products and money.[19] Typically, the traditional channel achieves its conscious coordination of effort through the mutual expectations of profit. In addition, each firm in the channel may influence the degree of cooperation and compliance of its partners by offering inducements in the form of services, deals, or other benefits or by persuading each link in the channel that it is in its own best interest to cooperate. A firm may also affect the behavior or decisions of another firm through the use of the power it may possess. Wilkinson has studied five bases of power in the channel of distribution – reward, coercive, legitimate, referent, and expert power – and has tested aspects of these relationships between firms.[20] Finally, a firm may remind a delinquent member in the channel of its contractual obligations or even threaten the member with legal action for a breach of agreement. This influence medium is known as the activation of commitments.

The Meaning of Exchange

Human behavior is more than the outward responses or reactions of people to stimuli. Man not only reacts to events or the actions of others but he self-generates his own acts.[21] His behavior is purposeful, intentional. It is motivated. Man is an information seeker and generator as well as an information processor. In short, human behavior is a conjunction of meaning with action and reaction.

Similarly, exchange is more than the mere transfer of a product or service for money. To be sure, most marketing exchanges are characterized by such a transfer. But the reasons behind the exchange – the explanation of its occurrence – lie in the social and psychological significance of the experiences, feelings, and meanings of the parties in the exchange. In general, marketing exchanges may exhibit one of three classes of meanings: utilitarian, symbolic, or mixed.

Utilitarian exchange. A utilitarian exchange is an interaction whereby goods are given in return for money or other goods and the motivation behind the actions lies in the anticipated use or tangible characteristics commonly associated with the objects in the exchange. The utilitarian exchange is often referred to as an economic exchange, and most treatments of exchange in marketing implicitly rely on this usage. As Bartels notes with regard to the identity crisis in marketing:

> Marketing has initially and generally been associated exclusively with the distributive part of the *economic* institution and function. . . .
>
> The question, then, is whether marketing is identified by the *field* of economics in which the marketing techniques have been developed and generally applied, or by the socalled marketing *techniques,* wherever they may be applied.
>
> If marketing relates to the distributive function of the economy, providing goods and services, that *physical* function differentiates it from all other social institutions.[22]

Most marketers have traditionally conceptualized the subject matter of the discipline in these terms, and they have proceeded from the assumptions embodied in utilitarian exchange.

In general, utilitarian exchange theory is built on the foundation of *economic man.*[23] Thus, it is assumed that:

1. Men are rational in their behavior.
2. They attempt to maximize their satisfaction in exchanges.

3. They have complete information on alternatives available to them in exchanges.
4. These exchanges are relatively free from external influence.

Coleman has developed an elaborate mathematical framework for representing exchange behavior that assumes many of the features of economic man.[24] His model is based on the theory of purposive action, which posits that each "actor will choose that action which according to his estimate will lead to an expectation of the most beneficial consequences."[25] Among other things, the theory may be used to predict the outcomes and degree of control social actors have for a set of collective actions in an exchange system.

Symbolic exchange. Symbolic exchange refers to the mutual transfer of psychological, social, or other intangible entities between two or more parties. Levy was one of the first marketers to recognize this aspect of behavior, which is common to many everyday marketing exchanges:

> . . . *symbol* is a general term for all instances where experience is mediated rather than direct; where an object, action, word, picture, or complex behavior is understood to mean not only itself but also some *other* ideas or feelings.
>
> The less concern there is with the concrete satisfactions of a survival level of existence, the more abstract human responses become. As behavior in the market place is increasingly elaborated, it also becomes increasingly symbolic. This idea needs some examination, becaue it means that sellers of goods are engaged, whether willfully or not, in selling *symbols*, as well as practical merchandise. It means that marketing managers must attend to more than the relatively superficial facts with which they usually concern themselves when they do not think of their goods as having symbolic significance. . . . *People buy things not only for what they can do, but also for what they mean.*[26]

Mixed exchange. Marketing exchanges involve both utilitarian and symbolic aspects, and it is often very difficult to separate the two. Yet, the very creation and resolution of marketing exchanges depend on the nature of the symbolic and utilitarian mix. It has only been within the past decade or so that marketers have investigated this deeper side of marketing behavior in their studies of psychographics, motivation research, attitude and multiattribute models, and other aspects of buyer and consumer behavior. Out of this research tradition has emerged a picture of man in his true complexity as striving for both economic and symbolic rewards. Thus, we see the emergence of *marketing man,* perhaps based on the following assumptions:

1. Man is sometimes rational, sometimes irrational.
2. He is motivated by tangible as well is intangible rewards, by internal as well as external forces.[27]
3. He engages in utilitarian as well as symbolic exchanges involving psychological and social aspects.
4. Although faced with incomplete information, he proceeds the best he can and makes at least rudimentary and sometimes unconscious calculations of the costs and benefits associated with social and economic exchanges.
5. Although occasionally striving to maximize his profits, marketing man often settles for less than optimum gains in his exchanges.
6. Finally, exchanges do not occur in isolation but are subject to a host of individual and social constraints: legal, ethical, normative, coercive, and the like.

The important research question to answer is: *What are the forces and conditions creating and resolving marketing exchange relationships?* The processes involved in the creation and resolution of exchange relationships constitute the subject matter of marketing, and these processes depend on, and cannot be separated from, the fundamental character of human and organizational needs.

SOCIAL MARKETING

The marketing literature is replete with conflicting definitions of *social marketing.* Some have defined the term to signify the *use* of marketing skills in social causes,[28] while others have meant it to refer also to "the *study* of markets and marketing activities within a total social system."[29] Bartels recently muddied the waters with still a new definition that is vastly different from those previously suggested. For him, social marketing designates "the *application* of marketing techniques to *nonmarketing* fields."[30] Since these definitions cover virtually everything in marketing and even some things outside of marketing, it is no wonder that one author felt compelled to express his "personal confusion" and "uncomfortable" state of mind regarding the concept.[31]

But what is social marketing? Before answering this question, we must reject the previous definitions for a number of reasons. First, we must reject the notion that social marketing is merely the "use" or "application" of marketing techniques or skills to other areas. A science or discipline is something more than its technologies. "Social marketing" connotes what is social and what is marketing, and to limit the definition to the tools of a discipline is to beg the question of the meaning of marketing. Second, social marketing is not solely the study of marketing within the frame of the total social system, and it is even more than the subject matter of the discipline. Rather, the meaning of social marketing – like that of marketing itself – is to be found in the unique *problems* that confront the discipline. Thus, as the philosopher of science, Popper, notes:

> The belief that there is such a thing as physics, or biology, or archaeology, and that these "studies" or "disciplines" are distinguishable by the subject matter which they investigate, appears to me to be a residue from the time when one believed that a theory had to proceed from a definition of its own subject matter. But subject matter, or kinds of things, do not, I hold, constitute a basis for distinguishing disciplines. Disciplines are distinguished partly for historical reasons and reasons of administrative convenience (such as the organization of teaching and of appointments), and partly because the theories which we construct to solve our problems have a tendency to grow into unified systems. But all this classification and distinction is a comparatively unimportant and superficial affair. *We are not students of some subject matter but students of problems.* And problems may cut right across the borders of any subject matter or discipline.[32]

Social marketing, then, addresses a particular type of problem which, in turn, is a subset of the generic concept of marketing. That is, social marketing is the answer to a particular question: Why and how are *exchanges* created and resolved in *social* relationships? Social relationships (as opposed to economic relationships) are those such as family planning agent-client, welfare agent-indigent, social worker-poor person, and so on.[33] Social marketing attempts to determine the dynamics and nature of the exchange behavior in these relationships.

But is there an exchange in a social relationship? Luck, for example, feels that "a person who receives a free service is not a buyer and has conducted no exchange of values with the provider of the service."[34] It is the contention in this article that there is most definitely an exchange in social marketing relationships, but the exchange is not the simple *quid pro quo* notion characteristic of most economic exchanges. Rather, social marketing relationships exhibit what may be called generalized or complex exchanges. They involve the symbolic transfer of both tangible and intangible entities, and they invoke various media to influence such exchanges.

Figure 7-2 illustrates a typical social marketing exchange. In this system, society authorizes

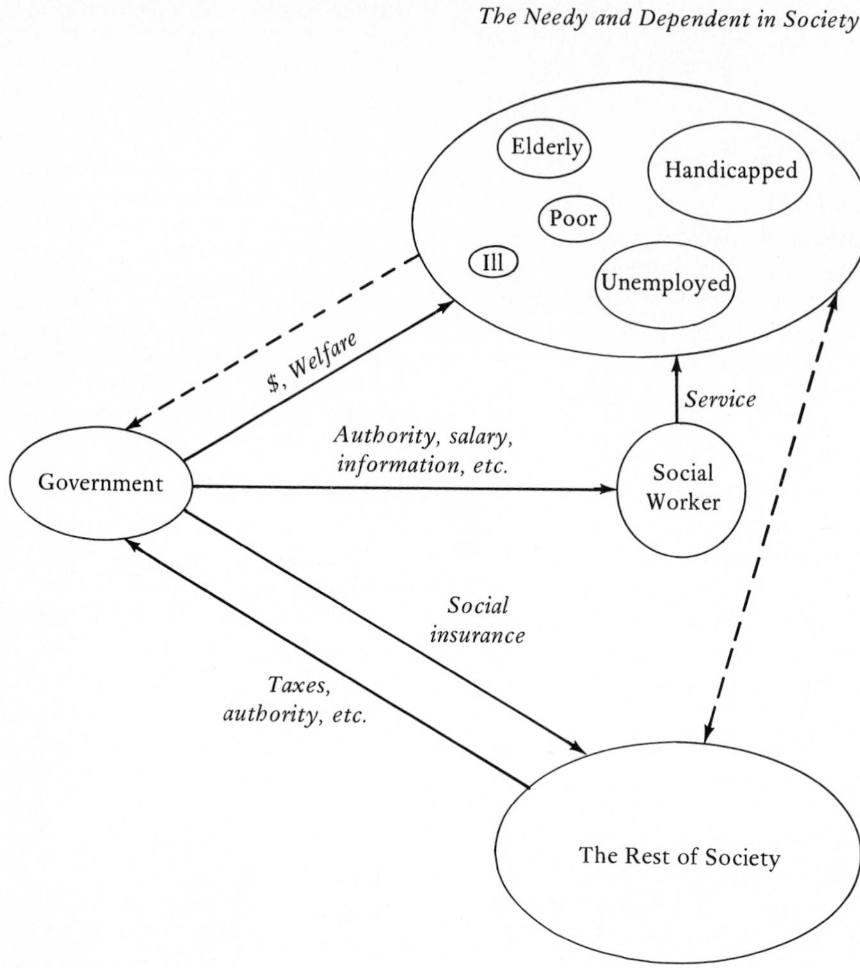

FIGURE 7-2 *Social Marketing and Exchange*

government – through its votes and tax payments – to provide needed social services such as welfare. In return, the members of society receive social insurance against common human maladies. Government, in turn, pays the salaries of social workers, gives them authority to provide social services, and so on. It also distributes welfare payments directly to the needy. These relatively contemporaneous transfers make this marketing system one of generalized exchange. In addition, a number of symbolic and delayed transfers occur that make the system also one of complex exchange. For example, as shown by dotted lines in the figure, in many cases the needy and dependent have given to the government in the past, since they may have paid taxes and voted. Moreover, members of society anticipate that they, or a number of their members, will become dependent and that social services represent an investment as well as an obligation. Hence, in one sense there is a mutual exchange between society and the needy separated, in part, by the passage of time. Finally, it should be noted that there are other tangential exchanges and forces occurring in this social marketing system that, depending on their balance, give it stability or promote change. The system achieves stability due, first, to the presence of the exchanges described above, which create mutual dependencies and univocal reciprocities; and, second, to symbolic exchanges, which reinforce the overt transfers. For example, the social worker gives to the needy but also receives back gratitude and feelings of accomplishment. The system undergoes change due to the dynamics of competing interests, as is exemplified in the efforts of lobbies and pressure groups to bring their needs to bear on the legislative process.

Thus, social marketing is really a subset of the generic concept of marketing in that it deals with the creation and resolution of exchanges in social relationships. Marketers can make contributions to other areas that contain social exchanges by providing theories and techniques for the understanding and control of such transactions. They do not usurp the authority of specialists in areas such as social work, but rather they aid and complement the efforts of these social scientists. It is not so much the fact that the subject matter of marketing overlaps with that of other disciplines as it is that the problems of marketing are universal. In answer to Bartels' query, "Is marketing a specific function with general applicability or a general function that is specifically applied?"[35] – one may state that it is neither. Rather, marketing is a general function of universal applicability. It is the discipline of exchange behavior, and it deals with problems related to this behavior.

CONCLUSIONS AND IMPLICATIONS

A number of broad research questions may be posed:

1. Why do marketing exchanges emerge? How do people and organizations satisfy their needs through exchange?
2. Why do some marketing exchanges persist in ongoing relationships while others fall apart?
3. What are the processes leading to changes in marketing exchange relationships? How do the social actors or third parties influence or control an exchange?
4. What are the consequences of imbalances in power, resources, knowledge, and so on, in a marketing exchange? What is an equitable exchange?
5. What are the relationships between conflict, cooperation, competition, and exchange?
6. At what level may marketing exchanges be analyzed? What are the consequences of viewing exchanges as single dyads or complex systems of relationships? What are the consequences of employing the individualistic reductionism of Homans versus the collectivistic orientation of Levi-Strauss for understanding exchange behavior?
7. Is the exchange paradigm universal? Does it apply to the free-enterprise countries of the western world, the planned economies of the communist countries, and the primitive economies of the third world?
8. How well does the exchange paradigm meet the requirements for theory as specified by philosophy of science criteria?

Although marketing seems to defy simple definition and circumspection, it is essential that marketers locate the distinctive focus (or foci) of the discipline. Failure to do so impedes both the growth of the discipline and the character of its performance. Exchange is a central concept in marketing, and it may well serve as the foundation for that elusive "general theory of marketing." This article has attempted to explore some of the key concepts in the exchange paradigm. Future research and discussion must search for specific social and psychological processes that create and resolve marketing exchanges.

NOTES

1. See, for example, Marketing Staff of The Ohio State University, "A Statement of Marketing Philosophy," *Journal of Marketing,* Vol. 29 (January 1965), pp. 43–44; E. Jerome McCarthy, *Basic Marketing,* 5th ed. (Homewood, Ill.: Richard D. Irwin, 1975); Philip Kotler, *Marketing Management,* 2nd ed. (Englewood Cliffs, N.J.: Prentice-Hall, 1972), p. 12; and Ben M. Enis, *Marketing Principles* (Pacific Palisades, Calif.: Goodyear Publishing Co., 1974), p. 21.
2. Philip Kotler, "A Generic Concept of Marketing," *Journal of Marketing,* Vol. 36 (April 1972), pp. 46–54; and Philip Kotler and Sidney J. Levy, "Broadening the Concept of Marketing," *Journal of Marketing,* Vol. 33 (January 1969), pp. 10–15.
3. Thomas S. Kuhn, *The Structure of Scientific Revolutions,* 2nd ed. (Chicago: The University of Chicago Press, 1970).
4. The distinction between restricted and generalized exchange was first made by anthropologist Claude Levi-Strauss in *The Elementary Structure of Kinship* (Boston: Beacon Press, 1969). An extended critical analysis of restricted and generalized exchange may be found in Peter P. Ekeh, *Social Exchange Theory: The Two Traditions* (Cambridge, Mass.: Harvard University Press, 1974), Chap. 3.
5. Ekeh, same reference as footnote 4, p. 50.
6. Ekeh, same reference as footnote 4, pp. 51–52.
7. David J. Luck, "Broadening the Concept of Marketing—Too Far," *Journal of Marketing,* Vol. 33 (January 1969), pp. 10–15; and Luck, "Social Marketing: Confusion Compounded," *Journal of Marketing,* Vol. 38 (October 1974), pp. 70–72.
8. Ekeh, same reference as footnote 4, pp. 48, 50.
9. Kotler, same reference as footnote 2, p. 48.
10. James M. Carman, "On the Universality of Marketing," *Journal of Contemporary Business,* Vol. 2 (Autumn 1973), p. 5; and Luck, "Social Marketing," same reference as footnote 7, p. 72.
11. A form of circular exchange in primitive societies was first suggested by Bonislaw Malinowski in *Argonauts of the Western Pacific* (London: Routledge and Kegan Paul, 1922), p. 93; but in his concept the same physical items were transmitted to all parties, while in complex circular exchange as defined here different tangible or symbolic entities may be transferred.
12. Wroe Alderson, *Dynamic Marketing Behavior* (Homewood, Ill.: Richard D. Irwin, 1965), Chap. 1.
13. For a modern treatment of Adam Smith's contribution to exchange theory, see Walter Nord, "Adam Smith and Contemporary Social Exchange Theory," *The American Journal of Economics and Sociology,* Vol. 32 (October 1974), pp. 421–436.
14. Sir James G. Frazer, *Folklore in the Old Testament,* Vol. 2 (London: Macmillan & Co., 1919).
15. George C. Homans, *Social Behavior: Its Elementary Forms,* rev. ed. (New York: Harcourt Brace Jovanovich, 1974); and Peter M. Blau, *Exchange and Power in Social Life* (New York: John Wiley & Sons, 1964).
16. Levi-Strauss, same reference as footnote 4. See also, Ekeh, same reference as footnote 4, Chaps. 3 and 4.
17. Talcott Parsons, "On the Concept of Influence," *Public Opinion Quarterly,* Vol. 27 (Spring 1963), pp. 37–62; and Parsons, "On the Concept of Political Power," *Proceedings of the American Philosophical Society,* Vol. 107 (June 1963), pp. 232–262. See also, Richard Emerson, "Power Dependence Relations," *American Sociological Review,* Vol. 27 (February 1962), pp. 31–40.
18. Richard P. Bagozzi, "Marketing as an Organized Behavioral System of Exchange," *Journal of Marketing,* Vol. 38 (October 1974), pp. 77–81.
19. See, for example, Louis W. Stern, *Distribution Channels: Behavioral Dimensions* (New York: Houghton Mifflin Co., 1969).
20. Ian Wilkinson, "Power in Distribution Channels," *Cranfield Research Papers in Marketing and Logistics,* Session 1973–1974 (Cranfield School of Management, Cranfield, Bedfordshire, England); and Wilkinson, "Researching the Distribution Channels for Consumer and Industrial Goods: the Power Dimension," *Journal of the Market Research Society,* Vol. 16 (No. 1, 1974), pp. 12–32.
21. This dynamic, as opposed to mechanistic, image of human behavior is described nicely in R. Harré and P. F. Secord, *The Explanation of Social Behavior* (Totawa, N.J.: Littlefield, Adams & Co., 1973).
22. Robert Bartels, "The Identity Crisis in Marketing," *Journal of Marketing,* Vol. 38 (October 1974), p. 75. Emphasis added.
23. For a modern treatment of economic man, see Harold K. Schneider, *Economic Man* (New York: The Free Press, 1974).
24. James S. Coleman, "Systems of Social Exchange," *Journal of Mathematical Sociology,* Vol. 2 (December 1972).
25. James S. Coleman, *The Mathematics of Collective Action* (Chicago: Aldine-Atherton, 1973).
26. Sidney J. Levy, "Symbols for Sale," *Harvard Business Review,* Vol. 37 (July–August 1959), pp. 117–119.
27. It should be stressed that man is motivated by the hope or anticipation of *future* rewards, and these may consist of classes of benefits not necessarily experienced in the past. See Homans's individualistic exchange theory, a learning perspective, same reference as footnote 15; Levi-Strauss's collectivistic, symbolic perspective, same reference as footnote 4; and Ekeh, same reference as footnote 4, pp. 118–124, 163.
28. Philip Kotler and Gerald Zaltman, "Social Marketing:

An Approach to Planned Social Change," *Journal of Marketing,* Vol. 35 (July 1971), p. 5.

29. William Lazer and Eugene J. Kelley, eds., *Social Marketing: Perspectives and Viewpoints* (Homewood, Ill.: Richard D. Irwin, 1973), p. 4. Emphasis added.
30. Same reference as footnote 22. Emphasis added.
31. Luck, "Social Marketing," same reference as footnote 7, p. 70.
32. Karl R. Popper, *Conjectures and Refutations* (New York: Harper & Row, 1963), p. 67.
33. For a conceptual framework comparing marketing and other social relationships, see Richard P. Bagozzi, "What is a Marketing Relationship?" *Der Markt,* No. 51, 1974, pp. 64-69.
34. Luck, "Social Marketing," same reference as footnote 7, p. 71.
35. Same reference as footnote 22, p. 73.

8

Shelby D. Hunt

The Nature and Scope of Marketing

During the past three decades, two controversies have overshadowed all others in the marketing literature. The first is the "Is marketing a science?" controversy sparked by an early *Journal of Marketing* article by Converse entitled "The Development of a Science of Marketing."[1] Other prominent writers who fueled the debate included Bartels, Hutchinson, Baumol, Buzzell, Taylor, and Halbert.[2] After raging throughout most of the '50s and '60s, the controversy has since waned. The waning may be more apparent than real, however, because many of the substantive issues underlying the marketing science controversy overlap with the more recent "nature of marketing" (broadening the concept of marketing) debate. Fundamental to both controversies are some radically different perspectives on the essential characteristics of both *marketing* and *science.*

The purpose of this article is to develop a conceptual model of the scope of marketing and to use that model to analyze (1) the approaches to the study of marketing, (2) the "nature of marketing" controversy, and (3) the marketing science debate. Before developing the model, some preliminary observations on the controversy concerning the nature of marketing are appropriate.

THE NATURE OF MARKETING

What is marketing? What kinds of phenomena are appropriately termed *marketing phenomena*? How do marketing activities differ from non-marketing activities? What is a marketing system? How can marketing processes be distinguished from other social processes? Which institutions should one refer to as marketing

"The Nature and Scope of Marketing," Shelby D. Hunt, Vol. 40 (July 1976), pp. 17–28. Reprinted from the *Journal of Marketing,* published by the American Marketing Association. This article won the Maynard Award as best theoretical article of the year.
Shelby Hunt is Professor of Marketing at Texas Technological University. He received his Ph.D. from Michigan State University and has written extensively in the area of marketing theory.
The author wishes to gratefully acknowledge the constructive criticisms of earlier drafts of this article by Professors George W. Brooker and John R. Nevin, both of the University of Wisconsin-Madison.

institutions? *In short, what is the proper conceptual domain of the construct labeled "marketing"?*

The American Marketing Association defines marketing as "the performance of business activities that direct the flow of goods and services from producer to consumer or user."[3] This position has come under attack from various quarters as being too restrictive and has prompted one textbook on marketing to note: "Marketing is not easy to define. No one has yet been able to formulate a clear, concise definition that finds universal acceptance."[4]

Although vigorous debate concerning the basic nature of marketing has alternately waxed and waned since the early 1900s, the most recent controversy probably traces back to a position paper by the marketing staff of the Ohio State University in 1965. They suggested that marketing be considered "the process in a society by which the demand structure for economic goods and services is anticipated or enlarged and satisfied through the conception, promotion, exchange, and physical distribution of goods and services."[5] Note the conspicuous absence of the notion that marketing consists of a set of *business activities* (as in the AMA definition). Rather, they considered marketing to be a *social process.*

Next to plunge into the semantical battle were Kotler and Levy. Although they did not specifically propose a new definition of marketing, Kotler and Levy in 1969 suggested that the concept of marketing be broadened to include nonbusiness organizations. They observed that churches, police departments, and public schools have products and customers, and that they use the normal tools of the marketing mix. Therefore, Kotler and Levy conclude that these organizations perform marketing, or at least marketing-like, activities. Thus,

> the choice facing those who manage nonbusiness organizations is not whether to market or not to market, for no organization can avoid marketing. The choice is whether to do it well or poorly, and on this necessity the case for organizational marketing is basically founded.[6]

In the same issue of the *Journal of Marketing,* Lazer discussed the changing boundaries of marketing. He pleaded that: "What is required is a broader perception and definition of marketing than has hitherto been the case – one that recognizes marketing's societal dimensions and perceives of marketing as more than just a technology of the firm."[7] Thus, Kotler and Levy desired to broaden the notion of marketing by including not-for-profit organizations, and Lazer called for a definition of marketing that recognized the discipline's expanding societal dimensions.

Luck took sharp issue with Kotler and Levy by insisting that marketing be limited to those business processes and activities that ultimately result in a *market* transaction.[8] Luck noted that even thus bounded, marketing would still be a field of enormous scope and that marketing specialists could still render their services to nonmarketing causes. Kotler and Levy then accused Luck of a new form of myopia and suggested that, "The crux of marketing lies in a *general idea of exchange* rather than the narrower thesis of market transactions."[9] They further contended that defining marketing "too narrowly" would inhibit students of marketing from applying their expertise to the most rapidly growing sectors of the society.

Other marketing commentators began to espouse the dual theses that (1) marketing be broadened to include nonbusiness organizations, and (2) marketing's societal dimensions deserve scrutiny. Thus, Ferber prophesied that marketing would diversify into the social and public policy fields.[10] And Lavidge sounded a similar call to arms by admonishing marketers to cease evaluating new products solely on the basis of whether they *can* be sold. Rather, he suggested, they should evaluate new products from a societal perspective, that is, *should* the product be sold?

> The areas in which marketing people can, and must, be of service to society have broadened. In addition, marketing's functions have been broadened. Marketing no longer can be defined adequately in terms of the activites involved in buying, selling, and transporting goods and services.[11]

The movement to expand the concept of marketing probably became irreversible when the *Journal of Marketing* devoted an entire issue to marketing's changing social/environmental role. At that time, Kotler and Zaltman coined the term *social marketing,* which they defined as "the design, implementation and control of programs calculated to influence the acceptability of social ideas and involving considerations of product planning, pricing, communication, distribution, and marketing research."[12] In the same issue, marketing technology was applied to fund raising for the March of Dimes, health services, population problems, and the recycling of solid waste.[13] Further, Dawson chastised marketers for ignoring many fundamental issues pertaining to the social relevance of marketing activities:

> Surely, in these troubled times, an appraisal of marketing's actual and potential role in relation to such [societal] problems is at least of equal importance to the technical aspects of the field. Yet, the emphasis upon practical problem-solving within the discipline far outweighs the attention paid to social ramifications of marketing activity.[14]

Kotler has since reevaluated his earlier positions concerning broadening the concept of marketing and has articulated a "generic" concept of marketing. He proposes that the essence of marketing is the *transaction,* defined as the exchange of values between two parties. Kotler's generic concept of marketing states: "Marketing is specifically concerned with how transactions are created, stimulated, facilitated and valued."[15] Empirical evidence indicates that, at least among marketing educators, the broadened concept of marketing represents a *fait accompli.* A recent study by Nichols showed that 95% of marketing educators believed that the scope of marketing should be broadened to include nonbusiness organizations. Similarly 93% agreed that marketing goes beyond just economic goods and services, and 83% favored including in the domain of marketing many activities whose ultimate result is not a market transaction.[16]

Although the advocates of extending the notion of marketing appear to have won the semantical battle, their efforts may not have been victimless. Carman notes that the definition of marketing plays a significant role in directing the research efforts of marketers. He believes that many processes (e.g., political processes) do not involve an exchange of values and that marketing should not take such processes under its "disciplinary wing."[17] Bartels has also explored the so-called identity crises in marketing and has pointed out numerous potential disadvantages to broadening the concept of marketing. These *potential* disadvantages include: (1) turning the attention of marketing researchers away from important problems in the area of physical distribution, (2) emphasizing methodology rather than substance as the content of marketing knowledge, and (3) an increasingly esoteric and abstract marketing literature. Bartels concluded: "If 'marketing' is to be regarded as so broad as to include both economic and noneconomic fields of application, perhaps marketing as originally conceived will ultimately reappear under another name."[18]

Similarly, Luck decries the "semantic jungle" that appears to be growing in marketing.[19] Citing conflicting definitions of *marketing* and *social marketing* in the current literature, Luck suggests that this semantic jungle has been impeding the efforts of marketers to think clearly about their discipline. He has challenged the American Marketing Association to create a special commission to clear up the definitional problems in marketing. Finally, a recent president of the American Marketing Association set the development of a consistent standard definition of marketing as a primary goal of the association.[20]

Three questions appear to be central to the "nature [broadening the concept] of marketing" controversy. First, what kinds of phenomena and issues *do* the various marketing writers perceive to be included in the scope of marketing? Second, what kinds of phenomena and issues *should* be included in the scope of marketing? Third, how can marketing be defined to both systematically encompass all the phenomena and issues that should be included and, at the same time, systematically exclude all other phenomena and issues? That is, a good definition of marketing must be both properly inclusive and exclusive. To rigorously evaluate these questions requires a conceptual model of the scope of marketing.

THE SCOPE OF MARKETING

No matter which definition of marketing one prefers, the scope of marketing is unquestionably broad. Often included are such diverse subject areas as consumer behavior, pricing, purchasing, sales management, product management, marketing communications, comparative marketing, social marketing, the efficiency/productivity of marketing systems, the role of marketing in economic development, packaging, channels of distribution, marketing research, societal issues in marketing, retailing, wholesaling, the social responsibility of marketing, international marketing, commodity marketing, and physical distribution. Though lengthy, this list of topics and issues does not exhaust the possibilities. Not all writers would include all the topics under the general rubric of marketing. The point deserving emphasis here, however, is that different commentators on marketing would *disagree* as to which topics should be excluded. The disagreement stems from fundamentally different perspectives and can best be analyzed by attempting to develop some common ground for classifying the diverse topics and issues in marketing.

The most widely used conceptual model of the scope of marketing is the familiar "4 Ps" model popularized by McCarthy in the early '60s.[21] The model is usually represented by three concentric circles. The inner circle contains the consumer, since this is the focal point of marketing effort. The second circle contains the marketing mix ("controllable factors") of price, place, promotion, and product. Finally, the third circle contains the uncontrollable factors of political and legal environment, economic environment, cultural and social environment, resources and objectives of the firm, and the existing business situation. As is readily apparent, many of the subject areas previously mentioned have no "home" in the 4 Ps model. For example, where does social marketing or efficiency of marketing systems or comparative marketing belong?

During a presentation at the 1972 Fall Conference of the American Marketing Association, Kotler made some observations concerning the desirability of classifying marketing phenomena using the concepts of *micro, macro, normative,* and *positive.*[22] These observations spurred the development of the conceptual model detailed in Table 8-1. The schema proposes that all marketing phenomena, issues, problems, models, theories, and research can be categorized using the three categorical dichotomies of (1) profit sector/nonprofit sector, (2) micro/macro, and (3) positive/normative. The three categorical dichotomies yield 2 x 2 x 2 = 8 classes or cells in the schema. Thus, the first class includes all marketing topics that are micro-positive and in the profit sector. Similarly, the second class includes all marketing activities that are micro-normative and in the profit sector, and so on throughout the table.

Some definitions are required to properly interpret the schema presented in Table 8-1. *Profit sector* encompasses the study and activities of organizations or other entities whose stated objectives include the realization of profit. Also applicable are studies that adopt the *perspective* of profit-oriented organizations. Conversly, *nonprofit* sector encompasses the study and perspective of all organizations and entities whose stated objectives do not include the realization of profit.

The *micro/macro* dichotomy suggests a classification based on the level of aggregation. *Micro* refers to the marketing activities of in-

TABLE 8-1 *The Scope of Marketing*

		Positive	Normative
Profit Sector	Micro	(1) Problems, issues, theories, and research concerning: a. Individual consumer buyer behavior b. How firms determine prices c. How firms determine products d. How firms determine promotion e. How firms determine channels of distribution f. Case studies of marketing practices	(2) Problems, issues, normative models, and research concerning how firms *should:* a. Determine the marketing mix b. Make pricing decisions c. Make product decisions d. Make promotion decisions e. Make packaging decisions f. Make purchasing decisions g. Make international marketing decisions h. Organize their marketing departments i. Control their marketing efforts j. Plan their marketing strategy k. Apply systems theory to marketing problems l. Manage retail establishments m. Manage wholesale establishments n. Implement the marketing concept
	Macro	(3) Problems, issues, theories, and research concerning: a. Aggregate consumption patterns b. Institutional approach to marketing c. Commodity approach to marketing d. Legal aspects of marketing e. Comparative marketing f. The efficiency of marketing systems g. Whether the poor pay more h. Whether marketing spurs or retards economic development i. Power and conflict relationships in channels of distribution j. Whether marketing functions are universal k. Whether the marketing concept is consistent with consumers' interests	(4) Problems, issues, normative models, and research concerning: a. How marketing can be made more efficient b. Whether distribution costs too much c. Whether advertising is socially desirable d. Whether consumer sovereignty is desirable e. Whether stimulating demand is desirable f. Whether the poor should pay more g. What kinds of laws regulating marketing are optimal h. Whether vertical marketing systems are socially desirable i. Whether marketing should have special social responsibilities

marketing using the three categorical dichotomies of profit sector/nonprofit sector, positive/normative, and micro/macro. This is not meant to imply that reasonable people cannot disagree as to which topics should fall within the scope of marketing. Nor does it even imply that reasonable people cannot disagree as to which cell in Table 8-1 is most appropriate for each issue or particular piece of research. For example, a study of the efficiency of marketing systems may have *both* positive and normative aspects; it may both *describe* existing marketing practices and *prescribe* more appropriate practices. Rather, the conceptual model of the scope of marketing presented in Table 8-1 provides a useful framework for analyzing fundamental differences among the various approaches to marketing and, as shall be demonstrated, the nature of marketing and marketing science controversies.

ANALYZING THE NATURE OF MARKETING AND MARKETING SCIENCE

The previous discussion on the scope of marketing now enables us to clarify some of the issues with respect to the "nature [broadening the concept] of marketing" controversy and the "Is marketing a science?" debate. Most marketing practitioners and some marketing academicians perceive the entire scope of marketing to be profit/micro/normative (cell 2 of Table 8-1). That is, practitioners often perceive the entire domain of marketing to be the analysis of how to improve the decision-making processes of marketers. This perspective is exemplified by the definition of marketing Canton has suggested[34] and, somewhat surprisingly, by the definition proffered by Kotler in the first edition of *Marketing Management:* "Marketing is the analyzing, organizing, planning, and controlling of the firm's customer-impinging resources, policies, and activities with a view to satisfying the needs and wants of chosen customer groups at a profit."[35]

Most marketing academicians would chafe at delimiting the entire subject matter of marketing to simply the profit/micro/normative dimensions. Most would, at the very least, include all the phenomena, topics, and issues indicated in the top half of Table 8-1 (that is, cells 1 through 4). Kotler and others now wish to include in the definition of marketing *all* eight cells in Table 8-1.

Other fields have experienced similar discipline-definitional problems. Several decades ago, a debate raged in philosophy concerning the definition of philosophy and philosophy of science. Some philosophers chose a very narrow definition of their discipline. Popper's classic rejoinder should serve to alert marketers to the danger that narrowly circumscribing the marketing discipline may trammel marketing inquiry:

> . . . the theory of knowledge was inspired by the hope that it would enable us not only to know more about knowledge, but also to contribute to the advance of knowledge – of scientific knowledge, that is . . . . Most of the philosophers who believe that the characteristic method of philosophy is the analysis of ordinary language seem to have lost this admirable optimism which once inspired the rationalist tradition. Their attitude, it seems, has become one of resignation, if not despair. They not only leave the advancement of knowledge to the scientists: they even define philosophy in such a way that it becomes, by definition, incapable of making any contribution to our knowledge of the world. The self-mutilation which this so surprisingly persuasive definition requires does not appeal to me. There is no such thing as an essence of philosophy, to be distilled and condensed into a definition. *A definition of the word* philosophy *can only have the character of a convention, of an agreement; and I, at any rate, see no merit in the arbitrary proposal to define the word* philosophy *in a way that may well prevent a student of philosophy from trying to contribute,* qua *philosopher, to the advancement of our knowledge of the world.*[36]

Four conclusions seem warranted. First,

definitions of the nature of marketing differ in large part because their authors perceive the total scope of marketing to be different portions of Table 8-1. Second, there is a growing consensus that the total scope of marketing should appropriately include all eight cells of Table 8-1. Third, it may be very difficult to devise a definition of marketing that would both systematically *include* all eight cells of Table 8-1 and, at the same time, systematically *exclude* all other phenomena. Especially difficult will be the task of including in a single definition both the normative dimensions of the *practice* of marketing and the positive dimensions of the *discipline* or *study* of marketing.

The fourth conclusion deserves special emphasis and elaboration. There is now a consensus among marketers that most nonprofit organizations, such as museums, zoos, and churches, engage in numerous activities (pricing, promoting, and so forth) that are very similar to the marketing activities of their profit-oriented cousins. There is also consensus that the marketing procedures that have been developed for profit-oriented organizations are equally applicable to nonprofit concerns. These are the two major, substantive issues involved in the debate over the nature (broadening the concept) of marketing. On these two issues there now exists substantial agreement.

The remaining two points of *disagreement* among marketers concerning the nature of marketing are minor when compared to the points of agreement. Issue one is essentially whether the activities of nonprofit organizations should be referred to as *marketing* activities or *marketing-like* activities. Given the agreement among marketers concerning the two previously cited substantive issues, the problem of distinguishing between marketing activities and marketing-like activities must be considered trivial to the extreme. The second issue on which disagreement exists concerns developing a definition of marketing. Although certainly nontrivial in nature, on this issue marketers would be well advised to take a cue from the discipline of philosophy, which has been around much longer and has yet to develop a consensus definition. That is, the discipline of marketing should not be overly alarmed about the difficulty of generating a consensus *definition* of marketing as long as there appears to be a developing consensus concerning its total *scope*.

The preceding analysis notwithstanding, there does remain a major, unresolved, substantive issue concerning the nature of marketing. Although *marketers* now recognize that nonprofit organizations (1) have marketing or marketing-like problems, (2) engage in marketing or marketing-like activities to solve these problems, and (3) can use the marketing policies, practices, and procedures that profit-oriented organizations have developed to solve marketing problems, we must candidly admit that most *nonmarketers* have yet to perceive this reality. Sadly, most administrators of nonprofit organizations and many academicians in other areas still do not perceive that many problems of nonprofit organizations are basically marketing in nature, and that there is an extant body of knowledge in marketing academia and a group of trained marketing practitioners that can help resolve these problems. Until administrators of nonprofit organizations perceive that they have marketing problems, their marketing decision making will inevitably suffer. Thus, the major *substantive* problem concerning broadening the concept of marketing lies in the area of *marketing* marketing to nonmarketers.

IS MARKETING A SCIENCE?

Returning to the "Is marketing a science?" controversy, the preceding analysis suggests that a primary factor explaining the nature of the controversy is the widely disparate notions of marketing held by the participants. The common element shared by those who hold that marketing is not (and cannot) be a science is the belief that the entire conceptual domain of marketing is cell 2: profit/micro/normative. Hutchinson clearly exemplifies this position:

> There is a real reason, however, why the field of marketing has been slow to develop an unique body of theory. It is a simple one: marketing is not a science. It is rather an art or a practice, and as such much more closely resembles engineering, medicine and architecture than it does physics, chemistry or biology. The medical profession sets us an excellent example, if we would but follow it; its members are called "practitioners" and not scientists. It is the work of physicians, as it is of any practitioner, to apply the findings of many sciences to the solution of problems . . . . It is the drollest travesty to relate the scientist's search for knowledge to the market research man's seeking after customers.[37]

If, as Hutchinson implies, the entire conceptual domain of marketing is profit/micro/normative, then marketing is not and (more importantly) probably *cannot* be a science. If, however, the conceptual domain of marketing includes both micro/positive and macro/positive phenomena, then marketing *could* be a science. That is, if phenomena such as consumer behavior, marketing institutions, marketing channels, and the efficiency of systems of distribution are included in the conceptual domain of marketing (and there appears to be a concensus to so include them), there is no reason why the study of these phenomena could not be deserving of the designation science.

Is marketing a science? Differing perceptions of the scope of marketing have been shown to be a primary factor underlying the debate on this question. The second factor contributing to the controversy is differing perceptions concerning the basic nature of science, a subject that will now occupy our attention.

The Nature of Science

The question of whether marketing is a science cannot be adequately answered without a clear understanding of the basic nature of science. So, what is a science? Most marketing writers cite the perspective proposed by Buzzell. A science is:

> . . . a classified and systematized body of knowledge, . . . organized around one or more central theories and a number of general principles, . . . usually expressed in quantitative terms, . . . knowledge which permits the prediction and, under some circumstances, the control of future events.[38]

Buzzell then proceeded to note that marketing lacks the requisite central theories to be termed a science.

Although the Buzzell perspective on science has much to recommend it, the requirement "organized around one or more central theories" seems overly restrictive. This requirement confuses the *successful culmination* of scientific efforts with *science itself.* Was the study of chemistry not a science before discoveries like the periodic table of elements? Analogously, would not a pole vaulter still be a pole vaulter even if he could not vault fifteen feet? As Homans notes, "What makes a science are its aims, not its result."[39] The major purpose of science is to discover (create? invent?) laws and theories to explain, predict, understand, and control phenomena. Withholding the label *science* until a discipline has "central theories" would not seem reasonable.

The previous comments notwithstanding, requiring a science to be organized around one or more central theories is not completely without merit. There are strong *honorific* overtones in labeling a discipline a science.[40] These semantical overtones are so positive that, as Wartofsky has observed, even areas that are nothing more than systematized superstition attempt to usurp the term.[41] Thus, there are treatises on such subjects as the "Science of Numerology" and the "Science of Astrology." In part, the label *science* is conferred upon a discipline to signify that it has "arrived" in the eyes of other scientists, and this confirmation usually occurs only when a discipline has matured to the extent that it contains several "central theories."[42] Thus, chronologically, physics achieved the status of science before psychology, and psychology before sociology. However, the total conceptual content of the term *science* is decidedly not just honorific. Marketing does not, and should not, have to wait to be knighted by others to be a science. How, then, do sciences differ from other disciplines, if not by virtue of having central theories?

Consider the discipline of chemistry—unquestionably a science. Chemistry can be defined as "the science of substances—their structure, their properties, and the reactions that change them into other substances."[43] Using chemistry as an illustration, three observations will enable us to clarify the distinguishing characteristics of sciences. First, a science must have a distinct subject matter, a set of real-world phenomena that serve as a focal point for investigation. The subject matter of chemistry is *substances,* and chemistry attempts to understand, explain, predict, and control phenomena related to substances. Other disciplines, such as physics, are also interested in substances. However, chemistry can meaningfully lay claim to being a separate science because physics does not *focus* on substances and their reactions.

What is the basic subject matter of marketing? Most marketers now perceive the ultimate subject matter to be the *transaction.* Some subscribe to the *narrower thesis of marketing* and wish to delimit the basic subject matter to the *market* transaction. Others propose the *liberalized thesis of marketing* and wish to include within the subject matter of marketing all transactions that involve any form of *exchange of values* between parties.

Harking back to the chemistry analogue, marketing can be viewed as the *science of transactions*—their structure, their properties, and their relationships with other phenomena. Given this perspective, the subject matter of marketing would certainly overlap with other disciplines, notably economics, psychology, and sociology. The analysis of transactions is considered in each of these disciplines. Yet, only in marketing is the transaction the focal point. For example, transactions remain a tangential issue in economics, where the primary focus is on the allocation of scarce resources.[44] Therefore, the first distinguishing characteristic is that any science must have a distinct subject matter. Given that the *transaction* is the basic subject matter of marketing, marketing would seem to fulfill this requirement. Note that this conclusion is *independent* of whether one subscribes to the narrower or more liberal thesis of marketing.

A distinct subject matter alone is not sufficient to distinguish sciences from other disciplines, because all disciplines have a subject matter (some less distinct than others). The previously cited perspective of chemistry provides a second insight into the basic nature of science. Note the phrase, "their structure, their properties, and their reactions." Every science seeks to describe and classify the structure and properties of its basic subject matter. Likewise, the term *reactions* suggests that the phenomena comprising the basic subject matter of chemistry are presumed to be systematically interrelated. Thus, another distinguishing characteristic: *Every science presupposes the existence of underlying uniformities or regularities among the phenomena that comprise its subject matter. The discovery of these underlying uniformities yields empirical regularities, lawlike generalizations (propositions), and laws.*

Underlying uniformities and regularities are necessary for science because (1) a primary goal of science is to provide responsibly supported explanations of phenomena,[45] and (2) the scientific explanation of phenomena requires the existence of laws or lawlike generalizations.[46] Uniformities and regularities are also a requisite for theory development since theories are systematically related sets of statements, *including some lawlike generalizations,* that are empirically testable.[47]

The basic question for marketing is not whether there presently exist several "central theories" that serve to unify, explain, and predict marketing phenomena, as Buzzell suggests. Rather, the following should be asked: "Are there underlying uniformities and regularities among the phenomena comprising the subject matter of marketing?" This question can be answered affirmatively on two grounds—one *a priori* and one empirical. Marketing is a discipline that investigates human behavior. Since numerous uniformities and regularities have been observed in other behavioral sciences,[48] there is no *a priori* reason for believing that the subject matter of marketing will be devoid of uniformities and regularities. The second ground for believing that the uniformities exist is empirical. The quantity of scholarly research conducted on marketing phenomena during the past three decades probably exceeds the total of *all* prior research in marketing. Substantial research has been conducted in the area of channels of distribution. Also, efforts in the consumer behavior dimension of marketing have been particularly prolific. Granted, some of the research has been less than profound, and the total achievements may not be commensurate with the efforts expended. Nevertheless, who can deny that some progress has been made or that *some* uniformities have been identified? In short, who can deny that there exist uniformities and regularities interrelating the subject matter of marketing? I, for one, cannot.

The task of delineating the basic nature of science is not yet complete. Up to this point we have used chemistry to illustrate that all sciences involve (1) a distinct subject matter and the description and classification of that subject matter, and (2) the presumption that underlying the subject matter are uniformities and regularities that science seeks to discover. The chemistry example provides a final observation. Note that "chemistry is the *science* of . . . ." This suggests that sciences can be differentiated from other disciplines by the method of analysis. At the risk of being somewhat tautologous: sciences employ a set of procedures commonly referred to as the scientific method. As Bunge suggests, "No scientific method, no science."[49] The historical significance of the development and acceptance of the method of science cannot be overstated. It has been called "the most significant intellectual contribution of Western civilization."[50] Is the method of science applicable to marketing?

Detailed explication of the scientific method is beyond the scope of this article and is discussed elsewhere.[51] Nevertheless, the cornerstone requirement of the method of science must be monitored. The word *science* has its origins in the Latin verb *scire,* meaning "to know." Now, there are many ways *to know* things. The methods of tenacity, authority, faith, intuition, and science are often cited.[52] The characteristic that separates scientific knowledge from other ways to "know" things is the notion of *intersubjective certification.*

Scientific knowledge, in which theories, laws, and explanations are primal, must be *objective* in the sense that its truth content must be *intersubjectively certifiable.*[53] Requiring that theories, laws, and explanations be empirically testable ensures that they will be intersubjectively certifiable since different (but reasonably competent) investigators with differing attitudes, opinions, and beliefs will be able to make observations and conduct experiments to ascertain their truth content. "Science strives for objectivity in the sense that its statements are to be capable of public tests with results that do not vary essentially with the tester."[54] Scientific knowledge thus rests on the bedrock of empirical testability.

There is no reason whatsoever to presume that the scientific method of analysis is any less appropriate to marketing phenomena than to other disciplines. Similarly, scholarly researchers in marketing, although sometimes holding rather distorted notions concerning such topics as the role of laws and theories in research, seem to be at least as technically proficient as researchers in other areas. Finally, although some marketing researchers continue to cite "proprietary studies" as evidentiary support for their positions, the extent of this practice is now extremely small.

In summary, sciences (1) have a distinct subject matter drawn from the real world which is described and classified, (2) presume underlying uniformities and regularities interrelating the subject matter, and (3) adopt intersubjectively certifiable procedures for studying the subject matter. This perspective can be appropriately described as a consensus composite of philosophy of science views on science.[55] For example, Wartofsky suggests that a science is

> . . . an organized or systematic body of knowledge, using general laws or principles; that it is knowledge about the world; and that it is that kind of knowledge concerning which universal agreement can be reached by scientists sharing a common language (or languages) and common criteria for the *justification* of knowledge claims and beliefs.[56]

Is Marketing a Science? A Conclusion

The scope of the area called marketing has been shown to be exceptionally broad. Marketing has micro/macro dimensions, profit sector/nonprofit sector dimensions, and positive/normative dimensions. Reasonable people may disagree as to which combination of these dimensions represents the *appropriate* total scope of marketing, although a consensus seems to be developing to include all eight cells in Table 8-1. If marketing is to be restricted to *only* the profit/micro/normative dimension (as many practitioners would view it), then marketing is not a science and could not become one. All sciences involve the explanation, prediction, and understanding of phenomena.[57] These explanations and predictions frequently serve as useful guides for developing normative decision rules and normative models. Such rules and models are then *grounded* in science.[58] Nevertheless, any discipline that is *purely* evaluative or prescriptive (normative) is not a science. At least for marketing academe, restricting the scope of marketing to its profit/micro/normative dimension is unrealistic, unnecessary, and, without question, undesirable.

Once the appropriate scope of marketing has been expanded to include at least some *positive* dimensions (cells 1, 3, 5, and 7 in Table 8-1), the explanation, prediction, and understanding of these phenomena could be a science. The question then becomes whether the study of the positive dimensions of marketing has the requisite characteristics of a science. Aside from the strictly honorific overtones of *nonmarketers* accepting marketing as a science, the substantive characteristics differentiating sciences from other disciplines have been shown to be (1) a distinct subject matter drawn from the real world and the description and classification of that subject matter, (2) the presumption of underlying uniformities and regularities interrelating the subject matter, and (3) the adoption of the method of science for studying the subject matter.

The *positive* dimensions of marketing have been shown to have a subject matter properly distinct from other sciences. The marketing literature is replete with description and classification. There have been discoveries (however tentative) of uniformities and regularities among marketing phenomena. Finally, although Longman deplores "the rather remarkable lack of scientific method employed by scientists of marketing,"[59] researchers in marketing are at least as committed to the method of science as are researchers in other disciplines. Therefore, the study of the *positive* dimensions of marketing can be appropriately referred to as *marketing science.*

NOTES

1. Paul D. Converse, "The Development of a Science of Marketing," *Journal of Marketing,* Vol. 10 (July 1945), pp. 14-23.
2. Robert Bartels, "Can Marketing Be a Science?" *Journal of Marketing,* Vol. 15 (January 1951), pp. 319-328; Kenneth D. Hutchinson, "Marketing as a Science: An Appraisal," *Journal of Marketing,* Vol. 16 (January 1952), pp. 286-293; W.J. Baumol, "On the Role of Marketing Theory," *Journal of Marketing,* Vol. 21 (April 1957), pp. 413-419; Robert D. Buzzell, "Is Marketing a Science?" *Harvard Business Review,* Vol. 41 (January-February 1963), pp. 32-48; Weldon J. Taylor, "Is Marketing a Science? Revisited," *Journal of Marketing,* Vol. 29 (July 1965), pp. 49-53; and M. Halbert, *The Meaning and Sources of Marketing Theory* (New York: McGraw-Hill Book Co., 1965).
3. Committee on Terms, *Marketing Definitions: A Glossary of Marketing Terms* (Chicago: American Marketing Assn., 1960).
4. Stewart H. Rewoldt, James D. Scott, and Martin R. Warshaw, *Introduction to Marketing Management* (Homewood, Ill.: Richard D. Irwin, 1973), p. 3.
5. Marketing Staff of the Ohio State University, "Statement of Marketing Philosophy," *Journal of Marketing,* Vol. 29 (January 1965), pp. 43-44.
6. Philip Kotler and Sidney J. Levy, "Broadening the Concept of Marketing," *Journal of Marketing,* Vol. 33 (January 1969), p. 15.
7. William Lazer, "Marketing's Changing Social Relationships," *Journal of Marketing,* Vol. 33 (January 1969), p. 9.
8. David Luck, "Broadening the Concept of Marketing – Too Far," *Journal of Marketing,* Vol. 33 (July 1969), p. 54.
9. Philip Kotler and Sidney Levy, "A New Form of Marketing Myopia: Rejoinder to Professor Luck," *Journal of Marketing,* Vol. 33 (July 1969), p. 57.
10. Robert Ferber, "The Expanding Role of Marketing in the 1970's," *Journal of Marketing,* Vol. 34 (January 1970), pp. 29-30.
11. Robert J. Lavidge, "The Growing Responsibilities of Marketing," *Journal of Marketing,* Vol. 34 (January 1970), p. 27.
12. Philip Kotler and Gerald Zaltman, "Social Marketing: An Approach to Planned Social Change," *Journal of Marketing,* Vol. 35 (July 1971), p. 5.
13. *Journal of Marketing,* Vol. 35 (July 1971): William A. Mindak and Malcolm H. Bybee, "Marketing's Application to Fund Raising," pp. 13-18; Gerald Zaltman and Ilan Vertinsky, "Health Services Marketing: A Suggested Model," pp. 19-27; John U. Farley and Harold J. Leavitt, "Marketing and Population Problems," pp. 28-33; and William G. Zikmund and William J. Stanton, "Recycling Solid Wastes: A Channels-of-Distribution Problem," pp. 34-39.
14. Leslie Dawson, "Marketing Science in the Age of Aquarius," *Journal of Marketing,* Vol. 35 (July 1971), p. 71.
15. Philip Kotler, "A Generic Concept of Marketing," *Journal of Marketing,* Vol. 36 (April 1972), p. 49.
16. William G. Nichols, "Conceptual Conflicts in Marketing," *Journal of Economics and Business,* Vol. 26 (Winter 1974), p. 142.
17. James M. Carman, "On the Universality of Marketing," *Journal of Contemporary Business,* Vol. 2 (Autumn 1973), p. 14.
18. Robert Bartels, "The Identity Crisis in Marketing," *Journal of Marketing,* Vol. 38 (October 1974), p. 76.
19. David J. Luck, "Social Marketing: Confusion Compounded," *Journal of Marketing,* Vol. 38 (October 1974), pp. 2-7.
20. Robert J. Eggert, "Eggert Discusses Additional Goals for His Administration, Seeks Help in Defining Marketing," *Marketing News,* September 15, 1974.
21. E.J. McCarthy, *Basic Marketing* (Homewood, Ill.: Richard D. Irwin, 1960).
22. These observations were apparently extemporaneous since they were not included in his published paper: Philip Kotler, "Defining the limits of Marketing," in *Marketing Education and the Real World,* Boris W. Becker and Helmut Becker, eds. (Chicago: American Marketing Assn., 1972).
23. L.D.H. Weld, *The Marketing of Farm Products* (New York: Macmillan, 1920).
24. Paul W. Stewart, *Does Distribution Cost Too Much?* (New York: Twentieth Century Fund, 1939).
25. Harold Barger, *Distribution's Place in the Economy Since 1869* (Princeton: Princeton University Press, 1955); Reavis Cox, *Distribution in a High Level Economy* (Englewood Cliffs, N.J.: Prentice-Hall, 1965); and Neil Borden, *The Economic Effects of Advertising* (Chicago: Richard D. Irwin, 1942).
26. Virgil Read, *Planned Marketing* (New York: Ronald Press, 1930); and P. White and W.S. Hayward, *Marketing Practice* (New York: Doubleday, Page & Co., 1924).
27. Same reference as footnote 21.
28. William Lazer and Eugene Kelley, "Systems Perspective of Marketing Activity," in *Managerial Marketing: Perspectives and Viewpoints,* rev. ed. (Homewood, Ill.: Richard D. Irwin, 1962); Lee Adler, "Systems Approach to Marketing," *Harvard Business Review,* Vol. 45 (May-June, 1967); and George Fisk, *Marketing Systems: An Introductory Analysis* (New York: Harper & Row, 1967).
29. Fisk, same reference as footnote 28; p. 3.
30. Robert J. Holloway and Robert S. Hancock, *The Environment of Marketing Behavior* (New York: John Wiley & Sons, 1964); Robert J. Holloway and Robert S. Hancock, *Marketing in a Changing Environment* (New York: John Wiley & Sons, 1968); and Richard A. Scott and

Norton E. Marks, *Marketing and Its Environment* (Belmont: Wadsworth, 1968).
31. Kotler and Levy, same reference as footnote 6; Kotler and Zaltman, same reference as footnote 12; and Kotler, same reference as footnote 15.
32. Mindak and Bybee, same reference as footnote 13; Farley and Leavitt, same reference as footnote 13; Zikmund and Stanton, same reference as footnote 13; Carman, same reference as footnote 17; and Donald P. Robin, "Success in Social Marketing," *Journal of Business Research,* Vol. 3 (July 1974), pp. 303-310.
33. Lazer, same reference as footnote 7; Dawson, same reference as footnote 14; David S. Aaker and George Day, *Consumerism* (New York: Free Press, 1971); Norman Kangun, *Society and Marketing* (New York: Harper & Row, 1972); Frederick E. Webster, Jr., *Social Aspects of Marketing* (Englewood Cliffs, N.J.: Prentice-Hall, 1974); Reed Moyer, *Macro-Marketing* (New York: John Wiley & Sons, 1972); John R. Wish and Stephen H. Gamble, *Marketing and Social Issues* (New York: John Wiley & Sons, 1971); Ross L. Goble and Roy Shaw, *Controversy and Dialogue in Marketing* (Englewood Cliffs, N.J.: Prentice-Hall, 1975); Ronald R. Gist, *Marketing and Society* (New York: Holt, Rinehart & Winston, 1971); and William Lazer and Eugene Kelley, *Social Marketing* (Homewood, Ill.: Richard D. Irwin, 1973).
34. Irving D. Canton, "A Functional Definition of Marketing," *Marketing News,* July 15, 1973.
35. Philip Kotler, *Marketing Management* (Englewood Cliffs, N.J.: Prentice-Hall, 1967), p. 12.
36. Karl R. Popper, *The Logic of Scientific Discovery* (New York: Harper & Row, 1959), p. 19. [Emphasis added.]
37. Hutchinson, same reference as footnote 2.
38. Buzzell, same reference as footnote 2, p. 37.
39. George C. Homans, *The Nature of Social Science* (New York: Harcourt, Brace & World, 1967), p. 4
40. Ernest Nagel, *The Structure of Science* (New York: Harcourt, Brace & World, 1961), p. 2.
41. Marx W. Wartofsky, *Conceptual Foundations of Scientific Thought* (New York: Macmillan Co., 1968), p. 44.
42. Thomas S. Kuhn, *The Structure of Scientific Revelations* (Chicago: University of Chicago Press, 1970), p. 161.
43. Linus Pauling, *College Chemistry* (San Francisco: W.H. Freeman & Co., 1956), p. 15.
44. Richard H. Leftwich, *The Price System and Resource Allocation* (New York: Holt, Rinehart & Winston, 1966), p. 2.
45. Same reference as footnote 40, p. 15.
46. Carl G. Hempel, *Aspects of Scientific Explanation* (New York: Free Press, 1965), pp. 354-364.
47. Richard S. Rudner, *The Philosophy of Social Science* (Englewood Cliffs, N.J.: Prentice-Hall, 1966), p. 10; and Shelby D. Hunt, "The Morphology of Theory and the General Theory of Marketing," *Journal of Marketing,* Vol. 35 (April 1971), pp. 65-68.
48. Bernard Berelson and Gary Steiner, *Human Behavior: An Inventory of Scientific Findings* (New York: Harcourt, Brace & World, 1964).
49. Mario Bunge, *Scientific Research I: The Search for System* (New York: Springer-Verlag, 1967), p. 12.
50. Charles W. Morris, "Scientific Empiricism," in *Foundations of the Unity of Science,* Vol. 1, Otto Newrath, Rudolf Carnap and Charles Morris, eds. (Chicago: University of Chicago Press, 1955), p. 63.
51. Shelby D. Hunt, *Marketing Theory: Conceptual Foundation of Research in Marketing* (Columbus, Ohio: Grid Publishing Co., 1976).
52. Morris R. Cohen and Ernest Nagel, *Logic and the Scientific Method* (New York: Harcourt, Brace & World, 1934), p. 193.
53. Same reference as footnote 36, p. 44.
54. Carl G. Hempel, "Fundamentals of Concept Formation in Empirical Science," in *Foundations of the Unity of Science,* Vol. 2, Otto Newrath, ed. (Chicago: University of Chicago Press, 1970), p. 695.
55. See, for example: Nagel, same reference as footnote 40, p. 4; May Brodbeck, *Readings in the Philosophy of the Social Sciences* (New York: Macmillan Co., 1968), pp. 1-11; Richard B. Braithwaite, *Scientific Explanation* (Cambridge: Cambridge University Press, 1951), pp. 1-21; B.F. Skinner, *Science and Human Behavior* (New York: Macmillan Co., 1953), pp. 14-22; Rudner, same reference as footnote 47, pp. 7-9; Abraham Kaplan, *The Conduct of Inquiry* (Scranton, Pa.: Chandler Publishing Co., 1964), p. 32; Popper, same reference as footnote 36, pp. 44-48; and Hempel, same reference as footnote 54, p. 672.
56. Same reference as footnote 41, p. 23.
57. Nagel, same reference as footnote 40, p. 15; Henry E. Kyburg, Jr., *Philosophy of Science* (New York: Macmillan Co., 1968), p. 3; Carl G. Hempel, "The Theoretician's Dilemma," in *Aspects of Scientific Explanation* (New York: Free Press, 1965), p. 173; and Nicholas Rescher, *Scientific Explanation* (New York: Free Press, 1970), p. 4.
58. Mario Bunge, *Scientific Research II: The Search for Truth* (New York: Springer-Verlag, 1967), p. 132.
59. Kenneth A. Longman, "The Management Challenge to Marketing Theory," in *New Essays in Marketing Theory,* George Fisk, ed. (Boston: Allyn & Bacon, 1971), p. 10.

II

Buyer Behavior

The marketing objectives of any firm are to identify potential customers and to convince them that the firm's products will satisfy their needs. These objectives imply an understanding of human behavior, especially the behavioral role of buyer, for production, resale, or consumption. The articles in Part II represent some of marketing's most significant attempts to analyze buyer behavior.

The normative framework for analyzing the buyer, as Alderson pointed out in Part I, is provided by economic theory. But marketing scholars have never been satisfied with the sterility of economics. George Katona led the movement to integrate economic theory and the behavioral sciences. His early paper remains the best overview of what has come to be known as the new theory of consumer economics.

A number of marketing scholars have elaborated, with comprehensive conceptualizations, on the economic foundations of buyer behavior. Two of the best of such papers are included here in Part II. First is "The Theory of Buyer Behavior" by John Howard and Jagdish Sheth. This article presents the most widely acknowledged general model of buyer behavior; it has been extensively debated and subjected to many empirical tests. Frederick Webster and Yoram Wind offer an essentially similar construct but focus on the behavior of the organizational buyer rather than of the consumer.

Marketing scholars are increasingly recognizing the influence of people and other factors not directly involved in the exchange transaction on its participants. Russell Belk provides an overview of situational effects, and Scott Ward concentrates on the impact of other people. Similarly, Everett Rogers's lifetime of work in the diffusion of innovations focuses attention on the dynamics of behavioral change over time. These papers have added precision to our thinking about the contexts within which buyer behavior occurs in marketing.

Much of our understanding of buyer behavior has been attained through rigorous empirical research. There are many such significant studies but few are so outstanding as to be classics. Two classic studies illustrate approaches of interest as well as useful results. Mason Haire's instant coffee study remains the definitive operationalization of behavioral constructs thought to be unmeasurable. William Wells's review paper shows that this tradition remains alive and well in marketing research.

9

George Katona

Rational Behavior and Economic Behavior

While attempts to penetrate the boundary lines between psychology and sociology have been rather frequent during the last few decades, psychologists have paid little attention to the problems with which another sister discipline, economics, is concerned. One purpose of this paper is to arouse interest among psychologists in studies of economic behavior. For that purpose it will be shown that psychological principles may be of great value in clarifying basic questions of economics and that the psychology of habit formation, of motivation, and of group belonging may profit from studies of economic behavior.

A variety of significant problems, such as those of the business cycle or inflation, of consumer saving or business investment, could be chosen for the purpose of such demonstration. This paper, however, will be concerned with the most fundamental assumption of economics, the principle of rationality. In order to clarify the problems involved in this principle, which have been neglected by contemporary psychologists, it will be necessary to contrast the most common forms of methodology used in economics with those employed in psychology and to discuss the role of empirical research in the social sciences.

THEORY AND HYPOTHESES

Economic theory represents one of the oldest and most elaborate theoretical structures in the social sciences. However, dissatisfaction with the achievements and uses of economic theory has grown considerably during the past few decades on the part of economists who are interested in what actually goes on in economic life. And yet leading sociologists and psychologists have recently declared, "Economics is today, in a theoretical sense, probably the most

Reprinted from *Psychological Review* (September, 1953), pp. 307–318.
The late George Katona, a native of Hungary, received a Ph.D. in psychology from Gottingen University and pioneered in combining psychology and economics. He was program director of the Survey Research Center and professor of economics and psychology at the University of Michigan. His two best-known books are The Powerful Consumer *and* Mass Consumption Society. Psychological Economics, *published in 1975, synthesizes his contributions.*

highly elaborated, sophisticated, and refined of the disciplines dealing with action."[1]

To understand the scientific approach of economic theorists, we may divide them into two groups. Some develop an a priori system from which they deduce propositions about how people *should* act under certain assumptions. Assuming that the sole aim of businessmen is profit maximization, these theorists deduce propositions about marginal revenues and marginal costs, for example, that are not meant to be suited for testing. In developing formal logics of economic action, one of the main considerations is elegance of the deductive system, based on the law of parsimony. A wide gap separates these theorists from economic research of an empirical-statistical type which registers what they call aberrations or deviations, due to human frailty, from the norm set by theory.

A second group of economic theorists adheres to the proposition that it is the main purpose of theory to provide hypotheses that can be tested. This group acknowledges that prediction of future events represents the most stringent test of theory. They argue, however, that reality is so complex that it is necessary to begin with simplified propositions and models which are known to be unreal and not testable.[2] Basic among these propositions are the following three which traditionally have served to characterize the economic man or the rational man:

1. The principle of complete information and foresight. Economic conditions—demand, supply, prices, etc.—are not only given but also known to the rational man. This applies as well to future conditions about which there exists no uncertainty, so that rational choice can always be made. (In place of the assumption of certainty of future developments, we find nowadays more frequently the assumption that risks prevail but the probability of occurrence of different alternatives is known; this does not constitute a basic difference.)
2. The principle of complete mobility. There are no institutional or psychological factors which make it impossible, or expensive, or slow, to translate the rational choice into action.
3. The principle of pure competition. Individual action has no great influence on prices because each man's choice is independent from any other person's choice and because there are no "large" sellers or buyers. Action is the result of individual choice and is not group-determined.

Economic theory is developed first under these assumptions. The theorists then introduce changes in the assumptions so that the theory may approach reality. One such step consists, for instance, of introducing large-scale producers, monopolists, and oligopolists, another of introducing time lags, and still another of introducing uncertainty about the probability distribution of future events. The question raised in each case is this: Which of the original propositions needs to be changed, and in what way, in view of the new assumptions?

The fact that up to now the procedure of gradual approximation to reality has not been completely successful does not invalidate the method. It must be acknowledged that propositions were frequently derived from unrealistic economic models which were susceptible to testing and stimulated empirical research. In this paper, we shall point to a great drawback of this method of starting out with a simplified a priori system and making it gradually more complex and more real—by proceeding in this way one tends to lose sight of important problems and to disregard them.

The methods most commonly used in psychology may appear at first sight to be quite similar to the methods of economics which have just been described. Psychologists often start with casual observations, derive from them hypotheses, test those through more systematic observations, reformulate and revise their hypotheses accordingly, and test them again. The process of hypotheses-observations-hypotheses-observations often goes on with no end in sight. Differences from the approach of economic theory may be found in the absence in psychological research of detailed systematic elaboration prior to any observation. Also, in psychological research, findings and generalizations in one field of behavior are often considered as hypotheses in another field of behavior. Accordingly, in analyzing economic behavior[3] and trying to understand rationality, psychologists can draw on (a) the theory of learning and thinking, (b) the theory of group belonging, and (c) the theory of motivation. This will be done in this paper.

HABITUAL BEHAVIOR AND GENUINE DECISION MAKING

In trying to give noneconomic examples of "rational calculus," economic theorists have often referred to gambling. From some textbooks one might conclude that the most rational place in the world is the Casino in Monte Carlo where odds and probabilities can be calculated exactly. In contrast, some mathematicians and psychologists have considered scientific discovery and the thought processes of scientists as the best examples of rational or intelligent behavior.[4] An inquiry about the possible contributions of psychology to the analysis of rationality may then begin with a formulation of the differences between (a) associative learning and habit formation and (b) problem solving and thinking.

The basic principle of the first form of behavior is repetition. Here the argument of Guthrie holds: "The most certain and dependable information concerning what a man will do in any situation is information concerning what he did in that situation on its last occurrence."[5] This form of behavior depends upon the frequency of repetition as well as on its recency and on the success of past performances. The origins of habit formation have been demonstrated by experiments about learning nonsense syllables, lists of words, mazes, and conditioned responses. Habits thus formed are to some extent automatic and inflexible.

In contrast, problem-solving behavior has been characterized by the arousal of a problem or question, by deliberation that involves reorganization and "direction," by understanding of the requirements of the situation, by weighing of alternatives and taking their consequences into consideration and, finally, by choosing among alternative courses of action.[6] Scientific discovery is not the only example of such procedures; they have been demonstrated in the psychological laboratory as well as in a variety of real-life situations. Problem solving results in action which is new rather than repetitive; the actor may have never behaved in the same way before and may not have learned of any others having behaved in the same way.

Some of the above terms, defined and analyzed by psychologists, are also being used by economists in their discussion of rational behavior. In discussing, for example, a manufacturer's choice between erecting or not erecting a new factory, or raising or not raising his prices or output, reference is usually made to deliberation and to taking the consequences of alternative choices into consideration. Nevertheless, it is not justified to identify problem-solving behavior with rational behavior. From the point of view of an outside observer, habitual behavior may prove to be fully rational or the most appropriate way of action under certain circumstances. All that is claimed here is that the analysis of two forms of behavior – habitual versus genuine decision making—may serve to clarify problems of rationality. We shall proceed therefore by deriving six propositions from the psychological principles. To some extent, or in certain fields of behavior, these are findings or empirical generalizations; to some extent, or in other fields of behavior, they are hypotheses.

1. Problem-solving behavior is a relatively rare occurrence. It would be incorrect to assume that everyday behavior consistently manifests such features as arousal of a problem, deliberation, or taking consequences of the action into consideration. Behavior which does not manifest these characteristics predominates in everyday life and in economic activities as well.
2. The main alternative to problem-solving behavior is not whimsical or impulsive behavior (which was considered the major example of "irrational" behavior by nineteenth-century philosophers). When genuine decision making does not take place, habitual behavior is the most usual occurrence: people act as they have acted before under similar circumstances, without deliberating and choosing.
3. Problem-solving behavior is recognized most commonly as a deviation from habitual behavior. Observance of the established routine is abandoned when in driving home from my office, for example, I learn that there is a parade in town and choose a different route, instead of automatically taking the usual one. Or, to mention an example of economic behavior: Many businessmen have rules of thumb concerning the timing for reorders of merchandise; yet sometimes they decide to place new orders even though their inventories have not reached the usual level of depletion (for instance, because they anticipate price increases), or not to order merchandise even though that level has been reached (because they expect a slump in sales).
4. Strong motivational forces—stronger than those which elicit habitual behavior—must be present to call forth problem-solving behavior. Being in a "crossroad situation," facing "choice points," or perceiving that something new has occurred are typical instances in which we are motivated to deliberate and choose. Pearl Harbor and the Korean aggression are extreme examples of "new" events; economic behavior of the problem-solving type was found to have prevailed widely after these events.
5. Group belonging and group reinforcement play a substantial role in changes of behavior due to problem solving. Many people become aware of the same events at the same time; our mass media provide the same information and often the same interpretation of events to groups of people (to businessmen, trade union members, sometimes to all Americans). Changes in behavior resulting from new events may therefore occur among very many people at the same time. Some economists[7] argued that consumer optimism and pessimism are unimportant because usually they will cancel out; in the light of sociopsychological principles, however, it is probable, and has been confirmed by recent surveys, that a change from optimistic to pessimistic attitudes, or vice versa, sometimes occurs among millions of people at the same time.
6. Changes in behavior due to genuine decision making will tend to be substantial and abrupt, rather than small and gradual. Typical examples of action that results from genuine decisions are cessation of purchases or buying waves, the shutting down of plants or the building of new plants, rather than an increase or

decrease of production by 5 or 10 percent.[8]

Because of the preponderance of individual psychological assumptions in classical economics and the emphasis placed on group behavior in this discussion, the change in underlying conditions which has occurred during the last century may be illustrated by a further example. It is related – the author does not know whether the story is true or fictitious – that the banking house of the Rothschilds, still in its infancy at that time, was one of the suppliers of the armies of Lord Wellington in 1815. Nathan Mayer Rothschild accompanied the armies and was present at the Battle of Waterloo. When he became convinced that Napoleon was decisively defeated, he released carrier pigeons so as to transmit the news to his associates in London and reverse the commodity position of his bank. The carrier pigeons arrived in London before the news of the victory became public knowledge. The profits thus reaped laid, according to the story, the foundation to the outstanding position of the House of Rothschild in the following decades.

The decision to embark on a new course of action because of new events was then made by one individual for his own profit. At present, news of a battle, or of change of government, or of rearmament programs, is transmitted in short order by press and radio to the public at large. Businessmen – the manufacturers or retailers of steel or clothing, for instance – usually receive the same news about changes in the price of raw materials or in demand, and often consult with each other. Belonging to the same group means being subject to similar stimuli and reinforcing one another in making decisions. Acting in the same way as other members of one's group or of a reference group have acted under similar circumstances may also occur without deliberation and choice. New action by a few manufacturers will, then, frequently or even usually not be compensated by reverse action on the part of others. Rather the direction in which the economy of an entire country moves – and often the world economy as well – will tend to be subject to the same influences.

After having indicated some of the contributions which the application of certain psychological principles to economic behavior may make, we turn to contrasting that approach with the traditional theory of rationality. Instead of referring to the formulations of nineteenth-century economists, we shall quote from a modern version of the classical trend of thought. The title of a section in a recent article by Kenneth J. Arrow is "The Principle of Rationality." He describes one of the criteria of rationality as follows: "We can imagine the individual as listing, once and for all, all conceivable consequences of his actions in order of his preference for them."[9] We are first concerned with the expression "all conceivable consequences." This expression seems to contradict the principle of selectivity of human behavior. Yet habitual behavior is highly selective since it is based on (repeated) past experience, and problem-solving behavior likewise is highly selective since reorganization is subject to a certain direction instead of consisting of trial (and error) regarding all possible avenues of action.

Secondly, Arrow appears to identify rationality with consistency in the sense of repetition of the same choice. It is part and parcel of rational behavior, according to Arrow, that an individual "makes the same choice each time he is confronted with the same set of alternatives."[10] Proceeding in the same way on successive occasions appears, however, a characteristic of habitual behavior. Problem-solving behavior, on the other hand, is flexible. Rationality may be said to reflect adaptability and ability to act in a new way when circumstances demand it, rather than to consist of rigid or repetitive behavior.

Thirdly, it is important to realize the differences between the concepts, action, decision, and choice. It is an essential feature of the approach derived from considering problem-solving behavior that there is action without deliberate decision and choice. It then becomes one of the most important problems of research to determine under what conditions genuine decision and choice occur prior to an action. The three concepts are, however, used without differentiation in the classical theory of rationality and also, most recently, by Parsons and Shils. According to the theory of these authors, there are "five discrete choices (explicit or implicit) which every actor makes before he can act;" before there is action "a decision must always be made (explicitly or implicitly, consciously or unconsciously)."[11]

There exists, no doubt, a difference in terminology, which may be clarified by mentioning a simple case: Suppose my telephone rings: I lift the receiver with my left hand and say, "Hello." Should we then argue that I made several choices, for instance, that I decided not to lift the receiver with my right hand and not to say, "Mr. Katona speaking"? According to our use of the terms decision and choice, my action was habitual and did not involve "taking consequences into consideration."[12] Parsons and Shils use the terms *decision* and *choice* in a different sense, and Arrow may use the terms *all conceivable consequences* and *same set of alternatives* in a different sense from the one employed in this paper. But the difference between the two approaches appears to be more far-reaching. By using the terminology of the authors quoted, and by constructing a theory of rational action on the basis of this terminology, fundamental problems are disregarded. If every action by definition presupposes decision making, and if the malleability of human behavior is not taken into consideration, a one-sided theory of rationality is developed and empirical research is confined to testing a theory which covers only some of the aspects of rationality.

This was the case recently in experiments devised by Mosteller and Nogee. These authors attempt to test basic assumptions of economic theory, such as the rational choice among alternatives, by placing their subjects in a gambling situation (a variation of poker dice) and compelling them to make a decision, namely, to play or not to play against the experimenter. Through their experiments the authors prove that "it is feasible to measure utility experimentally,"[13] but they do not shed light on the conditions under which rational behavior occurs or on the inherent features of rational behavior. Experiments in which making a choice among known alternatives is prescribed do not test the realism of economic theory.

MAXIMIZATION

Up to now we have discussed only one central aspect of rationality – means rather than ends. The end of rational behavior, according to economic theory, is maximization of profits in the case of business firms and maximization of utility in the case of people in general.

A few words, first, on maximizing profits. This is usually considered the simpler case because it is widely held (*a*) that business firms are in business to make profits and (*b*) that profits, more so than utility, are a quantitative, measurable concept.

When empirical research, most commonly in the form of case studies, showed that businessmen frequently strove for many things in addition to profits or in place of profits, most theorists were content with small changes in their systems. They redefined profits so as to include long-range profits and what has been called nonpecuniary or psychic profits. Striving for security or for power was identified with striving for profits in the more distant future; purchasing goods from a high bidder who was a member of the same fraternity as the purchaser, rather than from the lowest bidder – to cite an example often used in textbooks – was thought to be maximizing of nonpecuniary profits. Dissatisfaction with this type of theory construction is rather widespread. For example, a leading theorist wrote recently:

> If *whatever* a business man does is explained by the principle of profit maximization – because he does what he likes to do, and he likes to do what maximizes the sum of his pecuniary and nonpecuniary profits – the analysis acquires the character of a system of definitions and tautologies, and loses much of its value as an explanation of reality.[14]

The same problem is encountered regarding maximization of utility. Arrow defines rational behavior as follows: " . . . among all the combinations of commodities an individual can afford, he chooses that combination which maximizes his utility or satisfaction"[15] and speaks of the "traditional identification of rationality with maximization of some sort."[16] An economic theorist has recently characterized this type of definition as follows:

> The statement that a person seeks to maximize utility is (in many versions) a tautology: it is impossible to conceive of an observational phenomenon that contradicts it. . . . What if the theorem is contradicted by observation: Samuelson says it would not matter much in the case of utility theory; I would say that it would not make the slightest difference. For there is a free variable in his system: the tastes of consumers. . . . Any contradiction of a theorem derived from utility theory can always be attributed to a change of tastes, rather than to an error in the postulates or logic of the theory.[17]

What is the way out of this difficulty? Can psychology, and specifically the psychology of motivation, help? We may begin by characterizing the prevailing economic theory as a single-motive theory and contrast it with a theory of multiple motives. Even in case of a single decision of one individual, multiplicity of motives (or of vectors or forces in the field), some reinforcing one another and some conflicting with one another, is the rule rather than the exception. The motivational patterns prevailing among different individuals making the same decision need not be the same; the motives of the same individual who is in the same external situation at different times may likewise differ. This approach opens the way (*a*) for a study of the relation of different motives to different forms of behavior and (*b*) for an investigation of changes in motives. Both problems are disregarded by postulating a single-motive theory and by restricting empirical studies to attempts to confirm or contradict that theory.

The fruitfulness of the psychological approach may be illustrated first by a brief reference to business motivation. We may rank the diverse motivational patterns of businessmen by placing the striving for high immediate profits (maximization of short-run profits, to use economic terminology; charging whatever the market can bear, to use a popular expression) at one extreme of the scale. At the other extreme we place the striving for prestige or power. In between we discern striving for security, for larger business volume, or for profits in the more distant future. Under what kinds of business conditions will motivational patterns tend to conform with the one or the other end of the scale? Preliminary studies would seem to indicate that the worse the business situation is, the more frequent is striving for high immediate profits, and the better the business situation is, the more frequent is striving for nonpecuniary goals.[18]

Next we shall refer to one of the most important problems of consumer economics as well as of business-cycle studies, the deliberate choice between saving and spending. Suppose a college professor receives a raise in his salary or makes a few hundred extra dollars through a publication. Suppose, furthermore, that he suggests thereupon to his wife that they should buy a television set while the wife argues that the money should be put in the bank as a reserve against a "rainy day." Whatever the final decision may be, traditional economic theory would hold that the action which gives the greater satisfaction was chosen. This way of theorizing is of little value. Under what conditions will one type of behavior (spending) and under what conditions will another type of behavior (saving) be more frequent? Psychological hypotheses according to which the strength of vectors is related to the immediacy of needs have been put to a test through nationwide surveys over the past six years.[19] On the basis of survey findings the following tentative generalization was established: Pessimism, insecurity, expectation of income declines or bad times in the near future promote saving (putting the extra money in the bank), while optimism, feeling of security, expectation of income increases, or good times promote spending (buying the television set, for instance).

Psychological hypotheses, based on a theory of motivational patterns which change with circumstances and influence behavior, thus stimulated empirical studies. These studies, in turn, yielded a better understanding of past developments and also, we may add, better predictions of forthcoming trends than did studies based on the classical theory. On the other hand, when conclusions about utility or rationality were made on an a priori basis, researchers lost sight of important problems.[20]

DIMINISHING UTILITY, SATURATION, AND ASPIRATION

Among the problems to which the identification of maximizing utility with rationality gave rise, the measurability of utility has been prominent. At present the position of most economists appears to be that while interpersonal comparison of several consumers' utilities is not possible, and while cardinal measures cannot be attached to the utilities of one particular consumer, ordinal ranking of the utilities of each individual can be made. It is asserted that I can always say either that I prefer *A* to *B*, or that I am indifferent to having *A* or *B*, or that I prefer *B* to *A*. The theory of indifference curves is based on this assumption.

In elaborating the theory further, it is asserted that rational behavior consists not only of preferring more of the same goods to less ($2 real wages to $1, or two packages of cigarettes to one package, for the same service performed) but also of deriving diminishing increments of satisfaction from successive units of a commodity.[21] In terms of an old textbook example, one drink of water has tremendous value to a thirsty traveler in a desert; a second, third, or fourth drink may still have some value but less and less so; an *n*th drink (which he is unable to carry along) has no value at all. A generalization derived from this principle is that the more of a commodity or the more money a person has, the smaller are his needs for that commodity or for money, and the smaller his incentives to add to what he has.

In addition to using this principle of saturation to describe the behavior of the rational man, modern economists applied it to one of the most pressing problems of contemporary American economy. Prior to World War II the American people (not counting business firms) owned about 45 billion dollars in liquid assets (currency, bank deposits, government bonds) and these funds were highly concentrated among relatively few families; most individual families held no liquid assets at all (except for small amounts of currency). By the end of the year 1945, however, the personal liquid-asset holdings had risen to about 140 billion dollars and four out of every five families owned some bank deposits or war bonds. What is the effect of this great change on spending and saving? This question has been answered by several leading economists in terms of the saturation principle presented above. "The rate of saving is . . . a diminishing function of the wealth the individual holds"[22] because "the availability of liquid assets raises consumption generally by reducing the impulse to save."[23] More specifically: a person who owns nothing or very little will exert himself greatly to acquire some reserve funds, while a person who owns much will have much smaller incentives to save. Similarly, incentives to increase one's income are said to weaken with the amount of income. In other words, the strength of motivation is inversely correlated with the level of achievement.

In view of the lack of contact between economists and psychologists, it is hardly surprising that economists failed to see the relevance for their postulates of the extensive experimental work performed by psychologists on the problem of levels of aspiration. It is not necessary in this paper to describe these studies in detail. It may suffice to formulate three generalizations as established in numerous studies of goal-striving behavior:[24]

1. Aspirations are not static, they are not established once for all time.
2. Aspirations tend to grow with achievement and decline with failure.
3. Aspirations are influenced by the performance of other members of the group to which one belongs and by that of reference groups.

From these generalizations hypotheses were derived about the influence of assets on saving which differed from the postulates of the saturation theory. This not the place to describe the extensive empirical work undertaken to test the hypotheses. But it may be reported that the saturation theory was not confirmed; the level-of-aspiration theory likewise did not suffice to explain the findings. In addition to the variable "size of liquid-asset holdings," the studies had to consider such variables as income level, income change, and saving habits. (Holders of large liquid assets are primarily people who have saved a high proportion of their income in the past!)[25]

The necessity of studying the interaction of a great number of variables and the change of choices over time leads to doubts regarding the universal validity of a one-dimensional ordering of all alternatives. The theory of measurement of utilities remains an empty frame unless people's established preferences of *A* over *B* and of *B* over *C* provide indications about their probable future behavior. Under what conditions do people's preferences give us such clues and under what conditions do they not? If at different times *A* and *B* are seen in different contexts – because of changed external conditions or the acquisition of new experiences – we may have to distinguish among several dimensions.

The problem may be illustrated by an analogy. Classic economic theory postulates a one-dimensional ordering of all alternatives; Gallup asserts that answers to questions of choice can always be ordered on a yes-uncertain (don't know)-no continuum; are both arguments subject to the same reservations? Specifically, if two persons give the same answer to a poll question (e.g., both say "Yes, I am for sending American troops to Europe" or "Yes, I am for the Taft-Hartley Act") may they mean different things so that their identical answers do not permit any conclusions about the similarity of their other attitudes and their behavior? Methodologically it follows from the last argument that yes-no questions need to be supplemented by open-ended questions to discern differences in people's level of information and motivation. It also follows that attitudes and preferences should be ascertained through a multi-question approach (or scaling) which serves to determine whether one or several dimensions prevail.

ON THEORY CONSTRUCTION

In attempting to summarize our conclusions about the respective merits of different scientific approaches, we might quote the conclusions of Arrow which he formulated for social science in general rather than for economics:

> To the extent that formal theoretical structures in the social sciences have not been based on the hypothesis of rational behavior, their postulates have been developed in a manner which we may term *ad hoc*. Such propositions . . . depend, of course, on the investigator's intuition and common sense.[26]

The last sentence seems strange indeed. One may argue the other way around and point out that such propositions as "the purpose of business is to make profits" or "the best businessman is the one who maximizes profits" are based on intuition or supposed common sense, rather than on controlled observation. The main problem raised by the quotation concerns the function of empirical research. There exists an alternative to developing an axiomatic system into a full-fledged theoretical model in advance of testing the theory through observations. Controlled observations should be based on hypotheses, and the formulation of an integrated theory need not be delayed until all observations are completed. Yet theory construction is part of the process of hypothesis-observation-revised hypothesis and prediction-observation, and systematization should rely on some empirical research. The proximate aim of scientific research is a body of empirically validated generalizations and not a theory that is valid under any and all circumstances.

The dictum that "theoretical structures in the social sciences must be based on the hypothesis of rational behavior" presupposes that it is established what rational behavior is. Yet, instead of establishing the characteristics of rational behavior a priori, we must first determine the conditions a^1, b^1, c^1 under which behavior of the type x^1, y^1, z^1, and the conditions a^2, b^2, c^2 under which behavior of the type x^2, y^2, z^2 is likely to occur. Then, if we wish, we may designate one of the forms of behavior as rational. The contributions of psychology to this process are not solely methodological; findings and principles about noneconomic behavior provide hypotheses for the study of economic behavior. Likewise, psychology can profit from the study of economic behavior because many aspects of behavior, and among them the problems of rationality, may be studied most fruitfully in the economic field.

This paper was meant to indicate some promising leads for a study of rationality, not to carry such study to its completion. Among the problems that were not considered adequately were the philosophical ones (rationality viewed as a value concept), the psychoanalytic ones (the relationships between rational and conscious, and between irrational and unconscious), and those relating to personality theory and the roots of rationality. The emphasis was placed here on the possibility and fruitfulness of studying forms of rational behavior, rather than the characteristics of *the* rational man. Motives and goals that change with and are adapted to circumstances, and the relatively rare but highly significant cases of our becoming aware of problems and attempting to solve them, were found to be related to behavior that may be called truly rational.

NOTES

1. T. Parsons and E.A. Shils, (Editors), *Toward a General Theory of Action* (Cambridge, Mass.: Harvard University Press, 1951).
2. A variety of methods used in economic research differ, of course, from those employed by the two groups of economic theorists. Some research is motivated by dissatisfaction with the traditional economic theory; some is grounded in a systematization greatly different from traditional theory (the most important example of such systematization is national income accounting); some research is not clearly based on any

theory; finally, some research has great affinity with psychological and sociological studies.

3. The expression "economic behavior" is used in this paper to mean behavior concerning economic matters (spending, saving, investing, pricing, etc.). Some economic theorists use the expression to mean the behavior of the "economic man," that is, the behavior postulated in their theory of rationality.
4. Reference should be made first of all to Max Wertheimer who in his book *Productive Thinking* uses the terms "sensible" and "intelligent" rather than "rational." Since we are mainly interested here in deriving conclusions from the psychology of thinking, the discussion of psychological principles will be kept extremely brief. See M. Wertheimer, *Productive Thinking* (New York: Harper, 1945); G. Katona, *Organizing and Memorizing* (New York: Columbia University Press, 1940); and G. Katona, *Psychological Analysis of Economic Behavior* (New York: McGraw-Hill, 1951), especially Chapters 3 and 4.
5. E.R. Guthrie, *Psychology of Learning* (New York: Harper, 1935), p. 228.
6. Cf. the following statement by a leading psychoanalyst: "Rational behavior is behavior that is effectively guided by an understanding of the situation to which one is reacting." French adds two steps that follow the choice between alternative goals, namely, commitment to a goal and commitment to a plan to reach a goal. See T.M. French, *The Integration of Behavior* (Chicago: University of Chicago Press, 1952).
7. J.M. Keynes, *The General Theory of Employment, Interest and Money* (New York: Harcourt, Brace, 1936), p. 95.
8. Some empirical evidence supporting these six propositions in the area of economic behavior has been assembled by the Survey Research Center of the University of Michigan. See G. Katona, "Psychological Analysis of Business Decisions and Expectations," *American Economic Review* (1946), pp. 44-63.
9. K.J. Arrow, "Mathematical Models in the Social Sciences," in D. Lerner and H.D. Lasswell (Editors), *The Policy Sciences* (Stanford: Stanford University Press, 1951), p. 135.
10. In his recent book Arrow adds after stating that the economic man "will make the same decision each time he is faced with the same range of alternatives": "The ability to make consistent decisions is one of the symptoms of an integrated personality." See K.J. Arrow, *Social Choice and Individual Values* (New York: Wiley, 1951), p. 2.
11. T. Parsons and E.A. Shils, *op. cit.*
12. If I have reason not to make known that I am at home, I may react to the ringing of the telephone by fright, indecision, and deliberation (should I lift the receiver or let the telephone ring?) instead of reacting in the habitual way. This is an example of problem-solving behavior characterized as deviating from habitual behavior. The only example of action mentioned by Parsons and Shils, "a man driving his automobile to a lake to go fishing," may be habitual or may be an instance of genuine decision making.
13. F. Mosteller and P. Nogee, "An Experimental Measurement of Utility;" *Journal of Political Economy* (1951), pp. 371-405.
14. F. Machlup, "Marginal Analysis and Empirical Research," *American Economic Review* (1946), p. 526.
15. K.J. Arrow, *op cit.*
16. K.J. Arrow, *Social Choice and Individual Values* (New York: Wiley, 1951). The quotation refers specifically to Samuelson's definition but also applies to that of Arrow.
17. G.J. Stigler, "Review of P.A. Samuelson's Foundations of Economic Analysis," *Journal of American Statistical Association* (1948), p. 603.
18. G. Katona, *Psychological Analysis of Economic Behavior* (New York: McGraw-Hill, 1951), pp. 193-213.
19. In the Surveys of Consumer Finances, conducted annually since 1946 by the Survey Research Center of the University of Michigan for the Federal Reserve Board and reported in the *Federal Reserve Bulletin*. See a forthcoming publication of the Survey Research Center on consumer buying and inflation during 1950–52.
20. It should not be implied that the concepts of utility and maximization are of no value for empirical research. Comparison between maximum utility as determined from the vantage point of an observer with the pattern of goals actually chosen (the "subjective maximum"), which is based on insufficient information, may be useful. Similar considerations apply to such newer concepts as "minimizing regrets" and the "minimax."
21. This principle of diminishing utility was called a "fundamental tendency of human nature" by the great nineteenth century economist, Alfred Marshall.
22. G. Haberler, *Prosperity and Depression,* 3rd ed. (Geneva: League of Nations, 1941), p. 199.
23. The last quotation is from the publication of the U.S. Department of Commerce, *Survey of Current Business,* May 1950, p. 10.
24. K. Lewin, et al., "Level of Aspiration," in J. Hunt (Editor), *Personality and the Behavior Disorders* (New York: Ronald, 1944).
25. The empirical work was part of the economic behavior program of the Survey Research Center under the direction of the author.
26. K.J. Arrow, "Mathematical Models in the Social Sciences," in D. Lerner and H.D. Lasswell (Editors), *The Policy Sciences* (Stanford: Stanford University Press, 1951), p. 137.

10

John A. Howard
Jagdish N. Sheth

A Theory of Buyer Behavior

In the last fifteen years, considerable research on consumer behavior both at the conceptual and empirical levels has accumulated. This can be gauged by reviews of the research.[1] As a consequence we believe that sufficient research exists in both the behavioral sciences and consumer behavior to attempt a comprehensive theory of buyer behavior. Furthermore, broadly speaking, there are two major reasons at the basic research level which seem to have created the need to take advantage of this opportunity. The first reason is that a great variety exists in today's effort to understand the consumer, and unfortunately there is no integration of this variety. The situation resembles the seven blind men touching different parts of the elephant and making inferences about the animal which differ, and occasionally contradict one another. A comprehensive theory of buyer behavior would hopefully not only provide a framework for integrating the existing variety but also would prepare the researcher to adopt appropriate research designs which would control sources of influences other than those he is immediately interested in. The difficulty of replicating a study and the possibility of getting contradictory findings will be minimized accordingly.

The second major basic research reason for a comprehensive theory is the potential application of research in buying behavior to human behavior in general. In asserting the need to validate psychological propositions in a real

Reprinted from Reed Moyer, (ed.) *Changing Marketing Systems . . . Consumer, Corporate and Government Interfaces: Proceedings of the 1967 Winter Conference of the American Marketing Association,* 1967, published by the American Marketing Association.

John A Howard is George E. Warren Professor of Business in the Graduate School of Business, Columbia University. He is a distinguished marketing scholar who has directed studies of consumer behavior for both company and public policy purposes. In addition to The Theory of Consumer Behavior, *his books include* Marketing Management: Analysis and Control *and* Marketing Theory.

Jagdish N. Sheth is Professor of Business Administration at Southern California. He received his Ph.D. from Columbia University and has served on the faculties of Columbia University, Sloan School of Management, M.I.T., and the University of Illinois. He is a prolific author in areas of consumer psychology, multivariate methods, and international marketing.

world context Sherif has repeatedly and eloquently argued for applied research.[2] Also, McGuire argues that social psychology is moving toward theory-oriented research in *natural settings* because a number of forces are encouraging the movement away from laboratory research, and he cites the current work in buyer behavior as one of these forces.[3]

Again, one way that we can contribute to "pure" areas of behavioral science is by attempting a comprehensive theory which would help to identify and to iron out our own inconsistencies and contradictions. Such an attempt looks ambitious on the surface, but after several years of work and drawing upon earlier work,[4] we are confident that it can be achieved.

A BRIEF SUMMARY OF THE THEORY

Before we describe each component of the theory in detail, it will be helpful to discuss briefly the essentials of our view of the consumer choice process.

Much of buying behavior is more or less repetitive brand choice decisions. During his life cycle, the buyer establishes purchase cycles for various products which determine how often he will buy a given product. For some products, this cycle is very lengthy, as for example in buying durable appliances, and, therefore, he buys the product quite infrequently. For many other products, however, the purchase cycle is short and he buys the product frequently as is the case for many grocery and personal care items. Since there is usually the element of repeat buying, we must present a theory which incorporates the dynamics of purchase behavior over a period of time if we wish to capture the central elements of the empirical process.

In the face of repetitive brand choice decisions, the consumer simplifies his decision process by storing relevant information and routinizing his decision process. What is crucial, therefore, is to identify the elements of decision making, to observe the structural or substantive changes that occur in them over time due to the repetitive nature, and show how a combination of the decision elements affect search processes and the incorporation of information from the buyer's commercial and social environment.

The buyer, having been motivated to buy a product class, is faced with a brand choice decision. The elements of his decision are: (1) a set of motives, (2) several courses of action, and (3) decision mediators by which the motives are matched with the alternatives. Motives are specific to a product class, and they reflect the underlying needs of the buyer. The alternative courses of actions are the purchase of one of the various brands with their potential to satisfy the buyer's motives. There are two important notions involved in the definition of alternatives as brands. First, the brands which are alternatives of the buyer's choice decision at any given time are generally a small number, collectively called his "evoked set." The size of the evoked set is only two or three, a fraction of the brands he is aware of and still smaller fraction of the total number of brands actually available in the market. Second, any two consumers may have quite different alternatives in their evoked sets.

The decision mediators are a set of rules that the buyer employs to match his motives and his means of satisfying those motives. They serve the function of ordering and structuring the buyer's motives and then ordering and structuring the various brands based on their potential to satisfy these ordered motives. The decision mediators develop by the process of learning about the buying situation. They are, therefore, influenced by information from the buyer's environment and even more importantly by the actual experience of purchasing and consuming the brand.

When the buyer is just beginning to purchase a product class such as when a purchase is precipitated by a change in his life cycle, he lacks experience. In order, therefore, to develop the decision mediators, he *actively seeks information* from his commercial and social environments. The information that he either actively seeks or accidentally receives is subject to perceptual processes which not only limits the intake of information (magnitude of information is affected) but modifies it to suit his own frame of reference (quality of information is affected). These modifications are significant since they distort the neat "marketing stimulus-consumer response" relation.

Along with active search for information, the buyer may, to some extent, generalize from past similar experiences. Such generalization can be due to physical similarity of the new product class to the old product class. For example, in the initial purchases of Scotch whisky, the buyer may generalize his experiences in buying of gin. Generalization can also occur even when the two product classes are physically dissimilar but have a common meaning such as deriving from a company-wide brand name. For example, the buyer could generalize his experiences in buying a refrigerator or range to his first purchase of a dishwasher of the same brand.

Whatever the source, the buyer develops sufficient decision mediators to enable him to choose a brand which seems to have the best potential for satisfying his motives. If the brand proves satisfactory, the potential of that brand to satisfy his motives is increased. The result is that the probability of buying that brand is likewise increased. With repeated satisfactory purchases of one or more brands, the buyer is likely to manifest a routinized decision process whereby the sequential steps in buying are well structured so that some event which triggers the process may actually complete the choice decision. Routinized purchasing implies that his decision mediators are well established and that the buyer has strong brand preferences.

The phase of repetitive decision making, in which the buyer reduces the complexity of a buying situation with the help of information and experience, is called the *psychology of simplification*. Decision making can be divided into three stages and used to illustrate the psychology of simplification: Extensive Problem Solving, Limited Problem Solving and Routinized Response Behavior. The further he is along in simplifying his environment, the less is the tendency toward active search behavior. The environmental stimuli related to the purchase situation become more meaningful and less ambiguous. Furthermore, the buyer establishes more cognitive consistency among the brands as he moves toward routinization and the incoming information is then screened both with regard to its magnitude and quality. He becomes less attentive to stimuli which do not fit his cognitive structure and he distorts those stimuli which are forced upon him.

A surprising phenomenon, we believe, occurs in many instances of frequently purchased products such as in grocery and personal care items. The buyer, after attaining routinization of his decision process, may find himself in too simple a situation. He is likely to feel the monotony or boredom associated with such repetitive decision making. It is also very likely that he is dissatisfied with even the most preferred brand. In both cases, he may feel that all existing alternatives including the preferred brand are unacceptable. He therefore feels a need to *complicate* his buying situation by considering new brands, and this process can be called the *psychology of complication*. The new situation causes him to identify a new brand, and so he begins again to simplify in the manner described earlier. Thus with a frequently purchased item buying is a continuing process with its ups and downs in terms of information seeking analogous to the familiar cyclical fluctuations in economic activity.

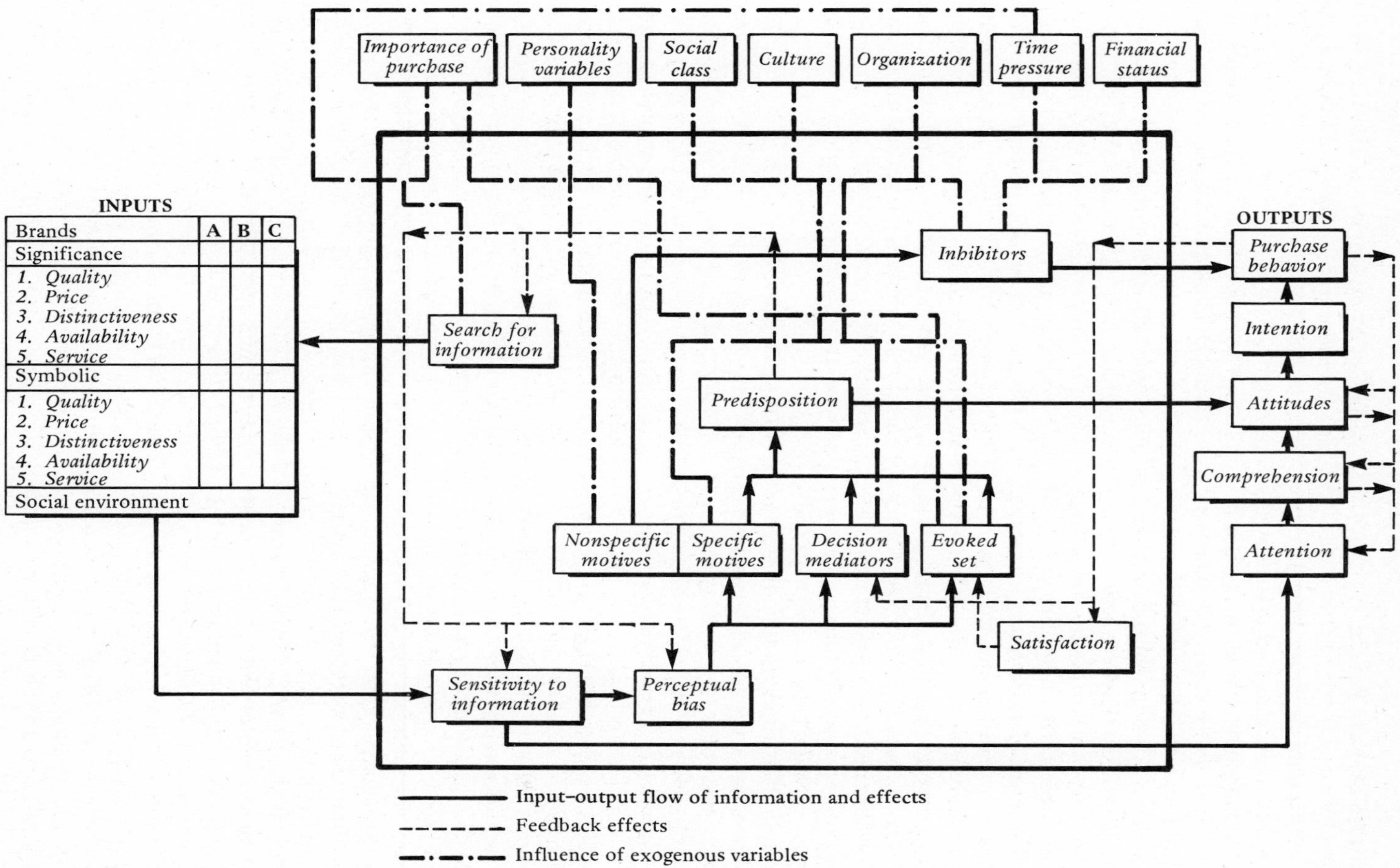

FIGURE 10–1 *A Theory of Buyer Behavior*

ELEMENTS OF THEORY

Any theory of human behavior needs some means for explaining individual differences. The marketing manager also is interested in differentiated masses of buyers. He wants to understand and separate individual differences so that he can classify or segment the total market based upon individual differences. By understanding the psychology of the individual buyer we may achieve this classification. Depending on the internal state of the buyer, a given stimulus may result in a given response. For example, one buyer who urgently needs a product may respond to the ad of a brand in that product class by buying it whereas another buyer who does not need the product may simply notice the ad and store the information or ignore the ad. A construct such as "level of motivation" will then explain the divergent reactions to the same stimulus. Alternatively, two buyers may both urgently need a product, but they buy two different brands. This can be explained by another construct: predisposition toward a brand.

Figure 10-1 represents the theory of buyer behavior. The central rectangular box isolates the various internal state variables and processes which combined together show the state of the buyer. The inputs to the rectangular box are the stimuli from the marketing and social environments. The outputs are a variety of responses that the buyer is likely to manifest based on the interaction between the stimuli and his internal state. Besides the inputs and outputs, there are a set of seven influences which affect the variables in the rectangular box.[5] These variables appear at the top of the diagram and are labelled "exogenous variables." Their function is to provide a means of adjusting for the interpersonal differences discussed above. The variables within the rectangular box serve the role of endogenous variables in the sense that changes in them are explained but they are something less than endogenous variables. They are not well defined and hence are not measurable. They are hypothetical constructs. Their values are inferred from relations among the output intervening variables. Several of the exogenous variables such as personality, social class and culture have traditionally been treated as part of the endogenous variables. We believe that they affect more specific variables, and by conceptualizing their effect as via the hypothetical constructs, we can better understand their role.

Thus it will be seen that the theory of buyer behavior has four major components; the stimulus variables, the response variable, the hypothetical constructs and the exogenous variables. We will elaborate on each of the components below both in terms of their substance and their interrelationships.

Stimulus Variables

At any point in time, the hypothetical constructs which reflect the buyer's internal state are affected by numerous stimuli from the environment. The environment is classified as Commercial or Social. The commercial environment is the marketing activities of various firms by which they attempt to communicate to the buyer. From the buyer's point of view, these communications basically come either via the physical brands themselves or some linguistic or pictorial representations of the attributes of the brands. If the elements of the brands such as price, quality, service, distinctiveness or availability are communicated through the physical brands (significates) then the stimuli are defined and classified as significative stimuli. If, on the other hand, the attributes are communicated in linguistic or pictorial symbols such as in mass media, billboards, catalogs, salesmen, etc., then the stimuli from commercial sources are classified as symbolic stimuli. We view the marketing mix as the optimum allocation of funds between the two major channels of communication – significative or symbolic – to the buyer.

Each commercial input variable is hypothesized to be multivariate. Probably the five major dimensions of a brand – price, quality, distinctiveness, availability and service – summarize the various attributes. The same dimensions are present in both significative or symbolic communication which become the input stimuli for the buyer. However, certain dimensions may be more appropriately conveyed by significative rather than symbolic communication and vice versa. For example, price is easily communicated by both channels; shape may best be communicated by two-dimensional pictures rather than verbal communication. Finally, size may not be easily communicated by any symbolic representation: the physical product (significate) may be necessary.

The third stimulus input variable is social stimuli. It refers to the information that the buyer's social environment provides regarding a purchase decision. The most obvious is word of mouth communication.

The inputs to the buyer's mental state from the three major sources are then processed and stored by their interaction with a series of hypothetical constructs, and the buyer may react immediately or later.

Hypothetical Constructs

The hypothetical constructs and their interrelationships are the result of an integration of Hull's learning theory,[6] Osgood's cognitive theory,[7] and Berlyne's theory of exploratory behavior[8] along with other ideas.

We may classify the constructs into two classes: (i) those that have to do with perception, and (ii) those having to do with learning. Perceptual constructs serve the function of information processing while the learning constructs serve the function of concept formation. It is interesting that, after years of experience in advertising, Reeves has a very similar classification:[9] his "penetration" is analogous to perceptual variables and his "unique selling propositions" is analogous to learning variables. We will at first describe the learning constructs since they are the major components of decision making; the perceptual constructs which serve the important role of obtaining and processing information are more complex and will be described later.

Learning constructs. The learning constructs are labeled as: (1) Motives – Specific and Nonspecific, (2) Brand Potential of Evoked Set, (3) Decision Mediators, (4) Predisposition toward the brands, (5) Inhibitors, and (6) Satisfaction with the purchase of the brand.

Motive is the impetus to action. Motives or goals may be thought of as constituting a means-end chain and hence, as being general or specific depending upon their position in the chain. Motives can refer to the buyer's specific goals in purchasing a product class. The buyer is motivated by the expectation or anticipation due to past learning of outcome from the purchase of each of the brands in his evoked set.

The specific motives – lower level motives in the means-end chain – are very closely anchored to the attributes of a product class and in this way they become purchase criteria. Examples of specific motives for buying a dietary product such as Metrecal or Sego are low calories, nutrition, taste, and value.

Very often, several specific motives are nothing more than indicators of some underlying more general motive, that is, some motive that is higher in the means-end chain. In the above example, the specific motives of nutrition and low calories might be merely indicators of the common motive of good health.

Motives also serve the important function of raising the buyer's general motivational state or arousal and thereby tuning up the buyer, causing him to pay attention to environmental stimuli. Examples of nonspecific motives are probably anxiety, fear, many of the personality variables such as authoritarianism, exhibitionism, aggressiveness, etc., and social motives of power, status, prestige, etc. Although they are nonspecific, they are not innate, but rather learned, mostly due to acculturation. The nonspecific motives also possess a hierarchy within themselves. For example, anxiety is considered to be the source of another motive, that of the need of money.[10]

Brand Potential of Evoked Set is the second learning construct. A buyer who is familiar with a product class has an evoked set of alternatives to satisfy his motives. The elements of his evoked set are some of the brands that make up the product class. The concept is important because for this buyer the brands in his evoked set constitute competition for the seller.

A brand is, of course, a class concept like many other objects or things. The buyer attaches a *word* to this concept – a label – which is the brand name such as "Campbell's Tomato Soup." Whenever he sees a can of Campbell's Tomato Soup or hears the phrase, the image conveys to him certain satisfactions, procedures for preparation, etc. In short, it conveys certain meaning including its potential to satisfy his motives.

Various brands in the buyer's evoked set will generally satisfy the goal structure differently. One brand may possess potential to the extent that it is an ideal brand for the buyer. Another brand, on the other hand, may satisfy motives just enough to be part of his evoked set. By the process of learning the buyer obtains and stores knowledge regarding each brand's potential and then rank orders them in terms of their want-satisfying potential. The evoked set, in short, is a set of alternatives with each alternative's payoff. Predisposition mentioned below enables the buyer to choose one among them.

Decision Mediator is the third learning construct and it brings together motives and alternatives. The brand potential of each of the brands in his evoked set are the decision alternatives with their payoffs. Decision mediators are the buyer's mental rules for matching the alternatives with his motives, for rank-ordering them in terms of their want-satisfying capacity. As mental rules, they exhibit reasons wherein the cognitive elements related to the alternatives and the motives are structured. The words that he uses to describe these attributes are also the words that he thinks with and that he finds are easy to remember. The criterial attributes are important to the manufacturer because if he knows them he can deliberately build into his brand and promotion those characteristics which will differentiate his brand from competing brands.

The decision mediators thus represent enduring cognitive rules established by the process of learning, and their function is to obtain meaningful and congruent relations among brands so that the buyer can manifest goal-directed behavior. The aim of the theory of buyer behavior is not just the identification of motives and the respective brands but to show their structure as well. It is the decision mediators which provide this structure.

In view of the fact that decision mediators are learned, principles of learning become crucial in their development and change over time. There are two broad sources of learning: (1) actual experiences, and (2) information. Actual experience can be either with the *same* buying situation in the past or with a *similar* buying situation. The latter is generally labelled as generalization as discussed earlier. Similarly, information as a source of learning can be from: (1) the buyer's commercial environment, or (2) his social environment. Later, we will elaborate on each of the sources of learning.

Predisposition, the fourth construct, is the summary effect of the previous three constructs. It refers to the buyer's preference toward brands in his evoked set. It is, in fact, an aggregate index which is reflected in attitude which, in turn, is measured by attitude scales. It might be visualized as the "place" where brands in Evoked Set are compared with Mediator's choice criteria to yield a judgment on the relative contribution of the brands to the buyer's motives. This judgment includes not only an estimate of the value of the brand to him but also an estimate of the confidence with which he holds that position. This uncertainty aspect of Predisposition can be called "brand ambiguity," in that, the more confident he holds it, the less ambiguous is the connotative meaning of the brand to the buyer and the more likely he is to buy it.[11]

Inhibitors, the fifth learning construct, are forces in the environment which create important disruptive influences in the actual purchase of a brand even when the buyer has reasoned out that that brand will best satisfy his motives. In other words, when the buyer is both predisposed to buy a brand and has the motivation to buy some brand in the product class, he may not buy it because several environmental forces inhibit its purchase and prevent him from satisfying his preferences.

We postulate at least four types of inhibitors. They are: (1) high price of the brand, (2) lack of availability of the brand, (3) time pressure on the buyer, and (4) the buyer's financial status. The first two are part of the environmental stimuli, and therefore, they are part of the input system. The last two come from the two exogenous variables of the same name. It should be pointed out that social constraints emanating from other exogenous variables may also create temporary barriers to the purchase of a brand.

An essential feature of all inhibitors is that they are *not internalized* by the buyer because their occurrence is random and strictly situational. However, some of the inhibitors may persist systematically over time as they concern a given buyer. If they persist long enough, the buyer is likely to incorporate them as part of his decision mediators and thus to internalize them. The consequence is that they may affect even the structure of alternatives and motives.

Satisfaction, the last of the learning constructs, refers to the degree of congruence between the actual consequences from purchase and consumption of a brand and what was expected from it by the buyer at the time of purchase. If the actual outcome is adjudged by the buyer as *at least* equal to the expected, the buyer will feel satisfied. If, on the other hand, the actual outcome is adjudged as less than what he expected, the buyer will feel dissatisfied and his attitude will be less favorable. Satisfaction or dissatisfaction with a brand can exist with respect to any one of the different attributes. If the brand proves more satisfactory than he expected, the buyer has a tendency to enhance the attractiveness of the brand. Satisfaction will, therefore, affect the reordering of the brands in the evoked set for the next buying decision.

Relations among learning constructs. Underlying Predisposition toward the brands and related variables, several important notions are present. The simplest way to describe them is to state that we may classify a decision process as either Extensive Problem Solving, Limited Problem Solving or Routinized Response Behavior depending on the strength of Predisposition toward the brands. In the early phases of buying, the buyer has not yet developed decision mediators well enough; specifically his product class concept is not well formed and predisposition is low. As he acquires information and gains experience in buying and consuming the brand, Decision Mediators become firm and Predisposition toward a brand is generally high.

In Extensive Problem Solving, Predisposition toward the brands is low. None of the brands is discriminated enough based on their criterial attributes for the buyer to show greater brand preference toward any one brand. At this state of decision making, brand ambiguity is high with the result that the buyer actively seeks information from his environment. Due to greater search for information, there exists a greater *latency of response* – the time interval from the initiation of a decision to its completion. Similarly, deliberation or reasoning will be high since he lacks a well-defined product class concept which is the denotative aspect of mediator. He is also likely to consider many brands as part of Evoked Set, and stimuli coming from the commercial environment are less likely to trigger any immediate purchase reaction.

When Predisposition toward the brands is moderate, the buyer's decision process can be called Limited Problem Solving. There still exists brand ambiguity since the buyer is not able to discriminate and compare brands so that he may prefer one brand over others. He is likely to seek information but not to the extent that he seeks it in Extensive Problem Solving. More importantly, he seeks information more on a relative basis to compare and discriminate various brands rather than to compare them absolutely on each of the brands. His deliberation or thinking is much less since Decision Mediators are tentatively well defined. Evoked Set will consist of a small number of brands, each having about the same degree of preference.

In Routinized Response Behavior, the buyer will have a high level of Predisposition toward brands in his evoked set. Furthermore, he has now accumulated sufficient experience and information to have little brand ambiguity. He will in fact discriminate among brands enough to show a strong preference toward one or two brands in the evoked set. He is unlikely to actively seek any information from his environment since such information is not needed. Also, whatever information he passively or accidentally receives, he will subject it to selective perceptual processes so that only congruent information is allowed. Very often, the congruent information will act as "triggering cues" to motivate him to manifest purchase behavior. Much of impulse purchase, we believe, is really the outcome of a strong predisposition and such a facilitating commercial stimulus as store display. The buyer's evoked set will consist of a few brands toward which he is highly predisposed. However, he will have greater preference toward one or two brands in his evoked set and less toward others.

As mentioned earlier, Predisposition is an aggregate index of decision components. Thus, any changes in the components due to learning from experience or information imply some change in Predisposition. The greater the learning, the more the predisposition toward the brands in the evoked set. The exact nature of learning will be described later when we discuss the dynamics of buying behavior.

Perceptual constructs. Another set of constructs serves the function of information procurement and processing relevant to a purchase decision. As mentioned earlier, information can come from any one of the three stimulus inputs – significative commercial stimuli, symbolic commercial stimuli, and social stimuli. Once again we will here only describe the constructs; their utilization by the buyer will be explained when we discuss the dynamics of buying behavior. The perceptual constructs in Figure 10-1 are: (a) Sensitivity to Information, (b) Perceptual Bias, and (c) Search for Information.

A perceptual phenomenon implies either ignoring a physical event which could be a stimulus, seeing it attentively or sometimes imagining what is not present in reality. All perceptual phenomena essentially create some change in quantity or quality of objective information.

Sensitivity to Information refers to the opening and closing of sensory receptors which control the intake of information. The manifestation of this phenomenon is generally called perceptual vigilance (paying attention) or perceptual defense (ignoring the information). Sensitivity to Information, therefore, primarily serves as a gatekeeper to information entering into the buyer's mental state. It thus controls the quantity of information input.

Sensitivity to Information, according to Berlyne,[12] is a function of the degree of ambiguity of the stimuli to which the buyer is exposed. If the stimulus is very familiar or too simple, the ambiguity is low and the buyer will not pay attention unless he is predisposed to such information from past learning. Furthermore, if ambiguity of the stimulus continues to be low, the buyer feels a sense of monotony and actually seeks other information, and this act can be said to *complicate* his environment. If the stimulus is very complex and ambiguous, the buyer finds it hard to comprehend and, therefore, he ignores it by resorting to perceptual defense. Only if the stimulus is in the moderate range of ambiguity is the buyer motivated to pay attention and to freely absorb the objective information.

In a single communication, the buyer may at first find the communication complex and ambiguous and so he will resort to perceptual defense and tend to ignore it. As some information enters, however, he finds that it is really at the medium level of ambiguity and so pays attention. On the other hand, it might be that the more he pays attention to it, the more he finds the communication too simple and, therefore, ignores it as the process of communication progresses.

A second variable which governs Sensitivity to Information is the buyer's predisposition toward the brand about which the information is concerned. The more interesting the information, the more likely the buyer is to open up his receptors and therefore to pay attention to the information. Hess has recently measured this by obtaining the strength of pupil dilation.

Perceptual Bias is the second perceptual construct. The buyer not only selectively attends to information, but he may actually distort it once it enters his mental state. In other words, quality of information can be altered by the buyer. This aspect of the perceptual process is summarized in Perceptual Bias. The buyer may distort the cognitive elements contained in information to make them congruent with his own frame of reference as determined by the amount of information he already has stored. A series of cognitive consistency theories have been recently developed to explain how this congruency is established and what the consequences are in terms of the distortion of information we might expect.[13] Most of the qualitative change in information arises because of feedback from various decision components such as Motives, Evoked Set and Decision Mediators. These relations are too complex, however, to describe in the summary.

The perceptual phenomena described above are likely to be less operative if the information is received from the buyer's social environment. This is because: (i) the source of social information, such as a friend, is likely to be favorably regarded by the buyer and therefore proper, undistorted reception of information will occur, and (ii) the information itself is modified by the social environment (the friend) so that it conforms to the needs of the buyer and, therefore, further modification is less essential.

Search for Information is the third perceptual construct. During the total buying phase which extends over time and involves several repeat purchases of a product class, there are stages when the buyer *actively* seeks information. It is very important to distinguish the times when he passively receives information from the situations where he actively seeks it. We believe that perceptual distortion is less operative in the latter instances and that a commercial communication, therefore, at that stage has a high probability of influencing the buyer.

The active seeking of information occurs when the buyer senses ambiguity of the brands in his evoked set. As we saw earlier, this happens in the Extensive Problem Solving and Limited Problem Solving phases of the decision process. The ambiguity of brand exists because the buyer is not certain of the outcomes from each brand. In other words, he has not yet learned enough about the alternatives to establish an expectancy of potential of the brands to satisfy his motives. This type of brand ambiguity is essentially confined to initial buyer behavior which we have called Extensive Problem Solving. However, ambiguity may still exist despite knowledge of the potential of alternative brands. This ambiguity is with respect to his inability to discriminate because his motives are not well structured: he does not know how to order them. He may then seek information which will resolve the conflict among goals, a resolution that is implied in his learning of the appropriate product class aspect of decision mediators that we discussed earlier.

There is yet another stage of total buying behavior in which the buyer is likely to seek information. It is when the buyer has not only routinized his decision process but he is so familiar and satiated with repeat buying that he feels bored. Then, all the existing alternatives in his evoked set including the most preferred brand become unacceptable to him. He seeks change or variety in that buying situation. In order to obtain this change, he actively searches for information on other alternatives (brands) that he never considered before. At this stage, he is particularly receptive to any information about new brands. Incidentally, here is an explanation for advertising in a highly stable industry. This phenomenon has long baffled both the critics and defenders of the institution of advertising. Newcomers to the market and forgetting do not provide a plausible explanation.

We have so far described the stimulus input variables and the hypothetical constructs. Now we proceed to describe the output of the system – the responses of the buyer.

Response Variables

The complexity of buyer behavior does not stop with the hypothetical constructs. Just as there is a variety of inputs, there exists a variety of buyer responses which becomes relevant for different areas of marketing strategy. This variety of consumer responses can be easily appreciated from the diversity of measures to evaluate advertising effectiveness. We have attempted to classify and order this diversity of buyer responses in the output variables. Most of the output variables are directly related to some and not other constructs. Each output variable serves different purposes both in marketing practice and fundamental research. Let us at first describe each variable and then provide a rationale for their interrelationships.

Attention. Attention is related to Sensitivity to Information. It is a response of the buyer which indicates the magnitude of his information intake. Attention is measured continuously during the time interval when the buyer receives information. There are several psychophysical methods of quantifying the degree of attention that the buyer pays to a message. The pupil dilation is one.

Comprehension. Comprehension refers to the store of knowledge about the brand that the buyer possesses at any point in time. This knowledge could vary from his simply being aware of a single brand's existence to a complete description of the attributes of the product class of which the brand is an element. It reflects the denotative meaning of the brand and in that sense it is strictly in the cognitive realm. It lacks the motivational aspects of behavior. Some of the standard measures of advertising effectiveness such as awareness, aided or unaided recall, and recognition may capture different aspects of the buyer's comprehension of the brand.

Attitude toward a brand. Attitude toward a brand is the buyer's evaluation of the brand's potential to satisfy his motives. It, therefore, includes the connotative aspects of the brand concept: it contains those aspects of the brand which are relevant to the buyer's goals. Attitude is directly related to Predisposition and so it consists of both the evaluation of a brand in terms of the criteria of choice from Mediator and the confidence with which that evaluation is held.

Intention to buy. Intention to buy is the buyer's forecast of his brand choice some time in the future. Like any forecast, it involves assumptions about future events including the likelihood of any perceived inhibitors creating barriers over the buyer's planning horizon. Intention to buy has been extensively used in the purchases of durable goods with some recent refinements in terms of the buyer's confidence in his own forecast; these studies are in terms of broadly defined product classes.[14] We may summarize this response of the buyer as something short of actual purchase behavior.

Purchase behavior. Purchase Behavior refers to the overt act of purchasing a brand. What becomes a part of company's sales or what the consumer records in a diary as a panel member, however, is only the terminal act in the sequence of shopping and buying. Very often, it is useful to observe the complete movement of the buyer from his home to the store and his purchase in the store. Yoell, for example, shows several case histories where a time and motion study of consumer's purchase behavior have useful marketing implications.[15] We think that at times it may be helpful to go so far as to incorporate the act of consumption into the definition of Purchase Behavior. We have, for example, developed and used the technique of sequential decision making where the buyer verbally describes the sequential pattern of his purchase behavior in a given buying situation. Out of this description a "flow chart" of decision making is obtained which reveals the number and the structure of the decision rules that the buyer employs.

Purchase Behavior is the overt manifestation of the buyer's Predisposition in conjunction with any Inhibitors that may be present. It differs from Attitude to the extent that Inhibitors are taken into consideration. It differs from Intention to the extent that it is the actual manifestation of behavior which the buyer only forecasted in his intention.

Several characteristics of Purchase Behavior become useful if we observe the buyer in a repetitive buying situation. These include the incidence of buying a brand, the quantity bought, and the purchase cycle. Several stochastic models of brand loyalty, for example, have been developed in recent years.[16] Similarly, we could take the magnitude purchased and compare light buyers with heavy buyers to determine if heavy buyers are more loyal buyers.

Interrelationship of response variables. In Figure 10-1, it will be seen that we have ordered the five response variables to create a hierarchy. The hierarchy is similar to the variety of hierarchies used in practice such as AIDA (Attention, Interest, Desire and Action), to the Lavidge and Steiner hierarchy of advertising effectiveness,[17] as well as to the different mental states that a person is alleged by the anthropologists and sociologists to pass through when he adopts an innovation.[18] There are, however, some important differences which we believe will clarify certain conceptual and methodological issues raised by Palda and others.[19]

First, we have added a response variable called Attention which is crucial since it reflects whether a communication is received by the buyer. Secondly, several different aspects of the cognitive realm of behavior such as awareness, recall, recognition, etc., are lumped into one category called Comprehension to suggest that they all are varying indicators of the buyer's storage of information about a brand which can be extended to *product class,* and in this way we obtain leverage toward understanding buyer innovation. Third, we have defined Attitude to include both affective and conative aspects since anyone who wants to establish causal relations between attitude and behavior must bring the motivational aspects into attitude. Furthermore, we separate the perceptual and the preference maps of the buyer into Comprehension and Attitude respectively. Fourth, we add another variable, Intention to Buy, because there are several product classes in both durable and semi-durable goods where properly defined and measured intentions have already proved useful. To the extent that Intention incorporates the buyer's forecast of his inhibitors, it might serve the useful function of informing the firm how to remove the inhibitors before the actual purchase behavior is manifested.

Finally, and most importantly, we have incorporated several feedback effects which were described when we discussed the hypothetical constructs. We will now show the relations as direct connections among response variables but the reader should bear in mind that these "outside" relations are merely the reflection of relations among the hypothetical constructs. For example, Purchase Behavior via Satisfaction entails some consequences which affect Decision Mediators and brand potential in Evoked Set; any change in them can produce change in Predisposition. Attitude is related to Predisposition and, therefore, it can also be changed in the period from pre-purchase to post-purchase. In incorporating this feedback, we are opening the way to resolving the controversy whether Attitude causes Purchase Behavior or Purchase Behavior causes Attitude. Over a period of time, the relation is interdependent, each affecting the other. Similarly, we have a feedback from Attitude to Comprehension and Attention, the rationale for which was given when we described the perceptual constructs.

DYNAMICS OF BUYING BEHAVIOR

Let us now explain the changes in the hypothetical constructs which occur due to learning.

The learning constructs are, of course, directly involved in the change that we label "learning." Since some of the learning constructs indirectly govern the perceptual constructs by way of feedbacks, there is also an indirect effect back upon the learning constructs themselves. As mentioned earlier, learning of Decision Mediators which structure Motives and Evoked Set of Brands which contain brand potentials can occur from two broad sources: (i) past experience and (ii) information. Experience can be further classified as having been derived from buying a specified product or buying some similar product. Similarly, information can come from the buyer's commercial environment or his social environment, and if commercial, it can be significative or symbolic.

We will look at the development and change in learning constructs as due to: (i) generalization from similar buying situations, (ii) repeat buying of the same product class, and (iii) information.

Generalization from Similar Purchase Situations

Some decision mediators are common across several product classes because many motives are common to a wide variety of purchasing activity. For example, a buyer may satisfy his health motive from many product classes by looking for nutrition. Similarly, many product classes are all bought at the same place which very often leads to spatial or contiguous generalization. The capacity to generalize provides the buyer with a truly enormous range of flexibility in adapting his purchase behavior to the myriad of varying market conditions he faces.

Generalization refers to the transfer of responses and of the relevance of stimuli from past situations to new situations which are similar. It saves the buyer time and effort in seeking information in the face of uncertainty that is inevitable in a new situation. Generalization can occur at any one of the several levels of purchase activity, but we are primarily interested in generalization of those decision mediators which only involve brand choice behavior in contrast to store choice or choice of shopping time and day. In other words, we are concerned with brand generalization.

Repeat Purchase Experiences

Another source of change in the learning constructs is the repeated purchase of the same product class over a period of time.

In Figure 10-1 the purchase of a brand entails two types of feedbacks, one affecting the decision mediators and the other affecting the brand potential of the evoked set. First, the experience of buying with all its cognitive aspects of memory, reasoning, etc., has a learning effect on the decision mediators. This occurs irrespective of which specific brand the buyer chooses in any one purchase decision because the decision mediators like the motives are product-specific and not limited to any one brand. Hence every purchase has an incremental effect in firmly establishing the decision mediators. This is easy to visualize if we remember that buying behavior is a series of mental and motor steps while the actual choice is only its terminal act.

Purchase of a brand creates certain satisfactions for the buyer which the consumer compares with his expectations of the brand's potential and this expectation is the basis on which he made his decision in the first place. This comparison of expected and actual consequences causes him to be satisfied or dissatisfied with his purchase of the brand. Hence, the second feedback from Purchase Behavior to Satisfaction changes the attractiveness of the brand purchased. If the buyer is satisfied with his consumption, he enhances the potential of the brand and this is likely to result in greater probability of its repeat purchase. If he is dissatisfied, the potential of the brand is diminished, and its probability of repeat purchase is also similarly reduced.

If there are no inhibitory forces which influence him, the buyer will continue to buy a brand which proves satisfactory. In the initial stages of decision making he may show some tendency to oscillate between brands in order to formulate his decision mediators. In other words, he may learn by trial-and-error at first and then settle on a brand and thereafter he may buy the brand with such regularity to suggest that he is brand loyal. Unless a product is of very high risk, however, there is a limit as to how long this brand loyalty will continue: he may become bored with his preferred brand and look for something new.

Information as a Source of Learning

The third major source by which the learning constructs are changed is information from the buyer's (i) commercial environment consisting of advertising, promotion, salesmanship and retail shelf display of the competing companies, and (ii) his social environment consisting of his family, friends, reference group and social class.

We will describe the influence of information at first as if the perceptual constructs were absent. In other words, we assume that the buyer receives information with perfect fidelity as it exists in the environment. Also, we will discuss separately the information from the commercial and social environments.

Commercial environment. The company communicates about its offerings to the buyers either by the physical brand (significates) or by symbols (pictorial or linguistic) which represent the brand. In other words, significative and symbolic communication are the two major ways of interaction between the sellers and the buyers.

In Figure 10-1, the influence of information is shown on Motives, Decision Mediators, Evoked Set, and Inhibitors. We believe that the influence of commercial information on motives (specific and nonspecific) is limited. The main effect is primarily to *intensify* whatever motives the buyer has rather than to create new ones. For example, physical display of the brand may intensify his motives above the threshold levels which combined with strong predisposition can result in impulse (unplanned) purchase. A similar reaction is possible when an ad creates sufficient intensity of motives to provide an impetus for the buyer to go to the store. A second way to influence motives is to show the *perceived instrumentality* of the brand and thereby make it a part of the buyer's defined set of alternatives. Finally, to a very limited extent, marketing stimuli may change the *content of the motives.* The general conception both among marketing men and laymen is that marketing stimuli change the buyer's motives. However, on a closer examination it would appear that what is changed is the *intensity* of buyer's motives already provided by the social environment. Many dormant or latent motives may become stimulated. The secret of success very often lies in identifying the change in motives created by social change and intensifying them as seems to be the case in the recent projection of youthfulness in many buying situations.

Marketing stimuli are also important in determining and changing the buyer's evoked set. Commercial information tells him of the existence of the brands (awareness), their identifying characteristics (Comprehension plus brand name) and their relevance to the satisfaction of the buyer's needs (Attitude).

Marketing stimuli are also important in creating and changing the buyer's decision mediators. They become important sources for learning decision mediators when the buyer has no prior experience to rely upon. In other words, when he is in the extensive problem-solving (EPS) stage, it is marketing and social stimuli which are the important sources of learning. Similarly, when the buyer actively seeks information because all the existing alternatives are unacceptable to him, marketing stimuli become important in *changing* his decision mediators.

Finally, marketing stimuli can unwittingly create inhibitors. For example, a company feels the need to emphasize price-quality association, but it may result in high-price inhibition in the mind of the buyer. Similarly, in emphasizing the details of usage and consumption of a product, the communication may create the inhibition related to time pressure.

Social environment. The social environment of the buyer – family, friends, reference groups – is another major source of information in his buying behavior. Most of the inputs are likely to be symbolic (linguistic) although at times the physical product may be shown to the buyer.

Information from his social environment also affects the four learning constructs: Motives, Decision Mediators, Evoked Set and Inhibitors. However, the effect on these constructs is different from that of the commercial environment. First, the information about the brands will be considerably modified by the social environment before it reaches the buyer. Most of the modifications are likely to be in the nature of adding connotative meanings to brand descriptions, and of the biasing effects of the communication's perceptual variables like Sensitivity to Information and Perceptual Bias. Second, the buyer's social environment will probably have a very strong influence on the content of his motives and their ordering to establish a goal structure. Several research studies have concentrated on such influences.[20] Third, the social environment may also affect his evoked set. This will be particularly true when the buyer lacks experience. Furthermore, if the product class is important to the buyer and he is technically incompetent or uncertain in evaluating the consequences of the brand for his needs, he may rely more on the social than on the marketing environment for information. This is well documented by several studies using the perceived risk hypothesis.[21]

Exogenous Variables

Earlier we mentioned that there are several influences operating on the buyer's decisions which we treat as exogenous, that is, we do not explain their formation and change. Many of these influences come from the buyer's social environment and we wish to separate the effects of his environment which have occurred in the past and are not related to a specific decision from those which are current and directly affect the decisions that occur during the period the buyer is being observed. The inputs during the observation period provide information to the buyer to help his current decision making. The past influences are already imbedded in the values of the perceptual and learning constructs. Strictly speaking, therefore, there is no need for some of the exogenous variables which have influenced the buyer in the past. We bring them out explicitly, however, for the sake of research design where the research may control or take into account individual differences among buyers due to such past influences. Incorporating the effects of these exogenous variables will reduce the size of the unexplained variance or error in estimation which it is particularly essential to control under field conditions. Figure 10-1 presents a set of exogenous variables which we believe provide the control essential to obtaining satisfactory predictive relations between the inputs and the outputs of the system. Let us briefly discuss each of the exogenous variables.

Importance of Purchase refers to differential degrees of ego-involvement or commitment in different product classes. It, therefore, provides a mechanism which must be carefully examined in interproduct studies. Importance of Purchase will influence the size of the Evoked Set and the magnitude of Search for Information. The more important the product class, the larger the Evoked Set.

Time Pressure is a current exogenous variable and, therefore, specific to a decision situation. It refers to the situation when a buyer feels pressed for time due to any of several environmental influences and so must allocate his time among alternative uses. In this process a re-allocation unfavorable to the purchasing activity can occur. Time pressure will create inhibition as mentioned earlier. It will also unfavorably affect Search for Information.

Financial Status refers to the constraint the buyer may feel because of lack of financial resources. This affects his purchase behavior to the extent that it creates a barrier to purchasing the most preferred brand. For example, a buyer may want to purchase a Mercedes-Benz but lacks sufficient financial resources and, therefore, he will settle for some low-priced American automobile such as a Ford or Chevrolet. Its effect is via Inhibitor.

Personality Traits take into consideration many of the variables such as self-confidence, self-esteem, authoritarianism and anxiety which have been researched to identify individual differences. It will be noted that these individual differences are "topic free" and, therefore, are supposed to exert their effect across product classes. We believe their effect is felt on: (i) nonspecific Motives and (ii) Evoked Set. For example, the more anxious a person, the greater the motivational arousal; dominant personalities are more likely by a small margin to buy a Ford instead of a Chevrolet; the more authoritarian a person, the narrower the category width of his evoked set.

Social and Organizational Setting (Organization) takes us to the group, to a higher level of social organization than the individual. It includes both the informal social organization such as family and reference groups which are relevant for *consumer behavior* and the formal organization which constitutes much of the environment for *industrial purchasing.* Organizational variables are those of small group interaction such as power, status and authority. We believe that the underlying process of intergroup conflicts in both industrial and consumer buying behavior are in principle very similar and that the differences are largely due to the formalization of industrial activity. Organization, both formal and social, is a crucial variable because it influences all the learning constructs.

Social Class refers to a still higher level of social organization, the social aggregate. Several indices are available to classify people into various classes. The most common perhaps is the Warner classification of people into upper-upper, lower-upper, upper-middle, lower-middle, upper-lower, and lower-lower classes. Social class mediates the relation between the input and the output by influencing: (i) specific Motives, (ii) Decision Mediators, (iii) Evoked Set, and (iv) Inhibitors. The latter influence is important particularly in the adoption of innovations.

Culture provides an even more comprehensive social framework than social class. Culture consists of patterns of behavior, symbols, ideas and their attached values. Culture will influence Motives, Decision Mediators, and Inhibitors.

CONCLUSIONS

In the preceding pages we have summarized a theory of buyer brand choice. It is complex. We strongly believe that complexity is essential to adequately describe buying behavior, from the point of view of both marketing practice and public policy.

We hope that the theory can provide new insights into past empirical data and guide future research so as to instill with coherence and unity current research which now tends to be atomistic and unrelated. We are vigorously pursuing a large research program aimed at testing the validity of the theory. The research was designed in terms of the variables specified by the theory and our most preliminary results cause us to believe that it was fruitful to use the theory in this way. Because it specifies a number of relationships, it has clearly been useful in interpreting the preliminary findings. Above all, it is an aid in communication among the researchers and with the companies involved.

Finally, a number of new ideas are set forth in the theory, but we would like to call attention to three in particular. The concept of evoked set provides a means of reducing the noise in many analyses of buying behavior. The product class concept offers a new dimension for incorporating many of the complexities of innovations and especially for integrating systematically the idea of innovation into a framework of psychological constructs. Anthropologists and sociologists have been pretty much content to deal with peripheral variables in their investigations of innovation. The habit-perception cycle in which perception and habit respond inversely offers hope for explaining a large proportion of the phenomenon that has long baffled both the critics and defenders of advertising: large advertising expenditures in a stable market where, on the surface, it would seem that people are already sated with information.

NOTES

1. Jagdish N. Sheth, "A Review of Buyer Behavior," *Management Science,* Vol. 13 (August, 1967),

pp. B718–B756; John A Howard, *Marketing Theory* (Boston, Mass.: Allyn and Bacon, 1965).

2. Musafer Sherif and Carolyn Sherif, "Interdisciplinary Coordination as a Validity Check: Retrospect and Prospects," in M. Sherif (ed.), *Problems of Interdisciplinary Relationships in the Social Sciences* (Chicago: Aldine Publishing Company, 1968).
3. William J. McGuire, "Some Impending Reorientations in Social Psychology," *Journal of Experimental Social Psychology,* Vol. 3 (1967), pp. 124–139.
4. Patrick Suppes, *Information Processing and Choice Behavior* (Technical Paper No. 9: Institute for Mathematical Studies in the Social Sciences, Stanford University, January 31, 1966), p. 27; John A. Howard, *op. cit.*
5. Terminology in a problem area that cuts across both economics and psychology is different because each discipline has often defined its terms differently from the other. We find the economists definitions of exogenous versus endogenous, and theory versus model more useful than those of the psychologist. The psychologists' distinction of hypothetical constructs and intervening variables, however, provides a helpful breakdown of endogenous variables. Finally, for the sake of exposition we have often here not clearly distinguished between the theory and its emirical counterparts. Although this practice encourages certain ambiguities, and we lay ourselves open to the charge of reifying our theory, we believe that for most readers it will simplify the task of comprehending the material.
6. Clark C. Hull, *Principles of Behavior* (New York: Appleton-Century-Crofts, Inc., 1943); Clark C. Hull, *A Behavior System* (New Haven: Yale University Press, 1952).
7. Charles E. Osgood, "A Behavioristic Analysis of Perception and Meaning as Cognitive Phenomena," *Symposium on Cognition, University of Colorado, 1955* (Cambridge, Harvard University Press, 1957), pp. 75–119; Charles E. Osgood, "Motivational Dynamics of Language Behavior," in J.R. Jones (ed.), *Nebraska Symposium on Motivation,* 1957 (Lincoln: University of Nebraska Press, 1957), pp. 348–423.
8. D.E. Berlyne, "Motivational Problems Raised by Exploratory and Epistemic Behavior," in Sigmund Koch (ed.), *Psychology: A Study of a Science,* Vol. 5 (New York: McGraw-Hill Book Company, 1963).
9. Rosser Reeves, *Reality in Advertising* (New York: Alfred A. Knopf, Inc., 1961).
10. J.S. Brown, *The Motivation of Behavior* (New York: McGraw-Hill Book Company, 1961).
11. George S. Day, "Buyer Attitudes and Brand Choice Behavior." Unpublished Ph.D. Dissertation, Graduate School of Business, Columbia University, 1967.
12. Berlyne, *op. cit.*
13. S. Feldman (ed.), *Cognitive Consistency: Motivational Antecedents and Behavioral Consequents* (Academic Press, 1966); Martin Fishbein (ed.), *Readings in Attitude Theory and Measurement* (New York: John Wiley & Sons, 1967).
14. Thomas F. Juster, *Anticipations and Purchases: An Analysis of Consumer Behavior* (Princeton University Press, 1964).
15. William Yoell, *A Science of Advertising through Behaviorism.* Unpublished manuscript, December, 1965.
16. Sheth, *op. cit.*
17. R.J. Lavidge and G.A. Steiner, "A Model for Predictive Measurements of Advertising Effectiveness," *Journal of Marketing* (October, 1961), pp. 50–68.
18. Everett M. Rogers, *The Diffusion of Innovations* (New York: Free Press, 1962).
19. Kristian S. Palda, "The Hypothesis of a Hierarchy of Effects: A Partial Evaluation," *Journal of Marketing Research* (February, 1966), pp. 13–24.
20. Sheth, *op. cit.*
21. Donald F. Cox, *Risk Taking and Information Handling in Consumer Behavior* (Boston, Mass.: Graduate School of Business Administration, Harvard University, 1967).

11

Frederick E. Webster, Jr.
Yoram Wind

A General Model for Understanding Organizational Buying Behavior

Industrial and institutional marketers have often been urged to base their strategies on careful appraisal of buying behavior within key accounts and in principal market segments. When they search the available literature on buyer behavior, however, they find virtually exclusive emphasis on consumers, not industrial buyers. Research findings and theoretical discussions about consumer behavior often have little relevance for the industrial marketer. This is due to several important differences between the two purchase processes. Industrial buying takes place in the context of a formal organization influenced by budget, cost, and profit considerations. Furthermore, organizational (i.e., industrial and institutional) buying usually involves many people in the decision process with complex interactions among people and among individual and organizational goals.

Similar to his consumer goods counterpart, the industrial marketer could find a model of buyer behavior useful in identifying those key factors influencing response to marketing effort. A buyer behavior model can help the marketer to analyze available information about the market and to identify the need for additional information. It can help to specify targets for marketing effort, the kinds of information needed by various purchasing decision makers, and the criteria that they will use to make these decisions. A framework for analyzing organizational buying behavior could aid in the design of marketing strategy.

The model to be presented here is a *general* model. It can be applied to all organizational buying and suffers all the weaknesses of general models. It does not describe a specific buying situation in the richness of detail required to make a model operational, and it cannot be

"A General Model for Understanding Organizational Buying Behavior," Frederick E. Webster, Jr., and Yoram Wind, Vol. 36 (April 1972), pp. 12–19. Reprinted from the *Journal of Marketing*, published by the American Marketing Association.

Frederick Webster is professor of marketing at Dartmouth College. He received his Ph.D. from Stanford University and has taught at Columbia University and Stanford University. He is an expert in the area of industrial marketing.

Yoram Wind is professor of marketing at the Wharton School, University of Pennsylvania. He received his Ph.D. from Stanford University. A prolific author, Wind's latest book is Product Policy.

quantified. However, generality offers a compensating set of benefits. The model presents a comprehensive view of organizational buying that enables one to evaluate the relevance of specific variables and thereby permits greater insight into the basic processes of industrial buying behavior. It identifies the *classes* of variables that must be examined by any student of organizational buying, practitioner, or academician. Although major scientific progress in the study of organizational buying will come only from a careful study of specific relationships among a few variables within a given class, this general model can help to identify those variables that should be studied. It can be useful in generating hypotheses and provides a framework for careful interpretation of research results that makes the researcher more sensitive to the complexities of the processes he is studying.

TRADITIONAL VIEWS

Traditional views of organizational buying have lacked comprehensiveness. The literature of economics, purchasing, and, to a limited degree, marketing has emphasized variables related to the buying task itself and has emphasized "rational," economic factors. In these economic views, the objective of purchasing is to obtain the minimum price or the lowest total cost-in-use (as in the materials management model[1]). Some of the models focussing on the buying task have emphasized factors that are not strictly economic such as reciprocal buying agreements[2] and other constraints on the buyer such as source loyalty.[3]

Other traditional views of organizational buying err in the opposite direction, emphasizing variables such as emotion, personal goals, and internal politics that are involved in the buying decision process but not related to the goals of the buying task. This "nontask" emphasis is seen in models which emphasize the purchasing agent's interest in obtaining personal favors,[4] in enhancing his own ego,[5] or in reducing perceived risk.[6] Other nontask models have emphasized buyer-salesman interpersonal interaction[7] and the multiple relationships among individuals involved in the buying process over time.[8] The ways in which purchasing agents attempt to expand their influence over the buying decision have also received careful study.[9] These views have contributed to an understanding of the buying process, but none of them is complete. To the extent that these models leave out task or nontask variables they offer incomplete guidelines for the industrial market strategist and researcher. The tendency in interpreting research results based on these simple models is to overemphasize the importance of some variables and to understate or ignore the importance of others.

AN OVERVIEW OF A GENERAL MODEL

The fundamental assertion of the more comprehensive model to be presented here is that organizational buying is a decision-making process carried out by individuals, in interaction with other people, in the context of a formal organization.[10] The organization, in turn, is influenced by a variety of forces in the environment. Thus, the four classes of variables determining organizational buying behavior are *individual, social, organizational* and *environmental.* Within each class, there are two broad categories of variables: Those directly related to the buying problem, called *task* variables; and those that extend beyond the buying problem, called *nontask* variables. This classification of variables is summarized and illustrated in Table 11-1.

The distinction between task and nontask variables applies to all of the classes of variables, and subclasses, to be discussed below. It is seldom possible to identify a given set of vari-

TABLE 11-1 *Classification and Examples of Variables Influencing Organizational Buying Decisions*

	Task	Nontask
Individual	Desire to obtain lowest price	Personal values and needs
Social	Meetings to set specifications	Informal, off-the-job interactions
Organizational	Policy regarding local supplier preference	Methods of personnel evaluation
		Political climate in an election year
Environmental	Anticipated changes in prices	

ables as exclusively task or nontask; rather, any given set of variables will have both task and nontask dimensions although one dimension may be predominant. For example, motives will inevitably have both dimensions – those relating directly to the buying problem to be solved and those primarily concerned with personal goals. These motives overlap in many important respects and need not conflict; a strong sense of personal involvement can create more effective buying decisions from an organizational standpoint.

Organizational buying behavior is a complex *process* (rather than a single, instantaneous act) and involves many persons, multiple goals, and potentially conflicting decision criteria. It often takes place over an extended period of time, requires information from many sources, and encompasses many interorganizational relationships.

The organizational buying process is a form of problem-solving, and a *buying situation* is created when someone in the organization perceives a problem – a discrepancy between a desired outcome and the present situation – that can potentially be solved through some buying action. Organizational buying behavior includes all activities of organizational members as they define a buying situation and identify, evaluate, and choose among alternative brands and suppliers. The *buying center* includes all members of the organization who are involved in that process. The roles involved are those of user, influencer, decider, buyer, and gatekeeper (who controls the flow of information into the buying center). Members of the buying center are motivated by a complex interaction of individual and organizational goals. Their relationships with one another involve all the complexities of interpersonal interactions. The formal organization exerts its influence on the buying center through the subsystems of tasks, structure (communication, authority, status, rewards, and work flow), technology, and people. Finally, the entire organization is embedded in a set of environmental influences including economic, technological, physical, political, legal, and cultural forces. An overview of the model and a diagrammatic presentation of the relationships among these variables are given in Figure 11-1.

ENVIRONMENTAL INFLUENCES

Environmental influences are subtle and pervasive as well as difficult to identify and to measure. They influence the buying process by providing information as well as constraints and opportunities. Environmental influences include physical (geographic, climate, or ecological), technological, economic, political, legal, and cultural factors. These influences are exerted through a variety of institutions including business firms (suppliers, competitors, and

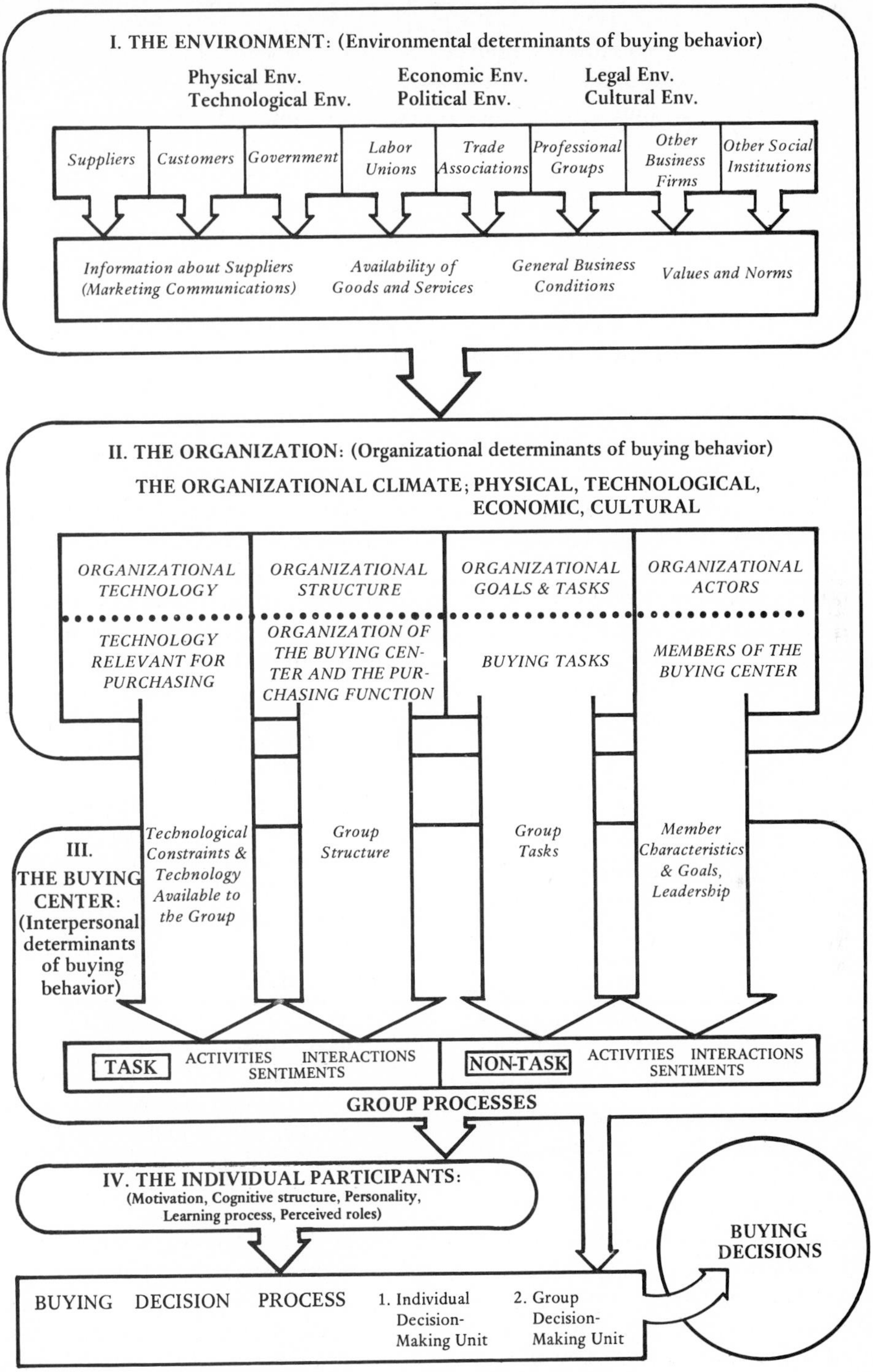

FIGURE 11-1 *A Model of Organizational Buying Behavior*

customers), governments, trade unions, political parties, educational and medical institutions, trade associations, and professional groups. The nature of these institutional forms will vary significantly from one country to another, and such differences are critical to the planning of multinational marketing strategies.

As Figure 11-1 illustrates, environmental influences have their impact in four distinct ways. First, they define the availability of goods and services. This function reflects especially the influence of physical, technological, and economic factors. Second, they define the general conditions facing the buying organization including the rate of economic growth, the level of national income, interest rates, and unemployment. Economic and political forces are the dominant influences on general business conditions. Some of these forces, such as economic factors, are predominantly (but not exclusively) task variables whereas others such as political variables may be more heavily nontask in nature. Third, environmental factors determine the values and norms guiding interorganizational and interpersonal relationships between buyers and sellers as well as among competitors, and between buying organizations and other institutions such as governments and trade associations. Such values and norms may be codified into laws, or they may be implicit. Cultural, social, legal, and political forces are the dominant sources of values and norms. Finally, environmental forces influence the information flow into the buying organization. Most important here is the flow of marketing communications from potential suppliers, through the mass media and through other personal and impersonal channels. Information flows reflect a variety of physical, technological, economic, and cultural factors.

The marketing strategist, whose customers are organizations, must carefully appraise each set of environmental factors and identify and analyze the institutions that exert those influences in each of the market segments served. This kind of analysis is especially important in entering new markets. For example, economic factors as revealed in measures of general business conditions must be continually assessed where market prices fluctuate and buyers make decisions to build or reduce inventories based on price expectations. Similarly, the impact of technological change in markets served must be considered as the basis for strategic decisions in the areas of product policy and promotion. The necessity of analyzing institutional forms is most readily apparent when markets are multinational in scope and require specific consideration of government policies and trade union influences. Environmental factors are important determinants of organizational buying behavior, but they can be so basic and pervasive that it is easy, and dangerous, to overlook them in analyzing the market.

ORGANIZATIONAL INFLUENCES

Organizational factors cause individual decision makers to act differently than they would if they were functioning alone or in a different organization. Organizational buying behavior is motivated and directed by the organization's goals and is constrained by its financial, technological, and human resources. This class of variables is primarily task-related. For understanding the influence of the formal organization on the buying process, Leavitt's classification of variables is most helpful.[11] According to Leavitt's scheme, organizations are multivariate systems composed of four sets of interacting variables:

Tasks—the work to be performed in accomplishing the objectives of the organization.

Structure—subsystems of communication, authority, status, rewards, and work flow.

Technology—problem-solving inventions used by the firm including plant and equipment and programs for organizing and managing work.

People—the actors in the system.

Each of these subsystems interacts with, and is dependent upon, the others for its functioning. Together, these four interacting sets of factors define the information, expectations, goals, attitudes, and assumptions used by each of the individual actors in their decision making. This general model defines four distinct but interrelated sets of variables that must be carefully considered in the development of marketing strategies designed to influence that process: buying tasks, organization structure, buying technology, and the buying center.

Buying Tasks

Buying tasks are a subset of organizational tasks and goals that evolves from the definition of a buying situation. These are pure task variables by definition. The specific tasks that must be performed to solve the buying problem can be defined as five stages in the buying decision process. (1) Identification of need; (2) establishment of specifications; (3) identification of alternatives; (4) evaluation of alternatives; and (5) selection of suppliers.[12] Buying tasks can be further defined according to four dimensions:

1. The *organizational purpose* served—e.g., whether the reason for buying is to facilitate production, or for resale, or to be consumed in the performance of other organizational functions.
2. The *nature of demand,* especially whether demand for the product is generated within the buying organization or by forces outside of the organization (i.e., "derived" demand) as well as other characteristics of the demand pattern such as seasonal and cyclical fluctuations.
3. The *extent of programming,* i.e., the degree of routinization at the five stages of the decision process.
4. The *degree of decentralization* and the extent to which buying authority has been delegated to operating levels in the organization.

Each of these four dimensions influences the nature of the organizational buying process and must be considered in appraising market opportunities. At each of the five stages of the decision process, different members of the buying center may be involved, different decision criteria are employed, and different information sources may become more or less relevant. Marketing strategies must be adjusted accordingly. There are rich research opportunities in defining the influence of different members of the buying center at various stages of the buying process.[13]

Organizational Structure

The formal organizational structure consists of subsystems of communication, authority, status, rewards, and work flow, all of which have important task and nontask dimensions. Each of these subsystems deserves careful study by researchers interested in organizational buying. The marketing literature does not include studies in this area. A beginning might be several rigorous observational or case studies.

The *communication* subsystem performs four essential functions: (1) Information; (2) command and instruction; (3) influence and persuasion; and (4) integration.[14] The marketer must understand how the communication system in customer organizations *informs* the members of the buying center about buying problems, evaluation criteria (both task and nontask related), and alternative sources of supply. He must appraise how *commands* and *instructions* (mostly task-related) flow through the hierarchy defining the discretion and latitude of individual actors. The pattern of *influence* and *persuasion* (heavily nontask in nature) defines the nature of interpersonal interactions within the buying center. Organizational members may differ in the extent to which they prefer either commands and instructions or more subtle influence and persuasion to guide the actions of subordinates. The *integrative* functions of communication become critical in coordinating the functioning of the buying center and may be one of the primary roles of the purchasing manager.

The *authority* subsystem defines the power of organizational actors to judge, command, or otherwise act to influence the behavior of others along both task and nontask dimensions. No factor is more critical in understanding the organizational buying process because the authority structure determines who sets goals and who evaluates (and therefore determines rewards for) organizational performance. The authority structure interacts with the communication structure to determine the degree of decentralization in the decision process.

The *status* system is reflected in the organization chart and defines the hierarchical structure of the formal organization. It also expresses itself in an informal structure. Both the formal and the informal organization define each individual's position in a hierarchy with respect to other individuals. Job descriptions define positions within the organization and the associated dimensions of responsibility and authority. Knowing the responsibility, authority, and the position in the internal status hierarchy of each member of the buying center is a necessary basis for developing an account strategy for the organizational customer. A complete theory of organizational buying will permit accurate predictions of an organizational actor's influence based upon his position and role.

The *rewards* system defines the payoffs to the individual decision maker. It is intimately related to the authority system which determines the responsibilities of organizational actors for evaluating other individuals. Here is the mechanism for relating organizational task accomplishment to individual nontask objectives. Persons join organizations in anticipation of the rewards given by the organization and agree to work toward organizational objectives in return for those rewards. A careful analysis of the formal and social reward structure of the organization as it affects and is perceived by the members of the buying center can be most helpful in predicting their response to marketing effort. The key fact is that people work for organizations in order to earn rewards related to personal goals, both economic and noneconomic.[15]

Every buying organization develops task-related procedures for managing the *work flow* of paperwork, samples, and other items involved in the buying decision process. The flow of paperwork also has nontask aspects which reflect the composition of the buying center as well as the authority and communication subsystems of an organizational structure. Needless to say, marketers must understand the mechanical details of buying procedures. Such procedures also provide documentation of the buying process that can provide useful data for the academic researcher.

Buying Technology

Technology influences both what is bought and the nature of the organizational buying process itself. In the latter respect, technology defines the management and information systems that are involved in the buying decision process, such as computers and management science approaches to such aspects of buying as "make or buy" analysis. More obviously, technology defines the plant and equipment of the organization, and these, in turn, place significant constraints upon the alternative buying actions available to the organization. It is a common failing of industrial marketing strategy, especially for new product introductions, to underestimate the demands that will be placed upon existing technology in customer organizations.[16] A new material, for example, may require new dies and mixing equipment, new skills of production personnel, and substantial changes in methods of production.

Buying Center

The buying center is a subset of the organizational actors, the last of the four sets of variables in the Leavitt scheme. The buying center was earlier defined as consisting of five roles: users, influencers, deciders, buyers, and gatekeepers. Since people operate as part of the total organization, the behavior of members of the buying center reflects the influence of others as well as the effect of the buying task, the organizational structure, and technology.

This interaction leads to unique buying behavior in each customer organization. The marketing strategist who wishes to influence the organizational buying process must, therefore, define and understand the operation of these four sets of organizational variables – tasks, structure, technology, and actors – in each organization he is trying to influence. The foregoing comments provide only the skeleton of an analytical structure for considering each of these factors and its implications for marketing action in a specific buying situation. The marketer's problem is to define the locus of buying responsibility within the customer organization, to define the composition of the buying center, and to understand the structure of roles and authority within the buying center.

SOCIAL (INTERPERSONAL) INFLUENCES

The framework for understanding the buying decision process must identify and relate three classes of variables involved in group functioning in the buying center. First, the various roles in the buying center must be identified. Second, the variables relating to interpersonal (dyadic) interaction between persons in the buying center and between members of the buying center and "outsiders" such as vendors' salesmen must be identified. Third, the dimensions of the functioning of the group as a whole must be considered. Each of these three sets of factors is discussed briefly in the following paragraphs.

Within the organization as a whole only a subset of organizational actors is actually involved in a buying situation. The buying center includes five roles:

Users – those members of the organization who use the purchased products and services.

Buyers – those with formal responsibility and authority for contracting with suppliers.

Influencers – those who influence the decision process directly or indirectly by providing information and criteria for evaluating alternative buying actions.

Deciders – those with authority to choose among alternative buying actions.

Gatekeepers – those who control the flow of information (and materials) into the buying center.

Several individuals may occupy the same role; e.g., there may be several influencers. Also, one individual may occupy more than one role; e.g., the purchasing agent is often both buyer and gatekeeper.

To understand interpersonal interaction within the buying center, it is useful to consider three aspects of role performance: (1) Role *expectations* (prescriptions and prohibitions for the behavior of the person occupying the role and for the behavior of other persons toward a given role); (2) role *behavior* (actual behavior in the role); and (3) role *relationships* (the multiple and reciprocal relationships among members of the group). Together, these three variables define the individual's *role set*. An awareness of each of these dimensions is necessary for the salesman responsible for contacting the various members of the buying center. It is especially important to understand how each member expects the salesman to behave toward him and the important ongoing relationships among roles in the buying center.

As illustrated in Figure 11-1, the nature of group functioning is influenced by five classes of variables – the individual members' goals and personal characteristics, the nature of leadership within the group, the structure of the group, the tasks performed by the group, and external (organizational and environmental) influences. Group processes involve not only activities but also interactions and sentiments among members, which have both task and nontask dimensions. Finally, the output of the group is not only a task-oriented problem solution (a buying action) but also nontask satisfaction and growth for the group and its members.

In analyzing the functioning of the buying center, it helps to focus attention on the buyer role, primarily because a member of the purchasing department is most often the marketer's primary contact point with the organization. Buyers often have authority for managing the contacts of suppliers with other organizational actors, and thus also perform the "gatekeeper" function. While the buyer's authority for selection of suppliers may be seriously constrained by decisions at earlier stages of the decision process (especially the development of specifications), he has responsibility for the terminal stages of the process. In other words, the buyer (or purchasing agent) is in most cases the final decision maker and the target of influence attempts by other members of the buying center.

In performing their task, purchasing agents use a variety of tactics to enhance their power which vary with the specific problems, the conditions of the organization, and the purchasing agent's personality. The tactics used by purchasing agents to influence their relationships with other departments can be viewed as a special case of the more general phenomenon of "lateral" relationships in formal organizations – those among members of approximately equal status in the formal organizational hierarchy.[17] These include *rule-oriented* tactics (e.g., appealing to the boss for the enforcement of organizational policy; appealing to rules and formal statements of authority); *rule-evading* tactics (e.g., compliance with requests from users that violate organizational policies); *personal-political* tactics (e.g., reliance on informal relationships and friendships to get decisions made and an exchange of favors with other members of the buying center); *educational* tactics (e.g., persuading other members of the organization to think in purchasing terms and to recognize the importance and potential contribution of the purchasing function); and finally, *organizational-interactional* tactics (e.g., change the formal organizational structure and the pattern of reporting relationships and information flows).

Buyers who are ambitious and wish to extend the scope of their influence will adopt certain tactics and engage in bargaining activities in an attempt to become more influential at earlier stages of the buying process. These tactics or bargaining strategies define the nature of the buyer's relationships with others of equal organizational status and structure the social situation that the potential supplier must face in dealing with the buying organization. An understanding of the nature of interpersonal relationships in the buying organization is an important basis for the development of marketing strategy.

THE INFLUENCE OF THE INDIVIDUAL

In the final analysis, all organizational buying behavior is individual behavior. Only the individual as an individual or a member of a group can define and analyze buying situations, decide, and act. In this behavior, the individual is motivated by a complex combination of personal and organizational objectives, constrained by policies and information filtered through the formal organization, and influenced by other members of the buying center. The individual is at the center of the buying process, operating within the buying center that is in turn bounded by the formal organization which is likewise embedded in the influences of the broader environment. It is the specific individual who is the target for marketing effort, not the abstract organization.

The organizational buyer's personality, perceived role set, motivation, cognition, and learning are the basic psychological processes which affect his response to the buying situation and marketing stimuli provided by potential vendors. Similar to consumer markets, it is important to understand the organizational buyer's psychological characteristics and especially his predispositions, preference structure, and decision model as the basis for marketing strategy decisions. Some initial attempts to develop categories of buying decision makers according to characteristic decision styles ("normative" and "conservative") have been reported.[18] Cultural, organizational, and social factors are important influences on the individual and are reflected in his previous experiences, awareness of, attitudes and preference toward particular vendors and products and his particular buying decision models.

The organizational buyer can, therefore, be viewed as a constrained decision maker. Although the basic mental processes of motivation, cognition, and learning as well as the buyer's personality, perceived role set, preference structure, and decision model are uniquely individual; they are influenced by the context of interpersonal and organizational influences within which the individual is embedded. The organizational buyer is motivated by a complex combination of individual and organizational objectives and is dependent upon others for the satisfaction of these needs in several ways. These other people define the role expectations for the individual, they determine the payoffs he is to receive for his performance, they influence the definition of the goals to be pursued in the buying decision, and they provide information with which the individual attempts to evaluate risks and come to a decision.

Task and Nontask Motives

Only rarely can the organizational buyer let purely personal considerations influence his buying decisions: In a situation where "all other things are equal," the individual may be able to apply strictly personal (nontask) criteria when making his final decision. In the unlikely event that two or more potential vendors offer products of comparable quality and service at a comparable price, then the organizational buyer may be motivated by purely personal, nontask variables such as his personal preferences for dealing with a particular salesman, or some special favor or gift available from the supplier.

The organizational buyer's motivation has both task and nontask dimensions. Task-related motives relate to the specific buying problem to be solved and involve the general criteria of buying "the right quality in the right quantity at the right price for delivery at the right time from the right source." Of course, what is "right" is a difficult question, especially to the extent that important buying influencers have conflicting needs and criteria for evaluating the buyer's performance.

Nontask-related motives may often be more important, although there is frequently a rather direct relationship between task and nontask motives. For example, the buyer's desire for promotion (a nontask motive) can significantly influence his task performance. In other words, there is no necessary conflict between task and nontask motives and, in fact, the pursuit of nontask objectives can enhance the attainment of task objectives.

Broadly speaking, nontask motives can be placed into two categories; achievement motives and risk-reduction motives. Achievement motives are those related to personal advancement and recognition. Risk-reduction motives are related, but somewhat less obvious, and provide a critical link between the individual and the organizational decision-making process. This is also a key component of the behavior theory of the firm[19] where uncertainty avoidance is a key motivator of organizational actors.

The individual's perception of risk in a decision situation is a function of uncertainty (in the sense of a probabilistic assessment) and of the value of various outcomes. Three kinds of uncertainty are significant: Uncertainty about available alternatives; uncertainty about the outcomes associated with various alternatives; and uncertainty about the way relevant other persons will react to various outcomes.[20] This uncertainty about the reaction of other persons may be due to incomplete information about their goals or about how an outcome will be evaluated and rewarded.

Information gathering is the most obvious tactic for reducing uncertainty, while decision avoidance and lowering of goals are means of reducing the value of outcomes. A preference for the status quo is perhaps the most common mode of risk reduction, since it removes uncertainty and minimizes the possibility of negative outcomes. This is one explanation for the large amount of source loyalty found in organizational buying and is consistent with the "satisficing" postulate of the behavioral theory of the firm.

The individual determinants of organizational buyer behavior and the tactics which buyers are likely to use in their dealings with potential vendors must be clearly understood by those who want to affect their behavior.

SUMMARY

This article has suggested the major dimensions and mechanisms involved in the complex organizational buying process. The framework presented here is reasonably complete although the details clearly are lacking. It is hoped that these comments have been sufficient to suggest a general model of the organizational buying process with important implications for the development of effective marketing and selling strategies as well as some implicit suggestions for scholarly research. The model is offered as a skeleton identifying the major variables that must be appraised in developing the information required for planning strategies. Hopefully, the model has also suggested some new insights into an important area of buying behavior presently receiving inadequate attention in the marketing literature.

NOTES

1. Dean S. Ammer, *Materials Management* (Homewood, Illinois: Richard D. Irwin, Inc., 1962), pp. 12 and 15.
2. Dean S. Ammer, "Realistic Reciprocity," *Harvard Business Review,* Vol. 40 (January–February, 1962), pp. 116–124.
3. Yoram Wind, "Industrial Source Loyalty," *Journal of Marketing Research,* Vol. 7 (November, 1970), pp. 450–457.
4. For a statement of this view, see J.B. Matthews, Jr., R.D. Buzzell, T. Levitt, and R. Frank, *Marketing: An Introductory Analysis* (New York: McGraw-Hill Book Company, Inc., 1964), p. 149.
5. For an example, see William J. Stanton, *Fundamentals of Marketing,* Second Ed. (New York: McGraw-Hill Book Company, Inc., 1967) p. 150.
6. Theodore Levitt, *Industrial Purchasing Behavior: A Study of Communications Effects* (Boston: Division of Research, Graduate School of Business Administration, Harvard University, 1965).
7. Henry L. Tosi, "The Effects of Expectation Levels and Role Consensus on the Buyer-Seller Dyad," *Journal of Business,* Vol. 39 (October, 1966), pp. 516–529.
8. Robert E. Weigand, "Why Studying the Purchasing Agent is Not Enough," *Journal of Marketing,* Vol. 32, (January, 1968), pp. 41–45.
9. George Strauss, "Tactics of Lateral Relationship," *Administrative Science Quarterly,* Vol. 7 (September, 1962) pp. 161–186.

10. The complete model is presented and discussed in detail in Frederick E. Webster, Jr. and Yoram Wind, *Organizational Buying Behavior* (Englewood Cliffs, New Jersey: Prentice-Hall, Inc., in press).
11. Harold J. Leavitt, "Applied Organization Change in Industry: Structural, Technical, and Human Approaches," in *New Perspectives in Organization Research,* W.W. Cooper, H.J. Leavitt, and M.W. Shelly, II, eds. (New York: John Wiley and Sons, Inc., 1964), pp. 55–71.
12. A modified version of this model is presented in P.J. Robinson, C.W. Faris, and Y. Wind, *Industrial Buying and Creative Marketing* (Boston: Allyn & Bacon, Inc., 1967), p. 14.
13. For research on the influence of organizational actors and information sources at various stages of the decision process, see Urban B. Ozanne and Gilbert A. Churchill, "Adoption Research: Information Sources in the Industrial Purchasing Decision," in *Marketing and the New Science of Planning,* Robert L. King, ed. (Chicago, Ill.: American Marketing Association, Fall, 1968), pp. 352–359; and Frederick E. Webster, Jr., "Informal Communication in Industrial Markets," *Journal of Marketing Research,* Vol. 7 (May, 1970), pp. 186–189.
14. Lee Thayer, *Communication and Communication Systems* (Homewood, Ill.: Richard D. Irwin, Inc., 1968), pp. 187–250.
15. Yoram Wind, "A Reward-Balance Model of Buying Behavior in Organizations," in *New Essays in Marketing Theory,* G. Fisk ed. (Boston: Allyn & Bacon, 1971).
16. Frederick E. Webster, Jr., "New Product Adoption in Industrial Markets: A Framework for Analysis," *Journal of Marketing,* Vol. 33 (July, 1969), pp. 35–39.
17. Same reference as footnote 9.
18. David T. Wilson, H. Lee Mathews, and Timothy W. Sweeney, "Industrial Buyer Segmentation: A Psychographic Approach," paper presented at the Fall, 1971 Conference of the American Marketing Association. See also Richard N. Cardozo, "Segmenting the Industrial Market," in *Marketing and the New Science of Planning,* Robert L. King ed. (Chicago: American Marketing Association, 1969), pp. 433–440.
19. Richard M. Cyert and James G. March, *A Behavioral Theory of the Firm* (Englewood Cliffs, N.J.: Prentice-Hall, 1963).
20. Donald F. Cox, ed., *Risk Taking and Information Handling in Consumer Behavior* (Boston: Division of Research, Graduate School of Business Administration, Harvard University, 1967).

12

Russell W. Belk

Situational Variables and Consumer Behavior

Growing recognition of limitations in the ability of individual consumer characteristics to explain variation in buyer behavior has prompted a number of appeals to examine situational influences on behavior. Ward and Robertson argued that "situational variables may account for considerably more variance than actor-related variables" (1973, p. 26). Lavidge (1966) cautioned that many buyer behaviors may be enacted only under specific conditions and necessitate situational investigations of intra-individual variability. Engel, Kollat, and Blackwell (1969) urged that *both* individual and situational factors must be considered in order to explain consumer choices. Nevertheless, these and other suggestions to include situational variables in research on consumer behavior have gone largely unheeded. The primary obstacle has been the absence of an adequate conception of the variables which comprise a situation. It is the purpose of the following discussion to explore such concepts and to suggest directions for the study of situational influence in consumer behavior.

CONSUMER SITUATIONS AND RELATED CONCEPTS

Situations, Behavioral Settings, and Environments

As a starting point for a definition, most theoreticians would agree that a situation comprises a point in time and space (Belk, 1975). For students of human behavior, a discrete time and place occupied by one or more persons identifies a situation of potential interest. A somewhat larger alternative unit of analysis would be Barker's (1968) "behavioral setting." A behavioral setting is not only bounded in time and space, but also by a complete sequence of behavior or an "action pattern." For example, a basketball game or a piano lesson is a behavioral setting because each involves an interval in time and space in which certain behaviors can be expected regardless of the particular persons present. But such patterns of behavior require stretching the time and place dimensions to broader and more continu-

Reprinted by permission from the *Journal of Consumer Research* (December 1975), pp. 157–164.
Russell Belk is a Professor of Marketing at the University of Utah and has taught at the University of Illinois. He received his Ph.D. from the University of Minnesota.

ous units than those defining a situation. While a behavioral setting might be a store which is open from 8:00 AM to 6:00 PM (Barker, 1968, p. 19), the current perspective would recognize a number of discrete situations which may occur within this setting.

The concept of an "environment" extends the time, place, and behavioral dimensions still further. Although there is less agreement as to what bounds and defines an environment,[1] it is clear that situations and behavioral settings are subunits within an environment. In one of his early formulations Lewin pointed out that an environment may be thought of as the chief characteristics of a more or less permanent "situation" (Lewin, 1933). In this sense situations represent momentary encounters with those elements of the total environment which are available to the individual at a particular time. Environment is also broader in terms of the geographic area over which it applies. For example, while the "legal environment" may be described to consist of laws, legal institutions, and interpretive tendencies within a governmental territory, and the behavioral setting may refer to a certain courtroom, the specific experience of individual *A* being cross-examined by attorney *G* during trial *M* in city *R* at 4:00 on day *X*, can only be described from a narrower situational perspective. It is this latter view of the conditions for experiences and the effect of these conditions on specific behavioral outcomes which the current perspective seeks to develop.

Situational Versus Non-situational Determinants of Consumer Behavior

A second group of concepts from which situations must be distinguished are the nonsituational determinants of a particular consumer behavior. Figure 12-1 shows a familiar stimulus-organism-response paradigm which has been modified to divide the stimulus into an object and a situation. This split is analogous to the perceptual distinctions between figure and ground or focal and contextual cues (Helson, 1964). That is, because behavior with respect to a product or service object is of primary significance in consumer behavior, the object to which the consumer is directly responding will be regarded as a unique source of behavioral influence. In not including personal and object characteristics within the concept of the situation there is also a purposeful departure from Lewin's (1935) formulation of the life space. The rationale for this more limited view of situation is the greater possibility of operationalizing a construct which has an existence apart from the individual's total consciousness. For there to be a hope of really adding to the ability to explain consumer behavior, this separate existence is essential.[2]

It might seem that a clear distinction may be made between persons, objects, and situations as separate sources of influence on behavior, but some potential for confusion exists in attempting to separate the characteristics of each determinant. R. L. Thorndike's (1947) concept of "lasting and general characteristics of the individual" is a useful device in distinguishing personal and situational characteristics. These individual features, including personality, intellect, sex, and race, are stable over times and places of observation and may therefore be attributed consistently to the individual. Where the feature is more transitory, such as having a headache, it must be considered to be at least partly a function of the situation. It is necessary to impose similar constraints on the conception of object characteristics in order to categorize a description such as a brand of soda being 10¢ less than competing brands. In cases where the characteristic tends to be a lasting and general feature of the brand it may be attributed to the object. Where the characteristic is specific to a time and place (e.g., a special sale) it should be regarded as a characteristic of the situation.

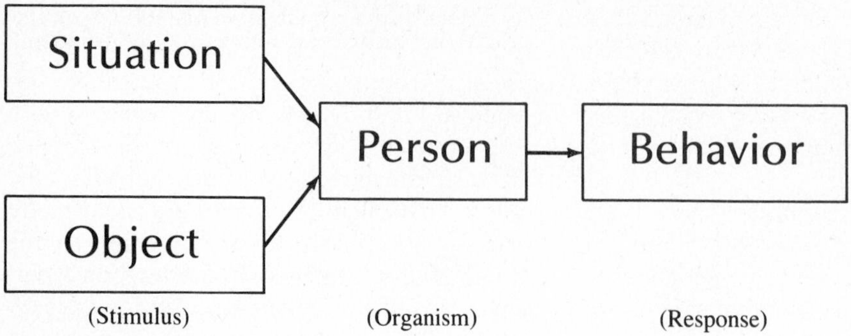

FIGURE 12-1 *A Revised S-O-R Paradigm*

Characteristics of Consumer Situations

Consistent with the previous distinctions, a consumer situation may be viewed as comprising ". . . all those factors particular to a time and place of observation which do not follow from a knowledge of personal (intra-individual) and stimulus (choice alternative) attributes and which have a demonstrable and systematic effect on current behavior" (Belk, 1974a). The greatest problem in operationalizing this view lies in defining "all those factors." Several attempts have been made to develop comprehensive taxonomies of situational characteristics. Using general guidelines suggested by Sherif and Sherif (1956), Sells (1963) constructed a subjective classification of over 200 situational variables including gravity, temperature, group structure, role requirements, and novelty of the situation in relation to prior experiences. Unfortunately, from the point of view of the current conception of situation, Sell's classification also includes some characteristics of the individual (e.g., age, sex, race) and environment (e.g., sources of food, erosion, language), and excludes certain descriptors of the physical locale (e.g., noises, colors, room or area size). Classification attempts by Bellows (1963), Wolf (1966), and Moos (1973), are less complete and suffer from similar drawbacks. Although also incomplete and parochial in its focus, a limited taxonomy by Allen (1965) of the situational factors found to affect conformity highlights several important social dimensions (e.g., public/private, interdependence of participants) and task dimensions (e.g., difficulty, importance) of the situation. These features contrast sharply with the taxonomy of 66 bipolar adjectival scales constructed by Kasmar (1970) to measure situations. From an initial list of 300 characteristics generated through room description protocols obtained from architecture students, scales were developed to describe 13 aspects of the situation; size, volume, scale, mood, color, texture, function, illumination, esthetic quality, climate, color, acoustical quality, and miscellaneous. Such characteristics provide a comprehensive description of the design features of the situation, but they completely neglect the social and task attributes which Allen's review (1965) emphasized. Furthermore a higher order factor analysis of data from Kasmar's scales has shown them to be highly redundant in terms of an underlying affective dimension (Mehrabian and Russell, 1974). Mehrabian and Russell's own (1974) attempt to develop three comprehensive situational descriptors (pleasure, arousal, and dominance) is also not very satisfying to depict the array of possible situational dimensions. However, by selectively combining features suggested in the various taxonomies cited, a skeletal notion of what is meant by "all those factors" comprising a situation may be offered. The following five groups of situational characteristics represent the general features from these taxonomies which are consistent with the current definition of situation.

1. *Physical Surroundings* are the most readily apparent features of a situation. These features include geographical and institutional location, decor, sounds, aromas, lighting, weather, and visible configurations of merchandise or other material surrounding the stimulus object.

2. *Social Surroundings* provide additional depth to a description of a situation. Other persons present, their characteristics, their apparent roles, and interpersonal interactions occurring are potentially relevant examples.

3. *Temporal Perspective* is a dimension of situations which may be specified in units ranging from time of day to season of the year. Time may also be measured relative to some past or future event for the situational participant. This allows conceptions such as time since last purchase, time since or until meals or payday, and time constraints imposed by prior or standing commitments.

4. *Task Definition* features of a situation include an intent or requirement to select, shop for, or obtain information about a general or specific purchase. In addition, task may reflect different buyer and user roles anticipated by the individual. For instance, a person shopping for a small appliance as a wedding gift for a friend is in a different situation than he would be in shopping for a small appliance for personal use.

5. *Antecedent States* make up a final group of features which characterize a situation. These are momentary moods (such as acute anxiety, pleasantness, hostility, and excitation) or momentary conditions (such as cash on hand, fatigue, and illness) rather than chronic individual traits. These conditions are further stipulated to be immediately antecedent to the current situation in order to distinguish states which the individual brings to the situation from states of the individual which result from the situation. For instance, a person may select a certain motion picture because he feels depressed (an antecedent state and a part of the choice situation), but the fact that the movie causes him to feel happier is a response to the consumption situation.[3] This altered state may then become antecedent for behavior in the next choice situation encountered, such as passing a street vendor on the way out of the theater.

Given a conception of the dimensions characterizing a situation, the final element of the definition of a situation requiring clarification is the requirement that these features have a "demonstrable and systematic effect on current behavior." To a greater extent than the problem of situational dimensions, this is an empirical question which has been the subject of some research. The following section reviews this research and examines the extent to which situational knowledge can be expected to add to our ability to explain consumer behavior.

ASSESSMENTS OF SITUATIONAL EFFECTS ON CONSUMER BEHAVIOR

Inventory Evidence

In the past six or seven years a small but growing number of empirical tests of situational influence in consumer behavior have been conducted using inventories of situational scenarios and choice alternatives. These inventories ask subjects to rate the likelihood that they would choose each of several alternative products or services under each of several sets of situational conditions. Summary descriptions of seven of these inventories are provided in the Appendix. It may well be argued that the situations investigated in these studies do not constitute random samples of possible situations and do not always reflect the full range of situational dimensions just outlined. Despite the fact that most of the inventories have relied on pretests to generate familiar situations, the argument is undoubtedly valid. Even so, any demonstration that behavior differs widely between the situations specified is evidence that there are important situational determinants for the class of choices considered.

Results comparing the relative influence from persons, products (responses), situations, and their interactions are presented in Table 12-1 for the six product categories that have been examined.[4] For all inventories the effects explaining the smallest proportions of variance are those which reflect superfluous response styles. For instance, a sizable interaction term for persons by situations would only indicate that some subjects view using any of the products in certain situations as more likely than do other subjects. Similarly, sizable main effects for persons or situations would have little meaning since they do not involve preference differences by product. A more dominant influence is the responses by situations interaction, especially for the meat and beverage inventories. This is the variance component which directly reflects the influence of systematic situational differences in product preferences. Furthermore, the lower contributions from the responses main effect in all inventories except motion pictures, suggest that general product popularity is a substantially less important determinant of consumer preferences than are situational conditions. For the meat and beverage inventories the small interaction terms for persons by responses reveal that in these categories situational influence also outstrips *individual* product preferences. For other inventories, again excepting motion pictures, the effects of situational and individual influences are jointly dominant. Motion pictures is the only category examined in which situational effects appear to be minimal. In this case individual preferences appear to be the consistent choice determinant with the general popularity of the movies following in importance.

A recent challenge to the validity of these inventory-based findings has been presented

TABLE 12-1 *Analysis of Consumer Behavior Variance*[a] *(percents of total variance)*

	Response Category[b]					
Source	*Beverage Products*	*Meat Products*	*Snack Products A*	*Fast Foods*[c]	*Leisure Activities*[d]	*Motion Pictures*
Persons (*P*)	0.5%	4.6%	6.7%	8.1%	4.5%	0.9%
Situations (*S*)	2.7%	5.2%	0.4%	2.2%	2.0%	0.5%
Products (Responses: *R*)	14.6%	15.0%	6.7%	13.4%	8.8%	16.6%
$R \times S$	39.8%	26.2%	18.7%	15.3%	13.4%	7.0%
$P \times S$	2.7%	2.9%	6.1%	2.2%	4.0%	1.9%
$P \times R$	11.8%	9.7%	22.4%	20.1%	21.2%	33.7%
$P \times S \times R$	—[e]	—[e]	3.4%	—[e]	—[e]	—[e]
Residual	27.8%[f]	36.4%	35.6%	38.7%	46.1%	39.4%
Total	100.0%	100.0%	100.0%	100.0%	100.0%	100.0%

[a] Components of variance analyses for mixed effects model with subjects random. For computational details, see Gleser, Chronbach and Rajaratnam (1965) and Endler and Hunt (1966).
[b] Inventories are described in Appendix.
[c] Variance components from this inventory have not previously been presented.
[d] Means of four samples.
[e] Not obtained due to single presentations of each situation-response combination.
[f] Incorrectly reported as entirely $P \times S \times R$.

by Lutz and Kakkar (1975). They argued that the experimental procedure of having subjects rate the same choice alternatives under all situational conditions may have spuriously inflated the situations by products interaction term. In order to test this possibility they replicated Belk's (1974a) snack product inventory, but exposed each subject to only one level of the situation factor (see Appendix for a description of their experiment). Their analysis obtained a contribution of less than 6 percent for the situations by products interaction, with a residual term which accounted for over 86 percent of the variance.[5] Unfortunately, their analysis assumed an inappropriate completely randomized factorial design rather than the split plot factorial design which was actually employed (Winer, 1971, pp. 366–371, Kirk, 1968, pp. 245–318). This problem renders their analysis meaningless and leaves the question of artifactual situational influence open. By altering the numbers of situations or responses by a factor of one half, Belk (1974b) has shown the variance component estimates of this inventory to be relatively stable across the resulting formats. Comparable results have been found by Endler and Hunt (1969) for a similar anxiety inventory. However, since these examinations do not reduce the number of situations to one per subject, the possibility that situational influence has been overestimated by these inventories still exists.

Other Evidence

Evidence of the importance of consumer situations has been found using other approaches which lend additional credence to a conclusion that situational influence is a pervasive factor in consumer behavior. Using multidimensional scaling Green and Rao (1972) found that consumer perceptions of and preferences for various bread and pastry items changed markedly over differing meal and menu situations. In a series of experimental choice simulations Hansen (1972) found that selection of a hairdryer as a gift depended upon characteristics of the supposed recipient, and that information seeking and choices from a fixed menu varied according to the description of the restaurant. Grønhaug (1972) found that buyers of tableware utilized different types and sources of information depending upon whether the purchase was for personal use or for a gift. By having subjects reconstruct word of mouth incidents, Belk (1971) found that one-third of the conversations about a new freeze dried coffee took place where the prior conversation concerned food, and that another third of the conversations began while drinking coffee. Sandell (1968b) was able to condition choice of specific cigarette brands to either stressful or boring situations and to consumption of a specific brand of beer.

Anecdotal evidence of situational influence abounds as well. For example, in retail settings the mere presence of children (Wells and LoSciuto, 1966), friends (Bell, 1967), and sales personnel (Albaum, 1967) have been observed to alter purchase outcomes; as time since last meal increased so did the total food bill of nonobese supermarket shoppers in a study by Nisbett and Kanouse (1968); Pennington (1965) found appliance sales were most frequent when customer and salesman were similar in their propensity to bargain; and greater risk was found to be perceived in buying the same good by mail than at a retail store (Spence, Engel and Blackwell, 1970).

From the variety of methods employed in these studies it appears that situational effects can be demonstrated both descriptively and experimentally. Although the amount of research specifically focused on situational influence is still quite small, a number of instances have been found in which situations can be shown to affect consumer behavior systematically. There is further encouragement for situational research from the refreshing fact that analyses of the behavioral inventories specifying situa-

Situations and products were chosen as in the meat inventory.

6. *Snack Products B.* Lutz and Kakkar (1975) replicated Belk's snack product inventory except that subjects in each of ten groups of from 24 to 36 students responded within only one of the situations and on only one occasion. Each group rated products in a different situation and a total of 306 subjects were employed.
7. *Fast Foods.* Using data collected by Leo Burnett U.S.A., Belk (1975) analyzed the effect of ten different situations (e.g., too tired to cook dinner, unexpected dinner guests, having a few friends over for a casual get-together) on responses to a six-point likelihood scale for each of ten (confidential) fast food outlets and related meal choices. Subjects were 98 housewives in a single community.

NOTES

1. A great deal of the effort in the emerging discipline of environmental or ecological psychology has been spent in debating boundaries. See for example Barker (1963), Craik (1970), Proshansky, Ittelson, and Rivlin (1970), Ittelson (1973), and Rivlin (1973).
2. This point is elaborated by Belk (1975). Mausner (1963) captured the argument in stating that "if one specifies the stimulus in terms of the nature of the receiver, lawfulness becomes impossible."
3. Hansen (1972) distinguishes between purchase, consumption, and communication situations. Comments in this paper concentrate primarily on consumer purchase choices.
4. The research reported generally employed a situations by products by persons repeated measures experimental design. While nearly all main effects and two way interactions yielded significant *F*-ratios, proportions of variance accounted for by each effect are more revealing (Belk, 1974a).
5. Hay's Omega squared statistic (Hays, 1964) was employed to derive these estimates. Since this statistic assumes a completely fixed effects model, results are not strictly comparable to those of the mixed effects components of variance method employed in the other studies reported.

REFERENCES

Albaum, G. "Exploring Interaction in a Marketing Situation," *Journal of Marketing Research,* 4 (May, 1967), 168–72.

Allen, B.L. "Situational Factors in Conformity," in Leonard Berkowitz, *Advances in Experimental Social Psychology,* Vol. 2, New York: Academic Press, 1965.

Barker, R.G. *The Stream of Behavior.* New York: Appleton-Century-Crofts, 1963.

———. *Ecological Psychology: Concepts and Methods for Studying the Environment of Human Behavior.* Stanford University Press, 1968.

Belk, R.W. "Occurrence of Word of Mouth Buyer Behavior as a Function of Situation and Advertising Stimuli," *Proceedings,* American Marketing Association Fall Conference, 1971, 419–22.

———. "An Exploratory Assessment of Situational Effects in Buyer Behavior," *Journal of Marketing Research,* 11 (May, 1974a), 156–163.

———. "Application and Analysis of the Behavior Differential Inventory for Assessing Situational Effects in Consumer Behavior," in Scott Ward and Peter Wright (eds.), *Advances in Consumer Research,* Vol. 1. Urbana: Association for Consumer Research, 1974b.

———. "The Objective Situation as a Determinant of Consumer Behavior," in Mary Jane Schlinger (ed.) *Advances in Consumer Research,* Vol. 2. Chicago: Association for Consumer Research, 1975.

Bell, G.D. "Self-Confidence and Persuasion in Car Buying," *Journal of Marketing Research,* 4 (February, 1967), 46–52.

Bellows, R. "Toward a Taxonomy of Social Situations," in Stephen B. Sells (ed.), *Stimulus Determinants of Behavior,* New York: Ronald, 1963.

Bishop, D.W. and P.A. Witt, "Sources of Behavioral Variance During Leisure Time," *Journal of Personality and Social Psychology,* 16 (October, 1970), 352–60.

Craik, K.H. "Environment Psychology," in Kenneth H. Craik, et al. *New Directions in Psychology,* Vol. 4, New York: Holt, Rinehart and Winston, 1970.

Endler, N.S. and J. McV. Hunt. "Sources of Behavioral Variance as Measured by the S-R Inventory of Anxiousness," *Psychological Bulletin,* 65 (1966), 336–46.

Engel, J.F., D.T. Kollat, and R.D. Blackwell. "Personality Measures and Market Segmentation," *Business Horizons,* 12 (June, 1969), 61–70.

Gleser, G.L., L.J. Cronbach, and N. Rajaratnam. "Generalizability of Scores Influenced by Multiple Sources of Variance," *Psychometricka,* 30 (1965), 395–418.

Green, P.E. and V.R. Rao, "Configural Synthesis in Multidimensional Scaling," *Journal of Marketing Research,* 9 (February, 1972), 65–68.

Grønhaug, K. "Buying Situation and Buyer's Information Behavior," *European Marketing Research Review,* 7 (September, 1972), 33–48.

Hansen, F. *Consumer Choice Behavior.* New York: The Free Press, 1972.

Hays, W. L. *Statistics for Psychologists.* New York: Rinehart and Winston, 1964.

Helson, H. "Current Trends and Issues in Adaptation-Level Theory," *American Psychologist,* 19 (1964), 26–38.

Ittelson, W.H. *Environment and Cognition.* New York: Seminar Press, 1973.

Kasmar, J.V. "The Development of a Usable Lexicon of Environmental Descriptors," *Environment and Behavior,* 2 (1970), 133–169.

Kirk, R.E. *Experimental Design: Procedures for the Behavior Sciences,* Belmont, California: Wadsworth Publishing, 1968.

Lavidge, R.J. "The Cotton Candy Concept: Intra-Individual Variability," in Lee Adler and Irving Crespi, *Attitude Research at Sea,* Chicago: American Marketing Association, 1966, 39–50.

Lewin, K. "Environmental Forces in Child Behavior and Development," in Carl C. Murchison, *Handbook of Child Psychology,* second edition, revised. Worcester, Massachusetts: Clark University Press, 1933, 94–127.

Lewin, K. *A Dynamic Theory of Personality.* New York: McGraw-Hill, 1935.

Lutz, R.J. and P.K. Kakkar. "The Psychological Situation as a Determinant of Consumer Behavior," in Mary Jane Schlinger (ed.), *Advances in Consumer Research,* Vol. 2. Chicago: Association for Consumer Research, 1975.

Mausner, B.M. "The Specification of the Stimulus Situation in a Social Interaction," in Stephen B. Sells, *Stimulus Determinants of Behavior.* New York: Ronald, 1963.

Mehrabian, A. and J.A. Russell. *An Approach to Environmental Psychology.* Cambridge: M.I.T. Press, 1974.

Moos, R.H. "Conceptualizations of Human Environments," *American Psychologist,* 28 (1973), 652–663.

Muse, M. "Time Expenditures in Homemaking Activities in 183 Vermont Farm Homes," *Vermont Agricultural Experimental Station Bulletin,* No. 530, 1946.

Nisbett, R.E. and D.E. Kanouse, "Obesity, Food Deprivation and Supermarket Shopping Behavior," *Journal of Personality and Social Psychology,* 12 (August, 1969), 289–94.

Pennington, A.L. "Customer-Salesman Bargaining Behavior in Retail Transactions," *Journal of Marketing Research,* 5 (August, 1965), 255–62.

Proshansky, H.M., W.H. Ittelson, and L.G. Rivlin. (eds.) *Environmental Psychology,* New York: Holt, Rinehart and Winston, 1970.

Sandell, R.G. "Effects of Attitudinal and Situational Factors on Reported Choice Behavior," *Journal of Marketing Research,* 4 (August, 1968a), 405–08.

———. "The Effects of Attitude Influence and Representational Conditioning on Choice Behavior," Stockholm: The Economic Research Institute, Stockholm School of Economics, 1968b.

Sells, S.B. "Dimensions of Stimulus Situations Which Accounts for Behavioral Variance," in Stephen B. Sells (ed.), *Stimulus Determinants of Behavior,* New York: Ronald, 1963.

Sherif, M. and C.W. Sherif. *An Outline of Social Psychology,* Rev. Ed. New York: Harper and Row, 1956.

Spence, H.E., J.R. Engel, and Roger D. Blackwell. "Perceived Risk in Mail-Order and Retail Store Buying," *Journal of Marketing Research,* 7 (August, 1970), 364–69.

Szali, A. et al. (eds) *The Use of Time.* The Hague: Mouten, 1973.

Thomas. W.I. "The Behavior Pattern and the Situation," *Proceedings,* Twenty-second Annual Meeting, American Sociological Society, 22 (1927), 1–13.

Thorndike, R.L. *Research Problems and Techniques.* Washington: U.S. Government Printing Office, Report No. 3 AAF Aviation Psychology Program, 1947.

Ward, S. and T.S. Robertson. "Consumer Behavior Research: Promise and Prospects," in Scott Ward and Thomas S. Robertson, *Consumer Behavior: Theoretical Sources.* Englewood Cliffs: Prentice-Hall, 1973, 3–42.

Wells, W.D. and A. LoSciuto. "A Direct Observation of Purchasing Behavior," *Journal of Marketing Research,* (August, 1966), 227–33.

Winer, B.J. *Statistical Principles in Experimental Design,* Second Edition. New York: McGraw-Hill, 1971.

Wolf, R. "The Measurement of Environments," in Anne Anastasi (ed.), *Testing Problems in Perspective,* Washington, D.C.: American Council on Education, 1966, 491–503.

13 Scott Ward

Consumer Socialization

Historically, market and consumer researchers have not been much interested in the consumer behavior of young people. Children, after all, have relatively little disposable income, and the major problems underlying consumer behavior research have to do with adults—the targets of most promotional activities.

On the other hand, child development and socialization researchers have virtually ignored consumer learning and behavior among children, focusing instead on the acquisition of fundamental orientations relevant to a wide range of behavior, such as sex-role learning and moral development.

Recently, however, some research attention has been devoted to effects of advertising on children, children's purchase decision-making, their influence on parental purchases, and the cumulative process by which children become socialized to the consumer environment. The primary impetus for these studies has been the charges made by various consumer's groups concerning the effects of marketing activities on children (especially TV advertising), and the subsequent need for empirical data as a basis for effective corporate and public policy formulation. These studies have in turn stimulated other research interests in the consumer behavior of young people. The general interest is in understanding the development of patterns of thinking and behaving which comprise consumer behavior, and this interest in "consumer socialization" is the focus of this paper.

It is a widely held belief in behavioral science that childhood experiences are of paramount importance in shaping patterns of cognition and behavior in later life, and this belief is supported by much research in clinical psychiatry, child development, criminology, and political socialization. Whether or not childhood experiences somehow influence later patterns of consumer behavior is an important hypothesis, for two reasons. First, we may be able to predict some aspects of adult behavior by knowing something about childhood experiences. Second, understanding processes by which children acquire consumption-related

Reprinted by permission from the *Journal of Consumer Research* (September 1974), pp. 1-14.
Scott Ward is Professor of Marketing at the University of Pennsylvania, and he previously taught at Harvard University. He has written extensively in the area of children's socialization.

skills, knowledge and attitudes is important to public policy formulation, and the development of consumer education programs. Partly as a by-product of the public policy issues surrounding effects of promotion on children, there is renewed interest in consumer education, as a means of preparing young people to evaluate and process marketing information.

There are other reasons for studying the consumer behavior of young people, and the processes by which consumer skills, knowledge and attitudes are developed. One reason is that research in this area may aid in the development of more effective and efficient marketing and information campaigns directed at young people. If one can judge by published materials from marketing practitioners, many marketing efforts aimed at young people are more the results of practitioner's trial and error experiences rather than research (Schiele, 1974). Although some large scale industry sponsored research is currently being done (Gene Reilly Group, Inc., 1973), the lack of a hard, empirical basis for the development of promotional efforts directed at young people is also reflected in the failure of information and persuasion campaigns sponsored by nonprofit organizations and government agencies (Ray, Ward, and Lesser, 1973). Research might help to increase the success-failure ratio among those interested in communicating with young people.

Other important reasons for studying consumer socialization stem from the need to understand family consumer behavior, intergenerational consistency and change, and the impact of social trends on buying patterns of young people and on family consumer behavior. Socialization research focuses on influences affecting children's development, but research on consumer socialization necessarily involves analysis of children's influence on intra-family patterns. Moreover, what kinds of consumer behaviors are "transmitted" across generations? Which are modified as a function of contemporaneous social trends and technological developments? And how do early learning experiences facilitate or inhibit these changes in consumption patterns?

A final reason for studying consumer socialization is that research in this area can potentially extend theoretical notions, developed in socialization and child development research. For example, stage theories of cognitive development provide useful explanatory concepts for assessing age-related differences in children's perceptions and understandings of television advertising. Conversely, applications of these stage-theory notions to this aspect of consumer socialization may usefully extend the theory itself.

The central purpose of this paper is to propose conceptual notions for research in the area of "consumer socialization." The term is first defined, and some important conceptual distinctions are made between consumer socialization and more general socialization processes. Three central issues are then discussed, for which data are needed in order to understand consumer socialization processes more adequately, and in order to bring evidence to bear on the areas of interest discussed earlier. The issues are: (1) the processes by which children acquire consumer skills, knowledge and attitudes; (2) the content of these socialization processes; and (3) how early learning influences later cognitions and behavior related to consumption. Research from relevant behavioral science areas is reviewed and assessed in terms of implications for these issues, and, finally, directions for future research in the area of consumer socialization are proposed.

Defining Consumer Socialization

One must understand what is meant by "socialization" before attempting to define the specific subspecies, "consumer socialization."[1] The term is usually broadly defined to refer to processes by which individuals learn to participate effectively in the social environment. Zigler and Child (1969) use the term this way:

> Socialization is a broad term for the whole process by which an individual develops, through transaction with other people, his specific patterns of socially relevant behaviors and experience.

Brim (1966) takes a more circumscribed view, referring specifically to the content of learning:

> [Socialization is] the process by which individuals acquire the knowledge, skills, and dispositions that enable them to participate as more or less effective members of groups and the society.

"Socialization" frequently refers to the learning of social roles and the behavior associated with those roles. Thus, studies have examined the socialization of newly married couples (Hill and Aldous, 1971), new employees (Moore, 1971), and prison inmates (Wheeler, 1971).

While "socialization" refers to processes affecting present and eventual behavior (e.g., parental influences on a child's achievement motivation and his later striving in the work environment), "anticipatory socialization" refers particularly to implicit, often unconscious learning for roles which will be assumed sometime in the future (Merton and Kitt, 1950; Riley et al., 1969).

Hess and Torney (1967) identify three types of anticipatory socialization. First, children acquire attitudes and values about adult roles which have limited relevance for the child but which form the basis for subsequent learning of specific behavior. Second, anticipatory socialization can refer to information which cannot be applied until later life: a child may have rudimentary understanding of "life insurance," but such information is normally not relevant until adulthood. Third, the concept can refer to general and specific skills which can be practiced in the immediate childhood situation, and which will be "called into play throughout life when appropriate occasions arise" (Hess and Torney, 1967).

"Consumer socialization" is defined here as processes by which young people acquire skills, knowledge, and attitudes relevant to their functioning as consumers in the marketplace. Several aspects of this definition deserve some explanation.

First, the focus here is on childhood socialization (although not exclusively), recognizing that not all learning takes place during this period of time, and that the impact of new roles – such as those adopted during adolescence – may greatly alter patterns of earlier learning.

Second, the discussion is limited to marketplace transactions, even though it is recognized that these are only a subspecies of transactions in general. That is, the focus is on consumption-relevant skills, knowledge, and attitudes, so the content of learning differentiates interest in consumer socialization from interest in other aspects of socialization.

Third, a distinction is necessary between skills, knowledge and attitudes that are directly relevant to consumption behavior, and skills, knowledge and attitudes that are indirectly relevant to consumption behavior. Directly relevant skills, knowledge and attitudes are those which are necessary for enactment of the consumer role – for example, skills at budgeting, pricing, knowledge of brand attitudes and shopping outlets, and attitudes toward products, brands, and sales people. However, it would be inaccurate to suggest that all consumer behavior occurs as a function of consumer role enactment. The notion of "role" implies interaction between positions of statuses in society, such as husband-wife, employer-employee. Consumer role enactment may be said to occur during the physical act of purchasing, or consumer role can refer to the set of physical and mental activities specifically involved in purchase decisions – shopping, talking to others about products and brands, and weighing purchase criteria. At such times, skills, knowledge and attitudes directly relevant to the transaction are quite useful.

However, more important for much consumption behavior are indirectly-relevant skills, knowledge and attitudes, which motivate purchases, but are not directly useful in the purchase decision or transaction itself. For example, a college student who purchases a dark suit for a business interview is acting in response to perceived norms and role requirements associated with job interviews. What is important for understanding his purchase is the knowledge and attitudes of the student concerning the interview situation norms, and associated role requirements. Other acts of consumer behavior may be motivated by a desire to acquire some of the trappings needed for successful enactment of particular roles (for example, an adolescent boy's purchase of cigarettes, or a razor).

Similarly, consumer socialization does not only prepare individuals to meet society's "requirements" or "expectations" regarding their behavior as consumers. In fact, society makes very few demands on people in terms of their consumer behavior. There are, however, social expectations that influence the behavior associated with various roles, which, in turn, influence consumer behavior, but in such cases consumer behavior is a second-order consequence of more fundamental aspects of social learning.

CONCEPTUALIZING CONSUMER SOCIALIZATION PROCESSES AND OUTCOMES

Conceptualizations of consumer socialization should take into account the content of children's learning about marketplace interaction, the processes by which learning takes place, and the changes in content and learning processes that occur over time.

Moreover, drawing on the distinction made above, it is also necessary to understand the influence of social role enactment on consumption behavior. In the broadest sense, this implies that one needs to understand how children acquire attitudes about the "social significance" of goods, or, more precisely, how people learn to perceive that the acquisition of some kinds of products or brands of goods can be instrumental to successful social role enactment.

Learning Processes

At the basis of much of the criticism of promotional practices directed at children is the implicit assumption that such practices are quite "powerful" in their influence on children (Action for Children's Television, 1971). On the other hand, defenders of such practices argue that parents modify the impact of promotions, and, in any case, much influence is exerted by peer groups (Banks, 1971). These differences of opinion exist at least partly because research has not focused on the relative influences of various socialization agents.

Greater understanding of consumer socialization processes could potentially provide useful input to consumer education programs. For example, what socialization processes occur within low-income subcultures? One could argue from a learning theory point of view that since children from low-income homes have less experience with money, and may be less aware of the range of consumer goods, their learning of some aspects of consumer skills should be less adequate than that of children from upper-income homes, who have more opportunities for consumption. On the other hand, one could argue that children from low-income homes are more likely to become highly skilled consumers, because they have had to learn disciplined uses of scarce resources. Again, data are lacking to support either view, and one would undertake different kinds of consumer education efforts depending on which view accurately characterizes socialization processes among low-income children.

Other questions can be raised about consumer socialization processes. Aside from the issue of the impact of advertising relative to other influences, what processes characterize the development of children's abilities to process information in advertising? Some argue that stage in cognitive development predicts children's abilities to handle advertising; others argue that more subtle effects occur as a function of modeling influences and portray response consequences. At a more general level, are parents purposive and systematic in their attempts to provide consumer training for their offspring, or is learning of consumer behavior more a matter of trial and error, observational learning, or identification with parents by offspring?

Finally, questions may be posed concerning how children develop social attitudes that may have implications for consumption, e.g., social reinforcement explanations for development of dependence behavior (Bandura and Walters, 1963; Walters and Parke, 1964); development of approval motivation (Crowne and Marlowe, 1964); and achievement motivation (McClelland, et al., 1953). It would be useful to know to what extent these general social orientations relate to consumption behavior. It seems reasonable to expect that young people who are highly motivated to seek achievements, or approval, may learn to evaluate material goods differently and differ in consumer behavior in other ways from young people who reflect lower levels of these social motivations.

Content of Learning

Any parent can attest that even young children learn some things relevant to consumer behavior, even if such learning merely involves recitation of advertising jingles, or development of brand preferences. But what aspects of learning are important in terms of the issues for consumer socialization research? For example, marketers and government policy-makers share an interest in understanding children's learning as it relates to their skills in evaluating advertising messages. The policy-maker is interested in learning which skills are necessary for children to "cognitively filter" puffery in advertising; the marketer is interested in designing messages which are geared to different levels of children's ability to process information in advertising.

Children's consumer behavior is limited, but what basic skills and knowledge do they acquire? For example, under what circumstances, and by what agents, do children learn skills at matching purchase criteria to product and brand alternatives? How do they learn advantages and disadvantages of shopping at various kinds of retail outlets, and when do they learn resource allocation habits, and understand notions of saving, spending, and investment?

Aside from these aspects of knowledge and behavior relatively directly related to consumption, we would like to know more about the formation of broad social attitudes relevant to consumption behavior, and how children learn that consumption of various products or brands can be a means of self-expression? What factors influence various motivational bases of consumption which are operative in different situations?

Permanence of Learning and Implications for Future Behavior

Basic to concern with content and processes of learning, research in consumer socialization must address the issue of what early learning experiences imply for later patterns of cognition and behavior.

There are three inter-related sub-issues:

(a) how "permanent" are various aspects of consumer socialization?

(b) what influences serve to modify previous learning?
(c) what aspects of early consumer socialization have the most direct implications for later behavior?

Obviously, one cannot simply assume that what is learned during childhood somehow "transfers intact" to adult life. Additional learning, extinction of earlier learning, the impact of new roles, all modify early learning. However, it is not evident whether what is learned in childhood is somehow "basic" to later behavior, i.e., whether later behavior is simply an extension and elaboration of more fundamental aspects of learning. For example, a child growing up in a lower class home may acquire certain orientations toward spending. How are these orientations modified later in life, as a consequence, say, of going to college, taking a similar–or different–status spouse, occupying a high-status social position?

REVIEW OF RESEARCH ON CONSUMER SOCIALIZATION

Reflecting the fact that concern with consumer socialization is relatively recent, few studies are precisely addressed to the kinds of conceptual issues discussed to this point. It is possible to take a broad view, however, and assess theoretical notions and empirical research in various disciplines and fields of study. The following review of research draws on investigations from various theoretical and research perspectives: child psychology, marketing research, home economics, and communications research.

Theoretical Perspectives

The point of view in this paper is that children's consumer behavior is best studied as a developmental phenomenon, and the working definition of "consumer socialization" focuses on children's development of skills, knowledge, and attitudes relevant to consumption behavior. The interest is in content, meaning the particular kinds of knowledge, skills and attitudes; the processes by which they are acquired; and the modification of learning over time.

Other writers have treated consumer socialization in somewhat similar theoretical perspectives. Sociologists Riesman and Roseborough (1955), for example, speculated that children learn "consumption necessities" from their parents, but "affective consumption" ("styles and moods of consumption") from peers. They observed, in 1955, that there is considerable uniformity throughout American society in the "standard package" of dwelling unit, furniture, appliances, standard brands, and they suggested that variations on this standard package are a function of both the content and processes of early learning and the changing social context. For example, the authors speculated that

> . . . the child who has been somewhat permissively brought up, who has had a hand in family consumer choice, who has earned and spent substantial sums in the teen-age period of ersatz grownup culture, will as a young married person assume as a right many of the items that for his parents were delayed and planned-for luxuries. (Riesman and Roseborough, 1955, p. 5)

They stressed notions of "conspicuous consumption"–i.e., particular patterns of consumption adopted as a means of demonstrating upward shifts in social status–although they were not specific about how such consumption norms develop in society or are learned by individuals.

In a similar vein, Parsons et al. (1953, Ch. 3) speculated that children learn basic seemingly "rational" aspects of consumption from parents, but "expressive elements of consumption" from peers and mass media; schools provide training in the "adaptive functions of consumption," meaning the functions of consumption in the context of broader social roles. However, Parsons and his colleagues suggested a contemporary decline in consumer skills; they speculated, in 1953, that young people learn less than in previous years about "integrative purchasing," e.g., allocation of savings to insurance and other investments. This trend was presumably a function of the increasing consumer affluence that characterized the early 1950's.

These early sociological essays provide some useful speculation about the general nature of consumer socialization processes. The failure of these authors or others to undertake empirical research based on these notions may stem from the fact that it is difficult to translate these very general ideas into testable propositions. For example, Riesman, Parsons, and their colleagues seemingly relegate all learning to social processes; however, they are less than explicit about what the consequences of various kinds of social learning processes might be. Moreover, they do not explicitly deal with differences in socialization that may occur as a consequence of cultural, sex, or social class differences, or, in the case of Parsons at least, changes in economic conditions.

From a quite different perspective, marketing academics have posed theories and models of consumer behavior that focus on an individual consumer's brand choice (Howard and Sheth, 1969), or on comparison or decision processes (Nicosia, 1966; Engel et al., 1968). These models focus on intra-individual processes. More relevant for consumer socialization research are models explicitly accounting for patterns of interpersonal influence in families. Such a model is Sheth's "theory" of family buying decisions, based on a review and synthesis of literature in several fields (Sheth, 1970). In contrast to the earlier model of brand choice behavior (Howard and Sheth, 1969), Sheth posed a series of variables and relationships in an attempt to account for the "total consumption of a family." An extensive review of this model (or the potential of modeling approaches to consumer socialization research) is beyond the scope of this paper. Suffice it to say that the primary utility of the model may be to stimulate research in the area by suggesting some of the variables involved in children's influence on parental buying decisions. As such, the model is relevant to only a portion of interests in consumer socialization; it has nothing to say about the influence of the family environment on children over time. Moreover, researchers using the model for research in family decision-making or consumer socialization must take care in interpreting some of the relationships depicted. For example, "other family members" (i.e., offspring), are posed in the model as equal partners in decisions with parents, and the model provides no basis for determining when this state of affairs may or may not exist. Furthermore, no elaboration is offered concerning the influence of birth order, age, and other factors that may have important consequences for processes depicted in the model.

To summarize, sociologists have discussed consumer socialization, but in the context of general essays, rather than theoretical propositions which could stimulate programmatic research. Moreover, their speculations might not be as appropriate to social and family environments of the 1970's, as they were to those of the 1950's (Roszak, 1969; Keniston, 1970). Sheth's more recent model is considerably more useful, although it is only indirectly relevant to consumer socialization issues.

Learning Processes and the Content of Learning

Research in consumer socialization requires understanding of two kinds of learning processes: those directly related to acquisition of consumption-related skills, knowledge and attitudes, and processes by which children acquire social motivations having consequences for consumption behavior.

Few studies have directly examined the first kinds of learning processes, but one exploratory, qualitative study is suggestive of the range of processes that may be involved in consumer socialization. McNeal (1964) individually interviewed 20 middle-class children in each of three age groups (5, 7, 9 years). The objective of the study was to "explore the attitudes, knowledge and involvement" of children in selected aspects of "the consumer role." "Consumer role" was defined as "all the activities associated with the acquisition of goods and services." As we have indicated, serious conceptual difficulties attend the notion of "consumer role," but McNeal was primarily interested in learning skills specifically associated with consumption, and only secondarily interested in learning social motivations having consequences for consumption behavior.

McNeal speculated that such role learning occurs through "observation, participation and training." Small sample sizes and the qualitative nature of his study presumably precluded more precise specification of the independent and dependent variables. McNeal suggested that much learning among the youngest children about "the shopping process" may occur by observation, since five-year olds could recall shopping trips with parents in great detail. He noted that most nine-year olds shop "independently" (presumably meaning shopping for themselves with discretionary personal funds, rather than shopping as an errand for parents), but he did not comment on the frequency of independent shopping, how this may relate to other aspects of learning, or what the implications are for later learning and behavior. McNeal found that younger children usually accompany parents on shopping trips, and over half were reported to be permitted occasionally to make purchase selections. The author suggested such activities are an important aspect of early learning through "participation."

McNeal found that older children demonstrated understanding of "marketing and retail functions" but notes that the school these children attended treated such matters in course work. He also suggested that children do not indicate "status motives" as a basis for imaginary purchases (e.g., cars), but he gave no description of how this information was elicited or how the data were interpreted to arrive at this conclusion. Unfortunately, McNeal did not attempt to summarize his qualitative data in terms of implications for the general "consumer role" framework he sought.

While McNeal did not explicitly interpret his findings in terms of the socialization literature, his data could be interpreted in terms of three areas of theory and research: cognitive development, imitation and observational learning, and interpersonal influence.

Many of the age-related differences he suggested can be explained in cognitive developmental terms: for example, his observation concerning children's lack of "status motives" for buying can be attributed to the difficulty young children have in "taking the role of another," which would be required for such status motives to be operative. Similarly, his findings regarding learning by "observation, participation and training" suggest the relevance of theories of interpersonal influence and observational and imitation learning.

Theories of Cognitive Development

These theories, typified by the work of Piaget (1928, 1952, 1954), Kohlberg (1971), and others, seek to explain development as a function of qualitative changes (stages) in cognitive organization that occur between infancy and childhood. Stages are defined in terms of the formal systems – primarily cognitive structures – the child is able to use in perceiving and dealing with the environment at different ages. Thus, cognitive developmental theories differ from classic learning theory interpretations of child development in that they focus on the interaction of personal and environmental factors, while learning theories characteristically view behavior as a function of forces applied to the child.

An example is provided by the work of Strauss and his colleagues, who used economic objectives and concepts in a series of experiments to test Piagetian notions of stages and conceptual development (Schuessler and Strauss, 1950; Strauss and Schuessler, 1951; Strauss, 1952; also, Danziger, 1958). The fact that Strauss chose "money concepts" as a stimulus material for studies among 4- to 11-year olds produced the partially unintended result of making an early contribution to our conceptual knowledge of how economic concepts and relationships are learned. Since such concepts are basic to consumer socialization, Strauss' results have important implications for several areas of research interest.

Strauss tested the development of children's understanding with respect to recognition (naming coins by various criteria); comparative value (which money is worth more); and equivalence (making change). In a later exploratory study, he examined children's perceptions and understanding of more complex phenomena; customer-storekeeper relations, relationship of customer payments to store expenses, and conceptual understanding of credit, retail markup, and the role of middlemen.

His data suggest that children's logical and reasoning processes are qualitatively different from those of adults – not simply "less developed," as some early developmental theorists suggested (Jersild, 1947). Rather, progression of conceptual learning appears to occur according to stages, and what is learned at one stage is a necessary condition for progression to the next. Schuessler and Strauss (1950, p. 762) argue that the stages may be conceptualized in Piaget's terms:

> The progression of conceptual learning moved, in each of the three areas (recognition, comparative value, equivalence) . . . from simple responses to complex ones, from concrete to abstract, from discrete to systematic, from undifferentiated to differentiated, from rigid to flexible, from egocentric (absolute) to nonegocentric (relative). (Parentheses mine.)

The authors find that understanding of these economic concepts and relationships increases with age; moreover, they report little difference between sexes, and among children from different social classes, in grasping these rudimentary aspects of learning.[2] Similar results are reported by Danziger in a qualitative study among Australian children (1958). Williams (1970), however, found that knowledge of economic concepts was greater among children from upper socioeconomic family backgrounds than among children from lower socioeconomic status backgrounds, at least among children from first through sixth grades.

Other studies have employed developmental notions to explain age-related differences in children's attention to television commercials (Ward, Levinson and Wackman, 1972) and their perceptions, explanations, and evaluations of them (Ward, 1972; Wackman and Ward, 1973; Blatt, Spencer and Ward, 1972; Robertson and Rossiter, 1974).

The general findings are that younger children (i.e., preoperational stage, roughly ages 2–7), exhibit greater stability in attention to television programs and commercials. Older children (i.e., concrete operational stage, roughly 7 or 8–12 or 13), exhibit greater differentiation between programs and commercials, as indexed by attention behavior. When television stimuli vary mainly in perceptual as opposed to auditory complexity, pre-operational children exhibit greater differentiation in their attention behavior (Wartella and Ettema, 1974). Similarly, the older the child, the more likely he is to differentiate program and advertising stimuli, to attribute selling motives to advertising, to exhibit multi-dimensional recall of television advertising, and to express skepticism about the validity of advertising claims.

These findings are explained in terms of cognitive developmental notions that characterize differences between children at preoperational and concrete operational developmental stages.

Interpersonal Influence, Observational and Imitation Learning

A series of studies have examined the nature and extent of children's influences on parental consumer behavior. Fewer studies have focused on parent's influences on children's developing attitudes, skills and knowledge relevant to consumption, and fewer still have examined relative influences of parents, peers, and mass media on consumer socialization processes. In contrast to studies relating responses to advertising to stages in cognitive development, these studies are normally only suggestive of patterns of intrafamily influence, rather than relatively explicit tests of theoretical propositions.

Consumer socialization processes would seem to proceed more through subtle interpersonal processes than through direct, purposive "consumer training" in families or schools. Ward and Wackman (1973) interviewed over 600 working- and middle-class mothers (and a subsample of fathers) of kindergarten, third and sixth grade children, and found that purposive consumer training by parents occurs infrequently. Parents of older children are somewhat more likely to report purposive teaching, and "setting an example," than parents of younger children. Parents have only general "consumer goals" for their children, most often related to teaching children about price-quality relationships. Few differences were found in teaching modes, frequency of purposive teaching, and consumer goals for children, depending on social class, age of child, and, perhaps surprisingly, sex of child.

If purposive consumer training rarely occurs in families, children may learn certain consumer skills through observation and imitation. The Ward and Wackman data (1973) indicate that mothers and fathers even *expect* their children to learn through observation. Bandura (1971) argues that such learning processes explain how material objects acquire social meaning through mass media advertising:

> As a rule, observed rewards increase, and observed punishments decrease, imitative behavior. This principle is widely applied in advertising appeals. In positive appeals, following the recommended action results in a host of rewarding outcomes. Smoking a certain brand of cigarettes or using a particular hair lotion wins the loving admiration of voluptuous belles, enhances job performance, masculinizes one's self-concept, tranquilizes irritable nerves, invites social recognition and amicable responsiveness from total strangers, and arouses affectionate reactions in spouses. The depicted outcome can be readily tailored to whatever is in vogue at a given time. When the importance of self-actualization was widely proclaimed, television viewers were told that simply by purchasing a certain brand of cigarettes one differentiated himself from the crowd. At the present time advertisements are capitalizing on ecological concerns, implying that purchasing certain products produces any number of ecological benefits.

To date, however, the implications of theories of observational and imitation learning have not been applied explicitly to studies of consumer socialization.

Other studies have examined the nature and extent of children's influence on parental purchases. Berey and Pollay (1968) examined the influence of 8- to 11-year old children on breakfast cereal purchases in middle and upper-middle class families (n = 48). Contrary to prediction, they found that highly child-centered mothers tend to purchase their child's requested cereal less frequently than less child-centered mothers. The authors speculate that the result may indicate that mothers with a high degree of concern for their children are more likely to buy what they perceive as "good" cereals, rather than those requested by their children, which may not always be "good." Also contrary to prediction, they found that the child's assertiveness was not related to the mother's brand recall. However, the small sample, and the measures, render these findings inconclusive. In particular, child's "assertiveness" was measured by teacher's ratings, which may not be a valid measure of assertiveness in the family.

Ward and Wackman (1972) studied parental perceptions of the frequency of 5- to 12-year old's purchase influence attempts and parental yielding among middle and upper-middle class families. Data are based on mail questionnaires obtained from mothers (n = 109). Contrary to Berey and Pollay's results, the authors found a moderate correlation between children's influence attempts (across more than 20 products) and parental yielding (r = .35) regardless of age. In general, influence attempts decline with age, but parental yielding increases with the child's age. This increase in yielding may mean that mothers become increasingly trusting of their children's judgment as their children get older.

Ward and Wackman also found that frequency of influence attempts was related to parent-child conflict, suggesting that purchase-influence attempts may be part of general patterns of disagreement between parents and children. Moreover, while mothers who placed restrictions on their children's viewing were less likely to yield to influence attempts (r – .24), but viewing restrictions were not related to perceived frequency of purchase influence attempts, suggesting that lesser amounts of television viewing does not necessarily dampen children's purchase influence attempts. Finally, the data indicate that mothers who have favorable attitudes toward advertising are more likely to yield to purchase influence attempts than mothers with less favorable attitudes. This result may suggest that, at least in families in which parental attitudes toward advertising are generally positive, parent-child interaction patterns reinforce mass media inputs to consumer socialization processes.

Wells (1966) suggested that children may influence their parent's purchases by "passive dictation," i.e., where other criteria are lacking or unimportant, a parent may purchase an item on the basis of the perceived wishes of the child. This hypothesis is supported by data from a national study of 6–14-year olds and their mothers (Gene Reilly Group, 1973). It was found that mothers of older children reported knowing their child's "favorite brands" for a variety of products, more than mothers of younger children. Data in this study also confirmed Ward and Wackman's findings that frequency of purchase influence attempts decrease, but mother's buying child's favorite brands increases with age. No major sex or social class differences were found.

Coulson suggested in a pilot study (1966) that housewives are aware of spouses' and children's brand preferences for various products, but that this awareness and "taking preferences into account" (presumably, buying these brands) decreases when brand names are not "visible," and when substantial product changes have occurred. Unfortunately, the data are most difficult to interpret, since brand "visibility" seems to be confounded with salience of brand appeal for various family members (e.g, cigarettes are classified as visible, and canned peas are "less visible").

Perhaps a general weakness of all of these studies of parent-child influence patterns is that they fail to suggest what learning may occur as a consequence of the reinforcement histories they imply. Such consequences are important for understanding consumer socialization.

Extending research by Dickens and Ferguson (1957), Marshall and Magruder (1960) investigated another area of intrafamily influence in an investigation of parental practices affecting children's knowledge and use of money. The author's stated intention was to test the validity of "truisms" and assumptions found in consumer education textbooks.[3] The sample consisted of 512 7, 8, 11, and 12-year-old children in predominantly rural areas of Kentucky. In the course of their analysis, they found positive linear relationships between knowledge of money use and "money experience," with age, IQ, and socioeconomic status background.[4]

The findings concerning experience with money extend Strauss' findings, although Marshall and Magruder do not interpret their findings in terms of a developmental framework, and questions may be raised concerning the validity and reliability of their scales. For example, Marshall and Magruder failed to find parent-child overlap on several aspects of consumption attitudes and practices, but the choice of variables and measures may have made parent-child comparisons difficult (e.g., "materialism," "money-centered" attitudes). They did find significant correlations between children's experiences with money and the extent to which parents "spent money wisely." The latter was measured by a "recommended practices scale," consisting of items concerning the extent to which expenditures are planned, the amount of joint decision-making, the practice of keeping financial records, and the frequency of communication with children about money practices. The fact that some of the items in the scale concern interaction with children about money practices may contaminate the observed relationship between wise spending and children's money experience; moreover, there may be considerable differences among social classes which were not identified with regard to the amount and kind of parent-child interaction about money.

To summarize these studies, it seems that consumer socialization proceeds more through subtle social learning processes, rather than through purposive and systematic parental training. Some learning may occur through observation of response consequences to models, as Bandura suggests, and learning no doubt occurs as a function of patterns of intrafamily influence which emerge as children attempt to acquire goods and services for themselves by requesting them of parents. It is not clear, however, just what children learn through these various processes, that contributes to their acquisition of skills, knowledge or attitudes important in consumer socialization.

Relative Influences of Socialization Agents

Several studies have attempted to assess relative influences of family, peers and mass media on aspects of consumer socialization. A few have used self-reported estimates as a means of measuring family, peer, and media influences on responses to advertising (James, 1971), purchase acts (Teter, 1966) or on drug attitudes and use (Kanter, 1970). The general finding is that parental influence decreases, and peer influence increases, with age, for a variety of purchase acts. Mass media influences are reported to be low and constant. Obviously, however, the adequacy of self-report measures of influence are suspect in terms of validity and reliability.

Ward and Wackman (1971) examined relative influence of parents and media on four aspects of "consumer learning": recall of TV commercial slogans, attitudes toward commercials, materialistic attitudes, and self-reported effects of advertising on specific purchases. They report that learning of slogans is a function of intelligence, rather than of TV exposure time; however, learning cognitive orientations – attitudes toward advertising and materialistic attitudes – is a function of reasons for watching commercials. Particularly important were "social utility" reasons (operationally defined as a motivation to watch commercials as a means of gathering information about life styles and behaviors associated with uses of specific consumer products). They found that younger adolescents talked more with parents about specific consumption practices and acts, but such intra-family communication appeared to mediate between exposure to advertising and purchasing for all adolescents. In a partial replication of this study, Stephens and Moore (1974) and Moore and Stephens (1974) report findings similar to the Ward and Wackman (1971) data, but in contrast to the earlier study only marginal differences were found in parent-child communication about consumption, and this communication was infrequent. This may be due to different family characteristics in their semi-rural sample, in contrast to Ward and Wackman's suburban sample.

Fauman (1966) studied relative influences of parents and peers on brand preferences and brand loyalty among 250 10, 11, and 12th grade boys from predominantly working-class families. Both peer and parental influence on brand preferences were found to decrease with intelligence, but were not related to media exposure time. Peer influence remained constant with age suggesting that this source of influence is established by early adolescence (10th grade). However, parental influence decreased with age. Brand loyalty was found to increase with age, but decrease with intelligence and with increasing media exposure. The results with respect to intelligence are not immediately clear; perhaps intelligence is correlated with decreased respect for others' opinions, or simply with increased knowledge of consumption alternatives, but Fauman did not explore these possibilities. Moreover, the data are based on the subject's reports of father's and friend's product and brand usage. Apparently no reliability checks were made of these data; more importantly, the direction of influence is not clear. If the son is correct that he and his father use the same brand, it may be that the son has influenced his father's brand preferences, rather than vice-versa.

Cateora (1963) analyzed general characteristics of teenage consumption patterns and the relative influences of peers and parents on some of these patterns. Data are based on 189 self-administered questionnaires completed by juniors and seniors in one high school in a "small" city. Cateora finds considerable homogeneity among adolescents concerning various "consumer values and goals,"[5] and that these values were relatively independent of social class. However, inspection of the data reveals several curvilinear relationships between social class and consumer attitudes and practices – upper-lower class students and lower-upper class students often expressed similar attitudes, but these differed from the attitudes of middle class adolescents. Such results may indicate that different experiences may lead to expression of the same attitude. For example, regarding attitudes toward quality vs. quantity in buying apparel, the responses of upper-middle class adolescents who said they preferred to buy one pair of good-quality shoes rather than several pairs of lesser quality shoes may reflect their having been in a position to make this choice, whereas the same attitudes expressed by lower-middle class adolescents may reflect their desire to be able to make this kind of purchase selection.

To summarize these studies of relative influence of socialization influences, it appears that the aspects of consumer socialization examined here reflect the conventional wisdom that parents become less important as children enter adolescence, and peers become more important. However, studies have examined only a few aspects of consumer socialization, and more data are needed before definitive statements can be made about the relative effectiveness of different socialization agents.

Learning Social Orientations Having Implications for Consumer Behavior

The position in this paper is that a conceptual distinction must be made between consumer socialization processes of acquisition of attitudes, knowledge and skills relatively directly related to consumption behavior (which may or may not have important implications for later behavior) and acquisition of more general attitudes, knowledge and skills relevant to role-enactment, which may have implications for consumption behavior. In the latter case, we must also understand when and why enactment of some social roles involves consumer behavior, and how children come to acquire attitudes about the social significance of material goods.[6]

A child's earliest experience with consumption may consist of learning how he should behave in order to receive material goods as a reward and to avoid having them withheld as punishment. Children also acquire skills in influencing parental purchases of products which they will use but which they do not consider a "reward."[7]

At some point, it would seem that material goods acquire "social meaning"—more accurately, that children begin to see goods as being instrumental in achieving social goals, rather than as simply fulfilling a functional need or as being the consequence of social behavior. That is, a child can obtain a candy bar as a reward for good behavior, or he can ask his mother to buy it simply because he is hungry and wants something sweet, or because he feels it will (temporarily, at least) place him a "cut above" his friends. These motivations are different, are acquired by different processes, and involve quite different kinds of skills, attitudes, and knowledge. Moreover, consumption as "reward" and consumption as "status symbol" are both social in nature; functional consumption is asocial.[8]

How does consumption acquire its "affective embroidery" or "expressive elements," as Riesman and Roseborough put it (1955)? Research suggests that cultural, family, peer group, and mass media influences may all affect such learning. Despite some signs of rejection of traditional values, research continues to indicate that adolescents in American culture are highly achievement oriented. Compared with Danish adolescents, Kandel and Lesser (1972) found American adolescents to be much more concerned with "getting somewhere, establishing oneself, and in this way gaining the respect or recognition of the community. What seems central here is a deep motivating concern for the regard of other . . ." (1972, p. 15). It may be that "regard for others" and "achievement" are sometimes demonstrated through consumption practices.

That children's aspirations for material goods reflect cultural values is demonstrated in a study by Kuhn (1954) who found marked differences between "most desired things" among Amish and other rural children. Social class may also affect children's perceptions of material goods and their implications for role-enactment (Katz, 1964). Certain studies suggest that "materialistic" attitudes are prevalent among blue collar workers, and it seems plausible that such attitudes may influence their children (Chinoy, 1955; Goldthorpe et al., 1969). Other socialization studies suggest kinds of family organization and parental relationships which may have implications for consumer socialization (Miller and Swanson, 1958; Davis et al., 1969; Hill et al., 1970; Davis, 1974; Hill and Aldous, 1971).

Finally, as noted earlier, research on development of dependence behavior (Bandura and Walters, 1963; Walters and Parke, 1964); approval motivation (Crowne and Marlowe, 1964) and achievement motivation (McClelland et al., 1953) is suggestive of social orientations which may have implications for consumer socialization. Research exploring the relationship between these orientations and consumer socialization processes however, is lacking.

Permanence of Early Learning

Socialization is a lifelong process, but most research on socialization focuses on learning during childhood and adolescence. In the behavioral science literature, there are few longitudinal studies to permit detailed analysis of the precise effects of early learning on many later patterns of cognition and behavior. In fact, the lack of extensive longitudinal data forces Brim to observe (1966, p. 21):

> The potency and durability of . . . [early childhood learning] are assumed on the basis of the frequency of learning situations, their primacy in the career of the organism, and the intensity of the rewards and punishments administered. Moreover, what is learned in childhood is difficult to change because much of it was learned under conditions of partial reinforcement.

Longitudinal research is currently being done, however (Bachman, 1969) and recent results of longitudinal investigations have supported the socialization hypothesis, as have earlier findings concerning relationships between childhood learning and adult behavior in such fields as clinical psychiatry and criminology (Short, 1966). In perhaps the best known research, Kagan and Moss (1962), in a 25-year longitudinal study, found consistency of a variety of social behaviors over the period of the study. Similarly, Lefkowitz et al. (1972) having followed children from third to thirteenth grade, concluded that aggressive behavior in early and late adolescence is predictable from aggressive behavior in childhood.

A crucial question for consumer socialization research is the extent to which early learning experiences influence later patterns of consumer behavior. One might assume that changes in the context of consumption from childhood to adulthood, and changes in the role requirements encountered in various stages of the life cycle, would "wash out" early learning. Two studies are relevant to this issue.

In one of the few longitudinal studies in consumer research, Guest (1955) interviewed a group of subjects regarding brand loyalty 12 years after he had first interviewed them. At the time of the original interviews, the subjects were children in grades 3–12 in the Washington, D.C. area who had indicated "favorite brands" (Guest, 1942). Guest suggests that his data indicate a strong degree of "brand loyalty," since about one-third of the subjects preferred the earlier-named brands even when present use, age at which original data were collected, IQ, and socioeconomic status were controlled. However, since only 20 percent of the original subjects were located and returned the mail re-interview questionnaire, and since brand availability was not controlled, the data are not conclusive. Moreover, it is not clear that a child's "favorite brands" should necessarily be correlated with later brand loyalty.

Another study, by Arndt (1971) examines long-term parental influence on offspring's consumer behavior. Arndt found significant relationships between college freshmen and sophomores and their parents regarding favorite stores, brand loyalty, opinion leadership, and innovativeness. Arndt reported that college students and their parents differ concerning "perceptual variables " (perceived product importance and perceived brand differences), but it is not clear whether this difference is simply a function of the different kinds of items or different patterns of use of the same items, which are purchased by college students and by their parents. He also reported parent-offspring similarity in "behavioral variables" (favorite store type pattern, opinion leadership, innovativeness), but these findings may correlate with other variables, since the students lived at home. Moreover, the small sample size (n = 55) does not permit generalizations to the large population of college-aged students who do not live with parents.

It is clear that longitudinal research is needed to address the issues of the extent to which early learning affects later consumer behavior. One extreme view would hold that role changes which occur with age would render early learning meaningless. (Even if this were literally true, studying consumer socialization would be necessary, in order to characterize adequately children's consumer behavior, and the influence of children on purchases by others in the family.) On the other hand, early learning may be an important determinant of later patterns of cognition and behavior. Virtually all behavioral research assumes that people are in some way influenced by earlier learning. The question may not be "how much" early learning experiences influence later consumer patterns, but "what aspects" of consumer socialization are important in influencing various specific patterns of adult consumer behavior.

DIRECTIONS FOR RESEARCH

The research reviewed in this paper is drawn from several different fields, and many different research interests are reflected. Nonetheless, the attempt has been to summarize findings which may be useful to investigators interested in undertaking research on consumer socialization.

The particular priorities for research in the field of consumer socialization depend, in part, on the investigator's particular interests. For example, consumer educators may be interested in knowing the kind of knowledge and skills that children learn imperfectly, or are not taught in the home or in consumer education courses. Corporate and government officials interested in policy formulation should be more interested in children's abilities to evaluate marketing stimuli adequately, and how these abilities develop.

Certain basic issues go across parochial research interests, however. Our present understanding of consumer socialization processes is based largely on inferences from research in other areas – most notably, socialization and child development research in psychology. Analyses of specific consumer socialization processes indicate that little purposive "consumer training" occurs in the home, so an important need is for research to determine the relevance of these processes described in research in other fields, for understanding consumer socialization.

We would like to know more precisely, for example, just what processes characterize children's acquisition of knowledge, attitudes and skills relating to consumption behavior, how these vary by factors such as family environment and social class, and how these processes change over time. Longitudinal research would be most useful in addressing these concerns.

Another pressing need is for research to determine how learning of basic social orientations affects consumer socialization. That is, how do children learn about the social significance of goods? Are children differentially motivated to acquire goods on the basis of their "social meaning?" Early sociological essays stressed such notions of "conspicuous consumption." But in light of contemporary social trends, are these notions still relevant in describing consumer behavior of young people?

The issues for consumer socialization research, and the findings reviewed here, suggest that certain approaches to research in the field may have relatively low payoff. It may be tempting, for example, simply to identify age-related differences in certain gross aspects of children's consumer behavior – how much allowance they receive, how many brand names they can identify, how accurate they are in pricing consumer goods and services, and so forth. The major issues, however, center around consumer socialization as a developmental phenomenon, and it may be most fruitful to focus on the *processes* rather than the *elements* of consumer socialization. For example, it would seem to be more useful to know how children evaluate brands rather than simply how many brands they know. Similarly, it is more important to know how children process information in advertising rather than simply how many advertisements they see in a given time.

Two other issues deserve some research attention. First, much behavioral science literature suggests that socialization processes differ according to social class as well as such factors as sex, intelligence, and birth-order (Hess, 1970). The influence of these social structure factors and related factors regarding the economic climate may have important implications for consumer socialization, but virtually no research has been done in this area. Second, while some studies reviewed here examined children's influences on parental purchasing behavior, the focus was on such influencing behavior as an aspect of children's goal achievement. Some research attention should be given to "reverse socialization," meaning processes by which children may influence their parents' knowledge, skills and attitudes relating to consumption. Such research might also address the impact of various contemporary social trends which are particularly relevant to young people, and the impact of these trends on the consumer behavior of young people, and on second-order effects on parents.

A final issue – and one which would seem to require conceptual thinking more than empirical research – is the problem of specifying dependent variables. The basis of interest in consumer socialization is a desire to influence developing processes of knowledge, skills and attitudes relating to consumption behavior. But what are the goals of such influence? Marketers and government communication campaign planners, for example, are interested in influencing children's specific consumer acts but in a larger sense, the impact of research on consumer socialization research would be magnified if longer-term consequences of consumer socialization processes are specified, and research oriented around these outcomes. One step in this direction is provided by Reuben Hill and his colleagues, in their classic study of resource allocation and consumption goals in three generations of families (Hill et al., 1970). While not explicitly concerned with socialization processes, the study suggests broad dimensions of consumer behavior that may be considered as "outcomes" of consumer socialization processes (e.g., planning, decision process efficiency, planfulness of consumer actions, satisfaction).

In summary, interest in consumer socialization has developed largely due to various contemporary issues relating to corporate and public policy formulation. Research in the field can profitably address these issues, and extend theory and research in other disciplines. It is suggested that consumer socialization be viewed as a lifelong process of acquisition of skills, knowledge and attitudes relating to consumption. The critical research needs center around the processes of socialization, the content of learning, and the modification of early learning over time. Finally, conceptual thinking is needed concerning the dependent variables – the ultimate goals of research in this area. It is suggested that these goals may center around the developing information-processing capabilities of consumers, or around ultimate consumer effectiveness in families.

NOTES

1. A complete primer or critical review of the socialization literature is beyond the scope of this paper. For excellent reviews see Zigler and Child, 1969; Goslin, 1971; Clausen, 1968; Hess, 1970; Brim, 1960, 1966, 1968. Specific applications of socialization notions are well-illustrated in the literature on political socialization. The interested reader may wish to see Hess and

Torney, 1967; Chaffee, Ward and Tipton, 1970.

2. Detailed analysis of findings is precluded by space considerations. Probably the best summary of this important series of studies is in Strauss, "The Development and Transformation of Monetary Meanings in the Child," *American Sociological Review,* 17 (1952), pp. 275-286.
3. While a plethora of textbooks and instructional materials purport to deal with "consumer education," few are based on any kind of research (Diamond, 1974). Marshall and Magruder found evidence which contradicted five of nine prescriptions for parental money education practices found in such "consumer education" texts. While this finding may not suggest that all formal consumer education efforts are based on false notions (the findings of Marshall and Magruder may be called into question as well), it may raise questions about the validity of some consumer education materials and practices.
4. Scale of "knowledge of money use" consisted of number of times child gave correct amount for dime-store items ranging in price from one cent to fifty cents. It is not clear, then, what this scale actually measures. "Money experience" scale consisted of items concerning frequency of specific purchases, number of specific choices of products in last week, if child had independently purchased a gift, and so forth. Again, the rationale or conceptual basis for the scale is not discussed. Procedures for deriving scales, information about scale distributions, or internal consistency of scale items are also not discussed.
5. Aspects of "consumer goals and values" examined included: attitudes toward credit and saving, "shopping patterns" (specifically, attitudes toward comparison shopping), perceived relationships between quality, quantity, and price, and attitudes toward merchants and toward advertising.
6. These attitudes would seem to underlie notions of "conspicuous consumption." The conceptual bases of such notions can be traced to Cooley's discussion of the "looking glass self" (1902) and Mead's "generalized other" (1934). The basic idea is that self is defined to some extent by how an individual feels others perceive him. To the extent that such learning occurs in socialization, our argument is that material goods, as well as behaviors, define the "self." More generally, consumer behavior may be considered one of many self-defining behaviors.
7. Presumably, the phenomenon of material goods as a reward or punishment varies with age. Infants may not understand the significance of material symbols as well as more expressive signs; conversely, except for special circumstances, material objects may lose rewarding properties among older children.
8. The distinction is similar to that made between "normative" and "informational" influence in groups conformity studies (Deutsch and Gerard, 1955) and between "psychosocial" and "problem-solving" influences on responses to persuasive communication (Bauer, 1967). More generally, the distinction is similar to Riesman's "other-directed" and "inner-directed" typology (Riesman, 1950).

REFERENCES

Action for Children's Television. Testimony before the Federal Trade Commission, November 10, 1971.

Arndt, J. "A Research Note on Intergenerational Overlap of Selected Consumer Variables," *Markeds Kommunikasjon,* 3 (1971), 1-8.

Bachman, J.G., Robert L. Kahn, Martha T. Mednick, Terrence N. Davidson, and Lloyd D. Johnston. *Youth in Transition,* 1, Ann Arbor: University of Michigan, Institute for Social Research, 1969.

Bandura, A. "Modeling Influences on Children," Testimony to the Federal Trade Commission, November, 1971.

Bandura, A. and R.H. Walters. *Adolescent Aggression.* New York: Ronald Press, 1959.

Banks, S. Testimony before the Federal Trade Commission, October 28, 1971.

Bauer, R.A. "Games People and Audiences Play," Paper read to seminar on Communication in Contemporary Society, University of Texas, March 26, 1967.

Berey, L.A. and R.W. Pollay. "Influencing Role of the Child in Family Decision Making," *Journal of Marketing Research,* V (February 1968); 70-72.

Blatt, J., Lyle Spencer, and Scott Ward. "A Cognitive Developmental Study of Children's Reactions to Television Advertising," in E.A. Rubinstein, G.A. Comstock, John P. Murray (Eds.), *Television and Social Behavior,* vol. 3: *Television in Day to Day Life: Patterns of Use.* Washington, U.S. Department of Health, Education and Welfare, 1972, 452-468.

Brim, O.G., Jr. "Personality Development as Role Learning," in I. Iscoe and H.W. Stevenson (Ed.), *Personality Development in Children.* Austin: University of Texas Press, 1960.

———. *"Adult Socialization,"* in J. Clausen (Ed.), *Socialization and Society.* Boston: Little, Brown, Inc., 1968.

Brim, O.G. and S. Wheller. *Socialization after Childhood: Two Essays.* New York: John Wiley & Sons, Inc., 1966.

Cateora, P.R. *An Analysis of the Teen-age Market.* Austin, Texas: University of Texas Bureau of Business Research, 1963.

Chaffee, S., S. Ward, and L. Tipton. "Mass Communication and Political Socialization," *Journalism Quarterly,* Winter (1970), 647-659.

Chinoy, E. *Automobile Workers and the American Dream.* New York: Doubleday Book Company, Inc., 1955.

Clausen, J.A. *Socialization and Society.* Boston: Little, Brown & Co., 1968.

Cooley, C.H. *Human Nature and the Social Order.* Boston: Scribner, 1902.

Coulson, J.S. "Buying Decisions within the Family and the Consumer Brand Relationship," in J.W. Newman (Ed.), *On Knowing the Consumer.* New York: John Wiley & Sons, Inc., 1966.

Crowne, D.P. and D. Marlowe. *The Motive for Approval: Studies in Evaluative Dependence.* New York: John Wiley & Sons, 1964.

Danziger, K. "Children's Earliest Conceptions of Economic Relationships (Australia)," *Journal of Social Psychology,* 47 (1958), 231-240.

Davis, H.L. "Family Decision-Making as Conflict Management," in S. Ward and P. Wright (Eds.), *Advances in Consumer Research,* vol. 1, Proceedings of the 4th Annual Conference of the Association for Consumer Research, 1974.

Davis, H.L., J.E. Denis, J.M. Lefebvre, and P. Peacock. "Determinants of Marital Roles in Consumer Decision Making." Unpublished paper, University of Chicago Graduate School of Business, 1969.

Deutsch, M. and H.B. Gerard. "A Study of the Normative and Informational Social Influences upon Individual Judgment," *Journal of Abnormal and Social Psychology,* 51 (1955), 629-636.

Diamond, S.L. "Consumer Education: Perspectives on the State of the Art." Harvard University, Graduate School of Business Administration, unpublished paper, 1974.

Dickins, D. and Virginia Gerguson. "Practices and Attitudes of Rural White Children and Parents Concerning Money," Mississippi State College Agricultural Experiment Station, technical bulletin no. 43 (April 1957).

Engel, F., D. Kollat, and R. Blackwell. *Consumer Behavior.* New York: Holt, Rinehart & Winston, 1968.

Fauman, B.C. "Determinants of Adolescents' Brand Preferences," unpublished paper (thesis), Sloan School of Management, Massachusetts Institute of Technology, June, 1966.

Gene Reilly Group, Inc. The Assumption by the Child of the Role of Consumer. Darien, Connecticut: The Gene Reilly Group, Inc., 1973.

Goldthorpe, J.H. *The Affluent Worker in the Class Structure.* Cambridge: Cambridge University Press, 1969.

Goslin, D.A. *Handbook of Socialization Theory and Research.* Chicago: Rand McNally & Co., 1971.

Guest, L.P. "The Genesis of Brand Awareness," *Journal of Applied Psychology,* 26 (1972), 800-808.

———. "Brand Loyalty – Twelve Years Later," *Journal of Applied Psychology* 39 (1955), 405-408.

Hess, R.D. and Judith V. Torney. *The Development of Political Attitudes in Children.* Chicago: Aldine Publishing Company, 1967.

———. "Social Class and Ethnic Influences on Socialization," in Paul H. Mussen (Ed.), *Manual of Child Psychology,* Vol. 2, third edition, New York: John Wiley & Sons, Inc., 1970, 457-559.

Hill, R. and Joan Aldous. "Socialization for Marriage and Parenthood," in D. Goslin (Ed.), *Handbook of Socialization Theory and Research.* Chicago: Rand McNally & Co., 1971, 951-983.

Hill, R., N. Foote, J. Aldous, R. Carlson, and R. MacDonald. *Family Development in Three Generations.* Cambridge, Mass: Schenkman Publishing Company, 1970.

Howard, J.A. and J. Sheth. *The Theory of Buyer Behavior.* New York: John Wiley & Sons, 1969.

James, L. *Youth, Media and Advertising.* Austin: University of Texas Bureau of Business Research, 1971.

Jersild, A. *Child Psychology.* New York: Macmillan, 1947.

Kagan, J. and H.A. Moss. *Birth to Maturity: A Study in Psychological Development.* New York: John Wiley & Sons, Inc., 1962.

Kandel, D.B. and G.S. Lesser. *Youth in Two Worlds.* San Francisco: Jossey-Bass, Inc., 1972.

Kanter, Donald L. "Pharmaceutical Advertising and Youth," unpublished paper, Coronado Unified School District, Coronado, California, 1970.

Katz, F.M. "The Meaning of Success: Some Differences in Value Systems of Social Classes," *Journal of Social Psychology,* 62 (1964), 141-148.

Keniston, K. "Youth: A 'New' Stage of Life," *American Scholar,* 39 (Autumn 1970), 631-654.

Kohlberg, L. "The Cognitive-Developmental Approach to Socialization," in D.A. Goslin (Ed.), *Handbook of Socialization Theory and Research.* Chicago: Rand McNally and Co., 1971.

Kuhn, M.H. "Factors in Personality: Socio-Cultural Determinants as Seen through the Amish," in F.L.K. Hsu (Ed.), *Aspects of Culture and Personality.* New York: Abelard-Schumann, Inc., 1954.

Lefkowitz, M.M., L.D. Eron, L.O. Walder, and L.R. Huesmann. "Television Violence and Child Aggression: A Follow-Up Study," in G. Comstock and E. Rubinstein (Eds.), *Television and Social Behavior,* Vol. III: *Television and Adolescent Aggressivess,* Washington: U.S. Department of Health, Education and Welfare, 1972, 35-135.

Marshall, H.R. and Lucille Magruder. "Relations Between Parent Money Education Practices and Children's Knowledge and Use of Money," *Child Development,* 31 (1960), 253-284.

McClelland, D.C., J.W. Atkinson, R.A. Clark, and E.L. Lowell. *The Achievement Motive.* New York: Appleton-Century, 1953.

McNeal, J.U. *Children as Consumers.* Austin, Texas: University of Texas Bureau of Business Research, 1964.

Mead, G.H. *Mind, Self, and Society.* Chicago: University of Chicago Press, 1934.

Merton, R.K. and Alice S. Kitt, "Contributions to the Theory of Reference Group Behavior," in R.K. Merton and P.F. Lazarsfeld (Ed.), *Continuities in Social Research: Studies in the Scope and Method of "The American Soldier."* Glencoe, Ill.: The Free Press, 1950, 87-89.

Miller, D.R. and G.E. Swanson. *The Changing American Parent.* New York: John Wiley & Sons, 1958.

Moore, R.L. and Lowndes F. Stephens. "Some Communication and Demographic Determinants of Consumer Learning among Older and Younger Adolescents," paper presented to Mass Communication Division of the International Communication Association, New Orleans, April 1974.

Moore, W.E. "Occupational Socialization," in D. Goslin (Ed.), *Handbook of Socialization Theory and Research.* Chicago: Rand McNally and Co., 1971, 861-885.

Nicosia, F. *Consumer Decision Processes: Marketing and Advertising Implications.* Englewood Cliffs, N.J.: Prentice-Hall, Inc., 1966.

Parsons, T., R.F. Bales, and E.A. Shils. *Working Papers in the Theory of Action.* Glencoe, Ill.: The Free Press, 1953.

Piaget, J. *The Child's Conception of the World.* New York: Harcourt, Brace, 1928.

———. *The Origins of Intelligence in Children.* New York: International Universities Press, 1952.

———. *The Construction of Reality in the Child.* New York: Basic Books, 1954.

Ray, M. and S. Ward. "Experimentation to Improve Pretesting Methods for Anti-Drug Abuse Information and Education Campaigns." Cambridge, Mass: Marketing Science Institute, 1973.

Riesman, D. *The Lonely Crowd.* New Haven, Conn.: Yale University Press, 1950.

Riesman, D. and H. Roseborough. "Careers and Consumer Behavior," in Lincoln Clark (Ed.), *Consumer Behavior,* Vol. II: *The Life Cycle and Consumer Behavior.* New York: New York University Press, 1955.

Riley, M.W., Anne Foner, Beth Hess, and M.L. Toby. "Socialization for the Middle and Later Years," in D. Goslin (Ed.), *Handbook of Socialization Theory and Research.* Chicago: Rand McNally and Co., 1971, 951-983.

Robertson, T.S. and J. Rossiter, "Children and Commercial Persuasion: An Attribution Theory Analysis," *Journal of Consumer Research,* 1 (June 1974).

Roszak, T. *The Making of a Counter Culture.* Garden City, New York: Double Day and Company, Inc., 1969.

Schiele, G.W., "How to Reach the Young Consumer," *Harvard Business Review,* 52 (March/April 1974), 77-86.

Schuessler, K. and Anselm Strauss, "A Study of Concept Learning by Scale Analysis," *American Sociological Review,* 15 (1950), 752-762.

Sheth, J.N. "A Theory of Family Buying Decision," paper read to American Psychological Association, Division of Consumer Psychology, September 5, 1970.

Short, J.F., Jr. *Juvenile Delinquency: The Socio-cultural Context.* New York: Russell Sage Foundation, 1966, 423-469.

Stephens, L.F. and Roy L. Moore. "Price Accuracy as a Consumer Skill Among Younger and Older Adolescents," paper submitted to Theory and Methodology Division, Association for Education in Journalism, San Diego, August 1974.

Strauss, A.L. "The Development and Transformation of Monetary Meanings in the Child," *American Sociological Review,* Vol. 17, 1952, 275-286.

Strauss, A.L. and K. Schuessler. "Socialization, Logical Reasoning, and Concept Development in the Child," *American Sociological Review,* 16 (1951), 514-523.

Teter, J.W. "The Family, Peers and Media Influence on Youth's Present and Future Consumption Preferences," unpublished thesis, Oklahoma State University, Stillwater, Oklahoma: 1966.

Wackman, D. and S. Ward. "Children's Information Processing of Television Commercial Messages," paper read to American Psychological Association, Division 23, Montreal, Canada, August 30, 1973.

Walters, R.H. and R.D. Parke. "Social Motivation, Dependency, and Susceptibility to Social Influence," in L. Berkowitz (Ed.), *Advances in Experimental Social Psychology,* Vol. 1. New York: Academic Press, 1964, 232-276.

Ward, S. "Children's Reactions to Commercials," *Journal of Advertising Research,* 12 (April 1972), 37-45.

Ward, S., David Levinson and Daniel Wackman. "Children's Attention to Television Advertising," in E.A. Rubinstein, G.A. Comstock, John P. Murray (Eds.), *Television and Social Behavior,* Vol. 3: *Television in Day to Day Life: Patterns of Use.* Washington: U.S. Dept. of Health, Education and Welfare, 1972, 491-516.

Ward, S. and D. Wackman, "Effects of Television Advertising on Consumer Socialization," Cambridge, Mass.: Marketing Science Institute, 1973.

Ward, S. and Daniel Wackman, "Family and Media Influences on Adolescent Consumer Learning," *American Behavioral Scientist,* 14 (January and February 1971), 415-427.

———. "Children's Purchase Influence Attempts and Parental Yielding," *Journal of Marketing Research,* 9 (August, 1972), 316-319.

Wartella, E. and James S. Ettma. "A Cognitive Developmental Study of Children's Attention to Television Commercials," *Communication Research,* 1 January 1974), pp. 44-69.

Wells, W.D. "Children as Consumers," in J.W. Newman (Ed.), *On Knowing the Consumer.* New York: John Wiley & Sons, Inc., 1966.

Wheeler, S. "Socialization in Correctional Institutions," in D. Goslin (Ed.), *Handbook of Socialization Theory and Research.* Chicago: Rand McNally & Co., 1971, 1005-1025.

William, J.W. "A Gradient of the Economic Concepts of Elementary School Children and Factors Associated with Cognition," *Journal of Consumer Affairs,* 4 (Winter 1970), 113-123.

Zigler, E. and I.L. Child. "Socialization," in G. Lindzey and E. Aronson (Eds.), *The Handbook of Social Psychology,* second ed.; Vol. 2: *The Individual in a Social Context.* Reading, Mass: Addison-Wesley Publishing Co., 1969.

14

Everett M. Rogers

New Product Adoption and Diffusion

The studies of the diffusion of innovations, including the part played by mass communication, promise to provide an empirical and quantitative basis for developing more rigorous approaches to theories of social change.

Melvin L. De Fleur (1966, p. 138)

Diffusion of innovations has the status of a bastard child with respect to the parent interests in social and cultural change: too big to ignore but unlikely to be given full recognition.

Frederick C. Fliegel and Joseph E. Kivlin (1966, p. 235n)

Diffusion research is thus emerging as a single, integrated body of concepts and generalizations, even though the investigations are conducted by researchers in several scientific disciplines.

Everett M. Rogers (1971, p. 47)

The purposes of this paper are (1) to summarize what we have learned from research on the diffusion of innovations that contributes to our understanding of new product adoption and diffusion, (2) to discuss how the academic history and the intellectual structuring of the diffusion field have affected its contributions and its shortcomings, and (3) to indicate future research priorities on the diffusion of innovations.

Our focus here is especially on the last 10-year period and on the diffusion of a particular type of innovation (new products), but for historical and comparative purposes, we also must briefly deal with the origins of diffusion research.

Since about the mid-1960s, there has been considerable interest in diffusion research on the part of consumer researchers and a certain degree of integration of diffusion frameworks and research findings into the literature on consumer behavior. For example, the leading textbook on consumer behavior today features a chapter on the diffusion and adoption of innovations. Many marketing texts these days have

Everett M. Rogers, "New Product Adoption and Diffusion," Reprinted from *Journal of Consumer Research* (March 1979), pp. 290–301, published by The Journal of Consumer Research, Inc.

Everett Rogers is a professor in the Institute for Communication Research at Stanford University. His landmark book, Diffusion of Innovations, *helped him win the Paul D. Converse award for contribution to the theory and science of marketing.*

a chapter on diffusion, or at least give considerable coverage to such topics as the innovation-decision process, adopter categories, opinion leadership, and the S-shaped diffusion curve.

Further, about 8 percent of the 1,800 publications dealing with empirical research on the diffusion of innovations, available to date, were authored by researchers associated with the field of marketing. These studies, mostly conducted since the mid-1960s, focus on new products as innovations. The present paper deals not only with these 8 percent of all diffusion publications but also with the other 92 percent, since I believe that the findings, methodologies, and theoretic frameworks from research on various types of innovations has applicability to consumer's adoption of new products. The adoption of most innovations entails the purchase of a new product, although this fact has often not been recognized by diffusion scholars.

THE RISE OF DIFFUSION RESEARCH AS AN INVISIBLE COLLEGE

From Revolutionary Paradigm to Classical Model

The origins of research on the diffusion of innovations trace from (1) the German-Austrian and the British schools of diffusionism in anthropology (whose members claimed that most changes in a society resulted from the introduction of innovations from other societies) and (2) the French sociologist Gabriel Tarde (1903), who pioneered in proposing the S-shaped diffusion curve and the role of opinion leaders in the process of "imitation." But the "revolutionary paradigm" for diffusion research occurred in the early 1940s when two sociologists, Bryce Ryan and Neal Gross (1943), published their seminal study of the diffusion of hybrid seed corn among Iowa farmers.

Any given field of scientific research begins with a major breakthrough or reconceptualization that provides a new way of looking at some phenomenon (Kuhn, 1962). This revolutionary paradigm typically sets off a furious amount of intellectual effort as promising young scientists are attracted to the field, either to advance the new conceptualization with their research or to disprove certain of its aspects. Gradually, a scientific consensus about the field is developed, and perhaps after several generations of academic scholars, the "invisible college" (composed of researchers on a common topic who are linked by communication ties) declines in scientific interest as fewer findings of an exciting nature are turned up. These are the usual stages in the normal growth of science, Kuhn (1962) claims.

Research on the diffusion of innovations has followed these rise-and-fall stages rather closely, although the final stage of demise has not yet begun (Crane, 1972).The hybrid corn study set forth a new approach to the study of communication and change that was soon followed up by an increasing number of scholars in a wide variety of scientific fields. Within 10 years (by 1952), over 100 diffusion researches were completed; during the next decade (by 1962), another 450; and by the end of 1974, another 1,250. So today there are over 2,700 publications about the diffusion of innovations, including about 1,800 empirical research reports and 900 other writings (Figure 14–1).[1] The amount of scientific activity in investigating the diffusion of innovations has increased at an exponential rate (doubling almost every two years) since the revolutionary paradigm appeared 32 years ago, as Kuhn's (1962) theory of the growth of science would predict.

The main elements in the "classical model" of the diffusion of new ideas that emerged are (1) the *innovation,* defined as an idea, practice, or object perceived as new by an individual or other relevant unit of adoption, (2) which is *communicated* through certain *channels* (3) over

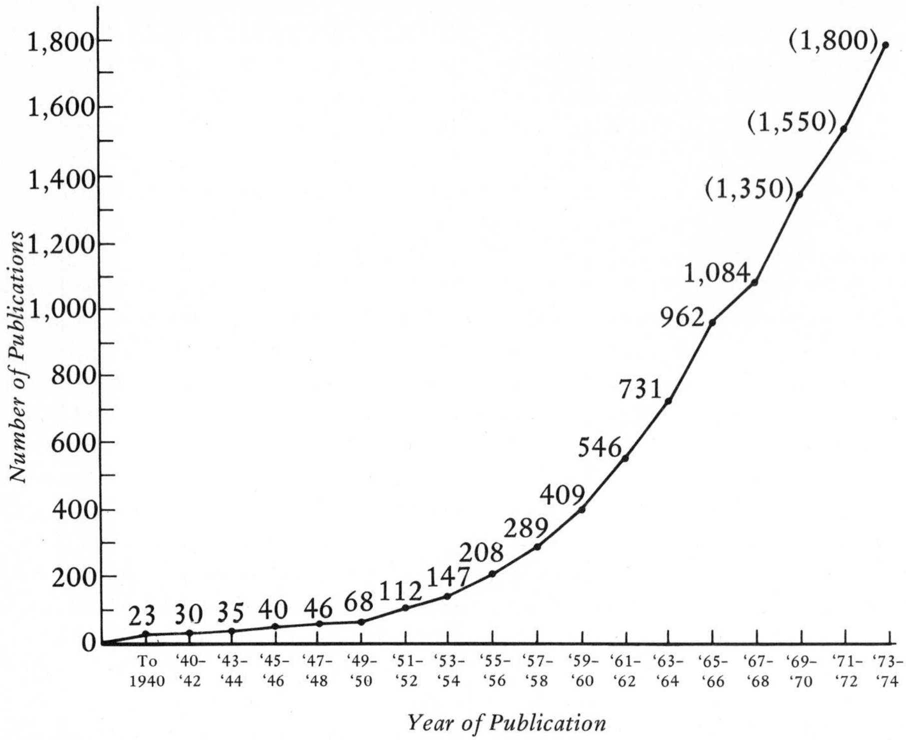

FIGURE 14-1 *Cumulative Number of Empirical Diffusion Research Publications, by Year of Publication.*

time (4) among the members of a *social system.* The Ryan and Gross (1943) study focused on hybrid corn, one of the most important innovations in midwestern agriculture. Data were gathered by personal interviews with all the Iowa farmers in two communities. The rate of adoption of the agricultural innovation followed an S-shaped, normal curve when plotted on a cumulative basis over time. The first farmers to adopt (the innovators) were more cosmopolite (indicated by traveling more frequently to Des Moines) and of higher socioeconomic status than later adopters. The typical Iowa farmer first heard about the innovation from a seed corn salesman, but interpersonal communication with peers was the most frequent channel leading to persuasion. The innovation process from awareness/knowledge to final adoption averaged about nine years, indicating that considerable time was required for adoption to occur.

Diffusion research is a particular type of communication research, but it began outside the academic field of communication. This was mostly a matter of timing, since the Ryan and Gross (1943) study preceded the first university centers or departments of communication by a good dozen years. Research on persuasion and attitude change, on nonverbal communication, and on most of the other important topics for communication research also began in psychology, anthropology, sociology, or other social sciences and then came to flower in the hands of communication scholars. The diffusion research approach was taken up in a variety of fields: education, anthropology, medical sociology, marketing, geography, and, most of all, rural sociology. Each of these disciplines pursued diffusion research in its specialized way and, for some time, without much interchange with the other diffusion research traditions.

The Intellectual Watershed of 1960

The year 1960 was in several respects a turning point for research on the diffusion of innovations. For one thing, the old disciplinary boundaries began to break down, and diffusion research began to emerge as "a single, integrated body of concepts and generalizations" (Rogers, 1971, p. 47). This emergence did not necessarily mean that all diffusion scholars completely agreed on definitions of concepts or on the most appropriate methods of inquiry, but at least the scholars generally recognized that they were investigating the same basic type of human behavior. Evidence of this recognition is shown in the works cited in their publications, as well as in the methods and models that they followed.

Second, researchers in the academic field of mass communication began to engage in diffusion research, at first by investigating the diffusion of major news events carried by the mass media: Alaskan statehood, the launching of Sputnik, and President Kennedy's assassination. The most noted news-event diffusion study, itself representing a "mini-revolutionary paradigm," was by Deutschmann and Danielson (1960). Today there are over 100 such news-event diffusion studies. Communication scholars soon began to study many types of other innovations, including technological innovations in agriculture, health, and family planning, especially in the developing nations of Latin America, Africa, and Asia.[2]

The early 1960s marked the beginning of a sharp takeoff in the number of diffusion studies in developing countries. Pioneering ventures in this direction by S.A. Rahim (1961) in Bangladesh and by Paul J. Deutschmann and Orlando Fals Borda (1962a, b) in Colombia suggested that new ideas spread among peasants in villages in a generally similar pattern to their diffusion in more media-saturated settings like the United States and Europe. The diffusion process, and the concepts and models utilized to analyze it, seemed to be cross-culturally valid, at least in the sense that comparable results were found in the new settings.

There were compelling reasons for the fast growth of diffusion studies in developing countries after 1960. Technology was assumed to be at the heart of development, at least in the dominant paradigm of development popular until very recent years.[3] In fact, innovativeness was thought to be the best single indicant of the multifaceted dimension called "modernization," the individual-level equivalent of development at the societal or system level (Rogers, 1969). Therefore, microlevel investigations of the diffusion of technological innovations among villagers were of direct relevance to development planners and other government officials in developing nations. These research results, and the general framework of diffusion, provided development agencies with both a kind of theoretical approach and an evaluation procedure.

The number of diffusion researches in developing nations totaled only about 54 in 1960 (13 percent of all diffusion studies), but rose steeply to over 800 or so by 1975, when about half of all diffusion studies were conducted in Latin America, Africa, and Asia. The major developing country of study is India, with over 450 of the 800 diffusion researches in developing countries.

An important boost to the internationalization of the diffusion field was the rise of KAP surveys in developing countries during the 1960s. KAP studies are sample surveys of knowledge (K), attitudes (A), and practice (P)—that is, adoption—of family planning innovations. K, A, and P are the logical dependent variables in evaluations of family planning communication campaigns, and, as national family planning programs arose after 1960 in many developing nations (especially in Asia) to cope with the population problem, KAP-type diffusion researches blossomed on all sides. Over 500 such KAP surveys were conducted in 72 nations by 1973 (Rogers, 1973, p. 377); India alone was the location for over half these investigations.

With the exception of the Taichung experiment in Taiwan (Freedman and Takeshita, 1969), the intellectual contribution of these KAP surveys "to scientific understanding of human behavior change has been dismal" (Rogers, 1973, p. 378). However, the KAP studies have provided a useful function by generally showing that most parents in developing countries want fewer children than they actually have, and that the majority desire a government family planning program. Even the harshest critic of KAP studies, Professor Philip M. Hauser (1967, p. 405), stated: "KAP survey results, erroneous or not, have helped to persuade prime ministers, parliaments, and the general population to move in a desirable direction and have provided family planning program administrators with 'justification' for budgets and programs."

Intellectually speaking, the family planning diffusion studies were generally disappointing, although several modifications in the "classical diffusion model" (such as the payment of incentives to promote diffusion and the use of nonprofessional change agent aides to help overcome the taboo nature of family planning communication) did emerge when family planning programs found the model wanting (Rogers, 1973). Also, the family planning diffusion studies gave a boost to field experimental research designs,[4] for over a dozen such experiments in various nations followed the Taichung study (Rogers and Agarwala-Rogers, 1975).

The rise of these field experiments, in place of one-shot survey designs, helped to overcome some of the methodological difficulties of diffusion studies in coming to grips with the "over-time" aspects of the communication of new ideas.

MARKETING RESEARCH ON DIFFUSION

While many of the field experimental designs in the diffusion field were conducted in developing nations and were concerned with family planning innovations, a number of other field experiments were carried out in the United States by marketing researchers.

The marketing tradition of diffusion research has come on strong since the early 1960s. Marketing managers of firms have long been concerned with how to launch new products more efficiently. One reason for this interest is the high failure rate of new consumer products, estimated at 92 percent of the approximately 6,000 new consumer items introduced each year (Connor, 1964).

The adoption of most innovations involves sale of a new product, of course, and it was easy for commercial firms to conceive of their new products as innovations and to adapt the theoretical and methodological framework of diffusion research to marketing problems. University faculty members in graduate schools of business led the way into diffusion research (Zaltman, 1965), to be followed soon after by marketing researchers in the employ of commercial firms. Unfortunately, a large proportion of these research reports lie only in the secret files of the sponsoring companies because of competitive threat, and they are thus unavailable to attempts at academic synthesis and the progress of scientific understanding of the diffusion process.

Much of the diffusion research in the marketing field was conducted either by the commercial manufacturers of the new product or by university professors with the sponsorship, or at least the cooperation, of the manufacturers. One advantage of this close relationship was that the diffusion researchers in the field of marketing often had some degree of control over the diffusion strategies that were used to promote the new products. This is a particularly important ingredient in the conduct of field experiments on diffusion. In fields other than marketing, diffusion scholars have seldom been able to manipulate the "treatment" variables, and it has therefore been impossible to conduct field experiments.

Perhaps a somewhat typical illustration of the field experimental approach by marketing researchers is provided by Arndt's (1967) study of the diffusion of a new food product. A letter about this innovation, enclosing a coupon allowing its purchase at one-third price, was sent to 495 housewives living in a married-student apartment complex. Personal interviews were carried out with these consumers 16 days after the diffusion campaign was launched. Arndt found that interpersonal communication about the new product frequently led to its initial purchase. Housewives who perceived the innovation as risky were more likely to seek the advice of their neighborhood opinion leaders about it. Naturally, this type of field experiment allowed determination of the impact of the reduced-price sample offer; the measure of impact was the rate of adoption (that is, purchase) of the new food product.

The diffusion research tradition of marketing has displayed an especially strong bias toward producing research results of use to the innovation's source (that is, the manufacturer of the new product) rather than to the consumers. This pro-innovation and pro-source orientation is also characteristic of other branches of diffusion research (a point to which we shall return), but less so than in the field of marketing.

One cannot help but wonder how the research approach (and the understandings that were obtained) might have been different if the Ryan and Gross (1943) hybrid corn study had been sponsored by the Iowa Farm Bureau Federation rather than by the Iowa Agricultural Extension Service and if the Coleman, Katz, and Menzel (1966) investigation of a new medical drug had been conducted under the auspices of the American Medical Association rather than Pfizer Drug Company. Perhaps "diffusion" research would have been called something like "innovation-seeking" or the "evaluation of innovations" had the receivers been in control (Rogers, 1971, p. 79).

The source-bias in marketing research on diffusion is especially surprising since this scientific specialty is often called "*consumer* research" in graduate schools of marketing, and it is often inspired by the "marketing concept," an approach that puts the consumer in control of the marketing process, at least in principle (Kotler and Zaltman, 1971). In diffusion researches following the marketing concept, the customer has often been studied, but usually to the advantage of the seller of the new product or service.

Even though the studies were usually commissioned by the selling agencies, consumers have often benefited from the diffusion researches in which they were respondents if their needs were met by the new products that emerged from such diffusion researches. These investigations *can* put the consumer in the driver's seat regarding new products, especially through a variant of diffusion inquiry called "acceptability research," in which the consumers' desires are determined and then a new product is designed to meet these previously unmet needs. Acceptability research began at the hands of marketing researchers and is now also followed in wider contexts. For example, the World Health Organization is currently involved in a research program in which the desired qualities of contraceptives are determined for the fertile audience in Latin America, Africa, and Asia to guide WHO biomedical researchers in the invention and development of future methods of family planning. This acceptability approach puts the potential consuming couples in the position, via survey research, of helping design more acceptable contraceptives.

Nevertheless, certain basic consumer-oriented research questions have not been asked in diffusion research, such as, How can the consumer be protected against the influence of advertising (or other promotional) messages? What information does the consumer need to know in order to make intelligent innovation decisions?

LACK OF A PROCESS ORIENTATION

We shall now consider the first of three important conceptual/methodological biases in diffusion research, which also characterize other types of communication research:

1. Lack of a process orientation.
2. A pro-innovation bias (and an associated ignoring of causality).
3. A psychological orientation, leading to shortchanging structure.

Every textbook definition of the concept of communcation either states or directly implies that it is a *process.*[5] Thus, one might expect an overwhelming emphasis in research and theory on the conceptualization of communcation as process. However, a recent analysis by Arundale (1971) shows that the research designs and measurements of communication almost never allow analysis of the over-time aspects of communication that would be necessary to explore process adequately. Very little communication research includes data at more than one observation point, and almost none at more than two such points in time. Therefore, almost all communication research is unable to trace the change in a variable over time; it deals only with the present tense of behavior. Communication thus becomes, in the actuality of communication research, an artificially halted snapshot.

Why has communication research not dealt more adequately with the change-over-time aspects of process?

1. We lack concepts and propositions that reflect a process orientation.
2. Time-series data are expensive to gather, unless one depends on respondent recall, a procedure that is often less than satisfactory.
3. Data gathering repeated over time leads to problems of respondent sensitization (unless one uses unobtrusive and nonreactive measurement methods), since communication research itself is a communication process.
4. Communication researchers are often pressured by research sponsors, doctoral requirements, and other logistic forces to produce immediate results; this is a strong discouragement to over-time research designs.

Thus, unfortunately, we define communication as process, but then proceed in communication research to treat communication as a one-shot affair.

Diffusion research is only slightly "less bad" in this respect than other types of communication research. Because *time* is one of the four essential elements in the diffusion process, and thus receives more explicit attention than in other types of communication research, it should be stressed in the research designs utilized in diffusion research.

These designs consist mainly of correlational analyses of cross-sectional data gathered in one-shot surveys of the respondents, thus following exactly the method pioneered by Ryan and Gross (1943). By 1968 (the last time a tabulation was made of the methodologies used in diffusion studies), only 65 of the then 1,084 empirical diffusion publications (about 6 percent) reported results from field experiments, and most of these field experiments had been done since 1960 (our turning-point year in the diffusion field, as mentioned earlier). Even allowing for the 67 diffusion publications (another 6 percent) that reported longitudinal panel studies at two or more points in time, the vast majority (about 88 percent) of all diffusion researches are one-shot surveys permitting only cross-sectional data analysis. Such research designs cannot tell us very much about the *process* of diffusion over time other than what can be reconstructed from recall data.

Diffusion studies are particularly able to rely on "moving pictures" of behavior rather than on "snapshots" because of their unique capacity to trace the sequential flow of an innovation through a social system. However, diffusion researchers mainly have relied on their respondents' ability to recall their date of awareness or adoption of a new idea. Essentially, the respondent is asked to look back over his shoulder and mentally reconstruct his past history of innovation experiences. This hindsight ability is not very accurate and undoubtedly varies on the basis of (1) the innovations' salience to the respondents; (2) the length of time over which recall is requested; and (3) individual differences in education, mental ability, etc.

Future diffusion research ought to develop improved methods for tracer studies, in which alternative sources of data are used to provide validity checks on recall data over time.[6] Much greater use should be made of field experiments and longitudinal panel studies, which, by their research designs, are able to take "moving pictures" of the diffusion process.

THE PRO-INNOVATION BIAS AND CAUSALITY

The second important bias found in most diffusion research is an inherent pro-change bias, which assumes that the innovations studied are "good" and should be adopted by everyone. Undoubtedly hybrid corn was profitable for each of the Iowa farmers in the Ryan and Gross (1943) study, but most other innovations that have been studied do not have this high degree of relative advantage. Many individuals, for their own good, should *not* adopt them.

The pro-innovation bias, coupled with the unfortunate and overwhelming dependence on survey research designs, means that diffusion research has mostly studied "what is" instead of "what could be" about diffusion processes. Therefore, method has followed the assumption that innovation is good, that the present process of diffusion is satisfactory and needs only minor tune-up rather than a major overhaul. Röling, Ascroft, and Chege (1974) have heavily scored diffusion research on this count, arguing that it has often led to increased inequity; field experimental designs are needed to test alternatives to current practice instead of replicating more surveys of "what is."

The pro-innovation bias in diffusion research, and its overwhelming reliance on correlational analysis of survey data, often led in the past to avoiding or ignoring the issue of causality. We often speak of "independent" and "dependent" variables in diffusion research, having taken these terms from experimental designs and then used them rather loosely with correlational analysis. A dependent variable thus means little more than the main variable in which the investigator is interested. In about 60 percent of all diffusion researches, the dependent variable is *innovativeness,* defined as the degree to which a responding unit is relatively earlier in adopting an innovation than other units in the system. It is implied that the

TABLE 14–1 *A Classification of Stages in Social Science Research*

Research Stages	Research Purpose	Research Method
1. Problem delineation	To define what we are looking for, and the extent to which it is a social problem	Qualitative analysis, such as case studies, observation, unstructured interviews, and literature review
2. Variable identification	To identify variables which might be linked to the problem, and to describe possible interconnections between these variables	Exploratory case studies, and other qualitative methods that are low on structure
3. Determination of relationships among the variables	To determine the clusters of relevant variables required for prediction, and to analyze their patterns of relationships	Cross-sectional, correlational analysis of quantitative survey data
4. Establishment of causality among the variables	To determine which factors are critical in promoting or inhibiting the problem	Longitudinal studies, and small-scale experiments with (1) over-time data, (2) in which at least one variable changes prior to the others, so as to determine time order
5. Manipulation of causal variables for policy-formation purposes	To determine the correspondence between a theoretical problem solution and the manipulable factors	Field experiments
6. Evaluation of alternative policies/programs	To assess the expected, as well as the unanticipated consequences of various programs/policies before and after they are applied on a large scale, and to determine the effectiveness of such programs in overall problem solution	Controlled field comparisons, such as the interrupted time-series field experiment

Source: Based on Gordon, MacEachron, and Fisher, "A Contingency Model for the Design of Problem-Solving Research Problems," *Millbank Memorial Fund Quarterly,* Spring 1974, p. 193. Permission for use granted by the Millbank Memorial Fund.

independent variables "lead to" innovativeness, although it is often unstated or uncertain whether this really means that an independent variable *causes* innovativeness.

In order for variable *X* to be the cause of variable *Y*, (1) *X* must precede *Y* in time order, (2) they must be related or covary, and (3) *X* must have a "forcing quality" on *Y*. Most diffusion researches have only determined that various independent variables covary with innovativeness; correlational analysis of one-shot survey data does not allow the determination of time order. Diffusion research has tarried too long at step 3 in Table 14–1 and should move on to step 4.

Correlational studies face a particular problem of time order that might be called "yesterday's innovativeness": In most diffusion surveys, innovativeness is measured "today" with recall data about past adoption behavior, while the independent variables are measured in the present tense. It is obviously impossible for an individual's attitudes, formed and measured now, to cause his adoption of an innovation three years previously (this would amount to *X* following *Y* in time order, thus making it impossible for *X* to cause *Y*).

So again we see the importance of research designs that allow us to learn the over-time aspects of diffusion. Field experiments are ideally suited to the purpose of assessing the effect of various independent variables (the treatments) on the dependent variable of innovativeness.

In order for *X* to cause *Y*, they must covary. If such covariance is very low, *X* is probably not a cause of *Y*. If their common variance is high, *X may* be a cause of *Y*. Diffusion research has specialized in determining the correlates of innovativeness.

Forcing quality, the way in which *X* acts on *Y*, is a theoretical rather than an empirical issue. The theoretical reasoning why certain variables might have a forcing quality on others needs to be given much greater attention in diffusion research. Theoretical approaches from other fields of communication study may have application to conceptualizing the forcing quality of certain independent variables on innovativeness and other dependent variables.

THE PSYCHOLOGICAL BIAS THAT SHORT-CHANGES STRUCTURE

The psychological bias in diffusion research stems from (1) its historical roots in academe and (2) the researchers' acceptance of how social problems are defined. Several early communication scholars came from psychological backgrounds, and it was only natural that their models of communication (and diffusion) largely ignored social-structural variables that affect communication. The transactional and relational nature of human communication tended to be overlooked, and this shortcoming was also characteristic of diffusion research, at least until fairly recently.

The Individual as the Unit of Analysis

The overwhelming focus on the *individual* as the unit of analysis in communication research (while largely ignoring the importance of communication *relationships* between sources and receivers) is often due to the assumption that the individual, as the unit of response, must consequently be the unit of analysis (Coleman, 1958–59). The monadic view of human behavior determined that "the kinds of substantive problems on which such research focused tended to be problems of 'aggregate psychology,' that is, *within*-individual problems, and never problems concerned with relations between people" (Coleman, 1958–59, p. 28). The use of survey methods in communication research has "de-structured" behavior:

> Using random sampling of individuals, the survey is a sociological meatgrinder, tearing the individual from his social context and guaranteeing that nobody in the study interacts with anyone else in it. It is a little like a biologist putting his experimental animals through a hamburger machine and looking at every hundredth cell through a microscope; anatomy and physiology get lost; structure and function disappear and one is left with cell biology. [Barton, 1968, p.1]

The main focus in diffusion research on the individual as the unit of analysis has only recently shifted to the dyad, clique, network, or system of individuals, centering on the communication relationships between individuals rather than on the individuals themselves. Encouraging attempts to overcome the psychological bias in diffusion research are provided by network analysis and by the open-systems approach.

These conceptual/methodological approaches suggest that even when the individual is the unit of response, the communication relationship (even though *it* can't "speak") can be the unit of analysis via some type of sociometric measurement. Sampling and data analysis procedures for relational analysis are being worked out,[7] but we still lack relational concepts and theories linking these concepts. Until diffusion scholars begin to think in relational terms, there will not be much relational analysis.

Person-Blame

The second reason for the artificially "destructured" psychological bias in communication research is the acceptance of a *person-blame-causal-attribution* definition of the social problems that we study: Individual-blame is the tendency to hold an individual responsible for his problems. Obviously, what is done about a social problem, including research, depends on how it is defined. Since communication scientists seldom participate in the identification and definition of social problems, they borrow or accept these definitions from alarmists, government officials, and other scientists.

Many illustrations of individual-blame can be cited in behavioral research. Caplan and Nelson (1973) found a high degree of individual-blame in psychological research on such problems as highway safety and race relations. They asked, "Why do we constantly study the poor rather than the nonpoor in order to understand the origins of poverty?"

An example of individual-blame is the poster produced by a pharmaceutical manufacturer: "LEAD PAINT CAN KILL!" The poster blamed mothers for allowing their children to eat paint. In New Haven, Connecticut, with the highest reported rates of lead paint poisoning of children in the U.S., landlords are legally prohibited from using lead paint on the inside of residences (W. Ryan, 1971). But the poster blames the mother, not the paint manufacturers or the landlords. And this tendency toward stressing individual-blame rather than system-blame is very common in communication research.

Diffusion research was originally (and for many years) as guilty as other types of communication research in following an individual-blame approach:

> We note an assumption in diffusion writings that the rate of adoption should be speeded up, that the innovation should be adopted by receivers, etc. [This is a consequence of the pro-innovation bias of diffusion research.] Seldom is it implied in diffusion documents that the source or the channels may be at fault for not providing more adequate information, for promoting inadequate or inappropriate innovations, etc. [Rogers, 1971, p. 79)

This psychological bias in diffusion research began with the hybrid seed corn study. Strangely, Ryan and Gross (1943) did not gather sociometric data about the interpersonal diffusion of the innovation within their two Iowa communities of study even though (1) they found that interpersonal communication from neighbors was essential in clinching adoption decisions and (2) their sampling design of a complete census of farmers in the two communities was ideal for gathering relational data for network-analysis purposes.

RESTORING SOCIAL STRUCTURE TO DIFFUSION RESEARCH

The refocusing of diffusion researches had to wait until later investigations, especially the drug study among medical doctors by Coleman et al. (1966). Then it became a common procedure for diffusion scholars to ask their respondents sociometric questions of the general form, "From whom in this system did you obtain information that led you to adopt this innovation?" The sociometric dyad represented by each answer to this question could consequently be punched on an IBM card (including data on the characteristics of the seeker *and* the sought), which then became the unit of analysis.

The relational data thus obtained were utilized to provide deeper insight into the role of opinion leaders in the two-step flow of communication, a conceptualization that was originated by Lazarsfeld, Berelson, and Gaudet (1944) prior to most diffusion research. Later research showed that the two-step flow hypothesis was mainly a gross oversimplification, since the flow of communication may actually have any number of steps, but the concept of opinion leadership has much theoretical and practical utility. Diffusion researches were able to advance understandings of opinion leadership because of their unique capacity to focus on the *flow* of innovations, new messages (to the receiver) that seem to leave deeper (and hence more recallable) scratches on men's minds. The tracer quality of an innovation's diffusion pathways aids the investigation of the flow of communication messages, and especially the role of certain individuals such as opinion leaders in this flow. For instance, the complicated relationship of leadership and group norms, first raised theoretically by George Homans (1961, p. 339), has received rather definite empirical elucidation by diffusion scholars, resulting in the proposition: *"When the system's norms favor change, opinion leaders are more innovative, but when the norms are traditional, opinion leaders are not especially innovative"* (Rogers, 1971, p. 219).

Network Analysis of Diffusion

Most communication research has largely ignored the effect of social structure on communication behavior, as we pointed out earlier, and diffusion research to date has only partly realized its full potential in this regard. *Network analysis* is a method of research for identifying the communication structure of a system in which sociometric data about communication flows or patterns are analyzed by using interpersonal relationships as the units of analysis (Rogers and Agarwala-Rogers, 1976). This tool promises to capitalize on the unique ability of diffusion inquiry to reconstruct specific message flows in a system and then to overlay the social structure of the system on these flows. The innovation's diffusion brings life to the otherwise static nature of the structural variables; network analysis permits understanding the social structure as it channels the process of diffusion. About the only other place in communication research where network analysis has been used to restore social structure to the communication process is in a few recent investigations of organizational communication.

The first, and very partial, attempts toward network analysis of the diffusion process simply identified opinion leaders in a system and determined their mass media and interpersonal communication behavior. This approach was only a slight extension of the usual monadic analysis, moving toward a relation type of analysis.

Next, diffusion scholars began to plot sequential-over-time sociograms of the diffusion of an innovation among the members of a system. Tentative steps were taken toward using communication relationships (such as sociometric dyads) as the units of analysis. This advance allowed data analysis of a "who-to-whom" communication matrix and facilitated inquiry into the identification (1) of cliques within the total system[8] and how such structural subgroupings affected the diffusion of an innovation and (2) of specialized communication roles such as liaisons, bridges, and isolates,[9] thus allowing communication research to proceed far beyond the relatively simpler is-

TABLE 14-2 *Comparison of Monadic and Relational Analysis in Research on the Diffusion of Innovations*

Characteristics of the Research Approach	Type of Diffusion Research Approach	
	Monadic Analysis	*Relational Analysis*
1. Unit of analysis	The individual	The communication relationship between two (or more) individuals
2. Most frequent sample design	Random samples of scattered individuals in a large sample (in order to maximize the generalizability of the research results)	Complete census of all eligible respondents in a system (such as a village), or a sample of such intact systems
3. Types of data utilized	Personal and social characteristics of individuals, and their communication behavior	Same as for monadic analysis, plus sociometric data about communication relationships
4. Main type of data analysis methods	Correlational analysis of cross-sectional survey data	Various types of network analysis of cross-sectional survey data
5. Main purpose of the research	To determine the variables (usually characteristics of individuals) related to innovativeness	To determine how social-structural variables affect diffusion flows in a system

sue of studying just opinion leadership. Further, the measurement of various structural indexes (such as system connectedness and system openness[10]) for individuals, cliques, or entire systems (such as organizations or communities) now became possible. Generally, system innovativeness is positively related to connectedness and to system openness.

These network analyses necessitated a new kind of sampling, as well as a shift to relational units of analysis. Instead of random samples of scattered individuals in a large population, the network studies usually depended on gathering data from *all* the eligible respondents in a system (such as a village) or a sample of such systems (Table 14-2). Usually these sample designs meant less emphasis on the ability to generalize the research results, which was traded off for a greater focus on understanding the role of social structures on diffusion flows. If such research were to study social structure, it had to sample intact social structures, or at least the relevant parts of them.

The Strength of Weak Ties

Out of the network analysis of interpersonal diffusion grew a research issue that came to be called "the strength of weak ties" (Granovetter, 1973; Liu and Duff, 1972).[11] The proposition summarizing this research is, *The informational strength of dyadic communication relationships is inversely related to the degree of homophily (and the strength of the attraction) between the source and the receiver.* Or, in other words, an innovation is diffused to a larger number of individuals and traverses a greater social distance when passed through weak ties rather than strong ones (Granovetter, 1973).

For any given topic, each individual operates in his/her particular communication environment consisting of a number of friends and acquaintances with whom the topic is discussed most frequently. These friends are usually highly homophilous (or similar) with the individual and with each other, and most of the individual's friends are friends of each other, thus constituting an "interlocking network" (Laumann, 1973; Rogers, 1973). This homophily and close attraction facilitate effective communication, but they act as a barrier preventing new ideas from entering the network. There is thus not much informational strength in the interlocking network; some heterophilous ties into the network are needed to give it more openness. These "weak ties" enable innovations to flow from clique to clique via liaisons and bridges. There is a cohesive power to the weak ties.

Laumann (1973) found important differences in political behavior, organizational participation, and consumer behavior between Detroit men with interlocking networks and those with radial networks. Thus the nature of these personal communication networks is perhaps one important way to distinguish consumers, at least in their receptivity to innovations. Innovators have more radial personal networks, and interlocking networks are more likely centered on later adopters.

Network analysis of the diffusion of the IUD in the Philippines demonstrated this strength of weak ties: The innovation spread most easily within interlocking cliques among housewives of very similar social status (Liu and Duff, 1972). But heterophilous flows were necessary to link these cliques; usually these "weak ties" connected two women who were not close friends and allowed the IUD to travel from a higher-status to a somewhat lower-status housewife. Therefore, at least occasional heterophilous dyadic communication in a network was a structural prerequisite for effective diffusion.

The case of network analysis on the strength of weak ties illustrates an important recent trend in diffusion research: The concepts used in this analysis are *relational* constructs. Perhaps we are seeing the real beginning of relational thinking in communication research.

CONCLUSIONS

Our quick tour of the past 32 years of diffusion research provides many examples of Thorstein Veblen's concept of "trained incapacity": By being taught to "see" innovativeness, opinion leadership, and other aspects of the classical model of diffusion, we failed to "see" much else. Acceptance of a revolutionary paradigm by scholars in a field enables them to cope with uncertainty and information overload through the simplification of reality that the paradigm represents. It also imposes and standardizes a set of assumptions and conceptual biases that, once begun, are difficult to recognize and overcome.

In my opinion the research designs, concepts, and measurement procedures of diffusion research have been very stereotyped. This similarity has facilitated the synthesis of diffusion findings, a task to which I have contributed; in fact, all diffusion studies look a good deal alike. But such standardization of research approaches has also greatly limited the contribution of diffusion research to more effective social programs and to furthering the scientific understanding of communication and human behavior change. Presumably this indictment is what one dean of a U.S. school of communication had in mind when he characterized the diffusion field as "a mile wide and an inch deep."

Nevertheless, I believe that *research on the diffusion of innovations has played an important role in helping put social structure back in the communication process.* Focus on structural variables has increasingly characterized diffusion research in the past decade, and the techniques of network analysis promise exciting further steps in this direction. Eventually this trend may help communication research shed its psychological bias and person-blame orientation.

For network analysis to fulfill its potential, however, I feel we must improve the methods of data gathering and measurement. Sociometric questions about communication behavior leave much to be desired; adequate evidence of their accuracy and stability over time are presently lacking. Unobtrusive, nonreactive measures are needed to provide validity checks on sociometry, leading to a multiple-measurement approach. At present, I believe our data-analysis techniques for relational analysis of communication behavior have far outrun the quality of our measurement.

Longitudinal panel designs for network analysis of diffusion processes are also needed; along with field experiments, they help secure the necessary data to illuminate the over-time process aspects of diffusion (and communication) and to facilitate exploration of the causal relationships involved in communication behavior.

Time is an explicit element in all diffusion research. But the measurement of time is one of the most egregious methodological weaknesses of past diffusion inquiry through its overwhelming dependence on recall data.

Thus, network analysis of over-time data and field experiments are robust tools offering promise for research on the diffusion of innovations in the years ahead.

Consumer researchers have already made important contributions to understanding the diffusion of innovations, and the diffusion model has extended the scope of investigations of the consumption of new products.

NOTES

1. All of these 1,800 empirical research publications, plus another 900 nonempirical, publications (bibliographies, theoretical works, etc.), are held in the Diffusion Documents Center in the Department of Population Planning at the University of Michigan. A bibliography of these 2,700 items (Rogers and Thomas, 1975) is available from the Department at no cost.
2. Detail on the convergence of diffusion research with communication research is provided by Katz (1960) and Rogers (1967).
3. In addition to assuming that capital-intensive technology was the vital ingredient in development, the dominant paradigm assumed that a nation had to pass through an industrial revolution en route to development, and that economic growth (guided by central planning agencies and quantified in aggregate terms like GNP) largely constituted the nature of development. After the paradigm shift, the newer conceptions of development stressed (1) the *equality* of distribution, (2) popular *participation* in decentralized development planning and execution, (3) *self-reliance* and independence in development, and (4) *integration of* traditional with modern systems (Rogers, 1975a).
4. A *field experiment* is an active intervention by an experimenter who administers a treatment (in the form of a program, project, or activity) to randomly selected respondents arranged in groups that are equivalent in the way they are chosen, with at least one treatment group and one control group (who do not receive the treatment).
5. A common definition of *communication* is the process by which an idea is transferred from a source to a receiver with the intent to change his/her behavior.
6. For example, in a study of the diffusion of a new drug among medical doctors, the physicians' recall data were checked against pharmacists' sales records for each doctor (Coleman et al., 1966).
7. *Relational analysis* is a research approach in which the unit of analysis is a relationship between two or more individuals (Rogers and Bhowmik, 1970–71).
8. A *clique* is a subsystem whose elements interact with each other relatively more frequently than with other members of the communication system.
9. A *liaison* is an individual who interpersonally connects two or more cliques within a system, without belonging to any clique. A *bridge* is an individual who is a member of a communication clique and has a link to an individual who is a member of a different communication clique. An *isolate* is an individual who has few communication contacts with the rest of the system.

10. *System connectedness* is the degree to which the members of a system as a whole are linked with each other in communication flows. *System openness* is the degree to which a system exchanges information with its environment.
11. These two sets of authors independently discovered the diffusion strength of weak sociometric ties, and although approaching the issue in somewhat different ways, they published articles with virtually identical titles within a few months of each other in 1972-73. Professors Liu, Duff, and Granovetter were well read in the diffusion literature but had not previously published on this topic, and their articles showed a relatively fresh approach to analyzing diffusion networks. Perhaps this relative newness in working with the classical diffusion model was one requisite for the originality of their contribution.

REFERENCES

Arndt, J. "Role of Product-Related Conversations in the Diffusion of a New Product," *Journal of Marketing Research,* 4 (August 1967), 291-95.

Arundale, R. B. *The Concept of Process in Human Communication Research.* Unpublished doctoral dissertation, Michigan State University, 1971.

Barton, A. H. "Bringing Society Back In: Survey Research and Macro-Methodology," *American Behavioral Scientist,* 12 (November-December 1968), 1-9.

Caplan, N. and S. D. Nelson. "On Being Useful: The Nature and Consequences of Psychological Research on Social Problems," *American Psychologist,* 28 (March 1973), 199-211.

Coleman, J. S. "Relational Analysis: The Study of Social Organization with Survey Methods," *Human Organization,* 17, (Winter 1958-59), 28-36.

Coleman, J. S., E. Katz, and H. Menzel. *Medical Innovation: A Diffusion Study.* Indianapolis: Bobbs-Merrill, 1966.

Connor, J. T. "Needed: New Economics for a New Era," *Printers' Ink,* 287 (May 29, 1964), 35-37.

Crane, D. *Invisible Colleges: Diffusion of Knowledge in Scientific Communities.* Chicago: University of Chicago Press, 1972.

De Fleur, M. L. *Theories of Mass Communication.* New York: McKay, 1966.

Deutschmann, P. J. and O. F. Borda. *Communication and Adoption Patterns in an Andean Village.* San José, Costa Rica: Programa Interamericano de Información Popular and Facultad de Sociologia, Universidad Nacional de Colombia, 1962a.

Deutschmann, P. J. and O. F. Borda. *La Comunicación de las Ideas entre los Campesinos Colombianos: Un Análisis Socio-Estadistico. Monografias Sociologicas* 14. Bogota: Universidad Nacional de Colombia, 1962b.

Deutschmann, P. J. and W. A. Danielson. "Diffusion of Knowledge of the Major News Story," *Journalism Quarterly,* 37 (Summer 1960), 345-55.

Fliegel, F. C. and J. E. Kivlin. "Attributes of Innovations as Factors in Diffusion," *American Journal of Sociology,* 72 (November 1966), 235-48.

Freedman, R. and J. Y. Takeshita. *Family Planning in Taiwan: An Experiment in Social Change.* Princeton: Princeton University Press, 1969.

Gordon, G., A. E. MacEachron, and G. L. Fisher. "A Contingency Model for the Design of Problem-Solving Research Problems: A Perspective on Diffusion Research," *Milbank Memorial Fund Quarterly/Health and Society,* 52 (Spring 1974) 185-220.

Granovetter, M. "The Strength of Weak Ties," *American Journal of Sociology,* 78 (May 1973), 1360-80.

Hauser, P. M. " 'Family Planning and Population Programs': A Book Review Article," *Demography,* 4 (no. 1, 1967), 397-414.

Homans, G. C. *Social Behavior: Its Elementary Forms.* New York: Harcourt, Brace and World, 1961.

Katz, E. "Communication Research and the Image of Society: Convergence of Two Traditions," *American Journal of Sociology,* 65 (March 1960), 435-40.

Kotler, P., and G. Zaltman. "Social Marketing: An Approach to Planned Social Change," *Journal of Marketing,* 35 (July 1971), 3-12.

Kuhn, T. K. *The Structure of Scientific Revolutions.* Chicago: University of Chicago Press, 1962.

Laumann, E. O. *Bonds of Pluralism: The Form and Substance of Urban Social Networks.* New York: Wiley, 1973.

Lazarsfeld, P. F., B. Berelson, and H. Gaudet. *The People's Choice.* New York: Duell, Sloan, and Pearce, 1944.

Liu, W. T. and R. W. Duff. "The Strength in Weak Ties," *Public Opinion Quarterly,* 36 (Fall 1972), 361-66.

Rahim, S. A. *Diffusion and Adoption of Agricultural Practices: A Study of Pattern of Communication, Diffusion and Adoption of Improved Agricultural Practice in a Village in East Pakistan.* Technical publication no. 7. Comilla, Pakistan: (Bangladesh) Academy for Village Development, 1961.

Robertson, T. S. *Innovative Behavior and Communication.* New York: Holt, Rinehart & Winston, 1971.

Rogers, E. M. "Mass Communication and the Diffusion of Innovations: Conceptual Convergence of Two Research Traditions." Paper presented at the Association for Education in Journalism, Boulder, Colorado, 1967.

———. *Modernization among Peasants: The Impact of Communication.* New York: Holt, Rinehart & Winston, 1969.

———. *Communication of Innovations: A Cross-Cultural Approach.* (2nd ed.) New York: Free Press, 1971.

———. *Communication Strategies for Family Planning.* New York: Free Press, 1973.

15

Mason Haire

Projective Techniques in Marketing Research

It is a well accepted maxim in merchandizing that, in many areas, we are selling the sizzle rather than the steak. Our market research techniques, however, in many of these same areas, are directed toward the steak. The sizzle is the subjective reaction of the consumer; the steak the objective characteristics of the product. The consumer's behavior will be based on the former rather than the latter set of characteristics. How can we come to know them better?

When we approach a consumer directly with questions about his reaction to a product we often get false and misleading answers to our questions. Very often this is because the question which we heard ourselves ask was not the one (or not the only one) that the respondent heard. For example: a brewery made two kinds of beer. To guide their merchandizing techniques they wanted to know what kind of people drank each kind, and particularly, what differences there were between the two groups of consumers. A survey was conducted which led up to the questions "Do you drink – – beer?" (If *yes*) "Do you drink the *Light* or *Regular?*" (These were the two trade names under which the company marketed.) (After identifying the consumers of each product it was possible to find out about the characteristics of each group so that appropriate appeals could be used, media chosen, etc.

An interesting anomaly appeared in the survey data, however. The interviewing showed (on a reliable sample) that consumers drank *Light* over *Regular* in a ratio of 3 to 1. The company had been producing and selling Regular over Light for some time in a ratio of 9 to 1. Clearly, the attempt to identify characteristics of the two kinds was a failure. What made them miss so far?

Reprinted from the *Journal of Marketing*, published by the American Marketing Association (April, 1950), pp. 649–656.

Mason Haire is a professor of organizational psychology and management at the Massachusetts Institute of Technology, in the Alfred P. Sloan School of Management. A much-published writer on psychology in management and social science research applications in business, his M.A. and Ph.D. in psychology are from Harvard University. Among his many books is Psychology in Management.

When we say "Do you drink *Light* or *Regular?*" we are at once asking which brand is used, but also, to some extent, saying "Do you drink the regular run-of-the-mill product or do you drink the one that is more refined and shows more discrimination and taste?" The preponderance of "Light" undoubtedly flows from this kind of distortion.

When we ask questions of this sort about the product we are very often asking also about the respondent. Not only do we say "What is – – product like?" but, indirectly "What are *you* like?" Our responses are often made up of both elements inextricably interwoven. The answers to the second question will carry clichés and stereotypes, blocks, inhibitions, and distortions, whenever we approach an area that challenges the person's idea of himself.

There are many things that we need to know about a consumer's reaction to a product that he can not tell us because they are to some extent socially unacceptable. For instance, the snob appeal of a product vitally influences its sale, but it is a thing that the consumer will not like to discuss explicitly. In other cases the consumer is influenced by motives of which he is, perhaps, vaguely aware, but which he finds difficult to put into words. The interviewer-respondent relationship puts a good deal of pressure on him to reply and to make sense in his reply. Consequently, he gives us stereotypical responses that use clichés which are commonly acceptable but do not necessarily represent the true motives. Many of our motives do not, in fact, "make sense," and are not logical. The question-answer relation demands sense above all. If the response does not represent the true state of affairs the interviewer will never know it. He will go away. If it does not make sense it may represent the truth, but the respondent will feel like a fool and the interviewer will not go away. Much better produce a cliché and be rid of him.

THE NATURE OF PROJECTIVE TESTS

Still other kinds of motives exist of which the respondent may not be explicitly conscious himself. The product may be seen by him as related to things or people or values in his life, or as having a certain role in the scheme of things, and yet he may be quite unable, in response to a direct question, to describe these aspects of the object. Nevertheless, these characteristics may be of great importance as motives. How can we get at them?

Clinical psychologists have long been faced with a parallel set of problems. It is quite usual for a patient to be unable or unwilling to tell the therapist directly what kinds of things are stirring in his motivational pattern. Information about these drives is of vital importance to the process of cure, so a good deal of research has been directed towards the development of techniques to identify and define them. The development of projective techniques as diagnostic tools has provided one of the most useful means to uncover such motivations, and the market-researcher can well afford to borrow their essentials from the therapist.

Basically, a projective test involves presenting the subject with an ambiguous stimulus – one that does not quite make sense in itself – and asking him to make sense of it. The theory is that in order to make it make sense he will have to add to it – to fill out the picture – and in so doing he projects part of himself into it. Since we know what was in the original stimulus we can quite easily identify the parts that were added, and, in this way, painlessly obtain information about the person.

Examples of these tests come readily to hand. Nearly everyone is familiar with the Rorschach Test, in which a subject is shown a series of ink-blots and asked to tell what they look like. Here the stimulus is incomplete in itself, and the interpretation supplied by the patient provides useful information. This test yields fairly general answers about the personality, however, and often we would like to narrow down the area in which the patient is supplying information.

The Thematic Apperception Test offers a good example of this function. Let us suppose that with a particular patient we have reason to suppose that his relation to figures of authority is crucial to his therapeutic problem. We can give him a series of pictures where people are shown, but where the relationship of authority or the characteristics of the authoritarian figure are not complete. He is asked to tell a story about each picture. If in each story the subordinate finally kills the figure of authority we have certain kinds of knowledge; if, on the other hand, he always builds the story so the subordinate figure achieves a secure and comfortable dependence, we have quite different information. It is often quite impossible to get the subject to tell us these things directly. Either he cannot or will not do so. Indirectly, however, he will tell us how he sees authority. Can we get him, similarly, to tell us how a product looks to him in his private view of the world?

APPLICATION OF PROJECTIVE TEST IN MARKET RESEARCH

Let us look at an example of this kind of thing in market research. For the purposes of experiment a conventional survey was made of attitudes toward Nescafé, an instant coffee. The questionnaire included the questions "Do you use instant coffee?" (If *No*) "What do you dislike about it?" The bulk of the unfavorable responses fell into the general area "I don't like the flavor." This is such an easy answer to a complex question that one may suspect it is a stereotype, which at once gives a sensible response to get rid of the interviewer and conceals other motives. How can we get behind this facade?

In this case an indirect approach was used. Two shopping lists were prepared. They were identical in all respects, except that one list specified Nescafé and one Maxwell House Coffee. They were administered to alternate subjects, with no subject knowing of the existence of the other list. The instructions were "Read the shopping list below. Try to project yourself into the situation as far as possible until you can more or less characterize the woman who bought the groceries. Then write a brief description of her personality and character. Wherever possible indicate what factors influenced your judgment."

Shopping list 1

Pound and a half of hamburger
2 loaves Wonder bread
bunch of carrots
1 can Rumford's Baking Powder
Nescafé instant coffee
2 cans Del Monte peaches
5 lbs. potatoes

Shopping list 2

Pound and a half of hamburger
2 loaves Wonder Bread
bunch of carrots
1 can Rumford's Baking Powder
1 lb. Maxwell House Coffee (Drip Ground)
2 cans Del Monte peaches
5 lbs. potatoes

Fifty people responded to each of the two shopping lists given above. The responses to these shopping lists provided some very interesting material. The following main characteristics of their descriptions can be given:

1. 48 per cent of the people described the woman who bought Nescafé as lazy; 4 percent described the woman who bought Maxwell House as lazy.
2. 48 percent of the people described the

woman who bought Nescafé as failing to plan household purchases and schedules well; 12 per cent described the woman who bought Maxwell House this way.

3. 4 percent described the Nescafé woman as thrifty; 16 per cent described the Maxwell House woman as thrifty. 12 per cent described the Nescafé woman as spendthrift; 0 per cent described the Maxwell House woman this way.
4. 16 per cent described the Nescafé woman as not a good wife; 0 per cent described the Maxwell House woman this way. 4 percent described the Nescafé woman as a good wife; 16 percent described the Maxwell House woman as a good wife.

A clear picture begins to form here. Instant coffee represents a departure from "home-made" coffee, and the traditions with respect to caring for one's family. Coffee-making is taken seriously, with vigorous proponents for laborious drip and filter-paper methods, firm believers in coffee boiled in a battered sauce pan, and the like. Coffee drinking is a form of intimacy and relaxation that gives it a special character.

On the one hand, coffee making is an art. It is quite common to hear a woman say, "I can't seem to make good coffee," in the same way that one might say, "I can't learn to play the violin." It is acceptable to confess this inadequacy, for making coffee well is a mysterious touch that belongs, in a shadowy tradition, to the plump, aproned figure who is a little lost outside her kitchen but who has a sure sense in it and among its tools.

On the other hand, coffee has a peculiar role in relation to the household and the home-and-family character. We may well have a picture, in the shadowy past, of a big black range that is always hot with baking and cooking, and has a big enamelled pot of coffee warming at the back. When a neighbor drops in during the morning, a cup of coffee is a medium of hospitality that does somewhat the same thing as cocktails in the late afternoon, but does it in a broad sphere.

These are real and important aspects of coffee. They are not physical characteristics of the product, but they are real values in the consumer's life, and they influence his purchasing. We need to know and assess them. The "labor-saving" aspect of instant coffee, far from being an asset, may be a liability in that it violates these traditions. How often have we heard a wife respond to "This cake is delicious!" with a pretty blush and "Thank you – I made it with such and such a prepared cake mix." This response is so invariable as to seem almost compulsive. It is almost unthinkable to anticipate a reply "Thank you, I made it with Pillsbury's flour, Fleischman's yeast, and Borden's milk." Here the specifications are unnecessary. All that is relevant is the implied "I made it" – the art and the credit are carried directly by the verb that covers the process of mixing and processing the ingredients. In ready-mixed foods there seems to be a compulsive drive to refuse credit for the product, because the accomplishment is not the housewife's but the company's.

In this experiment, as a penalty for using "synthetics" the woman who buys Nescafé pays the price of being seen as lazy, spendthrift, a poor wife, and as failing to plan well for her family. The people who rejected instant coffee in the original direct question blamed its flavor. We may well wonder if their dislike of instant coffee was not to a large extent occasioned by a fear of being seen by one's self and others in the role they projected onto the Nescafé woman in the description. When asked directly, however, it is difficult to respond with this. One can not say, "I don't use Nescafé because people will think I am lazy and not a good wife." Yet we know from these data that the feeling regarding laziness and shiftlessness was there. Later studies (reported below) showed that it determined buying habits, and that something could be done about it.

ANALYSIS OF RESPONSES

Some examples of the type of response received will show the kind of material obtained and how it may be analyzed. Three examples of each group are given below.

Descriptions of a Woman Who Bought, among Other Things, Maxwell House Coffee

> "I'd say she was a practical, frugal woman. She bought too many potatoes. She must like to cook and bake as she included baking powder. She must not care much about her figure as she does not discriminate about the food she buys."
>
> "The woman is quite influenced by advertising as signified by the specific name brands on her shopping list. She probably is quite set in her ways and accepts no substitutes."
>
> "I have been able to observe several hundred women shoppers who have made very similar purchases to that listed above, and the only clue that I can detect that may have some bearing on her personality is the Del Monte peaches. This item when purchased singly along with the other more staple foods indicates that she may be anxious to please either herself or members of her family with a 'treat.' She is probably a thrifty, sensible housewife."

Descriptions of a Woman Who Bought, among Other Things, Nescafé Instant Coffee

> "This woman appears to be either single or living alone. I would guess that she had an office job. Apparently, she likes to sleep late in the morning, basing my assumption on what she bought such as Instant Coffee which can be made in a hurry. She probably also has can [sic] peaches for breakfast, cans being easy to open. Assuming that she is just average, as opposed to those dazzling natural beauties who do not need much time to make up, she must appear rather sloppy, taking little time to make up in the morning. She is also used to eating supper out, too. Perhaps alone rather than with an escort. An old maid probably."
>
> "She seems to be lazy, because of her purchases of canned peaches and instant coffee. She doesn't seem to think, because she bought two loaves of bread, and then baking powder, unless she's thinking of making cake. She probably just got married."
>
> "I think the woman is the type who never thinks ahead very far—the type who always sends Junior to the store to buy one item at a time. Also she is fundamentally lazy. All the items, with the possible exception of the Rumford's, are easily prepared items. The girl may be an office girl who is just living from one day to the next in a sort of haphazard sort of life."

As we read these complete responses we begin to get a feeling for the picture that is created by Nescafé. It is particularly interesting to notice that the Nescafé woman is protected, to some extent, from the opprobrium of being lazy and haphazard by being seen as a single "office girl"—a role that relieves one from guilt for not being interested in the home and food preparation.

The references to peaches are significant. In one case (Maxwell House) they are singled out as a sign that the woman is thoughtfully preparing a "treat" for her family. On the other hand, when the Nescafé woman buys them it is evidence that she is lazy, since their "canned" character is seen as central.

In terms of the sort of results presented above, it may be useful to demonstrate the way these stories are coded. The following items are extracted from the six stories quoted:

Maxwell House

1. practical, frugal, likes to cook
2. influenced by advertising, set in her ways
3. interested in family, thrifty, sensible

Nescafé

1. single, office girl, sloppy, old maid
2. lazy, does not plan, newlywed
3. lazy, does not plan, office girl

Items such as these are culled from each of the stories. Little by little categories are shaped by the content of the stories themselves. In this way the respondent furnishes the dimensions of analysis as well as the scale values on these dimensions.

Second Test

It is possible to wonder whether it is true that the opprobrium that is heaped on the Nescafé woman comes from her use of a device that represents a short-cut and labor-saver in an area where she is expected to embrace pains-taking time-consuming work in a ritualistic way. To test this a variation was introduced into the shopping lists. In a second experiment one hundred and fifty housewives were tested with the form given above, but a sample was added to this group which responded to a slightly different form. It we assume that the rejection in the first experiment came from the presence of a feeling about synthetic shortcuts we might assume also that the addition of one more shortcut to both lists would bring the Maxwell House woman more into line with the Nescafé woman, since the former would now have the same guilt that the Nescafé woman originally had, while the Nescafé woman, already convicted of evading her duties, would be little further injured.

In order to accomplish this a second prepared food was added to both lists. Immediately after the coffee in both lists the fictitious item, "Blueberry Fill Pie Mix" was added. The results are shown in the accompanying table.

It will be seen immediately, in the first two columns, that the group to whom the original form of the list were given showed the same kind of difference as reported above in their estimates of the two women. The group with an additional prepared food, however, brought the Maxwell Coffee woman down until she is virtually undistinguishable from the Nescafé. There seems to be little doubt but that the prepared-food-character, and the stigma of avoiding house-wifely duties is responsible for the projected personality characteristics.

Relation to Purchasing

It is still relevant to ask whether the existence of these feelings in a potential consumer is related to purchasing. It is hypothesized that these personality descriptions provide an opportunity for the consumer to project hopes and fears and anxieties that are relevant to the way the product is seen, and that they represent important parts of her motivation in buying or not buying. To test this hypothesis, a small sample of fifty housewives, comparable in every way to the group just referred to, was given the original form of the shopping list (Nescafé only). In addition to obtaining the personality description, the interviewer, on a pretext, obtained permission to look at her pantry

TABLE 15-1 *Personality Characteristics Ascribed to Users of Prepared Foods*

If They Use	**No Prepared Food (Maxwell House alone)**		**Nescafé (alone)**		**Maxwell House (plus Pie Mix)**		**Nescafé (plus Pie Mix)**	
They are seen as:	*Number*	*Per Cent*	*Number*	*Per Cent*	*Number*	*Per Cent*	*Number*	*Per Cent*
Not economical	12	17	24	32	6	30	7	35
Lazy	8	11	46	62	5	25	8	40
Poor personality and appearance	28	39	39	53	7	35	8	40
N =	72		74		20		20	

shelves and determine personally whether or not she had instant coffee of any brand. The results of this investigation are shown in the accompanying table.

The trend of these data shows conclusively that if a respondent sees the woman who buys Nescafé as having undesirable traits, she is not likely to buy instant coffee herself. The projected unacceptable characteristics go with failure to buy, and it does not seem unwarranted to assume that the association is causal.

Furthermore, these projected traits are, to some extent, additive. For instance, if a respondent describes the woman as having one bad trait only, she is about twice as likely not to have instant coffee. However, if she sees her as having two bad traits, and no good ones (e.g., lazy, cannot cook), she is about three times as likely not to have instant coffee as she is to have it. On the other hand, if she sees her as having two good traits (e.g., economical, cares for family), she is about six times as likely to have it as not.

It was pointed out earlier that some women felt it necessary to "excuse" the woman who bought Nescafé by suggesting that she lived alone and hence could not be expected to be interested in cooking, or that she had a job and did not have time to shop better. Women who had instant coffee in the house found excuses almost twice as often as those who did not use instant coffee (12 out of 32, or 42 per cent, against 4 out of 18, or 22 per cent). These "excuses" are vitally important for merchandizing. The need for an excuse shows there is a barrier to buying in the consumer's mind. The presence of excuses shows that there is a way around the barrier. The content of the excuses themselves provides valuable clues for directing appeals toward reducing buying resistance.

CONCLUSIONS

There seems to be no question that in the experimental situation described here:

TABLE 15-2

The woman who buys Nescafé is seen as:	**By Women Who Had Instant Coffee in the House (N = 32)**		**By Women Who Did Not Have Instant Coffee in the House (N = 18)**	
	Number	*Per Cent*	*Number*	*Per Cent*
Economical**	22	70	5	28
Not economical	0	0	2	11
Cannot cook or does not like to**	5	16	10	55
Plans balanced meals*	9	29	2	11
Good housewife, plans well, cares about family**	9	29	0	0
Poor housewife, does not plan well, does not care about family*	5	16	7	39
Lazy*	6	19	7	39

* A single asterisk indicates that differences this great would be observed only 5 times out of 100 in repeated samplings of a population whose true difference is zero.

** A double asterisk indicates that the chances are 1 in 100. We are justified in rejecting the hypothesis that there is no difference between the groups.

1. Motives exist which are below the level of verbalization because they are socially unacceptable, difficult to verbalize cogently, or unrecognized.
2. These motives are intimately related to the decision to purchase or not to purchase, and
3. It is possible to identify and assess such motives by approaching them indirectly.

Two important general points come out of the work reported. The first is in the statement of the problem. It is necessary for us to see a product in terms of a set of characteristics and attributes which are part of the consumer's "private world," and as such may have no simple relationship to characteristics of the object in the "real" world. Each of us lives in a world which is composed of more than physical things and people. It is made up of goals, paths to goals, barriers, threats, and the like, and an individual's behavior is oriented with respect to these characteristics as much as to the "objective" ones. In the area of merchandizing, a product's character of being seen as a path to a goal is usually very much more important as a determinant of purchasing than its physical dimensions. We have taken advantage of these qualities in advertising and merchandizing for a long time by an intuitive sort of "playing-by-ear" on the subjective aspects of products. It is time for a systematic attack on the problem of the phenomenological description of objects. What kinds of dimensions are relevant to this world of goals and paths and barriers? What kind of terms will fit the phenomenological characteristics of an object in the same sense that the centimetre-gram-second system fits its physical dimensions? We need to know the answers to such questions, and the psychological definitions of valued objects.

The second general point is the methodological one that it is possible, by using appropriate techniques, to find out from the respondent what the phenomenological characteristics of various objects may be. By and large, a direct approach to this problem in terms of straightforward questions will not yield satisfactory answers. It is possible, however, by the use of indirect techniques, to get the consumer to provide, quite unselfconsciously, a description of the value-character of objects in his environment.

16

William D. Wells

Psychographics: A Critical Review

Among the standard fixtures in marketing research, the demographic profile is probably the most familiar. Age, income, education, and other indications of position in life space have so much influence on so many kinds of consumer behavior that users of a product or a brand, viewers of a TV program, or readers of a magazine are virtually certain to differ from the rest of the population on one or more of the common demographic dimensions. Marketing researchers collect demographics as a matter of routine, and marketers feel comfortable using them.

But demographic profiles, essential though they may be, have not been deemed sufficient. Especially since the end of World War II researchers have engaged in a continuous search for new, more comprehensive, and more exciting descriptions. It is as though demographics provided only a nodding acquaintance, and marketers wanted to know their customers much better.

Until recently this search has followed two somewhat different directions. Starting with the classic study by Koponen [74], investigators have repeatedly tried to correlate consumer behavior with scores obtained from standardized personality inventories. And, starting with Dichter's innovative studies of consumers' motivations [31], students of the consumer's mind have tried to apply the concepts and methods of clinical psychology to virtually every aspect of marketing.

From Koponen's study on, the work with personality inventories has been judged "equivocal" [65]. The correlations have almost invariably been low, and the relationships uncovered have often been so abstract that they could not be used with confidence in making real-world marketing decisions.

Motivation research has fared much better. In spite of severe criticisms on both ethical and methodological grounds, motivation research enjoyed a tremendous vogue; in its current

William D. Wells, "Psychographics: A Critical Review," Vol. 12 (May 1975), pp. 196–213. Reprinted from *Journal of Marketing Research*. Published by the American Marketing Association. Reprinted by permission of the publisher.

William Wells is Senior Vice President for Needham Harper and Steers advertising agency. He previously taught at the University of Chicago and has pioneered studies in the area of psychographics. He received his Ph.D. in psychology from Stanford University.

form – the small scale "qualitative study" – it still has many busy practitioners. It is somewhat ironic that the more rigorous of these two approaches has proved relatively sterile, while the sloppier methodology continues to produce results that intelligent people judge to be of great value.

Sometime during the 1960s a blend of these two traditions began to take shape. Variously called "life style" [102, 104], "psychographic" [29, 89, 90, 91, 95, 109], or "activity and attitude" [54, 55] research, this blend combines the objectivity of the personality inventory with the rich, consumer-oriented, descriptive detail of the qualitative motivation research investigation. This new blend has attracted considerable attention, both among "academics" and among "real-world" marketers. It has also attracted its share of criticism, and its share of skeptical questions as to its true usefulness and value [26, 33, 45, 86, 110, 120, 124, 142].

This review attempts to take stock of the present status and future prospects of psychographic research, including consumer-oriented research with standardized personality inventories. It begins with a definition of the field. It continues with examples of five somewhat different approaches to psychographic analysis. And it concludes with a critical discussion of the reliability, validity, and usefulness of psychographic measurements.

DEFINITIONS

Although the need for a common definition of psychographics is obvious, no single definition has met with general approval. Twenty-four articles on psychographics contain no less than 32 definitions, all somewhat different [29, 30, 33, 45, 53, 68, 79, 83, 89, 92, 95, 100, 105, 108, 109, 110, 111, 119, 120, 134, 140, 142, 143, 146], and each new publication seems to produce still another version of what psychographic research is or is not. Within this diversity, however, certain common elements are clearly visible.

Something More Than Demographics

All psychographic researchers have attempted to move beyond demographics into areas that are relatively untried and unfamiliar. Depending upon the investigator's objectives and to some extent upon his taste, the added dimensions have run from one or two [11, 23, 44, 67, 80] to several hundred [1, 102, 125, 136, 145] and have embraced a wide range of content, including activities, interests, opinions, needs, values, attitudes, and personality traits. In some cases the variables have been "homemade," and in others they have been borrowed from standardized attitude scales or personality inventories. In all cases, however, the common theme has been that demographic attributes alone are not enough.

Quantitative, Not Qualitative

Second, most psychographic researchers have employed precoded, objective questionnaires that can be self-administered or administered by ordinary survey interviewers. Precoding makes the data amenable to complex multivariate statistical analysis; ease of administration encourages – or at least permits – use of large, representative samples. Both practices distinguish psychographic studies from studies in the qualitative motivation research tradition.

Operationally, then, psychographic research can be defined as quantitative research intended to place consumers on psychological – as distinguished from demographic – dimensions. Because it goes beyond the standard and the accepted, it offers the possibility of new insights and unusual conclusions. Because it is quantitative rather than discursive, it opens the way to large, representative samples of respondents, and to multivariate statistical analysis of findings.

FIVE EXAMPLES

A Psychographic Profile Based on General "Life-Style" Dimensions

The need for good descriptions of consumers is well expressed in the following comment by an advertising copy writer:

> . . . Imagine that I've got to write an ad on a Sunday afternoon, and I want to feel sure I'm on the right track. I want to double check myself that people will understand it/react to it/remember it, plus a few subtleties like will they like it, dislike it, etc.
>
> So, I trudge all the way around the block, talking to the neighbors, and forty houses later I have a slight idea of what will happen to my ad when it reaches the world. That's what I understand Research does, only a lot more intelligently and a lot more thoroughly and in a lot more neighborhoods.
>
> A writer writes out of his personal collection of life experiences and his knowledge of people, and he imagines and projects them and he tries to translate them into his viewer's or his reader's terms. But he's feeding off himself. He's just one person. He can't afford to trust just his own experience. Research extends the writer. Information is his life blood. He can't write out of thin air. Anything that adds to his storehouse of information is necessary and vital [75].

Similar needs are felt by all others who must create products, services, or messages for customers they cannot meet in person. Just as the writer knows that he cannot feed only off himself, so also the product designer and the marketing manager know that they run grave risks when they rely solely on their own assumptions. Almost all of marketing is communication; marketers are most effective when they know their audiences.

As an example of the descriptive value of psychographic dimensions, consider the somewhat esoteric problem of communicating with consumers who are heavy users of shotgun ammunition. Persons of this sort would be of special interest to anyone who manufactures, markets, or advertises shotguns, ammunition, or associated hunting paraphernalia; to operators of hunting lodges and private hunting areas; to publishers of hunting magazines; and to government officials who promote or regulate this form of recreation.

A demographic profile of the heavy user of shotgun ammunition appears in Table 16-1. The man who spends at least $11 per year on shotgun shells differs from the nonbuyer in that he tends to be younger, lower in income and education, and more concentrated in blue collar occupations. He is also more apt to be living in rural areas, especially in the South.

TABLE 16-1 *Demographic Profile of the Heavy User of Shotgun Ammunition*

	Percent Who Spend $11+ Per Year on Shotgun Ammunition (141)	Percent Who Don't Buy (395)
Age		
Under 25	9	5
25-34	33	15
35-44	27	22
45-54	18	22
55+	13	36
Occupation		
Professional	6	15
Managerial	23	23
Clerical-Sales	9	17
Craftsman	50	35
Income		
Under $6,000	26	19
$6,000-$10,000	39	36
$10,000-$15,000	24	27
$15,000+	11	18
Population Density		
Rural	34	12
2,500-50,000	11	11
50,000-500,000	16	15
500,000-2 million	21	27
2 million +	13	19
Geographic Division		
New England–Mid-Atlantic	21	33
Central (N, W)	22	30
South Atlantic	23	12
E. South Central	10	3
W. South Central	10	5
Mountain	6	3
Pacific	9	15

Source: [107].

Now reflect upon the implication of this pattern. Hunting is a risky sport. Is the hunter a risk taker? Is he likely to follow rules on his own, or does he require external control? Hunting is a violent sport. Is the hunter attracted by violence in general? What other products would make good tie-in sales with hunting equipment? Is the hunter also a fisherman or a camper? Is he especially interested in food? Is he a regular newspaper reader? Is he a regular patron of discount stores? From the demographic profile alone, a marketer with a thorough knowledge of young, blue-collar, nonurban life styles might be able to guess the answers to at least some of these questions, but few would guess them all.

The data in Table 16-2 show how psychographic information can put flesh on demographic bones. These data came from a general life-style study that happened to contain a question about shotgun ammunition along with questions about approximately 100 other products and services. The questionnaire also contained questions about a wide range of activities, interests, and opinions; about reading of major magazines; and viewing of a large number of television programs. The study was not designed around shotgun users, or around the users of any other single product.

In spite of this lack of focus, the data in Table 16-2 show some interesting patterns. First, it is obvious that hunting is not an isolated phenomenon but rather is associated with other rugged outdoor endeavors. Shotgun shell buyers not only like to hunt, they also like to fish and to go camping. They even like to work outdoors. These relationships are interesting and useful because they suggest activities and

TABLE 16-2 *Psychographic Profile of the Heavy User of Shotgun Ammunition*

Base	Percent Who Spend $11+ Per Year on Shotgun Ammunition (141)	Percent Who Don't Buy (395)
I like hunting	88	7
I like fishing	68	26
I like to go camping	57	21
I love the out-of-doors	90	65
A cabin by a quiet lake is a great place to spend the summer	49	34
I like to work outdoors	67	40
I am good at fixing mechanical things	47	27
I often do a lot of repair work on my own car	36	12
I like war stories	50	32
I would do better than average in a fist fight	38	16
I would like to be a professional football player	28	18
I would like to be a policeman	22	8
There is too much violence on television	35	45
There should be a gun in every home	56	10
I like danger	19	8
I would like to own my own airplane	35	13
I like to play poker	50	26
I smoke too much	39	24
I love to eat	49	34
I spend money on myself that I should spend on the family	44	26
If given a chance, most men would cheat on their wives	33	14
I read the newspaper every day	51	72

Source: [107].

settings, other than hunting scenes, that might be appropriate for shotgun ammunition advertising. They suggest products that might be especially appropriate for joint promotions or other cooperative marketing ventures, such as displaying shotgun ammunition near camping or fishing equipment in retail outlets. Table 16-2 also shows that ammunition buyers are apt to be do-it-yourselfers, which suggests that hunters are apt to be buyers of hardware and tools.

Items in the third group in Table 16-2 suggest some hypotheses about the psychological makeup of the shotgun ammunition buyer. Compared with the nonbuyer he is definitely more attracted by violence, suggesting that detective, war, and violent Western TV programs ought to draw audiences with disproportionate numbers of shotgun users, and that action and adventure magazines ought to be considered when placing advertising associated with hunting. Relationships between product use and media exposure are always best documented by direct cross-tabulation, but when these data are not available (and they often are not) relationships suggested by life-style patterns can provide helpful direction.

The relatively high levels of agreement with the fourth section of Table 16-2 suggest that the hunter is generally less risk-averse than is his nonhunting counterpart. To policy makers charged with keeping hunters from shooting themselves and each other, this willingness to accept risk would suggest that sober warnings about the dangers of firearms may well be ineffective. Lest this conclusion seem hopelessly naive, let it be noted that sober warnings about the dangers of firearms are exactly what some policy makers have attempted.

The relatively high levels of agreement with the fifth section suggest a combination of self-indulgence and lack of internal control that seems congruent with the attitude toward risk just noted. If the hunter is in fact self-indulgent and relatively conscienceless, it would seem unwise to rely on appeals to fair play and conservation to regulate his activities. Again, such appeals have been tried with less success than expected.

The level of agreement with "I love to eat" and the hunter's professed willingness to spend money on himself suggest markets for premium foods designed to be taken along on hunting expeditions. These two findings also suggest the suitability of game-preparation recipes for hunting magazines, and they indicate that quantity and quality of food should get particular attention from proprietors of hunting lodges. Hunters don't mind roughing it, but they want it to be a well-fed roughness.

Finally, the relatively low level of agreement with "I read the newspaper every day" should serve as a warning to shotgun ammunition advertisers. This is not to assert that media decisions, positive or negative, should ever be based on responses to a single survey item. Rather, it suggests that any shotgun ammunition advertiser who is spending his budget in newspapers should think twice about alternatives.

This brief example shows how a psychographic profile obtained almost incidentally in the context of a large, general life-style survey can provide suggestions and hypotheses that bear on a wide range of marketing and policy decisions. A demographic profile alone would perhaps have provided some of these inferences, but surely not all of them.

This example also shows how a psychographic profile can help the marketer avoid some traps a demographic profile would have set for him. Knowing that heavy users of shotgun ammunition tend to be younger, more in blue collar occupations, and less urban than nonusers might suggest that they would be heavier users of beer, more interested in television, more interested in spectator sports, more prone to use credit, and more apt to shop at discount stores. Yet buyers of shotgun ammunition do not differ significantly from nonbuyers on any of these dimensions.

Other psychographic life-style profiles that have appeared in the literature include carryout foods [130]; eye makeup, shortening, oranges, and lemons [133, 136]; beer [103, 127]; mouthwash [127]; heavy duty hand soap [103]; bank charge cards [102]; department stores [83]; and air travel [11]. They also include profiles of the readers of magazines [117, 128] and of viewers of various television programs [104, 128]. In all these cases the psychographic data have provided rich, descriptive detail that could not have been inferred from demographics. See also [1, 47, 50, 58, 77, 118, 132, 136, 138].

A Product-Specific Psychographic Profile

In the previous example, the psychographic profile was drawn from a large set of general life-style items. Because the item list was large and diverse, some of the items happened to be related to consumption of shotgun ammunition. When a psychographic study is devoted to a single product category, it is not necessary to depend on item diversity to get useful relationships. Rather, the investigator can focus upon a limited set of relevant, product-related dimensions.

An excellent example of this use of psychographics is provided in a report by Young [144] on the "positioning" of the Ford Pinto. According to Young, the introductory Pinto advertising portrayed the car as "carefree, small (and) romantic." The strategy was "to sell to small car prospects; to compete against imported small cars; to say that the car was carefree, trouble free, beautifully styled, and economical" [144, p. 15].

As the introduction of the Pinto proceeded, psychographic research disclosed that potential Pinto buyers had a less romantic orientation toward cars and driving. They endorsed statements like "I wish I could depend on my car more," "I am more practical in car selection," "A car offers me a chance to tinker with machinery," "I like to feel how powerful my car is" and "The only function for a car is transportation." They rejected statements like "The kind of car you have is important as to how people see you" and "Taking care of a car is too much trouble."

As a result of this research, the Pinto was repositioned (in advertising, by its new agency) as "The epitomy of function, exemplifying basic economical transportation, trading on Ford's heritage of the Model A." Consequently, "Today Pinto is the largest selling subcompact, outselling Volkswagen by a sizeable margin" [144, p. 15].

Now it is admittedly farfetched to assume that all (or maybe even most) of Pinto's success was due to this change in position. But it does seem reasonable to believe that emphasis on economics and practicality appealed to the salient needs of potential subcompact buyers, and that the revised message communicated ideas that potential customers would find most persuasive.

Personality Traits as Descriptors

A report on "Ecologically Concerned Consumers: Who Are They?" [72] provides a third example of psychographic analysis. In this report the dependent variable was an "index of ecological concern" that included both attitudes toward ecological issues and conservationist behavior. The independent variables were 7 demographic characteristics, 12 personality traits taken from standardized personality inventories, and a variable called "perceived consumer effectiveness." This attribute was measured by degree of disagreement with "It is futile for the individual consumer to try to do anything about pollution."

The 20 independent variables were first screened by analysis of variance to determine which of them discriminated between respondents who were high and respondents who were low in ecological concern. The 10 variables that survived the screening were then input to Multiple Classification Analysis to "predict" the degree of ecological concern expressed by each respondent. To avoid confusion it should be noted that in this study, as in most psychographic studies, the term "predict" cannot be taken literally. Since the data were all collected at the same point in time, "prediction" really means correlation.

The MCA coefficients for the "factors that were found to be most significant" in "predicting" ecological concern are shown in Table 16-3. The coefficients show how much the members of each category differ in ecological concern from the total sample. Thus, respondents who were low in perceived consumer effectiveness were 2.49 points below average in ecological concern, respondents who were medium were 4.04 points below average, and so on.

TABLE 16-3 *MCA Profile of the Ecologically Concerned Consumer*

Factor	Level	Regression Coefficient
Perceived consumer effectiveness	Very low	–
	Low	–2.49
	Medium	–4.04
	High	–1.04
	Very high	2.54
Tolerance	Very low	.15
	Low	–.79
	Medium	–.39
	High	–.04
	Very High	1.00
Understanding	Very low	–.92
	Low	–.81
	Medium	.22
	High	.27
	Very high	1.25
Harm avoidance	Very low	–.59
	Low	.13
	Medium	.27
	High	.73
	Very high	–1.22
Annual family income	Under $5,000	–.39
	$5,000 to $6,999	–.24
	$7,000 to $9,999	.10
	$10,000 to $14,999	–.15
	$15,000 and over	.74

Mean = 11.31.
R^2 = .28.

This study differs from the ammunition study and the Pinto study in two important ways. First, in the ammunition and Pinto studies the descriptions of the target groups were developed by considering *all* the psychographic items that discriminated between the target group and the remainder of the population. In this study, on the other hand, the answers that respondents gave to the personality scale questions were summed to produce higher level, more abstract scores on "tolerance," "understanding," and "harm avoidance." This procedure had the effect of eliminating much of the rich descriptive detail that might have been provided by the individual questions. We do not know what answers produced high scores or low scores on the personality dimensions.

Second, in the ammunition and Pinto studies the profiles were developed by cross-tabulating *all* of the psychographic items with the dependent variable. In this study, the independent variables were linked to the dependent variable by a type of multiple regression. Like all other forms of multiple regression, MCA suppresses variables that are closely related to variables that are allowed to enter the equation. As a result, variables closely related to each other could not all have entered the description of the ecologically concerned consumer, even though they might have discriminated sharply in a cross-tabulation.

Many other examples of this general approach are to be found in the literature. In one of the earliest psychographic studies, Koponen regressed Edwards Personal Preference Schedule scores on consumption of cigarettes and readership of several magazines [74]. A group of investigators from the Advertising Research Foundation regressed the same set of independent variables against consumption of toilet paper, with predictable and poetically just results [5]. Frank, Massy, and Lodahl did the same for coffee, tea, and beer [41]. Wilson [139] factor analyzed an activity, interest, and opinion inventory and regressed various AIO factors against consumption of a list of products that included soft drinks, lipstick, and stomach remedies. And Darden and Reynolds [27] used scales representing fashion interest, fashion venturesomeness, cognitive style, information seeking, relative popularity and relative self-confidence to "predict" fashion opinion leadership. See also [21, 25, 39, 46, 69, 85, 87, 100, 123].

In all these cases a large set of descriptive items was reduced to a smaller number of more abstract scores, and this reduced set of independent variables was then linked to the dependent variable by means of some form of multiple regression. The descriptions thus provided were therefore more abstract and less redundant than the descriptions that would have been provided by simple cross-tabulation of the uncondensed raw data.

A General Life-Style Segmentation Study

A report of a major study by the Newspaper Advertising Bureau [109] provides an example of still another approach to psychographics. In this study a national sample of approximately 4,000 respondents completed questionnaires containing 300 psychographic questions, several dozen questions about product use, and questions about exposure to various media. The psychographic questions were reduced to a smaller set of scales by R-type factor analysis, and the resulting factor scores were input to Q-type factor analysis to place the respondents into relatively homogeneous groups. Condensed descriptions of the eight male groups are given in Figure 16-1.

This study differs from the first three in that it did not assume that members of any target group are all very similar. Instead of attempting to discover what hunters, Pinto buyers, or ecologically concerned consumers have in common, this study admitted the possibility that users of a product might fall into several quite different segments.

The wisdom of this approach is illustrated in Table 16-4. There it can be seen that the heavy users of several products and several brands, the readers of some magazines and the viewers of some TV programs tend to be concentrated in two or more segments that differ quite significantly from each other. When that is the case, any attempt to discover the characteristics of an undifferentiated target group—e.g., "the heavy beer drinker," "the user of Brand X deodorant," "the *Playboy* reader," or "the TV news viewer"—whether by simple cross-tabulation or by multiple regression—will be sure to underestimate the importance of the attributes upon which the segments differ. In extreme cases, when one segment of the target group is above average on a particular attribute and another segment is below average, merging the two segments into one target group can make the target group appear to be not different from the remainder of the population. (See [54, 55] for a neat example of this phenomena.)

A Product-Specified Segmentation

In the preceding example, the segmentation was based on general—as opposed to product related—psychographic items. When the investigation is devoted to one product, the investigator can focus upon product-related material. An example of the latter approach is given in a report by Pernica [95] of a stomach remedy segmentation. Pernica developed a list of 80 items that included symptom frequency, end benefits provided by different brands, attitudes toward treatment, and beliefs about ailments.

FIGURE 16-1 *Eight Male Psychographic Segments*

Group I. *"The Quiet Family Man"* (8% of total males)

He is a self-sufficient man who wants to be left alone and is basically shy. Tries to be as little involved with community life as possible. His life revolves around the family, simple work and television viewing. Has a marked fantasy life. As a shopper he is practical, less drawn to consumer goods and pleasures than other men.

Low education and low economic status, he tends to be older than average.

Group II. *"The Traditionalist"* (16% of total males)

A man who feels secure, has self-esteem, follows conventional rules. He is proper and respectable, regards himself as altruistic and interested in the welfare of others. As a shopper he is conservative, likes popular brands and well-known manufacturers.

Low education and low or middle socio-economic status; the oldest age group.

Group III. *"The Discontented Man"* (13% of total males)

He is a man who is likely to be dissatisfied with his work. He feels bypassed by life, dreams of better jobs, more money and more security. He tends to be distrustful and socially aloof. As a buyer, he is quite price conscious.

Lowest education and lowest socio-economic group, mostly older than average.

Group IV. *"The Ethical Highbrow"* (14% of total males)

This is a very concerned man, sensitive to people's needs. Basically a puritan, content with family life, friends, and work. Interested in culture, religion and social reform. As a consumer he is interested in quality, which may at times justify greater expenditure.

Well educated, middle or upper socio-economic status, mainly middle aged or older.

Group V. *"The Pleasure Oriented Man"* (9% of total males)

He tends to emphasize his masculinity and rejects whatever appears to be soft or feminine. He views himself a leader among men. Self-centered, dislikes his work or job. Seeks immediate gratification for his needs. He is an impulsive buyer, likely to buy products with a masculine image.

Low education, lower socio-economic status, middle aged or younger.

Group VI. *"The Achiever"* (11% of total males)

This is likely to be a hardworking man, dedicated to success and all that it implies, social prestige, power and money. Is in favor of diversity, is adventurous about leisure time pursuits. Is stylish, likes good food, music, etc. As a consumer he is status conscious, a thoughtful and discriminating buyer.

Good education, high socio-economic status, young.

Group VII. *"The He-Man"* (19% of total males)

He is gregarious, likes action, seeks an exciting and dramatic life. Thinks of himself as capable and dominant. Tends to be more of a bachelor than a family man, even after marriage. Products he buys and brands preferred are likely to have a "self-expressive value," especially a "Man of Action" dimension.

Well educated, mainly middle socio-economic status, the youngest of the male groups.

Group VIII. *"The Sophisticated Man"* (10% of total males)

He is likely to be an intellectual, concerned about social issues, admires men with artistic and intellectual achievements. Socially cosmopolitan, broad interests. Wants to be dominant, and a leader. As a consumer he is attracted to the unique and fashionable.

Best educated and highest economic status of all groups, younger than average.

TABLE 16-4 *Product and Media Use by Psychographic Group*

	Psychographic Group[a] Percentages							
	I	II	III	IV	V	VI	VII	VIII
Drink beer	45	56	57	51	75	59	80	72
Smoke cigarettes	32	40	40	29	54	42	51	38
Air travel outside U.S.	4	4	6	7	5	8	12	19
Air travel, domestic	14	15	14	26	19	32	20	42
Use Brand X deodorant	7	7	6	8	14	10	9	12
Used headache remedy in past four weeks	53	60	66	61	61	64	65	67
Read current issue of:								
Playboy	8	11	8	13	25	27	36	30
National Geographic	21	13	11	30	13	28	16	27
Time	17	8	7	16	9	26	17	29
Newsweek	17	14	8	20	11	18	13	22
Field & Stream	10	12	14	8	12	9	13	3
Popular Mechanics	11	6	9	9	9	9	8	6
Viewed in past week:								
Sanford & Son	32	35	29	19	26	25	27	23
Sonny & Cher	17	24	22	19	14	24	30	22
Marcus Welby	26	25	26	23	20	16	20	18
Rowan & Martin	21	23	17	15	22	20	23	21
New Dick Van Dyke	19	15	16	13	11	8	10	12

[a] Described in Figure 1.

Items tapping general personality traits were recast so as to be product specific. For instance, "I worry too much" was translated into "I seem to get stomach problems if I worry too much."

The 80 product-specific items were reduced to 13 factors by R factor analysis, and scores on the 13 factors were input into Q factor analysis to assign the respondents to homogeneous groups. The segments were described both in terms of the variables that went into the segmentation and in terms of personality traits, life-style attributes, and demographic characteristics (Figure 16-2). The ability of this procedure to discriminate among the brands in this product category is shown in Table 16-5.

Note that the discrimination produced by the product-specific approach is somewhat sharper than the discrimination produced by the more general segmentation. This outcome is common. When the segmentation is based upon the dimensions upon which brands differ, it is almost certain to discriminate more sharply among brands than when it is based upon more general considerations [54, 55, 143, 146]. Other examples of the product-specific approach can be found in [12, 30, 42, 52, 145–8].

This case history, and the four that precede it, provide five different examples of psychographic analysis. Collectively they show how psychographics can supplement demographics in interesting and useful ways. Individually they show the range of capabilities of these techniques, and they provide previews of some problems and ambiguities. We now turn to critical discussion of the problems that have arisen in the application of psychographic methods.

CRITICAL DISCUSSION

Questions about psychographics can be classified under four major headings: reliability, validity, applications to real-world marketing problems, and contributions to the study of consumer behavior. These topics will be dis-

FIGURE 16-2 *Segmentation of Stomach Remedy Users*

The Severe Sufferers. The Severe Sufferers are the extreme group on the potency side of the market. They tend to be young, have children, and be well educated. They are irritable and anxious people, and believe that they suffer more severely than others. They take the ailment seriously, fuss about it, pamper themselves, and keep trying new and different products in search of greater potency. A most advanced product with new ingredients best satisfies their need for potency and fast relief, and ties in with their psychosomatic beliefs.

The Active Medicators. The Active Medicators are on the same side of the motivational spectrum. They are typically modern suburbanites with average income and education. They are emotionally well adjusted to the demands of their active lives. They have learnt to cope by adopting the contemporary beliefs of seeking help for every ill, and use remedies to relieve even minor signs of ailments and every ache and pain. In a modern product, they seek restoration of their condition and energy, mental recovery, and a lift for their active lives. They are influenced by a brand's reputation and by how well it is advertised. They tend to develop strong brand loyalties.

The Hypochondriacs. The Hypochondriacs are on the opposite side of the motivational spectrum. They tend to be older, not as well educated, and women. They have conservative attitudes toward medication and a deep concern over health. They see possible dangers in frequent use of remedies, are concerned over side effects, and afraid of remedies with new ingredients and extra potency. To cope with these concerns, they are strongly oriented toward medical authority, seeking guidance in treatment, and what products they should use. They hold rigid beliefs about the ailment and are disciplined in the products they use, and how frequently. They want a simple, single-purpose remedy, which is safe and free from side effects, and backed by doctors or a reputable company.

The Practicalists. The Practicalists are in the extreme position on this side of the motivational spectrum. They tend to be older, well educated, emotionally the most stable, and least concerned over their ailment or the dangers of remedies. They accept the ailment and its discomforts as a part of life, without fuss and pampering. They use a remedy as a last resort, and just to relieve the particular symptom. They seek simple products whose efficacy is well proven, and are skeptical of complicated modern remedies with new ingredients and multiple functions.

TABLE 16-5 *Brand Use of Stomach Remedy Segments (Percent Use Brand Most Often)*

Brand	Severe Sufferers	Active Medicators	Hypochondriacs	Practicalists
A	6	3	1	1
B	32	23	10	8
C	16	17	12	5
D	16	19	24	8
E	5	29	37	51

cussed in turn, with special reference to the five case histories just given.

Reliability of Individual Terms and Scales

Here the term *reliability* is used in the restricted technical sense – i.e., freedom from *random* error [84, 93]. Although reliability of this sort is quite important, it is far from being the sole determinant of what a marketer is likely to be thinking about when he asks, "Can I rely on this study to guide my actions?" The other factors involved in that difficult and much more general question will be discussed in subsequent sections of this article.

When assessing reliability, it is important to distinguish between two major uses for psychographic measurements. One use is as a public opinion poll. An investigator might want to know, for example, how many people agree with "There should be a gun in every home," "Television commercials put too much emphasis on sex," or "I consider myself to be a member of the silent majority." In this use, when samples are of the size typically found in marketing surveys, *random* errors tend to cancel, and overall averages and percentages tend to be quite stable.

The other use of psychographics is in relationships, either in cross-tabulations – as in the shotgun and Pinto examples – or in "predictions" of dependent variables like ecological concern. Reliability is particularly important in studies of relationships because unreliable measurements can, in and of themselves, make strong relationships appear to be weak [84, 93].

Very little has been published on the reliability of "homemade" psychographic items and scales. In a review of the evidence available in 1971, Pessemier and Bruno [16, 98] reported a range of six-month test-retest reliability coefficients for individual items from "under .30" to "over .80" with a median between .60 and .69. And they reported reliability coefficients for multi-item scales ranging from .64 to .90, with a median of about .80. More recently, Darden and Reynolds [28] reported split-half reliabilities for 13 psychographic dimensions ranging from .60 to .89, with a median of .80.

Authors of standardized personality scales, like the scales used to identify the ecologically concerned consumer, normally provide evidence on scale reliability in their test manuals. Additional reliability data can often be found in *The Mental Measurements Yearbook* [18] and in literature reviews in such journals as *Psychological Bulletin.* These sources show that the standardized scales most often used by psychographic researchers have reliabilities that run from about .70 to about .90 – somewhat higher than the reported reliabilities of homemade variables.

What all this says is that both homemade and standardized psychographic measurements *can* have reliability high enough to support fairly strong relationships. However, it also says that the reliability of some psychographic measurements – especially some individual homemade items – may well be low enough to put a rather severe limitation on accuracy of "prediction."

Reliability of Dependent Variables

The maximum possible correlation between two variables is fully as dependent upon the reliability of what is being predicted as it is upon the reliability of the predictor [84, 93]. In psychographic studies, where the dependent variable is normally some form of consumer behavior, this means that strong relationships cannot be obtained unless the consumer behavior itself is measured accurately, no matter how reliable the psychographic measurements may be. This limitation is compounded by the fact that some kinds of consumer behavior – such as choice of a specific brand on a given occasion or exposure to a particular television program – may be so unstable that accurate prediction is virtually impossible, quite apart from any random measurement errors. Indeed, Bass [9] has gone so far as to assert that individual brand choice is so unstable that it can *never* be accurately predicted, by psychographics or by anything else.

With a few exceptions, psychographic researchers have not investigated the reliability of dependent variables. Successful prediction implies (but does not certify) adequate reliability. But unsuccessful prediction leaves the researcher in a quandry. Unsuccessful prediction can be due to unreliability in the psychographic measurements, to unreliability in the dependent variables, to lack of any "real" relationships between the psychographics and the behavior in question, or to some combination of all three. In the absence of reliability data it is impossible to determine which is the case.

Reliability of Relationships

In psychographic studies, as in other forms of marketing research, it is normal to find painstaking analysis of relationships that may be due at least in part to chance. In the shotgun ammunition study, for example, it is not possible to be sure that the same differences between buyers and nonbuyers would be found in a new sample drawn from the same population of respondents. Similarly, one cannot be sure that the same attitudes would identify subcompact car buyers if the Pinto study were repeated; or that, on replication, ecologically concerned consumers would differ from people in general as indicated by the data in Table 16-3. In the ecology study, some of the findings are particularly suspect. It does not seem at all likely that ecological concern really increases with income up to $10,000, drops between $10,000 and $14,999 and then resumes its upward climb. A much more probable explanation for that particular irregular relationship is some chance quirk in the data.

The only sure safeguard against being deceived by chance relationships is replication. When replication is impossible, the best procedure is to divide the sample into random parts, complete the analysis on one part, and then determine whether the same conclusions would have been reached via an identical analysis of the holdout group [6, 7, 14, 22, 34, 94, 141]. It is indeed unfortunate that this procedure has been the exception rather than the rule.

Reliability of Structure

Closely related to the question of reliability of relationships is the question of reliability of structure: do psychographic variables relate to each other in much the same way from study to study? In their reliability review Pessemier and Bruno compared factor analysis results from five large scale studies, including one conducted in Canada. They concluded that "the wide range of variables employed and the constructs to which they relate appear to be sufficiently reliable for both practical and theoretical purposes" [98, p. 397]. This conclusion is encouraging because it asserts that items tend to hang together in much the same way when studies are repeated. If that were not the case, it would be hard to put much credence in their relationship to anything else.

A further and more difficult question concerns the stability of the segments produced by various clustering procedures. If the Newspaper Advertising Bureau's general life-style segmentation or Pernica's segmentation of stomach remedy users were repeated on new samples of consumers, would the same conclusions be reached as to segment content and segment size? The answer to that question is of the utmost practical importance. If segments vary greatly in size, or disappear altogether, from one analysis to another, it makes no sense at all to develop products, messages, or media schedules on the assumption that the segments are real.

In a caveat that has gone largely unheeded,

Appel and Warwick noted in 1969 that: "Although Q-analysis is capable of reliably classifying people into relatively homogeneous groups based on psychographic data, there is a real question as to how many such groups can be reliably specified. . . . Unless the analyst is able to certify the reliability of the Q-group designations, the study findings are in serious question" [4, p. 25].

In the same vein, Johnson has more recently stated, "It has been the sad experience of many researchers that cluster analysis has produced interpretable groups differing dramatically in meaningful ways – and then subsequent analysis of new data has obtained equally convincing but entirely unrelated results. There are some uses of cluster analysis with which this would not be troublesome; but more frequently it would be an indication that neither solution is to be trusted" [62, p. 8].

The reliability of segments produced by empirical clustering procedures depends on several factors. First, and probably most important, reliability depends upon whether sharply differing, relatively homogeneous groups of consumers actually exist in the respondent population. The more segmented the population really is, the more the segmentation will be influenced by real structure, and not by adventitious bleeps [57]. Second, reliability will be influenced by the number of variables used, the size of the respondent sample, the accuracy with which the respondents answered the questions, and anything else that influences the stability of the correlations upon which the segmentation is based. Reliability will be influenced by the number of segments extracted. The larger the number of segments, the less likely they are to be reproducible [4]. And finally, reliability will depend upon the segmentation technique employed. Hierarchical clustering [61], a technique that has been used in a number of proprietary studies, may be much less reliable than alternative methods.

At this point in the development of psychographics, techniques for deriving segments are still primitive. We need to know much more about the conditions under which they succeed and the conditions under which they fail. We know for sure, however, that cluster solutions can be quite unstable, especially when the number of clusters is large. For this reason, it is especially important to compute the analysis on randomly selected halves of the sample and to reject solutions that do not match. This minimum requirement has often not been met. (See, for example [3, 12, 25, 39, 42, 76, 100].)

Reliability Summary

The available data indicate that psychographic measurements and analytic procedures can have satisfactory reliability. But, generally satisfactory reliability does not imply adequate reliability in all cases, and it may well be that some of the failures to find useful relationships between psychographics and consumer behavior have been due to instability in the measurements themselves. This may be especially true of the dependent variables, which can be unreliable both in the sense that they contain substantial amounts of random error, and in the sense that the behavior being measured is intrinsically unstable.

Unreliability also reduces the confidence one can place in relationships revealed by cross-tabulations or regressions, and the confidence one can place in clusters, both as to content and as to size. When important decisions are to be made on the basis of psychographics, it is essential that cross-tabulations, regressions, or clusters be cross-validated against holdout samples. It is all too easy to overanalyze findings that may be partially due to chance.

Validity

The term *validity* is used here in the traditional way. That is, a measurement is "valid" to the degree that it really does measure what it was intended to measure. Like other measurements, psychographic measurements can be reliable without being valid. They can be relatively free of random error but so full of irrelevancies and biases that conclusions based on them are partly (or even completely) false.

The question of the validity of psychographics is difficult and complex and cannot be answered simply. Here it is pursued under four headings: (1) construct validity of "homemade" psychographic variables, (2) construct validity of standardized scales, (3) construct validity of segments, and (4) predictive validity.

Construct Validity of Homemade Psychographic Variables

The construct validity of a measurement is established by showing that it relates to other variables to which it should be related, and does not relate to other variables to which it should not be related [19, 48, 93]. The process of establishing construct validity is normally spread out over time. It involves gradual accumulation of evidence, often by independent investigators, rather than a single finding of valid or not.

Pessemier and Bruno's review of the stability of certain psychographic constructs [16, 98] provides some evidence that bears upon the construct validity question. The fact that similar factors did indeed emerge when similar sets of items were answered by independent samples of respondents provides some assurance that individual psychographic items tend to relate to each other in internally consistent ways. While that finding is far from conclusive evidence of construct validity, it is a beginning. It shows that items which should go together do go together, while items that should not do not.

Further evidence of internal consistency can be found in the relationships between psychographics and demographics. Frequently one finds that the relationship between demographic and psychographic variables makes perfectly good sense. The evidence is not always conclusive, but when young people differ from old people in expected ways, or when more college graduates than nongraduates agree with "most of my friends have had a college education," the responses to the psychographic items seem right.

Beyond internal consistency, evidence for the construct validity of homemade items and scales is hard to find. The most general practice is to assume, unless there is evidence to the contrary, that the respondent is reporting accurately. Stated this baldly, the assumption sounds naive, but it is common in marketing research. When respondents are asked about brand preferences, exposure to media, or consumption of products, the general practice is to take answers at face value, even though it is known that such answers are sometimes wrong.

Much stronger evidence on construct validity would come from painstaking item-by-item and scale-by-scale convergent and discriminant validation [19]. That process has scarcely even begun, and it is so vastly complex that it will surely never be completed. In the meantime, users of homemade variables must be content with the assumption that respondents' answers contain a useful amount of valid information.

The Construct Validity of Standardized Scales

The psychographic researcher who uses standardized scales is less dependent upon face validity than is the researcher who assembles his own set of independent variables. Almost all published attitude scales and personality inventories are accompanied by at least some validity data, and some instruments are accompanied by quite a lot. If the scale has been widely used, the results of construct validity studies can be found in the *Mental Measurements Yearbook* and in reviews in psychological journals.

It is virtually impossible to make a valid generalization about the construct validity of standardized personality and attitude scales. Indeed, it often seems that the more a scale is investigated the less agreement there is as to its true meaning. (See for example [36, 38].)

It is safe to say, however, that the information that is available has frequently been ignored. In a recent review of personality inventories in consumer research, Kassarjian observed, "Typically a convenient, available, easily scored, and easy-to-administer personality inventory is selected and administered along with questionnaires on purchase data and preferences. The lack of proper scientific method and hypothesis generation is supposedly justified by the often-used disclaimer that the study is exploratory" [65, p. 416]. He followed that observation with a quote from Jacoby that also bears repeating: ". . . in most cases, no *a priori* thought is directed to *how,* or especially *why,* personality should or should not be related to that aspect of consumer behavior being studied. Moreover, the few studies which do report statistically significant findings usually do so on the basis of post-hoc 'picking and choosing' out of large data arrays" [60, p. 244].

Failure to make sensible use of construct validity data has been all too common. Its implications will be discussed in the next to the last section of this review.

The Construct Validity of Segments

Anyone who makes policy decisions on the basis of segmentations like those shown in Figures 16-1 and 16-2 must necessarily assume that relatively homogeneous groups of consumers fitting those descriptions actually exist. As noted in the reliability discussion, one way to check on this assumption is to determine whether the segments hold up under cross-validation with a held out sample of respondents. If segments disappear or change dramatically in size from one sample to another, the notion that the segments are "real" would appear to be tenuous indeed.

But even when segments hold up under cross-validation, there is still the question of how accurately the descriptions fit each member of each group. The "Traditionalist" described in Figure 16-1 is said to represent 16% of the adult male population – about 10 million people. How many of these 10 million really do differ from other consumers in all of those ways?

At present, questions about the reality of psychographic segments have no good answers, and with rare exceptions [40, 61, 62, 63, 81, 82, 86], such questions have scarcely even been approached. Few aspects of psychographics are more in need of basic research.

Predictive Validity

In econometrics, the validity of a model is established by its ability to predict the summed or averaged behavior of large numbers of individuals. In psychometrics, the validity of a test is established by its ability to predict the behavior of separate individuals. This distinction is important because the degree of accuracy that can be expected of predictions at the aggregate level is much higher than the degree of accuracy that can be expected of predictions at the individual level. One can predict with virtual certainty that there will be a traffic jam on the George Washington Bridge on a pleasant summer Friday afternoon; but one cannot be sure Arbuthnot will be in it.

The results of individual level predictions with psychographic instruments have paralleled the experience in research on personality. In the absence of good reason to believe that the psychographic construct would be closely related to the specific consumer behavior being studied, correlations have usually run between +.20 and −.20, with many close to zero [5, 15, 41, 49, 51, 70, 73, 76, 87, 88, 99, 100, 101, 131, 137]. When the psychographic constructs have been clearly relevant to the behavior being studied, individual correlations have been in the .20s and .30s [13, 20, 27, 102, 128]. And when relevant dimensions have been linked together in multiple regression, multiple correlations have been in the .50s and .60s [2, 43, 69, 96, 139].

Whether this record is good or bad depends greatly upon one's point of view. Many critics have declared that low correlations are of no practical value and have dismissed them out of hand [5, 7, 35, 64, 66]. But, as Bass, Tigert, and Lonsdale [10] have cogently argued, accounting for differences among groups of consumers, rather than explaining the variance in individual behavior, is often the real object of psychographic analysis. From that standpoint, the record looks much better.

The data in Table 16-2 are typical of the group differences that can be produced by psychographic items. Some of the differences are quite large, and many of them are larger than the differences produced by the demographic variables in Table 16-1. The data in Table 16-3 are typical of the discriminating power of more abstract general personality traits. The differences produced by the personality traits are rather small; but, as in the shotgun example, the differences produced by psychographics are larger than the differences produced by demographics.

Other comparisons of psychographics and demographics can be found in reports by Wilson [139], Good and Suchland [46], King and Sproles [69], Nelson [89], Pessemier and Tigert [96], and Berger and Schott [17]. These reports all show that the predictive validity of psychographic variables is likely to be substantially higher than the predictive validity of the demographic attributes that have long been accepted as good, true, and beautiful in marketing research.

Validity Summary

It is difficult to give a concise answer to the question: "Are psychographic measurements valid?" The answer would depend greatly upon exactly what type of validity the questioner had in mind. Even within a single type of validity the answer would vary greatly from study to study. The evidence does show that psychographic variables generally relate to each other, to demographics, and to use of products and media in ways that make perfectly good sense. That is not a very strong statement, but at least it says that the patterns in the data are consistent with what we believe to be true about consumer behavior.

The evidence on predictive validity shows that psychographic variables seldom account for large portions of the variance of individual behavior. However, this evidence also shows that psychographic variables are capable of producing substantial differences between groups of consumers, and that these differences are often larger than the differences produced by the standard demographic profile.

From a policy point of view, the most immediately pressing question concerns the reality of psychographic segments. Marketers who make important decisions on the basis of segmentation studies urgently need ways to determine when the products of cluster analysis or Q factor analysis represent real groups of real consumers, and when they represent figments of the computer's imagination.

APPLICATIONS TO MARKETING PROBLEMS

The last two sections of this review bear upon usefulness—first in the context of real-world marketing problems, then in the context of present and potential contributions to a more general understanding of consumer behavior. The real-world discussion will argue that reliability and validity are neither necessary nor sufficient to insure that psychographic data can be used. The remainder of the discussion will argue that psychographic methods have already made significant contributions to the understanding of consumer behavior, and these contributions are likely to become more important as time goes on.

How to Get Valid, Useless Results

The results of psychographic research can be reliable and valid, and still not useful, when relationships that should not have been expected fail to appear. This may seem like a perfectly obvious observation, yet—as Kassarjian and Jacoby have already indicated—the literature is full of attempts to predict consumer behavior from personality test scores in the absence of any good reason to believe that the two should be related [59]. Perhaps the classic example of this shot-in-the-dark approach is an early psychographic effort in which scales from The Edwards Personal Preference Schedule—scales intended to measure such needs as autonomy, dominance, order, and endurance—were correlated with purchases of single- and double-ply toilet tissue [5]. Even if it were true that all of the measurements in this study were perfectly reliable and perfectly valid, the failure to find a significant correlation between need for dominance, for example, and purchase of toilet paper, could hardly come as much of a surprise. The same general comment applies to Evans's finding that the Edwards scales cannot separate Ford owners from Chevrolet owners [37]; to Robertson and Myers's finding that California Psychological Inventory scores do not account for much of the variance in innovativeness or opinion leadership [116]; to Kollat and Willett's finding that a set of general personality traits including optimism, belief in fate, and belief in multiple causation of events did not predict impulse purchasing [73]; and to many other negative findings that have not been published. The general proposition is: when one has no reason to believe that the psychographic constructs should be related to the consumer behavior in question, a negative finding—even though all the measurements may be highly reliable and highly valid—is not worth much.

Another way to circumvent usefulness is to be too abstract. A grand example of abstraction carried to extremes is provided in a study by Sparks and Tucker [122]. This study found that a latent canonical root with heavy positive loadings on sociability and emotional stability, and a heavy negative loading on responsibility, accounted for much of the variance of a dimension that represents heavy consumption of alcoholic beverages, cigarettes, and shampoo. The study also found that a second latent dimension represented by a heavy positive loading on emotional stability and a heavy negative loading on cautiousness accounted for much of the variance of a dimension that represents heavy consumption of after-shave lotion, light consumption of headache remedies, light consumption of mouthwash and coffee, and disinclination to adopt new fashions. Assuming for the moment that this finding is both reliable and valid, just what does one do with it?

Third, psychographic measurements may be reliable and valid but so close to the behavior being studied that the relationship is essentially redundant. In Table 16-2, the best predictor of shotgun ammunition use is "I like to hunt." In Table 16-3, the best predictor of low ecological concern is agreement with "It is futile for the individual consumer to try to do anything about pollution." In Darden and Reynolds's study of men's fashions [27], the best predictors of fashion opinion leadership were two scales measuring "fashion interest" and "fashion venturesomeness." Findings of this sort are useful in the very restricted sense that they point to the construct validity of the psychographic items, but they are hardly likely to be greeted by marketing managers as world-shaking revelations.

To be useful in making real-world marketing decisions, psychographic data must be in some middle range between being almost totally redundant and being entirely unrelated to the behavior being studied. They must contain just the right amount of surprise. When that is the case, they can be very useful indeed, even when correlations are not high and even when questions about reliability and validity cannot be completely answered. This principle applies to profiles and to segmentations, for the same basic reason.

Why Psychographic Profiles Are Useful

To see why psychographic profiles are useful even in the absence of assured reliability and validity, it is necessary to consider the alternatives. Consider, for example, the copy writer quoted toward the beginning of this review. Confronted with a deadline for creating an advertisement, he could sit in his office and imagine his audience. But he might be wrong. As he said, he can't afford to trust just his own experience. He might do his own informal psychographic study – trudge all the way around the block talking to the neighbors. But to the degree that his neighbors are different from his customers, this informal research might easily be misleading.

The copy writer might depend upon a qualitative motivation study. If he did, he would be looking at findings from a small unrepresentative sample, and he would be depending upon the subjective judgment of the motivation research analyst. He might examine a demographic profile obtained from a large scale quantitative market survey. But, as the shotgun study illustrates, he would almost surely miss some valid relationships, and he would almost surely make some false inferences. Given these alternatives, it is easy to see why psychographic profiles have seen wide use in spite of legitimate questions as to reliability and validity. The copy writer cannot wait for convergent and discriminant validation. He must produce an advertisement, and to do that, he must use whatever information he can get.

The same basic problem confronts product designers, package designers, product managers, and media analysts. What product features will fit the life style of the potential customer? To what sort of person should the package be designed to appeal? Is the customer for this product or service unusually price conscious? Fashion conscious? Concerned about pollution? Concerned about his health? What are consumers' attitudes and opinions about what appears in magazines, newspapers, radio, and TV? All of these questions are regularly answered by some combination of intuition and quantitative and qualitative research. In many cases psychographic profiles add information that would not otherwise be available.

Why Psychographic Segmentations Are Useful

General segmentations like the Newspaper Advertising Bureau study offer the opportunity to tailor new products and services to the needs of different groups within the consumer population. It is easy to see that the "Quiet Family Man," the "Traditionalist," the "Ethical Highbrow," and the "Pleasure Oriented Man" (Figure 16-1) ought to have quite different requirements in automobiles, entertainment, vacations, insurance policies, food, and clothing. The life-style descriptions show those need patterns in considerable detail, and the media data normally collected in such studies show how to reach each group [121].

Product-specific segmentations like the stomach remedy study offer the opportunity to position and reposition existing brands. They show what needs the product meets within each group, and which brands are best at meeting them. With this information the marketer can appeal directly and efficiently to those groups most apt to find his brand appealing, and he can create new brands to fit need patterns his brand cannot satisfy. Parallel values accrue to marketers of services.

But the question remains – are the descriptions of the segments reliable and valid? Do real groups of real consumers fitting these descriptions actually exist? If the answer is yes, the user of a psychographic segmentation has at his disposal a new and superior way of understanding his customers. If the answer is no, the marketer who takes a segmentation study seriously is marketing to a family of fictions.

In view of the reservations already expressed as to the reliability and validity of segmentation procedures it might seem that the wisest course would be to ignore psychographics until the procedures have been thoroughly validated. But again, one must consider the alternatives. Marketers know that the customers for a product or a service are frequently not much alike. They know that empirical segmentation procedures hold out the possibility of new insights into how consumers may be divided into groups. And they know that the reliability and validity of segmentation procedures have not been established beyond all doubt. Given that dilemma, many marketers have elected to conduct and to use segmentation studies even when fully aware of the art's imperfections.

UNDERSTANDING CONSUMER BEHAVIOR

Finally, psychographic methods have contributed to more general knowledge of consumer behavior in at least three ways. Psychographic profiles have shed new light on some of the familiar and recurring topics in consumer research. Trend data now becoming available have shown how consumers are changing and how they are not. And general segmentations of the consumer population have created new typologies within which consumer behavior might be more efficiently described and better understood. This review concludes with brief descriptions of studies in each of these fields.

Profiles

Psychographic profiles have already contributed to our understanding of opinion leadership [69, 113, 126], innovativeness [23, 32, 60, 97, 126], retail out-shopping [114], private brand buying [17], social class [129], consumerist activism [56], catalog buying behavior [112], store loyalty [115], differences between Canada and the United States [8], differences between French-speaking and English-speaking Canadians [125], and concern for the environment [71, 72]. In all these cases the value added by the psychographic profile was much the same as the value added to the description of the shotgun ammunition buyer. Sometimes psychographics confirmed the existence of attributes that might have been inferred from demographic profiles. Sometimes they revealed the existence of attributes that a demographic profile did show. And sometimes they disconfirmed inferences that would have been incorrect. It seems certain that the trend toward psychographic descriptions of interesting groups of consumers will continue, and that such descriptions will become accepted as necessary components of studies of this kind.

Trend Data

As studies are repeated, it becomes possible to accumulate trend data that show how consumers are changing and how they are not changing. Such data are particularly valuable in an era when every other observer is prepared to describe "the changing consumer" and to make predictions about the effects of these changes upon markets for goods and services. In monitoring trends, the task of empirical psychographic analysis is to separate the changes that are actually happening from the changes that are not [24, 106].

New Typologies

The third application of psychographics to the study of consumer behavior is just now beginning to take shape. General segmentations, like the Newspaper Advertising Bureau study and the series of life-style studies conducted by the Leo Burnett Company [24, 92, 105, 106], have begun to produce the outlines of a new consumer typology. As groupings like those shown in Figure 16-1 are identified and confirmed by independent sets of investigators, it is at least possible that marketers will begin to think routinely in terms of segments marked off by common sets of activities, interests, needs, and values, and to develop products, services, and media schedules specifically to meet them.

At present, agreement among general segmentation studies is pretty far from complete. Differences in item content, sampling procedure and analytic technique have produced different sets of findings, each claiming to be real. Yet, even though the segments produced by various general segmentation studies differ in a number of ways, there is enough similarity among them to suggest that eventual consensus is not a vain hope. If consensus eventually is reached, there will be a new way of thinking about consumers as like-style groups.

Summary of Uses

To the marketing practitioner, psychographic methods have offered a way of describing consumers that has many advantages over alternative methods, even though much work on reliability and validity remains to be done. To researchers with more general interests, psychographic methods have offered new ways of looking at old problems, new dimensions for charting trends, and a new vocabulary in which consumer typologies may be described.

From the speed with which psychographics have diffused through the marketing community, it seems obvious that they are perceived as meeting a keenly felt need. The problem now is not so much one of pioneering as it is one of sorting out the techniques that work best. As that process proceeds, it seems extremely likely that psychographic methods will gradually become more familiar and less controversial, and eventually will merge into the mainstream of marketing research.

REFERENCES

1. *A Psychographic View of the Los Angeles Marketing Area.* Los Angeles, Calif.: Los Angeles Times, 1972.
2. Ahmed, Sadrudin A. "Prediction of Cigarette Consumption Level With Personality and Socioeconomic Variables," *Journal of Applied Psychology,* 56 (October 1972), 437–8.
3. Alpert, Mark I. "Personality and the Determinants of Product Choice," *Journal of Marketing Research,* 9 (February 1972), 89–92.
4. Appel, Valentine and Kenneth Warwick. *Procedures for Defining Consumer Market Targets.* New York: Grudin/Appel Research Corporation, 1969.
5. *Are There Consumer Types?* New York: Advertising Research Foundation, 1964.
6. Armstrong, J. Scott. "Derivation of Theory by Means of Factor Analysis, or Tom Swift and His Electric Factor Analysis Machine," *American Statistician,* 21 (December 1967), 17–21.
7. Arndt, Johan. *Market Segmentation.* Bergen, Norway: Universitetsforlaget, 1974.
8. Arnold, Stephen J. and Douglas J. Tigert. "Canadians and Americans: A Comparative Analysis," paper delivered at the Annual Convention of the American Psychological Association, Montreal, Canada, 1973.
9. Bass, Frank M. "The Theory of Stochastic Preference and Brand Switching," *Journal of Marketing Research,* 11 (February 1974), 1–20.
10. ———, Douglas J. Tigert, and Ronald F. Lonsdale. "Market Segmentation: Group Versus Individual Behavior," *Journal of Marketing Research,* 5 (August 1968), 264–70.
11. Behavior Science Corporation. *Developing the Family Travel Market.* Des Moines, Iowa: Better Homes and Gardens, 1972.
12. Bernay, Elayn K. "Life Style Analysis as a Basis for Media Selection," in Charles King and Douglas Tigert, eds., *Attitude Research Reaches New Heights.* Chicago: American Marketing Association, 1971, 189–95.
13. Birdwell, Al B. "A Study of the Influence of Image Congruence on Consumer Choice," *Journal of Business,* 41 (January 1968), 76–88.
14. Bither, Steward W. and Ira J. Dolich. "Personality as a Determinant Factor in Store Choice," *Proceedings.* Third Annual Conference, Association for Consumer Research, 1972, 9–19.
15. Brody, Robert P. and Scott M. Cunningham. "Personality Variables and the Consumer Decision Process," *Journal of Marketing Research,* 5 (February 1968), 50–7.
16. Bruno, Albert V. and Edgar A. Pessemier. "An Empirical Investigation of the Validity of Selected Attitude and Activity Measures," *Proceedings.* Third Annual Conference, Association for Consumer Research, 1972, 456–74.
17. Burger, Philip C. and Barbara Schott. "Can Private Brand Buyers Be Identified?" *Journal of Marketing Research,* 9 (May 1972), 219–22.

18. Buros, Oscar K. *The Seventh Mental Measurements Yearbook.* Highland Park, N.J.: The Gryphon Press, 1972.
19. Campbell, Donald T. and Donald W. Fiske. "Convergant and Discriminant Validation by the Multitrait-Multimethod Matrix," *Psychological Bulletin,* 56 (March 1959), 81-105.
20. Carman, James M. "Correlates of Brand Loyalty: Some Positive Results," *Journal of Marketing Research,* 7 (February 1970), 67-76.
21. Claycamp, Henry J. "Characteristics of Owners of Thrift Deposits in Commercial Banks and Savings and Loan Associations," *Journal of Marketing Research,* 2 (May 1965), 163-70.
22. Cooley, W.W. and P.R. Lohnes. *Multivariate Procedures in the Behavioral Sciences.* New York: John Wiley, 1962.
23. Coney, Kenneth A. "Dogmatism and Innovation; A Replication," *Journal of Marketing Research,* 9 (November 1972), 453-5.
24. Coulson, John S. "How Much Has The Consumer Changed?" paper presented at the Meeting of the American Association for Public Opinion Research, 1974.
25. Cunningham, William H. and William J.E. Crissy. "Market Segmentation by Motivation and Attitude," *Journal of Marketing Research,* 9 (February 1972), 100-2.
26. Danzig, Fred. "Int'l Marketing Congress Hears Psychographics Criticized, Defended," *Advertising Age,* 3 (June 1969), 104-5.
27. Darden, William R. and Fred D. Reynolds. "Predicting Opinion Leadership for Men's Apparel Fashions," *Journal of Marketing Research,* 9 (August 1972), 324-8.
28. ———. "Backward Profiling of Male Innovators," *Journal of Marketing Research,* 11 (February 1974), 79-85.
29. Demby, Emanuel. "Psychographics: Who, What, Why, When, Where and How," in Charles King and Douglas Tigert, eds., *Attitude Research Reaches New Heights.* Chicago: American Marketing Association, 1971, 196-9.
30. ———. "Psychographics and From Whence It Came," in William D. Wells, ed., *Life Style and Psychographics.* Chicago: American Marketing Association, 1974, 9-30.
31. Dichter, Ernest. *Handbook of Consumer Motivations.* New York: McGraw-Hill, 1964.
32. Donnelly, James H., Jr. "Social Character and Acceptance of New Products," *Journal of Marketing Research,* 7 (February 1970), 111-3.
33. Dorny, Lester R. "Observations on Psychographics," in Charles King and Douglas Tigert, eds., *Attitude Research Reaches New Heights.* Chicago: American Marketing Association, 1971, 200-1.
34. Einhorn, Hillel J. "Alchemy in the Behavioral Sciences," *Public Opinion Quarterly,* 36 (Fall 1972), 367-78.
35. Engel, James F., David T. Kollat, and Roger D. Blackwell. "Personality Measures and Market Segmentation," *Business Horizons,* 12 (June 1969), 61-70.
36. Entwisle, Doris R. "To Dispel Fantasies about Fantasy-Based Measures of Achievement Motivation," *Psychological Bulletin,* 77 (June 1972), 377-91.
37. Evans, Franklin B. "Psychological and Objective Factors in the Prediction of Brand Choice: Ford vs. Chevrolet," *Journal of Business,* 32 (October 1959), 340-69.
38. Fiske, Donald W. "Can A Personality Construct Be Validated? *Psychological Bulletin,* 80 (August 1973), 89-92.
39. Frank, Ronald E. "Predicting New Product Segments," *Journal of Advertising Research,* 12 (June 1972), 9-13.
40. Frank, Ronald E. and Paul E. Green. "Numerical Taxonomy in Marketing Analysis: A Review Article," *Journal of Marketing Research,* 5 (February 1968), 83-94.
41. Frank, Ronald E., William F. Massy, and Thomas M. Lodahl., "Purchasing Behavior and Personal Attributes," *Journal of Advertising Research,* 9 (December 1969), 15-24.
42. Frank, Ronald E. and Charles E. Strain. "A Segmentation Research Design Using Consumer Panel Data," *Journal of Marketing Research,* 9 (November 1972), 385-90.
43. Fry, Joseph N. "Personality Variables and Cigarette Brand Choice," *Journal of Marketing Research,* 8 (August 1971), 298-304.
44. Gardner, David M. "An Exploratory Investigation of Achievement Motivation Effects on Consumer Behavior," *Proceedings.* Third Annual Conference, Association for Consumer Research, 1972, 20-33.
45. Garfinkle, Norton. "The Value and Use of Psychographic Information in Decision Making," in Charles W. King and Douglas Tigert, eds., *Attitude Research Reaches New Heights.* Chicago: American Marketing Association, 1971, 206-210.
46. Good, Walter S. and Otto Suchland. *Consumer Life Styles and Their Relationship to Market Behavior Regarding Household Furniture.* East Lansing, Mich.: Michigan State University Research Bulletin, No. 26, 1970.
47. Gottlieb, Morris J. "Segmentation by Personality Types," in Lynne H. Stockman, ed., *Advancing Marketing Efficiency.* Chicago: American Marketing Association, 1959, 148-58.
48. Green, Paul E. and Donald S. Tull. *Research for Marketing Decisions,* second edition. Englewood Cliffs, N.J.: Prentice-Hall, 1970.
49. Greeno, Daniel W., Montrose S. Sommers, and Jerome B. Kernan. "Personality and Implicit Behavior Patterns," *Journal of Marketing Research,* 10 (February 1973), 63-9.
50. Grubb, Edward L. and Gregg Hupp. "Perception of Self, Generalized Stereotypes and Brand Selection," *Journal of Marketing Research,* 5 (February 1968), 58-63.
51. Gruen, Walter. "Preference for New Products and Its Relationship to Different Measures of Conformity," *Journal of Applied Psychology,* 44 (December 1960), 361-4.

52. Heller, Harry E. "Defining Target Markets by Their Attitude Profiles," in Lee Adler and Irving Crespi, eds., *Attitude Research on the Rocks.* Chicago: American Marketing Association, 1968, 45-57.
53. "How Nestle Uses Psychographics," *Media Decisions,* (July 1973), 68-71.
54. Hustad, Thomas P. and Edgar A. Pessemier. "Segmenting Consumer Markets with Activity and Attitude Measures," Institute Paper No. 298, Krannert Graduate School of Industrial Administration, Purdue University, 1971.
55. ———. "The Development and Application of Psychographic, Life-Style and Associated Activity and Attitude Measures," in W.D. Wells, ed., *Life Style and Psychographics.* Chicago: American Marketing Association, 1974, 31-70.
56. ———. "Will the Real Consumer Activist Please Stand Up: An Examination of Consumers' Opinions about Marketing Practices," *Journal of Marketing Research,* 10 (August 1973), 319-24.
57. Inglis, Jim and Douglas Johnson, "Some Observations on, and Developments in, the Analysis of Multivariate Survey Data," *Journal of the Market Research Society,* 12 (April 1970), 75-98.
58. Jacobson, Eugene and Jerome Kossoff. "Self-Percept and Consumer Attitudes Toward Small Cars," *Journal of Applied Psychology,* 47 (August 1963), 242-5.
59. Jacoby, Jacob. "Personality and Consumer Behavior: How Not to Find Relationships," Purdue Papers in Consumer Psychology, No. 102, 1969.
60. ———. "Personality and Innovation Proneness," *Journal of Marketing Research,* 8 (May 1971), 244-7.
61. Johnson, Richard M. "How Can You Tell if Things are 'Really' Clustered?" Paper read at a joint meeting of the New York chapters of the American Statistical Association and American Marketing Association, New York, 1972.
62. ———. *Using Q Analysis in Marketing Research.* Chicago: Market Facts, Inc., 1974.
63. Joyce, Timothy and C. Channon. "Classifying Market Survey Respondents," *Applied Statistics,* 5 (November 1966), 191-215.
64. Kassarjian, Harold H. "Social Character and Differential Preference for Mass Communication," *Journal of Marketing Research,* 2 (May 1965), 146-53.
65. ———. "Personality and Consumer Behavior: A Review," *Journal of Marketing Research,* 8 (November 1971), 409-18.
66. ———. "Personality and Consumer Behavior: A Way out of the Morass," paper presented at the 1973 meeting of the American Psychological Association.
67. Kay, Herbert. *Important News about Prime-Prospect Service.* Montclair, N.J.: Herbert Kay Research, Inc., 1969.
68. King, Charles W. "Social Science, Pragmatic Marketing Research and Psychographics," in Charles W. King and Douglas J. Tigert, eds., *Attitude Research Reaches New Heights.* Chicago: American Marketing Association, 1971, 228-31.
69. ——— and George B. Sproles. "The Explanatory Efficacy of Selected Types of Consumer Profile Variables in Fashion Change Agent Identification," Institute Paper No. 425, Krannert Graduate School of Industrial Administration, Purdue University, 1973.
70. King, Charles W. and John O. Summers. "Attitudes and Media Exposure," *Journal of Advertising Research,* 11 (February 1971), 26-32.
71. Kinnear, Thomas C., James R. Taylor, and Sadrudin A. Ahmed. "Socioeconomic and Personality Characteristics as They Relate to Ecologically-Constructive Purchasing Behavior," *Proceedings.* Third Annual Conference, Association for Consumer Research, 1972, 34-60.
72. ———. "Ecologically Concerned Consumers: Who Are They?" *Journal of Marketing Research,* 38 (April 1974), 20-4.
73. Kollat, David T. and Ronald P. Willett. "Customer Impulse Purchasing Behavior," *Journal of Marketing Research,* 1 (September 1960), 6-12.
74. Koponen, Arthur. "Personality Characteristics of Purchasers," *Journal of Advertising Research,* 1 (September 1960), 6-12.
75. Kuelper, Robert. "The Pit and the Pendulum," internal memo, Chicago: Leo Burnett Company, 1970.
76. Lessig, V. Parker and John O. Tollefson. "Market Segmentation Through Numerical Taxonomy," *Journal of Marketing Research,* 8 (November 1971), 480-7.
77. *Life Style of the WWD Subscriber.* New York: Women's Wear Daily, 1971.
78. "Life Style Portrait of the Hunter," *Journal of Leisure Research,* in press.
79. Lovell, M.R.C. "European Developments in Psychographics," in W.D. Wells, ed., *Life Style and Psychographics.* Chicago: American Marketing Association, 1974, 257-76.
80. Lunn, J.A. "Psychological Classification," *Commentary,* 8 (July 1966), 161-73.
81. ———. "Empirical Techniques in Consumer Research," in D. Pym, ed., *Industrial Society: Social Sciences in Management.* Baltimore: Penguin Books, 1968, 401-25.
82. Massy, William F., Ronald E. Frank, and Yoram Wind. *Market Segmentation.* Englewood Cliffs, N.J.: Prentice-Hall, 1972.
83. May, Eleanor G. "Psychographics in Department Store Imagery," Working Paper P-65. Cambridge, Mass.: Marketing Science Institute, 1971.
84. McNemar, Quinn. *Psychological Statistics,* second edition. New York: John Wiley & Sons, 1955.
85. Michaels, Peter W. "Life Style and Magazine Exposure," in Boris W. Becker and Helmut Becker, eds., *Combined Proceedings: Marketing Education and the Real World and Dynamic Marketing in a Changing World.* Chicago: American Marketing Association, 1973, 324-31.
86. Monk, Donald. "Burnett Life Style Research," *European Research: Marketing Opinion Advertising,* 1 (January 1973), 14-19.
87. Montgomery, David B. "Consumer Characteristics Associated with Dealing: An Empirical Example," *Jour-*

nal of Marketing Research, 8 (February 1971), 118-20.

88. Myers, John G. "Determinants of Private Brand Attitude," *Journal of Marketing Research,* 4 (February 1967), 73-81.
89. Nelson, Alan R. "A National Study of Psychographics," paper delivered at the International Marketing Congress, American Marketing Association, June 1969.
90. ———. "New Psychographics: Action-Creating Ideas, Not Lifeless Statistics," *Advertising Age,* 1 (June 28, 1971), 34.
91. ———. "Psyching Psychographics: A Look at Why People Buy," in Charles W. King and Douglas J. Tigert, eds., *Attitude Research Reaches New Heights.* Chicago: American Marketing Association, 1971, 181-8.
92. *New Information on Sugar User Psychographics.* Chicago: Leo Burnett, 1972.
93. Nunnally, Jim C. *Psychometric Theory.* New York: McGraw-Hill, 1967.
94. Overall, J.E. and C.J. Klett. *Applied Multivariate Analysis.* New York: McGraw-Hill, 1971.
95. Pernica, Joseph. "The Second Generation of Market Segmentation Studies: An Audit of Buying Motivation," in W.D. Wells, ed., *Life Style and Psychographics.* Chicago: American Marketing Association, 1974, 277-313.
96. Pessemier, Edgar A. and Douglas J. Tigert, "A Taxonomy of Magazine Readership Applied to Problems in Marketing Strategy and Media Selection," Institute Paper No. 195, Krannert Graduate School of Industrial Administration, Purdue University, 1967.
97. Pessemier, Edgar A., Philip C. Burger, and Douglas J.Tigert. "Can New Product Buyers Be Identified?" *Journal of Marketing Research,* 4 (November 1967), 349-54.
98. Pessemier, Edgar A. and Albert Bruno. "An Empirical Investigation of the Reliability and Stability of Activity and Attitude Measures," Reprint Series No. 391, Krannert Graduate School of Industrial Administration, 1971.
99. Peters, William H. and Neil M. Ford. "A Profile of Urban In-Home Shoppers: The Other Half," *Journal of Marketing,* 36 (January 1972), 62-4.
100. Peterson, Robert A. "Psychographics and Media Exposure," *Journal of Advertising Research,* 12 (June 1972), 17-20.
101. ——— and Allan L. Pennington. "SVIB Interests and Product Preferences," *Journal of Applied Psychology,* 53 (August 1969), 304-8.
102. Plummer, Joseph T. "Life Style Patterns and Commercial Bank Credit Card Usage," *Journal of Marketing,* 35 (April 1971), 35-41.
103. ———. "Learning About Consumers as Real People: The Application of Psychographic Data," paper presented to the Montreal Chapter, American Marketing Association, November 1971.
104. ———. "Life Style Patterns: A New Constraint for Mass Communications Research," *Journal of Broadcasting,* 16 (Winter 1971-72), 79-89.
105. ———. "The Theory and Uses of Life Style Segmentation," *Journal of Marketing,* 38 (January 1974), 33-7.
106. ———. "Life Style and Social Change: Evolutionary–Not Revolutionary," paper read at the 20th Annual AMA Management Seminar, Toronto, 1973.
107. ———. "Life Style Portrait of the Hunter," *Journal of Leisure Research* (in press).
108. ———. "Application of Life Style Research to the Creation of Advertising Campaigns," in W.D. Wells, ed., *Life Style and Psychographics.* Chicago: American Marketing Association, 1974, 157-69.
109. *Psychographics: A Study of Personality, Life Style, and Consumption Patterns.* New York: Newspaper Advertising Bureau, 1973.
110. Reiser, Richard J. "Psychographics: Marketing Tool or Research Toy?" *Chicago Marketing Scene,* (October 1972), 8-9.
111. Reynolds, Fred D. *Psychographics: A Conceptual Orientation.* Research Monograph No. 6. Athens, Ga.: Division of Research, University of Georgia, College of Business Administration, 1973.
112. ———. "An Analysis of Catalog Buying Behavior," *Journal of Marketing,* 38 (July 1974), 47-51.
113. ——— and William R. Darden. "Mutually Adaptive Effects of Interpersonal Communication," *Journal of Marketing Research,* 8 (November 1971), 449-54.
114. ———. "Intermarket Patronage: A Psychographic Study of Consumer Outshoppers," *Journal of Marketing,* 36 (October 1972), 50-4.
115. ——— and Warren S. Martin. "The Store Loyal Consumer: A Life Style Analysis," *Journal of Retailing,* in press.
116. Robertson, Thomas S. and James H. Myers. "Personality Correlates of Opinion Leadership and Innovative Buying Behavior," *Journal of Marketing Research,* 6 (May 1969), 164-8.
117. Roper, Elmo and associates. *Movers and Shakers.* New York: Harper-Atlantic Sales, 1970.
118. Ross, Ivan. "Self-Concept and Brand Preference," *The Journal of Business,* 44 (January 1971), 38-50.
119. Segnit, Susanna and Simon Broadbent. "Life Style Research," *European Research: Marketing Opinion Advertising,* 1 (January 1973), 6-13.
120. Simmons, W.R. "Overall Impressions of Psychographics," in Charles A. King and Douglas J. Tigert, eds., *Attitude Research Reaches New Heights.* Chicago: American Marketing Association, 1971, 215-9.
121. Skelly, Florence and Elizabeth Nelson. "Market Segmentation and New Product Development," *Scientific Business,* 4 (Summer 1966), 13-22.
122. Sparks, David L. and W.T. Tucker. "A Multivariate Analysis of Personality and Product Use," *Journal of Marketing Research,* 8 (February 1971), 67-70.
123. Summers, John O. "The Identity of Women's Clothing Fashion Opinion Leaders," *Journal of Marketing Research,* 7 (May 1970), 178-85.
124. Teleki, Margot. "The Research Go-Round," *Media-Scope,* (March 1970), 27-32, 38-40.
125. *The Lifestyles of English and French Canadian Women.* Toronto: Vickers and Benson Ltd., Marketing Services Department, 1972.

126. Tigert, Douglas J. "Psychometric Correlates of Opinion Leadership and Innovation," unpublished working paper, University of Chicago, 1969.
127. ———. "A Research Project in Creative Advertising Through Life-Style Analysis," in Charles W. King and Douglas J. Tigert, eds., *Attitude Research Reaches New Heights.* Chicago: American Marketing Association, 1971, 223-7.
128. ———. "Life Style Analysis as a Basis for Media Selection," in W.D. Wells, ed., *Life Style and Psychographics.* Chicago: American Marketing Association, 1974, 171-201.
129. ——— and William D. Wells. "Life Style Correlates of Age and Social Class," paper presented at the First Annual Meeting, Association for Consumer Research, Amherst, 1970.
130. Tigert, Douglas J., Richard Lathrope, and Michael Bleeg. "The Fast Food Franchise: Psychographic and Demographic Segmentation Analysis," *Journal of Retailing,* 47 (Spring 1971), 81-90.
131. Tucker, W.T. and John J. Painter. "Personality and Product Use," *Journal of Applied Psychology,* 45 (October 1961), 325-9.
132. Vitz, Paul C. and Donald Johnston. "Masculinity of Smokers and the Masculinity of Cigarette Images," *Journal of Applied Psychology,* 49 (June 1965), 155-9.
133. Wells, William D. "Segmentation by Attitude Types," in Robert L. King, ed., *Marketing and the New Science of Planning.* Chicago: American Marketing Association, 124-6.
134. ———. "Life Style and Psychographics: Definitions, Uses and Problems," in W.D. Wells, ed., *Life Style and Psychographics.* Chicago: American Marketing Association, 1974, 315-63.
135. ——— and Arthur D. Beard. "Personality and Consumer Behavior," in Scott Ward and Thomas S. Robertson, eds., *Consumer Behavior: Theoretical Sources.* Englewood Cliffs, N.J.: Prentice-Hall, 1973, 141-99.
136. Wells, William D. and Douglas J. Tigert. "Activities, Interests, and Opinions," *Journal of Advertising Research,* 11 (August 1971), 27-35.
137. Westfall, Ralph. "Psychological Factors in Predicting Product Choice," *Journal of Marketing,* 26 (April 1962), 34-40.
138. "What's Their Life Style?" *Media Decisions,* (September 1969), 34-35, 70, 72.
139. Wilson, Clark L. "Homemaker Living Patterns and Marketplace Behavior – A Psychometric Approach," in J.S. Wright and J.L. Goldstucker, eds., *New Ideas for Successful Marketing.* Chicago: American Marketing Association, 1966, 305-47.
140. Wind, Yoram and Paul E. Green. "Some Conceptual, Measurement, and Analytical Problems in Life Style Research," in W.D. Wells, ed., *Life Style and Psychographics.* Chicago: American Marketing Association, 1974, 97-126.
141. Wind, Yoram, Paul E. Green and Arun K. Jain. "Higher Order Factor Analysis in the Classification of Psychographic Variables," *Journal of the Market Research Society,* 15 (October 1973), 224-32.
142. Yoell, William. "Causes of Buying Behavior: Mythology or Fact? in Mernard A. Morin, ed., *Marketing in a Changing World.* Chicago: American Marketing Association, 1969, 241-8.
143. Young, Shirley. "Psychographics Research and Marketing Relevancy," in Charles A. King and Douglas J. Tigert, eds., *Attitude Research Reaches New Heights.* Chicago: American Marketing Association, 1971, 220-2.
144. ———. "Research Both for Strategic Planning and for Tactical Testing," *Proceedings.* 19th Annual Conference, Advertising Research Foundation, New York, 1973, 13-16.
145. ———. "The Dynamics of Measuring Unchange," in Russell Haley, ed., *Attitude Research in Transition.* Chicago: American Marketing Association, 1972, 49-82.
146. Ziff, Ruth. "Psychographics for Market Segmentation," *Journal of Advertising Research,* 11 (April 1971), 3-10.
147. ———. "Closing the Consumer-Advertising Gap through Psychographics," *Combined Proceedings: Marketing Education and the Real World and Dynamic Marketing in a Changing World.* Chicago: American Marketing Association, 1973, 457-61.
148. ———. "The Role of Psychographics in The Development of Advertising Strategy," in W.D. Wells, ed., *Life Style and Psychographics.* Chicago: American Marketing Association, 1974, 127-55.

III

Marketing Strategy

The dominant trend in the marketing discipline during the last ten to fifteen years has no doubt been the increasing emphasis on strategic analysis and planning. By late 1983, *Business Week,* the premier business newsweekly, headlined: "Marketing: The New Priority." Articles in Part III present some of the discipline's best scholarly thinking about marketing strategy.

Frederick Webster's seminal study of the views of thirty top managers keynotes this part. He found that "these chief executives and operating officers believe that marketing is the most important management in their businesses, and they see it becoming more important in the future." That importance, and the problems it portends, were emphasized in negative fashion by Robert Hayes and William Abernathy, who ascribe a key role to the marketing function in "managing our way to economic decline."

These articles provide a foundation for an in-depth analysis of marketing strategy. Derek Abell's strategic windows highlight the importance of anticipating and responding to changes in the marketplace. David Montgomery and Charles Weinberg demonstrate the development of strategic intelligence systems for identifying these changes. Philip Kotler, William Gregor, and William Rogers show how to use such information along with organizational analysis to prepare marketers to take advantage of marketplace change.

Since marketing begins with understanding customers, the next articles present the concept of market segmentation. The original statement is by Wendell Smith, who distinguishes between segmentation and product differentiation. Russell Haley offered the seminal view of benefit segmentation; much of the subsequent empirical work in perception and preference mapping builds on this concept. Jack Trout and Al Ries carried the segmentation idea into definite strategy in their work on positioning – winning a place for a product in the buyer's mind.

The final set of papers in this part explores the relationship between marketing strategy and organizational objectives. Robert Buzzell, Bradley Gale, and Ralph Sultan, using a large empirical data base, demonstrate the significant and enduring connections among marketing strategy, market share, and profitability; this work continues today under the auspices of the nonprofit Strategic Planning Institute. George Day's paper amplifies these relationships by focusing on the factors involved in strategic product portfolio planning. This paper summarizes much of the important work on marketing planning contributed to the literature by marketing practitioners.

17

Frederick E. Webster, Jr.

Top Management's Concerns about Marketing: Issues for the 1980's

This article reports the findings of a study of top managers' views of the marketing function. The potential value of these findings lies in that they focus attention on a number of issues of concern to top management, helping to define research hypotheses and productive areas of inquiry. Many of these issues have not received the research attention they need and deserve.

It is valuable, from time to time, for marketing academicians to attempt a validity check on their own views of the field as compared with marketing managers who are an important set of beneficiaries, ultimately, of the results of research in marketing (and who frequently provide the financial support needed to conduct the research). How else can academicians be sure that their efforts are meaningful and useful? Are we concerned about and working in areas that management is interested in? It also is helpful to know which issues will be most likely to generate management interest and support in the future.

A recent study by the Marketing Science Institute identified marketing managers' principal areas of concern as: improving marketing productivity; government regulation and marketing practice; effective corporate communications with a variety of constituencies; and integrating marketing and strategic planning with a companywide marketing orientation (Greyser 1980). The current research suggests that top management has a somewhat different view of major issues facing marketing management in the 1980's.

PURPOSE OF THE RESEARCH

The research reported here was designed to determine how a sample of chief executive and operating officers in a variety of American corporations viewed the marketing function. It was intended that the interviews should reveal the major issues and concerns that these top managers see facing the marketing function.

Reprinted from the *Journal of Marketing* (Summer 1981), pp. 9–16, published by the American Marketing Association.

Frederick Webster is Professor of Marketing at Dartmouth College. He received his Ph.D. from Stanford University and has taught at Columbia University and Stanford University.

The purpose was not to gather data that would tell marketing managers how to do their job better or to determine the degree of acceptance of particular analytical and decision making techniques. Rather, the purpose was to report to marketing managers and scholars that set of issues that is currently foremost in the thinking of top managers as they direct and evaluate the marketing management function. These findings thus have some specific implications for marketing managers as they prepare for the challenges of the 1980's, and they suggest a number of areas and hypotheses for future research.

Sample and Interviews

Interviews were conducted by the author with chief executive officers, chief operating officers, or other members of top management (with titles such as Vice Chairman and Executive Vice President-Director) in a total of 21 corporations. Approximately one-third of these executives had marketing management backgrounds. While large, multinational firms dominated the sample, a number of smaller, primarily industrial products firms were also included. In addition, nine trustees of the Marketing Science Institute interviewed top management representatives of their own firms and reported the results to the author. These interviews were conducted using the same interview guide used by the author. The total sample, therefore, includes 30 top managers. The companies included in the sample are:

AMCA International Corporation
American Can Corporation
Champion International Corporation
Connecticut Mutual Life Insurance Company
DeLorean Motor Company
Donaldson Company
Eastman Kodak Company
Economics Laboratory
Emery Air Freight Corporation
General Electric Company
General Foods Corporation
General Mills, Inc.
Gillette Company
Gould, Inc.
Graco, Inc.
International Business Machines Corporation
International Paper Company
ITEK Corporation
S.C. Johnson & Sons, Inc.
Markem Corporation
Mobile Oil Corporation
Norton Company
Philip Morris Incorporated
Provident National Bank
Quaker Oats Company
Joseph E. Seagram & Sons, Inc.
Sentry Insurance
Toro Company
Union Carbide Corporation
Xerox Corporation

This is clearly a convenience sample. Although there was some attempt to obtain a sample that contained a reasonably broad variety of industries and functional backgrounds among the respondents, the sample is by no means representative in a statistical sense. Likewise, the interpretation of the research results is highly subjective and impressionistic. It is obviously improper to generalize from these findings to all top managers, and it must also be recognized that comments about the rank order of importance of issues discussed are based on the author's interpretation of comments, not on hard quantitative measures of importance. All the same, it is likely that these findings have value as indicators of current concerns and as guides to research questions and hypotheses of some importance, because of the nature of the executives interviewed, not easily accessible to academic researchers, and the companies they represent. More research with executives at this level of the corporate hierarchy was called for by Jerry Wind in a *JM* editorial considering research priorities in marketing for the 1980's (Wind 1980).

Each interview took from one to three hours. While each was conducted according to a standard interview guide, each also tended to follow its own logic. Themes once established were persistent. The respondents were cordial and open and in all instances, seemed truly interested in the research and the research questions. An important motive for participating in this research was an interest in comparing one's thoughts and opinions with others who have similar responsibilities.

These managers do not spend a great deal of time thinking about the marketing function in the abstract; they focus on the problems of their own businesses and see marketing, when asked to think about it, in that light. Thus, they were not talking about marketing as it is studied and taught so much as marketing as it is practiced, intertwined with other business problems and functions. A good portion of these executives had trouble separating marketing from corporate strategy and planning, which would seem to underscore the concern of some authors that marketing scholars in the 1980's need to examine more closely the relationships between marketing and corporate strategy, and to support the observation that academic marketing researchers have been too concerned about tactical decisions rather than truly important strategic issues (Day and Wind 1980).

MARKETING COMPETENCE MORE IMPORTANT IN THE FUTURE

Despite the tendency of the research questions to focus on issues and concerns, a large majority of the respondents found the opportunity to express positive opinions and support for the marketing function in their businesses. In those firms where marketing is well-established and professional marketing competence is longstanding, such as in the large consumer package goods firms, it is clear that marketing is the prime line management function and that marketing competence is the key competitive weapon. In some other large firms, often with a mix of consumer and industrial products and markets, marketing was seen as a critical strategic area that would become more important in the more competitive, slower growth markets of the 1980's. But, there was also a sense in many of these firms that marketing management competence would have to improve. The executives in this second group of companies, having been somewhat critical of their marketing managers' performance in the past, would typically add that the responsibility for marketing failures and disappointments had to be shared with top management – i.e., themselves. A third group of top managers, typically those in smaller companies serving industrial markets (although not all of the smaller companies are in this set and not all firms in this set are small), saw a lack of marketing orientation as a historical weakness of their firms, but still stressed that increased marketing competence was a key priority for them for the 1980's.

In summary, there was virtually unanimous agreement, expressed spontaneously in most instances, that the marketing management function was a critical strategic function and that it would become even more so in the 1980's. (Perhaps some of this represents a bias introduced by the respondents' perceptions that the interviewer was identified with the marketing function, but care was taken to avoid leading questions and to minimize this potential problem.) Several respondents expressed the opinion that the financial management orientation that tended to dominate corporate strategy in the 1970's may have created a relatively short-term orientation that left firms in a somewhat weakened position to meet market conditions of the 80's. In the words of one respondent, "This led to an overstatement of the financial considerations versus what you can accomplish with good marketing." Other writers have recently noted that management's excessive concern for short-term, financial performance has created a competitive weakness for American firms as they enter the more competitive world markets of the 1980's (Hayes and Abernathy 1980, Mauser 1980).

MAJOR ISSUES AND CONCERNS

Although a given individual's major concerns were usually expressed in ways specific to his business, there was a surprising degree of consensus in the interviews as to the major issues facing marketing management. These issues will be highlighted and summarized first, next discussed briefly, and then some underlying questions will be defined. The principal issues that were uppermost in the minds of the executives interviewed can be summarized, in order of priority, as follows:

- Marketing managers are not sufficiently innovative and entrepreneurial in their thinking and decision making.
- The productivity of marketing expenditures appears to be decreasing as marketing costs, especially for advertising media and field selling, rise.
- Marketing managers are generally unsophisticated in their understanding of the financial dimensions of marketing decisions and lack a bottom-line orientation. They tend to focus more on sales volume and market share changes than on profit contribution and return on assets.
- The product management system, and the marketing competence it brought, are no longer the exclusive properties of the firms that developed the system. For those firms who have used it the longest, the system may have become an inhibitor of innovative thinking.
- Marketing people with MBA degrees tend to think alike, to be risk averse, to want to move into general management too quickly, and not to want to pursue careers in sales and sales management.
- The acceptance of the marketing concept as a management philosophy is still incomplete, especially in smaller, more technically oriented, and industrial (vs. consumer) firms.

Each of these concerns, summarized here and asserted as conclusions supported by admittedly subjective data, has significant implications for marketing managers as well as for marketing teachers/scholars, in their roles as educators and researchers.

Lack of Innovative and Entrepreneurial Thinking

The lack of innovative and entrepreneurial thinking by marketing people was expressed as a major concern by a majority of these respondents and came up in the discussion in several different contexts, including:

- failure to provide proper stimulation and guidance for R&D and product development;
- failure to exploit and develop markets for new products developed by R&D;
- inability to define new methods for promoting products to customers in the face of major increases in the costs of media advertising and personal selling;
- a general unwillingness to stick one's neck out and take a necessary risk;
- a failure to innovate in distribution and other areas in order to keep up with the changing requirements of industrial cus-

tomers doing business on a multinational basis;

- a tendency for product managers and higher levels of management in the product management organization, all of whom have similar education, training, and experience, to approach problems in the same way;
- attempting to meet significant new competition with traditional ways of doing business;
- inability to refine and modify product positioning.

These observations about the lack of innovative and entrepreneurial thinking by marketing people echo a management concern expressed by other authors, that American managers in general have emphasized short-term financial results and developed an institutionalized aversion to risk (Hayes and Abernathy 1980). If it is indeed true that marketing managers do not often think in an innovative and entrepreneurial fashion, part of the problem must be found in the systems used to direct, evaluate, and control marketing performance. In addition, one must look to the organizational arrangements made to facilitate two-way communication between marketing and research and development. Several of the respondents noted these connections and commented that these were a top management responsibility. One chief executive observed that the budget planning and review process encouraged marketing managers to stick to the proven path; truly innovative and distinctive marketing approaches have a low probability of surviving the hierarchical budget planning process.

Marketing Productivity

The second major set of issues identified by these business leaders concerned the declining productivity of marketing expenditures in the face of increased costs of doing business and, as noted above, failure to find innovative, more efficient approaches for communicating with customers. For the large, consumer package goods marketers the issues centered around increased media costs, particularly the costs of broadcast media. For firms in such areas as insurance and business machines, the concern was for the increased costs of fielding a national sales organization, especially in those cases where unit product prices were decreasing significantly. While the use of sophisticated decision models and analytical techniques was not a major concern of these top executives, positive or negative, none of the respondents felt, when asked, that such models and techniques had made significant contributions to the efficiency of marketing expenditures. A few, however, did describe marketing experiments currently underway to assess the productivity of advertising expenditures.

These impressions held by this sample of top managers are not inconsistent with the conclusions of marketing scholars who have looked at the contributions of management science to marketing. Myers, Greyser, and Massy (1979, p. 27) in their report on the American Marketing Association's Commission on the Effectiveness of Research and Development for Marketing Management noted that "A significant amount of marketing research effort, new knowledge development, model-building, and theorizing has had relatively little impact on improving marketing management over the [1955–1980] period." It is possible that a major part of the problem is that significant developments of potentially high relevance have simply not been reported in the literature that top management reads, nor has it been adequately communicated to them by their marketing staffs. It may also be significant to note that the most frequently cited work on marketing productivity analysis is still a small textbook published over 15 years ago (Sevin 1965). (See also Bucklin 1978 and Heskett 1965). There appears to be little or no connection at the moment between marketing productivity analysis and concepts and techniques of management science developed in the last two decades.

Financial Performance

A third set of issues focussed on marketing managers' lack of understanding of the financial dimensions of corporate strategy and management decision making. The major criticism was that marketing managers do not understand basic concepts of financial management and are unable to consider the financial consequences of their decisions. As a result, they are said to concentrate on sales volume and market share objectives rather than such measures of profitability as profit contribution margin, R.O.I., and return on assets employed by business segment (i.e., product, customer, region, etc.).

There is much more to this concern than these most obvious issues. A central dimension is performance evaluation and the relationship between what marketing managers emphasize in their decision making and how they are evaluated and rewarded. A second dimension concerns how much emphasis should be placed on financial considerations by marketing managers. Some of these executives expressed a concern that marketing people could place too much emphasis on financial dimensions, worrying about things other than how to get orders, build market share, and improve competitive effectiveness, which should be their major concerns. Yet another consideration is the way in which top management has changed the signals as they relate to marketing management. In the words of one respondent. "We used to say to them, 'You get the sales and profit margins and we'll worry about how to finance them.' Not any more."

Related to this is the fact that some top managements have had difficulty assessing the tradeoffs between current, short-term financial performance – sales volume, contribution margin, and cash flow – and future, long-term financial performance – market share and long-range return on investment. As a result, their marketing organizations have been receiving confused, changing, and conflicting signals. Astute top managers do tend to recognize this problem and take a major share of the blame for the less than satisfactory marketing performance that often resulted.

The Product Manager System and the MBA

Concern about the functioning of the product management system of marketing organizations is relatively straightforward and is also intertwined with a concern about the nature of MBA-trained managers. The product manager system per se no longer conveys the inherent competitive advantage that it held for those large consumer package goods firms that innovated the concept. Their smaller and newer competitors have copied the system and hired away some of the talent developed by the leaders. As these systems mature, higher levels of management are staffed by persons who have been promoted from lower levels of the product management organization. Thus, several levels of management can have very similar training and experience. These former product managers can tend to continue to dabble in the details of product management to a degree that hinders the effectiveness of management at the lower levels.

According to some of the executives interviewed in the larger, consumer package goods firms, product managers used to come from many areas within the firm – sales, manufacturing, engineering, and others – as well as from outside. Today in contrast the standard source is the top 20 or 30 MBA programs in leading universities throughout the country. Among the opinions expressed by these top management representatives about the MBA talent being recruited by their organizations are that MBA's all tend to think alike, to approach problems the same way, to obscure a problem with excessive numbercrunching and analysis, to want to move into general management too quickly, to be unwilling to stay in a position long enough to develop competence and learn the details of the business, and to have no interest in sales and sales management careers. These are familiar concerns about MBA's, but that does not make them valid.

Not only do these concerns about MBA aspirations and performance relate to the performance of the product manager system. They also relate directly to the observation that marketing managers do not like to take risks and are unable to approach problems in an innovative and entrepreneurial fashion.

Incomplete Acceptance of the Marketing Concept

As noted earlier, there was virtual unanimity among these executives that marketing is the critical management function in their firms from a strategic viewpoint and that it is likely to become even more important in the current decade. In the most sophisticated marketing organizations (i.e., the consumer package goods firms primarily), marketing is the line management function and the marketing concept is the dominant and pervasive management philosophy. In the rest of the companies in the sample, however, there appeared to be an incomplete acceptance of the marketing concept.

In the most obvious situation, the respondent executive could point to an absence of any senior executive with clear responsibility for marketing within the organization. In these instances, there had been a history of strong production-, technical- (engineering or R&D), or sales-oriented thinking dominating the firm. Another symptom of the problem was an absence of any market segmentation strategy. There also were a few cases where the respondent executive felt that marketing weakness was due to a failure by top management to devote the necessary financial and managerial resources to the marketing task.

In the industrial products and services firms especially, and also in some of the consumer products firms, marketing and sales were organizationally distinct, with sales being seen as a line function and marketing as a staff responsibility, often associated with the corporate planning function. The marketing function in these circumstances was said to be responsible for long-range marketing planning and market development, whereas the sales function was responsible for current year sales volume and profit performance through the implementation of marketing plans through specific sales and promotion programs. Not all of these top managers would agree that the separation of marketing and sales within the organization is evidence of incomplete acceptance of the marketing concept.

One senior executive made the important observation that getting the marketing concept understood and accepted is still the biggest challenge faced by any organization, despite the fact that the concept is now more than a quarter-century old. In his extensive experience in the top ranks of both industrial and consumer products firms, he noted that marketing "tends to degenerate into a sales orientation and an exclusive concern for marketing communications." He felt that there was an inevitable tendency in industrial firms for large customers, because of their importance, to bring pressures on the firm that create a very short-term orientation and a concern for specific orders and problems. He also pointed to sheer numbers of sales personnel compared with marketing as another reason why sales tends to dominate marketing. While these particular observations are attributable to a single CEO, they capture a set of issues of concern to a significant portion of this sample.

SOME IMPLICATIONS AND SUGGESTIONS FOR FUTURE RESEARCH

Although these concerns of top management are interesting for their own sake, and suggest some directions in which the marketing profession might look to find areas for improved management effectiveness, they also point to some underlying basic issues. These issues can be phrased as questions requiring further research and discussion.

How Does Management Performance Evaluation Impact on Marketing Performance?

There has been only minimal cooperation between organizational behavior and marketing scholars as revealed in the research literature, yet some of the most interesting and important issues of marketing decision making may be those that relate to the human side of enterprise. Criticism of marketing for failure to innovate and take risks is an obvious area where behavioral issues are at the core, not technical issues of marketing science and decision making. Part of the issue here is to explore relationships between various corporate financial goals and marketing performance as they are mediated through formal and informal performance appraisal systems. While recent months have seen some discussion of this issue in the management literature, it is an area that needs a great deal more management attention and academic research. Investigators need to look at relationships between measures of a firm's innovativeness, such as the rate of new product introductions, and how management in that firm is evaluated and rewarded. Marketing scholars need to become familiar with the work of scholars in organizational behavior on such topics as risk taking, organizational structure, and innovativeness, and integrate this into their own investigations of marketing performance and organizational effectiveness.

How Serious Is the Problem of Decreasing Productivity of Marketing Expenditures?

The assertion that marketing productivity has declined needs to be tested by careful analysis of changes in marketing costs and marketing effectiveness. Expenditure patterns need to be documented, adjusted for inflation, and related to changes in market share, sales volume, profit margin, and other measures of performance. A concern for such macro issues of marketing strategy and marketing performance has largely been left to the economists. Marketers have tended to focus their attention on the nuances of inter-brand competition and the battle for market share, and have not addressed some of the broader issues defined and outlined in this study.

At the minimum, marketers should be able to sort out the effects of cost inflation per se from the rest of the equation of marketing effectiveness that relates marketing dollar expenditures to marketing performance measures, if they are to deal with the charge of declining productivity. It is not likely that most marketing managers can defend themselves adequately against this charge, whether warranted or not, because they probably could not demonstrate any relationship between expenditures on marketing activities and traceable sales and profit results. The real issue here may not be productivity per se but an inability to measure cause-effect relationships between marketing expenditures and results.

What Has Happened to the Product Manager System?

There are several projects here for ambitious marketing scholars. A first step would be simply to track changes that have occurred in the nature and scope of product manager organizations in those firms that first developed such systems. A second step could be to trace their diffusion to other firms in the consumer packaged goods area and then beyond that to industrial product firms, providers of financial services, and other types of organizations, looking for adaptations that reflected the new environment of application. A third stage could define problems inherent in the system as perceived by product managers and their superiors in the organization. These descriptive stages could provide the base from which to investigate some more subtle and complex issues such as whether these systems stifle innovation and discourage risk taking. One hypothesis worth testing is that the training programs used by companies to develop product managers (not MBA programs) tend to develop rote approaches to problem analysis and solution. The issues here clearly trace back to issues of performance evaluation.

What Are the Barriers to Implementation and Maintenance of a Marketing Viewpoint in an Organization?

The obvious wisdom of customer orientation, market segmentation, and long-term strategic thinking based on sound market information, which are the hallmarks of the marketing concept, is hardly ever questioned, yet a substantial portion of this sample of some of the nation's top managers report frustration in getting that viewpoint implemented. Students of organizations and human behavior are seldom surprised by the gap between theory and practice, concept and implementation, but the difficulties of implementing the market concept need to be understood in much greater detail. An important dimension to examine here is the central role played by the chief executive officer in promoting a marketing viewpoint, developing a truly integrated marketing organization, and supporting the marketing management team, especially as it competes with strong managers in engineering, R&D, production, sales, and other areas for scarce financial resources.

Some observers would argue that the emergence of strong strategic planning departments has weakened the position of the marketing department in the corporate hierarchy. That issue needs to be examined carefully. The conclusion will probably depend on the extent to which marketing is perceived to be a part of, if not completely absorbed by, strategic planning. Another interesting issue here is whether a strong planning function serves as a stimulus or a barrier to innovative thinking. A reasonable hypothesis would be that it is intended to be the former but usually proves to be the latter.

SUMMARY AND CONCLUSIONS

These chief executives and operating officers believe that marketing is the most important management function in their businesses, and they see it becoming more important in the future. Whether they come from a marketing background or not, they believe that the development and maintenance of an effective marketing organization is a major requirement for success in the economic environment of increased competition and slow growth that will be characteristic of most markets in the 1980's. Having said that, however, these executives are critical of their marketing managers for a failure to think creatively and innovatively and to understand the financial implications of their decisions. They see marketing costs increasing faster than the effectiveness of those expenditures. They worry that the product management system may be becoming obsolete and express frustration with the difficulties of instilling and maintaining a true marketing orientation in their businesses. As CEO's and COO's, they feel a personal responsibility for the quality of their marketing managers and their performance and suspect that they have been guilty of giving conflicting signals to the marketers in their organizations because they, the top executives, have not resolved the complex tradeoffs between short-term and long-term measures of financial performance.

Against this background of management concerns, marketing managers and teachers/scholars in the field can assess their own activities, interests, and priorities. There are suggestions here that managers need to become more willing to take risks and more innovative and entrepreneurial in their thinking. Marketing managers need to devote more attention to financial analysis relevant to their decisions, especially relating to measures of return on investment and return on assets employed. This is a question of developing the necessary knowledge of financial management concepts as well as an issue of management attitude and viewpoint.

Those marketing managers who have the benefit of an MBA education may wish, in addition, to examine their own priorities and career plans. Does the career plan allow for adequate time to develop the necessary skills and understanding of the business to progress toward higher levels of marketing and general management? Does it recognize the importance of understanding the customer, the marketplace, competition, and distribution – knowledge that can often best be gained by significant exposure to field sales situations? MBA's must be sensitive to the way they are perceived by other members of the organization and must take steps to change the basis for those perceptions as well as the perceptions themselves.

For marketing academicians, some sobering self-analysis may also be in order. Are we asking the right questions? Marketing is different from finance and production, the other areas of management decision making where operations research and econometrics have been applied so forcefully and effectively. Marketing management is still more art than science and has yielded slowly to attempts to make it more scientific. Marketing data are by their very nature less precise, and cause-and-effect relationships are usually time-lagged and hard to pin down. Yet marketers aspire to the same degree of rigor that has characterized the analysis of their colleagues in these other functions. The result may have been a significant sacrifice of relevance (Mauser 1980).

The issues identified in this research as central to the thinking of top management are, by and large, qualitative, messy issues relating to organization, management direction and control, performance evaluation, goal-setting, etc. There is a real need for marketing researchers to refocus their attention on issues such as these, not just increasingly sophisticated issues of research methodology.

REFERENCES

Bucklin, Louis P. (1978), *Productivity in Marketing,* Chicago: American Marketing Association.

Day, George S. and Yoram Wind (1980), "Strategic Planning and Marketing: Time for a Constructive Partnership," *Journal of Marketing,* 44 (Spring), 7–8.

Greyser, Stephen A. (1980), "Marketing Issues," *Journal of Marketing,* 44 (January), 89–92.

Hayes, Robert H. and William J. Abernathy (1980), "Managing Our Way to Economic Decline," *Harvard Business Review,* 58 (July–August), 67–77.

Heskett, J.L., ed. (1965), *Productivity in Marketing,* Columbus: College of Commerce and Administration, The Ohio State University.

Mauser, Ferdinand (1980), "Marketing Issues: The Marketing Fraternity's Shortfall," *Journal of Marketing,* 44 (Fall), 97–98.

Myers, John G., Stephen A. Greyser, and William F. Massy (1979), "The Effectiveness of Marketing's 'R&D' for Marketing Management: An Assessment," *Journal of Marketing,* 43 (January), 17–29.

Sevin, Chester H. (1965), *Marketing Productivity Analysis,* New York: McGraw-Hill.

Wind, Yoram (1980), "Marketing in the Eighties," *Journal of Marketing,* 44 (January), 7–9.

Robert H. Hayes
William J. Abernathy

18

Managing Our Way to Economic Decline

During the past several years American business has experienced a marked deterioration of competitive vigor and a growing unease about its overall economic well-being. This decline in both health and confidence has been attributed by economists and business leaders to such factors as the rapacity of OPEC, deficiencies in government tax and monetary policies, and the proliferation of regulation. We find these explanations inadequate.

They do not explain, for example, why the rate of productivity growth in America has declined both absolutely and relative to that in Europe and Japan. Nor do they explain why in many high-technology as well as mature industries America has lost its leadership position. Although a host of readily named forces—government regulation, inflation, monetary policy, tax laws, labor costs and constraints, fear of a capital shortage, the price of imported oil—have taken their toll on American business, pressures of this sort affect the economic climate abroad just as they do here.

A German executive, for example, will not be convinced by these explanations. Germany imports 95% of its oil (we import 50%), its government's share of gross domestic product is about 37% (ours is about 30%), and workers must be consulted on most major decisions. Yet Germany's rate of productivity growth has actually increased since 1970 and recently rose to more than four times ours. In France the situation is similar, yet today that country's productivity growth in manufacturing (despite current crises in steel and textiles) more than triples ours. No modern industrial nation is immune to the problems and pressures besetting U.S. business. Why then do we find a disproportionate loss of competitive vigor by U.S. companies?

Reprinted by permission of the *Harvard Business Review*. "Managing Our Way to Economic Decline" by Robert H. Hayes and William J. Abernathy (July-August 1980), pp. 67–77.
Robert Hayes is Professor of Business Administration at Harvard University and received his Ph.D. from Stanford University.
The late William Abernathy was Professor of Business Administration at Harvard University and also received his Ph.D. from Harvard.

Our experience suggests that, to an unprecedented degree, success in most industries today requires an organizational commitment to compete in the marketplace on technological grounds – that is, to compete over the long run by offering superior products. Yet, guided by what they took to be the newest and best principles of management, American managers have increasingly directed their attention elsewhere. These new principles, despite their sophistication and widespread usefulness, encourage a preference for (1) analytic detachment rather than the insight that comes from "hands on" experience and (2) short-term cost reduction rather than long-term development of technological competitiveness. It is this new managerial gospel, we feel, that has played a major role in undermining the vigor of American industry.

American management, especially in the two decades after World War II, was universally admired for its strikingly effective performance. But times change. An approach shaped and refined during stable decades may be ill suited to a world characterized by rapid and unpredictable change, scarce energy, global competition for markets, and a constant need for innovation. This is the world of the 1980s and, probably, the rest of this century.

The time is long overdue for earnest, objective self-analysis. What exactly have American managers been doing wrong? What are the critical weaknesses in the ways that they have managed the technological performance of their companies? What is the matter with the long-unquestioned assumptions on which they have based their managerial policies and practices?

A FAILURE OF MANAGEMENT

In the past, American managers earned worldwide respect for their carefully planned yet highly aggressive action across three different time frames:

- *Short term* – using existing assets as efficiently as possible.
- *Medium term* – replacing labor and other scarce resources with capital equipment.
- *Long term* – developing new products and processes that open new markets or restructure old ones.

The first of these time frames demanded toughness, determination, and close attention to detail; the second, capital and the willingness to take sizable financial risks; the third, imagination and a certain amount of technological daring.

Our managers still earn generally high marks for their skill in improving short-term efficiency, but their counterparts in Europe and Japan have started to question America's entrepreneurial imagination and willingness to make risky long-term competitive investments. As one such observer remarked to us: "The U.S. companies in my industry act like banks. All they are interested in is return on investment and getting their money back. Sometimes they act as though they are more interested in buying other companies than they are in selling products to customers."

In fact, this curt diagnosis represents a growing body of opinion that openly charges American managers with competitive myopia: "Somehow or other, American business is losing confidence in itself and especially confidence in its future. Instead of meeting the challenge of the changing world, American business today is making small, short-term adjustments by cutting costs and by turning to the government for temporary relief. . . . Success in trade is the result of patient and meticulous preparations, with a long period of market preparation before the rewards are available. . . . To undertake such commitments is hardly in the interest of a manager who is concerned with his or her next quarterly earnings reports."[1]

More troubling still, American managers

themselves often admit the charge with, at most, a rhetorical shrug of their shoulders. In established businesses, notes one senior vice president of research: "We understand how to market, we know the technology, and production problems are not extreme. Why risk money on new businesses when good, profitable low-risk opportunities are on every side?" Says another, "It's much more difficult to come up with a synthetic meat product than a lemon-lime cake mix. But you work on the lemon-lime cake mix because you know exactly what that return is going to be. A synthetic steak is going to take a lot longer, require a much bigger investment, and the risk of failure will be greater."[2]

These managers are not alone; they speak for many. Why, they ask, should they invest dollars that are hard to earn back when it is so easy – and so much less risky – to make money in other ways? Why ignore a ready-made situation in cake mixes for the deferred and far less certain prospects in synthetic steaks? Why shoulder the competitive risks of making better, more innovative products?

In our judgment, the assumptions underlying these questions are prime evidence of a broad managerial failure – a failure of both vision and leadership – that over time has eroded both the inclination and the capacity of U.S. companies to innovate.

FAMILIAR EXCUSES

About the facts themselves there can be little dispute. Exhibits 18-1 to 18-4 document our sorry decline. But the explanations and excuses commonly offered invite a good deal of comment.

It is important to recognize, first of all, that the problem is not new. It has been going on for at least 15 years. The rate of productivity growth in the private sector peaked in the mid-1960s. Nor is the problem confined to a few sectors of our economy; with a few exceptions, it permeates our entire economy. Expenditures on R&D by both business and government, as measured in constant (noninflated) dollars, also peaked in the mid-1960s – both in absolute terms and as a percentage of GNP. During the same period the expenditures on R&D by West

EXHIBIT 18-1 *Growth in Labor Productivity Since 1960 (United States and Abroad)*

	Average Annual Percent Change	
	Manufacturing 1960–1978	*All industries 1960–1976*
United States	2.8%	1.7%
United Kingdom	2.9	2.2
Canada	4.0	2.1
Germany	5.4	4.2
France	5.5	4.3
Italy	5.9	4.9
Belguim	6.9*	–
Netherlands	6.9*	–
Sweden	5.2	–
Japan	8.2	7.5

* 1960–1977.

Source: Council on Wage and Price Stability, *Report on Productivity* (Washington, D.C.: Executive Office of the President, July 1979).

EXHIBIT 18-2 *Growth of Labor Productivity by Sector, 1948-1978*

	Growth of Labor Productivity (annual average percent)		
Time Sector	*1948-65*	*1965-73*	*1973-78*
Private business	3.2%	2.3%	1.1%
Agriculture, forestry, and fisheries	5.5	5.3	2.9
Mining	4.2	2.0	-4.0
Construction	2.9	-2.2	-1.8
Manufacturing	3.1	2.4	1.7
Durable goods	2.8	1.9	1.2
Nondurable goods	3.4	3.2	2.4
Transportation	3.3	2.9	0.9
Communication	5.5	4.8	7.1
Electric, gas, and sanitary services	6.2	4.0	0.1
Trade	2.7	3.0	0.4
Wholesale	3.1	3.9	0.2
Retail	2.4	2.3	0.8
Finance, insurance, and real estate	1.0	-0.3	1.4
Services	1.5	1.9	0.5
Government enterprises	-0.8	0.9	-0.7

Note: Productivity data for services, construction, finance, insurance, and real estate are unpublished.

Source: Bureau of Labor Statistics.

Germany and Japan have been rising. More important, American spending on R&D as a percentage of sales in such critical research-intensive industries as machinery, professional and scientific instruments, chemicals, and aircraft had dropped by the mid-1970s to about half its level in the early 1960s. These are the very industries on which we now depend for the bulk of our manufactured exports.

Investment in plant and equipment in the United States displays the same disturbing trends. As economist Burton G. Malkiel has pointed out: "From 1948 to 1973 the [net book value of capital equipment] per unit of labor grew at an annual rate of almost 3%. Since 1973, however, lower rates of private investment have led to a decline in that growth rate to 1.75%. Moreover, the recent composition of investment [in 1978] has been skewed toward equipment and relatively short-term projects and away from structures and relatively long-lived investments. Thus our industrial plant has tended to age. . . ."[3]

Other studies have shown that growth in the incremental capital equipment-to-labor ratio has fallen to about one-third of its value in the early 1960s. By contrast, between 1966 and 1976 capital investment as a percentage of GNP in France and West Germany was more than 20% greater than that in the United States; in Japan the percentage was almost double ours.

To attribute this relative loss of technological vigor to such things as a shortage of capital in the United States is not justified. As Malkiel and others have shown, the return on equity of American business (out of which comes the capital necessary for investment) is about the

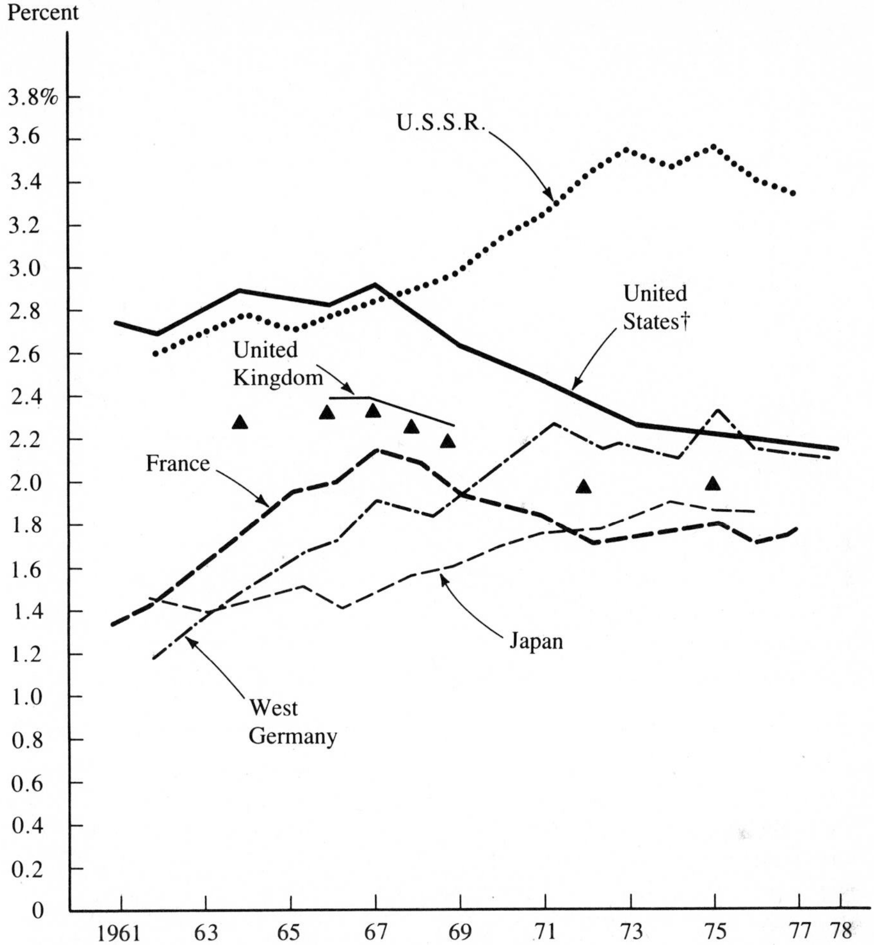

* Gross expenditures for performance of R&D including associated capital expenditures.
†Detailed information on capital expenditures for R&D is not available for the United States. Estimates for the period 1972–1977 show that their inclusion would have an impact of less than one-tenth of 1% for each year.
Note: The latest data may be preliminary or estimates.

Source: Science Indicators–1978, (Washington, D.C.: National Science Foundation, 1979), p. 6.

EXHIBIT 18-3 *National Expenditures for Performance of R&D as a Percent of GNP by Country, 1961–1978**

same today as 20 years ago, *even after adjusting for inflation.* However, investment in both new equipment and R&D, as a percentage of GNP, was significantly higher 20 years ago than today.

The conclusion is painful but must be faced. Responsibility for this competitive listlessness belongs not just to a set of external conditions but also to the attitudes, preoccupations, and practices of American managers. By their

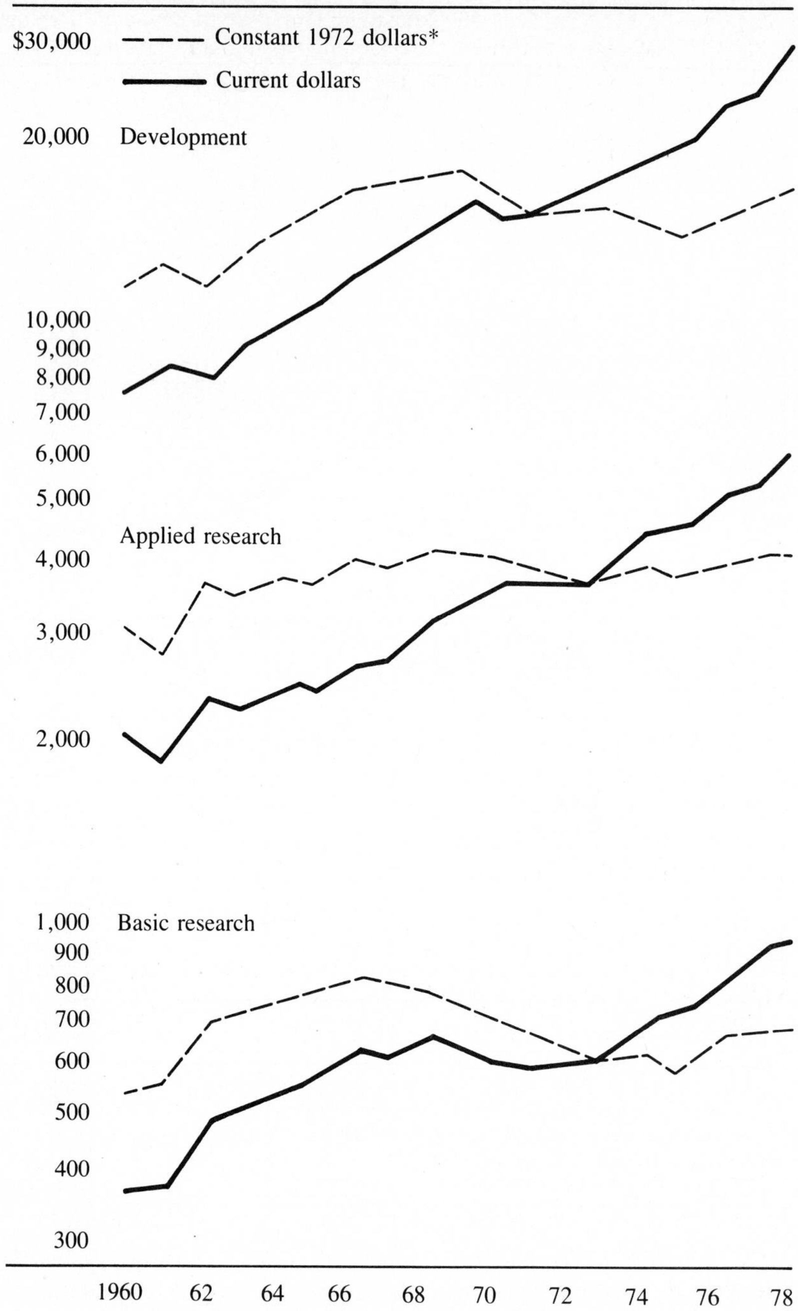

Note: Preliminary data are shown for 1977 and estimates for 1978.

* GNP implicit price deflators used to convert current dollars to constant 1972 dollars.

Source: Science Indicators-1978, p. 87.

EXHIBIT 18-4 *Industrial R&D Expenditures for Basic Research, Applied Research, and Development, 1960-1978 (in $ Millions)*

preference for servicing existing markets rather than creating new ones and by their devotion to short-term returns and "management by the numbers," many of them have efficiently forsworn long-term technological superiority as a competitive weapon. In consequence, they have abdicated their strategic responsibilities.

THE NEW MANAGEMENT ORTHODOXY

We refuse to believe that this managerial failure is the result of a sudden psychological shift among American managers toward a "super-safe, no risk" mind set. No profound sea change in the character of thousands of individuals could have occurred in so organized a fashion or have produced so consistent a pattern of behavior. Instead we believe that during the past two decades American managers have increasingly relied on principles which prize analytical detachment and methodological elegance over insight, based on experience, into the subtleties and complexities of strategic decisions. As a result, maximum short-term financial returns have become the overriding criteria for many companies.

For purposes of discussion, we may divide this *new* management orthodoxy into three general categories: financial control, corporate portfolio management, and market-driven behavior.

Financial Control

As more companies decentralize their organizational structures, they tend to fix on profit centers as the primary unit of managerial responsibility. This development necessitates, in turn, greater dependence on short-term financial measurements like return on investment (ROI) for evaluating the performance of individual managers and management groups. Increasing the structural distance between those entrusted with exploiting actual competitive opportunities and those who must judge the quality of their work virtually guarantees reliance on objectively quantifiable short-term criteria.

Although innovation, the lifeblood of any vital enterprise, is best encouraged by an environment that does not unduly penalize failure, the predictable result of relying too heavily on short-term financial measures – a sort of managerial remote control – is an environment in which no one feels he or she can afford a failure or even a momentary dip in the bottom line.

Corporate Portfolio Management

This preoccupation with control draws support from modern theories of financial portfolio management. Originally developed to help balance the overall risk and return of stock and bond portfolios, these principles have been applied increasingly to the creation and management of corporate portfolios – that is, a cluster of companies and product lines assembled through various modes of diversification under a single corporate umbrella. When applied by a remote group of dispassionate experts primarily concerned with finance and control and lacking hands-on experience, the analytic formulas of portfolio theory push managers even further toward an extreme of caution in allocating resources.

"Especially in large organizations," reports one manager, "we are observing an increase in management behavior which I would regard as excessively cautious, even passive; certainly overanalytical; and, in general, characterized by a studied unwillingness to assume responsibility and even reasonable risk."

Market-driven Behavior

In the past 20 years, American companies have perhaps learned too well a lesson they had long been inclined to ignore: businesses should be customer oriented rather than product oriented. Henry Ford's famous dictum that the public could have any color automobile it wished as long as the color was black has since given way to its philosophical opposite: "We have got to stop marketing makeable products and learn to make marketable products."

At last, however, the dangers of too much reliance on this philosophy are becoming apparent. As two Canadian researchers have put it: "Inventors, scientists, engineers, and academics, in the normal pursuit of scientific knowledge, gave the world in recent times the laser, xerography, instant photography, and the transistor. In contrast, worshippers of the marketing concept have bestowed upon mankind such products as new-fangled potato chips, feminine hygiene deodorant, and the pet rock. . . ."[4]

The argument that no new product ought to be introduced without managers undertaking a market analysis is common sense. But the argument that consumer analyses and formal market surveys should dominate other considerations when allocating resources to product development is untenable. It may be useful to remember that the initial market estimate for computers in 1945 projected total worldwide sales of only ten units. Similarly, even the most carefully researched analysis of consumer preferences for gas-guzzling cars in an era of gasoline abundance offers little useful guidance to today's automobile manufacturers in making wise product investment decisions. Customers may know what their needs are, but they often define those needs in terms of existing products, processes, markets, and prices.

Deferring to a market-driven strategy without paying attention to its limitations is, quite possibly, opting for customer satisfaction and lower risk in the short run at the expense of superior products in the future. Satisfied customers are critically important, of course, but not if the strategy for creating them is responsible as well for unnecessary product proliferation, inflated costs, unfocused diversification, and a lagging commitment to new technology and new capital equipment.

THREE MANAGERIAL DECISIONS

These are serious charges to make. But the unpleasant fact of the matter is that, however useful these new principles may have been initially, if carried too far they are bad for U.S. business. Consider, for example, their effect on three major kinds of choices regularly faced by corporate managers: the decision between imitative and innovative product design, the decision to integrate backward, and the decision to invest in process development.

Imitative vs. Innovative Product Design

A market-driven strategy requires new product ideas to flow from detailed market analysis or, at least, to be extensively tested for consumer reaction before actual introduction. It is no secret that these requirements add significant delays and costs to the introduction of new products. It is less well known that they also predispose managers toward developing products for existing markets and toward product designs of an imitative rather than an innovative nature. There is increasing evidence that market-driven strategies tend, over time, to dampen the general level of innovation in new product decisions.

Confronted with the choice between innovation and imitation, managers typically ask whether the marketplace shows any consistent preference for innovative products. If so, the additional funding they require may be economically justified; if not, those funds can more properly go to advertising, promoting, or reducing the prices of less-advanced products. Though the temptation to allocate resources so as to strengthen performance in existing products and markets is often irresistible, recent studies by J. Hugh Davidson and others confirm the strong market attractiveness of innovative products.[5]

Nonetheless, managers having to decide between innovative and imitative product design face a difficult series of marketing-related trade-offs. Exhibit 18-5 summarizes these trade-offs.

By its very nature, innovative design is, as Joseph Schumpeter observed a long time ago, initially destructive of capital – whether in the form of labor skills, management systems, technological processes, or capital equipment. It tends to make obsolete existing investments in both marketing and manufacturing organizations. For the managers concerned it represents the choice of uncertainty (about economic returns, timing, etc.) over relative predictability, exchanging the reasonable expectation of current income against the promise of high future value. It is the choice of the gambler, the person willing to risk much to gain even more.

Conditioned by a market-driven strategy and held closely to account by a "results now" ROI-oriented control system, American managers have increasingly refused to take the chance on innovative product/market development. As one of them confesses: "In the last year, on the basis of high capital risk, I turned down new products at a rate at least twice what I did a year ago. But in every case I tell my people to go back and bring me some new product ideas."[6] In truth, they have learned caution so well that many are in danger of forgetting that market-driven, follow-the-leader companies usually end up following the rest of the pack as well.

Backward Integration

Sometimes the problem for managers is not their reluctance to take action and make investments but that, when they do so, their action has the unintended result of reinforcing the status quo. In deciding to integrate backward because of apparent short-term rewards, managers often restrict their ability to strike out in innovative directions in the future.

Consider, for example, the case of a manufacturer who purchases a major component

EXHIBIT 18-5 *Trade-offs between Imitative and Innovative Design for an Established Product Line*

Imitative Design	Innovative Design
Market demand is relatively well known and predictable.	Potentially large but unpredictable demand; the risk of a flop is also large.
Market recognition and acceptance are rapid.	Market acceptance may be slow initially, but the imitative response of competitors may also be slowed.
Readily adaptable to existing market, sales, and distribution policies.	May require unique, tailored marketing distribution and sales policies to educate customers or because of special repair and warranty problems.
Fits with existing market segmentation and product policies.	Demand may cut across traditional marketing segments, disrupting divisional responsibilities and cannibalizing other products.

from an outside company. Static analysis of production economies may very well show that backward integration offers rather substantial cost benefits. Eliminating certain purchasing and marketing functions, centralizing overhead, pooling R&D efforts and resources, coordinating design and production of both product and component, reducing uncertainty over design changes, allowing for the use of more specialized equipment and labor skills—in all these ways and more, backward integration holds out to management the promise of significant short-term increases in ROI.

These efficiencies may be achieved by companies with commodity-like products. In such industries as ferrous and nonferrous metals or petroleum, backward integration toward raw materials and supplies tends to have a strong, positive effect on profits. However, the situation is markedly different for companies in more technologically active industries. Where there is considerable exposure to rapid technological advances, the promised value of backward integration becomes problematic. It may provide a quick, short-term boost to ROI figures in the next annual report, but it may also paralyze the long-term ability of a company to keep on top of technological change.

The real competitive threats to technologically active companies arises less from changes in ultimate consumer preference than from abrupt shifts in component technologies, raw materials, or production processes. Hence those managers whose attention is too firmly directed toward the marketplace and near-term profits may suddenly discover that their decision to make rather than buy important parts has locked their companies into an outdated technology.

Further, as supply channels and manufacturing operations become more systematized, the benefits from attempts to "rationalize" production may well be accompanied by unanticipated side effects. For instance, a company may find itself shut off from the R&D efforts of various independent suppliers by becoming their competitor. Similarly, the commitment of time and resources needed to master technology back up the channel of supply may distract a company from doing its own job well. Such was the fate of Bowmar, the pocket calculator pioneer, whose attempt to integrate backward into semiconductor production so consumed management attention that final assembly of the calculator, its core business, did not get the required resources.

Long-term contracts and long-term relationships with suppliers can achieve many of the same cost benefits as backward integration without calling into question a company's ability to innovate or respond to innovation. European automobile manufacturers, for example, have typically chosen to rely on their suppliers in this way; American companies have followed the path of backward integration. The resulting trade-offs between production efficiencies and innovative flexibility should offer a stern warning to those American managers too easily beguiled by the lure of short-term ROI improvement. A case in point: the U.S. auto industry's huge investment in automating the manufacture of cast-iron brake drums probably delayed by more than five years its transition to disc brakes.

Process Development

In an era of management by the numbers, many American managers—especially in mature industries—are reluctant to invest heavily in the development of new manufacturing processes. When asked to explain their reluctance, they tend to respond in fairly predictable ways. "We can't afford to design new capital equipment for just our own manufacturing needs" is one frequent answer. So is: "The capital equipment producers do a much better job, and they can amortize their development costs over sales to many companies." Perhaps most common is: "Let the others experiment in manufacturing; we can learn from their mistakes and do it better."

Each of these comments rests on the assumption that essential advances in process technology can be appropriated more easily through equipment purchase than through in-house equipment design and development. Our extensive conversations with the managers of European (primarily German) technology-based companies have convinced us that this assumption is not as widely shared abroad as in the United States. Virtually across the board, the European managers impressed us with their strong commitment to increasing market share through internal development of advanced process technology—even when their suppliers were highly responsive to technological advances.

By contrast, American managers tend to restrict investments in process development to only those items likely to reduce costs in the short run. Not all are happy with this. As one disgruntled executive told us: "For too long U.S. managers have been taught to set low priorities on mechanization projects, so that eventually divestment appears to be the best way out of manufacturing difficulties. Why?

"The drive for short-term success has prevented managers from looking thoroughly into the matter of special manufacturing equipment, which has to be invented, developed, tested, redesigned, reproduced, improved, and so on. That's a long process, which needs experienced, knowledgeable, and dedicated people who stick to their jobs over a considerable period of time. Merely buying new equipment (even if it is possible) does not often give the company any advantage over competitors."

We agree. Most American managers seem to forget that, even if they produce new products with their existing process technology (the same "cookie cutter" everyone else can buy), their competitors will face a relatively short lead time for introducing similar products. And as Eric von Hipple's studies of industrial innovation show, the innovations on which new industrial equipment is based usually originate with the user of the equipment and not with the equipment producer.[7] In other words, companies can make products more profitable by investing in the development of their own process technology. Proprietary processes are every bit as formidable competitive weapons as proprietary products.

THE AMERICAN MANAGERIAL IDEAL

Two very important questions remain to be asked: (1) Why should so many American managers have shifted so strongly to this new managerial orthodoxy? and (2) Why are they not more deeply bothered by the ill effects of those principles on the long-term technological competitiveness of their companies? To answer the first question, we must take a look at the changing career patterns of American managers during the past quarter century; to answer the second, we must understand the way in which they have come to regard their professional roles and responsibilities as managers.

The Road to the Top

During the past 25 years the American manager's road to the top has changed significantly. No longer does the typical career, threading sinuously up and through a corporation with stops in several functional areas, provide future top executives with intimate hands-on knowledge of the company's technologies, customers, and suppliers.

Exhibit 18-6 summarizes the currently available data on the shift in functional background of newly appointed presidents of the 100 largest U.S. corporations. The immediate significance of these figures is clear. Since the mid-1950s there has been a rather substantial increase in the percentage of new company

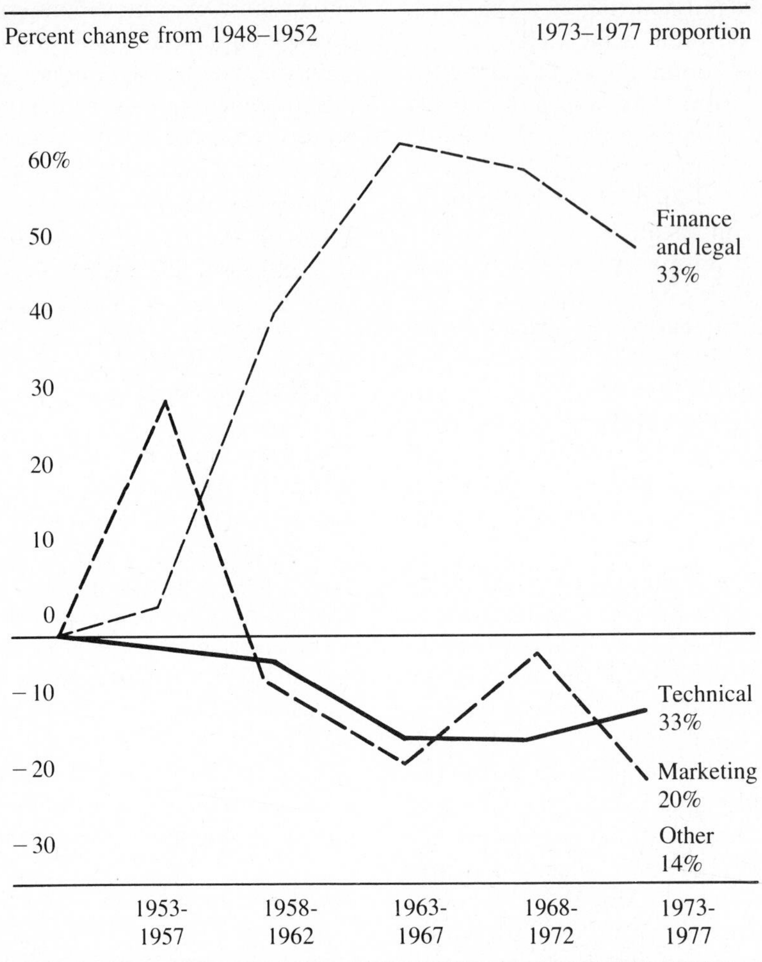

Source: Golightly & Co. International (1978). *© 1978 by Harbridge House, Inc.*

EXHIBIT 18-6 *Changes in the Professional Origins of Corporate Presidents (Percent Changes from Baseline Years [1948–1952] for 100 top U.S. Companies)*

presidents whose primary interests and expertise lie in the financial and legal areas and not in production. In the view of C. Jackson Grayson, president of the American Productivity Center, American management has for 20 years "coasted off the great R&D gains made during World War II, and constantly rewarded executives from the marketing, financial, and legal sides of the business while it ignored the production men. Today [in business schools] courses in the production area are almost nonexistent."[8]

In addition, companies are increasingly choosing to fill new top management posts from outside their own ranks. In the opinion of foreign observers, who are still accustomed to long-term careers in the same company or division, "High-level American executives . . .

seem to come and go and switch around as if playing a game of musical chairs at an Alice in Wonderland tea party."

Far more important, however, than any absolute change in numbers is the shift in the general sense of what an aspiring manager has to be "smart about" to make it to the top. More important still is the broad change in attitude such trends both encourage and express. What has developed, in the business community as in academia, is a preoccupation with a false and shallow concept of the professional manager, a "pseudo-professional" really – an individual having no special expertise in any particular industry or technology who nevertheless can step into an unfamiliar company and run it successfully through strict application of financial controls, portfolio concepts, and a market-driven strategy.

The Gospel of Pseudo-Professionalism

In recent years, this idealization of pseudo-professionalism has taken on something of the quality of a corporate religion. Its first doctrine, appropriately enough, is that neither industry experience nor hands-on technological expertise counts for very much. At one level, of course, this doctrine helps to salve the conscience of those who lack them. At another, more disturbing level it encourages the faithful to make decisions about technological matters simply as if they were adjuncts to finance or marketing decisions. We do not believe that the technological issues facing managers today can be meaningfully addressed without taking into account marketing or financial considerations; on the other hand, neither can they be resolved with the same methodologies applied to these other fields.

Complex modern technology has its own inner logic and developmental imperatives. To treat it as if it were something else – no matter how comfortable one is with that other kind of data – is to base a competitive business on a two-legged stool, which must, no matter how excellent the balancing act, inevitably fall to the ground.

More disturbing still, true believers keep the faith on a day-to-day basis by insisting that as issues rise up the managerial hierarchy for decision they be progressively distilled into easily quantifiable terms. One European manager, in recounting to us his experiences in a joint venture with an American company, recalled with exasperation that "U.S. managers want everything to be simple. But sometimes business situations are not simple, and they cannot be divided up or looked at in such a way that they become simple. They are messy, and one must try to understand all the facets. This appears to be alien to the American mentality."

The purpose of good organizational design, of course, is to divide responsibilities in such a way that individuals have relatively easy tasks to perform. But then these differentiated responsibilities must be pulled together by sophisticated, broadly gauged integrators at the top of the managerial pyramid. If these individuals are interested in but one or two aspects of the total competitive picture, if their training includes a very narrow exposure to the range of functional specialties, if – worst of all – they are devoted simplifiers themselves, who will do the necessary integration? Who will attempt to resolve complicated issues rather than try to uncomplicate them artificially? At the strategic level there are no such things as pure production problems, pure financial problems, or pure marketing problems.

Merger Mania

When executive suites are dominated by people with financial and legal skills, it is not surprising that top management should increasingly allocate time and energy to such concerns as cash management and the whole process of corporate acquisitions and mergers. This is indeed what has happened. In 1978 alone there were some 80 mergers involving companies with assets in excess of $100 million each; in 1979 there were almost 100. This represents roughly $20 billion in transfers of large companies from one owner to another – two-thirds of the total amount spent on R&D by American industry.

In 1978 *Business Week* ran a cover story on cash management in which it stated that "the 400 largest U.S. companies together have more than $60 billion in cash – almost triple the amount they had at the beginning of the 1970s." The article also described the increasing attention devoted to – and the sophisticated and exotic techniques used for – managing this cash hoard.

There are perfectly good reasons for this flurry of activity. It is entirely natural for financially (or legally) trained managers to concentrate on essentially financial (or legal) activities. It is also natural for managers who subscribe to the portfolio "law of large numbers" to seek to reduce total corporate risk by parceling it out among a sufficiently large number of separate product lines, businesses, or technologies. Under certain conditions it may very well make good economic sense to buy rather than build new plants or modernize existing ones. Mergers are obviously an exciting game; they tend to produce fairly quick and decisive results, and they offer the kind of public recognition that helps careers along. Who can doubt the appeal of the titles awarded by the financial community; being called a "gunslinger," "white knight," or "raider" can quicken anyone's blood.

Unfortunately, the general American penchant for separating and simplifying has tended to encourage a diversification away from core technologies and markets to a much greater degree than is true in Europe or Japan. U.S. managers appear to have an inordinate faith in the portfolio law of large numbers – that is, by amassing enough product lines, technologies, and businesses, one will be cushioned against the random setbacks that occur in life. This might be true for portfolios of stocks and bonds, where there is considerable evidence that setbacks *are* random. Businesses, however, are subject not only to random setbacks such as strikes and shortages but also to carefully orchestrated attacks by competitors, who focus all their resources and energies on one set of activities.

Worse, the great bulk of this merger activity appears to have been absolutely wasted in terms of generating economic benefits for stockholders. Acquisition experts do not necessarily make good managers. Nor can they increase the value of their shares by merging two companies any better than their shareholders could do individually by buying shares of the acquired company on the open market (at a price usually below that required for a takeover attempt).

There appears to be a growing recognition of this fact. A number of U.S. companies are now divesting themselves of previously acquired companies; others (for example, W.R. Grace) are proposing to break themselves up into relatively independent entities. The establishment of a strong competitive position through in-house technological superiority is by nature a long, arduous, and often unglamorous task. But it is what keeps a business vigorous and competitive.

THE EUROPEAN EXAMPLE

Gaining competitive success through technological superiority is a skill much valued by the seasoned European (and Japanese) managers with whom we talked. Although we were able to locate few hard statistics on their actual practice, our extensive investigations of more than 20 companies convinced us that European managers do indeed tend to differ significantly from their American counterparts. In fact, we found that many of them were able to articulate these differences quite clearly.

In the first place, European managers think

themselves more pointedly concerned with how to survive over the long run under intensely competitive conditions. Few markets, of course, generate price competition as fierce as in the United States, but European companies face the remorseless necessity of exporting to other national markets or perishing.

The figures here are startling: manufactured product exports represent more than 35% of total manufacturing sales in France and Germany and nearly 60% in the Benelux countries, as against not quite 10% in the United States. In these export markets, moreover, European products must hold their own against "world class" competitors, lower-priced products from developing countries, and American products selling at attractive devalued dollar prices. To survive this competitive squeeze, European managers feel they must place central emphasis on producing technologically superior products.

Further, the kinds of pressures from European labor unions and national governments virtually force them to take a consistently long-term view in decision making. German managers, for example, must negotiate major decisions at the plant level with worker-dominated works councils; in turn, these decisions are subject to review by supervisory boards (roughly equivalent to American boards of directors), half of whose membership is worker elected. Together with strict national legislation, the pervasive influence of labor unions makes it extremely difficult to change employment levels or production locations. Not surprisingly, labor costs in Northern Europe have more than doubled in the past decade and are now the highest in the world.

To be successful in this environment of strictly constrained options, European managers feel they must employ a decision-making apparatus that grinds very fine – and very deliberately. They must simply outthink and outmanage their competitors. Now, American managers also have their strategic options hedged about by all kinds of restrictions. But those restrictions have not yet made them as conscious as their European counterparts of the long-term implications of their day-to-day decisions.

As a result, the Europeans see themselves as investing more heavily in cutting-edge technology than the Americans. More often than not, this investment is made to create new product opportunities in advance of consumer demand and not merely in response to market-driven strategy. In case after case, we found the Europeans striving to develop the products and process capabilities with which to lead markets and not simply responding to the current demands of the marketplace. Moreover, in doing this they seem less inclined to integrate backward and more likely to seek maximum leverage from stable, long-term relationships with suppliers.

Having never lost sight of the need to be technologically competitive over the long run, European and Japanese managers are extremely careful to make the necessary arrangements and investments today. And their daily concern with the rather basic issue of long-term survival adds perspective to such matters as short-term ROI or rate of growth. The time line by which they manage is long, and it has made them painstakingly attentive to the means for keeping their companies technologically competitive. Of course they pay attention to the numbers. Their profit margins are usually lower than ours, their debt ratios higher. Every tenth of a percent is critical to them. But they are also aware that tomorrow will be no better unless they constantly try to develop new processes, enter new markets, and offer superior – even unique – products. As one senior German executive phrased it recently, "We look at rates of return, too, but only after we ask 'Is it a good product?' "[9]

CREATING ECONOMIC VALUE

Americans traveling in Europe and Asia soon learn they must often deal with criticism of our country. Being forced to respond to such criticism can be healthy, for it requires rethinking some basic issues of principle and practice.

We have much to be proud about and little to be ashamed of relative to most other countries. But sometimes the criticism of others is uncomfortably close to the mark. The comments of our overseas competitors on American business practices contain enough truth to require our thoughtful consideration. What is behind the decline in competitiveness of U.S. business? Why do U.S. companies have such apparent difficulties competing with foreign producers of established products, many of which originated in the United States?

For example, Japanese televisions dominate some market segments, even though many U.S. producers now enjoy the same low labor cost advantages of offshore production. The German machine tool and automotive producers continue their inroads into U.S. domestic markets, even though their labor rates are now higher than those in the United States and the famed German worker in German factories is almost as likely to be Turkish or Italian as German.

The responsibility for these problems may rest in part on government policies that either overconstrain or undersupport U.S. producers. But if our foreign critics are correct, the long-term solution to America's problems may not be correctable simply by changing our government's tax laws, monetary policies, and regulatory practices. It will also require some fundamental changes in management attitudes and practices.

It would be an oversimplification to assert that the only reason for the decline in competitiveness of U.S. companies is that our managers devote too much attention and energy to using existing resources more efficiently. It would also oversimplify the issue, although possibly to a lesser extent, to say that it is due purely and simply to their tendency to neglect technology as a competitive weapon.

Companies cannot become more innovative simply by increasing R&D investments or by conducting more basic research. Each of the decisions we have described directly affects several functional areas of management, and major conflicts can only be reconciled at senior executive levels. The benefits favoring the more innovative, aggressive option in each case depend more on intangible factors than do their efficiency-oriented alternatives.

Senior managers who are less informed about their industry and its confederation of parts suppliers, equipment suppliers, workers, and customers or who have less time to consider the long-term implications of their interactions are likely to exhibit a noninnovative bias in their choices. Tight financial controls with a short-term emphasis will also bias choices toward the less innovative, less technologically aggressive alternatives.

The key to long-term success – even survival – in business is what it has always been: to invest, to innovate, to lead, to create value where none existed before. Such determination, such striving to excel, requires leaders – not controllers, market analysts, and portfolio managers. In our preoccupation with the braking systems and exterior trim, we may have neglected the drive trains of our corporations.

NOTES

1. Ryohei Suzuki, "Worldwide Expansion of U.S. Exports – A Japanese View," *Sloan Management Review,* Spring 1979, p. 1.
2. *Business Week*, February 16, 1976, p. 57.
3. Burton G. Malkiel, "Productivity – The Problem Behind the Headlines," HBR May-June 1979, p. 81.
4. Roger Bennett and Robert Cooper, "Beyond the Marketing Concept," *Business Horizons,* June 1979, p. 76.
5. J. Hugh Davidson, "Why Most New Consumer Brands Fail," HBR March-April 1976, p. 117.
6. *Business Week,* February 16, 1976, p. 57.
7. Eric von Hippel, "The Dominant Role of Users in the Scientific Instrument Innovation Process," MIT Sloan School of Management Working Paper 75-764, January 1975.
8. *Dun's Review,* July 1978, p. 39.
9. *Business Week,* March 3, 1980, p. 76.

19 Derek F. Abell

Strategic Windows

Strategic Market Planning involves the management of any business unit in the dual tasks of *anticipating* and *responding* to changes which affect the marketplace for their products. This article discusses both of these tasks. Anticipation of change and its impact can be substantially improved if an organizing framework can be used to identify sources and directions of change in a systematic fashion. Appropriate responses to change require a clear understanding of the alternative strategic options available to management as a market evolves and change takes place.

DYNAMIC ANALYSIS

When changes in the market are only incremental, firms may successfully adapt themselves to the new situation by modifying current marketing or other functional programs. Frequently, however, market changes are so far-reaching that the competence of the firm to continue to compete effectively is called into question. And it is in such situations that the concept of "strategic windows" is applicable.

The term "strategic window" is used here to focus attention on the fact that there are only limited periods during which the "fit" between the key requirements of a market and the particular competencies of a firm competing in that market is at an optimum. Investment in a product line or market area should be timed to coincide with periods in which such a strategic window is open. Conversely, disinvestment should be contemplated if what was once a good fit has been eroded–i.e., if changes in market requirements outstrip the firm's capability to adapt itself to them.

Among the most frequent questions which management has to deal with in this respect are:

Should funds be committed to a proposed new market entry? Now? Later? Or not at all? If a commitment is to be made, how large should it be?

Reprinted from the *Journal of Marketing* (July 1978), pp. 21-26, published by the American Marketing Association.

Derek Abell is Professor of Business Administration at Harvard University. He has written extensively in the strategy area.

Should expenditures of funds of plant and equipment or marketing to support existing product lines be expanded, continued at historical levels, or diminished?

When should a decision be made to quit and throw in the towel for an unprofitable product line or business area?

Resource allocation decisions of this nature all require a careful assessment of the future evolution of the market involved and an accurate appraisal of the firm's capability to successfully meet key market requirements. The strategic window concept encourages the analysis of these questions in a dynamic rather than a static framework, and forces marketing planners to be as specific as they can about these future patterns of market evolution and the firm's capability to adapt to them.

It is unfortunate that the heightened interest in product portfolio analysis evident in the last decade has failed to adequately encompass these issues. Many managers routinely classify their various activities as "cows," "dogs," "stars," or "question marks" based on a *static* analysis of the *current* position of the firm and its market environment.

Of key interest, however, is the question not only of where the firm is today, but of how well equipped it is to deal with *tomorrow*. Such a *dynamic* analysis may foretell non-incremental changes in the market which work to disqualify market leaders, provide opportunities for currently low share competitors, and sometimes even usher in a completely new cast of competitors into the marketplace. Familiar contemporary examples of this latter phenomenon include such products as digital watches, women's pantyhose, calculators, charter air travel, office copiers, and scientific instrumentation.

In all these cases existing competitors have been displaced by new contenders as these markets have evolved. In each case changing market requirements have resulted in a *closing* strategic window for incumbent competitors and an *opening* window for new entrants.

MARKET EVOLUTION

The evolution of a market usually embodies more far-reaching changes than the relatively systematic changes in customer behavior and marketing mix due to individual product life cycles. Four major categories of change stand out:

1. The development of new primary demand opportunities whose marketing requirements differ radically from those of existing market segments.
2. The advent of new competing technologies which cannibalize the existing ones.
3. Market redefinition caused by changes in the definition of the product itself and/or changes in the product market strategies of competing firms.
4. Channel changes.

There may be other categories of change or variants in particular industries. That doesn't matter; understanding of how such changes may qualify or disqualify different types of competitors can still be derived from a closer look at examples within each of the four categories above.

New Primary Demand

In a primary demand growth phase, decisions have to be reached by existing competitors about whether to spend the majority of the resources fighting to protect and fortify market positions that have already been established, or whether to seek new development opportunities.

In some cases, it is an original entrant who ploughs new territory – adjusting his approach to the emergent needs of the marketplace; in other cases it is a new entrant who, maybe basing his entry on expertise developed elsewhere, sees a "strategic window" and leapfrogs over the original market leader to take advantage of the new growth opportunity. Paradoxically, pioneering competitors who narrowly focus their activities in the early stages of growth may have the most difficulty in making the transition to new primary demand growth opportunities later. Emery Air Freight provides an example of a company that did face up to a challenge in such a situation.

Emery Air Freight. This pioneer in the air freight forwarding business developed many of the early applications of air freight in the United States. In particular, Emery's efforts were focused on servicing the "emergency" segment of the market, which initially accounted for a substantial portion of all air freight business. Emery served this market via an extensive organization of regional and district offices. Among Emery's major assets in this market was a unique nationwide, and later worldwide, communications network; and the special competence of personnel located in the district offices in using scheduled carriers in the most efficient possible way to expedite deliveries.

As the market evolved, however, many new applications for air freight emerged. This included regular planned shipments of high value-low weight merchandise, shipments of perishables, "off-line" service to hard-to-reach locations, and what became known as the TCC (Total Cost Concept) market. Each of these new applications required a somewhat different approach than that demanded by the original emergency business.

TCC applications, for example, required detailed logistics planning to assess the savings and benefits to be obtained via lower inventories, quicker deliveries and fewer lost sales through the use of air freight. Customer decisions about whether or not to use air freight required substantially more analysis than had been the case for "emergency" use; furthermore, decisions which had originally been made by traffic managers now involved marketing personnel and often top management.

A decision to seek this kind of business thus implied a radical change in Emery's organization – the addition of capability to analyze complex logistics systems and to deal with upper echelons of management.

New Competing Technologies

When a fundamental change takes place in the basic technology of an industry, it again raises questions of the adaptability to new circumstances of existing firms using obsolete technology.

In many cases established competitors in an industry are challenged, not by another member of the same industry, but by a company which bases its approach on a technology developed outside that industry. Sometimes this results from forward integration of a firm that is eager to develop applications for a new component or raw material. Texas Instruments' entry into a wide variety of consumer electronic products from a base of semi-conductor manufacture is a case in point. Sometimes it results from the application by firms of a technology developed in one market to opportunities in another. Or sometimes a breakthrough in either product or process technology may remove traditional barriers to entry in an industry and attract a completely new set of competitors. Consider the following examples:

> Watchmakers have recently found that a new class of competitor is challenging their industry leadership – namely electronic firms who are seeking end market applications for their semiconductors, as well as a new breed of assemblers manufacturing digital watches.

> Manufacturers of mechanical adjustable speed drive equipment found their markets eroded by electrical speed drives in the early 1900's. Electrical drives were based on rotating motor-generator sets and electronic controls. In the late 1950's, the advent of solid state electronics, in turn, virtually obsoleted rotating equipment. New independent competitors, basing their approach on the assembly of electronic components, joined the large electrical equipment manufacturers in the speed drive market. Today, yet another change is taking place, namely the advent of large computer controlled drive systems. This is ushering yet another class of competitors into the market—namely, companies whose basic competence is in computers.

In each of these cases, recurrent waves of new technology fundamentally changed the nature of the market and usually ushered in an entirely new class of competitors. Many firms in most markets have a limited capability to master all the technologies which might ultimately cannibalize their business. The nature of technological innovation and diffusion is such that most *major* innovations will originate outside a particular industry and not within it.

In many cases, the upheaval is not only technological; indeed the nature of competition may also change dramatically as technology changes. The advent of solid state electronics in the speed drive industry, for example, ushered in a number of small, low overhead, independent assemblers who based their approach primarily on low price. Prior to that, the market had been dominated by the large electrical equipment manufacturers basing their approach largely on applications engineering coupled with high prices and high margins.

The "strategic window" concept does not preclude adaption when it appears feasible, but rather suggests that certain firms may be better suited to compete in certain technological waves than in others. Often the cost and the difficulty of acquiring the new technology, as well as the sunk-cost commitment to the old, argue against adaption.

MARKET REDEFINITION

Frequently, as markets evolve, the fundamental definition of the market changes in ways which increasingly disqualify some competitors while providing opportunities for others. The trend towards marketing "systems" of products as opposed to individual pieces of equipment provides many examples of this phenomenon. The situation of Docutel illustrates this point.

Docutel. This manufacturer of automatic teller machines (ATM's) supplied virtually all the ATM's in use up to late 1974. In early 1975, Docutel found itself losing market share to large computer companies such as Burroughs, Honeywell, and IBM as these manufacturers began to look at the banks' total EFTS (Electronic Funds Transfer System) needs. They offered the bank a package of equipment representing a complete system of which the ATM was only one component. In essence their success may be attributed to the fact that they redefined the market in a way which increasingly appeared to disqualify Docutel as a potential supplier.

Market redefinition is not limited to the banking industry; similar trends are underway in scientific instrumentation, process control equipment, the machine tool industry, office equipment, and electric control gear, to name but a few. In each case, manufacturers basing their approach on the marketing of individual hardware items are seeing their "strategic window" closing as computer systems producers move in to take advantage of emerging opportunities.

CHANNEL CHANGES

Changes in the channels of distribution for both consumer and industrial goods can have far reaching consequences for existing competitors and would-be entrants.

Changes take place in part because of product life cycle phenomena – the shift as the market matures to more intensive distribution, increasing convenience, and often lower levels of channel service. Changes also frequently take place as a result of new institutional development in the channels themselves. Few sectors of American industry have changed as fast as retail and wholesale distribution, with the result that completely new types of outlets may be employed by suppliers seeking to develop competitive advantage.

Whatever the origin of the change, the effect may be to provide an opportunity for a new entrant and to raise questions about the visability of existing competitors. Gillette's contemplated entry into the blank cassette tape market is a case in point.

Gillette. As the market for cassettes evolved due to increased penetration and new uses of equipment for automotive, study, business, letter writing, and home entertainment, so did distribution channels broaden into an increasing number of drug chains, variety stores, and large discount stores.

Presumably it was recognition of a possible "strategic window" for Gillette that encouraged executives in the Safety Razor Division to look carefully at ways in which Gillette might exploit the cassette market at this particular stage of its evolution. The question was whether Gillette's skill in marketing low-priced, frequently purchased package goods, along with its distribution channel resources, could be applied to marketing blank cassettes. Was there a place for a competitor in this market to offer a quality, branded product, broadly distributed and supported by heavy media advertising in much the same way that Gillette marketed razor blades?

Actually, Gillette decided against entry, apparently not because a "strategic window" did not exist, but because profit prospects were not favorable. They did, however, enter the cigarette lighter business based on similar analysis and reportedly have had considerable success with their *Cricket* brand.

PROBLEMS AND OPPORTUNITIES

What do all these examples indicate? *First,* they suggest that the "resource requirements" for success in a business – whether these be financial requirements, marketing requirements, engineering requirements, or whatever – may change radically with market evolution. *Second,* they appear to suggest that, by contrast, the firm's resources and key competencies often cannot be so easily adjusted. The result is a *predictable* change in the fit of the firm to its market – leading to defined periods during which a "strategic window" exists and can be exploited.

The "strategic window" concept can be useful to incumbent competitors as well as to would-be entrants into a market. For the former, it provides a way of relating future strategic moves to market evolution and of assessing how resources should be allocated to existing activities. For the latter, it provides a framework for diversification and growth.

Existing Businesses

Confronted with changes in the marketplace which potentially disqualify the firm from continued successful participation, several strategic options are available:

1. An attempt can be made to assemble the resources needed to close the gap between the new critical marketing requirements and the firm's competencies.
2. The firm may shift its efforts to selected segments, where the "fit" between requirements and resources is still acceptable.

3. The firm may shift to a "low profile" approach – cutting back severely on all further allocation of capital and deliberately "milking" the business for short-run profit.
4. A decision may be taken to exit from that particular market either through liquidation or through sale.

All too frequently, however, because the "strategic window" phenomenon is not clearly recognized, these strategic choices are not clearly articulated. Instead, "old" approaches are continued long after the market has changed with the result that market position is lost and financial losses pile up. Or, often only half-hearted attempts are made to assemble the new resources required to compete effectively; or management is simply deluded into believing that it can adapt itself to the new situation even where this is actually out of the question.

The four basic strategic choices outlined above may be viewed hierarchically in terms of *resource commitment,* with No. 1 representing the highest level of commitment. Only the company itself can decide which position on the hierarchy it should adopt in particular situations, but the following guideline questions may be helpful:

To what extent do the changes call for skills and resources completely outside the traditional competence of the firm? A careful analysis has to be made of the gap which may emerge between the evolving requirements of the market and the firm's profile.

To what extent can changes be anticipated? Often it is easier to adapt through a series of minor adjustments – a stepping stone approach to change – than it is to be confronted with a major and unexpected discontinuity in approach.

How rapid are the changes which are taking place? Is there enough time to adjust without forfeiting a major share of the market which later may be difficult to regain?

How long will realignment of the functional activities of the firm take? Is the need limited to only some functions, or are all the basic resources of the firm affected – e.g., technology, engineering, manufacturing, marketing, sales, and organization policies?

What existing commitments – e.g., technical skills, distribution channels, manufacturing approaches, etc. – constrain adaption?

Can the new resources and new approaches be developed internally or must they be acquired?

Will the changes completely obsolete existing ways of doing business or will there be a chance for coexistence? In the case of new technologies intruding from outside industry, the decision often has to be made to "join-em rather than fight-em." Not to do so is to risk complete obsolescence. In other cases, coexistence may be possible.

Are there segments of the market where the firm's existing resources can be effectively concentrated?

How large is the firm's stake in the business? To the extent that the business represents a major source of revenues and profit, a greater commitment will probably need to be made to adapt to the changing circumstances.

Will corporate management, in the event that this is a business unit within a multibusiness corporation, be willing to accept different goals for the business in the future than it has in the past? A decision not to adapt to changes may result in high short-run returns from that particular business. Looking at the problem from the position of corporate planners interested in the welfare of the total corporation, a periodic market-by-market analysis in the terms described above would appear to be imperative prior to setting goals, agreeing on strategies, and allocating resources.

New Entrants

The "strategic window" concept has been used implicitly by many new entrants to judge the direction, timing, and scale of new entry activities. Gillette's entry into cigarette lighters, major computer manufacturers' entry into ATM's, and Procter & Gamble's entry into many consumer markets *after* pioneers have laid the groundwork for a large scale, mass market approach to the specific product areas, all are familiar examples.

Such approaches to strategic market planning require two distinctly different types of analysis:

1. Careful assessment has to be made of the firm's strengths and weaknesses. This should include audits of all the key resources of the company as well as its various existing programs of activity.
2. Attention should be directed away from the narrow focus of familiar products and markets to a search for opportunities to put unique competencies to work. This requires a broader appreciation of overall environmental, technical and market forces and knowledge of many more markets, than is encountered in many firms today. It puts a particular burden on marketing managers, general managers, and business planners used to thinking in terms of existing activities.

Analysis of patterns of market evolution and diagnosis of critical market requirements in the future can also be of use to incumbent competitors as a forewarning of a potential new entry. In such cases, adjustments in strategy can sometimes be made in advance, which will ultimately deter would-be new competitors. Even where this is not the case, resource commitments may be adjusted to reflect the future changes in structure of industrial supply.

CONCLUSION

The "strategic window" concept suggests that fundamental changes are needed in marketing management practice, and in particular in strategic market planning activities. At the heart of these changes is the need to base marketing planning around predictions of future patterns of market evolution and to make assessments of the firm's capabilities to deal with change. Such analyses require considerably greater strategic orientation than the sales forecasting activities which underpin much marketing planning today. Users of product portfolio chart analysis, in particular, should consider the dynamic as opposed to the static implications in designating a particular business.

Entry and exit from markets is likely to occur with greater rapidity than is often the case today, as firms search for opportunities where their resources can be deployed with maximum effectiveness. Short of entry and exit, the allocation of funds to markets should be timed to coincide with the period when the fit between the firm and the market is at its optimum. Entering a market in its early stages and evolving with it until maturity may, on closer analysis, turn out to be a serious management error.

It has been said that while the life of the product is limited, a market has greater longevity and as such can provide a business with a steady and growing stream of revenue and profit if management can avoid being myopic about change. This article suggests that as far as any one firm is concerned, a market also is a temporary vehicle for growth, a vehicle which should be used and abandoned as circumstances dictate – the reason being that the firm is often slower to evolve and change than is the market in which it competes.

20

David B. Montgomery
Charles B. Weinberg

Toward Strategic Intelligence Systems

In the past 10 years, there has been a dramatic increase in the use of strategic planning tools such as BCG's growth/share matrix, AD Little's life cycle strategy, Shell's Directional Policy Matrix, and GE's stoplight strategy matrix. This has resulted from the much-needed perception by management that projecting yesteryear's trends into the future and then concentrating on day-to-day operating decisions is not enough for success. Strategic planning is rapidly being included in the definition of essential managerial tasks, and a tremendous amount of managerial interest has been focused on the techniques outlined above.

While this focus has been and should continue to be of great value, a critical point is often overlooked. *A strategic plan can be no better than the information on which it is based.* There has been little focus on strategic intelligence systems, the selection, gathering, and analysis of information needed for strategic planning. Yet it is obvious that without good market share information, a growth/share matrix will be unreliable, or that knowledge of a competitor's intentions can be the key determinant of a strategy.

This paper is designed first to present an overview of strategic intelligence systems (SIS) – their purpose and the kinds of information they gather. The second section discusses the collection of strategic intelligence. The final section provides a brief discussion of the analysis and processing of strategic intelligence.

Examples are provided describing different companies' approaches to SIS, based on a research project in which, in addition to an extensive literature review, more than 100 executives in over 30 companies were interviewed. Although corporate names need to be disguised, the firms interviewed come from a

Reprinted from the *Journal of Marketing* (Fall 1979), pp. 41–52, published by the American Marketing Association.
David Montgomery is the Robert Magowan Professor of Marketing at Stanford University and previously taught at M.I.T.
Charles Weinberg is Professor of Marketing at the University of British Columbia and received his Ph.D. from Columbia University.

broad range of industries and in most cases had sales in excess of $100 million. These examples are not intended to add up to "the" one complete, integrated approach to be copied, but rather are illustrations and stimuli for thought.

STRATEGIC INTELLIGENCE SYSTEMS – AN OVERVIEW

Purposes

It is important that the design of a SIS consider the purposes for which it is intended. Some method is needed to avoid collecting vast quantities of meaningless data, while simultaneously preventing a focus so narrow that crucial information is missed. An understanding of the purposes of a SIS is helpful in achieving this aim.

Defensive intelligence is oriented towards avoiding surprises. A company plans and manages itself on the basis of certain implicit and explicit assumptions about the world. A properly designed SIS should monitor the world to make certain that these assumptions continue to hold and to send up a flag if a major change (usually a threat) occurs. In one company which desired to implement this mode of thinking, a policy was made that unanticipated "surprises" would not be accepted as a reason for not meeting a strategic business unit's (SBU) targets. The view taken was that if an event was potentially so important, the manager should have a SIS watching for it and would therefore be able to prepare contingency plans.

Passive intelligence is designed to provide benchmark data for objective evaluation. An example of this is Dayton-Hudson's gathering of competitive retailer performance in order to reward management performance on a basis relative to competition.

Offensive intelligence is designed to identify opportunities. Often opportunities that would not otherwise be discovered can be identified through a SIS. For example, one company's strategic intelligence indicated that a major competitor was laying off R&D people of a certain type during a recession. From this, the company knew that the competitor would be unable to respond on a timely basis to a certain class of research-generated product improvements. The company used this knowledge to justify current R&D expenditures which enabled it to capture market position when the competitor was weakest. Another example was when a company's intelligence system indicated that a competitor had a serious service problem. From its own previous experience, the company recognized this as an inventory investment problem and knew that it would take the competitor about two years to straighten out its problems. Armed with this knowledge, the company substantially increased its market share.

Areas of Focus

In order to accomplish the three purposes of defensive, passive, and offensive intelligence, a SIS should focus on the following environments.

Competitive

The competitive environment is of critical importance. However, a firm should not simply monitor its current competitors, but should scan the environment for potential competitors. The price of ignoring potential competitors and neglecting to take proactive steps to avoid or blunt their effect can be extremely high. For example, Scott Paper's preoccupation with acquisitions apparently diverted its attention from the threat posed by Proctor and Gamble's potential and actual emergence as a substantial force in Scott's major paper markets (Hyatt and Coonly 1971).

Customers may also be potential competitors. One company which was heavily dependent upon a large customer analyzed that customer's incentives for backward integration. This analysis, triggered by an explicit requirement for contingency plans, suggested that, from the customer's viewpoint, backward integration was not in the customer's best interest. The next year, when the company's intelligence agents – its salespeople – learned about the customer's plans to integrate backward, the previous analysis was used to dissuade the customer from that course of action.

Technological

The technological environment is crucial not only because of its evolutionary impact on existing products but also because many innovations are introduced from outside a traditional industry – e.g., ball point pens, xerography, instant photography. Cooper and Schendel's (1976) study of 22 companies in seven industries (locomotives, vacuum receiving tubes, fountain pens, safety razors, fossil fuel boilers, propellers, and leather) found the first commercial introduction of an innovation occurred from outside the industry in four out of seven industries. The study further found that the old technologies did not decline immediately, but continued to expand in four out of the seven cases. In fact, it took anywhere from five to 14 years for the dollar volume of the new technology to exceed that of the old technology. The mode of penetration of the new technology tended to be the capturing of a series of submarkets. This study suggests that replacement technologies may emerge and develop even while companies engaged in the old technology are lulled into complacency by near term prosperity. From a strategic perspective, long-run survival requires at least a monitoring of emerging technology. In one company interviewed in our study, the corporate planning staff provides a list of emerging technologies and division managers then are required in their strategic plans to indicate the likely impact of these technologies upon their division. The purpose is not only to sensitize division managers, but the corporation as a whole to coming opportunities and threats.

Customer

Thorough analysis of a firm's customers and noncustomers is possibly the most valuable and most neglected area of strategic intelligence. Customer analysis means more than figuring out how to get Customer X to repeat or expand an order. Good customer and noncustomer analysis should reveal emerging technologies, competitive advantages and disadvantages, and new product ideas. Von Hippel's (1977) study of technological innovation in two industries found that in 74% of the 137 innovations studied, the source of the innovation was the supplier's customers. In these two industries, customers provided about three times as many new ideas as the company research departments.

Economic

The economic environment is of overriding importance to a company's future. Issues such as GNP, inflation, the money market, and interest rates are of obvious importance. Changes in the price of raw materials (e.g., oil) significantly affect most companies. It is also important to try to determine the secondary implications of these benchmark indicators. For example, a move towards balancing the federal budget may lower the amount of government-sponsored R&D forthcoming in a particular field. Government responses to continuing inflation, such as price and wage guidelines, should be anticipated and contingency plans prepared.

Examination of the effects of these issues on suppliers is also crucial. For example, many institutional food services on long-term, fixed price contracts have had profits severely hurt due to very sharp increases which their suppliers have imposed on certain products due to worldwide shortages.

Political and Regulatory

The political and regulatory environment is a difficult one as international companies are particularly aware. However, the increasing number of federal and state agencies which seek to impact on corporate policies, often with conflicting objectives, affects virtually all companies. In a recent survey of CEOs of the 1975 Fortune 500, government was cited as the number one area of concern (Burk 1976). Several companies such as Mobil and General Electric have adopted a proactive stance to try to improve the political climate within which private corporations must function (Ross 1976).

The fact that government agencies often do not correctly anticipate either the impact or the response to regulatory actions indicates the opportunity for a broadening of business/government contact. A recent example would be the FTC's de facto voiding (by unacceptable restrictions) the Bic purchase of American Safety Razor from Phillip Morris. The FTC rejected this acquisition on the grounds that it would be anticompetitive. This FTC action has been considered a remote possibility, and was apparently a surprise to the companies involved. Perhaps better intelligence would have identified the FTC as a potential major problem. Extensive advance briefing could have conceivably altered the outcome, or else the effort could have been abandoned before significant amounts of managerial time were expended.

Social

The final environment to be reviewed here relates to the rapidly changing social environment which has led to concerns with such issues as pollution control, conservation, and the rights of minorities. Again, appropriate intelligence may enable corporations to anticipate and react to such shifts in a more functional manner than has been typical of the past. As a case in point, GE claims that its environmental system led it to anticipate the emerging women's movement which enabled it to produce guidelines for women's employment one year ahead of the government (Wilson 1975). Anticipating social concerns generates a time advantage in which companies can provide positive, helpful input to government policy makers charged with establishing guidelines and regulations.

STRATEGIC INTELLIGENCE SYSTEMS IN THE STRATEGIC INTELLIGENCE CYCLE

Strategic intelligence systems can be seen as being part of the strategic intelligence cycle (see Figure 20-1). As mentioned above, most current work has been concerned with the latter stages of this cycle – processing and analysis, dissemination, and use. A SIS is essentially the feeder process to the analysis and use segments of the strategic intelligence cycle. The SIS performs two crucial functions, directing the intelligence function and collecting the information. This section will focus on these tasks.

Directing the Intelligence Function

This first stage of the intelligence cycle is concerned with establishing parameters for what information is needed, what priorities should be established, and what indicators should be monitored. Since a specific corporate application must account for idiosyncracies in the company's situation and its management style, the discussion in this section will not prescribe a formula, but rather will provide a broad outline of the issues and offer several specific illustrations.

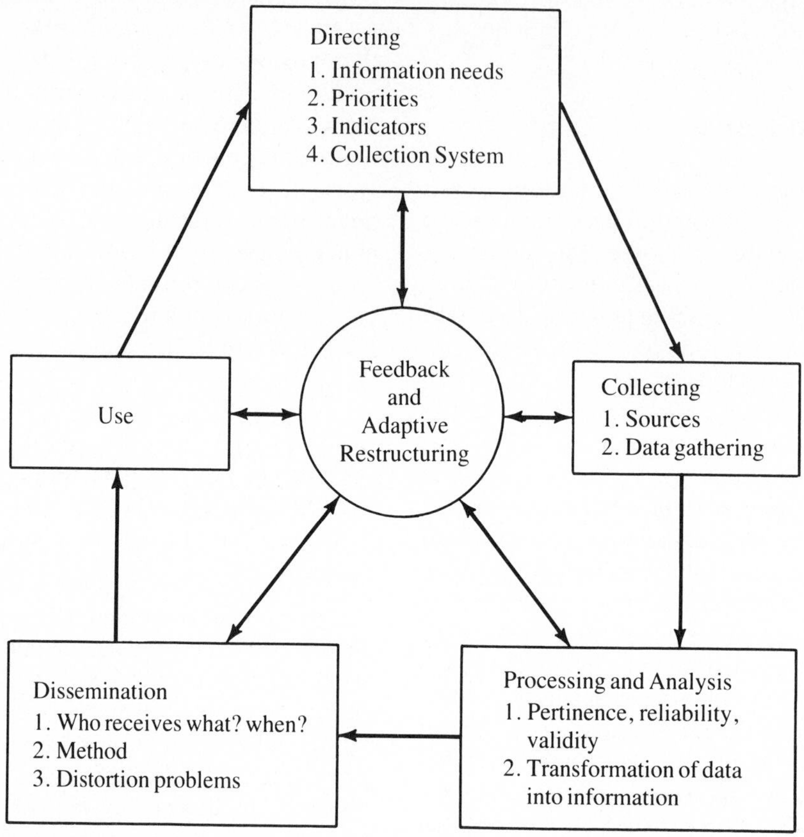

FIGURE 20-1 *The Intelligence Cycle*

Needs

There has been a substantial and praiseworthy increase in management's desires for environmental information. However, a word of caution is in order. The problem is not to generate data, but to determine what information is relevant and actionable. The emerging tools of strategic planning and analysis – product portfolios, competitive audits, etc. – provide a framework for ascertaining what information is needed and how it might be used if obtained. As the USE portion of the strategic intelligence cycle has become more sophisticated, the need for focused information also has increased.

A potentially useful framework for specifying information needs can be generated from the tripartite military paradigm of (1) areas of influence, (2) immediate zone, and (3) area of interest. The areas of influence would be the product/market segments in which the company is currently engaged. The immediate zone represents areas of competitive activity which are close to, but not directly competitive with, the company's current operations. The area of interest represents areas of potential opportunities or threats in the longer term. Generally there is less need for detail and a longer time horizon as the focus shifts outward from areas of influence.

Many companies fail to utilize available opportunities due to their exclusive concentration on their areas of influence and consequent lack of attention to their immediate zone and areas of interest. As an example of this kind of opportunity, Gillette noted that Bic, which had been a formidable competitor in the disposable lighter market, had pioneered disposable razors in Europe in 1975 (*Business Week* Feb. 28, 1977). When Gillette learned that Bic had introduced the disposable razor in Canada in early 1976, it became clear that a major potential competitor was drawing near to the U.S. market. In response, Gillette rushed its "Good News" disposable razor into production and onto the national market in early 1976. Bic followed with U.S. test markets in mid-1976, but Gillette had apparently already paved the way for its dominance of this market. It is clear that by paying attention to its immediate zone and area of interest, Gillette was able to capitalize on an opportunity it would have lost had it only focused on its domestic markets.

Priorities

A useful conceptual approach to establishing priorities may be stated as follows:

Importance of becoming aware of an event of interest =

f(1. Importance of event to the organization.
2. Speed with which the event can impact the organization.
3. Speed with which the organization can react to the event.)

Intelligence priorities should be established based upon (1) the importance of becoming aware of an event, (2) the likelihood the event will occur, and (3) the costs of anticipation and reaction. A SIS is justified if the costs of reacting to events exceed the costs of anticipating them and responding proactively. We believe that if companies were to carefully make such evaluations and trade-offs, then far more companies would attend to the development and nurturing of strategic intelligence systems.

Indicators

While a company might like to have some direct measures of a competitor's intentions, such measures are usually lacking. Hence firms must resort to using indicators or surrogate measures. For example, content analysis of corporate annual reports might be used in order to assess the extent to which a competitor's management is proactive or reactive in its approach to the world.

An indicator need not be unambiguous in its potential impact on the company. For example, if a competitor should make an unexpectedly low bid on a contract, this could be an indicator or one or more conditions such as: (1) the competitor's backlog is running dangerously low and he is getting desperate for work, (2) the persons in charge of the bid erred, or (3) the competitor has leap frogged existing technology. The indicator – an unusually low bid – may therefore relate to a variety of true states, each of which has substantially different strategic implications for the company.

Collecting Intelligence

Intelligence collection entails the notion of scanning the environments of a company in search of data which individually or collectively will provide decision relevant inputs to the firm.

Scanning can be subdivided into two subcomponents: surveillance and search. Surveillance is a viewing and monitoring function which does not focus upon a single target or objective, but rather observes multiple aspects of the environment being scanned in an effort to detect relevant changes. In contrast, search implies deliberate investigation and research. The detection of significant events in the environment by surveillance will often trigger a search for further answers. To illustrate, one of the companies interviewed learned, through its conventional competitive surveillance activities (e.g., attending to articles and announcements concerning competitors in the business press), that a major competitor had sold a particular manufacturing operation. Since the company knew from its own operations that this manufacturing activity was the most profitable portion of its own vertically integrated chain of activities, the question arose as to why the competitor had sold this operation. Two potential reasons seemed apparent: (1) the competitor, a closely held company, was in a serious cash bind and was forced to sell this profitable operation in order to improve its financial position or (2) the competitor had made a breakthrough that would render the sold technology either obsolete or at least substantially less valuable. Set against the background of data the company had, both answers seemed plausible. Learning the true answer had important strategic significance. If done for financial reasons, this could signal either competitor vulnerability or a reduction in his vulnerability depending upon the results of a further investigation. On the other hand, if the competitor had made some technological breakthroughs, then the company could no longer assume a stable environment. Clearly early resolution of these uncertainties was required. This example illustrates how a signal detected by the surveillance function of scanning can lead to questions which require search to answer.

There is some empirical evidence indicating that scanning can be beneficial. In his analysis of a contingency theory of strategy formulation, Miller (1975) concludes that successful firms tend to use more scanning. Or, to view the situation conversely, Schendel, Patten, and Riggs's (1976) study of corporate turn-around strategies in some 54 companies concluded that the original downturn typically resulted from the failure of the firm's scanning or management control procedure to identify more than one or two of the major problems confronting the firm. Thus, there can be both upscale reward and downside risk attached to environmental scanning. These results are consistent with Grinyer and Norburn's (1975) study which found that higher financial performance was positively associated with the use of more informal channels of communication and with the number of items of information used in reaching decisions.

Sources of Intelligence

Legitimate sources of intelligence are in abundant supply for the manager and company willing to apply imagination and effort in structuring a strategic intelligence system. Table 20-1 illustrates primary sources of intelligence along with selected examples of each. While it would be of doubtful value for any given company to pursue all sources on a continuing basis, a company should review a wide range of potential sources before choosing which one to use. The text will highlight some of the sources in Table 20-1 and examples of their use. Hopefully this will suggest the possibilities available to management.

Federal government. A significant recent development has been the emergence of the federal government as a source of strategic intelligence.[1] While the government has long been a source of commercially relevant information, recent amendments to the Freedom of Information Act (FOIA) have greatly expanded the potential role of the government as an intelligence source. The 1966 FOIA was amended in 1974 in order to give it greater

TABLE 20-1 *Sources of Intelligence*

Source	Examples	Comment
Government	Freedom of Information Act	1974 amendments have led to accelerating use.
	Government Contract Administration	Examination of competitor's bids and documentation may reveal competitor's technology and indicate his costs and bidding philosophy.
	Patent filings	Belgium and Italy publish patent applications shortly after they are filed. Some companies (e.g., pharmaceutical) patent their mistakes in order to confuse their competitors.
Competitors	Annual reports and 10Ks	FTC and SEC line of business reporting requirements will render this source more useful in the future.
	Speeches and public announcements of competitor's officers.	Reveal management philosophy, priorities, and self-evaluation systems.
	Products	Systematic analysis of a competitor's products via back engineering may reveal the competitor's technology and enable the company to monitor changes in the competitor's engineering and assembly operations. Forecasts of a competitor's sales may often be made from observing his serial numbers over time.
	Employment ads	May suggest the technical and marketing directions in which a competitor is headed.
	Consultants	For example, if a competitor has retained Boston Consulting, then portfolio management strategies become more likely.
Suppliers	Banks, advertising agencies, public relations firms, and direct mailers and catalogers, as well as hard goods suppliers.	Have a tendency to be more talkative than competitors since the information transmitted may enhance supplier's business. Can be effective sources of information on such items as competitor's equipment installations and on what retail competitors are already carrying certain product lines. Suppliers biases can usually be recognized.
Customers	Purchasing Agents	Generally regarded as self serving. Low reliability as a source.
	Customer engineers and corporate officers	Valued sources of intelligence. One company taught its salespersons to perform elementary service for customers in order to get the salespersons past the purchasing agent and on to the more valued sources of intelligence.
Professional Associations and Meetings	Scientific and technical society meetings, management association meetings	Examine competitor's products, research and development, and management approach as revealed in displays, brochures, scientific papers, and speeches.
Company Personnel	Executives, sales force, engineers and scientists, purchasing agents	Sensitize them to the need for intelligence and train them to recognize and transmit to the proper organizational location relevant intelligence which comes to their attention.
Other Sources	Consultants, management service companies, and the media	Wide variety of special purpose and syndicated reports available.

force. The amended Act provides that any person has the right of access to and can obtain copies of any document, file, or other record in the possession of any federal agency or department. To limit noncompliance by delay, the amended FOIA provides that requests must either be granted or denied within 10 working days in most cases. Nine specific discretionary exemptions are provided in the amended Act; exemption 4, which exempts "trade secrets and commercial or financial information obtained from a person and privileged or confidential," is of the greatest interest from the standpoint of corporate FOIA use.

It should be emphasized that the exemptions may be used at the discretion of the agency in question. Further, if the government is to use the exemptions to protect information, it must prove, if challenged, that the requested information is confidential and that its disclosure would result in substantial competitive injury to the company which originally supplied the information or would impair the agency's ability to obtain future information. Recent practice illustrates reluctance by some agencies to invoke the discretionary exemptions. For example, in response to FOIA requests, the Securities and Exchange Commission plans to release illegal or dubious payments information which had been voluntarily supplied by companies after a promise of confidentiality. Another example of this tendency to release information is the FTC's decision to make material submitted by a defendant publicly available whenever hearings are held on proposed consent degrees in antitrust or consumer protection actions.

In the years since FOIA amendments have taken effect, business has made increasing use of the FOIA as an intelligence source. The experience of Air Cruisers Co. illustrates both the threats and opportunities provided by the amended FOIA. In August 1975, Air Cruisers received Federal Aviation Administration (FAA) approval of its design for a 42-person inflatable life raft for commercial aircraft. As the largest raft ever to gain FAA approval, it constituted a substantial competitive advantage to Air Cruisers. Six months later, Air Cruisers learned that the FAA was about to release an 18-inch high stack of confidential technical documents to a competitor, Switlik Parachute Company, which had made an FOIA request for the documents. The material included results of performance tests and construction designs, which would enable Switlik to shortcut costly design, testing, and certification procedures. While Air Cruisers was able to block the FAA from releasing all of the data, it had to accept the release of some documents. This information helped Switlik design its own large raft with which it defeated Air Cruisers in a contest for an important European contract.

Additional examples abound. Consider the following which provide some notion of the breadth and type of competitive information potentially available from government agencies and departments under FOIA requests:

- A Washington, D.C. lawyer, presumably on behalf of a rival drug company, obtained an FDA inspector's report on conditions in the Midwestern plant of a large pharmaceutical company. It included such useful trade secrets as a description of proposed new products, manufacturing capabilities, and sterilization procedures at the inspected plant.
- Crown Zellerbach requested all FTC information on the Proctor & Gamble announcement that "New White Cloud bathroom tissue is the softest bathroom tissue on earth. We have been called on to prove this claim by the United States Government and have."
- Westinghouse received from the Department of Commerce 10 reports which had been paid for and submitted by other corporations on how Japanese nontariff barriers hurt sales in Japan.
- Both Honeywell and Burroughs requested

details of an $8 million Interior Department contract with Control Data Corporation.

Further evidence of substantial business use of FOIA may be found at the FTC and the FDA. In the nearly eight years between the July 1967 effective date of the original FOIA and the February 1975 effective date for the amendments, the FTC is estimated to have received less than 1,000 FOIA requests with 10% coming from business. Requests reached this same level, in the first 18 months after the amendments took effect, with almost 20% coming from business. To be sure, these figures understate total business use of FOIA because the original source of a request can often be masked by having attorneys and FOIA service companies make the direct request of a government agency. Nevertheless, the above usage data underscore the impact of the 1974 amendments on the functioning of the FOIA.

The agency with one of the largest volumes of FOIA requests and a substantial share from business is the FDA. In 1974, 2,000 FOIA requests were received by the FDA. The volume exploded to 13,052 in 1975, the year in which the amendments took effect, and doubled in 1976 to nearly 22,000. Over 70% of all requests were from industry or FOI service companies. One reason for this rapid growth has been this agency's liberal interpretation of the FOIA.

While a substantial amount of business use has been made of the FOIA, the potential has just begun to be realized. Although corporate attorneys often claim that their managers know about the operation of the Act (usually because the attorneys had circulated a memo about it), field research indicated that only a tiny minority of managers were at all well informed about the Act and its managerial significance. Managers must be made aware of both the opportunities and inherent threats in the FOIA. The opportunities for learning about competitors are amply illustrated in the above examples. On the other hand, it is imperative that managers become aware of just how vulnerable their own confidential data are when in the hands of the government. Companies should plan in advance, as part of any submission of confidential data to the government, for the defense of such data against a FOIA request from a competitor for these data. Not to do so will increasingly expose a company to the prospect of meeting a 10 working day deadline in which it must convince an agency not to release the company's data. So whether for offensive or defensive purposes, companies must learn to live with and utilize the FOIA as a source of strategic intelligence.

The amended FOIA along with the Sunshine Laws which took effect in March 1977 have broader strategic implications than competitive intelligence. Together they have the potential to reduce the uncertainty which plagues business and government relations by more fully opening government decision processes to outside scrutiny. As discussed earlier, this potential is particularly important because the CEOs of Fortune's 500 indicated that government is their most troublesome area.

Competitors. A second major source of strategic intelligence is competitors themselves. Use of strategic planning tools such as one of the variants of product portfolio analysis helps management focus on critical strategy issues. Some of the most important of these issues relate to the incentives and opportunities facing various competitors and their financial and managerial capacities for carrying out alternative strategies. In a very real sense, the introduction of these strategic planning tools has raised a host of questions relating to competitive response and reaction. A variety of intelligence sources are available for addressing such questions. Annual reports and 10Ks may provide considerable insight into the philosophy and management capability of a competitor as well as his financial capabilities and technological and product plans. For example, GE was stimulated to take a careful look at solid state controls on washers and dryers as a result of having seen both Whirlpool and Hitachi mention these devices in their annual reports (Allen 1978). The FTC and SEC requirements for line of business reporting should greatly enrich annual reports and 10Ks as a source of intelligence. Further, a careful perusal of the footnote to a competitor's annual report may reveal, for example, pension obligations which will drastically impact the ability of a competitor to respond flexibly.

The priorities and self-evaluation systems of a competitor may also be revealed by public announcements and speeches as well as in 10Ks and annual reports. Presidents often cannot resist the opportunity to "brag," and in so doing may reveal much about the firm's growth objectives, investment strategy, trade-offs between long-term and short-term results, and product/market policies. The advantage of knowing a competitor's personality was underlined in the field study at one company. This company knew that one of its major competitors tended to be extremely inconsistent in its marketing activities. This knowledge enabled the company to avoid overaction to any one of the competitor's scattered moves.

Much valuable competitive intelligence may be gleaned from scanning a competitor's personnel activities. For example, if technical personnel of a given type are being laid off, this can be indicative of the competitor's intentions and capabilities in that technical area. A company who observes a competitor taking such action may have an excellent opportunity to gain a technical and marketing edge on that competitor, as was discussed earlier. On the other hand, analysis of a competitor's employment ads may tell a great deal about that competitor's future plans. There is some evidence that such an approach may be valuable. In one case, an outside team was assigned to monitor the personnel ads of a company for one month. At the end of the month, the team reported on what they thought was going on. Not only were they accurate in most cases, but they spotted three problems in production and quality control which the firm's own top management didn't even know existed.

Own personnel. A company's own personnel can be invaluable sources of intelligence if they have been trained to be receptive to intelligence and if they are encouraged to transmit the intelligence to appropriate organizational locations. Sales call reports which explicitly encourage reporting of intelligence and debriefing reports submitted by scientists and engineers upon return from professional meetings are two of the more common methods used. In many instances, a firm's purchasing agents may play a key role in intelligence acquisition. The key issue in tapping this internal source is to sensitize personnel to the need for intelligence, train them to recognize it, and reward them for transmitting it. In this area, the firm should bear in mind Pasteur's statement that ". . . chance favors the prepared mind."

In summary, most firms have a large number of potential intelligence sources. Some of these are common and widely used, such as trade association data, but others, such as studies of competitor's want ads, may be less so. The proper choice of intelligence sources depends not only upon the data that it provides, but also how it interrelates with other aspects of the company's strategic intelligence system.

ANALYSIS AND PROCESSING OF STRATEGIC INTELLIGENCE

A firm and its managers use a variety of approaches to combine, sort, and process the environmental *data* in order to produce timely and relevant *information* for forming, monitoring, evaluating, and modifying strategy. The strategic data management problem is complicated by the considerable emphasis placed on personal communications by senior managers. For example, Rohlf and Wish (1974) found that managers spend an average of six hours a day in personal or telephone communications. Further, the unstructured nature of many strategic decisions, especially in the problem finding state, increases the difficulty of transforming data into strategic information.

Despite these difficulties, the process of intelligence derivation is a critical one in the formulation of strategies. After data are generated or enter the system, they should be evaluated. The formal evaluation of data, although frequently carried out in military intelligence systems, appears to be rarely done by business.

Evaluation of Data

Evaluation includes determining the pertinence, reliability, and validity (accuracy) of data obtained. Evaluation of pertinence can include pertinence to a number of people in the organization and specifically determines if the data are relevant to the company, if needed immediately, and, if so, by whom.

Reliability is an evaluation of the source or agency by which the data are gathered or transmitted. The principal basis for judging reliability is previous experience with a source. This is particularly relevant for businesses which use such recurrent sources as the sales force, security analysts, and suppliers. Although it would seem that a "track record" of these sources can be built up over time, for example, to identify the biases of salesmen in reporting only certain events or in being overly optimistic, such practices were rarely observed in the field interviews. It should be noted that suppliers recognize that they are being used as a source of data and try to draw a line between "providing something of value, but not too much."

Validity or accuracy means the probable truth of the data itself. Methods for assessing validity include comparison with other data which may be available from other sources, searching for associated indicators, and face validity. For example in a long-term policy study for the Environmental Protection Agency, 16 different futures studies were reviewed in a fixed format as one approach to convergent validity (Elgin, MacMichael, and Schwartz 1975).

Transformation of Data into Information

The six transformation functions—transmission, accumulation, aggregation, analysis, pattern recognition, and mixing—by which data can become information vary considerably in complexity (See Table 20-2). Although the six functions overlap, each has at its core a distinctive transformation. Obviously, the functions do not necessarily occur sequentially and can occur at several levels in an organization.

Transmission

Transmission, conceptually a very simple notion, is the movement of data from one point or person in the organization to another. Transmission can also occur simultaneously with some of the other processing functions. However, data which are received through many corporate entry points are often not communicated to those who can use them most effectively. In consequence, transmission should be at least conceptually considered as a separate function. Companies need to develop methods to facilitate ("force") the transmission of information by providing incentives for the reporting of certain types of information or by providing ways for a manager to know the information needs of others.

Accumulation

Accumulation is the storage of data in such a way that it can be retrieved by the managers

TABLE 20-2 *Six Transformation Functions*

Name	Description	Brief Examples
1. Transmission	1. Moving data from one point to another	1a) Manager in one company who receives information personally or by telephone from line managers and distributes information personally or by weekly newsletters 1b) Highly mechanized interactive computer system to make data base reachable by numerous managers
2. Accumulation	2. Storing data in one place; implies some notion of retrievability	2a) Corporate libraries or computer systems 2b) Not frequently observed in practice, managers tend to keep data in their heads or in individualized data bases ("little black book")
3. Aggregation	3. Many data points brought together into a smaller set which is usually more easily accessed	3a) Use of computer program to reduce thick Nielsen reports to much shorter documents 3b) Page length limitation on planning documents
4. Analysis	4. The analysis, usually formal, of data in order to seek and measure relations	4a) Use of econometric consulting firms to provide forecasts of the economy 4b) Use of Shell's Directional Policy Matrix to locate businesses for a portfolio analysis
5. Mix	5. Passing of data around to a variety of managers looking for possible links. The data is often not well ordered	5a) CEO insists on plans which show multiple inputs at each phase 5b) Open planning meetings in which managers must give and defend plans before colleagues
6. Pattern Recognition	6. A more informal, less analytic process than analysis (4) in which patterns or relations are sought. Can be a result of the other five functions described	6a) Combining plant closing, financial and product change information to recognize a competitor is short of cash 6b) Special purpose competitor studies & role playing or the use of adversary teams

in a company. A substantial data base provides a source from which the organization can learn about itself and its environment. This is particularly true when attempting to resolve unstructured strategic problems, for which information needs are difficult to define beforehand.

The field interviews revealed limited amounts of accumulation of strategic environmental data. Several reasons explain why this accumulation does not take place. First, because the data often originate from the personal sources of a manager, the effort required to record it and enter it into a more formal and permanent system may not seem worthwhile, especially for "soft data." The remedies would seem to be easing the transmission process and increasing the rewards. In one company, the central collector receives data varying from rumors to documented facts by telephone or in person. The central collector then alerts line managers on an individual basis of particularly significant events, publishes a weekly newsletter, prepares special reports, and maintains files on competitors. There are substantial behavioral advantages to this system. The managers do not fill out forms, they input data verbally and are rewarded, in turn, by receiving pertinent information.

Second, information accumulation may not take place because managers do not think the system works well. For instance, computer-based systems often concentrate on the easily quantified factors in formats which reflect the needs of accounting systems rather than those of operating or strategy managers.

Third, managers may have incentives for not wanting others to have their full data set. In a corporate budgeting system, a manager may be able to present plans which maximize his or her capital allocation or limit his or her performance goals based on his or her unique knowledge of the data.

One consumer durables manufacturer has a particularly interesting central collection system based on a substantial disaggregated data base which includes such factors as factory shipments, survey data on consumer habits, and construction reports. The system is unique because rather than distribution of a large number of reports (as had been done in the past), the main way to use it is for managers to visit the central facility, which is located in the marketing department. The location was chosen to provide user access and the overall style is casual and user oriented to create an environment "painless and pleasant for the harried marketing executive" (from a company brochure).

Aggregation

Aggregation is the function in which many data points are collapsed into a smaller set of pertinent information. It is the first of the functions in which something is done to the data beyond making it available to managers. Summarization of environmental data occurs in virtually all companies, although with various degrees of care and attention. Given the massive amounts of data potentially available and a manager's limited time for reviewing information, aggregation is a vital function.

Corporate staff groups are often responsible for the summarization of economic trends. In a relatively smaller number of companies, social, political, and regulatory factors are summarized as well. Thus, on a macro or corporate level, summarization or aggregation of data takes place. However, only limited aggregation of environmental data, especially competitive data, was observed on a SBU or product-market basis except as part of the annual planning process or, in a few cases, when special purpose competitive assessment reports were made.

Analysis

The analysis of data is a formal process which attempts to find and measure relations among variables. Although at times it may draw heavily on mathematics and numeric procedures, it is a logical and not a mathematical process. A number of companies employ econometric consulting firms and others do similar work on their own. Many consumer goods companies employ analytical approaches to measure relationships between sales and marketing mix variables. In several companies, the main focus of analysis is on predicting industry capacity.

The level of analysis of environmental data varies extensively across companies. For example, in some companies, competitive balance sheets are used primarily as a benchmark or "scoreboard" to rate the company as compared to its competition. In others, it is used more aggressively to anticipate threats or provide opportunities. As an illustration, when one company noticed that a competitor was highly leveraged and consequently would be unable to finance new product development, it gained considerable market share by improving its own product.

Pattern Recognition

Pattern recognition, although not as structured or formal as the analysis process just discussed, also attempts to find patterns or relations among variables. Human abilities to perceive and determine patterns among disparate sets of information and data are the critical distinctive elements in the process of pattern recognition. Although computerized systems can be of great assistance, in strategic analysis the "lack of simple alpha-numeric indicators, combined with enormous textural complexity, suggests that [pattern recognition] . . . will not be trival or automatic in the foreseeable future" (Webb 1969, p. 10). An example of pattern recognition occurred in one company when the information that a competitor was closing a plant and changing his product line was combined with balance sheet analysis to realize that the competitor was short of cash. This, of course, left the competitor vulnerable to a number of aggressive strategies. The generation and use of in-depth competitive assessment reports, the preparation of strategy documents from the viewpoint of a major competitor, and the formation of in-house competitor teams exemplify different organizational approaches to pattern recognition.

Mixing

The unstructured and often unstable nature of strategic problems requires that an additional transformation function be defined which brings together the apparently unrelated data spread throughout an organization in order to identify linkages. This function is termed "mixing."

A somewhat analogous notion is Cohen, March, and Olsen's (1972) garbage can model. In that conceptualization, an organization is conceived of as a collection of problems and solutions in which organizational members find ways either to enrich the collection of problems and solutions or to find links between the problems and solutions. The approach formulated here emphasizes two major factors. First, problems and solutions are viewed as being dynamic so that "windows" as to when linkages can be established are limited. Thus, problems and opportunities should be viewed as moving through a container rather than residing in a collection. Second, an active approach can be taken to ensure that problems and solutions are actively interchanged or mixed within an organization.

Companies appear to use a variety of techniques to force mixing including participative planning meetings across divisions and organizational levels, weekly senior executive sessions with invited presentations, and rejection of plans which do not reflect mixing. For example, in one company, the CEO rejected divisional plans out of hand because they did not show any evidence of interaction across divisions. In another, marketing managers were asked to write the finance plan, financial managers were asked to write the production plan, etc. In large companies, facing a broad variety of strategic options, mixing can help the company to become aware of the range of opportunties and threats facing it and to develop synergistic responses.

SUMMARY AND PERSPECTIVES

As more organizations implement strategic planning and management activities, there will be an increasing need for strategic intelligence systems which can help managers to learn about the important environments with which their organization interrelates and to become aware of threats and opportunities that are posed.

The construction of viable strategic intelligence systems is exceedingly complex because of the unstructured nature of strategic decisions, the difficultly of separating out important and relevant information from the vast amounts of data accessible to the manager, and the reliance of managers on personal information sources. As would be expected, in most of the companies interviewed tactical information systems were better articulated than strategic ones. On the other hand, a number of companies have developed effective means of learning about their environments and, most importantly, have implemented strategic decision systems which allow them to capitalize on opportunities and to defend themselves against threats. This article has developed a framework for examining intelligence systems which is sensitive to the character of the strategic process.

For a strategic intelligence system to be useful, a company must have a real commitment to strategic planning. Otherwise, the planning process, if carried out at all, becomes only an exercise and managers appear to place limited effort towards gathering and communicating accurate, relevant intelligence. There are a number of different organizational policies which can be utilized to promote the transformation of data into information and the utilization of this information. Elaboration on this issue is beyond the scope of this article. However, only in rare circumstances do effective intelligence systems emerge without organizational incentives to encourage their operation.

There appear to be a number of asymmetries in managers' perceptions about information collection. Four, in particular, stand out. (1) Companies tend to believe that their competitors nearly always detect and rapidly decide how to respond to company actions such as a price change. This perception persists in spite of knowledge of substantial delays in their own detection and response decision time in reacting to the competitors. This can lead a company to rescind prematurely an effort to lead a price increase based upon a belief competitors won't follow, when in fact the lack of response by the competitor may merely be symptomatic of a poor and slow intelligence system. (2) The government is viewed as an extensive collector of information, but not as a source; the discussion of the FOIA indicated how companies could access data held by the government. (3) Conversely, to the case of the government, suppliers are more often viewed as a source of information about competitors than as a source to the competitors. (4) Companies send engineers and managers to meetings with instructions to gather more information than they reveal; it would seem unlikely for this outcome to occur for all companies involved. These asymmetries, which obviously are not shared by all managers, suggest some of the potential available from a review of an organization's procedures to gather and process strategic data.

Information systems are a means to an end – decision making which leads to more profitable results. The concepts and structures for strategic intelligence systems discussed in this article are designed to help organizations make more profitable strategic decisions.

NOTE

1. The following discussion of the Freedom of Information Act is based on Montgomery, Peters, and Weinberg (1978).

REFERENCES

Allen, Michael G. (1978), "Strategic Planning With a Competitive Focus," *The McKinsey Quarterly* (Autumn), 2–13.

Burk, Charles G. (1976), "A Group Profile of the Fortune 500 Chief Executives," *Fortune,* 19 (May), 173.

Business Week (1977), "Gillette: after the Diversification that Failed," (February 28), 58.

Cohen, Michael D., James G. March, and Johan P. Olsen (1972), "A Garbage Can Model of Organizational Choice," *Administrative Science Quarterly* (March), 1.

Cooper, A. C. and D. Schendel (1976), "Strategic Responses to Technological Threats," *Business Horizons,* 19 (February), 61.

Elgin, D. S., D. C. MacMichael, and P. Schwartz (1975), "Alternative Futures for Environmental Policy Planning: 1975–2000," Environmental Protection Agency (October).

Grinyer, P. H. and D. Norburn (1975), "Planning for Existing Markets: Perceptions of Executives and Financial Performance," *Journal of the Royal Statistical Society A,* 138 (Part 1), 70.

Hyatt, J. and J. Coonly (1971), "How Proctor & Gamble Put the Big Squeeze on Scott Paper Company," *The Wall Street Journal* (October 20), 1.

Miller, D. (1975), "Toward a Contingency Theory of Strategy Formulation," paper presented at 35th annual Academy of Management Meeting (August).

Montgomery, David B., Anne H. Peters, and Charles B. Weinberg (1978), "The Freedom of Information Act: Strategic Opportunities and Threats," *Sloan Management Review,* 19 (Winter), 1–13.

Rohlf, J. and M. Wish (1974), "Analysis of Demand for Video Communication," Telecommunication Policy Research Conference, Airlie, Virginia (April 18).

Ross, I. (1976), "Public Relations Isn't Kid Gloves Stuff at Mobil," *Fortune,* 93 (September), 106.

Schendel, D. E., G. R. Patten, and J. Riggs (1976), "Corporate Turnaround Strategies: A Study of Profit, Decline, and Recovery," *Journal of General Management,* 3 (Spring), 3.

von Hippel, E. (1977), "Has a Customer Already Developed Your Next Product?" *Sloan Management Review,* 18 (Winter), 63.

Webb, Eugene J. (1969), "Individual and Organizational Forces Influencing the Interpretation of Indicators," unpublished working paper, Stanford: Graduate School of Business, Stanford University (April), 10.

Wilson, I. (1975), "Does GE Really Plan Better," *MBA,* 9 (November), 42.

Philip Kotler
William Gregor
William Rogers

21

The Marketing Audit Comes of Age

Comparing the marketing strategies and tactics of business units today versus ten years ago, the most striking impression is one of marketing strategy obsolescence. Ten years ago U.S. automobile companies were gearing up for their second postwar race to produce the largest car with the highest horsepower. Today companies are selling increasing numbers of small and medium-size cars and fuel economy is a major selling point. Ten years ago computer companies were introducing ever-more powerful hardware for more sophisticated uses. Today they emphasize mini- and micro-computers and software.

It is not even necessary to take a ten-year period to show the rapid obsolescence of marketing strategies. The growth economy of 1950–1970 has been superseded by a volatile economy which produces new strategic surprises almost monthly. Competitors launch new products, customers switch their business, distributors lose their effectiveness, advertising costs skyrocket, government regulations are announced, and consumer groups attack. These changes represent both opportunities and problems and may demand periodic reorientations of the company's marketing operations.

Many companies feel that their marketing operations need regular reviews and overhauls but do not know how to proceed. Some companies simply make many small changes that are economically and politically feasible, but fail to get to the heart of the matter. True, the company develops an annual marketing plan but management normally does not take a deep and objective look at the marketing strategies, policies, organizations, and operations on a recurrent basis. At the other extreme, companies install aggressive new top marketing management hoping to shake down the marketing cobwebs. In between there must be more orderly ways to reorient marketing operations to changed environments and opportunities.

Reprinted from "The Marketing Audit Comes of Age," by Philip Kotler, William Gregor, and William Rogers, *Sloan Management Review,* Vol. 18, No. 2, pp. 25–43, by permission of the publisher.
Philip Kotler is Harold T. Martin Professor of Marketing at Northwestern University and received his Ph.D. from M.I.T.
William Gregor and William Rogers are both Management Consultants with The Management Analysis Center.

ENTER THE MARKETING AUDIT

One hears more talk today about the *marketing audit* as being the answer to evaluating marketing practice just as the public accounting audit is the tool for evaluating company accounting practice. This might lead one to conclude that the marketing audit is a new idea and also a very distinct methodology. Neither of these conclusions is true.

The marketing audit as an idea dates back to the early fifties. Rudolph Dallmeyer, a former executive in Booz-Allen-Hamilton, remembers conducting marketing audits as early as 1952. Robert J. Lavidge, President of Elrick and Lavidge, dates his firm's performance of marketing audits to over two decades ago. In 1959, the American Management Association published an excellent set of papers on the marketing audit under the title *Analyzing and Improving Marketing Performance,* Report No. 32, 1959. During the 1960s, the marketing audit received increasing mention in the lists of marketing services of management consultant firms. It was not until the turbulent seventies, however, that it began to penetrate management awareness as a possible answer to its needs.

As for whether the marketing audit has reached a high degree of methodological sophistication, the answer is generally no. Whereas two certified public accountants will handle an audit assignment using approximately the same methodology, two marketing auditors are likely to bring different conceptions of the auditing process to their task. However, a growing consensus on the major characteristics of a marketing audit is emerging and we can expect considerable progress to occur in the next few years.

In its fullest form and concept, a marketing audit has four basic characteristics. The first and most important is that it is *broad* rather than narrow in focus. The term "marketing audit" should be reserved for a *horizontal (or comprehensive) audit* covering the company's marketing environment, objectives, strategies, organization, and systems. In contrast a *vertical (or indepth) audit* occurs when management decides to take a deep look into some key marketing function, such as sales force management. A vertical audit should properly be called by the function that is being audited, such as a sales force audit, an advertising audit, or a pricing audit.

A second characteristic feature of a marketing audit is that it is conducted by someone who is *independent* of the operation that is being evaluated. There is some loose talk about self-audits, where a manager follows a checklist of questions concerning his own operation to make sure that he is touching all the bases.[1] Most experts would agree, however, that the self-audit, while it is always a useful step that a manager should take, does not constitute a *bona fide* audit because it lacks objectivity and independence. Independence can be achieved in two ways. The audit could be an *inside audit* conducted by a person or group inside the company but outside of the operation being evaluated. Or it could be an *outside audit* conducted by a management consulting firm or practitioner.

The third characteristic of a marketing audit is that it is *systematic.* The marketing auditor who decides to interview people inside and outside the firm at random, asking questions as they occur to him, is a "visceral" auditor without a method. This does not mean that he will not come up with very useful findings and recommendations; he may be very insightful. However, the effectiveness of the marketing audit will normally increase to the extent that it incorporates an orderly sequence of diagnostic steps, such as there are in the conduct of a public accounting audit.

A final characteristic that is less intrinsic to a marketing audit but nevertheless desirable is that it be conducted *periodically.* Typically, evaluations of company marketing efforts are commissioned when sales have turned down sharply, sales force morale has fallen, or other problems have occurred at the company. The fact is, however, that companies are thrown into a crisis partly because they have failed to review their assumptions and to change them during good times. A marketing audit conducted when things are going well can often help make a good situation even better and also indicate changes needed to prevent things from turning sour.

The above ideas on a marketing audit can be brought together into a single definition:

> A marketing audit is a *comprehensive, systematic, independent,* and *periodic* examination of a company's–or business unit's–marketing environment, objectives, strategies, and activities with a view of determining problem areas and opportunities and recommending a plan of action to improve the company's marketing performance.

WHAT IS THE MARKETING AUDIT PROCESS?

How is a marketing audit performed? Marketing auditing follows the simple three-step procedure shown in Figure 21-1.

Setting the Objectives and Scope

The first step calls for a meeting between the company officer(s) and a potential auditor to explore the nature of the marketing operations and the potential value of a marketing audit. If the company officer is convinced of the potential benefits of a marketing audit, he and the auditor have to work out an agreement on the objectives, coverage, depth, data sources, report format, and the time period for the audit.

Consider the following actual case. A plumbing and heating supplies wholesaler with three branches invited a marketing consultant to prepare an audit of its overall marketing policies and operations. Four major objectives were set for the audit:

- determine how the market views the company and its competitors,
- recommend a pricing policy
- develop a product evaluation system,
- determine how to improve the sales activity in terms of the deployment of the sales force, the level and type of compensation, the measurement of performance, and the addition of new salesmen.

Furthermore, the audit would cover the marketing operations of the company as a whole and the operations of each of the three branches, with particular attention to one of the branches. The audit would focus on the marketing operations but also include a review of the purchasing and inventory systems since they intimately affect marketing performance.

The company would furnish the auditor with published and private data on the industry. In addition, the auditor would contact suppliers of manufactured plumbing supplies for additional market data and contact wholesalers outside the company's market area to gain further information on wholesale plumbing and heating operations. The auditor would interview all the key corporate and branch management, sales and purchasing personnel, and would ride with several of those salesmen on their calls. Finally, the

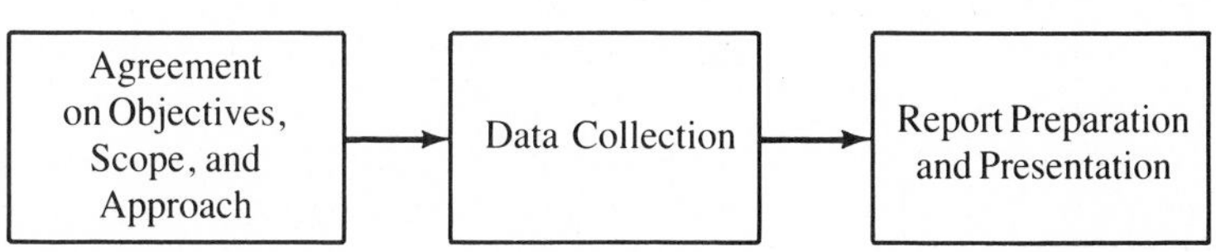

FIGURE 21-1 *Steps in a Marketing Audit*

auditor would interview a sample of the major plumbing and heating contractor customers in the market areas of the two largest branches.

It was decided that the report format would consist of a draft report of conclusions and recommendations to be reviewed by the president and vice-president of marketing, and then delivered to the executive committee which included the three branch managers. Finally, it was decided that the audit findings would be ready to present within six to eight weeks.

Gathering the Data

The bulk of an auditor's time is spent in gathering data. Although we talk of a single auditor, an audit team is usually involved when the project is large. A detailed plan as to who is to be interviewed by whom, the questions to be asked, the time and place of contact, and so on, has to be carefully prepared so that auditing time and cost are kept to a minimum. Daily reports of the interviews are to be written up and reviewed so that the individual or team can spot new areas requiring exploration, while data are still being gathered.

The cardinal rule in data collection is not to rely solely for data and opinion on those being audited. Customers often turn out to be the key group to interview. Many companies do not really understand how their customers see them and their competitors, nor do they fully understand customer needs. This is vividly demonstrated in Table 21-1, which shows the results of asking end users, company salesmen, and company marketing personnel for their views of the importance of different factors affecting the user's selection of a manufacturer. According to the table, customers look first and foremost at the quality of technical support services, followed by prompt delivery, followed by quick response to customer needs. Company salesmen think that company reputation, however, is the most important factor in customer choice, followed by quick response to customer needs and technical support services. Those who plan marketing strategy have a different opinion. They see company price and product quality as the two major factors in buyer choice, followed by quick response to customer needs. Clearly, there is lack of consonance between what buyers say they want, what company salesmen are responding to, and what company marketing planners are emphasizing. One of the major contributions of marketing auditors is to expose these discrepancies and suggest ways to improve marketing consensus.

TABLE 21-1 *Factors in the Selection of a Manufacturer*

Factor	All Users Rank	Company Salesmen Rank	Company Nonsales Personnel Rank
Reputation	5	1	4
Extension of Credit	9	11	9
Sales Representatives	8	5	7
Technical Support Services	1	3	6
Literature and Manuals	11	10	11
Prompt Delivery	2	4	5
Quick Response to Customer Needs	3	2	3
Product Price	6	6	1
Personal Relationships	10	7	8
Complete Product Line	7	9	10
Product Quality	4	8	2

Source: Marketing and Distribution Audit, A Service of Decision Sciences Corporation, p. 32. Used with permission of the Decision Sciences Corporation.

Preparing and Presenting the Report

The marketing auditor will be developing tentative conclusions as the data come in. It is a sound procedure for him to meet once or twice with the company officer before the data collection ends to outline some initial findings to see what reactions and suggestions they produce.

When the data gathering phase is over, the marketing auditor prepares notes for a visual and verbal presentation to the company officer or small group who hired him. The presentation consists of restating the objectives, showing the main findings, and presenting the major recommendations. Then, the auditor is ready to write the final report, which is largely a matter of putting the visual and verbal material into a good written communication. The company officer(s) will usually ask the auditor to present the report to other groups in the company. If the report calls for deep debate and action, the various groups hearing the report should organize into subcommittees to do follow-up work with another meeting to take place some weeks later. The most valuable part of the marketing audit often lies not so much in the auditor's specific recommendations but in the process that the managers of the company begin to go through to assimilate, debate, and develop their own concept of the needed marketing action.

MARKETING AUDIT PROCEDURES FOR AN INSIDE AUDIT

Companies that conduct internal marketing audits show interesting variations from the procedures just outlined. International Telephone and Telegraph, for example, has a history of forming corporate teams and sending them into weak divisions to do a complete business audit, with a heavy emphasis on the marketing component. Some teams stay on the job, often taking over the management.

General Electric's corporate consulting division offers help to various divisions on their marketing problems. One of its services is a marketing audit in the sense of a broad, independent, systematic look at the marketing picture in a division. However, the corporate consulting division gets few requests for a marketing audit as such. Most of the requests are for specific marketing studies or problem-solving assistance.

The 3M Company uses a very interesting and unusual internal marketing plan audit procedure. A marketing plan audit office with a small staff is located at corporate headquarters. The main purpose of the 3M marketing plan audit is to help the divisional marketing manager improve the marketing planning function, as well as come up with better strategies and tactics. A divisional marketing manager phones the marketing plan audit office and invites an audit. There is an agreement that only he will see the results and it is up to him whether he wants wider distribution.

The audit centers around a marketing plan for a product or product line that the marketing manager is preparing for the coming year. This plan is reviewed at a personal presentation by a special team of six company marketing executives invited by the marketing plan audit office. A new team is formed for each new audit. An effort is made to seek out those persons within 3M (but not in the audited division) who can bring the best experience to bear on the particular plan's problems and opportunities. A team typically consists of a marketing manager from another division, a national salesmanager, a marketing executive with a technical background, a few others close to the type of problems found in the audited plan, and another person who is totally unfamiliar with the market, the product, or the major marketing techniques being used in the plan. This person usually raises some important points others forget to raise, or do not ask because "everyone probably knows about that anyway."

The six auditors are supplied with a summary of the marketing manager's plan about ten days before an official meeting is held to review the plan. On the audit day, the six auditors, the head of the audit office, and the divisional marketing manager gather at 8:30 A.M. The marketing manager makes a presentation for about an hour describing the division's competitive situation, the long-run strategy, and the planned tactics. The auditors proceed to ask hard questions and debate certain points with the marketing manager and each other. Before the meeting ends that day, the auditors are each asked to fill out a marketing plan evaluation form consisting of questions that are accompanied by numerical rating scales and room for comments.

These evaluations are analyzed and summarized after the meeting. Then the head of the audit office arranges a meeting with the divisional marketing manager and presents the highlights of the auditor's findings and recommendations. It is then up to the marketing manager to take the next steps.

COMPONENTS OF THE MARKETING AUDIT

A major principle in marketing audits is to start with the marketplace first and explore the changes that are taking place and what they imply in the way of problems and opportunities. Then the auditor moves to examine the company's marketing objectives and strategies, organization, and systems. Finally he may move to examine one or two key functions in more detail that are central to the marketing performance of that company. However, some companies ask for less than the full range of auditing steps in order to obtain initial results before commissioning further work. The company may ask for a marketing environment audit, and if satisfied, then ask for a marketing strategy audit. Or it might ask for a marketing organization audit first, and later ask for a marketing environment audit.

We view a full marketing audit as having six major components, each having a semiautonomous status if a company wants less than a full marketing audit. The six components and their logical diagnostic sequence are discussed below. The major auditing questions connected with these components are gathered together in Appendix A at the end of this article.

Marketing Environment Audit

By marketing environment, we mean both the *macro-environment* surrounding the industry and the *task environment* in which the organization intimately operates. The macro-environment consists of the large-scale forces and factors influencing the company's future over which the company has very little control. These forces are normally divided into economic-demographic factors, technological factors, political-legal factors, and social-cultural factors. The marketing auditor's task is to asses the key trends and their implications for company marketing action. However, if the company has a good long-range forecasting department, then there is less of a need for a macro-environment audit.

The marketing auditor may play a more critical role in auditing the company's task environment. The task environment consists of markets, customers, competitors, distributors and dealers, suppliers, and marketing facilitators. The marketing auditor can make a contribution by going out into the field and interviewing various parties to assess their current thinking and attitudes and bringing them to the attention of management.

Marketing Strategy Audit

The marketing auditor then proceeds to consider whether the company's marketing strategy is well-postured in the light of the opportunities and problems facing the company. The starting point for the marketing strategy audit is the corporate goals and objectives followed by the marketing objectives. The auditor may find the objectives to be poorly stated, or he may find them to be well-stated but inappropriate given the company's resources and opportunities. For example, a chemical company had set a sales growth objective for a particular product line at 15 percent. However, the total market showed no growth and competition was fierce. Here the auditor questioned the basic sales growth objective for that product line. He proposed that the product line be reconsidered for a maintenance or harvest objective at best and that the company should look for growth elsewhere.

Even when a growth objective is warranted,

the auditor will want to consider whether management has chosen the best strategy to achieve that growth.

Marketing Organization Audit

A complete marketing audit would have to cover the question of the effectiveness of the marketing and sales organization, as well as the quality of interaction between marketing and other key management functions such as manufacturing, finance, purchasing, and research and development.

At critical times, a company's marketing organization must be revised to achieve greater effectiveness within the company and in the marketplace. Companies without product management systems will want to consider introducing them, companies with these systems may want to consider dropping them, or trying product teams instead. Companies may want to redefine the role concept of a product manager from being a promotional manager (concerned primarily with volume) to a business manager (concerned primarily with profit). There is the issue of whether decision-making responsibility should be moved up from the brand level to the product level. There is the perennial question of how to make the organization more market-responsive including the possibility of replacing product divisions with market-centered divisions. Finally, sales organizations often do not fully understand marketing. In the words of one vice-president of marketing: "It takes about five years for us to train sales managers to think marketing."

Marketing Systems Audit

A full marketing audit then turns to examine the various systems being used by marketing management to gather information, plan, and control the marketing operation. The issue is not the company's marketing strategy or organization per se but rather the procedures used in some or all of the following systems: sales forecasting, sales goal and quota setting, marketing planning, marketing control, inventory control, order processing, physical distribution, new products development, and product pruning.

The marketing audit may reveal that marketing is being carried on without adequate systems of planning, implementation, and control. An audit of a consumer products division of a large company revealed that decisions about which products to carry and which to eliminate were made by the head of the division on the basis of his intuitive feeling with little information or analysis to guide the decisions. The auditor recommended the introduction of a new product screening system for new products and an improved sales control system for existing products. He also observed that the division prepared budgets but did not carry out formal marketing planning and hardly any research into the market. He recommended that the division establish a formal marketing planning system as soon as possible.

Marketing Productivity Audit

A full marketing audit also includes an effort to examine key accounting data to determine where the company is making its real profits and what, if any, marketing costs could be trimmed. Decision Sciences Corporation, for example, starts its marketing audit by looking at the accounting figures on sales and associated costs of sales. Using marketing cost accounting principles,[2] it seeks to measure the marginal profit contribution of different products, end user segments, marketing channels, and sales territories.

We might argue that the firm's own controller or accountant should do the job of providing management with the results of marketing cost analysis. A handful of firms have created the job position of marketing controllers who report to financial controllers and spend their time looking at the productivity and validity of various marketing costs. Where an organization is doing a good job of marketing cost analysis, it does not need a marketing auditor to study the same. But most companies do not do careful marketing cost analysis. Here a marketing auditor can pay his way by simply exposing certain economic and cost relations which indicate waste or conceal unexploited marketing opportunities.

Zero-based budgeting[3] is another tool for investigating and improving marketing productivity. In normal budgeting, top management allots to each business unit a percentage increase (or decrease) of what it got last time. The question is not raised whether that basic budget level still makes sense. The manager of an operation should be asked what he would basically need if he started his operation from scratch and what it would cost. What would he need next and what would it cost? In this way, a budget is built from the ground up reflecting the true needs of the operation. When this was applied to a technical sales group within a large industrial goods company, it became clear that the company had three or four extra technical salesmen on its payroll. The manager admitted to the redundancy but argued if a business upturn came, these men would be needed to tap the potential. In the meantime, they were carried on the payroll for two years in the expectation of a business upturn.

Marketing Function Audit

The work done to this point might begin to point to certain key marketing functions which are performing poorly. The auditor might spot, for example, sales force problems that go very deep. Or he might observe that advertising budgets are prepared in an arbitrary fashion and such things as advertising themes, media, and timing are not evaluated for their effectiveness. In these and other cases, the issue becomes one of notifying management of the desirability of one or more marketing function audits if management agrees.

WHICH COMPANIES CAN BENEFIT MOST FROM A MARKETING AUDIT?

All companies can benefit from a competent audit of their marketing operations. However, a marketing audit is likely to yield the highest payoff in the following companies and situations:

Production-Oriented and Technical-Oriented Companies. Many manufacturing companies have their start in a love affair with a certain product. Further products are added that appeal to the technical interests of management, usually with insufficient attention paid to their market potential. The feeling in these companies is that marketing is paid to sell what the company decides to make. After some failures with its "better mousetraps," management starts getting interested in shifting to a market orientation. But this calls for more than a simple declaration by top management to study and serve the customer's needs. It calls for a great number of organizational and attitudinal changes that must be introduced carefully and convincingly. An auditor can perform an important service in recognizing that a company's problem lies in its production orientation, and in guiding management toward a market orientation.

Troubled Divisions. Multidivision companies usually have some troubled divisions. Top management may decide to use an auditor to assess the situation in a troubled division rather than rely solely on the division management's interpretation of the problem.

High Performing Divisions. Multidivision companies might want an audit of their top dollar divisions to make sure that they are reaching their highest potential, and are not on the verge of a sudden reversal. Such an audit may also yield insights into how to improve marketing in other divisions.

Young Companies. Marketing audits of emerging small companies or young divisions of large companies can help to lay down a solid marketing approach at a time when management faces a great degree of market inexperience.

Nonprofit Organizations. Administrators of colleges, museums, hospitals, social agencies, and churches are beginning to think in marketing terms, and the marketing audit can serve a useful educational as well as diagnostic purpose.

WHAT ARE THE PROBLEMS AND PITFALLS OF MARKETING AUDITS?

While the foregoing has stressed the positive aspects of marketing audits and their utility in a variety of situations, it is important to note some of the problems and pitfalls of the marketing audit process. Problems can occur in the objective-setting step, the data collection step, or the report presentation step.

Setting Objectives

When the marketing audit effort is being designed by the auditor and the company officer who commissioned the audit, several problems will be encountered. For one thing, the objectives set for the audit are based upon the company officer's and auditor's best *a priori* notions of what the key problem areas are for the audit to highlight. However, new problem areas may emerge once the auditor begins to learn more about the company. The original set of objectives should not constrain the auditor from shifting his priorities of investigation.

Similarly, it may be necessary for the auditor to use different sources of information than envisioned at the start of the audit. In some cases this may be because some information sources he had counted on became unavailable. In one marketing audit, the auditor had planned to speak to a sample of customers for the company's electro-mechanical devices, but the company officer who hired him would not permit him to do so. In other cases, a valuable new source of information may arise that was not recognized at the start of the audit. For example, the auditor for an air brake system manufacturer found as a valuable source of market intelligence a long-established manufacturers' representatives firm that approached the company after the audit had begun.

Another consideration at the objective-setting stage of the audit is that the management most affected by the audit must have full knowledge of the purposes and scope of the audit. Audits go much more smoothly when the executive who calls in the auditor either brings the affected management into the design stage, or at least has a general introductory meeting where the auditor explains his procedures and answers questions from the people in the affected business.

Data Collection

Despite reassurances by the auditor and the executive who brought him in, there will still be some managers in the affected business who will feel threatened by the auditor. The auditor must expect this, and realize that an individual's fears and biases may color his statements in an interview.

From the onset of the audit, the auditor must guarantee and maintain confidentiality of each individual's comments. In many audits, personnel in the company will see the audit as a vehicle for unloading their negative feelings about the company or other individuals. The auditor can learn a lot from these comments, but he must protect the individuals who make them. The auditor must question interviewees in a highly professional manner to build their confidence in him, or else they will not be entirely honest in their statements.

Another area of concern during the information collection step is the degree to which the company executive who brought in the auditor will try to guide the audit. It will be necessary for this officer and the auditor to strike a balance in which the executive provides some direction, but not too much. While overcontrol is the more likely excess of the executive, it is possible to undercontrol. When the auditor and the company executive do not have open and frequent lines of communication during the audit, it is possible that the auditor may place more emphasis on some areas and less on others than the executive might have desired. Therefore, it is the responsibility of both the auditor and the executive who brought him in to communicate frequently during the audit.

Report Presentation

One of the biggest problems in marketing auditing is that the executive who brings in the auditor, or the people in the business being audited, may have higher expectations about what the audit will do for the company than the actual report seems to offer. In only the most extreme circumstances will the auditor develop surprising panaceas or propose startling new opportunities for the company. More likely, the main value of his report will be that it places priorities on ideas and directions for the company, many of which have already been considered by some people within the audited organization. In most successful audits, the auditor, in his recommendations, makes a skillful combination of his general and technical marketing background (e.g., designs of salesman's compensation systems, his ability to measure the size and potential of markets) with some opportunistic ideas that people in the audited organization have already considered, but do not know how much importance to place upon them. However, it is only in the company's implementation of the recommendations that the payoff to the company will come.

Another problem at the conclusion of the audit stems from the fact that most audits seem to result in organizational changes. Organizational changes are a common outcome because the audit usually identifies new tasks to be accomplished and new tasks demand people to do them. One thing the auditor and the executive who brought him in must recognize, however, is that organizational promotions and demotions are exclusively the executive's decision. It is the executive who has to live with the changes once the auditor has gone, not the auditor. Therefore, the executive should not be lulled into thinking that organizational moves are any easier because the auditor may have recommended them.

The final problem, and this is one facing the auditor, is that important parts of an audit may be implemented incorrectly, or not implemented at all, by the executive who commissioned the audit. Non-implementation of key parts of the audit undermines the whole effectiveness of the audit.

SUMMARY

The marketing audit is one important answer to the problem of evaluating the marketing performance of a company or one of its business units. Marketing audits are distinguished from other marketing exercises in being *comprehensive, independent, systematic,* and *periodic.* A full marketing audit would cover the company's (or division's) external environment, objectives, strategies, organization, systems, and functions. If the audit covers only one function, such as sales management or advertising, it is best described as a marketing function audit rather than a marketing audit. If the exercise is to solve a current problem, such as entering a market, setting a price, or developing a package, then it is not an audit at all.

The marketing audit is carried out in three steps: developing an agreement as to objectives and scope; collecting the data; and presenting the report. The audit can be performed by a competent outside consultant or by a company auditing office at headquarters.

The possible findings of an audit include detecting unclear or inappropriate marketing objectives, inappropriate strategies, inappropriate levels of marketing expenditures, needed improvements in organization, and needed improvements in systems for marketing information, planning, and control. Companies that are most likely to benefit from a marketing audit include production-oriented companies, companies with troubled or highly vulnerable divisions, young companies, and nonprofit organizations.

Many companies today are finding that their premises for marketing strategy are growing obsolete in the face of a rapidly changing environment. This is happening to company giants such as General Motors and Sears as well as smaller firms that have not provided a mechanism for recycling their marketing strategy. The marketing audit is not the full answer to marketing strategy recycling but does offer one major mechanism for pursuing this desirable and necessary task.

APPENDIX A–COMPONENTS OF A MARKETING AUDIT

The Marketing Environment Audit

I. Macro-Environment

Economic-demographic

1. What does the company expect in the way of inflation, material shortages, unemployment, and credit availability in the short run, intermediate run, and long run?
2. What effect will forecasted trends in the size, age distribution, and regional distribution of population have on the business?

Technology

1. What major changes are occurring in product technology? In process technology?
2. What are the major generic substitutes that might replace this product?

Political-legal

1. What laws are being proposed that may affect marketing strategy and tactics?
2. What federal, state, and local agency actions should be watched? What is happening in the areas of pollution control, equal employment opportunity, product safety, advertising, price control, etc., that is relevant to marketing planning?

Social-cultural

1. What attitudes is the public taking toward business and toward products such as those produced by the company?
2. What changes are occurring in consumer life-styles and values that have a bearing on the company's target markets and marketing methods?

II. Task Environment

Markets

1. What is happening to market size, growth, geographical distribution and profits?
2. What are the major market segments? What are their expected rates of growth? Which are high opportunity and low opportunity segments?

Customers

1. How do current customers and prospects rate the company and its competitors, particularly with respect to reputation, product quality, service, sales force, and price?
2. How do different classes of customers make their buying decisions?
3. What are the evolving needs and satisfactions being sought by the buyers in this market?

Competitors

1. Who are the major competitors? What are the objectives and strategies of each major competitor? What are their strengths

and weaknesses? What are the sizes and trends in market shares?
2. What trends can be foreseen in future competition and substitutes for this product?

Distribution and dealers

1. What are the main trade channels bringing products to customers?
2. What are the efficiency levels and growth potentials of the different trade channels?

Suppliers

1. What is the outlook for the availability of different key resources used in production?
2. What trends are occurring among suppliers in their pattern of selling?

Facilitators

1. What is the outlook for the cost and availability of transportation services?
2. What is the outlook for the cost and availability of warehousing facilities?
3. What is the outlook for the cost and availability of financial resources?
4. How effectively is the advertising agency performing? What trends are occurring in advertising agency services?

Marketing Strategy Audit

Marketing objectives

1. Are the corporate objectives clearly stated and do they lead logically to the marketing objectives?
2. Are the marketing objectives stated in a clear form to guide marketing planning and subsequent performance measurement?
3. Are the marketing objectives appropriate, given the company's competitive position, resources, and opportunities? Is the appropriate strategic objective to build, hold, harvest, or terminate this business?

Strategy

1. What is the core marketing strategy for achieving the objectives? Is it a sound marketing strategy?
2. Are enough resources (or too much resources) budgeted to accomplish the marketing objectives?
3. Are the marketing resources allocated optimally to prime market segments, territories, and products of the organization?
4. Are the marketing resources allocated optimally to the major elements of the marketing mix, i.e., product quality, service, sales force, advertising, promotion, and distribution?

Marketing Organization Audit

Formal structure

1. Is there a high-level marketing officer with adequate authority and responsibility over those company activities that affect the customer's satisfaction?
2. Are the marketing responsibilities optimally structured along functional product, end user, and territorial lines?

Functional efficiency

1. Are there good communication and working relations between marketing and sales?
2. Is the product management system working effectively? Are the product managers able to plan profits or only sales volume?
3. Are there any groups in marketing that need more training, motivation, supervision, or evaluation?

Interface efficiency

1. Are there any problems between marketing and manufacturing that need attention?
2. What about marketing and R&D?

3. What about marketing and financial management?
4. What about marketing and purchasing?

Marketing Systems Audit

Marketing information system

1. Is the marketing intelligence system producing accurate, sufficient, and timely information about developments in the marketplace?
2. Is marketing research being adequately used by company decision makers?

Marketing planning system

1. Is the marketing planning system well-conceived and effective?
2. Is sales forecasting and market potential measurement soundly carried out?
3. Are sales quotas set on a proper basis?

Marketing control system

1. Are the control procedures (montly, quarterly, etc.) adequate to insure that the annual plan objectives are being achieved?
2. Is provision made to analyze periodically the profitability of different products, markets, territories, and channels of distribution?
3. Is provision made to examine and validate periodically various marketing costs?

New product development system

1. Is the company well-organized to gather, generate, and screen new product ideas?
2. Does the company do adequate concept research and business analysis before investing heavily in a new idea?
3. Does the company carry out adequate product and market testing before launching a new product?

Marketing Productivity Audit

Profitability analysis

1. What is the profitability of the company's different products, served markets, territories, and channels of distribution?
2. Should the company enter, expand, contract, or withdraw from any business segments and what would be the short- and long-run profit consequences?

Cost-effectiveness analysis

1. Do any marketing activities seem to have excessive costs? Are these costs valid? Can cost-reducing steps be taken?

Marketing Function Audit

Products

1. What are the product line objectives? Are these objectives sound? Is the current product line meeting these objectives?
2. Are there particular products that should be phased out?
3. Are there new products that are worth adding?
4. Are any products able to benefit from quality, feature, or style improvements?

Price

1. What are the pricing objectives, policies, strategies, and procedures? To what extent are prices set on sound cost, demand, and competitive criteria?
2. Do the customers see the company's prices as being in line or out of line with the perceived value of its offer?
3. Does the company use price promotions effectively?

Distribution

1. What are the distribution objectives and strategies?
2. Is there adequate market coverage and service?
3. Should the company consider changing its degree of reliance on distributors, sales reps, and direct selling?

Sales force

1. What are the organization's sales force objectives?

2. Is the sales force large enough to accomplish the company's objectives?
3. Is the sales force organized along the proper principle(s) of specialization (territory, market, product)?
4. Does the sales force show high morale, ability, and effort? Are they sufficiently trained and incentivized?
5. Are the procedures adequate for setting quotas and evaluating performances?
6. How is the company's sales force perceived in relation to competitors' sales forces?

Advertising, promotion, and publicity

1. What are the organization's advertising objectives? Are they sound?
2. Is the right amount being spent on advertising? How is the budget determined?
3. Are the ad themes and copy effective? What do customers and the public think about the advertising?
4. Are the advertising media well chosen?
5. Is sales promotion used effectively?
6. Is there a well-conceived publicity program?

NOTES

1. Many useful checklist questions for marketers are found in C. Eldridge, *The Management of the Marketing Function* (New York: Association of National Advertisers, 1967).
2. See P. Kotler, *Marketing Management Analysis, Planning and Control* (Englewood Cliffs, N.J.:Prentice-Hall, Inc., 1976), pp. 457–462.
3. See P.J. Stonich, "Zero-Base Planning – A Management Tool," *Managerial Planning,* July–August 1976, pp. 1–4.

22

Wendell R. Smith

Product Differentiation and Market Segmentation as Alternative Marketing Strategies

During the decade of the 1930's, the work of Robinson and Chamberlin resulted in a revitalization of economic theory. While classical and neoclassical theory provide a useful framework for economic analysis, the theories of perfect competition and pure monopoly had become inadequate as explanations of the contemporary business scene. The theory of perfect competition assumes homogeneity among the components of both the demand and supply sides of the market, but diversity or heterogeneity had come to be the rule rather than the exception. This analysis reviews major marketing strategy alternatives that are available to planners and merchandizers of products in an environment characterized by imperfect competition.

DIVERSITY IN SUPPLY

That there is a lack of homogeneity or close similarity among the items offered to the market by individual manufacturers of various products is obvious in any variety store, department store, or shopping center. In many cases the impact of this diversity is amplified by advertising and promotional activities. Today's advertising and promotion tends to emphasize appeals to *selective* rather than *primary* buying motives and to point out the distinctive or differentiating features of the advertiser's product or service offer.

The presence of differences in the sales offers made by competing suppliers produces a diver-

Reprinted from the *Journal of Marketing,* published by the American Marketing Association (July 1956), pp. 3–8. This article won the 1956 Alpha Kappa Psi Award as best article of the year.
Wendell R. Smith is Professor of Marketing and Dean of the School of Business Administration at the University of Massachusetts. He has been chairman of the national marketing advisory committee of the U.S. Department of Commerce and president of the American Marketing Association. For three years, Dean Smith was staff vice president for market development for Radio Corporation of America, and he was the first director of the Marketing Science Institute. He holds three degrees from the University of Iowa.

sity in supply that is inconsistent with the assumptions of earlier theory. The reasons for the presence of diversity in specific markets are many and include the following:

1. Variations in the production equipment and methods or processes used by different manufacturers of products designed for the same or similar uses.
2. Specialized or superior resources enjoyed by favorably situated manufacturers.
3. Unequal progress among competitors in design, development, and improvement of products.
4. The inability of manufacturers in some industries to eliminate product variations even through the application of quality control techniques.
5. Variations in producers' estimates of the nature of market demand with reference to such matters as price sensitivity, color, material, or package size.

Because of these and other factors, both planned and uncontrollable differences exist in the products of an industry. As a result, sellers make different appeals in support of their marketing efforts.

DIVERSITY OR VARIATIONS IN CONSUMER DEMAND

Under present-day conditions of imperfect competition, marketing managers are generally responsible for selecting the over-all marketing strategy or combination of strategies best suited to a firm's requirements at any particular point in time. The strategy selected may consist of a program designed to bring about the *convergence* of individual market demands for a variety of products upon a single or limited offering to the market. This is often accomplished by the achievement of product differentiation through advertising and promotion. In this way, variations in the demands of individual consumers are minimized or brought into line by means of effective use of appealing product claims designed to make a satisfactory volume of demand *converge* upon the product or product line being promoted. This strategy was once believed to be essential as the marketing counterpart to standardization and mass production in manufacturing because of the rigidities imposed by production cost considerations.

In some cases, however, the marketer may determine that it is better to accept *divergent* demand as a market characteristic and to adjust product lines and marketing strategy accordingly. This implies ability to merchandise to a heterogeneous market by emphasizing the precision with which a firm's products can satisfy the requirements of one or more distinguishable market segments. The strategy of product differentiation here gives way to marketing programs based upon measurement and definition of market differences.

Lack of homogeneity on the demand side may be based upon different customs, desire for variety, or desire for exclusiveness or may arise from basic differences in user needs. Some divergence in demand is the result of shopping errors in the market. Not all consumers have the desire or the ability to shop in a sufficiently efficient or rational manner as to bring about selection of the most needed or most wanted goods or services.

Diversity on the demand side of the market is nothing new to sales management. It has always been accepted as a fact to be dealt with in industrial markets where production to order rather than for the market is common. Here, however, the loss of precision in the satisfying of customer requirements that would be necessitated by attempts to bring about convergence of demand is often impractical and, in some cases, impossible. However, even in industrial marketing, the strategy of product differentiation should be considered in cases where products are applicable to several industries and may have horizontal markets of substantial size.

LONG-TERM IMPLICATIONS

While contemporary economic theory deals with the nature of product differentiation and its effects upon the operation of the total economy, the alternative strategies of product differentiation and market segmentation have received less attention. Empirical analysis of contemporary marketing activity supports the hypothesis that, while product differentiation and market segmentation are closely related (perhaps even inseparable) concepts, attempts to distinguish between these approaches may be productive of clarity in theory as well as greater precision in the planning of marketing operations. Not only do strategies of differentiation and segmentation call for differing systems of action at any point in time, but the dynamics of markets and marketing underscore the importance of varying degrees of diversity *through time* and suggest that the rational selection of marketing strategies is a requirement for the achievement of maximum functional effectiveness in the economy as a whole.

If a rational selection of strategies is to be made, an integrated approach to the minimizing of total costs must take precedence over separate approaches to minimization of production costs on the one hand and marketing costs on the other. Strategy determination must be regarded as an over-all management decision which will influence and require facilitating policies affecting both production and marketing activities.

DIFFERENCES BETWEEN STRATEGIES OF DIFFERENTIATION AND SEGMENTATION

Product differentiation and market segmentation are both consistent with the framework of imperfect competition.[1] In its simplest terms, *product differentiation* is concerned with the bending of demand to the will of supply. It is an attempt to shift or to change the slope of the demand curve for the market offering of an individual supplier. This strategy may also be employed by a group of suppliers such as a farm cooperative, the members of which have agreed to act together. It results from the desire to establish a kind of equilibrium in the market by bringing about adjustment of market demand to supply conditions favorable to the seller.

Segmentation is based upon developments on the demand side of the market and represents a rational and more precise adjustment of product and marketing effort to consumer or user requirements. In the language of the economist, segmentation is *disaggregative* in its effects and tends to bring about recognition of several demand schedules where only one was recognized before.

Attention has been drawn to this area of analysis by the increasing number of cases in which business problems have become soluble by doing something about marketing programs and product policies that overgeneralize both markets and marketing effort. These are situations where intensive promotion designed to differentiate the company's products was not accomplishing its objective—cases where failure to recognize the reality of market segments was resulting in loss of market position.

While successful product differentiation will result in giving the marketer a horizontal share of a broad and generalized market, equally successful application of the strategy of market segmentation tends to produce depth of market position in the segments that are effectively defined and penetrated. The differentiator seeks to secure a layer of the market cake, whereas one who employs market segmentation strives to secure one or more wedge-shaped pieces.

Many examples of market segmentation can be cited: the cigarette and automobile industries are well-known illustrations. Similar developments exist in greater or lesser degree in almost all product areas. Recent introduction of a refrigerator with no storage compartment for frozen foods was in response to the distinguishable preferences of the segment of the refrigerator market made up of home freezer owners whose frozen food storage needs had already been met.

Strategies of segmentation and differentiation may be employed simultaneously, but more commonly they are applied in sequence in response to changing market conditions. In one sense, segmentation is a momentary or short-term phenomenon in that effective use of this strategy may lead to more formal recognition of the reality of market segments through redefinition of the segments as individual markets. Redefinition may result in a swing back to differentiation.

The literature of both economics and marketing abounds in formal definitions of product differentiation. *From a strategy viewpoint*, product differentiation is securing a measure of control over the demand for a product by advertising or promoting differences between a product and the products of competing sellers. It is basically the result of sellers' desires to establish firm market positions and/or to insulate their business against price competition. Differentiation tends to be characterized by heavy use of advertising and promotion and to result in prices that are somewhat above the equilibrium levels associated with perfectly competitive market conditions. It may be classified as a *promotional* strategy or approach to marketing.

Market segmentation, on the other hand, consists of viewing a heterogeneous market (one characterized by divergent demand) as a number of smaller homogeneous markets in response to differing product preferences among important market segments. It is attributable to the desires of consumers or users for more precise satisfaction of their varying wants. Like differentiation, segmentation often involves substantial use of advertising and promotion. This is to inform market segments of the availability of goods or services produced for or presented as meeting their needs with precision. Under these circumstances, prices tend to be somewhat closer to perfectly competitive equilibrium. Market segmentation is essentially a *merchandising* strategy, merchandising being used here in its technical sense as representing the adjustment of market offerings to consumer or user requirements.

THE EMERGENCE OF THE SEGMENTATION STRATEGY

To a certain extent, market segmentation may be regarded as a force in the market that will not be denied. It may result from trial and error in the sense that generalized programs of product differentiation may turn out to be effective in some segments of the market and ineffective in others. Recognition of, and intelligent response to, such a situation necessarily involves a shift in emphasis. On the other hand, it may develop that products involved in marketing programs designed for particular market segments may achieve a broader acceptance than originally planned, thus revealing a basis for convergence of demand and a more generalized marketing approach. The challenge to planning arises from the importance of determining, preferably in advance, the level or degree of segmentation that can be exploited with profit.

There appear to be many reasons why formal recognition of market segmentation as a strategy is beginning to emerge. One of the most important of these is the decrease in the size of the minimum efficient producing or manufacturing unit required in some product areas. American industry has also established the technical base for product diversity by gaining release from some of the rigidities imposed by earlier approaches to mass production. Hence, there is less need today for generalization of markets in response to the necessity for long production runs of identical items.

Present emphasis upon the minimizing of

marketing costs through self-service and similar developments tends to impose a requirement for better adjustment of products to consumer demand. The retailing structure, in its efforts to achieve improved efficiency, is providing less and less sales push at point of sale. This increases the premium placed by retailers upon products that are presold by their producers and are readily recognized by consumers as meeting their requirements as measured by satisfactory rates of stock turnover.

It has been suggested that the present level of discretionary buying power is productive of sharper shopping comparisons, particularly for items that are above the need level. General prosperity also creates increased willingness "to pay a little more" to get "just what I wanted."

Attention to market segmentation has also been enhanced by the recent ascendancy of product competition to a position of great economic importance. An expanded array of goods and services is competing for the consumer's dollar. More specifically, advancing technology is creating competition between new and traditional materials with reference to metals, construction materials, textile products, and in many other areas. While such competition is confusing and difficult to analyze in its early stages, it tends to achieve a kind of balance as various competing materials find their markets of maximum potential as a result of recognition of differences in the requirements of market segments.

Many companies are reaching the stage in their development where attention to market segmentation may be regarded as a condition or cost of growth. Their *core* markets have already been developed on a generalized basis to the point where additional advertising and selling expenditures are yielding diminishing returns. Attention to smaller or *fringe* market segments, which may have small potentials individually but are of crucial importance in the aggregate, may be indicated.

Finally, some business firms are beginning to regard an increasing share of their total costs of operations as being fixed in character. The higher costs of maintaining market position in the channels of distribution illustrate this change. Total reliance upon a strategy of product differentiation under such circumstances is undesirable, since market share available as a result of such a promotion-oriented approach tends to be variable over time. Much may hinge, for example, upon week-to-week audience ratings of the television shows of competitors who seek to outdifferentiate each other. Exploitation of market segments, which provides for greater maximization of consumer or user satisfactions, tends to build a more secure market position and lead to greater over-all stability. While traditionally, high fixed costs (regarded primarily from the production viewpoint) have created pressures for expanded sale of standardized items through differentiation, the possible shifting of certain marketing costs into the fixed area of the total cost structure tends to minimize this pressure.

CONCLUSION

Success in planning marketing activities requires precise utilization of both product differentiation and market segmentation as components of marketing strategy. It is fortunate that available techniques of marketing research make unplanned market exploration largely unnecessary. It is the obligation of those responsible for sales and marketing administration to keep the strategy mix in adjustment with market structure at any given point in time and to produce in marketing strategy at least as much dynamism as is present in the market. The ability of business to plan in this way is dependent upon the maintenance of a flow of market information that can be provided by marketing research as well as the full utilization of available techniques of cost accounting and cost analysis.

Cost information is critical because the upper limit to which market segmentation can be carried is largely defined by production cost considerations. There is a limit to which diversity in market offerings can be carried without driving production costs beyond practical limits. Similarly, the employment of product differentiation as a strategy tends to be restricted by the achievement of levels of marketing costs that are untenable. These cost factors tend to define the limits of the zone within which the employment of marketing strategies or a strategy mix dictated by the nature of the market is permissive.

It should be emphasized that while we have here been concerned with the differences between product differentiation and market segmentation as marketing strategies, they are closely related concepts in the setting of an imperfectly competitive market. The differences have been highlighted in the interest of enhancing clarity in theory and precision in practice. The emergence of market segmentation as a strategy once again provides evidence of the consumer's preeminence in the contemporary American economy and the richness of the rewards that can result from the application of science to marketing problems.

NOTE

1. Imperfect competition assumes lack of uniformity in the size and influence of the firms or individuals that comprise the demand or supply sides of a market.

23

Russell I. Haley

Benefit Segmentation: A Decision-Oriented Research Tool

Market segmentation has been steadily moving toward center stage as a topic of discussion in marketing and research circles. Hardly a conference passes without at least one session devoted to it. Moreover, in March the American Management Association held a three-day conference entirely concerned with various aspects of the segmentation problem.

According to Wendell Smith, "segmentation is based upon developments on the demand side of the market and represents a rational and more precise adjustment of product and marketing effort to consumer or user requirements."[1] The idea that all markets can be profitably segmented has now received almost as widespread acceptance as the marketing concept itself. However, problems remain. In the extreme, a marketer can divide up his market in as many ways as he can describe his prospects. If he wishes, he can define a left-handed segment, or a blue-eyed segment, or a German-speaking segment. Consequently, current discussion revolves largely around which of the virtually limitless alternatives is likely to be most productive.

SEGMENTATION METHODS

Several varieties of market segmentation have been popular in the recent past. At least three kinds have achieved some degree of prominence. Historically, perhaps the first type to exist was geographic segmentation. Small manufacturers who wished to limit their investments, or whose distribution channels were not large enough to cover the entire country, segmented the U.S. market, in effect, by selling their products only in certain areas.

However, as more and more brands became national, the second major system of segmentation – demographic segmentation – became popular. Under this philosophy targets were

Reprinted from the *Journal of Marketing,* published by the American Marketing Association. Russell I. Haley, "Benefit Segmentation: A Decision-Oriented Research Tool," *Journal of Marketing,* Vol. 32, pp. 30–35, July 1968.

Russell I. Haley is president of Haley, Oberholtser and Associates, specialists in marketing research and advertising. He has long been associated with attitude research and market segmentation studies. Mr. Haley received his M.B.A. from Columbia University in statistics.

defined as younger people, men, or families with children. Unfortunately, a number of recent studies have shown that demographic variables such as age, sex, income, occupation and race are, in general, poor predictors of behavior and consequently, less than optimum bases for segmentation strategies.[2]

More recently, a third type of segmentation has come into increasing favor – volume segmentation. The so-called "heavy half" theory, popularized by Dik Twedt of the Oscar Mayer Company,[3] points out that in most product categories one-half of the consumers account for around 80% of the consumption. If this is true, the argument goes, shouldn't knowledgeable marketers concentrate their efforts on these high-volume consumers? Certainly they are the most *valuable* consumers.

The trouble with this line of reasoning is that not all heavy consumers are usually available to the same brand – because they are not all seeking the same kinds of benefits from a product. For example, heavy coffee drinkers consist of two types of consumers – those who drink chain store brands and those who drink premium brands. The chain store customers feel that all coffees are basically alike and, because they drink so much coffee, they feel it is sensible to buy a relatively inexpensive brand. The premium brand buyers, on the other hand, feel that the few added pennies which coffees like Yuban, Martinson's Chock Full O'Nuts, and Savarin cost are more than justified by their fuller taste. Obviously, these two groups of people, although they are both members of the "heavy half" segment, are not equally good prospects for any one brand, nor can they be expected to respond to the same advertising claims.

These three systems of segmentation have been used because they provide helpful guidance in the use of certain marketing tools. For example, geographic segmentation, because it describes the market in a discrete way, provides definite direction in media purchases. Spot TV, spot radio, and newspapers can be bought for a geographical segment selected for concentrated effort. Similarly, demographic segmentation allows media to be bought more efficiently since demographic data on readers, viewers, and listeners are readily available for most media vehicles. Also, in some product categories demographic variables are extremely helpful in differentiating users from non-users, although they are typically less helpful in distinguishing between the users of various brands. The heavy-half philosophy is especially effective in directing dollars toward the most important parts of the market.

However, each of these three systems of segmentation is handicapped by an underlying disadvantage inherent in its nature. All are based on an ex post facto analysis of the kinds of people who make up various segments of a market. They rely on *descriptive* factors rather than *causal* factors. For this reason they are not efficient predictors of future buying behavior, and it is future buying behavior that is of central interest to marketers.

BENEFIT SEGMENTATION

An approach to market segmentation whereby it is possible to identify market segments by causal factors rather than descriptive factors, might be called "benefit segmentation." The belief underlying this segmentation strategy is that the benefits which people are seeking in consuming a given product are the basic reasons for the existence of true market segments. Experience with this approach has shown that benefits sought by consumers determine their behavior much more accurately than do demographic characteristics or volume of consumption.

This does not mean that the kinds of data gathered in more traditional types of segmentation are not useful. Once people have been classified into segments in accordance with the benefits they are seeking, each segment is contrasted with all of the other segments in terms of its demography, its volume of consumption, its brand perceptions, its media habits, its personality and life-style, and so forth. In this way, a reasonably deep understanding of the people who make up each segment can be obtained. And by capitalizing on this understanding, it is possible to reach them, to talk to them in their own terms, and to present a product in the most favorable light possible.

The benefit segmentation approach is not new. It has been employed by a number of America's largest corporations since it was introduced in 1961.[4] However, case histories have been notably absent from the literature because most studies have been contracted for privately, and have been treated confidentially.

The benefit segmentation approach is based upon being able to measure consumer value systems in detail, together with what the consumer thinks about various brands in the product category of interest. While this concept seems simple enough, operationally it is very complex. There is no simple straightforward way of handling the volumes of data that have to be generated. Computers and sophisticated multivariate attitude measurement techniques are a necessity.

Several alternative statistical approaches can be employed, among them the so-called "Q" technique of factor analysis, multi-dimensional scaling, and other distance measures.[5] All of these methods relate the ratings of each respondent to those of every other respondent and then seek clusters of individuals with similar rating patterns. If the items related are potential consumer benefits, the clusters that emerge will be groups of people who attach similar degrees of importance to the various benefits. Whatever the statistical approach selected, the end result of the analysis is likely to be between three and seven consumer segments, each representing a potentially productive focal point for marketing efforts.

Each segment is identified by the benefits it is seeking. However, it is the *total configuration* of the benefits sought which differentiates one segment from another, rather than the fact that one segment is seeking one particular benefit and another a quite different benefit. Individual benefits are likely to have appeal for several segments. In fact, the research that has been done thus far suggests that most people would like as many benefits as possible. However, the *relative* importance they attach to individual benefits can differ importantly and, accordingly, can be used as an effective lever in segmenting markets.

Of course, it is possible to determine benefit segments intuitively as well as with computers and sophisticated research methods. The kinds of brilliant insights which produced the Mustang and the first 100-millimeter cigarette have a good chance of succeeding whenever marketers are able to tap an existing benefit segment.

However, intuition can be very expensive when it is mistaken. Marketing history is replete with examples of products which someone felt could not miss. Over the longer term, systematic benefit segmentation research is likely to have a higher proportion of successes.

But is benefit segmentation practical? And is it truly operational? The answer to both of these questions is "yes." In effect, the crux of the problem of choosing the best segmentation system is to determine which has the greatest number of practical marketing implications. An example should show that benefit segmentation has a much wider range of implications than alternative forms of segmentation.

An Example of Benefit Segmentation

While the material presented here is purely illustrative to protect the competitive edge of companies who have invested in studies of this kind, it is based on actual segmentation studies.

Consequently, it is quite typical of the kinds of things which are normally learned in the course of a benefit segmentation study.

The toothpaste market has been chosen as an example because it is one with which everyone is familiar. Let us assume that a benefit segmentation study has been done and four major segments have been identified – one particularly concerned with decay prevention, one with brightness of teeth, one with the flavor and appearance of the product, and one with price. A relatively large amount of supplementary information has also been gathered (Table 23-1) about the people in each of these segments.

The decay prevention segment, it has been found, contains a disproportionately large number of families with children. They are seriously concerned about the possibility of cavities and show a definite preference for fluoride toothpaste. This is reinforced by their personalities. They tend to be a little hypochondriacal and, in their life-styles, they are less socially-oriented than some of the other groups. This segment has been named The Worriers.

The second segment, comprised of people who show concern for the brightness of their teeth, is quite different. It includes a relatively large group of young marrieds. They smoke more than average. This is where the swingers are. They are strongly social and their life-style patterns are very active. This is probably the group to which toothpastes such as Macleans or Plus White or Ultra Brite would appeal. This segment has been named the Sociables.

In the third segment, the one which is particularly concerned with the flavor and appearance of the product, a large portion of the brand deciders are children. Their use of spearmint toothpaste is well above average. Stripe has done relatively well in this segment. They are more ego-centered than other segments, and their life-style is outgoing but not to the extent of the swingers. They will be called The Sensory Segment.

The fourth segment, the price-oriented segment, shows a predominance of men. It tends to be above average in terms of toothpaste usage. People in this segment see very few meaningful differences between brands. They switch more frequently than people in other segments and tend to buy a brand on sale. In terms of personality, they are cognitive and they are independent. They like to think for themselves and make brand choices on the basis of their judgment. They will be called The Independent Segment.

TABLE 23-1 *Toothpaste Market Segment Description*

Segment Name:	The Sensory Segment	The Sociables	The Worriers	The Independent Segment
Principal benefit sought:	Flavor, product appearance	Brightness of teeth	Decay prevention	Price
Demographic strengths:	Children	Teens, young people	Large families	Men
Special behavioral characteristics:	Users of spearmint-flavored toothpaste	Smokers	Heavy users	Heavy users
Brands disproportionately favored:	Colgate, Stripe	Macleans, Plus White, Ultra Brite	Crest	Brands on sale
Personality characteristics:	High self-involvement	High sociability	High hypochondriasis	High autonomy
Life-style characteristics	Hedonistic	Active	Conservative	Value-oriented

Marketing Implications of Benefit Segmentation Studies

Both copy directions and media choices will show sharp differences depending upon which of these segments is chosen as the target – The Worriers, The Sociables, The Sensory Segment, or The Independent Segment. For example, the tonality of the copy will be light if The Sociable Segment or The Sensory Segment is to be addressed. It will be more serious if the copy is aimed at The Worriers. And if The Independent Segment is selected, it will probably be desirable to use rational, two-sided arguments. Of course, to talk to this group at all it will be necessary to have either a price edge or some kind of demonstrable product superiority.

The depth-of-sell reflected by the copy will also vary, depending upon the segment which is of interest. It will be fairly intensive for The Worrier Segment and for The Independent Segment, but much more superficial and mood-oriented for The Sociable and Sensory Segments.

Likewise, the setting will vary. It will focus on the product for The Sensory Group, on socially-oriented situations for The Sociable Group, and perhaps on demonstration or on competitive comparisons for The Independent Group.

Media environments will also be tailored to the segments chosen as targets. Those with serious environments will be used for The Worrier and Independent Segments, and those with youthful, modern and active environments for The Sociable and The Sensory Groups. For example, it might be logical to use a larger proportion of television for The Sociable and Sensory Groups, while The Worriers and Independents might have heavier print schedules.

The depth-of-sell needed will also be reflected in the media choices. For The Worrier and Rational Segments longer commercials – perhaps 60-second commercials – would be indicated, while for the other two groups shorter commercials and higher frequency would be desirable.

Of course, in media selection the facts that have been gathered about the demographic characteristics of the segment chosen as the target would also be taken into consideration.

The information in Table 23-1 also has packaging implications. For example, it might be appropriate to have colorful packages for The Sensory Segment, perhaps aqua (to indicate fluoride) for The Worrier Group, and gleaming white for The Sociable segment because of their interest in bright white teeth.

It should be readily apparent that the kinds of information normally obtained in the course of a benefit segmentation study have a wide range of marketing implications. Sometimes they are useful in suggesting physical changes in a product. For example, one manufacturer discovered that his product was well suited to the needs of his chosen target with a single exception in the area of flavor. He was able to make a relatively inexpensive modification in his product and thereby strengthen his market position.

The new product implications of benefit segmentation studies are equally apparent. Once a marketer understands the kinds of segments that exist in his market, he is often able to see new product opportunities or particularly effective ways of positioning the products emerging from his research and development operation.

Similarly, benefit segmentation information has been found helpful in providing direction in the choice of compatible point-of-purchase materials and in the selection of the kinds of sales promotions which are most likely to be effective for any given market target.

Generalizations from Benefit Segmentation Studies

A number of generalizations are possible on the basis of the major benefit segmentation studies which have been conducted thus far. For example, the following general rules of thumb have become apparent:

- It is easier to take advantage of market segments that already exist than to attempt to create new ones. Some time ago the strategy of product differentiation was heavily emphasized in marketing textbooks. Under this philosophy it was believed that a manufacturer was more or less able to create new market segments at will by making his product somewhat different from those of his competitors. Now it is generally recognized that fewer costly errors will be made if money is first invested in consumer research aimed at determining the present contours of the market. Once this knowledge is available, it is usually most efficient to tailor marketing strategies to existing consumer-need patterns.
- No brand can expect to appeal to all consumers. The very act of attracting one segment may automatically alienate others. A corrollary to this principle is that any marketer who wishes to cover a market fully must offer consumers more than a single brand. The flood of new brands which have recently appeared on the market is concrete recognition of this principle.
- A company's brands can sometimes cannibalize each other but need not necessarily do so. It depends on whether or not they are positioned against the same segment of the market. Ivory Snow sharply reduced Ivory Flakes' share of the market, and the Ford Falcon cut deeply into the sales of the standard size Ford because, in each case, the products were competing in the same segments. Later on, for the same companies, the Mustang was successfully introduced with comparatively little damage to Ford; and the success of Crest did not have a disproportionately adverse effect on Gleem's market position because, in these cases, the segments to which the products appealed were different.
- New and old products alike should be designed to fit *exactly* the needs of some segment of the market. In other words, they should be aimed at people seeking a specific combination of benefits. It is a marketing truism that you sell people one at a time – that you have to get *someone* to buy your product before you get *anyone* to buy it. A substantial group of people must be interested in your specific set of benefits before you can make progress in a market. Yet, many products attempt to aim at two or more segments simultaneously. As a result, they are not able to maximize their appeal to any segment of the market, and they run the risk of ending up with a dangerously fuzzy brand image.
- Marketers who adopt a benefit segmentation strategy have a distinct competitive edge. If a benefit segment can be located which is seeking exactly the kinds of satisfactions that one marketer's brand can offer better than any other brand, the marketer can almost certainly dominate the purchases of that segment. Furthermore, if his competitors are looking at the market in terms of traditional types of segments, they may not even be aware of the existence of the benefit segment which he has chosen as his market target. If they are ignorant in this sense, they will be at a loss to explain the success of his brand. And it naturally follows that if they do not understand the reasons for his success, the kinds of people buying his brand, and the benefits they are obtaining from it, his competitors will find it very difficult to successfully attack the marketer's position.
- An understanding of the benefit segments which exist within a market can be used to advantage when competitors introduce new products. Once the way in which consumers are positioning the new prod-

uct has been determined, the likelihood that it will make major inroads into segments of interest can be assessed, and a decision can be made on whether or not counteractions of any kind are required. If the new product appears to be assuming an ambiguous position, no money need be invested in defensive measures. However, if it appears that the new product is ideally suited to the needs of an important segment of the market, the manufacturer in question can introduce a new competitive product of his own, modify the physical properties of existing brands, change his advertising strategy, or take whatever steps appear appropriate.

Types of Segments Uncovered through Benefit Segmentation Studies

It is difficult to generalize about the types of segments which are apt to be discovered in the course of a benefit segmentation study. To a large extent, the segments which have been found have been unique to the product categories being analyzed. However, a few types of segments have appeared in two or more private studies. Among them are the following:

The Status Seeker a group which is very much concerned with the prestige of the brands purchased.

The Swinger a group which tries to be modern and up to date in all of its activities. Brand choices reflect this orientation.

The Conservative a group which prefers to stick to large successful companies and popular brands.

The Rational Man a group which looks for benefits such as economy, value, durability, etc.

The Inner-Directed Man a group which is especially concerned with self-concept. Members consider themselves to have a sense of humor, to be independent and/or honest.

The Hedonist a group which is concerned primarily with sensory benefits.

Some of these segments appear among the customers of almost all products and services. However, there is no guarantee that a majority of them or, for that matter, any of them exist in any given product category. Finding out whether they do and, if so, what should be done about them is the purpose of benefit segmentation research.

CONCLUSION

The benefit segmentation approach is of particular interest because it never fails to provide fresh insight into markets. As was indicated in the toothpaste example cited earlier, the marketing implications of this analytical research tool are limited only by the imagination of the person using the information a segmentation study provides. In effect, when segmentation studies are conducted, a number of smaller markets emerge instead of one large one. Moreover, each of these smaller markets can be subjected to the same kinds of thorough analyses to which total markets have been subjected in the past. The only difference – a crucial one – is that the total market was a heterogeneous conglomeration of sub-groups. The so-called average consumer existed only in the minds of some marketing people. When benefit segmentation is used, a number of relatively homogeneous segments are uncovered. And, because they are homogeneous, descriptions of them in terms of averages are much more appropriate and meaningful as marketing guides.

NOTES

1. Wendell R. Smith, "Product Differentiation and Market Segmentation as Alternative Product Strategies," *Journal of Marketing,* Vol. XXI (July, 1956), pp. 3-8.
2. Ronald E. Frank, "Correlates of Buying Behavior for Grocery Products," *Journal of Marketing,* Vol. 31 (October, 1967), pp. 48-53; Ronald E. Frank, William Massey, and Harper W. Boyd, Jr., "Correlates of Grocery Product Consumption Rates," *Journal of Marketing Research,* Vol. 4 (May, 1968), pp. 184-190; and Clark Wilson, "Homemaker Living Patterns and Marketplace Behavior – A Psychometric Approach," in John S. Wright and Jac L. Goldstucker, Editors, *New Ideas for Successful Marketing,* Proceedings of 1966 World Congress (Chicago: American Marketing Association, June, 1966) pp. 305-331.
3. Dik Warren Twedt, "Some Practical Applications of the 'Heavy Half' Theory" (New York: Advertising Research Foundation 10th Annual Conference, October 6, 1964).
4. Russell I. Haley, "Experimental Research on Attitudes toward Shampoos," an unpublished paper (February, 1961).
5. Ronald E. Frank and Paul E. Green, "Numerical Taxonomy in Marketing Analysis: A Review Article," *Journal of Marketing Research,* Vol. V (February, 1968), pp. 83-98.

24

Jack Trout
Al Ries

Positioning Cuts through Chaos in Marketplace

As far as advertising is concerned, the good old days are gone forever.

As the president of a large consumer products company said recently, "Count on your fingers the number of successful new national brands introduced in the last two years. You won't get to your pinky."

Not that a lot of companies haven't tried. Every supermarket is filled with shelf after shelf of "half successful" brands. The manufacturers of these me-too products cling to the hope that they can develop a brilliant advertising campaign which will lift their offspring into the winner's circle.

Meanwhile, they hang in there with coupons, deals, point of purchase displays. But profits are hard to come by and that "brilliant" advertising campaign, even if it comes, doesn't ever seem to turn the brand around.

No wonder management people turn skeptical when the subject of advertising comes up. And instead of looking for new ways to put the power of advertising to work, management invents schemes for reducing the cost of what they are currently doing. Witness the rise of the house agency, the media buying service, the barter deal.

ADS DON'T WORK LIKE THEY USED TO

The chaos in the marketplace is a reflection of the fact that advertising just doesn't work like it used to. But old traditional ways of doing things die hard. "There's no reason that advertising can't do the job," say the defenders of the status quo, "as long as the product is good, the plan is sound and the commercials are creative."

But they overlook one big, loud reason. The marketplace itself. The noise level today is far too high. Not only the volume of advertising, but also the volume of products and brands.

Jack Trout is president and Al Ries is chairman of Ries, Cappiello, Colwell, Inc., an advertising agency. Both authors have published pioneering articles in the conceptual area of positioning products. Their concepts have heavily influenced practical marketing strategy.

To cope with this assault on his or her mind, the average consumer has run out of brain power and mental ability. And with a rising standard of living the average consumer is less and less interested in making the "best" choice. For many of today's more affluent customers, a "satisfactory" brand is good enough.

Advertising prepared in the old, traditional ways has no hope of being successful in today's chaotic marketplace.

In the past, advertising was prepared in isolation. That is, you studied the product and its features and then you prepared advertising which communicated to your customers and prospects the benefits of those features.

It didn't make much difference whether the competition offered those features or not. In the traditional approach, you ignored competition and made every claim seem like a preemptive claim. Mentioning a competitive product, for example, was considered not only bad taste, but poor strategy as well.

In the positioning era, however, the rules are reversed. To establish a position, you must often not only name competitive names, but also ignore most of the old advertising rules as well.

In category after category, the prospect already knows the benefits of using the product. To climb on his product ladder, you must relate your brand to the brands already there.

AVIS TOOK 'AGAINST' POSITION

In today's marketplace, the competitor's image is just as important as your own. Sometimes more important. An early success in the positioning era was the famous Avis campaign.

The Avis campaign will go down in marketing history as a classic example of establishing the "against" position. In the case of Avis, this was a position against the leader.

"Avis is only Number 2 in rent-a-cars, so why go with us? We try harder."

For 13 straight years, Avis lost money. Then they admitted they were No. 2 and have made money every year since. Avis was able to make substantial gains because they recognized the position of Hertz and didn't try to attack them head-on.

VW MADE "UGLY" POSITION WORK

A company can sometimes be successful by accepting a position that no one else wants. For example, virtually all automobile manufacturers want the public to think they make cars that are good looking. As a result, Volkswagen was able to establish a unique position for themselves. By default.

The strength of this position, of course, is that it communicates the idea of reliability in a powerful way. "The 1970 VW will stay ugly longer" was a powerful statement because it is psychologically sound. When an advertiser admits a negative, the reader is inclined to give them the position.

A similar principle is involved in Smucker's jams and jellies. "With a name like Smucker's," says the advertising, "you know it's got to be good."

BATTLE OF THE COLAS

The advantage of owning a position can be seen most clearly in the soft drink field. Three major cola brands compete in what is really not a contest. For every ten bottles of Coke, only four bottles of Pepsi and one bottle of Royal Crown are consumed.

While there may be room in the market for a No. 2 cola, the position of Royal Crown is weak. In 1970, for example, Coca-Cola's sales increase over the previous year (168,000,000 cases) was more than Royal Crown's entire volume (156,000,000 cases).

Obviously, Coke has a strong grip on the cola position. And there's not much room left for the other brands. But, strange as it might seem, there might be a spot for a reverse kind of product. One of the most interesting positioning ideas is the one currently being used by Seven-Up. It's the "Un-Cola" and it seems silly until you take a closer look.

"Wet and Wild" was a good campaign in the image era. But the "Un-Cola" is a great program in the positioning era. Sales jumped something like 10 per cent the first year the product was positioned against the cola field. And the increases have continued.

The brilliance of this idea can only be appreciated when you comprehend the intense share of mind enjoyed by the cola category. Two out of three soft drinks consumed in the U.S. are cola drinks.

By linking the product to what's already in the mind of the prospect, the Un-Cola position establishes Seven-Up as an alternative to a cola drink.

A somewhat similar positioning program is working in the media field. This is the "third newsweekly" concept being used by *Sports Illustrated* to get into the mind of the media buyer.

It obviously is an immensely successful program. But what may not be so obvious, is why it works. The "third newsweekly" certainly doesn't describe *Sports Illustrated.* (As the Un-Cola doesn't describe Seven-Up.)

What it does do, however, is to relate the magazine to a media category that is uppermost in the prospect's mind (as the Un-Cola relates to the soft drink category that is uppermost in the mind).

Both the Seven-Up and the *Sports Illustrated* programs are dramatic reminders that positioning is not something you do with the product. Positioning is something you do with the mind. That is, you position the product in the mind of the prospect.

YOU CAN REPOSITION COMPETITOR

In order to position your own brand, it's sometimes necessary to reposition the competitor.

In the case of Beck's beer, the repositioning is done at the expense of Lowenbrau: "You've tasted the German beer that's the most popular in America. Now taste the German beer that's the most popular in Germany."

This strategy works because the prospect had assumed something about Lowenbrau that wasn't true.

The current program for Raphael aperitif wine also illustrates this point. The ads show a bottle of "made in France" Raphael and a bottle of "made in U.S.A." Dubonnet. "For $1.00 a bottle less," says the headline, "you can enjoy the imported one." The shock, of course, is to find that Dubonnet is a product of the U.S.

PLIGHT OF AIRLINE X

In the positioning era, the name of a company or product is becoming more and more important. The name is the hook that allows the mind to hang the brand on its product ladder. Given a poor name, even the best brand in the world won't be able to hang on.

Take the airline industry. The big four domestic carriers are United, American, TWA and an airline we'll call Airline X.

Like all airlines, Airline X has had its ups and downs. Unfortunately, there have been more downs than ups. But unlike some of its more complacent competitors, Airline X has tried. A number of years ago, it brought in big league marketing people and pushed in the throttle.

Airline X was among the first to "paint the planes," "improve the food" and "dress up the stewardesses" in an effort to improve its reputation.

And Airline X hasn't been bashful when it

comes to spending money. Year after year, it has one of the biggest advertising budgets in the industry. Even though it advertises itself as "the second largest passenger carrier of all the airlines in the free world," you may not have guessed that Airline X is Eastern. Right up there spending with the worldwide names.

For all that money, what do you think of Eastern? Where do you think they fly? Up and down the East Coast, to Boston, Washington, Miami, right? Well, Eastern also goes to St. Louis, New Orleans, Atlanta, San Francisco, Acapulco. But Eastern has a regional name and their competitors have broader names which tell the prospect they fly everywhere.

Look at the problem from just one of Eastern's cities, Indianapolis. From Indianapolis, Eastern flies *north* to Chicago, Milwaukee and Minneapolis. And *south* to Birmingham and Mobile. They just don't happen to fly *east*.

And then there is the lush San Juan run which Eastern has been serving for more than 25 years. Eastern used to get the lion's share of this market. Then early last year American Airlines took over Trans Caribbean. So today, who is number one to the San Juan sun? Why American, of course.

No matter how hard you try, you can't hang "The Wings of Man" on a regional name. When the prospect is given a choice, he or she is going to prefer the national airline, not the regional one.

B.F. GOODRICH HAS IDENTITY CRISIS

What does a company do when its name (Goodrich) is similar to the name of a much larger company in the same field (Goodyear)?

Goodrich has problems. They could reinvent the wheel and Goodyear would get most of the credit.

If you watched the Super Bowl last January, you saw both Goodrich and Goodyear advertise their "American-made radial-ply tires." But which company do you think got their money's worth at $200,000 a pop?

We haven't seen the research, but our bet would be on Goodyear, the company that owns the tire position.

BEWARE OF THE NO-NAME TRAP

But even bad names like Eastern and Goodrich are better than no name at all.

In *Fortune's* list of 500 largest industrials, there are now 16 corporate nonentities. That is, 16 major American companies have legally changed their names to meaningless initials.

How many of these companies can you recognize: ACF, AMF, AMP, ATO, CPC, ESB, FMC, GAF, NVF, NL, PPG, RCA, SCM, TRW, USM and VF?

These are not tiny companies either. The smallest of them, AMP, has more than 10,000 employees and sales of over $225,000,000 a year.

What companies like ACF, AMF, AMP and the others fail to realize is that their initials have to stand for something. A prospect must know your name first before he or she can remember your initials.

GE stands for General Electric. IBM stands for International Business Machines. And everyone knows it. But how many people knew that ACF stood for American Car & Foundry?

Furthermore, now that ACF has legally changed its name to initials, there's presumably no way to even expose the prospect to the original name.

An exception seems to be RCA. After all, everyone knows that RCA stands for, or rather used to stand for, Radio Corp. of America.

That may be true today. But what about tomorrow? What will people think 20 years from now when they see those strange initials? Roman Catholic Archdiocese?

And take Corn Products Co. Presumably it changed its name to CPC International because it makes products out of lots of things besides corn, but you can't remember "CPC" without bringing Corn Products Co. to mind. The tragedy is CPC made the change to "escape" the past. Yet the exact opposite occurred.

LINE EXTENSION CAN BE TRAP, TOO

Names are tricky. Consider the Protein 21/29 shampoo, hair spray, conditioner, concentrate mess.

Back in 1970, the Mennen Co. introduced a combination shampoo conditioner called "Protein 21." By moving rapidly with a $6,000,000 introductory campaign (followed by a $9,000,000 program the next year), Mennen rapidly carved out a 13 per cent share of the $300,000,000 shampoo market.

Then Mennen hit the line extension lure. In rapid succession, the company introduced Protein 21 hair spray, Protein 29 hair spray (for men), Protein 21 conditioner (in two formulas), Protein 21 concentrate. To add to the confusion, the original Protein 21 was available in three different formulas (for dry, oily and regular hair).

Can you imagine how confused the prospect must be trying to figure out what to put on his or her head? No wonder Protein 21's share of the shampoo market has fallen from 13 per cent to 11 per cent. And the decline is bound to continue.

FREE RIDE CAN BE COSTLY

Another similar marketing pitfall recently befell, of all companies, Miles Laboratories.

You can see how it happens. A bunch of the boys are sitting around a conference table trying to name a new cold remedy.

"I have it," says Harry. "Let's call it Alka-Seltzer Plus. That way we can take advantage of the $20,000,000 we're already spending to promote the Alka-Seltzer name."

"Good thinking, Harry," and another money-saving idea is instantly accepted.

But lo and behold, instead of eating into the Dristan and Contac market, the new product turns around and eats into the Alka-Seltzer market.

And you know Miles must be worried. In every TV commercial, the "Alka-Seltzer" gets smaller and smaller and the "Plus" gets bigger and bigger.

Related to the free-ride trap, but not exactly the same, is another common error of judgment called the "well-known name" trap.

Both General Electric and RCA thought they could take their strong positions against IBM in computers. But just because a company is well known in one field doesn't mean it can transfer that recognition to another.

In other words, your brand can be on top of one ladder and nowhere on another. And the further apart the products are conceptually, the greater the difficulty of making the jump.

In the past when there were fewer companies and fewer products, a well-known name was a much greater asset than it is today. Because of the noise level, a "well-known" company has tremendous difficulty trying to establish a position in a different field than the one in which it built its reputation.

YOU CAN'T APPEAL TO EVERYONE

A human emotion called "greed" often leads an advertiser into another error. American Motors' introduction of the Hornet is one of the best examples of the "everybody" trap.

You might remember the ads, "The little rich car. American Motors Hornet: $1,994 to $3,589."

A product that tries to appeal to everyone winds up appealing to no one. People who want to spend $3,500 for a car don't buy the Hornet because they don't want their friends to think they're driving a $1,900 car. People who want to spend $1,900 for a car don't buy the Hornet because they don't want a car with $1,600 worth of accessories taken off of it.

AVOID THE F.W.M.T.S. TRAP

If the current Avis advertising is any indication, the company has "forgotten what made them successful."

The original campaign not only related No. 2 Avis to No. 1 Hertz, but also exploited the love that people have for the underdog. The new campaign (Avis is going to be No. 1) not only is conventional "brag and boast" advertising, but also dares the prospect to make the prediction not come true.

Our prediction: Avis ain't going to be No. 1. Further prediction: Avis will lose ground to Hertz and National.

Another company that seems to have fallen into the forgotten what made them successful trap is Volkswagen.

"Think small" was perhaps the most famous advertisement of the sixties. Yet last year VW ran an ad that said, "Volkswagen introduces a new kind of Volkswagen. Big."

O.K., Volkswagen, should we think small or should we think big?

Confusion is the enemy of successful positioning. Prediction: Rapid erosion of the Beetle's position in the U.S. market.

The world seems to be turning faster.

Years ago, a successful product might live 50 years or more before fading away. Today, a product's life cycle is much shorter. Sometimes it can be measured in months instead of years.

New products, new services, new markets, even new media are constantly being born. They grow up into adulthood and then slide into oblivion. And a new cycle starts again.

Yesterday, beer and hard liquor were campus favorites. Today it's wine.

Yesterday, the well-groomed man had his hair cut every week. Today, it's every month or two.

Yesterday, the way to reach the masses was the mass magazines. Today, it's network TV. Tomorrow, it could be cable.

The only permanent thing in life today is change. And the successful companies of tomorrow will be those companies that have learned to cope with it.

The acceleration of "change" creates enormous pressures on companies to think in terms of tactics rather than strategy. As one respected advertising man commented, "The day seems to be past when long-range strategy can be a winning technique."

But is change the way to keep pace with change? The exact opposite appears to be true.

The landscape is littered with the debris of projects that companies rushed into in attempting to "keep pace." Singer trying to move into the boom in home appliances. RCA moving into the boom of computers. General Foods moving into the boom in fast-food outlets. Not to mention the hundreds of companies that threw away their corporate identities to chase the passing fad to initials.

While the programs of those who kept at what they did best and held their ground have been immensely successful. Maytag selling their reliable appliances. Walt Disney selling his world of fantasy and fun. Avon calling.

And take margarine. Thirty years ago the first successful margarine brands positioned themselves against butter. "Tastes like the high-priced spread," said a typical ad.

And what works today? Why the same strategy. "It isn't nice to fool Mother Nature," says the Chiffon commercial, and sales go up 25 per cent. Chiffon is once again the best selling brand of soft margarine.

LONG-RANGE THINKING IMPORTANT

Change is a wave on the ocean of time. Short-term, the waves cause agitation and confusion, but long-term the underlying currents are much more significant.

To cope with change, it's important to take a long-range point of view. To determine your basic business. Positioning is a concept that is cumulative. Something that takes advantage of advertising's long-range nature.

In the seventies a company must think even more strategically than it did before. Changing the direction of a large company is like trying to turn an aircraft carrier. It takes a mile before anything happens. And if it was a wrong turn, getting back on course takes even longer.

To play the game successfully, you must make decisions on what your company will be doing not next month or next year, but in five years, ten years. In other words, instead of turning the wheel to meet each fresh wave, a company must point itself in the right direction.

You must have vision. There's no sense building a position based on a technology that's too narrow. Or a product that's becoming obsolete. Remember the famous *Harvard Business Review* article entitled "Marketing Myopia"? It still applies.

If a company has positioned itself in the right direction, it will be able to ride the currents of change, ready to take advantage of those opportunities that are right for it. But when an opportunity arrives, a company must be ready to move quickly.

Because of the enormous advantages that accrue to being the leader, most companies are not interested in learning how to *compete* with the leader. They want to be the leader. They want to be Hertz rather than Avis. *Time* rather than *Newsweek*. General Electric rather than Westinghouse.

Historically, however, product leadership is usually the result of an accident, rather than a preconceived plan.

The xerography process, for example, was offered to 32 different companies (including IBM and Kodak) before it wound up at the old Haloid Co. Renamed Haloid Xerox and then finally Xerox, the company has since dominated the copier market. Xerox now owns the copier position.

Were IBM and Kodak stupid to turn down xerography? Of course not. These companies reject thousands of ideas every year.

Perhaps a better description of the situation at the time was that Haloid, a small manufacturer of photographic supplies, was desperate, and the others weren't. As a result, it took a chance that more prudent companies couldn't be expected to take.

When you trace the history of how leadership positions were established, from Hershey in chocolate to Hertz in rent-a-cars, the common thread is not marketing skill or even product innovation. The common thread is seizing the initiative before the competitor has a chance to get established. In someone's oldtime military terms, the marketing leader "got there firstest with the mostest." The leader usually poured in the marketing money while the situation was still fluid.

IBM, for example, didn't invent the computer. Sperry Rand did. But IBM owns the computer position because they built their computer fortress before competition arrived.

And the position that Hershey established in chocolate was so strong they didn't need to advertise at all, a luxury that competitors like Nestle couldn't afford.

You can see that establishing a leadership position depends not only on luck and timing, but also upon a willingness to "pour it on" when others stand back and wait.

Yet all too often, the product leader makes the fatal mistake of attributing its success to marketing skill. As a result, it thinks it can transfer that skill to other products and other marketing situations.

Witness, for example, the sorry record of Xerox in computers. In May of 1969, Xerox exchanged nearly 10,000,000 shares of stock (worth nearly a billion dollars) for Scientific Data Systems Inc. Since the acquisition, the company (renamed Xerox Data Systems) has lost millions of dollars, and without Xerox's support would have probably gone bankrupt.

And the mecca of marketing knowledge, International Business Machines Corp., hasn't done much better. So far, the IBM plain-paper copier hasn't made much of a dent in Xerox's business. Touché.

The rules of positioning hold for all types of products. In the packaged goods area, for example, Bristol-Myers tried to take on Crest toothpaste with Fact (killed after $5,000,000 was spent on promotion). Then they tried to go after Alka-Seltzer with Resolve (killed after $11,000,000 was spent). And according to a headline in the February 7 [1972] issue of *Advertising Age,* "Bristol-Myers will test Dissolve aspirin in an attempt to unseat Bayer."

The suicidal bent of companies that go head-on against established competition is hard to understand. They know the score, yet they forge ahead anyway. In the marketing war, a "charge of the light brigade" happens every day. With the same predictable result.

ONE STRATEGY FOR LEADER

Successful marketing strategy usually consists of keeping your eyes open to possibilities and then strking before the product leader is firmly fixed.

As a matter of fact, the marketing leader is usually the one who moves the ladder into the mind with his or her brand nailed to the one and only rung. Once there, what can a company do to keep its top-dog position?

There are two basic strategies that should be used hand in hand. They seem contradictory, but aren't. One is to ignore competition, and the other is to cover all bets.

As long as a company owns the position, there's no point in running ads that scream "We're No. 1." Much better is to enhance the product category in the prospect's mind. Notice the current IBM campaign that ignores competition and sells the value of computers. All computers, not just the company's types.

Although the leader's advertising should ignore the competition, the leader shouldn't. The second rule is to cover all bets.

This means a leader should swallow his or her pride and adopt every new product development as soon as it shows signs of promise. Too often, however, the leader pooh-poohs the development, and doesn't wake up until it's too late.

ANOTHER STRATEGY FOR NON-LEADERS

Most companies are in the No. 2, 3, 4 or even worse category. What then?

Hope springs eternal in the human breast. Nine times out of ten, the also-ran sets out to attack the leader, a la RCA's assault on IBM. Result: Disaster.

Simply stated, the first rule of positioning is this: You can't compete head-on against a company that has a strong, established position. You can go around, under or over, but never head-to-head.

The leader owns the high ground. The No. 1 position in the prospect's mind. The top rung of the product ladder.

The classic example of No. 2 strategy is Avis. But many marketing people misread the Avis story. They assume the company was successful because it tried harder.

Not at all. Avis was successful because it related itself to the position of Hertz. Avis preempted the No. 2 position. (If trying harder were the secret of success, Harold Stassen would be president.)

Most marketplaces have room for a strong

No. 2 company provided they position themselves clearly as an alternative to the leader. In the computer field, for example, Honeywell has used this strategy successfully.

"The other computer company vs. Mr. Big," says a typical Honeywell ad. Honeywell is doing what none of the other computer companies seems to be willing to do. Admit that IBM is, in fact, the leader in the computer business. Maybe that's why Honeywell and Mr. Big are the only large companies reported to be making money on computers.

SOME 'STRONG' POSITIONS AREN'T

Yet there are positions that can be taken. These are positions that look strong, but in reality are weak.

Take the position of Scott in paper products. Scott has about 40 per cent of the $1.2 billion market for towels, napkins, toilet tissues and other consumer paper products. But Scott, like Mennen with Protein 21, fell into the line-extension trap.

ScotTowels, ScotTissue, Scotties, Scottkins, even BabyScott. All of these items undermined the Scott foundation. The more products hung on the Scott name, the less meaning the name had to the average consumer.

When Procter & Gamble attacked with Mr. Whipple and his tissue-squeezers, it was no contest. Charmin is now the No. 1 brand in the toilet-tissue market.

In Scott's case, a large "share of market" didn't mean they owned the position. More important is a large "share of mind." The housewife could write "Charmin," Kleenex, Bounty and Pampers" on her shopping list and know exactly what products she was going to get. "Scott" on a shopping list has no meaning. The actual brand names aren't much help either. Which brand, for example, is engineered for the nose, Scotties or ScotTissue?

In positioning terms, the name "Scott" exists in limbo. It isn't firmly ensconced on any product ladder.

ELIMINATE EGOS FROM DECISION MAKING

To repeat, the name is the hook that hangs the brand on the product ladder in the prospect's mind. In the positioning era, the brand name to give a product is probably a company's single, most important marketing decision.

To be successful in the positioning era, advertising and marketing people must be brutally frank. They must try to eliminate all ego from the decision making process. It only clouds the issue.

One of the most critical aspects of "positioning" is being able to evaluate objectively products and how they are viewed by customers and prospects.

As a rule, when it comes to building strong programs, trust no one, especially managers who are all wrapped up in their products. The closer people get to products, the more they defend old decisions or old promises.

Successful companies get their information from the marketplace. That's the place where the program has to succeed, not in the product manager's office.

A company that keeps its eye on Tom, Dick and Harry is going to miss Pierre, Hans and Yoshio.

Marketing is rapidly becoming a worldwide ball game. A company that owns a position in one country now finds that it can use that position to wedge its way into another.

IBM has 62 per cent of the German computer market. Is this fact surprising? It shouldn't be. IBM earns more than 50 per cent of its profits outside the U.S.

As companies start to operate on a worldwide basis, they often discover they have a name problem.

A typical example is U.S. Rubber, a worldwide company that marketed many products not made of rubber. Changing the name to Uniroyal created a new corporate identity that could be used worldwide.

CREATIVITY TAKES BACK SEAT

In the seventies, creativity will have to take a back seat to strategy.

Advertising Age itself reflects this fact. Today you will find fewer stories about individual campaigns and more stories about what's happening in an entire industry. Creativity alone isn't a worthwhile objective in an era where a company can spend millions of dollars on great advertising and still fail miserably in the marketplace.

Consider what Harry McMahan calls the "Curse of Clio." In the past, the American Festival has made special awards to "Hall of Fame Classics." Of the 41 agencies that won these Clio awards, 31 have lost some or all of these particular accounts.

But the cult of creativity dies hard. One agency president said recently, "Oh, we do positioning all the time. But after we develop the position, we turn it over to the creative department." And too often, of course, the creativity does nothing but obscure the positioning.

In the positioning era, the key to success is to run the naked positioning statement, unadorned by so-called creativity.

ASK YOURSELF THESE QUESTIONS

If these examples have moved you to want to apply positioning thinking to your own company's situation, here are some questions to ask yourself:

1. What position, if any, do we already own in the prospect's mind?

Get the answer to this question from the marketplace, not the marketing manager. If this requires a few dollars for research, so be it. Spend the money. It's better to know exactly what you're up against now than to discover it later when nothing can be done about it.

2. What position do we want to own?

Here is where you bring out your crystal ball and try to figure out the best position to own from a long-term point of view.

3. What companies must be out-gunned if we are to establish that position?

If your proposed position calls for a head-to-head approach against a marketing leader, forget it. It's better to go around an obstacle rather than over it. Back up. Try to select a position that no one else has a firm grip on.

4. Do we have enough marketing money to occupy and hold the position?

A big obstacle to successful positioning is attempting to achieve the impossible. It takes money to build a share of mind. It takes money to establish a position. It takes money to hold a position once you've established it.

The noise level today is fierce. There are just too many "me-too" products and too many "me-too" companies vying for the mind of the prospect. Getting noticed is getting tougher.

5. Do we have the guts to stick with one consistent positioning concept?

With the noise level out there, a company has to be bold enough and consistent enough to cut through.

The first step in a positioning program normally entails running fewer programs, but stronger ones. This sounds simple, but actually runs counter to what usually happens as corporations get larger. They normally run more programs, but weaker ones. It's this fragmentation that can make many large advertising budgets just about invisible in today's media storm.

6. Does our creative approach match our positioning strategy?

Creative people often resist positioning thinking because they believe it restricts their creativity. And it does. But creativity isn't the objective in the seventies. Even "communications" itself isn't the objective.

The name of the marketing game in the seventies is "positioning." And only the better players will survive.

RETROSPECTIVE COMMENTARY

THE POSITIONING ERA: A VIEW TEN YEARS LATER

If one word could be said to have marked the course of advertising in the decade of the '70s it is the word "positioning." Positioning has become the buzzword of advertising and marketing people, not only in this country, but around the world.

It was just 10 years ago that the word and the concept were introduced for the first time to the advertising community in the pages of *Industrial Marketing* and *Advertising Age*.

The article, written by Jack Trout, named names and made predictions, all based on the "rules" of a game Jack called positioning.

On positioning's 10th anniversary, it might be interesting to look back at that 1969 article and see what changes have taken place.

> Today's marketplace is no longer responsive to strategies that worked in the past. There are just too many products, too many companies and too much marketing noise. We have become an overcommunicated society. (1969)

The question most frequently asked us is "why"? Why do we need a new approach to advertising and marketing?

The answer today is the same as it was then. We have become an overcommunicated society. With only 5% of the world's population, America consumes 57% of the world's advertising output. The per capita consumption of advertising in the U.S. today is about $200 a year.

If you spend $1,000,000 a year on advertising, you are bombarding the average consumer with less than ½¢ of advertising, spread out over 365 days – a consumer who is already exposed to $200 worth of advertising from other companies.

In our overcommunicated society, to talk about the "impact" of advertising is to seriously overstate the potential effectiveness of your messages. It's an egocentric view that bears no relationship to the realities of the marketplace itself.

In the communication jungle out there, the only hope to score big is to be selective, to concentrate on narrow targets, to practice segmentation. In a word, "positioning" is still the name of the game today.

> The mind, as a defense against the volume of today's communications, screens and rejects much of the information offered it. In general, the mind accepts only that which matches prior knowledge or experience. (1969)

Millions of dollars have been wasted trying to change minds with advertising. Once a mind is made up, it's almost impossible to change it. Certainly not with a weak force like advertising.

The average person can tolerate being told something about which he or she knows nothing. (This is why "news" is an effective advertising approach.) But the average person can't tolerate being told he or she is "wrong." Mind-changing is the road to advertising disaster.

Back in 1969, Jack used the computer industry as an example of the folly of trying to change minds.

Company after company tried to tell people its computers were "better" than IBM's. Yet that doesn't "compute" in the prospect's mind. "If you're so smart," says the prospect, "how come you're not rich like IBM?"

The computer "position" in the minds of most people is filled with the name of a company called "IBM." For a competitive computer manufacturer to obtain a favorable position in the prospect's mind, he or she must somehow relate the company to IBM's position.

In other words, don't try to change the prospect's mind at all. Accept what's up there and work around it. It's the only hope in today's overcommunicated society.

> Positioning is a game where the competitor's image is just as important as your own. Sometimes more important. (1969)

The classic example is the famous Avis campaign.

"Avis is only No. 2 in rent-a-cars. So why go with us? We try harder." This program was extremely successful for Avis until corporate egos got in the way. Then the company launched a campaign which said "Avis is going to be No. 1."

No way.

Be honest. In the last 15 years, Avis has run many different advertising campaigns. "The wizard of Avis." "You don't have to run through airports." Etc. But what is the single theme that leaps into your mind when someone mentions Avis?

Of course, "Avis is only No. 2., etc." Yet Avis in the last few years has consistently ignored this No. 2 concept.

We call this the "F.W.M.T.S." trap. (Forgot What Made Them Successful.)

If you want to be successful today, you can't ignore the competitor's position. Nor can you walk away from your own. In the immortal words of Woody Allen, "Play it where it lies."

Another advertiser that fell into the F.W.M.T.S. trap is Seven-Up. With the "Uncola" campaign, the company successfully positioned its 7UP drink as an alternative to Coke and Pepsi. (Almost two-thirds of all the soft drinks consumed in the U.S. are cola drinks.)

But the current campaign says, "America is turning 7UP." America is doing no such thing. Seven-Up is advertising its aspirations. No different conceptually than the "Avis is going to be No. 1" campaign. And no more effective.

> In the positioning era, the name of your company or product is becoming more and more important. (1969)

No aspect of positioning has proved as controversial as the "importance of the name."

Our 1969 example was Eastern Airlines. Among the four largest domestic airlines, Eastern consistently ranks at the bottom on passenger surveys.

Why? Eastern has a "regional" name that puts them in a different category than the big nationwide carriers (American, United, Trans World Airlines). The name Eastern puts the airline in the same category with Southern, North Central, Piedmont, Allegheny. The regional airline category.

After 10 years of effort, Eastern still ranks at the bottom of the big four.

You see what you expect to see. The passenger who has a bad experience on American or United says, "It was just one of those things." An exception to the good service he or she was expecting.

The passenger who has a bad experience on Eastern says, "It's that darn Eastern Airlines again." A continuation of the bad service he or she was expecting.

One prime objective of all advertising is to heighten expectations. To create the illusion that the product or service will perform the miracles you expect. And presto, it does.

Recently, Allegheny Airlines has seen the light. The new name: USAir. Now watch them take off.

Yes, but that's consumer advertising and the industrial customer buys on reason, not emotion. On logic and facts.

As IBM's competitors. Or Xerox's or General Electric's.

Especially for high technology, high visibility products like computers and copiers, the average industrial customer tends to be far more emotional than your average Charmin-squeezing housewife. (Who, more often than not, is downright practical.)

Industrial customers are also cursed by a "play it safe" attitude.

You can't blame them. No housewife ever got fired for buying the wrong brand of coffee. But plenty of industrial buyers have been in deep trouble over a high-technology buy that went sour. (Babcock & Wilcox will have trouble pushing its nuclear power plants in the future no matter how "superior" its specs are.)

The trend in industrial products is toward more sophistication, more use of integrated circuits, fiber optics, lasers, etc. So you can expect the industrial buyer to buy more on feelings, hunches and especially reputation. And less on objective production comparisons.

Which is why "factual expository copy" is getting less important in industrial advertising and "positioning" more important.

> Your program has to go beyond just establishing a name. Too many programs start there and end there. To secure a worthwhile position for a corporate name, you need a thought to go with it. (1969)

Ten years ago, the Olin campaign was getting a lot of creative kudos. And the ads were beautifully done. But what is Olin? What is its position?

Even today, these questions have no clear-cut answer in the mind of the prospect.

Line Extension Trap

You can't hang a company on a name. You need an idea. Of all the positioning concepts suggested by the 1969 article, this one has proved to be the most useful. It led directly to what we call "the line extension trap."

When the marketing history of the '70s is written, the single most significant trend will have to be "line extension." Line extension has swept through the marketing community like Sherman through Georgia. And for some very sound reasons.

Logic is on the side of line extension. Arguments of economics. Trade acceptance. Customer acceptance. Lower advertising costs. Increased income. Reduced costs. The corporate image.

As we said, logic is on the side of line extension. Truth, unfortunately, is not. The paradox of marketing is that conventional wisdom is almost always wrong.

Xerox went out and bought a computer company with a perfectly good name. Scientific Data Systems.

And what was the first thing they did? They changed the name to Xerox Data Systems. Then they ran an ad that said, "This Xerox machine can't make a copy."

Any Xerox machine that couldn't make a copy was headed for trouble, believe us.

When Xerox folded their computer operations, it cost another $84,000,000 to sweep up the mess.

Singer went out and did the same thing with the old, respected Friden name. One of their introductory ads said, "Singer Business Machines introduces Touch & Know."

Get it? Touch and know, touch and sew.

This is the ultimate positioning mistake. To try to transfer a generic brand name to a different product sold to a different market. And then, to top it all off, to knock off your own sewing machine slogan.

Touch and Go would have been more appropriate. When they folded this operation, Singer set a record. They recorded one of the largest one quarter write-offs ever reported by any company anywhere in the world – $341,000,000.

If your corporate name is inappropriate for the new product you intend to market, create a new one. And a new position.

> One thing that's worse than a 'just a name' program is one without a name. That sounds like it

> could never happen, doesn't it? Well, it does when companies use initials instead of a name. (1969)

This idea was later developed into what we call "The no-name trap." Of all the positioning concepts outlined back in 1969, this one generated the most instant acceptance. The superiority of a name over a meaningless set of initials could generally be documented by market research.

The initialitus that struck American business in the late '60s and early '70s abated. Some companies even went back to their original names.

> A company has no hope to make progress head-on against the position that IBM has established. (1969)

This is perhaps the most quoted sentence from the original article—as true today as it was then.

IBM has an overwhelming position in the broad middle range of computers. So, how do you compete against IBM in computers? The 1969 article had a suggestion on how to do it.

> It's almost impossible to dislodge a strongly dug-in leader who owns the high ground. You're a lot better off to open up a new front or position—that is, unless you enjoy being shot-up. (1969)

A New Front

The big computer successes in the '70s were the companies that avoided going head-to-head with IBM—Digital Equipment Corp. and Data General, in particular, at the low end of the market.

Even Apple and Radio Shack have done profitable computer business, in the home market.

This "new front" idea has been developed in our marketing warfare seminars into a concept called "flanking warfare." You avoid the competitor's high ground by outflanking them.

> Another problem that occurs fairly often is represented by the one B.F. Goodrich faces. What do you do when your name (Goodrich) is similar to the name of a larger company in the same field [Goodyear]? (1969)
>
> Goodrich has problems. Our research indicates that they could reinvent the wheel and Goodyear would get most of the credit. If ever a company could benefit from a name change, they're one. (1969)

In 1968, Goodyear had sales of $2,926,000,000 while B.F. Goodrich's sales were $1,340,000,000. A ratio of 2.2 to 1.

Ten years later, in 1978, Goodyear had sales of $7,489,000,000 while B.F. Goodrich had sales of $2,594,000,000. A ratio of 2.9 to 1.

So the rich get richer. Fair enough.

But what is odd is that the loser's advertising continues to get all the publicity. "We're the other guys" got a lot of favorable attention in the press. But not a lot of favorable attention from the tire-buying public.

The Real Reckoning

But what really rattled the cages of the Madison Ave. mavens was positioning's implied attack on "creativity."

Even through creativity was not mentioned in the 1969 article, we didn't hesitate to attack it later on. By 1972, we were saying, "Creativity is dead. The name of the advertising game in the '70s is positioning."

In truth, the decade of the '70s might well be characterized as a "return to reality." White knights and black eyepatches gave way to such positioning concepts as Lite Beer's "Everything you've always wanted in a great beer. And less."

Poetic? Yes. Artful? Yes. But also a straightforward, clearly defined explanation of the basic positioning premise.

On the occasion of positioning's 10th anniversary, it might be appropriate to ask, where do we go from here?

If creativity belonged to the '60s and positioning to the '70s, where will we be in the '80s?

Would you believe us if we told you in the

next decade we will be burying the marketing concept?

Probably not, but we'll tell you anyway.

For at least 50 years now, astute advertising people have preached the marketing gospel. "The customer is king," said the marketing moguls. Over and over again, they used their wondrous presentations to warn top management that to be "production" oriented instead of "customer" oriented was to flirt with disaster.

But it's beginning to look like "King Customer" is dead. And that they're selling a corpse to their management.

Plenty of companies who have dutifully followed their marketing experts have seen millions of dollars disappear in valiant but disastrous customer-oriented efforts.

Who do you suppose masterminded those classic positioning mistakes? Not amateurs, but full-fledged marketing professionals with briefcases full of credentials.

General Electric in computers. Singer in business machines. Sara Lee in frozen dinners.

Of course, these marketing executives had excuses. "Product problems." "Not enough capital." Or the ever popular, "Not enough distribution" were often cited to explain these failures.

Can it be that marketing, itself, is the problem?

Many managers are beginning to realize that something is wrong—that the traditional definition of marketing (to be customer-oriented) is becoming an obsolete concept.

A New Perspective

To get a better perspective of the situation, you have to go back to the '20s, when industry started its dramatic march forward. It was then that business first became production oriented. This was the heyday of Henry Ford and his Model T.

You could have any color you wanted as long as it was black. Mr. Ford was more interested in keeping his production lines rolling (and his prices down) than in keeping his customers satisfied.

You might think that advertising was an unnecessary luxury in a production-oriented economy. Quite the contrary.

Advertising was an important ingredient in the scheme of things. Advertising's first commandment was "Mass advertising creates mass demand which makes mass production possible."

Neat. Except that General Motors tooled up its production lines to please its prospects rather than its production engineers and quickly grabbed the sales leadership from Ford.

Things haven't been the same since.

In the aftermath of World War II, business became customer-oriented with a vengeance.

The marketing man was in charge, no doubt about it, and his prime minister was marketing research.

But today, every company has become marketing oriented. Knowing what the customer wants isn't too helpful if a dozen other companies are already serving his or her wants.

American Motor's problem is not the customer. American Motor's problem is General Motors, Ford and Chrysler.

To be successful today, a company must be "competitor" oriented. It must look for weak points in the positions of its competitors and then launch marketing attacks against those weak points. For example, while others were losing millions in the computer business, DEC was making millions by exploiting IBM's weakness in small computers.

Similarly, Savin established a successful beachhead in small, inexpensive copiers. A weak point in the Xerox lineup.

And from out of nowhere came a product called Bubble Yum to take a big bite out of the bubble gum market. By exploiting the competitions' weakness of being hard to chew, they over-ran some strongly entrenched brands that had been around for years.

There are those who would say that competitors are always considered in a well-thought-out marketing plan. Indeed they are. Usually towards the back of the book under a heading entitled "Competitive Evaluation." Almost as an afterthought.

Upfront with prominence is the major part of the plan. The details of marketplace, the various demographic segments and a myriad of "customer" research statistics carefully gleaned from endless focus groups, test panels, concept and market tests.

The Battle Plan

The future marketing plan won't look like this. In fact, it won't be called a marketing plan at all. But a competitive plan, or a battle plan.

In the battle plan of the future, many more pages will be dedicated to the competition. The plan will carefully dissect each participant in the marketplace. It will develop a list of competitive strengths and weaknesses as well as a plan of action to either exploit or defend against them.

There might even come a day when this plan will contain a dossier on each of the competitors' key management people which will include their favorite tactics and style of operation. (Not unlike those Germans kept on the Allied commanders in World War II.)

And we're not talking about the distant future. Already the first signs of this trend are starting to appear in the professional journals.

In the August, 1978, issue of *Management Review*, is a report entitled, "Customer or competitor: Which guideline for marketing?" In the article, Alfred R. Oxenfeldt and William L. Moore spell out six "weaknesses" that can make a firm vulnerable to an attack from a competitor. The article's basic premise was that switching to a competitor orientation can provide a better payoff.

In the August, 1978, issue of *Business Horizons,* William S. Sachs and George Benson state the issue more directly: "Is it time to discard the marketing concept?"

These articles point out that a small, but growing, number of experts believe that the customer isn't what he or she used to be.

Confusion has set in. In many categories, customers no longer perceive any large differences in products. Thus brand choice will not be based on a rational search of all brands in the category but on a brand that was previously tried. Or the leader. Or the one positioned to the prospect's segment.

Once buying patterns are established, it has become more and more difficult to change them. The customer doesn't really want to accept any more information on a category that he or she has already cataloged in the mind. No matter how dramatically or how creatively this information is presented.

What does all this portend for the marketing people of the '80s? Or whatever they are going to be called.

In simple terms, it means that they have to be prepared to wage marketing warfare. Successful marketing campaigns will have to be planned like military campaigns.

Strategic planning will become more and more important. Companies will have to learn how to attack, defend and flank their competition. And when to resort to guerrilla warfare.

They will need better intelligence on how to anticipate competitive moves.

On the personal level, successful marketing people will have to exhibit many of the same virtues that make a great general—courage, boldness, loyalty and perseverance.

The winners in the marketing battles of the future will be those men and women who have best learned the lessons of military history—the marketing people who have learned to plan like Alexander the Great, maneuver like Napoleon Bonaparte and fight like George S. Patton.

They will also be the marketing people who know their competitors better than they know their own customers.

Robert D. Buzzell
Bradley T. Gale
Ralph G. M. Sultan

25

Market Share – A Key to Profitability

It is now widely recognized that one of the main determinants of business profitability is market share. Under most circumstances, enterprises that have achieved a high share of the markets they serve are considerably more profitable than their smaller-share rivals. This connection between market share and profitability has been recognized by corporate executives and consultants, and it is clearly demonstrated in the results of a project undertaken by the Marketing Science Institute on the Profit Impact of Market Strategies (PIMS). The PIMS project, on which we have been working since late 1971,[1] is aimed at identifying and measuring the major determinants of return on investment (ROI) in individual businesses. Phase II of the PIMS project, completed in late 1973, reveals 37 key profit influences, of which one of the most important is market share.

There is no doubt that market share and return on investment are strongly related. Exhibit 25-1 shows average pretax ROI figures for groups of businesses in the PIMS project that have successively increasing shares of their markets. (For an explanation of how businesses, markets, and ROI results are defined and measured in the PIMS project, see the ruled insert on pp. 319–320.) On the average, a difference of 10 percentage points in market share is accompanied by a difference of about 5 points in pretax ROI.

Authors' note: We wish to acknowledge the contributions of our associates in the PIMS project to the results reported in this paper. Sidney Schoeffler, Donald F. Heany, and James Conlin made valuable suggestions, and Paula Nichols carried out numerous analyses very efficiently and cheerfully. The authors are, of course, solely responsible for any errors or misrepresentations that remain.
Reprinted by permission of the Harvard Business Review. "Market Share – A Key to Profitability" by Robert D. Buzzell, Bradley T. Gale and Ralph G.M. Sultan (January-February 1975).

Robert Buzzell, professor of Business Administration at Harvard University, received his Ph.D. at Ohio State University. He is a former executive director of the Marketing Science Institute.
Bradley Gale is a professor of Economics at the University of Massachusetts. He directed the economic analysis of the PIMS project.
Ralph Sultan is chief economist of the Royal Bank of Canada in Montreal. He is a former faculty member at Harvard University.

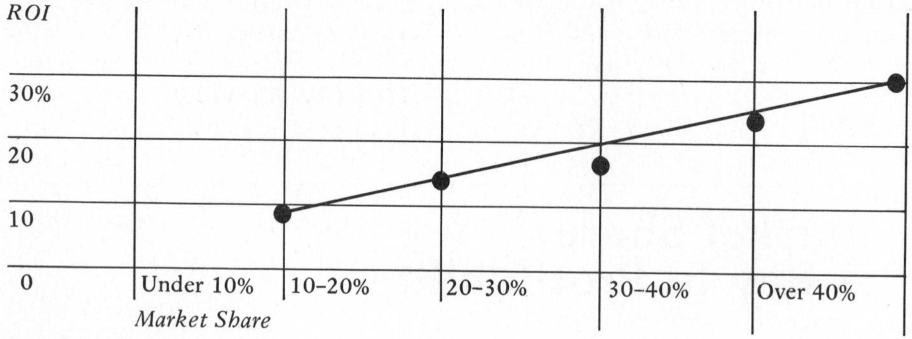

EXHIBIT 25-1 *Relationship between Market Share and Pretax ROI*

While the PIMS data base is the most extensive and detailed source of information on the profit/market-share relationship, there is additional confirming evidence of its existence. For instance, companies enjoying strong competitive positions in their primary product markets tend to be highly profitable. Consider, for example, such major companies as IBM, Gillette, Eastman Kodak, and Xerox, as well as smaller, more specialized corporations like Dr. Scholl (foot care products) and Hartz Mountain (pet foods and accessories).

Granted that high rates of return usually accompany high market share, it is useful to explore the relationship further. Why is market share profitable? What are the observed differences between low- and high-share businesses? Does the notion vary from industry to industry? And, what does the profitability/market-share relationship imply for strategic planning? In this article we shall attempt to provide partial answers to these questions by presenting evidence on the nature, importance, and implications of the links between market share and profit performance.

WHY MARKET SHARE IS PROFITABLE

The data shown in Exhibit 25-1 demonstrate the differences in ROI between high- and low-market-share businesses. This convincing evidence of the relationship itself, however, does not tell us why there is a link between market share and profitability. There are at least three possible explanations:

Economies of scale. The most obvious rationale for the high rate of return enjoyed by large-share businesses is that they have achieved economies of scale in procurement, manufacturing, marketing, and other cost components. A business with a 40% share of a given market is simply twice as big as one with 20% of the same market, and it will attain, to a much greater degree, more efficient methods of operation within a particular type of technology.

Closely related to this explanation is the so-called "experience curve" phenomenon widely publicized by the Boston Consulting Group.[2] According to BCG, total unit costs of producing and distributing a product tend to decline by a more or less constant percentage with each doubling of a company's cumulative output. Since, in a given time period, businesses with large market shares generally also have larger cumulative sales than their smaller competitors, they would be expected to have lower costs and correspondingly higher profits.

Market power. Many economists, especially among those involved in antitrust work, believe that economies of scale are of relatively little importance in most industries. These economists argue that if large-scale businesses earn higher profits than their smaller competitors, it is a result of their greater market power: their size permits them to bargain more effectively, "administer" prices, and, in the end, realize significantly higher prices for a particular product.[3]

Quality of management. The simplest of all explanations for the market-share/profitability relationship is that both share and ROI reflect a common underlying factor: the quality of management. Good managers (including, perhaps, lucky ones!) are successful in achieving high shares of their respective markets; they are also skillful in controlling costs, getting maximum productivity from employees, and so on. Moreover, once a business achieves a leadership position – possibly by developing a new field – it is much easier for it to retain its lead than for others to catch up.

These explanations of why the market-share/profitability relationship exists are not mutually exclusive. To some degree, a large-share business may benefit from all three kinds of relative advantages. It is important, however, to understand from the available information how much of the increased profitability that accompanies high market share comes from each of these or other sources.

HOW MARKET SHARE RELATES TO ROI

Analysis of the PIMS data base sheds some light on the reasons for the observed relationship between market share and ROI. Businesses with different market-share levels are compared as to financial and operating ratios and measures of relative prices and product quality in Exhibit 25-2. In examining these figures, remember that

EXHIBIT 25-2 *Relationships of Market Share to Key Financial and Operating Ratios for Overall PIMS Sample of Businesses*

Financial and Operating Ratios	Market Share Under 10%	10%-20%	20%-30%	30%-40%	Over 40%
Capital structure:					
Investment/sales	68.66	67.74	61.08	64.66	63.98
Receivables/sales	15.52	14.08	13.96	15.18	14.48
Inventory/sales	9.30	8.97	8.68	8.68	8.16
Operating results:					
Pretax profit/sales	-0.16	3.42	4.84	7.60	13.16
Purchases/sales	45.40	39.90	39.40	32.60	33.00
Manufacturing/sales	29.64	32.61	32.11	32.95	31.76
Marketing/sales	10.60	9.88	9.06	10.45	8.57
R&D/sales	2.60	2.40	2.83	3.18	3.55
Capacity/utilization	74.70	77.10	78.10	75.40	78.00
Product quality: average of percents superior minus inferior	14.50	20.40	20.40	20.10	43.00
Relative price*	2.72	2.73	2.65	2.66	2.39
Number of businesses	156	179	105	67	87

*Average value on 5-point scale:
5 = 10% or more lower than leading competitors' average;
3 = within 3% of competition;
1 = 10% or more higher than competition.

the PIMS sample of businesses includes a wide variety of products and industries. Consequently, when we compare businesses with market shares under 10%, say, with those having shares over 40%, we are not observing differences in costs and profits within a single industry. Each subgroup contains a diversity of industries, types of products, kinds of customers, and so on.

Differences between High-and-Low-Share Businesses

The data in Exhibit 25-2 reveal four important differences between high-share businesses and those with smaller shares. The samples used are sufficiently large and balanced to ensure that the differences between them are associated primarily with variations in market share, and not with other factors. These differences are:

1. *As market share rises, turnover on investment rises only somewhat, but profit margin on sales increases sharply.* ROI is, of course, dependent on both the rate of net profit on sales and the amount of investment required to support a given volume of sales. Exhibit 25-2 reveals that the ratio of investment to sales declines only slightly, and irregularly, with increased market share. The data show too that capacity utilization is not systematically related to market share.

On the surface then, higher investment turnover does not appear to be a major factor contributing to higher rates of return. However, this observation is subject to some qualification. Our analysis of the PIMS data base shows that investment intensity (investment relative to sales) tends to vary directly with a business's degree of vertical integration.

(The degree of vertical integration is measured as the ratio of the total value added by the business to its sales. Both the numerator and denominator of the ratio are adjusted by subtracting the pretax income and adding the PIMS average ROI, multiplied by the investment.)

Vertical integration thus has a strong negative relation to the ratio of purchases to sales. Since high market-share businesses are on the average somewhat more vertically integrated than those with smaller shares, it is likely that investment turnover increases somewhat more with market share than the figures in Exhibit 25-2 suggest. In other words, as shown in Exhibit 25-3, for a given degree of vertical integration, the investment-to-sales ratio declines significantly, even though overall averages do not.

Nevertheless, Exhibit 25-2 shows that the major reason for the ROI/market-share relationship is the dramatic difference in pretax profit margins on sales. Businesses with market shares under 10% had average pretax losses of 0.16%. The average ROI for businesses with under 10% market share was about 9%. Obviously, no individual business can have a negative profit-to-sales ratio and still earn a positive ROI. The apparent inconsistency between the averages reflects the fact that some businesses in the sample incurred losses that were very high in relation to sales but that were much smaller in relation to investment. In the PIMS sample, the average return on sales exhibits a strong, smooth, upward trend as market share increases.

EXHIBIT 25-3 *Effect of Vertical Integration on Investment/Sales Ratio*

Vertical Integration	Market Share Under 10%	10%-20%	20%-30%	30%-40%	Over 40%
Low	65	61	46	58	55
High	77	76	75	70	69

Why do profit margins on sales increase so sharply with market share? To answer this, it is necessary to look in more detail at differences in prices and operating expenses.

2. *The biggest single difference in costs, as related to market share, is in the purchases-to-sales ratio.* As shown in Exhibit 25-2, for large-share businesses – those with shares over 40% – purchases represent only 33% of sales, compared with 45% for businesses with shares under 10%.

How can we explain the decline in the ratio of purchases to sales as share goes up? One possibility, as mentioned earlier, is that high-share businesses tend to be more vertically integrated – they "make" rather than "buy," and often they own their own distribution facilities. The decline in the purchases-to-sales ratio is quite a bit less (see Exhibit 25-4) if we control for the level of vertical integration. A low purchases-to-sales ratio goes hand in hand with a high level of vertical integration.

Other things being equal, a greater extent of vertical integration ought to result in a rising level of manufacturing costs. (For the non-manufacturing businesses in the PIMS sample, "manufacturing" was defined as the primary value-creating activity of the business. For example, processing transactions is the equivalent of manufacturing in a bank.) but the data in Exhibit 25-2 show little or no connection between manufacturing expense, as a percentage of sales, and market share. This could be because, despite the increase in vertical integration, costs are offset by increased efficiency.

This explanation is probably valid for some of the businesses in the sample, but we believe that, in the majority of cases, the decline in costs of purchased materials also reflects a combination of economies of scale in buying and, perhaps, bargaining power in dealing with suppliers. Economies of scale in procurement arise from lower costs of manufacturing, marketing, and distributing when suppliers sell in large quantities. For very large-scale buyers, custom-designed components and special formulations of materials that are purchased on long-term contracts may offer "order of magnitude" economies.

Still another possible explanation of the declining purchases-to-sales ratio for large-share businesses might be that they charge higher prices, thus increasing the base on which the percentage is figured. This does not, however, appear to be the case.

In Exhibit 25-2 we give measures of price relative to competition for each group of businesses that indicate otherwise. Because of the great difficulty of computing meaningful relative price-index numbers, the measure we used here is rather crude. We asked the PIMS participants to indicate on a five-point scale whether their prices were "about the same" as major competitors, "somewhat" higher or lower, or "substantially" higher or lower for each business. The average values of this scale measure are virtually identical for each market-share group, except for those with shares over 40%.

Despite the similarity of relative prices for the first four share groups, the purchases-to-sales ratios decline in a regular, substantial fashion as share increases. In light of this, we do not believe that the decline in purchase costs is a reflection of higher price levels imposed by "market power."

EXHIBIT 25-4 *Purchase-to-Sales Ratio Corrected for Vertical Integration*

Vertical Integration	Market Share Under 10%	10%-20%	20%-30%	30%-40%	Over 40%
Low	54	51	53	52	46
High	32	27	29	24	23

3. *As market share increases, there is some tendency for marketing costs, as a percentage of sales, to decline.* The difference in marketing costs between the smallest and largest market-share groups amounts on the average to about 2% of sales. We believe that this reflects true scale economies, including the spreading of fixed marketing costs and the ability of large-share businesses to utilize more efficient media and marketing methods. In the case of industrial products, large scale permits a manufacturer to use his own sales force rather than commissioned agents and, at some point, to utilize specialized sales forces for specific product lines or markets. For consumer goods, large-scale businesses may derive an important cost advantage from their ability to utilize the most efficient mass-advertising media.

In addition, leading brands of consumer products appear to benefit to some extent from a "bandwagon effect" that results from the brand's greater visibility in retail stores or greater support from retail store sales personnel. For example, Anheuser-Busch has for some time enjoyed lower advertising costs per case of beer than its smaller rivals—just as the advertising expense per car of General Motors is significantly lower than that of other competing auto manufacturers.

4. *Market leaders develop unique competitive strategies and have higher prices for their higher-quality products than do smaller-share businesses.* The figures in Exhibit 25-2 do not show smooth, continuous relationships between market share and the various components of price, cost, and investment. Indeed, it appears that one pattern operates as share increases up to 40%, but a somewhat different pattern above that figure.

Particularly, there are substantial differences in relative price and product quality between market leaders and the rest of the sample. Market leaders obtain higher prices than do businesses with smaller market shares. A principal reason for this may be that market leaders also tend to produce and sell significantly higher-quality products and services than those of their lower-share competitors.

We measured quality as follows: We asked the participating companies to judge for each business the proportions of total sales comprised of products and services that were "superior," "equivalent," and "inferior" to those of leading competitors. The figures shown in Exhibit 25-2 are averages of the differences between the superior quality and the inferior quality percentages.

The measures we used for relative price and relative quality are not, of course, directly comparable. Thus it is impossible to determine which is greater—the price premiums earned by market leaders, or the differential in the quality of their products. But it is clear that the combination of significantly higher prices and quality represents a unique competitive position for market leaders.

Market leaders, in contrast to their smaller competitors, spend significantly higher amounts on research and development, relative to sales. As shown in Exhibit 25-2, the average ratio of R&D to sales for the highest-share group of businesses was 3.55%—nearly 40% greater than the ratio for the under-10% share group. This, combined with the quality advantage enjoyed by market leaders, suggests that they typically pursue a strategy of product leadership. Certainly this is consistent with what is known about innovative leaders such as Eastman Kodak, IBM, and Proctor & Gamble.

Given that market leaders have a high market share and thus the profitability that goes with it, it is natural to question whether the share and profitability ratio shifts from industry to industry. In other words, do businesses in some kinds of industries need a higher share than others to be profitable?

Variations among Industries

While our analyses of the PIMS data base clearly demonstrates a strong general relationship between ROI and market share, they also indicate that the importance of share varies considerably from one type of industry or market situation to another. Two of the more striking variations are summarized in Exhibit 25-4. These figures show that:

1. *Market share is more important for infrequently purchased products than for frequently purchased ones.* For infrequently purchased products, the ROI of the average market leader is about 28 percentage points greater than the ROI of the average small-share business. For frequently purchased products (those typically bought at least once a month), the corresponding ROI differential is approximately 10 points.

Why? Infrequently purchased products tend to be durable, higher unit-cost items such as capital goods, equipment, and consumer durables, which are often complex and difficult for buyers to evaluate. Since there is a bigger risk inherent in a wrong choice, the purchaser is often willing to pay a premium for assured quality.

Frequently purchased products are generally low unit-value items such as foods or industrial supplies. The risk in buying from a lesser-known, small-share supplier is lower in most cases, so a purchaser can feel free to shop around.

2. *Market share is more important to businesses when buyers are "fragmented" rather than concentrated.* As Exhibit 25-5 shows, when buyers are fragmented (i.e., no small group of consumers accounts for a significant proportion of total sales), the ROI differential is 27 percentage points for the average market leader. However, when buyers are concentrated, the leaders' average advantage in ROI is reduced to only 19 percentage points greater than that of the average small-share business.

A likely explanation for this is that when buyers are fragmented, they cannot bargain for the unit cost advantage that concentrated buyers receive, thus allowing higher profits for the large-share business. Obviously, then, the ROI differential is smaller when buyers are somewhat concentrated. In this case, powerful buyers tend to bargain away some of the seller's cost differential by holding out for low prices.

Clearly, the strategic implications of the market-share/profitability relationship vary according to the circumstances of the individual business. But there is no doubt that the relationship can be translated into dynamic strategies for all companies trying to set market goals.

WHAT THE ROI/MARKET SHARE LINK MEANS FOR STRATEGY

Because market share is so strongly related to profitability, a basic strategic issue for top management is to establish market-share objectives. These objectives have much to do with the rate of return that can reasonably be budgeted in the short and long runs, as well as the capital requirements and cash flow of a business.

Setting Market-Share Goals

What market-share goals are feasible, or even desirable, obviously depends on many things, including the strength of competitors, the resources available to support a strategy, and the willingness of management to forgo present earnings for future results. At the risk of oversimplification, we can classify market-share strategies into three rather broad groups:

1. Building strategies are based on active efforts to increase market share by means of new product introductions, added marketing programs, and so on.
2. Holding strategies are aimed at maintaining the existing level of market share.
3. Harvesting strategies are designed to achieve high short-term earnings and cash flow by permitting market share to decline.

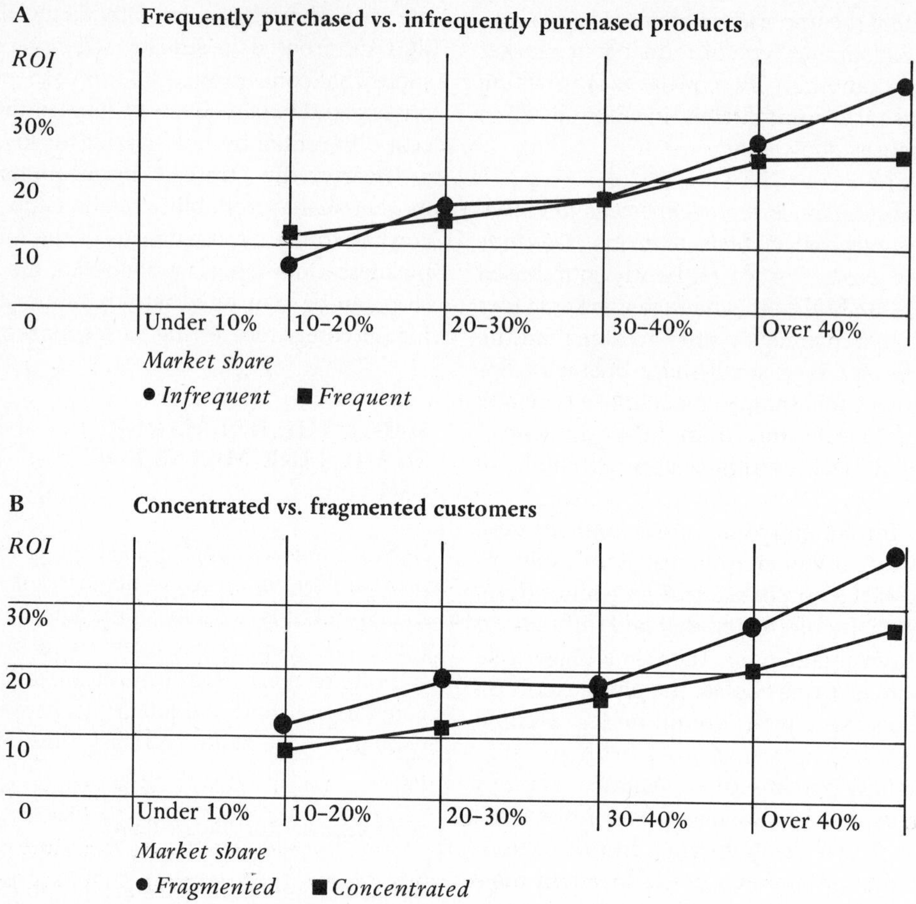

EXHIBIT 25-5 *Industry Variations in the Share/ROI Relationship*

When does each of these market-share strategies seem most appropriate? How should each be implemented? The experiences documented in the PIMS data base provide some clues.

Building strategies. The data presented in Exhibit 25-1 imply that, in many cases, even a marginally acceptable rate of return can be earned only by attaining some minimum level of market share. If the market share of a business falls below this minimum, its strategic choices usually boil down to two: increase share or withdraw. Of course there are exceptions to this rule.

But we are convinced that in most markets there is a minimum share that is required for viability. RCA and General Electric apparently concluded that they were below this minimum in the computer business, and they pulled out. Similarly, Motorola, with an estimated 6% to 7% share of U.S. TV-set sales, and a rumored loss of $20 million in the period from 1970 to 1973, announced its intention early in 1974 to sell the business to Matsushita.

On the other hand, when share is not so low as to dictate withdrawal, but is still not high enough to yield satisfactory returns, managers can consider aggressive share-building strategies. They should recognize, however, that (a) big increases in share are seldom achieved quickly; and (b) expanding share is almost always expensive in the short run.

Among the 600 businesses in the PIMS sample, only about 20% enjoyed market share gains of 2 points or more from 1970 to 1972. As might be expected, successful building strategies were most common among relatively new businesses. Of those that have begun operations since 1965, over 40% achieved share increases of 2 points or more – compared with only 17% of the businesses established before 1950.

Generally speaking, businesses that are building share pay for short-run penalty for doing so. Exhibit 25-6 compares ROI results for businesses with different beginning market shares and for businesses with decreasing, steady, and increasing shares over the period 1970 to 1972. Generally, the businesses that were "building" (i.e., had share increases of at least 2 points) had ROI results of 1 to 2 points lower than those that maintained more or less steady ("holding") positions. The short-term cost of building was greatest for small-share businesses, but even for market leaders, ROI was significantly lower when share was rising than it was when share was stable.

Schick's campaign to build sales of the "Flexamatic" electric shaver during 1972 and 1973 dramatically illustrates the cost of increasing market share. In late 1972 Schick introduced the Flexamatic by means of a controversial national advertising campaign in which direct performance comparisons were made with its leading competitors. Trade sources have estimated that Schick spent $4.5 million in 1972 and $5.2 million in 1973 on advertising, whereas the company's advertising expenditures in 1970 and 1971 had been under $1 million annually.

In one sense the effort was successful: by late 1972 Schick's market share had doubled from 8% to 16%. But the impact on company profits was drastic. Schick's operating losses for the fiscal year ending February 28, 1974 amounted to $14.5 million on sales of $93.8 million, and it appears that although it was not the only cause, the high promotional cost of the Flexamatic campaign was a major contributing factor. Only time can tell whether Schick's short-term losses will prove to be justified by increased future cash flows.

The Schick example is, no doubt, an extreme one. Nevertheless, a realistic assessment of any share-building strategy should take into account the strong likelihood that a significant price will have to be paid – at least in the short run. Depending on how great the gains are and how long it takes to achieve them, this cost may or may not be offset by the longer-term gains.

In a recent article, William Fruhan demon-

TABLE 25-6 *How ROI Is Affected by Market-Share Changes*

	Market-Share Strategies		
Market Share 1970	**Building: Up 2 Points or More**	**Holding: Less Than 2 Points Up or Down**	**Harvesting: Down 2 Points or More**
	Average ROI, 1970–1972		
Under 10%	7.5%	10.4%	10.0%
10%–20%	13.3	12.6	14.5
20%–30%	20.5	21.6	9.5
30%–40%	24.1	24.6	7.3
40% or over	29.6	31.9	32.6

strated that there was a positive relation between market share and rate of return for automobile manufacturers and for retail food chains.[4] Yet he also cited examples of disasters stemming from overambition in the market-share dimension from the computer industry, the retail food business, and the airline companies.

The main thrust of Fruhan's article was to encourage business strategists to consider certain questions before launching an aggressive market-share expansion strategy: (1) Does the company have the necessary financial resources? (2) Will the company find itself in a viable position if its drive for expanded market share is thwarted before it reaches its market share target? (3) Will regulatory authorities permit the company to achieve its objective with the strategy it has chosen to follow? Negative responses to these questions would obviously indicate that a company should forgo market-share expansion until the right conditions are created.

It is fairly safe for us to say, therefore, that whenever the market position of a business is reasonably satisfactory, or when further building of share seems excessively costly, managers ought to follow holding strategies.

Holding strategies. By definition, a holding strategy is designed to preserve the status quo. For established businesses in relatively mature markets – which is to say, for the majority of businesses in advanced economies – holding is undoubtedly the most common strategic goal with respect to market share.

A key question for businesses that are pursuing holding strategies is, "What is the most profitable way to maintain market position?" The answer to this question depends on many things, including the possibilities and costs of significant technological change and the strength and alertness of competitors. Because competitive conditions vary so much, few reliable generalizations can be made about profit-maximizing methods of maintaining market share.

Nevertheless, our analyses of the PIMS data base do suggest some broad relationships between ROI and competitive behavior. For example, our data indicate that large-share businesses usually earn higher rates of return when they charge premium prices. (Recall that this pricing policy is usually accompanied by premium quality.) Also, ROI is usually greater for large-share businesses when they spend more than their major competitors, in relation to sales, on sales force effort, advertising and promotion, and research and development.

For small-share businesses, however, the most profitable holding strategy is just the opposite: on the average, ROI is highest for these businesses when their prices are somewhat below the average of leading competitors and then their rates of spending on marketing and R&D are relatively low.

Harvesting strategies. Opposed to a share-building strategy is one of "harvesting" – deliberately permitting share to fall so that higher short-run earnings and cash flow may be secured. Harvesting is more often a matter of necessity than of strategic choice. Cash may be urgently needed to support another activity – dividends, for example, or management's earnings record. Whatever the motivation, corporate management sometimes does elect to "sell off" part of a market-share position.

The experience of the businesses in the PIMS data pool, summarized in Exhibit 25-6, indicates that only large-share businesses are generally able to harvest successfully. Market leaders enjoyed rates of return about three quarters of a point higher when they allowed market share to decline than when they maintained it over the period 1970–1972. For the other groups of businesses shown in Exhibit 25-6, differences in ROI between "holding" and "harvesting" are irregular. Of course, these comparisons also reflect the influence of factors other than strategic choice. Market share was lost by many businesses because of intensified competition, rising costs, or other changes which hurt both their profitability and their competitive positions. For this reason, it is impossible to derive a true measure of the profitability of harvesting. Nevertheless, the PIMS data support our contention that, under proper conditions, current profits can be increased by allowing share to slide.

When does harvesting make sense, assuming it is a matter of choice? A reduction in share typically affects profits in a way directly opposite to that of building: ROI is increased in the short run but reduced in the longer term. Here again, a trade-off must be made. The net balance will depend on management's assessment of the direction and timing of future developments such as technological changes, as well as on its preference for immediate rather than deferred profits.

Balancing Costs and Benefits

Evidence from the PIMS study strongly supports the proposition that market share is positively related to the rate of return on investment earned by a business. Recognition of this relationship will affect how managers decide whether to make or buy to decrease purchasing costs, whether to advertise in certain media, or whether to alter the price or quality of a product. Also, recognizing that emphasis on market share varies considerably among industries and types of market situations, decisions concerning product and customer are likely to be influenced. For instance, a small competitor selling frequently purchased, differentiated consumer products can achieve satisfactory results with a small share of the market. Under other conditions, it would be virtually impossible to earn satisfactory profits with a small share (e.g., infrequently purchased products sold to large, powerful buyers).

Finally, choices among the three basic market share strategies also involve a careful analysis of the importance of market share in a given situation. Beyond this, strategic choice requires a balancing of short-term and long-term costs and benefits. Neither the PIMS study nor any other empirical research can lead to a "formula" for these strategic choices. But we hope that the findings presented here will at least provide some useful insights into the probable consequences of managers' choices.

THE PIMS DATA BASE

The data on which this article is based come from the unique pool of operating experience assembled in the PIMS project, now in its third year of operations at the Marketing Science Institute. During 1973, 57 major North American corporations supplied financial and other information on 620 individual "businesses" for the three-year period 1970–1972.

Each business is a division, product line, or other profit center within its parent company, selling a distinct set of *products* or *services* to an identifiable group or groups of *customers,* in competition with a well-defined set of competitors. Examples of businesses include manufacturers of TV sets; man-made fibers; and nondestructive industrial testing apparatus.

Data were compiled for individual businesses by means of special allocations of exist-

ing company data and, for some items, judgmental estimates supplied by operating managers of the companies.

For each business, the companies also provided estimates of the total sales in the market served by the business. Markets were defined, for purposes of the PIMS study, in much narrower terms than the "industries" for which sales and other figures are published by the Bureau of the Census. Thus the data used to measure market size and growth rates cover only the specific products or services, customer types, and geographic areas in which each business actually operates.

The *market share* of each business is simply its dollar sales in a given time period, expressed as a percentage of the total market sales volume. The figures shown are average market shares for the three-year period 1970–1972. (The average market share for the businesses in the PIMS sample was 22.1%.)

Return on investment was measured by relating *pretax operating profits* to the *sum of equity and long-term debt.* Operating income in a business is after deduction of allocated corporate overhead costs, but *prior* to any capital charges assigned by corporate offices. As in the case of market share data, the ROI figures shown in Exhibits 25-1, 25-5, and 25-6 are averages for 1970–1972.

As explained in the earlier HBR article, the focus of the PIMS project has been primarily on ROI because this is the performance measure most often used in strategic planning. We recognize, however, that ROI results are often not entirely comparable between businesses. When the plant and equipment used in a business have been almost fully depreciated, for example, its ROI will be inflated. Also, ROI results are affected by patents, trade secrets, and other proprietary aspects of the products or methods of operation employed in a business. These and other differences among businesses should naturally be kept in mind in evaluating the reasons for variations in ROI performance.

NOTES

1. See the earlier article on Phases I and II of the project by Sidney Schoeffler, Robert D. Buzzell, and Donald F. Heany, "Impact of Strategic Planning on Profit Performance," HBR March–April 1974.
2. Boston Consulting Group, Inc., *Perspectives on Experience* (Boston, 1968 and 1970).
3. This general argument has been made in numerous books, articles, and speeches dealing with antitrust economics, see, for example, Joe S. Bain, *Industrial Organization,* 2nd edition (New York, John Wiley & Sons, 1968), especially Chapter 6.
4. "Pyrrhic Victories in Fights for Market Share," HBR September–October 1972.

26

George S. Day

A Strategic Perspective on Product Planning

INTRODUCTION

The past decade has seen growing recognition that the product planning function within diversified companies of all sizes involves tradeoffs among competing opportunities and strategies. During this period the combination of more complex markets, shorter product life cycles and social, legal and governmental trends put a premium on minimizing the degree of risk in the product mix. More recently, managers have had to cope with severe resource constraints, stemming partly from weaknesses in the capital markets and a general cash shortage, and the triple traumas of the energy crisis, materials shortages and inflation.

Some of the manifestations of the new climate for product planning are skepticism toward the value of full product lines, unwillingness to accept the risks of completely new products, an emphasis on profit growth rather than volume growth and active product elimination and divestment programs.[1] Yet managements cannot afford to turn their backs on all opportunities for change and attempt to survive simply by doing a better job with the established products and services. Eventually all product categories become saturated or threatened by substitutes and diversification becomes essential to survival. Consumer goods companies are especially feeling this pressure as the productivity of line extensions or product adaptations directed at narrow market segments declines. Also the likelihood of regulatory actions directed at products, such as aerosols and cyclamates, points up the risks of having a closely grouped product line.[2] More than ever, long-run corporate health is going to depend on the ability of product planners to juggle those conflicting pressures of diversification and consolidation.

The pervasive nature of the resource allocation problem in product planning is the focus of this article. The emphasis is on the basic issues of the role of new and established products and markets and the choice of areas of new product development to pursue. The first issue is addressed in the context of the product port-

Reprinted with permission from *Journal of Contemporary Business.* Copyright © 1975, pp. 1-34.
George Day is a professor of Marketing at the University of Toronto. He received his Ph.D. from Columbia University and has taught at Stanford University and Western Ontario.

folio, which describes the mixture of products that generate cash and in which the company can invest cash. A detailed examination of the product portfolio begins with its component parts, the product life cycle and the notion of market dominance, and then turns to the implications for strategic planning and resource allocation.

Once the role of new products has been established, the issue of where to look is addressed with an explicit statement of a search strategy. This statement defines the characteristics of desirable opportunities in terms that are meaningful to product planners.

STRATEGIC PLANNING AND PRODUCT PLANNING

There are as many concepts of strategy as writers on the subject.[3] Several of the more useful definitions for our immediate purposes are:

- Decisions today which affect the future (not future decisions)
- Major questions of resource allocation that determine a company's long-run results
- The calculated means by which the firm deploys its resources – i.e., personnel, machines and money – to accomplish its purpose under the most advantageous circumstances
- A competitive edge that allows a company to serve the customers better than its competitors
- The broad principles by which a company hopes to secure an advantage over competitors, an attractiveness to buyers and a full exploitation of company resources.

Following these definitions, the desired output of the strategic planning process is a long-run plan "that will produce an attractive growth rate and a high rate of return on investment by achieving a market position so advantageous that competitors can retaliate only over an extended time period at a prohibitive cost."[4]

Most strategic planning processes and the resulting plans show a distinct family resemblance, although the specifics obviously vary greatly. These specifics usually include[5]: (1) a statement of the mission of the strategic business unit (SBU),[6] (2) the desired future position the SBU and the corporation wants to attain, comprising measurable profitability, sales, market share, efficiency and flexibility objectives, (3) the key environmental assumptions and the opportunities and threats, (4) a statement of the strengths, weaknesses and problems of the SBU and its major competitors, (5) the strategic gap between the desired and forecasted position of the SBU, (6) actions to be taken to close the gap – the strategy and (7) the required resources and where they can be obtained, including financial resources such as net cash flow, the equity base and debt capacity and management capabilities. These are the main elements of the planning process that are relevant to product planning, leaving aside the issues of detailed implementation plans, contingency plans, which state in advance what modifications will be made if key environmental or competitor assumptions turn out to be false, and the monitoring procedures.

What is lacking in the planning process just described is a systematic procedure for generating and choosing strategic alternatives. One of the greatest weaknesses of current strategic plans is the lack of viable strategy alternatives which present very different approaches and outcomes. Too frequently top management sees only one strategy which the SBU has decided is best in terms of its own and the managers' personal needs and objectives. This ignores the interdependency among products (the portfolio aspect)[7] and the possibility that what is best for each SBU is not necessarily best for the entire company.[8] In recognition of this problem, the planning process shown in Figure 26-1 incorporates an analysis of the product portfolio. The remainder of this paper is devoted to the

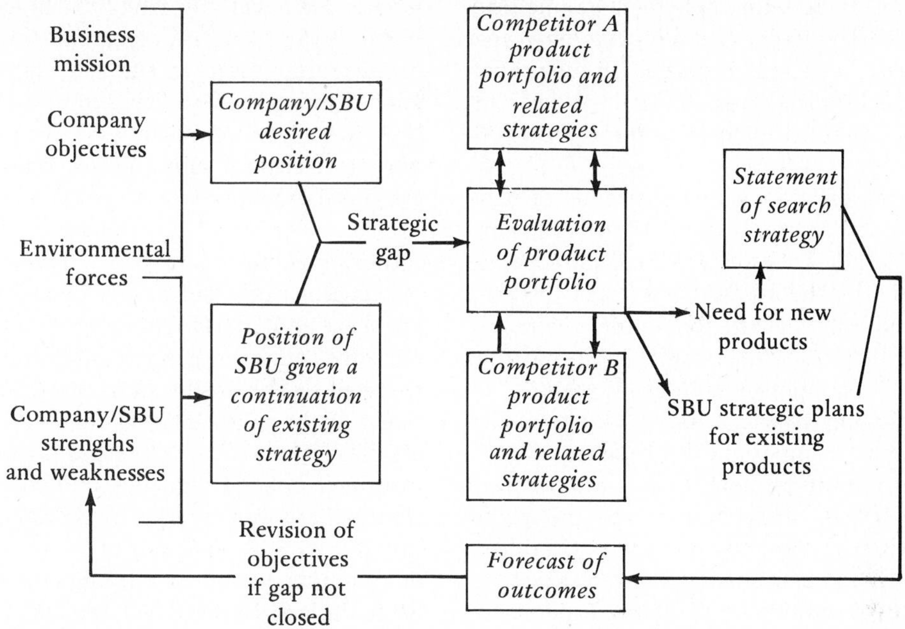

FIGURE 26-1 *Highlighting Product Planning Activities in the Strategic Planning Process*

uses and limitations of the product portfolio and the implications for developing strategy alternates that optimize the long-run position of the firm.

THE COMPONENTS OF THE PRODUCT PORTFOLIO

Market share and stage in the product life cycle have long been regarded as important determinants of profitability. The contribution of the product portfolio concept is that it permits the planner to consider these two measures simultaneously in evaluating the products of an entire company or a division or SBU.

The Value of Market Share Dominance

The belief in the benefits of a dominant market share is rooted deeply in the experience of executives. It is reinforced by the facts of life in most markets:

- The market leader is usually the most profitable
- During economic downturns, customers are likely to concentrate their purchases in suppliers with large shares, and distributors and retailers will try to cut inventories by eliminating the marginal supplier
- During periods of economic growth, there is often a bandwagon effect with a large share presenting a positive image to customers and retailers.[9]

Of course, market domination has its own pitfalls, beyond antitrust problems, ". . . monopolists flounder on their own complacency rather than on public opposition. Market domination produces tremendous internal resistance against any innovation and makes adaptation to change dangerously difficult. Also, it usually means that the enterprise has too many of its eggs in one basket and is too vulnerable to economic fluctuations."[10] The leader is also highly vulnerable to competitive actions, especially in the pricing area, since the leader establishes the basic industry price from which smaller competitors can discount.

The clearest evidence of the value of market share comes from a study of The Profit Impact of Market Strategies (PIMS) of 620 separate businesses by the Marketing Science Institute which, in turn, draws on earlier work by General Electric. Early results indicated that market share, investment intensity (ratio of total investment to sales) and product quality were the most important determinants of pretax return on investment, among a total of 37 distinct factors incorporated into the profit model.[11] On average it was found that a difference of 10 points in market share was accompanied by a difference of about 5 points in pretax ROI. As share declines from more than 40 percent to less than 10 percent, the average pretax ROI dropped from 30 percent to 9.1 percent.

The PIMS study also provided some interesting insights into the reasons for the link between market share and profitability.[12] The results point to economies of scale and, especially, the opportunities for vertical integration as the most important explanations. Thus high-share businesses (more than 40 percent) tend to have low ratios of purchases to sales because they make rather than buy and own their distribution facilities. The ratio of purchases to sales increases from 33 percent for high-share businesses to 45 percent for low-share (less than 10 percent) businesses. But because of economies of scale in manufacturing and purchasing there is no significant relationship between manufacturing expenses or the ratio of sales to investment and the market share. To some degree these results also support the market power argument of economists; market leaders evidently are able to bargain more effectively (either through the exercise of reciprocity or greater technical marketing skills) and obtain higher prices than their competition (but largely because they produce and sell higher-quality goods and services). The fact that market leaders spend a significantly higher percentage of their sales on R and D suggest that they pursue a conscious strategy of product leadership.

Experience curve analysis. The importance of economies of scale in the relationship of market share and profitability is verified by the experience curve concept. Research, largely reported by the Boston Consulting Group, has found that in a wide range of businesses (including plastics, semiconductors, gas ranges and life insurance policies), the total unit costs, in constant dollars, decline by a constant percentage (usually 20 to 30 percent) with each doubling of accumulated units of output or experience.[13] Since the experience effect applies to all value added, it subsumes economies of scale and specialization effects along with the well-known learning curve which applies only to direct labor costs.

An experience curve, when plotted on a log-log scale as in Figure 26-2, appears as a straight line. The locations of the competitors on this curve are determined approximately by their respective accumulated experience, for which relative market share is a good surrogate (this may not be true if some competitors recently have entered the market by buying experience through licenses or acquisitions). Then it follows that the competitor with the greatest accumulated experience will have the lowest relative costs and, if prices are similar between competitors, also will have the greatest profits. Of course, companies that fail to reduce costs along the product category experience curve and who are not dominant will be at an even greater competitive disadvantage.

Figure 26-2 shows a price prevailing at one point in time. Over the long run, prices also will decline at roughly the same rate as costs decline. The major exception to this rule occurs during the introduction and growth state of the life cycle, when the innovator and/or dominant competitor, is tempted to maintain prices at a high level to recoup the development costs. The high price umbrella usually achieves this immediate end because unit profits are high. The drawback is the incentive to higher cost competitors to enter the market and attempt to increase their market shares. In effect, the dominant competitor is trading future market share for current profits. This may be sensible if the early leader: (1) has a number of attractive new product opportunities requiring cash, (2) there are potential competitors whose basic business position will enable them eventually to enter the product category regardless of the pricing strategy[14] or (3) significant barriers to entry can be erected.

Product Life Cycle

That products pass through various stages between life and death (introduction → growth → maturity → decline) is hard to deny. Equally accepted is the notion that a company should have a mix of products with representation in each of these stages.

Thus the concept of a product life cycle would appear to be an essential tool for understanding product strategies.[15] Indeed this is true, but only *if* the position of the product and the duration of the cycle can be determined. This caveat should be kept in mind when considering the following summary of the important aspects of the product life cycle:

- Volume and profit growth attract competition during the early *growth* (or takeoff) stage of the life cycle. The product market is even more attractive if the innovator lacks the capacity to satisfy demand. However, these competitors may contribute to the growth of sales by their market development expenditures and product improvements.
- Purchase patterns and distribution channels are still fluid during the rapid *growth* stage. For this reason, market shares can be increased at relatively low cost over short periods of time by capturing a disproportionate share of incremental sales (especially where these sales come from new users rather than heavier usage by existing users).

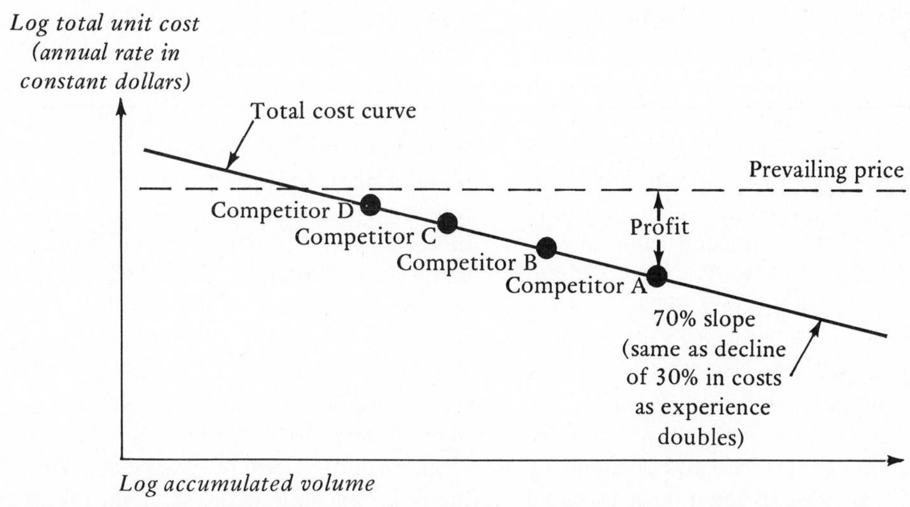

FIGURE 26-2 *Cost Experience Curve Showing Relative Profit Levels of Competitors*

- As a product reaches *maturity* there is evidence of saturation, finer distinctions in benefits surrounding the product and appeals to special segments.
- There is often an industry shake-out to signal the *end* of the rapid growth stage. The trigger might be an excessive number of competitors who have to resort to price cutting to survive; a dominant producer who seeks to regain share; or a large competitor buying into the market (and all these effects will be accentuated by an economic slow down). The result is a period of consolidation during which marginal competitors either drop out, merge with other small competitors or sell out to larger competitors.
- During the *maturity* stage, market-share relationships tend to stabilize; distribution patterns have been established and are difficult to change. This, in turn, contributes to inertia in purchasing relationships and selling oriented toward maintaining relationships. Any substantial increase in share of market will require a reduction in a competitor's capacity utilization which will be resisted vigorously. As a result, gains in share are both time-consuming and costly. This is not necessarily the case if the attempt to gain shares is spearheaded by a significant improvement in product value or performance which the competitor cannot easily match. A case in point is the growth in private labels, or distributor-controlled labels, in both food and general merchandising categories.
- As substitutes appear and/or sales begin to decline, the core product behaves like a commodity and is subject to intense and continuing price pressure. The result is further competitors dropping out of the market, since only those with extensive accumulated experience and cost-cutting capability are able to generate reasonable profits and ROI's.
- The *decline* stage can be forestalled by vigorous promotion (plus, a new creative platform) and product improvement designed to generate more frequent usage or new users and applications.[16] Of course, if these extensions are sufficiently different, a new product life cycle is launched.

Measurement and Interpretation Problems

The concepts underlying the product portfolio are much easier to articulate than to implement.

What is the product-market? The crux of the problem is well stated by Moran:

> In our complex service society there are no more product classes – not in any meaningful sense, only as a figment of file clerk imagination. There are only use classes – users which are more central to some products and peripheral to others – on a vast overlapping continuum. To some degree, in some circumstances almost anything can be a partial substitute for almost anything else. An eight-cent stamp substitutes to some extent for an airline ticket.[17]

Where does this leave the manager who relies on share of some (possibly ill-defined) market as a guide to performance evaluation and resource allocation. First he or she must recognize that most markets do not have neat boundaries. For example, patterns of substitution in industrial markets often look like continua, i.e., zinc, brass, aluminum and engineered plastics such as nylon and polycarbonates can be arrayed rather uniformly along dimensions of price and performance. A related complication, more pertinent to consumer product markets, is the possibility of segment differences in perceptions of product substitutability. For example, there is a timid, risk-averse segment that uses a different product for each kind of surface cleaning (i.e., surface detergents, scouring powders, floor cleaners, bleaches, lavatory cleaners and general-purpose wall cleaners). At the other extreme is the segment that uses detergent for every cleaning problem. Thirdly, product/markets may have to be defined in terms of distribution patterns. Thus, tire companies treat the OEM and replacement tire markets as separate and distinct, even though the products going through these two channels are perfect substitutes so far as the end customer is concerned.

Perhaps the most important consideration is the time frame. A long-run view, reflecting strategic planning concerns, invariably will reveal a larger product-market to account for: (1) changes in technology, price relationships and availability which may remove or reduce cost and performance limitations, e.g., the boundaries between minicomputers, programmable computers and time-sharing systems in many use situations are becoming very fuzzy; (2) the time required by present and prospective buyers to react to these changes, which includes modifying behavior patterns, production systems, etc. and (3) considerable switching among products over long periods of time to satisfy desires for variety and change, as is encountered in consumer goods with snacks, for example.

Despite these complexities, the boundaries of product markets usually are established by four-digit Standard Industrial Classification (SIC) categories and/or expert judgment. The limitations of the SIC are well known[18] but often do not outweigh the benefits of data availability in a convenient form that can be broken down further to geographic markets. In short, the measure is attractive on tactical grounds (for sales force, promotional budget, etc., allocation) but potentially misleading for strategic planning purposes.

What is market dominance? A measure of market share, per se, is not a good indicator of the extent to which a firm dominates a market. The value of a 30 percent share is very different in a market where the next largest competitor has 40 percent than in one where the next largest has only 20 percent. Two alternative measures which incorporate information on the structure of the competition are:

- Company share ÷ share of largest competitor
- Company share ÷ share of three largest competitors

The former measure is more consistent with the implications of the experience curve, while the latter is perhaps better suited to highly concentrated markets (where the four-firm concentration ratio is greater than 80 percent, for example). Regardless of which measure is used it is often the case that the dominant firm has to be at least 1.5 times as large as the next biggest competitor in order to ensure profitability. When there are two large firms of roughly equal shares, especially in a growth business such as nuclear power generators, the competition is likely to be severe. In this instance, both General Electric and Westinghouse have about 40 percent shares and don't expect to be profitable on new installations until after 1977. Conversely, when the two largest firms have small shares, say less than 5 percent, neither measure of market dominance is meaningful.

Evidence of market share dominance, no matter how it is measured, will not be equally meaningful in all product markets. Results from the PIMS study[19] suggest that importance of market share is influenced most strongly by the frequency of purchases.

While the full reasons for this difference in

Return on Investment

Share Market	**Infrequently Purchased (<once/mon)**	**Frequently Purchased (>once/mon)**
Under 10%	6.9%	12.4%
10–19	14.4	13.7
20–29	17.8	17.4
30–39	24.3	23.1
Over 40	34.6	22.9

profitability are obscure they probably relate to differences in unit costs and prior buyer experience with the available alternatives which, in turn, determine willingness to reduce risk by buying the market leader and/or paying a premium price. Also, the frequently purchased category is dominated by consumer goods where there is considerable proliferation of brand names through spin offs, flankers, fighting brands, etc. in highly segmented markets. Each of these brands, no matter how small, shares production facilities and will have low production and distribution costs, although they may be treated as separate businesses.[20] It is hardly surprising that the experience curve concept is difficult to apply to consumer goods. Most of the successful applications have been with infrequently purchased industrial products; relatively undifferentiated, with high value added compared to raw material costs and fairly stable rates of capacity utilization.

A further caveat regarding the experience curve concerns the extent to which costs ultimately can be reduced. The experience curve clearly does not happen according to some immutable law; it requires careful management and some degree of long-run product stability (and, ideally, standardization). These conditions cannot be taken for granted and will be threatened directly by the customer demand for product change and competitive efforts to segment the market. In effect, product innovation and cost efficiency are not compatible in the long-run.[21]

A related question concerns the relevance of the experience curve to a new competitor in an established market. It is doubtful that a new entrant with reasonable access to the relevant technology would incur the same level of initial costs as the developers of the market.

What is the stage in the product life cycle? It is not sufficient to simply know the current rate of growth of the product category. The strategic implications of the product life cycle often hinge on forecasting changes in the growth rate and, in particular, on establishing the end of the growth and maturity stages.

The first step in utilizing the life cycle is to ensure that the product class is identified properly. This may require a distinction between a broad product type (cigarettes) and a more specific product form (plain filter cigarettes). Secondly, the graph of product (type or form) sales needs to be adjusted for factors that might obscure the underlying life cycle, i.e., price changes, economic fluctuations and population changes. The third and most difficult step is to forecast when the product will move from one stage to another. The specific problems are beyond the scope of this article. However, the range of possibilities is illustrated by these various leading indicators of the "top-out" point.[22]

- Evidence of saturation; declining proportion of new trier versus replacement sales
- Declining prices and profits
- Increased product life
- Industry over capacity
- Appearance of new replacement product or technology
- Changes in export/import ratio
- Decline in elasticity of advertising and promotion, coupled with increasing price elasticity
- Changes in consumer preferences

These measures generally will indicate only the *timing* of the top-out point, and each is sufficiently imprecise that it is strongly advisable to use as many as possible in combination. Forecasts of the product sales *level* to be achieved at the top-out point may be obtained by astute incorporation of the leading indicators into: (1) technological forecasts, (2) similar product analysis (where sales patterns of products with analogous characteristics are used to estimate the sales pattern of the new product) or (3) epidemiological models whose parameters include initial sales rates and market saturation levels estimated with marketing research methods.[23]

ANALYZING THE PRODUCT PORTFOLIO

The product life cycle highlights the desirability of a variety of products/services with different present and prospective growth rates. However, this is not a sufficient condition for a well balanced portfolio of products that will ensure profitable long-run growth. Two other factors are market share position and the need to balance cash flows within the corporation. Some products should *generate* cash (and provide acceptable reported profits) and others should *use* cash to support growth; otherwise, the company will build up unproductive cash reserves or go bankrupt.[24] These issues are clarified by jointly considering share position and market growth rate, as in the matrix of Figure 26-3. The conceptualization used here is largely attributable to the Boston Consulting Group.[25]

It must be stressed that the growth-share matrix discussed here is simply one way of conceptualizing the product portfolio. It has been useful as a device for synthesizing the analyses and judgments of the earlier steps in the planning process, especially in facilitating an approach to strategic decision making that considers the firm to be a whole that is more than the sum of its separate parts. For these purposes, the arbitrary classifications of products in the growth-share matrix are adequate to differentiate the strategy possibilities.[26]

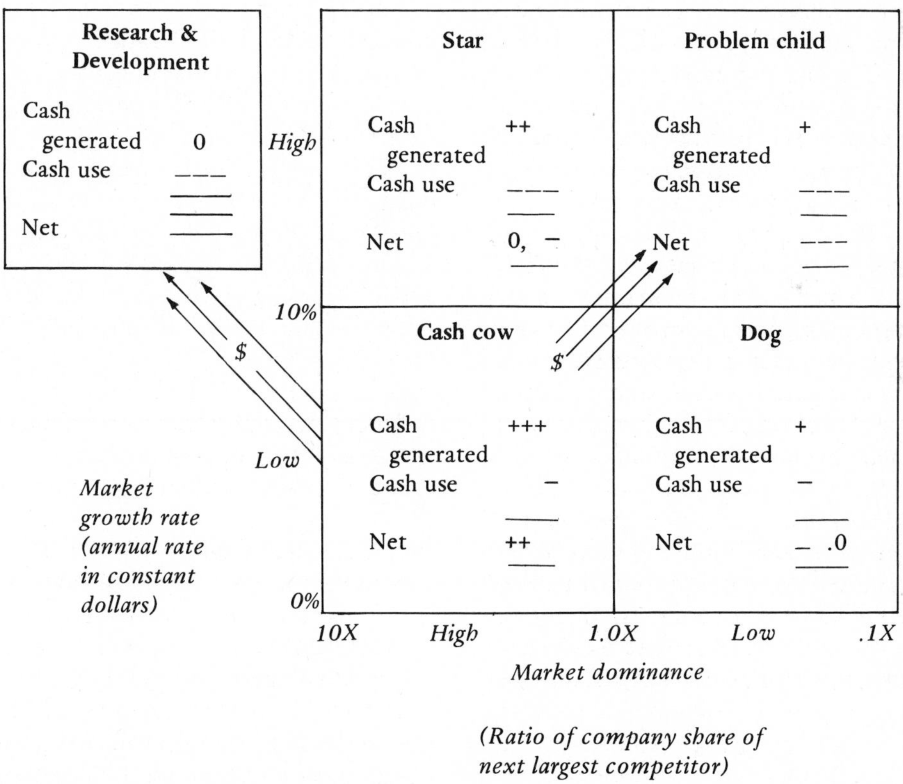

FIGURE 26-3 *Describing the Product Portfolio in the Market Share Growth Matrix. (Arrows indicate principal cash flows.)*

Product Portfolio Strategies

Each of the four basic categories in the growth-share matrix implies a set of strategy alternatives that generally are applicable to the portfolio entries in that category.[27]

Stars. Products that are market leaders, but also growing fast, will have substantial reported profits but need a lot of cash to finance the rate of growth. The appropriate strategies are designed primarily to protect the existing share level by reinvesting earnings in the form of price reductions, product improvement, better market coverage, production efficiency increases, etc. Particular attention must be given to obtaining a large share of the new users or new applications that are the source of growth in the market. Management may elect, instead, to maximize short-run profits and cash flow at the expense of long-run market share. This is highly risky because it usually is predicated on a continuing stream of product innovations and deprives the company of a cash cow which may be needed in the future.

Cash cows. The combination of a slow market growth and market dominance usually spells substantial net cash flows. The amount of cash generated is far in excess of the amount required to maintain share. All strategies should be directed toward maintaining market dominance – including investments in technological leadership. Pricing decisions should be made cautiously with an eye to maintaining price leadership. Pressure to overinvest through product proliferation and market expansion should be resisted unless prospects for expanding primary demand are unusually attractive. Instead, excess cash should be used to support research activities and growth areas elsewhere in the company.

Dogs. Since there usually can be only one market leader and because most markets are mature, the greatest number of products fall in this category.[28] Such products are usually at a cost disadvantage and have few opportunities for growth at a reasonable cost. Their markets are not growing, so there is little new business to compete for, and market share gains will be resisted strenuously by the dominant competition.

The product remains in the portfolio because it shows (or promises) a modest book profit. This accounting result is misleading because most of the cash flow must be reinvested to maintain competitive position and finance inflation.[29] Another characteristic of a dog is that individual investment projects (especially those designed to reduce production costs) show a high ROI. However, the competitive situation is such that these returns cannot be realized in surplus cash flow that can be used to fund more promising projects. In addition there are the potential hidden costs of unproductive demands on management time (and consequent missed opportunities) and low personnel morale because of a lack of achievement.

The pejorative label of dog becomes increasingly appropriate the closer the product is to the lower-right corner of the growth/share matrix.[30] The need for positive action becomes correspondingly urgent. The search for action alternatives should begin with attempts to alleviate the problem without divesting. If these possibilities are unproductive, attention then can shift to finding ways of making the product to be divested as attractive as possible; then to liquidation and, finally if need be, to abondonment:

- Corrective action. Naturally all reasonable cost-cutting possibilities should be examined, but, as noted above, these are not likely to be productive in the long-run. A related alternative is to find a market segment that can be dominated. The attractiveness of this alternative will depend on the extent to which the segment can be protected from competition – perhaps because of technology or distribution requirements.[31] What must be avoided is the natural tendency of operating managers to arbitrarily redefine their markets in order to improve their share position and thus change the classification of the product when, in fact, the economics of the business are unchanged. This is highly probable when the product-market boundaries are ambiguous.

- Harvest. This is a conscious cutback of all support costs to the minimum level to maximize the product's profitability over a foreseeable lifetime, which is usually short. This cutback could include reducing advertising and sales effort, increasing delivery time, increasing the acceptable order size and eliminating all staff support activities such as marketing research.
- Value added. Opportunities may exist for reparceling a product or business that is to be divested. This may involve dividing the assets into smaller units or participating in forming a "kennel of dogs" in which the weak products of several companies are combined into a healthy package. This latter alternative is especially attractive when the market is very fractionated.
- Liquidation. This is the most prevalent solution usually involving a sale as a going concern but, perhaps, including a licensing agreement. If the business/product is to be sold as a unit, the problem is to maximize the selling price–a function of the prospective buyers need for the acquisition (which will depend on search strategy) and their overhead rate. For example, a small company may find the product attractive and be able to make money because of low overhead.
- Abandonment. The possibilities here include giveaways and bankruptcy.

Problem children. The combination of rapid growth rate and poor profit margins creates an enormous demand for cash. If the cash is not forthcoming, the product will become a dog as growth inevitably slows. The basic strategy options are fairly clear-cut; either invest heavily to get a disproportionate share of the new sales or buy existing share by acquiring competitors and thus move the product toward the star category or get out of the business using some of the methods just described.

Consideration also should be given to a market segmentation strategy, but only if a defensible niche can be identified and resources are available to gain dominance. This strategy is even more attractive if the segment can provide an entree and experience base from which to push for dominance of the whole market.

Further Strategic Implications

While the product portfolio is helpful in suggesting strategies for specific products, it is equally useful for portraying the overall health of a multiproduct company. The issue is the extent to which the portfolio departs from the balanced display of Figure 26-4, both for the present and in 3 to 5 years.

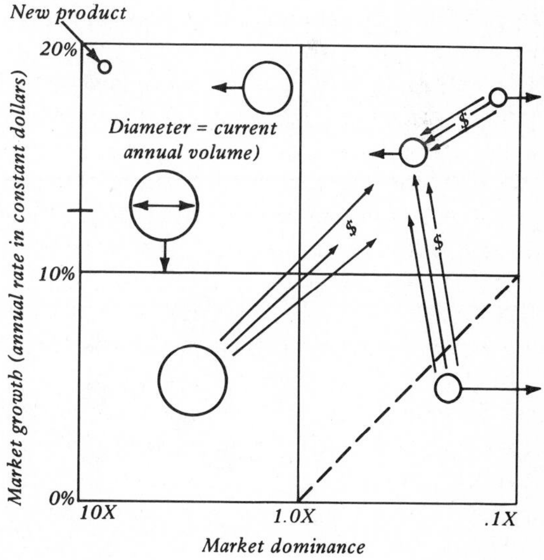

FIGURE 26-4 *A Balanced Product Portfolio*

Among the indicators of overall health are size and vulnerability of the cash cows (and the prospects for the stars, if any) and the number of problem children and dogs. Particular attention must be paid to those products with large cash appetites. Unless the company has abundant cash flow, it cannot afford to sponsor many such products at one time. If resources (including debt capacity) are spread too thin, the company simply will wind up with too many marginal products and suffer a reduced capacity to finance promising new product entries or acquisitions in the future. Some indication of this type of resource misallocation can be obtained from a comparison of the growth rates of the product class and the company's entrant (as illustrated in Figure 26-5). Ideally, nothing should be in the upper sector where market growth exceeds company growth—unless the product is being harvested.

Competitive analysis. Product portfolios should be constructed for each of the major competitors. Assuming competitive management follows the logic just described, they eventually will realize that they can't do everything. The key question is which problem children will be supported aggressively and which will be eliminated. The answer obviously will be difficult to obtain, but has an important bearing on the approach the company takes to its own problem children.

Of course, a competitive position analysis has many additional dimensions which must be explored in depth before specific competitive actions and reactions within each product category can be forecast.[32] This analysis, coupled with an understanding of competitive portfolios, becomes the basis for any fundamental strategy employing the military concept of concentration which essentially means to concentrate strength against weakness.[33]

Dangers in the pursuit of market share. Tilles has suggested a number of criteria for evaluating strategy alternatives.[34] The product portfolio is a useful concept for addressing the first three: (1) environmental consistency, (2) internal consistency and (3) adequacy of resources. A fourth criteria considers whether the degree of risk is acceptable, given the overall level of risk in the portfolio.

The experience of a number of companies, such as G.E. and RCA, in the mainframe com-

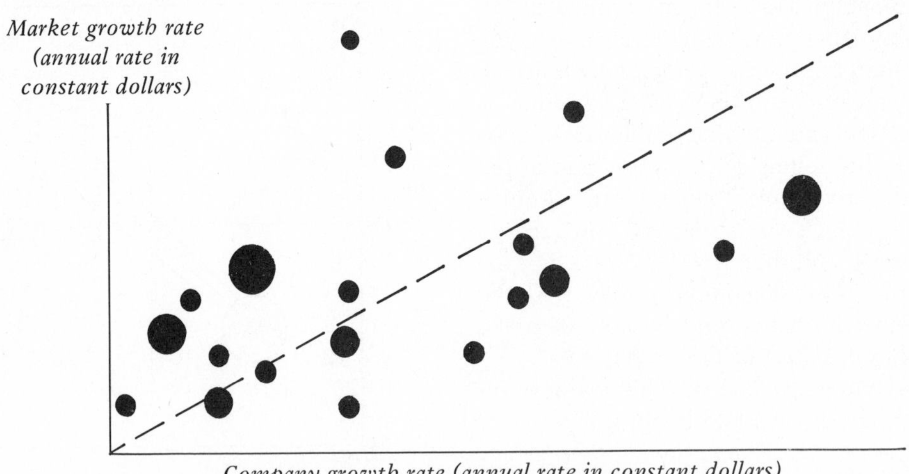

FIGURE 26-5 *Market Industry Versus Company Growth Rates. (Illustrative diversified company—diameters are proportional to current annual sales volume.)*

puter business, points to the particular risks inherent in the pursuit of a market share. An analysis of these "pyrrhic victories"[35] suggests that greatest risks can be avoided if the following questions can be answered affirmatively: (1) Are company financial resources adequate? (2) If the fight is stopped short for some reason, will the corporation's position be competitively viable? and (3) Will government regulations permit the corporation to follow the strategy it has chosen? The last question includes antitrust policies which now virtually preclude acquisitions made by large companies in related fields[36] and regulatory policies designed to proliferate competition, as in the airline industry.

Organizational implications. Although this discussion has focused on the financial and market position aspects of the product portfolio, the implications encompass the deployment of all corporate resources – tangible assets as well as crucial intangibles of management skills and time.

One policy that clearly must be avoided is to apply uniform performance objectives to all products, or SBU's, as is frequently attempted in highly decentralized profit-center management approaches. The use of flexible standards, tailored to the realities of the business, logically should lead to the recognition that different kinds of businesses require very different management styles. For example, stars and problem children demand an entrepreneurial orientation, while cash cows emphasize skills in fine tuning marketing tactics and ensuring effective allocation of resources. The nature of specialist support also will differ; e.g., R and D support being important for growth products and financial personnel becoming increasingly important as growth slows.[37] Finally, since good managers, regardless of their styles are always in short supply, the portfolio notion suggests that they not be expended in potentially futile efforts to turn dogs into profitable performers. Instead they should be deployed into situations where the likelihood of achievement and, hence, of reinforcement, is high.

Other methods of portraying the portfolio. The growth-share matrix is far from a complete synthesis of the underlying analyses and judgments as to the position of the firm in each of its product-markets. The main problem of the matrix concerns the growth rate dimension. While this is an extremely useful measure in that it can have direct implications for cash flows, it is only one of many possible determinants of the attractiveness of the market. A list of other possible factors is summarized in Table 26-1. (Not all these factors will be rele-

TABLE 26-1 *Factors Determining Market and Industry Attractiveness*

Market	• Size (present and potential) • Growth/stage in life cycle • Diversity of user segments • Foreign opportunities • Cyclicality
Competition	• Concentration ratio • Capacity utilization • Structural changes (e.g., entries and exits • Position changes • Vertical threats/opportunities • Sensitivity of shares and market size to price, service, etc. • Extent of "captive" business
Profitability	• Level and trend of leaders • Contribution rates • Changes/threats on key leverage factors (e.g., scale economies and pricing) • Barriers to entry
Technology	• Maturity/volatility • Complexity • Patent protection • Product/process opportunities
Other	• Social/environmental • Government/political • Unions • Human factors

vant to all markets.) The importance of each factor depends on the company's capabilities, but careful consideration will help to identify unusual threats, such as impending government regulations, that might significantly reduce future attractiveness. Similarly, market share may not provide a comprehensive indication of the company's position in each market; as in the case of a leader in a market that is rapidly fragmenting.

The qualitative aspects of overall attractiveness and position also can be incorporated into a matrix which portrays the product portfolio [see below]. This matrix does not have the immediate cash flow implication of the growth-share matrix, thus, it should be used as a complementary, rather than a replacement approach.

NEW PRODUCT PLANNING

A product portfolio analysis identifies the need for new products or new markets and the probable level of available resources but does not indicate where to look. This presents management with a number of difficult questions:

- What degree of relationship to the present business is necessary and desirable?
- What are the possibilities for internal development versus acquisition?
- When is an innovation preferred to an imitation and vice versa?
- What are the characteristics of desirable new products?

These and innumerable other questions have to be answered before personnel in the product planning, corporate development or other responsible functions can pursue their tasks efficiently. In short, top management must decide how much growth is desired and feasible, the contribution of new versus established products and the broad direction as to how the growth will be achieved.

What is needed is a strategy statement that specifies those areas where development is to proceed and identifies (perhaps by exclusion) those areas that are off-limits. As Crawford notes, "the idea of putting definitive restrictions on new product activity is not novel, but use of it, especially sophisticated use, is still not widespread."[38] The major criticisms of a comprehensive statement of new product development strategy are that it will inhibit or restrict creativity and that ideas with great potential will be rejected. Experience suggests that clear guidance improves creativity by focusing energy on those areas where the payoff is likely to be

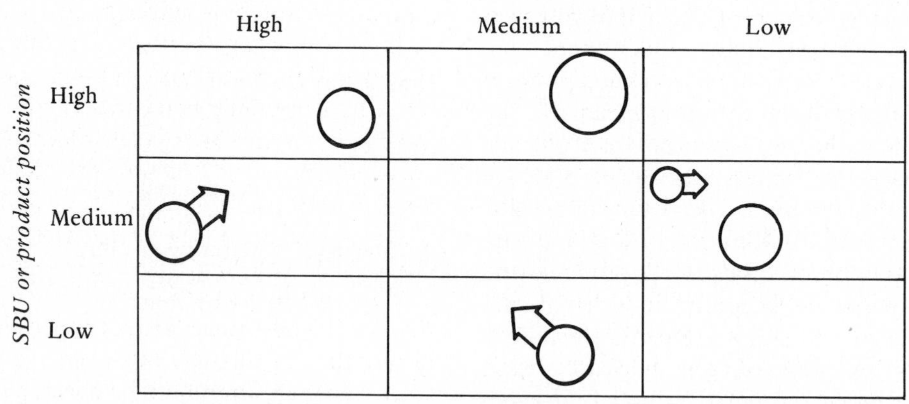

Industry or Market Attractiveness. (Arrow represents forecast of change in position. Diameter [of circles] is proportional to share of company sales contributed by product.)

greatest. Also, experience shows that significant breakthroughs outside the bounds of the product development strategy statement can be accommodated readily in an ongoing project evaluation and screening process.

The New Product Development Strategy Statement

The essential elements of this statement are the specification of the product-market scope, the basic strategies to be used for growing within that scope and the characteristics of desirable alternatives. These elements guide the search for new product ideas, acquisitions, licenses, etc., and form the basis for a formal screening procedure.

Product-market scope. This is an attempt to answer the basic question, "what business(es) do we want to be in" and is a specific manifestation of the mission of the SBU or company. There is no ready-made formula for developing the definition of the future business. One approach is to learn from definitions that have been useful in guiding successful strategies. For example, the General Electric Housewares SBU defines their present (circa 1973) business as "providing consumers with functional aids to increase the enjoyment or psychic fulfillment of selected lifestyles"—specifically those dealing with preparation of food, care of the person, care of personal surroundings and planning assistance. In the future their business will expand to include recreation, enhancement of security and convenient care of the home.

This statement of the future business satisfied one important criteria [*sic*]: that it be linked to the present product-market scope by a clearly definable common thread. In the case of G.E. Housewares, the common thread is with generic needs being satisfied (or problems being solved, as the case may be). Ansoff argues that the linkage also can be with product characteristics, distribution capability or underlying technology—as long as the firm has distinctive competency in these areas.[39]

Other criteria for appraising the usefulness of a description of the future business opportunities are: (1) specificity—if the definition of product-market scope is too general, it won't have an impact on the organization (e.g., consider the vagueness of being in the business of supplying products with a plug on the end); (2) flexibility—the definition should be adapted constantly to recognize changing environmental conditions (e.g., Gerber no longer can say that babies are their only business), (3) attainability—can be undertaken within the firm's resources and competencies and (4) competitive advantage—it always is preferable to protect and build on these strengths and competencies that are not possessed as fully by the competition.[40]

Basic strategies for growth. At the broad level of a new product development strategy, the basic issues are the *growth* vector, or the direction the firm is moving within the chosen product-market scope, and the emphasis on *innovation* versus *imitation.*

There are almost an infinite number of possibilities for growth vectors. The basic alternatives are summarized in Figure 26-6.[41] There is no intention here to suggest that these strategies are mutually exclusive; indeed, various combinations can be pursued simultaneously in order to close the strategic gaps identified in the overall planning process. Furthermore, most of the strategies can be pursued either by internal development or acquisition and coupled with vertical diversification (either forward toward a business that is a customer or backward toward a business that is a supplier).

The choice of growth vector will be influenced by all the factors discussed earlier as part of the overall corporate planning process. Underlying any choice is, by necessity, an appraisal of the risks compared with the payoffs. The essence of past experience is that growth

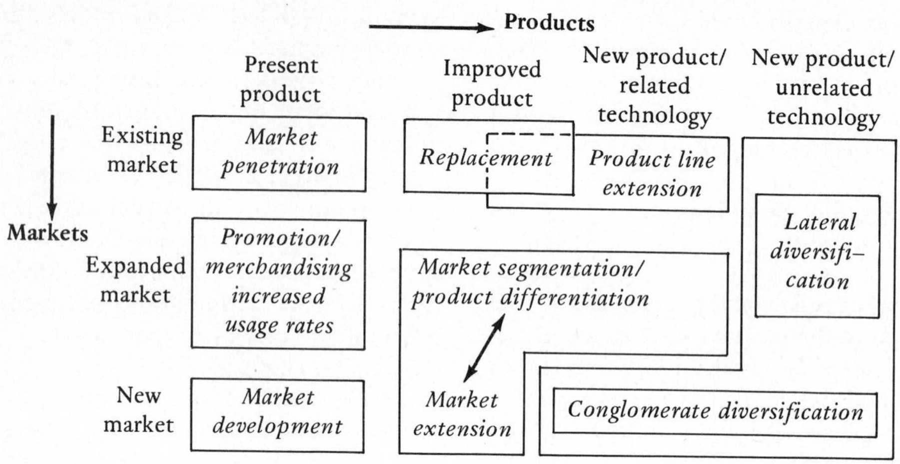

FIGURE 26-6 *Growth Vector Alternatives*

vectors within the existing market (or, at least, closely related markets) are much more likely to be successful than ventures into new markets.[42] Therefore, diversification is the riskiest vector to follow—especially if it is attempted by means of internal development. The attractiveness of acquisitions for diversification is the chance to reduce the risks of failure by buying a known entity with (reasonably) predictable performance.

An equally crucial basic strategy choice is the degree of emphasis on innovation versus imitation. The risks of being an innovator are well known so few, if any, diversified corporations can afford to be innovators in each product-market. There are compelling advantages to being first in the market if barriers to entry (because of patent protections, capital requirements, control over distributions, etc.) can be erected, the product is difficult to copy or improve on and the introductory period is short. The imitator, by contrast, is always put at a cost disadvantage by a successful innovator and must be prepared to invest heavily to build a strong market position. While profits over the life of the product may be lower for an imitator, the risks are much lower because the innovator has provided a full-scale market test which can be monitored to determine the probable growth in future sales. Also, the innovator may provide significant opportunities by not serving all segments or, more likely, by not implementing the introduction properly.

The conscious decision to lead or follow pervades all aspects of the firm. Some of the important differences that result can be seen from the various strategic orientations to high technology markets discussed by Ansoff and Steward:

- First to market . . . based on strong R and D, technical leadership and risk taking
- Follow the leader . . . based on strong development resources and the ability to act quickly as the market starts its growth phase
- Applications engineering . . . based on product modifications to fit needs of particular customers in mature markets
- Me-too . . . based on superior manufacturing efficiency and cost control.[43]

Characteristics of desirable alternatives. Three fundamental questions have to be asked of each new product or service being sought or considered: (1) How will a strong competitive advantage be obtained? The possibilities range from superiority in underlying technology or product quality, to patent protection, to marketing requirements. Another dimension of this question is the specification of markets or competitors to be avoided on the grounds that these situations would blunt the pursuit of a competitive advantage. (2) What is the potential for synergy? This asks about joint effects, or "the mutually reinforcing impact a product-market entry has on a firm's efficiency and effectiveness."[44] Synergy can be sought for defensive reasons, in order to supply a competence that the firm lacks or to spread the risks of a highly cyclical industry, as has motivated a number of mergers in the machine tool industry. Alternatively, synergy can utilize an existing competence such as a distribution system (notable examples here are Gillette and Coca Cola), a production capability, promotional skills, etc. In addition, "financial reinforcement may occur either because of the relative pattern of funds generation and demand . . . or because the combination is more attractive to the financial community than the pieces would be separately."[45] (3) What specific operating results are required? The possibilities here usually are expressed in terms of threshold or minimum desirable levels:

- Rate of market growth
- Payback period (despite its deficiencies it is a reflection of the risk level)
- Minimum sales level. (This is a function of fixed costs and scale of operations: the danger is that a product with good long-run potential will be rejected because of modest short-run sales possibilities.)
- Profit levels, cash flow and return on assets. (Each of these financial requirements must be developed in light of the firm's product portfolio.)

SUMMARY

Too often product planning is conducted as though each established product or service, and new product opportunity being sought or evaluated were independent of the other products of the firm. The implication is that corporate performance is the sum of the contributions of individual profit centers or product strategies.[46]

This article emphasizes the need to consider the interdependencies of products as parts of a portfolio described by market share dominance and market growth rate before overall corporate performance can be optimized. Only then can decisions as to resource allocation, growth and financial objectives and specific strategies be developed for established products and the need for new products identified.

There is little doubt that the future will see increasing acceptance of a broad systems approach to overall corporate strategy, in general, and to product planning, in particular. There are already a number of successful practitioners to emulate (who have gained a competitive edge that cannot be ignored).[47] More importantly, as the business environment becomes increasingly resource-constrained there may be no other choice for most firms.

NOTES

1. "The Squeeze on Product Mix," *Business Week* (5 January 1974), pp. 50–55, "Toward Higher Margins and Less Variety," *Business Week* (14 September 1974), pp. 98–99; E.B. Weiss, "We'll See Fewer New Products in 1975 – Culprit Is Shortage of Capital, Resources," *Advertising Age* (2 December 1974); "Corrective Surgery," *Newsweek* (27 January 1975), p. 50; and Jack Springer, "1975: Bad Year for New Products; Good Year for Segmentation," *Advertising Age* (10 February 1975), pp. 30–39.
2. Barry R. Linsky, "Which Way to Move with New Products," *Advertising Age* (22 July 1974), pp. 45–46.
3. George A. Steiner, *Top Management Planning* (London: Macmillan, 1969); H. Igor Ansoff, *Corporate Strategy* (New York: McGraw-Hill, 1965).
4. David T. Kollat, Roger D. Blackwell and James F. Robeson, *Strategic Marketing* (New York: Holt, Rinehart and Winston, 1972), p. 12.
5. This description of the planning process has been adapted from Kollat, et al., *Strategic Marketing;* Louis V. Gerstner, "The Practice of Business: Can Strategic Planning Pay Off?" *Business Horizons* (December 1972);

Herschner Cross, "New Directions in Corporate Planning," An address to Operations Research Society of America (Milwaukee, Wisconsin: 10 May 1973).

6. The identification of "strategic business units" is a critical first step in any analysis of corporate strategy. Various definitions have been used. Their flavor is captured by the following guidelines for defining a business: (1) no more than 60 percent of the expenses should represent arbitrary allocations of joint costs, (2) no more than 60 percent of the sales should be made to a vertically integrated (downstream) subsidiary and (3) the served market should be homogeneous; i.e., segments are treated as distinct if they represent markedly different shares, competitors and growth rates.
7. E. Eugene Carter and Kalman J. Cohen, "Portfolio Aspects of Strategic Planning," *Journal of Business Policy,* 2 (1972), pp. 8-30.
8. C.H. Springer, "Strategic Management in General Electric," *Operations Research* (November-December 1973), pp. 1177-1182.
9. Bernard Catry and Michel Chevalier, "Market Share Strategy and the Product Life Cycle," *Journal of Marketing,* 38 (October 1974), pp. 29-34.
10. Peter F. Drucker, *Management: Tasks, Responsibilities, Practices* (New York: Harper and Row, 1973), p. 106.
11. Sidney Schoeffler, Robert D. Buzzell and Donald F. Heany, "Impact of Strategic Planning on Profit Performance," *Harvard Business Review* (March-April 1974), pp. 137-145.
12. Robert D. Buzzell, Bradley T. Gale and Ralph G. M. Sultan, "Market Share, Profitability and Business Strategy," unpublished working paper (Marketing Science Institute, August 1974).
13. For more extended treatments and a variety of examples, see Patrick Conley, "Experience Curves as a Planning Tool," *IEEE Transactions* (June 1970); *Perspectives on Experience* (Boston: Boston Consulting Group, 1970); and "Selling Business a Theory of Economics," *Business Week* (8 September 1974).
14. "An example of this situation was DuPont's production of cyclohexane. DuPont was the first producer of the product but the manufacture of cyclohexane is so integrated with the operations of an oil refinery that oil refiners have an inherent cost advantage over companies, such as DuPont, without an oil refinery." Robert B. Stobaugh and Philip L. Townsend, "Price Forecasting and Strategic Planning: The Case of Petrochemicals," *Journal of Marketing Research,* 12 (February 1975), pp. 19-29.
15. Theodore Levitt, "Exploit the Product Life Cycle," *Harvard Business Review* (November-December 1965), pp. 81-94.
16. Harry W. McMahan, "Like Sinatra, Old Products Can, Too, Get a New Lease on Life," *Advertising Age* (25 November 1974), p. 32.
17. Harry T. Moran, "Why New Products Fail," *Journal of Advertising Research* (April 1973).
18. See Douglas Needham, *Economic Analysis and Industrial Structure* (New York: Holt, Rinehart and Winston); Sanford Rose, "Bigness Is a Numbers Game," *Fortune* (November 1969).
19. Buzzell, Gale and Sultan, "Market Share, Profitability."
20. An extreme example is Unilever in the UK with 20 detergent brands all sharing joint costs to some degree.
21. William J. Abernathy and Kenneth Wayne, "Limit of the Learning Curve," *Harvard Business Review,* 52 (September-October 1974), pp. 109-119.
22. Aubrey Wilson, "Industrial Marketing Research in Britain," *Journal of Marketing Research,* 6 (February 1969), pp. 15-28.
23. John C. Chambers, Satinder K. Mullick and Donald D. Smith, *An Executives' Guide to Forecasting* (New York: John Wiley and Sons, 1974); Frank M. Bass, "A New Product Growth Model for Consumer Durables," *Mangement Science,* 15 (January 1969), pp. 215-227.
24. Of course the cash flow pattern also may be altered by changing debt and/or dividend policies. (For most companies, the likelihood of new equity funding is limited.) Limits on growth are imposed when the additional business ventures to be supported have too high a business risk for the potential reward and/or the increase in debt has too high a (financial) risk for the potential rewards.
25. Among the publications of the Boston Consulting Group that describe the portfolio are: Perspectives on Experience (1970) and the following pamphlets authored by Bruce D. Henderson in the general perspectives series; "The Product Portfolio" (1970); "The Experience Curve Reviewed: The Growth Share Matrix or the Product Portfolio" (1973); and "Cash Traps" (1972).
26. A similar matrix reportedly is used by the Mead Corporation; see John Thackray, "The Mod Matrix of Mead," *Management Today* (January 1972), pp. 50-53, 112. This application has been criticized on the grounds of oversimplification, narrow applicability and the unwarranted emphasis on investment versus new investment. Indeed the growth-share matrix is regarded by Thackray as primarily a device for achieving social control.
27. William E. Cox, Jr., "Product Portfolio Strategy: An Analysis of the Boston Consulting Group Approach to Marketing Strategies," *Proceedings of the American Marketing Association,* 1974.
28. It is also typical that the weighted ratio of average market share versus the largest competitor is greater than 1.0. This reflects the contribution of the cash cows to both sales and profits. It also accounts for the familiar pattern whereby 20 percent of the products account for 80 percent of the dollar margin (a phenomena generally described as Pareto's Law).
29. The Boston Consulting Group defines such products as cash traps when the required reinvestment, including increased working capital, exceeds reported profit plus increase in permanent debt capacity: Bruce D. Henderson, "Cash Traps," *Perspectives,* Number 102 (Boston Consulting Group, 1972).
30. The label may be meaningless if the product is part of a product line, an integral component of a system or where most of the sales are internal.
31. It should be noted that full line/full service competitors may be vulnerable to this strategy if there are cus-

tomer segments which do not need all the services, etc. Thus, Digital Equipment Corp. has prospered in competition with IBM by simply selling basic hardware and depending on others to do the applications programming. By contrast, IBM provides, for a price, a great deal of service backup and software for customers who are not self-sufficient. "A Minicomputer Tempest," *Business Week* (27 January 1975), pp. 79-80.

32. Dimensions such as product and pricing policy, geographic and distributor strength, delivery patterns, penetration by account size and probable reaction to our company initiatives need to be considered. See C. Davis Fogg, "Planning Gains in Market Share," *Journal of Marketing,* 38 (July 1974), pp. 30-38.
33. This concept is developed by Harper Boyd, "Strategy Concepts" unpublished manuscript, 1974, and is based on B. H. Liddel Hart, *Strategy: The Indirect Approach* (London: Faber and Faber, 1951).
34. Seymour Tilles, "How to Evaluate Corporate Strategy," *Harvard Business Review,* 41 (July-August 1963).
35. William E. Fruhan, "Pyrrhic Victories in Fights for Market Share," *Harvard Business Review,* 50 (September-October 1972).
36. "Is John Sherman's Antitrust Obsolete?" *Business Week* (23 March 1974).
37. Stephen Dietz, "Get More Out of Your Brand Management," *Harvard Business Review* (July-August 1973).
38. C. Merle Crawford, "Strategies for New Product Development: Guidelines for a Critical Company Problem," *Business Horizons* (December 1972), pp. 49-58.
39. H. Igor Ansoff, *Corporate Strategy.*
40. Kenneth Simmonds, "Removing the Chains from Product Policy," *Journal of Management Studies* (February 1968).
41. This strategy matrix was influenced strongly by the work of David T. Kollat, Roger D. Blackwell and James F. Robeson, *Strategic Marketing* (New York: Holt, Rinehart and Winston, 1972), pp. 21-23 which, in turn, was adapted from Samuel C. Johnson and Conrad Jones, "How to Organize for New Products," *Harvard Business Review,* 35 (May-June 1957), pp. 49-62.
42. According to the experience of A. T. Kearney, Inc., the chances of success are a direct function of how far from home the new venture is aimed. Specifically, the likelihood of success for an improved product into the present market is assessed as 0.75, declines to 0.50 for a new product with unrelated technology into the present market and to 0.25 for an existing product into a new market. The odds of success for external diversification are as low as 0.05. These numbers are mainly provocative because of the difficulties of defining what constitutes a failure (is it a product that failed in test or after national introduction, for example). See "Analyzing New Product Risk," *Marketing for Sales Executives* (The Research Institute of America, January 1974).
43. H. Igor Ansoff and John Steward, "Strategies for a Technology-Based Business," *Harvard Business Review,* 45 (November-December 1967), pp. 71-83.
44. Kollat, Blackwell and Robeson, *Strategic Marketing,* p. 24.
45. Seymour Tilles, "Making Strategy Explicit," in H. Igor Ansoff (ed.) *Business Strategy* (London: Penguin Books, 1969), p. 203.
46. Bruce D. Henderson, "Intuitive Strategy," *Perspectives,* No. 96 (The Boston Consulting Group, 1972).
47. See "Selling Business a Theory of Economics," *Business Week* (8 September 1973), "G.E.'s New Strategy for Faster Growth," *Business Week* (8 July 1972), "First Quarter and Stockholders Meeting Report" (Texas Instruments, Inc., 8 April 1973); "The Winning Strategy at Sperry Rand," *Business Week* (24 February 1973), "How American Standard Cured Its Conglomeritis," *Business Week* (28 September 1974); "G.E. Revamps Strategy: Growth through Efficiency," *Advertising Age* (3 June 1974).

IV

The Marketing Program

After buyer behavior has been analyzed and basic strategy formulated, the marketing manager must operationalize that strategy by combining many different elements of marketing decision-making. In marketing parlance, the elements are combined into a marketing program. Part IV begins with Neil Borden's seminal statement of the combination of elements to form "the marketing mix." The remaining papers in this part focus on classic expositions of its elements.

The product life cycle is one of the discipline's key managerial frameworks. John Smallwood reviews the PLC and shows how it relates to other mix elements. Lynn Shostack's paper contends that too much of a marketer's thinking about products is restricted to tangible goods; she calls for a broader conception of the nature of benefits available to customers, emphasizing the intangible nature of many such benefits.

The distribution area is represented by three classic papers. The most venerable is Stanley Hollander's "The Wheel of Retailing," which argues that change in retailing institutions follows essentially a cyclical pattern. Louis Bucklin connects retail institutions to the types of goods they market; his paper thus not only addresses distribution, but also reviews the standard convenience/shopping/specialty good taxonomy introduced to the discipline in 1923 by Melvin Copeland. The third distribution paper is Louis Stern and Torger Reve's masterful synthesis of the concept of the channel of distribution (an idea unique to marketing thinking) and the vast literature on the socio-political marketing environment.

Pricing is an area of considerable significance to marketing decision-making. Most of the literature here is derived from price theory in economics, an area that assumes certainty of knowledge. Joseph Guiltinan addresses pricing issues under uncertainty—the usual situation in marketing.

The area of promotion in marketing is broad and diverse. Three papers explore aspects of promotion. First, Robert Lavidge and Gary Steiner present the definitive statement of the "hierarchy of effects" – the thinking stages through which a buyer must pass – and associated advertising objectives. Empirical research into the effectiveness of advertising is elegantly illustrated by Russell Ackoff and James Emshoff's work with a major client. Finally, the research stream conducted by Orville Walker, Gilbert Churchill and Neil Ford in the sales management area is summarized in their piece on motivation and performance.

27

Neil H. Borden

The Concept of The Marketing Mix

I have always found it interesting to observe how an apt or colorful term may catch on, gain wide usage, and help to further understanding of a concept that has already been expressed in less appealing and communicative terms. Such has been true of the phrase "marketing mix," which I began to use in my teaching and writing some 15 years ago. In a relatively short time it has come to have wide usage. This note tells of the evolution of the marketing mix concept.

The phrase was suggested to me by a paragraph in a research bulletin on the management of marketing costs, written by my associate, Professor James Culliton.[1] In this study of manufacturers' marketing costs he described the business executive as a

> "decider," an "artist"–a "mixer of ingredients," who sometimes follows a recipe as he goes along, sometimes adapts a recipe to the ingredients immediately available, and sometimes experiments with or invents ingredients no one else has tried.

I liked his idea of calling a marketing executive a "mixer of ingredients," one who is constantly engaged in fashioning creatively a mix of marketing procedures and policies in his efforts to produce a profitable enterprise.

For many years previous to Culliton's cost study the wide variations in the procedures and policies employed by managements of manufacturing firms in their marketing programs and the correspondingly wide variation in the costs of these marketing functions, which Culliton aptly ascribed to the varied "mixing of ingredients," had become increasingly evident as we had gathered marketing cases at the Harvard Business School. The marked differences in the patterns or formulae of the marketing programs not only were evident through facts disclosed in case histories, but also were reflected clearly

Reprinted from *Journal of Advertising Research,* © Advertising Research Foundation, Inc. (June, 1964), pp. 2–7.

The late Neil H. Borden, Professor Emeritus of Harvard, spent a summer lecturing in Australia, served for three years as a consultant in India, and lectured on management in Singapore. His M.B.A. degree is from Harvard. He was president of the American Marketing Association and published work on many phases of advertising. His 1942 study, The Economic Effects of Advertising, *is still recognized as a definitive work.*

in the figures of a cost study of food manufacturers made by the Harvard Bureau of Business Research in 1929. The primary objective of this study was to determine common figures of expenses for various marketing functions among food manufacturing companies, similar to the common cost figures which had been determined in previous years for various kinds of retail and wholesale businesses. In this manufacturer's study we were unable, however, with the data gathered to determine common expense figures that had much significance as standards by which to guide management, such as had been possible in the studies of retail and wholesale trades, where the methods of operation tended toward uniformity. Instead, among food manufacturers the ratios of sales devoted to the various functions of marketing such as advertising, personal selling, packaging, and so on, were found to be widely divergent, no matter how we grouped our respondents. Each respondent gave data that tended to uniqueness.

Culliton's study of marketing costs in 1947–48 was a second effort to find out, among other objectives, whether a bigger sample and a more careful classification of companies would produce evidence of operating uniformities that would give helpful common expense figures. But the result was the same as in our early study: there was wide diversity in cost ratios among any classifications of firms which were set up, and no common figures were found that had much value. This was true whether companies were grouped according to similarity in product lines, amount of sales, territorial extent of operations, or other bases of classification.

Relatively early in my study of advertising, it had become evident that understanding of advertising usage by manufacturers in any case had to come from an analysis of advertising's place as one element in the total marketing program of the firm. I came to realize that it is essential always to ask: what overall marketing strategy has been or might be employed to bring about a profitable operation in light of the circumstances faced by the management? What combination of marketing procedures and policies has been or might be adopted to bring about desired behavior of trade and consumers at costs that will permit a profit? Specifically, how can advertising, personal selling, pricing, packaging, channels, warehousing, and the other elements of a marketing program be manipulated and fitted together in a way that will give a profitable operation? In short, I saw that every advertising management case called for a consideration of the strategy to be adopted for the total marketing program, with advertising recognized as only one element whose form and extent depended on its careful adjustment to the other parts of the program.

The soundness of this viewpoint was supported by case histories throughout my volume, *The Economic Effects of Advertising.*[2] In the chapters devoted to the utilization of advertising by business, I had pointed out the innumerable combinations of marketing methods and policies that might be adopted by a manager in arriving at a marketing plan. For instance, in the area of branding, he might elect to adopt an individualized brand or a family brand. Or he might decide to sell his product unbranded or under private label. Any decision in the area of brand policy in turn has immediate implications that bear on his selection of channels of distribution, sales force methods, packaging, promotional procedure, and advertising. Throughout the volume the case materials cited show that the way in which any marketing function is designed and the burden placed upon the function are determined largely by the overall marketing strategy adopted by managements to meet the market conditions under which they operate. The forces met by different firms vary widely. Accordingly, the programs fashioned differ widely.

Regarding advertising, which was the function under focus in the economic effects volume, I said at one point:

> In all the above illustrative situations it should be recognized that advertising is not an operating method to be considered as something apart, as something whose profit value is to be judged alone. An able management does not ask, "Shall we use or not use advertising," without consideration of the product and of other management procedures to be employed. Rather the question is always one of finding a management formula giving advertising its due place in the combination of manufacturing methods, product form, pricing, promotion and selling methods, and distribution methods. As previously pointed out different formulae, i.e., different combinations of methods, may be profitably employed by competing manufacturers.

From the above it can be seen why Culliton's description of a marketing manager as a "mixer of ingredients" immediately appealed to me as an apt and easily understandable phrase, far better than my previous references to the marketing man as an empiricist seeking in any situation to devise a profitable "pattern" or "formula" of marketing operations from among the many procedures and policies that were open to him. If he was a "mixer of ingredients," what he designed was a "marketing mix."

It was logical to proceed from a realization of the existence of a variety of "marketing mixes" to the development of a concept that would comprehend not only this variety, but also the market forces that cause managements to produce a variety of mixes. It is the problems raised by these forces that lead marketing managers to exercise their wits in devising mixes or programs which they hope will give a profitable business operation.

To portray this broadened concept in a visual presentation requires merely:

1. A list of the important elements or ingredients that make up marketing programs.
2. A list of the forces that bear on the marketing operation of a firm and to which the marketing manager must adjust in his search for a mix or program that can be successful.

The list of elements of the marketing mix in such a visual presentation can be long or short, depending on how far one wishes to go in his classification and sub-classification of the marketing procedures and policies with which marketing managements deal when devising marketing programs. The list of elements which I have employed in my teaching and consulting work covers the principal areas of marketing activities which call for management decisions as revealed by case histories. I realize others might build a different list. Mine is as follows:

Elements of the Marketing Mix of Manufacturers

1. *Product Planning*—policies and procedures relating to:
   a. Product lines to be offered—qualities, design, etc.
   b. Markets to sell—whom, where, when, and in what quantity.
   c. New product policy—research and development program.
2. *Pricing*—policies and procedures relating to:
   a. Price level to adopt.
   b. Specific prices to adopt—odd-even, etc.
   c. Price policy—one price or varying price, price maintenance, use of list prices, etc.
   d. Margins to adopt—for company, for the trade.
3. *Branding*—policies and procedures relating to:
   a. Selection of trade marks.
   b. Brand policy—individualized or family brand.
   c. Sale under private label or unbranded.
4. *Channels of Distribution*—policies and procedures relating to:

   a. Channels to use between plant and consumer.
   b. Degree of selectivity among wholesalers and retailers.
   c. Efforts to gain cooperation of the trade.
5. *Personal Selling*—policies and procedures relating to:
   a. Burden to be placed on personal selling and the methods to be employed in:
      1. Manufacturer's organization.
      2. Wholesale segment of the trade.
      3. Retail segment of the trade.
6. *Advertising*—policies and procedures relating to:
   a. Amount to spend—i.e., the burden to be placed on advertising.
   b. Copy platform to adopt:
      1. Product image desired.
      2. Corporate image desired.
   c. Mix of advertising—to the trade, through the trade, to consumers.
7. *Promotions*—policies and procedures relating to:
   a. Burden to place on special selling plans or devices directed at or through the trade.
   b. Form of these devices for consumer promotions, for trade promotions.
8. *Packaging*—policies and procedures relating to:
   a. Formulation of package and label.
9. *Display*—policies and procedures relating to:
   a. Burden to be put on display to help effect sale.
   b. Methods to adopt to secure display.
10. *Servicing*—policies and procedures relating to:
   a. Providing service needed.
11. *Physical Handling*—policies and procedures relating to:
   a. Warehousing.
   b. Transportation.
   c. Inventories.
12. *Fact Finding and Analysis*—policies and procedures relating to:
   a. Securing, analysis, and the use of facts in marketing operations.

Also, if one were to make a list of all the forces which managements weigh at one time or another when formulating their marketing mixes, it would be very long indeed, for the behavior of individuals and groups in all spheres of life has a bearing, first, on what goods and services are produced and consumed, and second, on the procedures that may be employed in bringing about exchange of these goods and services. However, the important forces which bear on marketers, all arising from the behavior of individuals or groups, may readily be listed under four heads, namely, the behavior of consumers, the trade, competitors, and government.

The next outline contains these four behavior forces with notations of some of the important behavioral determinants within each force. These must be studied and understood by the marketer, if his marketing mix is to be successful. The great quest of marketing management is to understand the behavior of humans in response to the stimuli to which they are subjected. The skillful marketer is one who is a perceptive and practical psychologist and sociologist, who has keen insight into individual and group behavior, who can foresee changes in behavior that develop in a dynamic world, who has creative ability for building well-knit programs because he has the capacity to visualize the probable response of consumers, trade, and competitors to his moves. His skill in forecasting response to his marketing moves should well be supplemented by a further skill in devising and using tests and measurements to check consumer or trade response to his program or parts thereof, for no marketer has so much prescience that he can proceed without empirical check.

Here, then, is the suggested outline of forces which govern the mixing of marketing elements. This list and that of the elements taken together provide a visual presentation of the concept of the marketing mix.

Market Forces Bearing on the Marketing Mix

1. *Consumers' Buying Behavior*—as determined by their:
   a. Motivation in purchasing.
   b. Buying habits.
   c. Living habits.
   d. Environment (present and future, as revealed by trends, for environment influences consumers' attitudes toward products and their use of them).
   e. Buying power.
   f. Number (i.e., how many).
2. *The Trade's Behavior*—wholesalers' and retailers' behavior, as influenced by:
   a. Their motivations.
   b. Their structure, practices, and attitudes.
   c. Trends in structure and procedures that portend change.
3. *Competitors' Position and Behavior*—as influenced by:
   a. Industry structure and the firm's relation thereto.
      1. Size and strength of competitors.
      2. Number of competitors and degree of industry concentration.
      3. Indirect competition—i.e., from other products.
   b. Relation of supply to demand—oversupply or undersupply.
   c. Product choices offered consumers by the industry—i.e., quality, price, service.
   d. Degree to which competitors compete on price vs. nonprice bases.
   e. Competitors' motivations and attitudes—their likely response to the actions of other firms.
   f. Trends technological and social, portending change in supply and demand.
4. *Government Behavior*—controls over marketing:
   a. Regulations over products.
   b. Regulations over pricing.
   c. Regulations over competitive practices.
   d. Regulations over advertising and promotion.

When building a marketing program to fit the needs of his firm, the marketing manager has to weigh the behavioral forces and then juggle marketing elements in his mix with a keen eye on the resources with which he has to work. His firm is but one small organism in a large universe of complex forces. His firm is only a part of an industry that is competing with many other industries. What does the firm have in terms of money, product line, organization, and reputation with which to work? The manager must devise a mix of procedures that fit these resources. If his firm is small, he must judge the response of consumers, trade, and competition in light of his position and resources and the influence that he can exert in the market. He must look for special opportunities in product or method of operation. The small firm cannot employ the procedures of the big firm. Though he may sell the same kind of product as the big firm, his marketing strategy is likely to be widely different in many respects. Innumerable instances of this fact might be cited. For example, in the industrial goods field, small firms often seek to build sales on a limited and highly specialized line, whereas industry leaders seek patronage for full lines. Small firms often elect to go in for regional sales rather than attempt the national distribution practiced by larger companies. Again, the company of limited resources often elects to limit its production and sales to products whose potential is too small to attract the big fellows. Still again, companies with small resources in the cosmetic field not infrequently have set up introductory marketing programs employing aggressive personal selling and a "push" strategy with distribution limited to leading department stores. Their initially small advertising funds have been directed through these selected retail outlets, with the offering of the products and their story told over the signatures of the stores. The strategy has been to borrow kudos for their products from the leading stores' reputations and to gain a gradual radiation of distribution to smaller stores in all types of channels, such as often comes from the trade's follow-the-leader behavior. Only after resources have grown from mounting sales has a dense retail distribution been aggressively sought and a shift made to place the selling burden more and more on company-signed advertising.

The above strategy was employed for Toni products and Stoppette deodorant in their early marketing stages when the resources of their producers were limited (cf. case of Jules Montenier, Inc. in Borden and Marshall).[3] In contrast, cosmetic manufacturers with large resources have generally followed a "pull" strategy for the introduction of new products, relying on heavy campaigns of advertising in a rapid succession of area introductions to induce a hoped-for, complete retail coverage from the start (cf. case of Bristol-Myers Company in Borden and Marshall).[4] These introductory campaigns have been undertaken only after careful programs of product development and test marketing have given assurance that product and selling plans had high promise of success.

Many additional instances of the varying strategy employed by small versus large enterprises might be cited. But those given serve to illustrate the point that managements must fashion their mixes to fit their resources. Their objectives must be realistic.

LONG VS. SHORT TERM ASPECTS OF MARKETING MIX

The marketing mix of a firm in a large part is the product of the evolution that comes from day-to-day marketing. At any time the mix represents the program that a management has evolved to meet the problems with which it is constantly faced in an ever-changing, ever-challenging market. There are continuous tactical maneuvers: a new product, aggressive promotion, or price-change initiated by a competitor must be considered and met; the failure of the trade to provide adequate market coverage or display must be remedied; a faltering sales force must be reorganized and stimulated; a decline in sales share must be diagnosed and remedied; an advertising approach that has lost effectiveness must be replaced; a general business decline must be countered. All such problems call for a management's maintaining effective channels of information relative to its own operations and to the day-to-day behavior of consumers, competitors, and the trade. Thus, we may observe that short-range forces play a large part in the fashioning of the mix to be used at any time and in determining the allocation of expenditures among the various functional accounts of the operating statement.

But the overall strategy employed in a marketing mix is the product of longer-range plans and procedures dictated in part by past empiricism and in part, if the management is a good one, by management foresight as to what needs to be done to keep the firm successful in a changing world. As the world has become more and more dynamic, blessed is that corporation which has managers who have foresight, who can study trends of all kinds—natural, economic, social, and technological—and, guided by these, devise long-range plans that give promise of keeping their corporations afloat and successful in the turbulent sea of market change. Accordingly, when we think of the marketing mix, we need to give particular heed today to devising a mix based on long-range planning that promises to fit the world of five or ten or more years hence. Provision for effective long-range planning in corporate organization and procedure has become more and more recognized as the earmark of good management in a world that has become increasingly subject to rapid change.

To cite an instance among American marketing organizations which have shown foresight in adjusting the marketing mix to meet social and economic change, I look upon Sears Roebuck and Company as an outstanding example. After building an unusually successful mail order business to meet the needs of a rural America, Sears management foresaw the need to depart from its marketing pattern as a mail order company catering primarily to farmers. The trend from a rural to an urban United States was going on apace. The automobile and good roads promised to make town and city stores increasingly available to those who continued to be farmers. Relatively early, Sears launched a chain of stores across the land, each easily accessible by highway to both farmer and city resident, and with adequate parking space for customers. In time there followed the remarkable telephone and mail order plan directed at urban residents to make buying easy for Americans when congested city streets and highways made shopping increasingly distasteful. Similarly, in the areas of planning products which would meet the desires of consumers in a fast-changing world, of shaping its servicing to meet the needs of a wide variety of mechanical products, of pricing procedures to meet the challenging competition that came with the advent of discount retailers, the Sears organization has shown a foresight, adaptability, and creative ability worthy of emulation. The amazing growth and profitability of the company attest to the foresight and skill of its managements. Its history shows the wisdom of careful attention to market forces and their impending change in devising marketing mixes that may assure growth.

USE OF THE MARKETING MIX CONCEPT

Like many concepts, the marketing mix concept seems relatively simple, once it has been expressed. I know that before they were ever tagged with the nomenclature of "concept," the ideas involved were widely understood among marketers as a result of the growing knowledge about marketing and marketing procedures that came during the preceding half century. But I have found for myself that once the ideas were reduced to a formal statement with an accompanying visual presentation, the concept of the mix has proved a helpful device in teaching, in business problem solving, and, generally, as an aid to thinking about marketing. First of all, it is helpful in giving an answer to the question often raised as to "what is marketing?" A chart which shows the elements of the mix and the forces that bear on the mix helps to bring understanding of what marketing is. It helps to explain why in our dynamic world the thinking of management in all its functional areas must be oriented to the market.

In recent years I have kept an abbreviated chart showing the elements and the forces of the marketing mix in front of my classes at all times. In case discussion it has proved a handy device by which to raise queries as to whether the student has recognized the implications of any recommendation he might have made in the areas of the several elements of the mix. Or, referring to the forces, we can question whether all the pertinent market forces have been given due consideration. Continual reference to the mix chart leads me to feel that the students' understanding of "what marketing is" is strengthened. The constant presence and use of the chart leaves a deeper understanding that marketing is the devising of programs that successfully meet the forces of the market.

In problem solving the marketing mix chart is a constant reminder of:

1. The fact that a problem seemingly lying in one segment of the mix must be deliberated with constant thought regarding the effect of any change in that sector on the other areas of marketing operations. The necessity of integration in marketing thinking is ever present.
2. The need of careful study of the market forces as they might bear on problems in hand.

In short, the mix chart provides an ever-ready checklist as to areas into which to guide thinking when considering marketing questions or dealing with marketing problems.

MARKETING: SCIENCE OR ART?

The quest for a "science of marketing" is hard upon us. If science is in part a systematic formulation and arrangement of facts in a way to help understanding, then the concept of the marketing mix may possibly be considered a small contribution in the search for a science of marketing. If we think of a marketing science as involving the observation and classification of facts and the establishment of verifiable laws that can be used by the marketer as a guide to action with assurance that predicted results will ensue, then we cannot be said to have gotten far toward establishing a science. The concept of the mix lays out the areas in which facts should be assembled, these to serve as a guide to management judgment in building marketing mixes. In the last few decades American marketers have made substantial progress in adopting the scientific method in assembling facts. They have sharpened the tools of fact finding – both those arising within the business and those external to it. Aided by these facts and by the skills developed through careful observation and experience, marketers are better fitted to practice the art of designing marketing mixes than would be the case had not the techniques of gathering facts been advanced as they have been in recent decades. Moreover, marketers have made progress in the use of the scientific method in designing tests whereby the results from mixes or parts of mixes can be measured. Thereby marketers have been learning how to subject the hypotheses of their mix artists to empirical check.

With continued improvement in the search for and the recording of facts pertinent to marketing, with further application of the controlled experiment, and with an extension and careful recording of case histories, we may hope for a gradual formulation of clearly defined and helpful marketing laws. Until then, and even then, marketing and the building of marketing mixes will largely lie in the realm of art.

NOTES

1. James W. Culliton, *The Management of Marketing Costs* (Boston: Division of Research, Graduate School of Business Administration, Harvard University, 1948).
2. Neil H. Borden, *The Economic Effects of Advertising* (Homewood, Illinois: Richard D. Irwin, 1942).
3. Neil H. Borden and M. V. Marshall, *Advertising Management: Text and Cases* (Homewood, Illinois: Richard D. Irwin, 1959), pp. 498–518.
4. *Ibid.*, pp. 518–33.

28

John E. Smallwood

The Product Life Cycle: A Key to Strategic Marketing Planning

Modern marketing management today increasingly is being supported by marketing information services of growing sophistication and improving accuracy. Yet the task remains for the marketing manager to translate information into insights, insights into ideas, ideas into plans, and plans into reality and satisfactory programs and profits. Among marketing managers there is a growing realization of the need for concepts, perspectives, and for constructs that are useful in translating information into profits. While information flow can be mechanized and the screening of ideas routinized, no alternative to managerial creativity has yet been found to generate valuable marketing ideas upon which whole marketing programs can be based. The concept of the product life cycle has been extremely useful in focusing this creative process.

The product life cycle concept in many ways may be considered to be the marketing equivalent of the periodic table of the elements concept in the physical sciences; like the periodic table, it provides a framework for grouping products into families for easier predictions of reactions to various stimuli. With chemicals – it is a question of oxidation temperature and melting point; with products – it is marketing channel acceptance and advertising budgets. Just as like chemicals react in similar ways, so do like products. The product life cycle helps to group these products into homogeneous families.

The product life cycle can be the key to successful and profitable product management, from the introduction of new products to profitable disposal of obsolescent products. The fundamental concept of the product life cycle (PLC) is illustrated in Figure 28-1.

In application, the vertical scale often is measured in saturation of the product (percentage of customer units using), while the horizontal scale is calibrated to represent the passage of time. Months or years are usually the units of time used in calibration, although theoretically, an application along the same concept of much shorter or longer durations (milliseconds in physical sciences, millenia in ar-

Reprinted from *MSU Business Topics* (Winter 1973), pp. 29–35.
John Smallwood is director of economic and marketing research at Whirlpool Corporation.

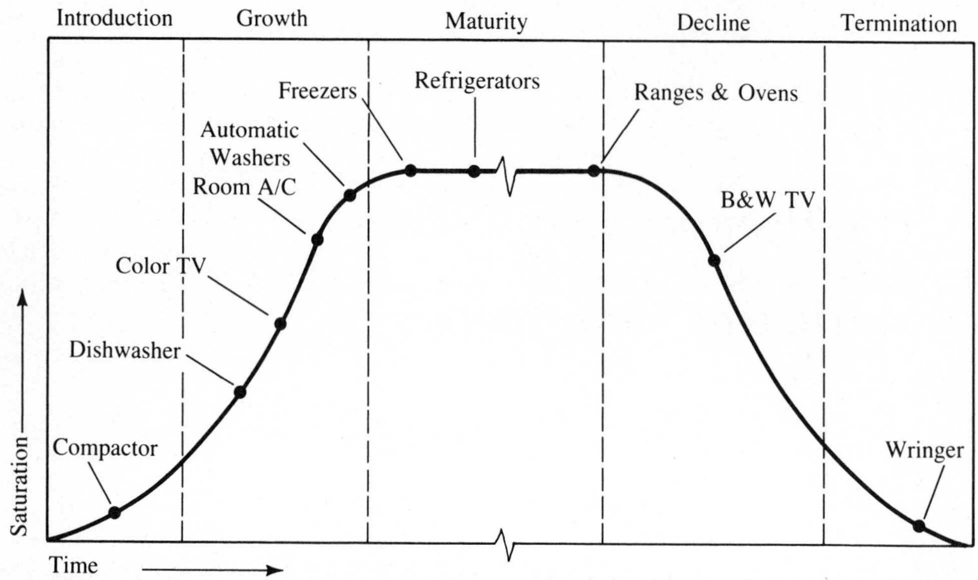

FIGURE 28-1 *Life Cycle Stages of Various Products*

chaeology) might be found. In Figure 28-1 the breakdown in the time scale is shown by stages in the maturity of product life. The saturation scale, however, is a guide only and must be used accordingly. When comparing one product with another, it is sometimes best treated by use of qualitative terms, not quantitative units. It is important to the user of the product life cycle concept that this limitation be recognized and conceptual provisions be made to handle it. For example, if the basic marketing unit chosen is "occupied U.S. households," one cannot expect a product such as room air conditioners to attain 100 percent saturation. This is because many households already have been fitted with central air conditioning; thus, the potential saturation attainment falls well short of 100 percent of the marketing measurement chosen.

To overcome this difficulty, marketing managers have two basic options. They can choose a more restrictive, specific marketing unit such as "all occupied U.S. households that do not have forced air heating"; homes without forced air heating are unlikely candidates for central air conditioning. It can be anticipated that room air conditioners will saturate not only *that* market, but portions of other markets as well. On the other hand, on the basis of informed judgment, management can determine the *potential* saturation of total households and convert the PLC growth scale to a measurement representing the degree of attainment of potential saturation in U.S. households. The author has found the latter approach to be the more useful one. By this device, automatic washers are considered to be at 100 percent saturation when they are at their full potential of an arbitrarily chosen 80 percent.

Consider Figure 28-1, where various products are shown positioned by life cycle stages: the potential saturations permit the grouping of products into like stages of life cycle, even when their actual saturation attainments are dissimilar. One can note that in Figure 28-1 automatic washers (which are estimated at 58 percent saturation) and room air conditioners (30 percent) are positioned in the same growth stage in Figure 28-1; freezers (29 percent) and refrigerators (99 percent), on the other hand, are in the maturity stage. This occurs because, *in our judgment,* freezers have a potential of only about one-third of "occupied households" and thus have attained almost 90 percent of that market. Automatic clothes washers, however, have a potential of about four-fifths of the occupied households and at about 70 percent of their potential still show some of the characteristics of the growth stage of the PLC. General characteristics of the products and their markets are summarized in Table 28-1.

The product life cycle concept is illustrated as a convenient scheme of product classification. The PLC permits management to assign given products to the appropriate stages of acceptance by a given market: *introduction, growth, maturity, decline,* and *termination.* The actual classification of products by appropriate stages, however, is more art than science. The whole process is quite imprecise; but unsatisfactory as this may be, a useful classification can be achieved with management benefits that are clearly of value. This can be illustrated by examining the contribution of the PLC concept in the following marketing activities: sales forecasting, advertising, pricing, and marketing planning.

APPLICATIONS OF THE PLC TO SALES FORECASTING

One of the most dramatic uses of the PLC in sales forecasting was its application in explaining the violent decline in sales of color TV during the credit crunch recession of 1969–70. This occurred after the experience of the 1966–67 mini-recession which had almost no effect on color TV sales that could be discerned

TABLE 28-1 *Product Life Cycle*

	Introduction	Growth	Maturity	Decline	Termination
MARKETING					
Customers	Innovative/ High income	High income/ Mass market	Mass market	Laggards/ Special	Few
Channels	Few	Many	Many	Few	Few
Approach	Product	Label	Label	Specialized	Availability
Advertising	Awareness	Label superiority	Lowest price	Psycho-graphic	Sparse
Competitors	Few	Many	Many	Few	Few
PRICING					
Price	High	Lower	Lowest	Rising	High
Gross margins	High	Lower	Lowest	Low	Rising
Cost Reductions	Few	Many	Slower	None	None
Incentives	Channel	Channel/ Consumer	Consumer/ Channel	Channel	Channel
PRODUCT					
Configuration	Basic	Second generation	Segmented/ Sophisticated	Basic	Stripped
Quality	Poor	Good	Superior	Spotty	Minimal
Capacity	Over	Under	Optimum	Over	Over

through the usual "noise" of the available product flow data. A similar apparent insensitivity was demonstrated in 1958, in 1961, and again in 1966–67, with sales of portable dishwashers. However, it too was followed by a noticeable sales reduction in the 1969–71 period, with annual factory shipments as shown in Figure 28-2.

In early 1972 sales of both portable dishwashers and color TV sets showed a positive response to an improving economic climate, raising the question as to why both products had become vulnerable to economic contractions after having shown a great degree of independence of the business cycle during previous years. The answer to the question seems to lie in their stage in the product life cycle. In comparing the saturation of color TV and dishwashers, as shown in Figure 28-2, consider first the case of color TV sales.

We can ascertain that as late as 1966, saturation of color TV was approximately 8 percent. By late in 1969, however, saturation had swiftly increased to nearly 40 percent.

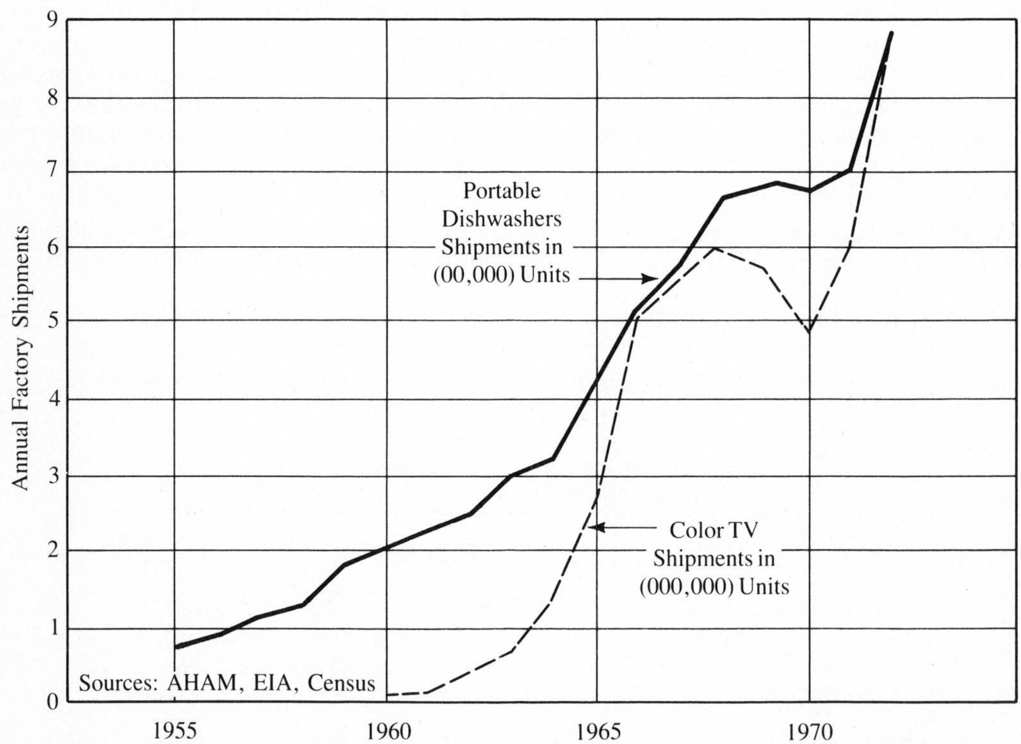

2%	5%	11%	40%	Dishwashers
NA	1%	6%	45%	Color TV
Household Saturation				

FIGURE 28-2 *Effect of Recession on Product Sales*

The same observation is true in the case of dishwashers—considered a mass market appliance only since 1965. This is the key to the explanation of both situations. At the early, introductory stages of their life cycles, both appliances were making large sales gains as the result of being adopted by consumers with high incomes. Later, when sales growth depended more upon adoption by the less affluent members of the mass market whose spending plans are modified by general economic conditions, the product sales began to correlate markedly to general economic circumstances.

It appears that big ticket consumer durables such as television sets and portable dishwashers tend to saturate as a function of customer income. This fact is illustrated by the data displayed in Figure 28-3, concerning refrigerators and compactors, where one can note the logical relationship between the two products as to the economic status of their most important customers and as to their position in the product life cycle. The refrigerator is a mature product while the compactor is the newest product in the major appliance family.

The refrigerator once was in the introduction stage and had marketing attributes similar to the compactor. The refrigerator's present marketing characteristics are a good guide to proper expectations for the compactor as it matures from the *introductory* stage through *growth* to *maturity.* One can anticipate that the compactor, the microwave oven, and even nondurables such as good quality wines will someday be included in the middle income consumption patterns, and we will find their sales to be much more coincident with general economic cycles.

Refrigerators, 1965–1969

		14–24	25–34	35–44	45–54	55–64	65 +
50	Under $5,000	6	6	5	7	7	19
56	$5,000–7,000	10	15	10	8	8	5
114	$7,000–10,000	12	32	27	24	13	6
82	$10,000–15,000	4	19	24	23	10	2
36	$15,000–25,000	1	6	11	12	5	1
8	$25,000–or More			3	3	2	
		33	78	89	77	45	33

346 dots—
each dot represents
10,000 refrigerators

Compactors, 1970–1971

	14–24	25–34	35–44	45–54	55–64	65 +	
Under $5,000							
$5,000–7,000		1	1	1			3
$7,000–10,000	1	2	2	2	2	1	10
$10,000–15,000	1	7	9	9	3	1	30
$15,000–25,000	1	10	16	14	5	1	47
$25,000–or More	1	10	23	18	8	3	63
	4	30	51	44	18	6	

153 dots—
each dot represents
1,000 compactors

FIGURE 28-3 *Purchase Patterns by Age and Income of Households*

PRODUCT LIFE STAGES AND ADVERTISING

The concept of a new product filtering through income classes, combined with long-respected precepts of advertising, can result in new perspectives for marketing managers. The resulting observations are both strategic and tactical. New advertising objectives and new insights for copy points and media selection may be realized. Consider the advertising tasks by the following phases:

Phase 1. Introduction

The first objective is to make the best customer prospects aware that the new product or service is now available; to tell him what it does, what are the benefits, why claims are to be believed, and what will be the conditions of consumption.

Phase 2. Growth

The next objective is to saturate the mass market with the same selling points as used in Phase 1. In addition, it is to recognize that a particular brand of the product is clearly superior to other "inferior" substitutes while, at the same time, to provide a rationalization that this purchase is not merely a wasteful, luxury indulging activity, but that it will make the consumer a better *something,* a better husband, mother, accountant, driver, and so forth.

Phase 3. Maturity

A new rationalization, respectability, is added, besides an intensification of brand superiority ("don't buy substitutes; get the real XYZ original, which incidentally, is *new* and *improved* . . . "). To a great extent, the *product* registration is dropped. Respectability is a strong requisite of the American lower class, which in this phase is the economic stratum containing the most important opportunities for sales gains. Companies do not abandon higher income customers, but they now match advertising to a variety of market segments instead of concentrating on only one theme for the market. Several distinct advertising programs are used. All elements of the marketing mix – product, price, sales promotion, advertising, trading and physical distribution channels – are focused on specific market segments.

Phase 4. Decline

Superior substitutes for a product generally will be adopted first by the people who before were the first to adopt the product in consideration. These people usually are from the upper economic and social classes. Advertising themes reflect this situation when they concentrate on special market segments such as West Coast families or "consumption societies" such as beer drinkers or apartment dwellers.

PRODUCT LIFE STAGES AND PRICING

As a product progresses through all five stages of the life cycle shown in Figure 28-1, the price elasticity can be expected to undergo dramatic changes. Generally speaking, price elasticity of a realtively simple product will be low at first. Thus, when customers are drawn from the higher income classes, demand is relatively inelastic. Later, when most customers are in the lower income categories, greater price elasticity will exist.

Of course, increased price elasticity will not automatically lower prices during the growth stage of the PLC. It is in this growth stage, however, that per unit costs *are* most dramatically reduced because of the effect of the learning curve in engineering, production, and marketing. Rising volume and, more important, the *forecasts* of higher volumes, justifies increased capital investments and higher fixed costs, which when spread over a larger number of units thereby reduce unit costs markedly. New competitors surface with great rapidity in this stage as profits tend to increase dramatically.

Pricing in the mature phase of the PLC usually is found to be unsatisfactory, with no one's profit margins as satisfactory as before. Price competition is keener within the distribution channel in spite of the fact that relatively small price differences seldom translate into any change in aggregate consumer activity.

PRODUCT PLANNING AND THE PLC

Curiously enough, the very configuration of the product takes on a classical pattern of evolution as it advances through the PLC. At first, the new device is designed for function alone; the initial design is sometimes crude by standards that will be applied in the future. As the product maturation process continues, performance sophistication increases. Eventually the product develops to the point where competitors are hardpressed to make meaningful differences which are perceptible to consumers.

As the product progresses through the product life cycle these modifications tend to describe a pattern of metamorphosis from "the ugly box" to a number of options. The adjustment cycle includes:

Part of house: the built-in look and function. Light fixtures, cooking stoves, wall safes, and furnaces are examples.

Furniture: a blending of the product into the home decor. This includes television, hi-fi consoles, radios, clocks, musical instruments, game tables, and so forth.

Portability: a provision for increased *presence* of the product through provisions for easier movement (rollers or compactness), or multiple unit ownership (wall clocks, radios, even refrigerators), or miniaturization for portability. Portability and *personalization,* such as the pocket knife and the wristwatch, can occur.

System: a combination of components into one unit with compatible uses and/or common parts for increased convenience, lower cost, or less space. Home entertainment centers including television, radio, hi-fi, refrigerator-freezers, combination clothes washer-dryers, clock radios, pocket knife-can-and-bottle openers are illustrative.

Similar changes can also be observed in the distribution channel. Products often progress from specialty outlets in the introductory stage to mass distribution outlets such as discount houses and contract buyers during the "maturity" and "decline" phases of the PLC. Interestingly enough, the process eventually is reversed. Buggy whips can still be found in some specialty stores and premium prices are paid for replicas of very old products.

CONCLUSION

The product life cycle is a useful concept. It is the equivalent of the periodic table of the elements in the physical sciences. The maturation of production technology and product configuration along with marketing programs proceeds in an orderly, somewhat predictable course over time with the merchandising nature and marketing environment noticeably similar between products that are in the same stage of their life cycle. Its use as a concept in forecasting, pricing, advertising, product planning, and other aspects of marketing management can make it a valuable concept, although considerable amounts of judgment must be used in its application.

29

G. Lynn Shostack

Breaking Free from Product Marketing

New concepts are necessary if service marketing is to succeed. Service marketing is an uncharted frontier. Despite the increasing dominance of services in the U.S. economy, basic texts still disagree on how services should be treated in a marketing context.[1]

The heart of this dispute is the issue of applicability. The classic marketing "mix," the seminal literature, and the language of marketing all derive from the manufacture of physical goods. Practicing marketers tend to think in terms of products, particularly mass-market consumer goods. Some service companies even call their output "products" and have "product" management functions modeled after those of experts such as Procter and Gamble.

Marketing seems to be overwhelmingly product-oriented. However, many service-based companies are confused about the applicability of product marketing, and more than one attempt to adopt product marketing has failed.

Merely adopting product marketing's labels does not resolve the question of whether product marketing can be overlaid on service businesses. Can corporate banking services really be marketed according to the same basic blueprint that made *Tide* a success? Given marketing's historic tenets, there is simply no alternative.

Could marketing itself be "myopic" in having failed to create relevant paradigms for the service sector? Many marketing professionals who transfer to the services arena find their work fundamentally "different," but have a difficult time articulating how and why their priorities and concepts have changed. Often, they also find to their frustration and bewilderment that "marketing" is treated as a peripheral function or is confused with one of its components, such as research or advertising, and kept within a very narrow scope of influence and authority.[2]

This situation is frequently rationalized as being due to the "ignorance" of senior management in service businesses. "Education" is usually recommended as the solution. However,

Reprinted from the *Journal of Marketing* (April 1977), pp. 73-80, published by the American Marketing Association.

G. Lynn Shostack is Senior Vice President at Bankers Trust Company and previously worked for Citibank in New York.

an equally feasible, though less comforting, explanation is that service industries have been slow to integrate marketing into the mainstream of decision-making and control because marketing offers no guidance, terminology, or practical rules that are clearly *relevant* to services.

MAKING ROOM FOR INTANGIBILITY

The American Marketing Association cites both goods *and* services as foci for marketing activities. Squeezing services into the Procrustean phrase, "intangible products,"[3] is not only a distortion of the AMA's definition but also a complete contradiction in terms.

It is wrong to imply that services are just like products "except" for intangibility. By such logic, apples are just like oranges, except for their "appleness." Intangibility is not a modifier; it is a state. Intangibles may come with tangible trappings, but no amount of money can buy physical ownership of such intangibles as "experience" (movies), "time" (consultants), or "process" (dry cleaning). A service is rendered. A service is experienced. A service cannot be stored on a shelf, touched, tasted or tried on for size. "Tangible" means "palpable," and "material." "Intangible" is an antonym, meaning "*im*palpable," and "*not* corporeal."[4] This distinction has profound implications. Yet marketing offers no way to treat intangibility as the core element it is, nor does marketing offer usable tools for managing, altering, or controlling this amorphous core.

Even the most thoughtful attempts to broaden the definition of "that which is marketed" away from product synonymity suffer from an underlying assumption of tangibility. Not long ago, Philip Kotler argued that "values" should be considered the end result of "marketing."[5] However, the text went on to imply that "values" were created by "objects," and drifted irredeemably into the classic product axioms.

To truly expand marketing's conceptual boundaries requires a framework which accommodates intangibility instead of denying it. Such a framework must give equal descriptive weight to the components of "service" as it does to the concept of "product."

THE COMPLEXITY OF MARKETED ENTITIES

What kind of framework would provide a new conceptual viewpoint? One unorthodox possibility can be drawn from direct observation of the marketplace and the nature of the market "satisfiers" available to it. Taking a fresh look, it seems that there are really very few, if any, "pure" products or services in the marketplace.

Examine, for instance, the automobile. Without question, one might say, it is a physical object, with a full range of tangible features and options. But another, equally important element is marketed in tandem with the steel and chrome—i.e., the service of transportation. Transportation is an *independent* marketing element; in other words, it is not car-dependent, but can be marketed in its own right. A car is only *one* alternative for satisfying the market's transportation needs.

This presents a semantic dilemma. How should the automobile be defined? Is General Motors marketing a *service*, a service that happens to include a *by*-product called a car? Levitt's classic "Marketing Myopia" exhorts businessmen to think in exactly this generic way about what they market.[6] Are automobiles "tangible services"? It cannot be denied that both elements—tangible and intangible—exist and are vigorously marketed. Yet they are, by definition, different qualities, and to attempt to compress them into a single word or phrase begs the issue.

Conversely, how shall a service such as airline transportation be described? Although the service itself is intangible, there are certain very real things that belong in any description of the total entity, including such important tangibles as interior decor, food & drink, seat design, and overall graphic continuity from tickets to attendants' uniforms. These items can dramatically affect the "reality" of the service in the consumer's mind. However, there is no accurate way to lump them into a one-word description.

If "either-or" terms (product vs. service) do not adequately describe the true nature of marketed entities, it makes sense to explore the usefulness of a new *structural* definition. This broader concept postulates that market entities are, in reality, *combinations of discrete elements* which are linked together in molecule-like wholes. Elements can be either tangible or intangible. The entity may have either a tangible or intangible nucleus. But the whole can only be described as having a certain dominance.

MOLECULAR MODEL

A "molecular" model offers opportunities for visualization and management of a total market entity. It reflects the fact that a market entity can be partly tangible *and* partly intangible, without diminishing the importance of either characteristic. Not only can the potential be seen for picturing and dealing with multiple *elements,* rather than *a thing,* but the concept of dominance can lead to enriched considerations of the priorities and approach that may be required of a marketer. Moreover, the model suggests the scientific analogy that if market entities have multiple elements, a deliberate or inadvertent change in a *single* element may completely alter the entity, as the simple switching of FE_3O_2 to FE_2O_3 creates a new substance. For this reason, a marketer must carefully manage all the elements, especially those for service-based entities, which may not have been considered previously within his domain.

DIAGRAMMING MARKET ENTITIES

A simplified comparison demonstrates the conceptual usefulness of a molecular modeling system. In Exhibit 29-1, automobiles and airline travel are broken down into their major elements. As shown, these two entities have different nuclei. They also differ in dominance.

Clearly, airline travel is intangible-dominant; that is, it does not yield physical ownership of a tangible good. Nearly all of the other important elements in the entity are intangible as well. Individual elements and their combinations represent unique satisfiers to different market segments. Thus:

- For some markets—students, for example—pure transport takes precedence over all other considerations. The charter flight business was based on this element. As might be expected during lean economic times, "no frills" flights show renewed emphasis on this nuclear core.
- For business travelers, on the other hand, schedule frequency may be paramount.
- Tourists, a third segment, may respond most strongly to the combination of inflight and post-flight services.

As the market entity of airline travel has evolved, it has become more and more complex. Ongoing reweighting of elements can be observed, for example, in the marketing of airline food, which was once a battleground of quasi-gourmet offerings. Today, some airlines have stopped marketing food altogether, while others are repositioning it primarily to the luxury markets.

AIRLINES VS. AUTOMOBILES

In comparing airlines to automobiles, one sees obvious similarities. The element of transportation is common to both, as it is to boats, trains, buses, and bicycles. Tangible decor also plays a role in both entities. Yet in spite of their similarities, the two entities are not the same, either in configuration or in marketing implications.

In some ways, airline travel and automobiles are mirror opposites. A car is a physical possession that renders a service. Airline travel, on the other hand, cannot be physically possessed. It can only be experienced. While the inherent "promise" of a car is service, airline transportation often promises a Lewis Carroll version of *"product,"* i.e., *destination,* which is marketed as though it were physically obtainable. If only tropical islands and redwood forests *could* be purchased for the price of an airline ticket!

The model can be completed by adding the remaining major marketing elements in a way that demonstrates their function vis-a-vis the organic core entity. First, the total entity is ringed and defined by a set value or price. Next, the valued entity is circumscribed by its distribution. Finally, the entire entity is encompassed, according to its core configuration, by its public "face," i.e., its positioning to the market.

The molecular concept makes it possible to describe and array market entities along a continuum, according to the weight of the "mix" of elements that comprise them. As Exhibit 29-2 indicates, teaching services might be at one end of such a scale, *intangible or I-dominant,* while salt might represent the other extreme, *tangible* or *T-dominant.* Such a scale accords intangible-based entities a place and weight commensurate with their true importance. The framework also provides a mechanism for comparison and market positioning.

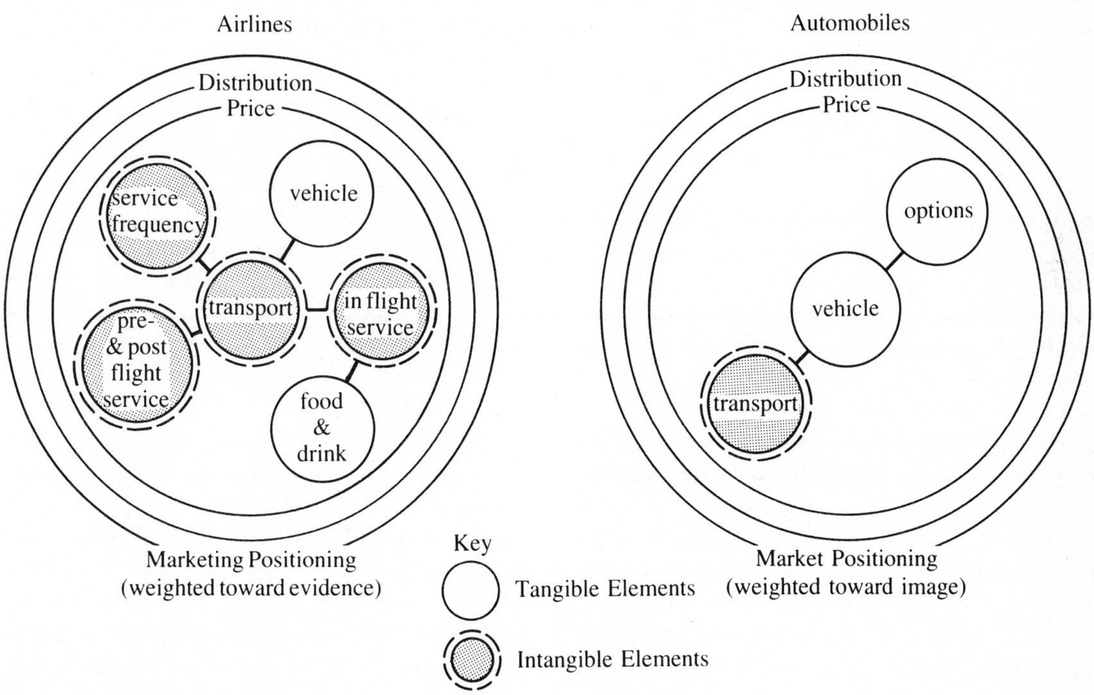

EXHIBIT 29-1 *Diagram of Market Entities*

In one of the handful of books devoted to services, the author holds that "the more intangible the service, the greater will be the difference in the marketing characteristics of the service."[7] Consistent with an entity scale, this axiom might now be amended to read: **the greater the weight of intangible elements in a market entity, the greater will be the divergence from product marketing in priorities and approach.**

IMPLICATIONS OF THE MOLECULAR MODEL

The hypothesis proposed by molecular modeling carries intriguing potential for rethinking and reshaping classic marketing concepts and practices. Recognition that service-dominant entities differ from product-dominant entities allows consideration of other distinctions which have been intuitively understood, but seldom articulated by service marketers.

A most important area of difference is immediately apparent – i.e., that service "knowledge" and product "knowledge" cannot be gained in the same way.

A *product* marketer's first task is to "know" his product. For tangible-dominant entities this is relatively straight-forward. A tangible object can be described precisely. It is subject to physical examination or photographic reproduction or quantitative measure. It can not only be exactly replicated, but also modified in precise and duplicate ways.

It is not particularly difficult for the marketer of *Coca-Cola*, for example, to summon all the facts regarding the product itself. He can and does make reasonable assumptions about the product's behavior, e.g., that it is consistent chemically to the taste, visually to the eye, and physically in its packaging. Any changes he might make in these three areas can be deliberately controlled for uniformity since they will be tangibly evident. In other words, the marketer can take the product's "reality" for granted and move on to considerations of price, distribution, and advertising or promotion.

To gain *service* "knowledge," however, or knowledge of a service element, where does one begin? It has been pointed out that intangible elements are dynamic, subjective, and ephemeral. They cannot be touched, tried on for size, or displayed on a shelf. They are exceedingly difficult to quantify.

Reverting to airline travel, precisely what *is* the service of air transportation to the potential purchaser? What "percent" of airline travel is comfort? What "percent" is fear or adventure? What *is* this service's "reality" to its market? And how does that reality vary from segment to segment? Since this service exists only during the time in which it is rendered, the entity's true "reality" must be defined experientially, not in engineering terms.

A NEW APPROACH TO SERVICE DEFINITION

Experiential definition is a little-explored area of marketing practice. A product-based marketer is in danger of assuming he understands an intangible-dominant entity when, in fact, he may only be projecting his *own* subjective version of "reality." And because there is no documented guidance on acquiring service-knowledge, the chances for error are magnified.

Case Example

One short-lived mistake (with which the author is familiar) occurred recently in the trust department of a large commercial bank. The department head, being close to daily operations, understood "investment management" as the combined work of hundreds of people, backed by the firm's stature, resources, and long history. With this "reality" in mind, he concluded that the service could be better represented by professional salesmen, than through the traditional, but interruptive use of the portfolio manager as main client contact.

Three salesmen were hired, and given a training course in investments. They failed dismally, both in maintaining current client relationships and in producing new business for the firm. In hindsight, it became clear that the department head misunderstood the service's "reality" as it was being experienced by his clients. To the clients, "investment *management*" was found to mean "investment *manager*"–i.e., a single human being upon whom they depended for decisions and advice. No matter how well prepared, the professional salesman was not seen as an acceptable substitute by the majority of the market.

Visions of Reality

Clearly, more than one version of "reality" may be found in a service market. Therefore, the crux of service-knowledge is the description of the major *consensus realities* that define the service entity to various market segments. The determination of consensus realities should be a high priority for service marketers, and marketing should offer more concrete guidance and emphasis on this subject than it does.

To define the market-held "realities" of a service requires a high tolerance for subjective, "soft" data, combined with a rigidly objective attitude toward that data. To understand what a service entity is to a market, the marketer must undertake more initial research than is common in product marketing. More important, it will be research of a different kind than is the case in product marketing. The marketer must rely heavily on the tools and skills of psychology, sociology and other behavioral sciences–tools that in product marketing usually come into play in determining *image,* rather than fundamental "reality."

In developing the blueprint of a service entity's main elements, the marketer might find, for instance, that although tax return preparation is analogous to "accurate mathematical computation" within his firm, it means "freedom from responsibility" to one segment of the consuming public, "opportunity for financial savings" to another segment, and "convenience" to yet a third segment.

Unless these "realities" are documented and ranked by market importance, no sensible plan can be devised to represent a service effectively or deliberately. And in *new* service development, the importance of the service-research function is even more critical, because the successful development of a new service–a molecular collection of

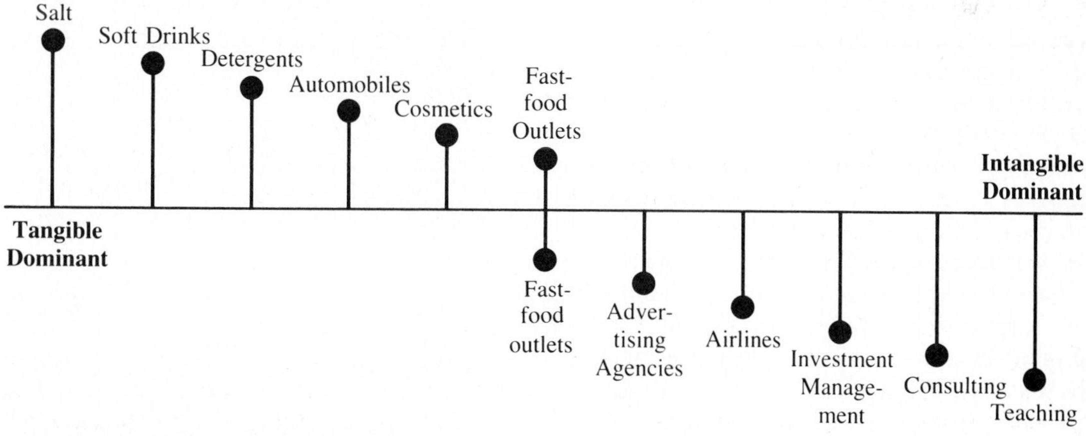

EXHIBIT 29–2 *Scale of Market Entities*

intangibles—is so difficult it makes new-product development look like child's play.

IMAGE VS. EVIDENCE—THE KEY

The definition of consensus realities should not be confused with the determination of "image." Image is a method of *differentiating* and *representing* an entity to its target market. Image is not "product;" nor is it "service." As was suggested in Exhibit 29-1, there appears to be a critical difference between the way tangible- and intangible-dominant entities are best represented to their markets. Examination of actual cases suggests a common thread among effective representations of services that is another mirror-opposite contrast to product techniques.

In comparing examples, it is clear that consumer product marketing often approaches the market by enhancing a physical object through abstract associations. *Coca-Cola*, for example, is surrounded with visual, verbal and aural associations with authenticity and youth. Although *Dr. Pepper* would also be physically categorized as a beverage, its *image* has been structured to suggest "originality" and "risk-taking;" while *7-up* is "light" and "buoyant." A high priority is placed on linking these abstract images to physical items.

But a service is already abstract. To compound the abstraction dilutes the "reality" that the marketer is trying to enhance. Effective service representations appear to be turned 180° *away* from abstraction. The reason for this is that service images, and even service "realities," appear to be shaped to a large extent by the things that the consumer can comprehend with his five senses—tangible things. But a service itself cannot be tangible, so reliance must be placed on **peripheral** clues.

Tangible clues are what allow the detective in a mystery novel to surmise events at the scene of a crime without having been present. Similarly, when a consumer attempts to judge a service, particularly before using or buying it, that service is "known" by the tangible clues, the tangible evidence, that surround it.

The management of tangible evidence is not articulated in marketing as a primary priority for service marketers. There has been little in-depth exploration of the *range* of authority that emphasis on tangible evidence would create for the service marketer. In product marketing, tangible evidence is primarily the product itself. But for services, tangible evidence would encompass broader considerations in contrast to product marketing, *different* considerations than are typically considered marketing's domain today.

Focusing on the Evidence

In *product* marketing, many kinds of evidence are beyond the marketer's control and are consequently omitted from priority consideration in the market positioning process. Product marketing tends to give first emphasis to creating *abstract* associations.

Service marketers, on the other hand, should be focused on enhancing and differentiating "realities" through manipulation of *tangible* clues. The management of evidence comes first for service marketers, because service "reality" is arrived at by the consumer mostly through a process of deduction, based on the total impression that the evidence creates. Because of product marketing's biases, service marketers often fail to recognize the unique forms of evidence that they *can* normally control and fail to see that they should be part of marketing's responsibilities.

MANAGEMENT OF THE ENVIRONMENT

Environment is a good example. Since product distribution normally means shipping to outside agents, the marketer has little voice in structuring the environment in which the product is sold. His major controllable impact on the environment is usually product packaging. Services, on the other hand, are often fully integrated with environment; that is, the setting in which the service is "distributed" *is* controllable. To the extent possible, management of the physical environment should be one of a service marketer's highest priorities.

Setting can play an enormous role in influencing the "reality" of a service in the consumer's mind. Marketing does not emphasize this rule for services, yet there are numerous obvious examples of its importance.

Physicians' offices provide an interesting example of intuitive environmental management. Although the quality of medical service may be identical, an office furnished in teak and leather creates a totally different "reality" in the consumer's mind from one with plastic slipcovers and inexpensive prints. Carrying the example further, a marketer could expect to cause change in the service's image simply by painting a physician's office walls neon pink or silver, instead of white.

Similarly, although the services may be identical, the consumer's differentiation between "Bank A Service" and "Bank B Service" is materially affected by whether the environment is dominated by butcher-block and bright colors or by marble and polished brass.

By understanding the importance of evidence management, the service marketer can make it his business to review and take control of this critical part of his "mix." Creation of environment can be deliberate, rather than accidental or as a result of leaving such decisions in the hands of the interior decorators.

Integrating Evidence

Going beyond environment, evidence can be integrated across a wide range of items. Airlines, for example, manage and coordinate tangible evidence, and do it better than almost any large service industry. Whether by intuition or design, airlines do *not* focus attention on trying to explain or characterize the service itself. One never sees an ad that attempts to convey "the slant of takeoff," "the feel of acceleration," or "the aerodynamics of lift." Airline transport is given shape and form through consistency of a firm's identification, its uniforms, the decor of its planes, its graphics, and its advertising. Differentiation among airlines, though they all provide the same service, is a direct result of differences in "packages" of evidence.

Some businesses in which tangible and intangible elements carry equal weight emphasize abstractions and evidence in about equal proportions. McDonald's is an excellent example. The food *product* is associated with "nutritious" (two all-beef, etc.), "fun" (Ronald McDonald) and "helpful" ("We Do it All for You," "You Deserve a Break Today"). The main *service* element, i.e., fast food preparation, is tangibly distinguished by uniformity of environment, color, and style of graphics and apparel, consistency of delivery (young employees), and the ubiquitous golden arches.

Using the scale developed in Exhibit 29-2, this concept can be postulated as a principle for service representation. As shown in Exhibit 29-3, once an entity has been analyzed and positioned on the scale, the degree to which the marketer will focus on either tangible evidence or intangible abstractions for market positioning will be found to be **inversely related to the entity's dominance.**

The more intangible elements there are, the more the marketer must endeavor to stand in the consumer's shoes, thinking through and gaining control of *all* the inputs to the consumer's mind that can be classified as material evidence.

Some forms of evidence can seem trivial until one recognizes how great their impact can be on service perception. Correspondence is

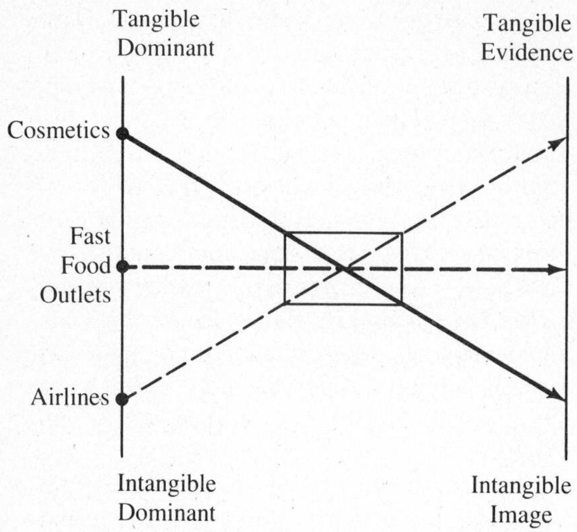

EXHIBIT 29-3 *Principle of Market Positioning Emphasis*

one example. Letters, statements, and the like are sometimes the main conveyers of the "reality" of a service to its market; yet often these are treated as peripheral to any marketing plan. From the grade of paper to the choice of colors, correspondence is visible evidence that conveys a unique message. A mimeographed, nonpersonalized, cheaply offset letter contradicts any words about service quality that may appear in the text of that letter. Conversely, engraved parchment from the local dry cleaner might make one wonder about their prices.

Profile as Evidence

As was pointed out in the investment management example, services are often inextricably entwined with their human representatives. In many fields, a person is perceived to *be* the service. The consumer cannot distinguish between them. Product marketing is myopic in dealing with the issue of *people as evidence* in terms of market positioning. Consumer marketing often stops at the production of materials and programs for salesmen to use. Some service industries, on the other hand, have long intuitively managed human evidence to larger ends.

Examples of this principle have been the basis for jokes, plays, and literature. "The Man in the Grey Flannel Suit," for example, was a synonym for the advertising business for many years. Physicians are uniformly "packaged" in smocks. Lawyers and bankers are still today known for pin-stripes and vests. IBM representatives were famous for adhering to a "White Shirt" policy. Going beyond apparel, as mentioned earlier, McDonald's even achieves age uniformity – an extra element reinforcing its total market image.

These examples add up to a serious principle when thoughtfully reviewed. They are particularly instructive for service marketers. None of the above examples were the result of deliberate market planning. McDonald's, for instance, backed into age consistency as a result of trying to keep labor costs low. Airlines are the single outstanding example of consciously-planned standards for uniformity in human representation. The power of the human evidence principle is obvious, and the potential power of more deliberately controlling or structuring this element is clear.

Lest this discussion be interpreted as an advocacy of regimentation, it should be pointed out that management of human evidence can be as basic as providing nametags to service representatives or as complex as the "packaging" of a political candidate, whose very words are often chosen by committee and whose hair style can become a critical policy issue. Or, depending upon what kind of service "reality" the marketer wishes to create, human representation can be encouraged to display *non*-conformity, as is the case with the "creative" departments of advertising agencies. The point is that service marketers should be charged with tactics and strategy in this area, and must consider it a management responsibility.

SERVICES AND THE MEDIA

As has been previously discussed, service elements are abstract. Because they are abstract, the marketer must work hard at making them "real," by building a case from tangible evidence. In this context, media advertising presents a particularly difficult problem.

The problem revolves around the fact that media (television, radio, print) are one step removed from tangibility. Media, by its McLuhanesque nature, abstracts the physical.

Even though product tangibility provides an anchor for media representation because a product can be *shown,* media still abstract products. A photograph is only a two-dimensional version of a physical object, and may be visually misleading. Fortunately, the consumer makes the mental connection between seeing a product in the media and recognizing it in reality. This is true even when a product is substantially distorted. Sometimes, only part of a product is shown. Occasionally, as in recent commercials for *7-up,* the product is *not* shown. However, the consumer remembers past experience. He has little difficulty recognizing *7-up* by name or remembered appearance when he sees it or wants to buy it.

Thus, media work *with* the creation of product image and *help* in adding abstract qualities to tangible goods. Cosmetics, for example, are often positioned in association with an airbrushed or soft-focus filmed *ideal* of beauty. Were the media truly accurate, the wrinkles and flaws of the flesh, to which even models are heir, might not create such an appealing product association.

Making Services More Concrete

Because of their abstracting capabilities, the media often make service entities more **hazy,** instead of more **concrete,** and the service marketer must work *against* this inherent effect. Unfortunately, many marketers are so familiar with product-oriented thinking that they go down precisely the wrong path and attempt to represent services by dealing with them in abstractions.

The pages of the business press are filled with examples of this type of misconception in services advertising. In advertisements for investment management, for instance, the worst examples attempt to describe the already intangible service with *more* abstractions such as "sound analysis," "careful portfolio monitoring," "strong research capability," etc. Such compounded abstractions do *not* help the consumer form a "reality," do *not* differentiate the service and do *not* achieve any credibility, much less any customer "draw."

The best examples are those which attempt to associate the service with some form of **tangible evidence,** working against the media's abstracting qualities. Merrill Lynch, for instance, has firmly associated itself with a clear visual symbol of bulls and concomitant bullishness. Where Merrill Lynch does not use the visual herd, it uses photographs of **tangible physical booklets,** and invites the consumer to write for them.

Therefore, the final principle offered for service marketers would hold that **effective media representation of intangibles is a function of establishing non-abstract manifestations of them.**

CONCLUSION

This article has presented several market-inspired thoughts toward the development of new marketing concepts, and the evolution of relevant service marketing principles. The hypotheses presented here do not by any means represent an exhaustive analysis of the subject. No exploration was done, for example, on product vs. service pricing or product vs. service distribution. Both areas offer rich potential for creative new approaches and analysis.

It can be argued that there are many grey areas in the molecular entity concept, and that diagramming and managing according to the multiple-elements schema could present considerable difficulties by virtue of its greater complexity. It might also be argued that some distinctions between tangible and intangible-dominant entities are so subtle as to be unimportant.

The fact remains that service marketers are in urgent need of concepts and priorities that are relevant to their actual experience and needs, and that marketing has failed in evolving to meet that demand. However unorthodox, continuing exploration of this area must be encouraged if marketing is to achieve stature and influence in the new post-Industrial Revolution services economy.

NOTES

1. See, for example, E. Jerome McCarthy, *Basic Marketing: A Managerial Approach,* 4th ed. (Homewood, IL: Richard D. Irwin, 1971) pg. 303 compared to William J. Stanton, *Fundamentals of Marketing,* 3rd ed. (New York: McGraw-Hill, 1971), pg. 567.
2. See William R. George and Hiram C. Barksdale, "Marketing Activities in the Service Industries," **Journal of Marketing**, Vol. 38 No. 4 (October 1974), pp. 65–70.
3. *The Meaning and Sources of Marketing Theory*– Marketing Science Institute Series (New York: McGraw-Hill, 1965), pg. 88.
4. *Webster's New Collegiate Dictionary* (Springfield, MA: G.&C. Merriam Company, 1974).
5. Philip Kotler, "A Generic Concept of Marketing," **Journal of Marketing**, Vol. 36 No. 2 (April 1972), pp. 46–54.
6. Theodore H. Levitt, "Marketing Myopia," *Harvard Business Review,* Vol. 38 (July–August 1960), pp. 45-46.
7. Aubrey Wilson, *The Marketing of Professional Services,* (New York: McGraw-Hill, 1972) pg. 8.

30

Stanley C. Hollander

The Wheel of Retailing

"The wheel of retailing" is the name Professor Malcolm P. McNair has suggested for the major hypothesis concerning patterns of retail development. This hypothesis holds that new types of retailers usually enter the market as low-status, low-margin, low-price operators. Gradually they acquire more elaborate establishments and facilities, with both increased investments and higher operating costs. Finally they mature as high-cost, high-price merchants, vulnerable to newer types who, in turn, go through the same pattern. Department-store merchants, who originally appeared as vigorous competitors to the smaller retailers and who have now become vulnerable to discount house and supermarket competition, are often cited as prime examples of the wheel pattern.[1]

Many examples of conformity to this pattern can be found. Nevertheless, we may ask: (1) Is this hypothesis valid for all retailing under all conditions? (2) How accurately does it describe total American retail development? (3) What factors cause wheel-pattern changes in retail institutions?

The following discussion assembles some of the slender empirical evidence available that might shed some light on these three questions: In attempting to answer the third question, a number of hypotheses should be considered that marketing students have advanced concerning the forces that have shaped retail development.

TENTATIVE EXPLANATIONS OF THE WHEEL

(A) Retail personalities. New types of retail institutions are often established by highly

Reprinted from the *Journal of Marketing*, published by the American Marketing Association (July, 1960), pp. 37–42.

Stanley C. Hollander is professor of marketing at Michigan State Univeristy. He has been an analyst for a chain of retail stores and has taught at the Universities of Buffalo, Pennsylvania, and Minnesota. His published work is in the field of retailing, and he holds a B.S. from New York University, an M.A. from the American University, and a Ph.D. in economics from the University of Pennsylvania. Explorations in Retailing, *which Professor Hollander edited, is a milestone in the academic progress of the retailing field.*

aggressive, cost-conscious entrepreneurs who make every penny count and who have no interest in unprofitable frills. But, as P. D. Converse has suggested, these men may relax their vigilance and control over costs as they acquire age and wealth. Their successors may be less competent. Either the innovators or their successors may be unwilling, or unable, to adjust to changing conditions. Consequently, according to this view, deterioration in management causes movement along the wheel.[2]

(B) Misguidance. Hermann Levy has advanced the ingenious, if implausible, explanation that retail trade journals, seduced by profitable advertising from the store equipment and supply industry, coax merchants into superfluous "modernization" and into the installation of overly elaborate facilities.[3]

(C) Imperfect competition. Although retail trade is often cited as the one type of business that approaches the Adam Smith concept of perfect competition, some economists have argued that retailing actually is a good example of imperfect competition. These economists believe that most retailers avoid direct price competition because of several forces, including resale price maintenance, trade association rules in some countries, and, most important, the fear of immediate retaliation. Contrariwise, the same retailers feel that service improvements, including improvements in location, are not susceptible to direct retaliation by competitors. Hence, through a ratchet process, merchants in any established branch of trade tend to provide increasingly elaborate services at increasingly higher margins.[4]

(D) Excess capacity. McNair attributes much of the wheel effect to the development of excess capacity, as more and more dealers enter any branch of retail trade.[5] This hypothesis rests upon an imperfect competition assumption, since, under perfect competition excess capacity would simply reduce margins until the excess vendors were eliminated.

(E) Secular trend. J. B. Jefferys has pointed out that a general, but uneven, long-run increase in the British standard of living provided established merchants with profitable opportunities for trading up. Jefferys thus credits adjustments to changing and wealthier market segments as causing some movement along the wheel. At the same time, pockets of opportunity have remained for new, low-margin operations because of the uneven distribution of living-standard increases.[6]

(F) Illusion. Professor B. Holdren has suggested in a recent letter that present tendencies toward scrambled merchandising may create totally illusory impressions of the wheel phenomenon. Store-wide average margins may increase as new, high-markup lines are added to the product mix, even though the margins charged on the original components of that mix remain unchanged.

DIFFICULTIES OF ANALYSIS

An examination of the actual development of retail institutions here and abroad does shed some light on both the wheel hypothesis and its various explanations. However, a number of significant difficulties hinder the process.

1. Statements concerning changes in retail margins and expenses are the central core of the wheel hypothesis. Yet valid information on historical retail expense rates is very scarce. Long-run changes in percentage margins probably do furnish fairly reliable clues to expense changes, but this is not true over short or intermediate periods. For example, 1957 furniture-store expense rates were about 5 percentage points higher than their

1949–1951 average, yet gross margins actually declined slightly over the same period.[7]

2. Historical margin data are somewhat more plentiful, but these also have to be dredged up from fragmentary sources.[8]
3. Available series on both expenses and margins merely note changes in retailers' outlays and receipts. They do not indicate what caused those changes and they do not report changes in the costs borne by suppliers, consumers, or the community at large.
4. Margin data are usually published as averages that may, and frequently do, mask highly divergent tendencies.
5. A conceptual difficulty presents an even more serious problem than the paucity of statistics. When we talk about "types" of retailers, we think of classifications based upon ways of doing business and upon differences in price policy. Yet census categories and other systems for reporting retail statistics are usually based upon major differences in commodity lines. For example, the "pineboard" druggists who appeared in the 1930s are a "type" of retailing for our purposes. Those dealers had cruder fixtures, charged lower prices, carried smaller assortments, gave more attention to turnover, and had less interest in prescriptions than did conventional druggists. Yet census reports for drugstores necessarily included all of the pineboards that maintained any sort of prescription department.

Discount houses provide another example of an important, but amorphous, category not reflected in census classifications. The label "discount house" covers a variety of retailers. Some carry stocks, others do not. Some have conventional store facilities, whereas others operate in office buildings, lofts, and warehouses. Some feature electrical appliances and hard goods, while others emphasize soft goods. Some pose as wholesalers, and others are practically indistinguishable from all other popular priced retailers in their fields. Consequently discount dealers' operating figures are likely to be merged into the statistics reported for other appliance, hardware, or apparel merchants.

EXAMPLES OF CONFORMITY

British

British retailing provides several examples of conformity to the wheel pattern. The grocery trade has gone through several wheel-like evolutions, according to a detailed analysis made by F. G. Pennance and B. S. Yamey.[9] Established firms did initiate some changes and some margin reductions, so that the pattern is obscured by many cross currents. But the major changes seem to have been due to the appearance and then the maturation, first, of department-store food counters; then of chain stores; and finally, of cut-price and cash-and-carry stores. Now supermarkets seem to be carrying the pattern through another evolution.[10]

Jefferys also has noted a general long-run upgrading in both British department stores and chains.[11] Vague complaints in the co-operative press and a decline in consumer dividend rates suggest that wheel-like changes may have occurred in the British co-operative movement.[12]

American

Very little is known about retail margins in this country before the Civil War. Our early retail history seems to have involved the appearance, first, of hawkers, walkers, and peddlers; then, of general stores; next, of specialty stores; and finally, of department stores. Each of these types apparently came in as a low-margin, lower-price competitor to the established outlets, and thus was consistent with the wheel pattern. We do not know, however, whether there was simply a long-run decline in retail margins through successive improvements in retail efficiency from one type to another (contrary to the wheel pattern), or whether each of the early types was started on a low-margin basis, gradually "up-graded," and so provided room for the next entrant (in accordance with the pattern).

The trends toward increasing margins can be more easily discerned in many branches of retailing after the Civil War. Barger has described increases over the years 1869–1947 among important retail segments, including department stores, mail-order firms, variety stores, and jewelry dealers. He attributes much of the pre-World War I rise in department-store margins to the absorption of wholesaling functions. Changes in merchandise mix, such as the addition of soda fountains and cafeterias to variety stores and the upgrading of mail-order merchandise, seem to have caused some of the other increases. Finally, he believes changes in customer services have been a major force in raising margins.[13] Fabian Linden has extended Barger's observations to note similar 1949–1957 margin increases for department stores, variety chains, and appliance dealers.[14]

Some other examples of at least partial conformity to the wheel pattern may be cited. Many observers feel that both discount-house services and margins have increased substantially in recent years.[15] One major discount-house operator has stated that he has been able to keep his average markup below 12%, in spite of considerable expansion in his facilities and commodity mix.[16] However, the consensus seems to be that this probably is an exception to the general rule.

A study of gasoline pricing has pointed out how many of the so-called "off-brand" outlets have changed from the "trackside" stations of pre-war days. The trackside dealers typically maintained unattractive and poorly equipped installations, at out-of-the-way locations where unbranded gasoline was sold on a price basis. Today many of them sell well-promoted regional and local brands, maintain attractive, efficient stations, and provide prompt and courteous service. Some still offer cut prices, but many have raised their prices and margins up to or above national brand levels.[17] Over time, many of the pine-board druggists also seem to have become converted to fairly conventional operations.[18]

NON-CONFORMING EXAMPLES

Foreign

In underdeveloped countries, the relatively small middle- and upper-income groups have formed the major markets for "modern" types of retailing. Supermarkets and other modern stores have been introduced in those countries largely at the top of the social and price scales, contrary to the wheel pattern.[19] Some non-conforming examples may also be found in somewhat more industrialized environments. The vigorous price competition that developed among Japanese department stores during the first three decades of this century seems directly contrary to the wheel hypothesis.[20] B. S. Yamey's history of resale price maintenance also reports some price-cutting by traditional, well-established British merchants who departed from the wheel pattern in the 1880s an 1890s.[21] Unfortunately, our ignorance of foreign retail history hinders any judgment of the representatives of these examples.

American

Automatic merchandising, perhaps the most "modern" of all American retail institutions, departed from the wheel pattern by starting as a high-cost, high-margin, high-convenience type of retailing.[22] The department-store branch movement and the concomitant rise of planned shopping centers also has progressed directly contrary to the wheel pattern. The early department-store branches consisted of a few stores in exclusive suburbs and some equally high-fashion college and resort shops.

Only in relatively recent years have the branches been adjusted to the changing and more democratic characteristics of the contemporary dormitory suburbs. Suburban shopping centers, too, seem to have appeared first as "Manhasset Miracle Miles" and "Ardmores" before reaching out to the popular price customers. In fact, complaints are still heard that the regional shopping centers have displayed excessive resistance to the entry of really aggressive, low-margin outlets.[23] E. R. A. Seligman and R. A. Love's study of retail pricing in the 1930s suggests that pressures on prices and margins were generated by all types of retailers. The mass retailing institutions, such as the department and chain stores, that had existed as types for many decades were responsible for a goodly portion of the price cutting.[24] As McNair has pointed out, the wheel operated very slowly in the case of department stores.

Finally, Harold Barger has described the remarkable stability of overall distributive margins during the years 1919–1947.[25] Some shifting of distributive work from wholesalers to retailers apparently affected their relative shares of the total margins during this period, but this is not the type of change contemplated by the wheel pattern. Of course, the stability Barger notes conceivably could have been the result of a perfectly smooth functioning of the pattern, with the entrance of low-margin innovators providing exactly the right balance for the upcreep of margins in the longer established types. But economic changes do not come in smooth and synchronized fashion, and Barger's data probably should indicate considerably wider oscillations if the wheel really set the mold for all retailing in the post-war period.

CONCLUSIONS

The number of non-conforming examples suggests that the wheel hypothesis is not valid for all retailing. The hypothesis, however, does seem to describe a fairly common pattern in industrialized, expanding economies. Moreover, the wheel is not simply an illusion created by scrambled merchandising, as Holdren suggests. Undoubtedly some of the recent "upcreep" in supermarket average margins is due to the addition of nonfood and other high margin lines. But in recent years the wheel pattern has also been characteristic of department-store retailing, a field that has been relatively unreceptive to new commodity groups.[26]

In some ways, Jefferys' secular trend explanation appears most reasonable. The tendency of many established retailers to reduce prices and margins during depressions suggests also that increases may be a result of generally prospering environments. This explanation helps to resolve an apparent paradox inherent in the wheel concept. Why should reasonably skilled businessmen make decisions that consistently lead their firms along seemingly profitable routes to positions of vulnerability? Jefferys sees movement along the wheel as the result of sensible, business-like decisions to change with prospering market segments and to leave the poorer customers to low-margin innovators. His explanation is supported by the fact that the vulnerability contemplated by the wheel hypothesis usually means only a loss of market share, not a loss of absolute volume. At least in the United States, though, this explanation is partially contradicted by studies showing that prosperous consumers are especially prone to patronize discount houses. Also they are equally as likely to shop in supermarkets as are poorer consumers.[27]

The imperfect competition and excess capacity hypotheses also appear highly plausible. Considerably more investigation is needed before their validity can be appraised properly. The wheel pattern developed very slowly, and very recently in the department-store field. Yet market imperfections in that field probably were greater before the automobile gave the consumer shopping mobility. Major portions of the supermarket growth in food retailing and discount-house growth in appliance distribution occurred during periods of vastly expanding consumption, when excess capacity probably was at relatively low levels. At the moment there is little evidence to suggest any clear-cut correlation between the degree of market imperfection and the appearance of the wheel pattern. However, this lack may well be the result of the scarcity of empirical studies of retail competition.

Managerial deterioration certainly must explain some manifestations of the wheel, but not all. Empires rise and fall with changes in the quality of their leadership, and the same thing seems true in business. But the wheel hypothesis is a hypothesis concerning types of retailing and not merely individual firms. Consequently, the managerial-deterioration explanation holds true only if it is assumed that new people entering any established type of retailing as the heads of both old and new companies are consistently less competent than the first generation. Again, the fact that the wheel has operated very slowly in some fields suggests that several successive managerial generations can avoid wheel-like maturation and decay.

NOTES

1. M. P. McNair, "Significant Trends and Developments in the Postwar Period," in A.B. Smith (editor), *Competitive Distribution in a Free, High-Level Economy and Its Implications for the University* (Pittsburgh: University of Pittsburgh Press, 1958), pp. 1-25, at pp. 17-18.
2. P .D. Converse, "Mediocrity in Retailing," *Journal of Marketing* (April, 1959), pp. 419-420.
3. Hermann Levy, *The Shops of Britain* (London: Kegan Paul, Trench, Trubner & Co., 1947), pp. 210-211.
4. D. L. Shawver, *The Development of Theories of Retail Price Determination* (Urbana: University of Illinois Press, 1956), p. 92.
5. Same reference as footnote 1.
6. J. B. Jefferys, *Retail Trading in Great Britain,* 1850-1950 (Cambridge: Cambridge University Press, 1954), various pages, especially p. 96.
7. Cited in Fabian Linden, "Department Store Operations," *Conference Board Business Record* (October, 1958), pp. 410-414, at p. 411.
8. See Harold Barger, *Distribution's Place in the American Economy Since 1869* (Princeton: Princeton University Press, 1955).
9. F. G. Pennance and B. S. Yamey, "Competition in the Retail Grocery Trade, 1850-1939," *Economica* (March, 1955), pp. 303-317.
10. "La Methode Americaine," *Time* (November 16, 1959), pp. 105-106.
11. Same reference as footnote 6.
12. "Battle of the Dividend," *Co-operative Review* (August, 1956), p. 183; "Independent Commission's Report," *Co-operative Review* (April, 1958), pp. 84-89; £52 Million Dividend in 1957," *Co-operative Review* (August 1958), pp. 171-172.
13. Same reference as footnote 8, p. 82.
14. See footnote 7.
15. D. A. Loehwing, "Resourceful Merchants," *Barron's* (November 17, 1958), p. 3.
16. S. Masters, quoted in "Three Concepts of Retail Service," *Stores* (July-August, 1959), pp. 18-21.
17. S. M. Livingston and T. Levitt, "Competition and Retail Gasoline Prices," *The Review of Economics and Statistics* (May, 1959), pp. 119-132, at p. 132.
18. Paul C. Olsen, *The Marketing of Drug Products* (New Brunswick: Rutgers University Press, 1948), pp. 130-132.
19. H. S. Hettinger, "Marketing in Persia," *Journal of Marketing* (January, 1951), pp. 289-297; H. W. Boyd, Jr., R. M. Clewett, & R. L. Westfall, "The Marketing Structure of Venezuela," *Journal of Marketing* (April, 1958), pp. 391-397; D. A. Taylor, "Retailing in Brazil," *Journal of Marketing* (July, 1959), pp. 54-58; J. K. Galbraith and R. Holton, *Marketing Efficiency in Puerto Rico* (Cambridge: Harvard University Press, 1955), p. 35.
20. G. Fukami, "Japanese Department Stores," *Journal of Marketing* (July, 1953), pp. 41-49, at p. 42.
21. "The Origins of Resale Price Maintenance," *The Economic Journal* (September, 1952), pp. 522-545.
22. W. S. Fishman, "Sense Makes Dollars," *1959 Directory of Automatic Merchandising* (Chicago: National Automatic Merchandising Association, 1959), p. 52; M. V. Marshall, *Automatic Merchandising* (Boston: Graduate School of Business Administration, Harvard University, 1954), pp. 108-109, 122.
23. P. E. Smith, *Shopping Centers* (New York: National Retail Merchant's Association, 1956), pp. 11-12; M. L.

Sweet, "Tenant-Selection Policies of Regional Shopping Centers," *Journal of Marketing* (April, 1959), pp. 399–404.
24. E. R. A. Seligman and R. A. Love, *Price Cutting and Price Maintenance* (New York: Harper & Brothers, 1932).
25. Same reference as footnote 8, pp. ix, x.
26. R. D. Entenberg, *The Changing Competitive Position of Department Stores in the United States by Merchandise Lines* (Pittsburgh: University of Pittsburgh Press, 1957), p. 52.
27. R. Holton, *The Supply and Demand Structure of Food Retailing Services, A Case Study* (Cambridge: Harvard University Press, 1954).

31

Louis P. Bucklin

Retail Strategy and the Classification of Consumer Goods

When Melvin T. Copeland published his famous discussion of the classification of consumer goods, shopping, convenience, and specialty goods, his intent was clearly to create a guide for the development of marketing strategies by manufacturers.[1] Although his dicussion involved retailers and retailing, his purpose was to show how consumer buying habits affected the type of channel of distribution and promotional strategy that a manufacturer should adopt. Despite the controversy which still surrounds his classification, his success in creating such a guide may be judged by the fact that through the years few marketing texts have failed to make use of his ideas.

The purpose of this article is to attempt to clarify some of the issues that exist with respect to the classification, and to extend the concept to include the retailer and the study of retail strategy.

CONTROVERSY OVER THE CLASSIFICATION SYSTEM

The starting point for the discussion lies with the definitions adopted by the American Marketing Association's Committee on Definitions for the classification system in 1948.[2] These are:

Convenience Goods: Those consumers' goods which the customer purchases frequently, immediately, and with the minimum of effort.

Shopping Goods: Those consumers' goods which the customer in the process of selection and purchase characteristically compares on such bases as suitability, quality, price and style.

Specialty Goods: Those consumers' goods on which a significant group of buyers are habitually willing to make a special purchasing effort.

Reprinted from the *Journal of Marketing,* published by the American Marketing Association (January, 1963), pp. 51-56.

Louis P. Bucklin has taught in business schools at the University of Colorado and Northwestern University and is now professor of marketing at the University of California at Berkeley. He received his bachelor's degree from Dartmouth, his M.B.A. from Harvard, and his Ph.D. from Northwestern. He is an authority on marketing channels and channel management.

This set of definitions was retained in virtually the same form by the Committee on Definitions in its latest publication.[3]

Opposing these accepted definitions stands a critique by Richard H. Holton.[4] Finding the Committee's definitions too imprecise to be able to measure consumer buying behavior, he suggested that the following definitions not only would represent the essence of Copeland's original idea, but be operationally more useful as well.

Convenience Goods: Those goods for which the consumer regards the probable gain from making price and quality comparisons as small compared to the cost of making such comparisons.

Shopping Goods: Those goods for which the consumer regards the probable gain from making price and quality comparisons as large relative to the cost of making such comparisons.

Specialty Goods: Those convenience or shopping goods, which have such a limited market as to require the consumer to make a special effort to purchase them.

Holton's definitions have particular merit because they make explicit the underlying conditions that control the extent of a consumer's shopping activities. They show that a consumer's buying behavior will be determined not only by the strength of his desire to secure some good, but by his perception of the cost of shopping to obtain it. In other words, the consumer continues to shop for *all goods* so long as he feels that the additional satisfaction from further comparisons are at least equal to the cost of making the additional effort. The distinction between shopping and convenience goods lies principally in the degree of satisfaction to be secured from further comparisons.

The Specialty Good Issue

While Holton's conceptualization makes an important contribution, he has sacrificed some of the richness of Copeland's original ideas. This is essentially David J. Luck's complaint in a criticism of Holton's proposal.[5] Luck objected to the abandonment of the *willingness* of consumers to make a special effort to buy as the rationale for the concept of specialty goods. He regarded this type of consumer behavior as based upon unique consumer attitudes toward certain goods and not the density of distribution of those goods. Holton, in a reply, rejected Luck's point; he remained convinced that the real meaning of specialty goods could be derived from his convenience goods, shopping goods continuum, and market conditions.[6]

The root of the matter appears to be that insufficient attention has been paid to the fact that the consumer, once embarked upon some buying expedition, may have only one of two possible objectives in mind. A discussion of this aspect of consumer behavior will make possible a closer synthesis of Holton's contributions with the more traditional point of view.

A Forgotten Idea

The basis for this discussion is afforded by certain statements, which the marketing profession has largely ignored over the years, in Copeland's original presentation of his ideas. These have regard to the extent of the consumer's awareness of the precise nature of the item he wishes to buy, *before* he starts his shopping trip. Copeland stated that the consumer, in both the case of convenience goods and specialty goods, has full knowledge of the particular good, or its acceptable substitutes, that he will buy before he commences his buying trip. The consumer, however, lacks this knowledge in the case of a shopping good.[7] This means that the buying trip must not only serve the objective of purchasing the good, but must enable the consumer to discover which item he wants to buy.

The behavior of the consumer during any

shopping expedition may, as a result, be regarded as heavily dependent upon the state of his decision as to what he wants to buy. If the consumer knows precisely what he wants, he needs only to undertake communication activities sufficient to take title to the desired product. He may also undertake ancillary physical activities involving the handling of the product and delivery. If the consumer is uncertain as to what he wants to buy, then an additional activity will have to be performed. This involves the work of making comparisons between possible alternative purchases, or simply search.

There would be little point, with respect to the problem of classifying consumer goods, in distinguishing between the activity of search and that of making a commitment to buy, if a consumer always performed both before purchasing a good. The crucial point is that he does not. While most of the items that a consumer buys have probably been subjected to comparison at some point in his life, he does not make a search before each purchase. Instead, a past solution to the need is frequently remembered and, if satisfactory, is implemented.[8] Use of these past decisions for many products quickly moves the consumer past any perceived necessity of undertaking new comparisons and leaves only the task of exchange to be discharged.

REDEFINITION OF THE SYSTEM

Use of this concept of problem solving permits one to classify consumer buying efforts into two broad categories which may be called shopping and nonshopping goods.

Shopping Goods

Shopping goods are those for which the consumer *regularly* formulates a new solution to his need each time it is aroused. They are goods whose suitability is determined through search before the consumer commits himself to each purchase.

The motivation behind this behavior stems from circumstances which tend to perpetuate a lack of complete consumer knowledge about the nature of the product that he would like to buy.[9] Frequent changes in price, style, or product technology cause consumer information to become obsolete. The greater the time lapse between purchases, the more obsolete will his information be. The consumer's needs are also subject to change, or he may seek variety in his purchases as an actual goal. These forces will tend to make past information inappropriate. New search, due to forces internal and external to the consumer, is continuously required for products with purchase determinants which the consumer regards as both important and subject to change.[10]

The number of comparisons that the consumer will make in purchasing a shopping good may be determined by use of Holton's hypothesis on effort. The consumer, in other words, will undertake search for a product until the perceived value to be secured through additional comparisons is less than the estimated cost of making those comparisons. Thus, shopping effort will vary according to the intensity of the desire of the consumer to find the right product, the type of product and the availability of retail facilities. Whether the consumer searches diligently, superficially, or even buys at the first opportunity, however, does not alter the shopping nature of the product.

Nonshopping Goods

Turning now to nonshopping goods, one may define these as products for which the consumer is both willing and able to use stored solutions to the problem of finding a product to answer a need. From the remarks on shopping goods it may be generalized that nonshopping goods have purchase determinants which do not change, or which are perceived as changing inconsequentially, between purchases.[11] The consumer, for example, may assume that price for some product never changes or that price is unimportant. It may be unimportant because either the price is low, or the consumer is very wealthy.

Nonshopping goods may be divided into convenience and specialty goods by means of the concept of a preference map. Bayton introduces this concept as the means to show how the consumer stores information about products.[12] It is a rough ranking of the relative desirability of the different kinds of products that the consumer sees as possible satisfiers for his needs. For present purposes, two basic types of preference maps may be envisaged. One type ranks all known product alternatives equally in terms of desirability. The other ranks one particular product as so superior to all others that the consumer, in effect, believes this product is the only answer to his need.

Distinguishing the Specialty Good

This distinction in preference maps creates the basis for discriminating between a convenience good and a specialty good. Clearly, where the consumer is indifferent to the precise item among a number of substitutes which he could buy, he will purchase the most accessible one and look no further. This is a convenience good. On the other hand, where the consumer recognizes only one brand of a product as capable of satisfying his needs, he will be willing to bypass more readily accessible substitutes in order to secure the wanted item. This is a specialty good.

However, most nonshopping goods will probably fall in between these two polar extremes. Preference maps will exist where the differences between the relative desirability of substitutes may range from the slim to the well marked. In order to distinguish between convenience goods and specialty goods in these cases, Holton's hypothesis regarding consumer effort may be employed again. A convenience good, in these terms, becomes one for which the consumer has such little preference among his perceived choices that he buys the item which is most readily available. A specialty good is one for which consumer preference is so strong that he bypasses, or would be willing to bypass, the purchase of more accessible substitutes in order to secure his most wanted item.

It should be noted that this decision on the part of the consumer as to how much effort he should expend takes place under somewhat different conditions than the one for shopping goods. In the nonshopping good instance the consumer has a reasonably good estimate of the additional value to be achieved by purchasing his preferred item. The estimate of the additional cost required to make this purchase may also be made fairly accurately. Consequently, the consumer will be in a much better position to justify the expenditure of additional effort here than in the case of shopping goods where much uncertainty must exist with regard to both of these factors.

THE NEW CLASSIFICATION

The classification of consumer goods that results from the analysis is as follows:

Convenience Goods: Those goods for which the consumer, before his need arises, possesses a preference map that indicates a willingness to purchase any of a number of known substitutes rather than to make the additional effort required to buy a particular item.

Shopping Goods: Those goods for which the consumer has not developed a complete preference map before the need arises, requiring him to undertake search to construct such a map before purchase.

Specialty Goods: Those goods for which the consumer, before his need arises, possesses a preference map that indicates a willingness to expend the additional effort required to purchase the most preferred item rather than to buy a more readily accessible substitute.

EXTENSION TO RETAILING

The classification of the goods concept developed above may now be extended to retailing. As the concept now stands, it is derived from consumer attitudes or motives toward a *product*. These attitudes, or product motives, are based upon the consumer's interpretation of a product's styling, special features, quality, and social status of its brand name, if any. Occasionally the price may also be closely associated with the product by the consumer.

Classification of Patronage Motives

The extension of the concept to retailing may be made through the notion of patronage motives, a term long used in marketing. Patronage motives are derived from consumer attitudes concerning the retail establishment. They are related to factors which the consumer is likely to regard as controlled by the retailer. These will include assortment, credit, service, guarantee, shopping ease and enjoyment, and usually price. Patronage motives, however, have never been systematically categorized. It is proposed that the procedure developed above to discriminate among product motives be used to classify consumer buying motives with respect to retail stores as well.

This will provide the basis for the consideration of retail marketing strategy and will aid in clearing up certain ambiguities that would otherwise exist if consumer buying motives were solely classified by product factors. These ambiguities appear, for example, when the consumer has a strong affinity for some particular brand of a product, but little interest in where he buys it. The manufacturer of the product, as a result, would be correct in defining the product as a specialty item if the consumer's preferences were so strong as to cause him to eschew more readily available substitutes. The retailer may regard it as a convenience good, however, since the consumer will make no special effort to purchase the good from any particular store. This problem is clearly avoided by separately classifying product and patronage motives.

The categorization of patronage motives by the above procedure results in the following three definitions. These are:

Convenience Stores: Those stores for which the consumer, before his need for some product arises, possesses a preference map that indicates a willingness to buy from the most accessible store.

Shopping Stores: Those stores for which the consumer has not developed a complete preference map relative to the product he wishes to buy, requiring him to undertake a search to construct such a map before purchase.

Specialty Stores: Those stores for which the consumer, before his need for some product arises, possesses a preference map that indicates a willingness to buy the item from a particular establishment even though it may not be the most accessible.

The Product-Patronage Matrix

Although this basis will not afford the retailer a means to consider alternative strategies, a finer classification system may be obtained by relating consumer product motives to consumer patronage motives. By cross-classifying each product motive with each patronage motive, one creates a three-by-three matrix, representing nine possible types of consumer buying behavior. Each of the nine cells in the matrix may be described as follows:

1. *Convenience Store–Convenience Good:* The consumer, represented by this category, prefers to buy the most readily available brand of product at the most accessible store.
2. *Convenience Store–Shopping Good:* The consumer selects his purchase from among the assortment carried by the most accessible store.
3. *Convenience Store–Specialty Good:* The consumer purchases his favored brand from the most accessible store which has the item in stock.
4. *Shopping Store–Convenience Good:* The consumer is indifferent to the brand of product he buys, but shops among different stores in order to secure better retail service and/or lower retail price.
5. *Shopping Store–Shopping Good:* The consumer makes comparisons among both retail controlled factors and factors associated with the product (brand).
6. *Shopping Store–Specialty Good:* The consumer has a strong preference with respect to the brand of the product, but shops among a number of stores in order to secure the best retail and/or price for this brand.
7. *Specialty Store–Convenience Good:* The consumer prefers to trade at a specific store, but is indifferent to the brand of product purchased.
8. *Specialty Store–Shopping Good:* The consumer prefers to trade at a certain store, but is uncertain as to which product he wishes to buy and examines the store's assortment for the best purchase.
9. *Specialty Store–Specialty Good:* The consumer has both a preference for a particular store and a specific brand.

Conceivably, each of these nine types of behavior might characterize the buying patterns of some consumers for a given product. It seems more likely, however, that the behavior of consumers toward a product could be represented by only three or four of the categories. The remaining cells would be empty, indicating that no consumers bought the product by these methods. Different cells, of course, would be empty for different products.

THE FORMATION OF RETAIL STRATEGY

The extended classification system developed above clearly provides additional information important to the manufacturer in the planning of his marketing strategy. Of principal interest here, however, is the means by which the retailer might use the classification system in planning his marketing strategy.

Three Basic Steps

The procedure involves three steps. The first is the classification of the retailer's potential customers for some product by market segment, using the nine categories in the consumer buying habit matrix to define the principal segments. The second requires the retailer to determine the nature of the marketing strategies necessary to appeal to each market segment. The final step is the retailer's selection of the market segment, and the strategy associated with it, to which he will sell. A simplified, hypothetical example may help to clarify this process.

A former buyer of dresses for a department store decided to open her own dress shop. She rented a small store in the downtown area of a city of 50,000, ten miles distant from a metropolitan center of several hundred thousand population. In contemplating her marketing strategy, she was certain that the different incomes, educational backgrounds, and tastes of the potential customers in her city meant that various groups of these women were using sharply different buying methods for dresses. Her initial problem was to determine, by use of the consumer buying habit matrix, what proportion of her potential market bought dresses in what manner.

By drawing on her own experience, discussions with other retailers in the area, census and other market data, the former buyer estimated that her potential market was divided, according to the matrix, in the proportions [shown in Table 31-1].

This analysis revealed four market segments that she believed were worth further consideration. (In an actual situation, each of these four should be further divided into submarket segments according to other possible factors such as age, income, dress size required, location of residence, etc.) Her next task was to determine the type of marketing mix which would most effectively appeal to each of these segments. The information for these decisions was derived from the characteristics of consumer behavior associated with each of the defined segments. The following is a brief description of her assessment of how elements of the marketing mix ought to be weighted in order to formulate a strategy for each segment.

TABLE 31-1 *Proportion of Potential Dress Market in Each Matrix Cell*

Buying Habit	% of Market
Convenience store–convenience good	0
Convenience store–shopping good	3
Convenience store–specialty good	20
Shopping store–convenience good	0
Shopping store–shopping good	35
Shopping store–specialty good	2
Specialty store–convenience good	0
Specialty store–shopping good	25
Specialty store–specialty good	15
	100

A Strategy for Each Segment

To appeal to the convenience store-specialty good segment she felt that the two most important elements in the mix should be a highly accessible location and selection of widely-accepted brand merchandise. Of somewhat lesser importance, she found, were depth of assortment, personal selling, and price. Minimal emphasis should be given to store promotion and facilities.

She reasoned that the shopping store-shopping good requires a good central location, emphasis on price, and a broad assortment. She ranked store promotion, accepted brand names and personal selling as secondary. Store facilities would, once again, receive minor emphasis.

The specialty store-shopping good market would, she believed, have to be catered to with an exceptionally strong assortment, a high level of personal selling and more elaborate store facilities. Less emphasis would be needed upon prominent brand names, store promotions, and price. Location was of minor importance.

The specialty store-specialty good category, she thought, would require a marketing mix heavily emphasizing personal selling and highly elaborate store facilities and service. She also felt that prominent brand names would be required, but that these would probably have to include the top names in fashion, including labels from Paris. Depth of assortment would be secondary, while least emphasis would be placed upon store promotion, price, and location.

Evaluation of Alternatives

The final step in the analysis required the former dress buyer to assess her abilities to implement any one of these strategies, given the degree of competition existing in each segment. Her considerations were as follows. With regard to the specialty store-specialty good market, she was unprepared to make the investment in store facilities and services that she felt would be necessary. She also thought, since a considerable period of time would probably be required for her to build up the necessary reputation, that this strategy involved substantial risk. Lastly, she believed that her experience in buying high fashion was somewhat limited and that trips to European fashion centers would prove burdensome.

She also doubted her ability to cater to the specialty store-shopping good market, principally because she knew that her store would not be large enough to carry the necessary assortment depth. She felt that this same factor would limit her in attempting to sell to the shopping store-shopping good market as well. Despite the presence of the large market in this segment, she believed that she would not be able to create sufficient volume in her proposed quarters to enable her to compete effectively with the local department store and several large department stores in the neighboring city.

The former buyer believed her best opportunity was in selling to the convenience store-specialty good segment. While there were already two other stores in her city which were serving this segment, she believed that a number of important brands were still not represented. Her past contacts with resources led her to believe that she would stand an excellent chance of securing a number of these lines. By stocking these brands, she thought that she could capture a considerable number of local customers who currently were purchasing them in the large city. In this way, she believed, she would avoid the full force of local competition.

Decision

The conclusion of the former buyer to use her store to appeal to the convenience store-specialty good segment represents the culmination to the process of analysis suggested here. It shows how the use of the three-by-three matrix of consumer buying habits may aid the retailer in developing his marketing strategy. It is a device which can isolate the important market segments. It provides further help in enabling the retailer to associate the various types of consumer behavior with those elements of the marketing mix to which they are sensitive. Finally, the analysis forces the retailer to assess the probability of his success in attempting to use the necessary strategy in order to sell each possible market.

NOTES

1. Melvin T. Copeland, "Relation of Consumers' Buying Habits to Marketing Methods," *Harvard Business Review* (April, 1923), pp. 282-289.
2. Definitions Committee, American Marketing Association, "Report of the Definitions Committee," *Journal of Marketing* (October, 1948), pp. 202-217, at p. 206, p. 215.
3. Definitions Committee, American Marketing Association, *Marketing Definitions,* (Chicago: American Marketing Association, 1960), pp. 11, 21, 22.
4. Richard H. Holton, "The Distinction between Convenience Goods, Shopping Goods, and Specialty Goods," *Journal of Marketing* (July, 1958), pp. 53-56.
5. David J. Luck, "On the Nature of Specialty Goods," *Journal of Marketing* (July, 1959), pp. 61-64.
6. Richard H. Holton, "What Is Really Meant by 'Specialty Goods'?" *Journal of Marketing* (July, 1959), pp. 64-67.
7. Melvin T. Copeland, same reference as footnote 1, pp. 283-284.
8. George Katona, *Psychological Analysis of Economic Behavior* (New York: McGraw-Hill Book Co., Inc., 1951), p. 47.
9. Same reference, pp. 67-68.
10. George Katona and Eva Mueller, "A Study of Purchase Decisions in Consumer Behavior," Lincoln Clark, editor, *Consumer Behavior* (New York: University Press, 1954), pp. 30-87.
11. Katona, same reference as footnote 8, p. 68.
12. James A. Bayton, "Motivation, Cognition, Learning—Basic Factors in Consumer Behavior," *Journal of Marketing* (January, 1958), pp. 282-289, at p. 287.

32

Louis W. Stern
Torger Reve

Distribution Channels as Political Economies: A Framework for Comparative Analysis

Published studies related to distribution channels present, collectively, a rather disjointed collage. This is due, in part, to the absence of a framework which can accommodate the various paradigms and orientations employed in performing research on distribution channel phenomena. What is needed is a comprehensive mapping of the field which depicts the various paths one could follow, the likely places where one might end up, and the boundaries of the various places within the entire conceptual space. If this mapping were successfully accomplished, then those individuals already within the field would have a better understanding of where their work stood relative to others' and would, hopefully, be encouraged to seek out complementary paradigms to those which they have adopted. The mapping would also indicate to many of those who perceive themselves as standing outside the field that much of what they are doing could easily have relevance to the substance of the field. They might even be motivated to advance the field themselves. And, most importantly, the mapping would be helpful to prospective scholars who, to a large extent, do not have a very solid understanding of the research opportunities available within the field. While no single article is ever likely to accomplish such a comprehensive mapping, there is clearly a strong need to make a beginning. If a meaningful start at ordering the field can be undertaken, then this will likely encourage others to pursue the completion and refinement of the ordering process.

Despite the centrality of distribution channels in marketing, there exist three major deficiencies in the current status of distribution channel theory and research. *First,* analyses of distribution channels have largely focused on the technologies (e.g., sales force incentive systems, pricing procedures, and the like) em-

Reprinted from the *Journal of Marketing* (Summer 1980), pp. 52–64, published by the American Marketing Association.

Louis W. Stern is a Montgomery Ward Professor of Marketing at Northwestern University and previously taught at Ohio State. He has written extensively in the area of distribution.
Torger Reve is a professor at the Norwegian School of Economics and Business Administration, and received his Ph.D. from Northwestern University.

ployed by individual organizations in their efforts to structure and control channel activities (cf., Gattorna 1978; McCammon and Little 1965; McCammon, Bates and Guiltinan 1971). These analyses have adopted a *micro* orientation in keeping with traditional problem-solving approaches in marketing management. Little attention has been given to questions of the maintenance, adaptation, and evolution of marketing channels as competitive entities.

Second, channel theory is fragmented into two seemingly disparate disciplinary orientations: an *economic* approach and a *behavioral* approach. The former attempts to apply microeconomic theory and industrial organization analysis to the study of distribution systems and has been essentially "efficiency" oriented, focusing on costs, functional differentiation, and channel design (cf., Baligh and Richartz 1967; Bucklin 1966; Bucklin and Carman 1974; Cox, Goodman, and Fichandler 1965). The latter borrows heavily from social psychology and organization theory and has been essentially "socially" oriented, focusing on power and conflict phenomena (cf., Alderson 1957; Stern 1969). Rarely have there been attempts to integrate these two perspectives. Indeed, they should be viewed as complementary, because the former deals mainly with economic "outputs" while the latter is concerned with behavioral "processes."

Third, empirical studies of distribution networks have been extremely limited in their scope and methodological sophistication. The vast majority of empirical works in the channels area has been purely descriptive in nature, with little or no testing of formal hypotheses derived from theory (cf., McCammon and Little 1965). Although more recent studies evidence a trend toward more systematic testing of theoretical relationships, these investigations have typically been confined to an analysis of a single distribution channel within a particular industry (exceptions include Etgar 1976a, 1978; Hunt and Nevin 1974; Porter 1974; Weik 1972).[1] Future channel research must focus on making systematic *comparisons* of different distribution networks within and between various environmental conditions, irrespective of whether the different networks are found in the same industry or across industries.

A promising framework for addressing these issues is provided by the *political economy* approach to the study of social systems (Benson 1975; Wamsley and Zald 1973, 1976; Zald 1970a, 1970b). Basically, the *political economy approach views a social system as comprising interacting sets of major economic and sociopolitical forces which affect collective behavior and performance.* The purpose of this article, therefore, is to present a political economy framework which can be applied to gain deeper understanding of the *internal* functioning of a distribution channel. Such a framework also permits comprehension of the processes where distribution channels are influenced by and adapt to environmental conditions. It is, however, recognized that this framework is only one of many that might be suggested. It has been selected because of its strong potential for comprehensively mapping this area of marketing inquiry.

The political economy framework outlined here should be viewed as the first step in the direction of identifying and dimensionalizing the major variables influencing and ordering channel structure and behavior. A premise of the framework as initially formulated is that complex socioeconomic interrelations involve multilateral interactions as opposed to "simple" cause-effect mechanisms, such as those between power use and conflict or between channel design and costs. Given the present state of channel theory development, the inital task to be performed in accomplishing methodological and interpretive rigor is to lay out the relevant channel dimensions in terms of "fields," e.g., external-internal; economic-sociopolitical; structural-process. Otherwise, theoretical research in the area will continue to suffer from ad hoc operationalizations, where researchers select independent measures and globally hypothesize some dependent outcome without indicating or even being aware of which other interacting variables are being held or assumed constant. Hence, the political economy framework should be seen as an attempt to *chart out* or classify the total field of channel interaction. The political economy perspective as an organizing framework impels the generation of significant research questions and, therefore, has the potential for producing new theoretical insights.

As an aid to exploring the promise of the framework, a number of *illustrative* propositions have been generated throughout this article. They should be helpful in stimulating future research because they provide some insights into the kinds of meaningful relationships among core concepts which are motivated by employing the framework. However, it should be noted that there has been no attempt to specify research designs to "test" the propositions. This is because the propositions can be operationalized in a variety of ways. Given the existing state of knowledge in the channels area, it might be misleading for us to suggest specific operationalizations and would, almost certainly, deflect attention from the main purpose of the article due to the controversy they might evoke. As an aid to the reader, we have provided an appendix which conceptually defines a few of the key constructs used. This "glossary" only serves to suggest the conceptual boundaries of the constructs; it is not intended to provide operation allegations.

In the following section, the full political economy framework is broadly outlined. Then, the remainder of the paper explores, in considerable detail, the *intra*-channel variables included in the framework.

THE POLITICAL ECONOMY FRAMEWORK

The political economy framework is capsulized in Figure 32-1. As indicated, there are two major systems: (I) the *internal political economy,* i.e., the internal structuring and functioning of the distribution channel, and (II) the *external political economy,* i.e., the channel's task environment. Both systems are divided into two component parts: an *economy* and a *polity*. The major relationships which need to be explored are indicated by arrows with capital letter notations (see Figure 32-1).

The Internal Political Economy

Distribution channels are interorganizational "collectivities" of institutions and actors simultaneously pursuing self-interest and collective

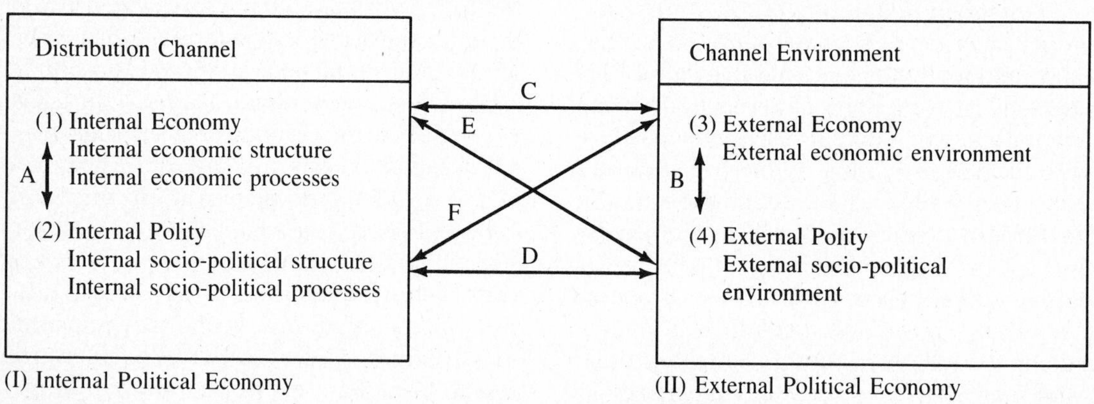

FIGURE 32-1 *A Political Economy Framework for Distribution Channel Analysis*

goals (Reve and Stern 1979; Van de Ven, Emmett, and Koenig 1974). As such, the actors interact in a socioeconomic setting of their own, called an internal political economy. To comprehend fully the relevant internal dimensions and interactions, the framework suggests that a channel be analyzed in relation to its (1) *internal economy,* i.e., the internal economic structure and processes and its (2) *internal polity,* i.e., the internal sociopolitical structure and processes.

The internal economic structure is described by the type of transactional form linking channel members, i.e., the vertical economic arrangement within the marketing channel, while the internal economic processes refer to the nature of the decision mechanisms employed to determine the terms of trade among the members. On the other hand, the internal sociopolitical structure is defined by the pattern of power-dependence relations which exist among channel members, while the internal sociopolitical processes are described in terms of the dominant sentiments (i.e., cooperation and/or conflict) within the channel.

Identifying that marketing channels consist of an internal economy and an internal polity is not a major departure from prior approaches to channel research. The contribution of the political economy framework is the explicit insistence that economic and sociopolitical forces not be analyzed in isolation. By considering the interactions between the economy and the polity, it is possible to understand and explain the internal structuring and functioning of distribution systems and to derive a number of illustrative propositions for channel research.

The 'External' Political Economy

Organizations always operate within an environment. The environment of a distribution channel is a complex of economic, physical, cultural, demographic, psychological, political, and technological forces. In the political economy framework, such forces are, as shown in Figure 32-1, incorporated in (3) *the external economy,* i.e., the prevailing and prospective economic environment and (4) *the external polity,* i.e., the external sociopolitical system in which the channel operates. The external economy of a distribution channel can be described by the nature of its vertical (input and output) and horizontal markets. The external polity can be described by the distribution and use of power resources among external actors (e.g., competitors, regulatory agencies, and trade associations) (cf., Palamountain 1955; Pfeffer and Salancik 1978; Thompson 1967; Yuchtman and Seashore 1967). An analysis of the external sociopolitical environment entails specification of the type of actors exercising power in the environment (Evan 1965), the power relations and means of control used between the external actors and the focal channel (Thompson 1967), the power relations between external actors (Terreberry 1968), and the extent to which the activities of channel members are actually controlled by environmental forces (Benson 1975).

The external economic and sociopolitical forces interact and define environmental conditions for the channel. The external political economy thus influences the internal political economy through adaptation and interaction processes (Aldrich 1979). Furthermore, channels not only adapt to their environments, but also influence and shape them (Pfeffer and Salancik 1978). The arrows in Figure 32-1 which indicate interactions between the component systems therefore point in both directions.

Attention is now turned to an elaboration of the internal political economy of distribution channels. The focus on intra-channel variables is a natural starting point, given that virtually all existing channel research has dealt with internal channel phenomena. Knowledge of environmental variables and their impact is fragmentary at best (Etgar 1977). Future examinations of the political economy framework must, however, focus on environmental variables and on the interactions between the internal and external economies.

THE INTERNAL POLITICAL ECONOMY OF DISTRIBUTION CHANNELS: AN ELABORATION OF THE FRAMEWORK

In this section the major internal economic and sociopolitical forces at work in distribution channels are described. These forces interact in shaping channel arrangements and in affecting marketing channel behavior and performance.

Internal Economy of Distribution Channels

Distribution channels are primarily set up to perform a set of essential *economic* functions in society, bridging the gap between production and consumption. Thus, it is no surprise that a substantial proportion of channel research, especially the earlier studies, has focused on an analysis of the *internal economy* of distribution channels (see Gattorna 1978; McCammon and Little 1965 for reviews).

As already indicated, the internal economy of a distribution channel may be divided into two components. The *internal economic structure* refers to the vertical economic arrangements or the transactional form in the channel. These arrangements range from a series of independently owned and managed specialized units which transact exchanges across markets to complete vertical integration where exchanges between wholly-owned units are conducted within a hierarchy (Williamson 1975). Whereas market transactions rely primarily on the use of the price mechanism, hierarchical transactions rely on administrative mechanisms. Between these two extreme economic arrangements lies a wide variety of structures in which the market mechanism is modified through some kind of formal or informal contractual arrangements between the parties involved (Blois 1972; Liebeler 1976).

Operating within each internal economic structure of a channel are certain *internal economic processes* or decision mechanisms. Thus, agreement on the terms of trade and the division of marketing functions among channel members may be reached in impersonal, routine, or habitual ways; through bargaining; or via centralized planning processes. The type of processes used to allocate resources in any given channel is likely to conform to or, at least, be constrained by the transactional form of the channel. Typically, competitive, price-mediated mechanisms are dominant in those market transactions where information is relatively complete and products are undifferentiated, as in soybean trading, while centralized planning is dominant in most hierarchical transactions. But competitive, price-mediated mechanisms have also been simulated in hierarchical structures through mathematical programming models using computed shadow prices as terms of transfer (Jennergren 1979). For other transactions which fall in between the two structural extremes, the allocation of many marketing activities is largely determined through bargaining among the parties.

Of critical importance for channel analysis is the need to compare the efficiency and effectiveness of various transactional forms or structures across each of the three decision making mechanisms. It is also important to consider cases where a specific economic process is employed across economic structures. For example, an illustrative proposition dealing with centralized planning processes might be:

P1. The more centralized planning processes predominate, irrespective of the transactional form, the more efficient and effective the marketing channel for a product or service is likely to be.

In this sense, efficiency could be defined in terms of output to input ratios (e.g., sales per square foot) and effectiveness could be some external market referent (e.g., market share). A number of theoretical rationales underlie P1: (1) the likely constraints on suboptimization within the channel derived from joint decision making, (2) the exploitation of potential scale economies, (3) the possible cost advantages gained via increased programming of distributive functions, and (4) the reduction of transaction costs due to reduced uncertainties and lessened opportunism (cf., Etgar 1976a, Gronhaug and Reve 1979).

There are, however, a number of rationales working against P1's central premise: (1) the satisficing modes which operate when centralized planning processes predominate, (2) the danger of bureaucratization and loss of cost consciousness, and (3) the curbing of initiative at "lower" levels. Therefore, P1 demands investigation in concert with a second, counter proposition.

P2. The more centralized planning processes predominate, irrespective of the transactional form, the less likely is the marketing channel to be able to react quickly to external threats.

This proposition has its roots in the criticism which has often been directed at vertically integrated systems (cf., Arndt and Reve 1979; Sturdivant 1966). However, it may also apply to market transactions, because the more that the exchange process among channel members is organized, the more severe become tradeoffs between efficiency and adaptiveness. On the other hand, while fast and specific adaptation to localized threats will likely be slow when centralized planning processes are prevalent, the adoption of such processes may permit better environmental scanning, more opportunities to influence external actors, and more ability to absorb shocks over the long run than those channels which are typified by bargaining or by routine or habitual decision making.

Analysis is also required within transactional forms across the various decision making mechanisms. Especially significant are the issues which Williamson (1975) raises in his markets and hierarchies framework. He shows how market transactions may become very costly due to human factors, such as bounded rationality and opportunism, coupled with environmental factors, such as uncertainty and economically concentrated input or output markets (i.e., small numbers bargaining). When information is unequally possessed, opportunistic behavior is likely to prevail, and exchange may be commercially hazardous. An illustrative proposition drawn from this line of reasoning is:

P3. Market transactions in oligopsonistic situations are likely to lead to information imbalances, opportunistic behavior, and high transaction costs. Impersonal, routine, or habitual decision making mechanisms in such situations will not suffice to overcome opportunistic behavior within the channel.

For example, when the members of atomistic industries, such as those found in the manufacture of maintenance, operating, and repair items, rely on open market forces to determine the terms of trade between themselves and the members of oligopolies, such as in the aerospace or automative industries, the latter may withhold relevant information regarding demand projections and manipulate the exchange process by distorting any information passed along in order to achieve inequitable advantages from their fragmented suppliers. Extensive theoretical rationales underlying P3 are provided by Williamson (1975), Arrow (1974), and Lindblom (1977). Empirical research, using this internal economy perspective, is required to test the large number of Williamsonian hypotheses dealing with why channel structures based on market transactions may tend to fail.

Internal Polity of Distribution Channels

As has been noted by several channel analysts (e.g., Alderson, Palamountain), distribution channels are not only economic systems but also social systems.[2] This observation has led to research on the behavioral aspects of distribution channels and the intrachannel sociopolitical factors (Stern 1969; Stern and El-Ansary 1977). In a political economy framework, these forces are referred to as the *internal polity* of distribution channels. The economy and the polity of channels are basically allocation systems, allocating scarce economic resources and power or authority, respectively. Both the economy and polity of channels can also be viewed as coordination systems (Hernes 1978) or ways of managing the economics and politics of interorganizational systems.

The polity of a marketing channel might be seen as oriented to the allocation and use of authority and power within the system. Similar to the internal economy, there are also structural and process variables which describe the working of the internal polity. Adopting Emerson's (1962, 1972) notion of power relationships as the inverse of the existing dependency relationships between the system's actors, the *internal sociopolitical structure* is given by the initial pattern of power-dependence relations within the channel. The limiting cases of dependence are minimal power and completely centralized power. Power is a relational concept inherent in exchange between social actors (Emerson 1962, 1972). There will always be *some* power existing within channels due to mutual dependencies which exist among channel members, even though that power may be very low (El-Ansary and Stern 1972). However, power can also be fully concentrated in a single organization which then appears as the undisputed channel administrator (e.g., Lusch 1976). Such a power constellation can be referred to as a unilateral power system (Bonoma 1976). Because of the numerous marketing flows which tie the channel members together, the more common case is a mixed power situation where different firms exercise control over different flows, functions, or marketing activities (e.g., Etgar 1976b). The latter can be referred to as a mixed power system (Bonoma 1976).[3] Careful analysis is required to assess correctly the power-dependency patterns in a marketing channel (cf., El-Ansary and Stern 1972; Etgar 1976b; Frazier and Brown 1978; Hunt and Nevin 1974; Wilkinson 1973), because sociopolitical structures alter over time. Changing bases of power, coalition formations, and evolving linkages with external actors are among the factors causing such dynamism and creating measurement problems.

The various patterns of power-dependence relationships in a distribution channel are thought to be associated with various *sociopolitical processes.* The sociopolitical processes primarily refer to the dominant sentiments and behaviors which characterize the interactions between channel members. Although channel sentiments and behaviors are multidimensional constructs, two major dimensions in channel analysis are cooperation and conflict. Cooperation can be represented as joint striving towards an object (Stern 1971)—the process of coalescing with others for a good, goal, or value of mutual benefit. Cooperation involves a combination of object- and collaborator-centered activity which is based on a compatibility of goals, aims, or values. It is an activity in which the potential collaborator is viewed as providing the means by which a divisible goal or object desired by the parties may be obtained and shared. Conflict, on the other hand, is opponent-centered behavior (Stern 1971) because in a conflict situation, the object is controlled by the opponent while incompatibility of goals, aims, or values exists. The major concern in such situations is to overcome the opponent or counterpart as a means of securing the object. Conflict is characterized by mutual interference or blocking behavior.[4]

While they are highly interrelated, cooperation and conflict are separate, distinguishable processes. Exchange between social actors generally contains a certain dialect varying between conflictual and cooperative behavior (Guetzkow 1966). A common example is found in customer-supplier relationships ordered by long-term contracts. They reflect basically cooperative sentiments, but conflicts regularly take place regarding the interpretation of contractual details and problem-solving approaches.

At one extreme, dysfunctional conflict processes – those aimed at injuring or destroying another party – will severely impede any existing or potential cooperative behaviors among the parties. However, the absence of confrontation will not necessarily produce maximal joint-striving, because the complacency and passivity which may be present in the relationship may cause the parties to overlook salient opportunities for coalescing (cf., Coser 1956; Thomas 1976). Indeed, because of the mutual dependencies which exist in channels, it is likely that conflict, in some form, will always be present (Schmidt and Kochan 1972; Stern and El-Ansary 1977; Stern and Gorman 1969). In addition, channels cannot exist without a minimum level of cooperation among the parties. Thus, conflictual and cooperative processes will exist simultaneously in all channels.

Having specified major structure and process variables in the internal polity, it now is possible to examine their interactions for illustrative propositions. For instance, there exists a relatively large number of situations in distribution where power is somewhat balanced, e.g., when department store chains deal with well-known cosmetic manufacturers, when large plumbing and heating wholesalers deal with major manufacturers of air conditioning equipment, and when supermarket chains deal with large grocery manufacturers. Drawing from political science theory, it can be proposed that:

P4. In marketing channels typified by balanced power relationships, interactions will be predominantly cooperative as long as the balance of strength is preserved (e.g., Kaplan 1957). However, the potential for dysfunctional conflict is higher than it would be if power were imbalanced (Gurr 1970).

The first part of P4 is primarily drawn from balance of power theories of international politics which predict peaceful coexistence as long as balance of strength remains. This position is congruent with the insights offered by bilateral oligopoly and duopoly theories in economics (Scherer 1970) which forecast the development of informal or formal interfirm agreements regarding pricing and competitive actions. The second part of P4 draws on relative deprivation theories of collective conflict (Gurr 1970) which predict that conflict potential and the magnitude of manifest dysfunctional conflict will be highest in balanced power situations.

Even though P4 is intuitively appealing, counter propositions can be offered which indicate that empirical verification is required. For example, Korpi (1974), a political scientist, argues that conflict potential is higher in slightly imbalanced than in balanced power constellations while Williamson (1975), an economist, posits that a centralized power pattern – the extreme form of imbalanced power – will tend to exhibit predominantly cooperative modes of exchange when compared to a more balanced pattern. Furthermore, in an imbalanced situation, ideology is often used as a unifying and cooperation-inducing force by the more powerful party. The seeming cooperation in a balanced power constellation may be of a deterrent nature. Thus, there is a need to distinguish between detente-type cooperation and ideologically-induced cooperation.

As with the variables specified for the internal economy, there is clearly a need to compare structural sociopolitical conditions across processes and vice versa in order to generate propositions which can permit predictions for channel management. At the same time, it is important to understand that conflict and cooperation processes are activities conducive to some economic end; they are not ends in themselves. Furthermore, the way in which power is used within a channel will clearly affect the sociopolitical processes. For example, it may be proposed that:

P5. In marketing channels characterized by imbalanced power, the use of coercive power will produce a dysfunctional level of conflict.

Additionally,

P6. Marketing channels characterized by imbalanced power and dominated by coercive influence strategies will be inherently unstable, resulting in decreased competitive viability.

To some extent, the works of Raven and Kruglanski (1970); Stern, Schulz, and Grabner (1973); and Lusch (1976) examining the relation between bases of power and resulting conflict point in the direction of these propositions.

Alternately, in line with findings generated by Wittreich (1962), Kriesberg (1952), and Weik (1972), it is possible to propose that:

P7. Marketing channels characterized by minimal power will exhibit low levels of cooperation.

This is supported by McCammon (1970) who has argued that conventional marketing channels, comprised of isolated and autonomous decision making units, are unable to program distribution activities successfully. If power is low, so is dependence. Thus, two or more relatively independent entities may not be motivated to cooperate.

The above propositions indicate a few of the expected relations within the internal polity of distribution channels. As mentioned, they are merely illustrative of the meaningful insights for channel theory and management available in this kind of analysis.

Interaction between Internal Economy and Internal Polity of Distribution Channels

The essence of the political economy framework for the analysis of marketing systems is that economic and sociopolitical forces are not analyzed in isolation. Therefore, it is imperative to examine the interactions between the economy and the polity. To illustrate the potency of the combination, it is again possible to generate a series of propositions. Each of these propositions draws upon the variables enumerated previously.

The constellation of a given economic structure with a certain sociopolitical structure within a marketing channel will influence the economic and sociopolitical processes which take place. Considered first is the intersection between various power structures and economic structures typified by market transactions.

P8. In marketing channels in which market transactions are the predominant mode of exchange and in which power is centralized, centralized planning processes will emerge.

A relative power advantage within a channel is often used to program channel activities, and in such situations, decision making with respect to at least certain functions (e.g., promotion, physical distribution) tends to be centralized. Indicative of these types of channel arrangements are those found in the food industry where manufacturers, such as Nabisco and Kraft, develop shelf or dairy case management plans for supermarket chains; in the automotive aftermarket where warehouse distributors, such as Genuine Parts Company, evoke inventory management programs for jobbers (e.g., NAPA); in lawn care products where manufacturers, such as O.M. Scott, engage in detailed merchandise programming with the various retailers of their products; and in general merchandise retailing where retailers, such as Sears, Wards, and Penneys, preprogram the activities of their private label suppliers.

In addition to economic efficiency considerations, several behavioral considerations underlie P8. Thus, following Williamson (1975), some form of organizing process (in this case, centralized planning or programming) is required in order to overcome the tendencies toward opportunistic behavior present in market transactions and to cope with the bounded rationality of each channel member. The means to achieve centralized planning may be centralized power, although this is not always likely to be the case. For example, even in cases where there are balanced power structures in channels, centralized planning processes have emerged. This was the case when the Universal Product Code was developed jointly by retailers and manufacturers operating through their food industry trade associations.

P8 can be elaborated by considering the sociopolitical processes which are likely to prevail in market transactions with centralized planning.

> P9. Under the conditions specified by P8, marketing channels will exhibit a relatively high level of conflict, but they will also exhibit highly cooperative processes. Such channels will tend to be more competitively effective than others where market transactions are also the predominant mode of exchange.

Following Korpi's (1974) reasoning, P9 predicts that conflict potential will be high due to the imbalanced power situation. The expectation with respect to cooperation is based on the ability of the channel administrator to mitigate opportunistic tendencies among the units in the channel and to establish superordinate goals. The overall effect of the combination of interacting variables in P9 will be to produce effective channel systems in which programmed merchandising is likely to be the rule rather than the exception. Such channels are likely to be more successful in improving their market shares relative to other channels typified by market transactions.

Anecdotal evidence supporting P8 and P9 can be found in the construction and farm equipment industries. In these industries, market transactions are the predominant means of exchange between the various manufacturers and their dealers. However, Caterpillar and Deere have gained sizable leads over their rivals by developing highly efficient and effective systems of distribution through the use of their considerable power in their channels. They have achieved an unusual amount of success by programming their networks and by managing conflict within them.

Another proposition in line with the discussion above is that:

> P10. In marketing channels in which hierarchical transactions are the predominant mode of exchange and in which power is centralized, conflict processes are more likely to be effectively managed, superordinate goals are more likely to be established, and efficiency is more likely to be achieved relative to any other marketing channel.

The underlying rationale for this proposition is supplied by Williamson (1975):

> Unlike autonomous contractors, internal divisions that trade with one another in a vertical integration relationship do not ordinarily have pre-emptive claims on their respective profit streams. Even though the divisions in question may have profit center standing, this is apt to be

> exercised in a restrained way. For one thing, the terms under which internal trading occurs are likely to be circumscribed. Cost-plus pricing rules, and variants thereof, preclude supplier divisions from seeking the monopolistic prices to which their sole supply position might otherwise entitle them. In addition, the managements of the trading divisions are more susceptible to appeals for cooperation. Since the aggressive pursuit of individual interests redounds to the disadvantage of the system and as present and prospective compensation (including promotions) can be easily varied by the general office to reflect noncooperation, simple requests to adopt a cooperative mode are more apt to be heeded. Altogether, a more nearly joint profit maximizing attitude and result is to be expected. (p. 29)

However, it should be noted that, even within a vertically integrated channel, opportunism and bounded rationality may still be found. In addition, the large size of many vertically integrated organizations often creates problems of bureaucratization and inflexibility. Thus, P10 isolates centralized, as opposed to decentralized, power. For example, the power which Sears' field operations held with regard to inventory levels within its stores was one of the major reasons for the disastrous inventory situation the company faced in 1974. In order to reduce the opportunistic behavior which existed among Sears' various divisions (e.g., the retail stores refused to hold their rightful share of the inventories which were building to abnormal levels in Sears' distribution centers), the entire company was reorganized and power was centralized more firmly in its Chicago headquarters. Now it remains to be seen whether Sears' management is equal to the task of successfully controlling the organization. Clearly, the advantages of such an internal political economy can dissipate as increasing degrees of vertical integration lead to more complex organization, more impersonal relationships, less perception of the relationships between actions and results, less moral involvement, generally more self-serving behavior, and greater toleration for substandard performance.

It should be noted that the political economy framework also encourages the examination of more narrowly focused propositions than those already stated. Given the difficulties associated with researching channel issues (due primarily to the lack of accessibility to and the sensitivity of the data involved), it is likely that research using the political economy framework should start with relatively manageable tasks. Illustrative of such propositions are:

P11. The more that relationships between channel members are characterized by cooperative behavior, the greater the level of profits attainable to the channel as a whole.

P12. The greater the proportion of relative power possessed by any channel member, the greater the proportion of the channel's profits that member will receive.

Central issues in political economies are (1) how surpluses are generated and (2) how they are distributed among the members. These "processes" provide critical links between the "political" and "economic" aspects of the system. P11 suggests a positive relationship between the level of cooperation within the channel and the joint profits obtained by it. The rationale is that cooperative behavior facilitates coordination and programming of activities within the channel which, in turn, provides potential cost advantages and improved competitive strength. In some cases, cooperation is likely to be informal, requiring a minimum of interaction. In these cases, environmental factors such as professional or trade norms, the role of trade associations, and the impact of government regulations may play significant roles in encouraging joint striving behavior. In other cases, cooperation may take the form of ad hoc consultations, the formation of committees, the establishment of federative coordination bodies, or the construction of bilateral contracts, joint ventures, or other types of formal long-term agreements (Pfeffer and Salancik 1978).

P12 addresses the critical issue of the allocation of joint profits within the marketing channel. The division of returns clearly is a matter of relative power and bargaining skill. Thus, the benefits obtained in the economic arena are divided in the political arena, a situation which is analogous to the income reallocation problem in welfare economics. Porter (1974) has found some empirical support for P12 using mainly secondary data.

Focusing on the interaction between the economy and polity of marketing channels may also produce insights into the evolution and adaptation of channel institutions. Innovative distributive institutions, such as limited line-limited service grocery stores (e.g., Aldi) and catalogue showrooms (e.g., McDade), may emerge due to differential cost advantages achieved by improved logistical systems or sharper positioning relative to specific consumer segments. The initiative for such innovations often comes from "outsiders" who are at odds with traditional channel norms and practices (Kriesberg 1955; McCammon and Bates 1965). Thus, the innovations result, at least in part, because of functional conflicts within existing channels. As the new institutions mature, they tend to hire personnel from competitors, thereby gradually changing their professional orientation. At the same time, they become preoccupied with quality, add services, and begin to cater to broader market segments, thus moving towards the same practices as their competitors. The functional conflicts with other channel members tend to disappear, and opportunities for new outsiders to innovate emerge. Such scenarios as the "wheel of retailing" simply illustrate how sociopolitical circumstances often influence economic activities within a marketing channel. In turn, the economic form influences the sociopolitical sentiments surrounding the emerging transactions which lead, in turn, to further changes in economic activities.

CONCLUSION

Analysis of distribution channels as political economies provides a framework in which to incorporate and integrate the variety of approaches and findings found in the existing channel literature. More importantly, the emergent framework provides a basis for future research by isolating the critical dimensions determining transactional effectiveness and efficiency in distribution. It also provides a conceptual mapping which may be useful to anyone with an interest in channel relationships.

The framework, including the illustrative propositions developed from it, presents a preliminary, general look at distribution channel structuring and functioning. In particular, the propositions advanced above serve to underscore the caveat that the economy and the polity of such systems are inseparably linked and cannot be studied in isolation (Frey 1978; Lindblom 1977; Thorelli 1965; Tivey 1978). Choosing an internal economic structure for a channel seems to have clear implications for the internal sociopolitical structure involved. The constellations formed by the intersection of the various economic and sociopolitical structures also have implications for the type of sociopolitical processes to be expected within channels. An internal economic structure may have certain benefits in terms of the economic performance and the competitive effectiveness of the channel. On the other hand, the sociopolitical processes associated with a given internal economy may vary both in the transaction costs and in the rationality of decision making for the channel as a whole. All of these factors directly influence channel performance. Another general implication which may be drawn from this type of analysis is that the various political economies of channels require different interorganizational management strategies for maintaining and expanding channel operations and for dealing with channel conflicts.

Clearly, factors in the external political economy will have a profound influence on a channel's internal political economy. Any propositions generated by adopting the political economy framework, including those outlined here, need to be modified by circumstances in the external economy and polity. A description of the impact of external forces and internal-external interactions then emerges as a topic for future work. However, this directive must be kept in proper perspective. In the only published empirical research focusing directly on the latter topic, Etgar (1977) has indicated that certain aspects of the internal political economy of channels can be expected to explain more of the variance in channel behavior than environmental factors. Following his findings, the strongest emphasis in future research should probably remain focused on achieving a deeper understanding of the internal political economy. The framework provided in this article should, hopefully, be of some assistance in this respect.

APPENDIX

Definitions of Key Concepts in the Political Economy Framework (See Fig. 32-A-1)

Political economy = collectivity comprised of an economic system (economy) and a sociopolitical system (polity) which jointly influence collective behavior and performance.

I. Internal political economy = the internal structuring and functioning of an organized collectivity (e.g., marketing chan-

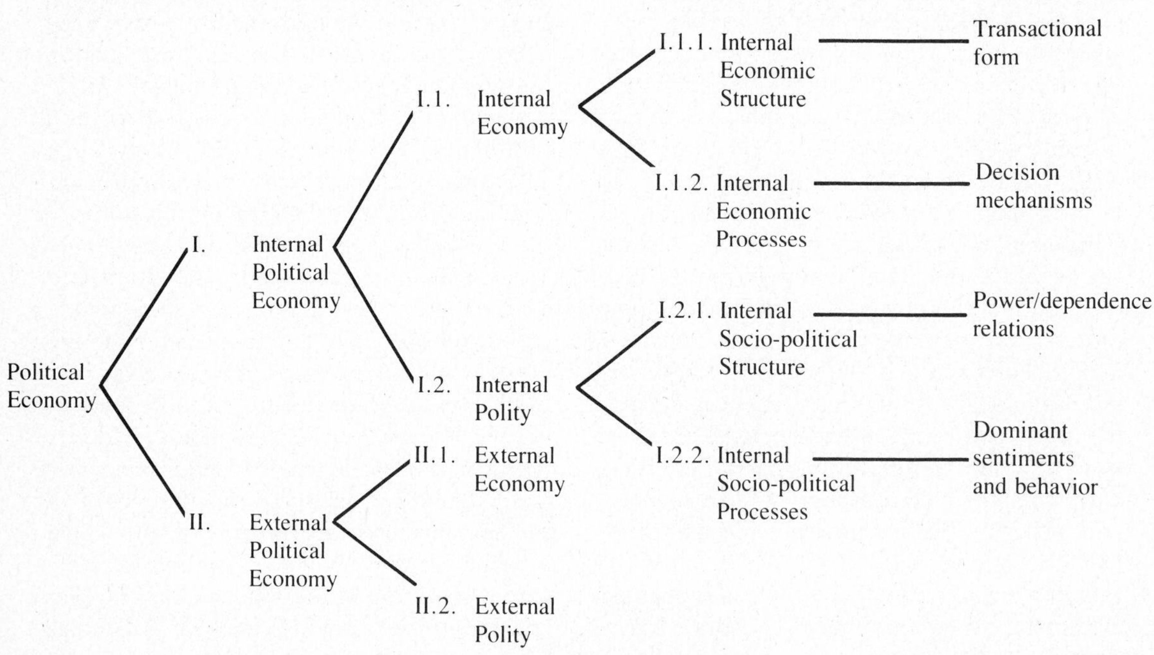

FIGURE 32-A-1 *Key Concepts in the Political Economy Framework*

nel) analyzed in terms of an internal economy and an internal polity and their interactions.

II. External political economy = the task environment of an organized collectivity (e.g., marketing channel) analyzed in terms of an external economy and an external polity and their interactions.

I.1. Internal economy = the internal economic allocation system analyzed in terms of the internal economic structure and processes.

I.2. Internal polity = the internal sociopolitical allocation system analyzed in terms of the internal sociopolitical structure and processes.

II.1. External economy = the economic task environment of an organized collectivity (e.g., marketing channel) described by the nature of its vertical (input and output) and horizontal markets.

II.2. External polity = the sociopolitical task environment of an organized collectivity (e.g., marketing channel) described by the distribution and use of power resources among external actors and their prevailing sentiments.

I.1.1. Internal economic structure = the economic arrangements or transactional form within an organized collectivity (e.g., marketing channel) set up to complete internal exchanges.

I.1.2. Internal economic processes = the decision making processes within an organized collectivity (e.g., marketing channel) which determine the terms of trade and the division of labor, functions, and activities among the internal actors.

I.2.1. Internal sociopolitical structure = the pattern of power/dependence relations within an organized collectivity (e.g., marketing channel).

I.2.2. Internal sociopolitical processes = the dominant sentiments and behaviors which characterize the interactions between actors within an organized collectivity (e.g., marketing channel).

I.1.1. Transactional form = internal economic arrangements ranging from markets to hierarchies (e.g., vertical integration).

I.1.2. Decision making processes = internal collective choice processes ranging from impersonal determination of terms of trade through the price mechanism, through bargaining processes, to centralized planning processes.

I.2.1 Power/dependence relations = internal power/dependence pattern ranging from minimal power (low dependence), through mixed power constellations of balanced and imbalanced power (mutual dependence), to centralized power (unilateral dependence).

I.2.2. Dominant sentiments and behaviors = internal sentiments and behaviors of cooperation and functional or dysfunctional conflict characterizing internal exchange, ranging from minimal cooperation, high dysfunctional conflict to maximal cooperation, functional conflict.

NOTES

1. Methodologically, many of the studies fall short due to the incorrect use of informant methodologies as well as insufficient and often single-item operationalizations of constructs, thus not allowing for reliability checks and construct validation. For an excellent critique, see Phillips (1980). Thus, more emphasis needs to be given to careful research designs and improved measurement.
2. Simply observing that many marketing channels are loosely aligned (e.g., McVey 1960) does not invalidate their systemic nature. For argumentation supporting the perspective that channels are social action systems, see Reve and Stern (1979).
3. Bonoma (1976) also proposes a third power constellation – the bilateral power system – in which the interactants are in a unit relation jointly determining unit policy for individual and group action. Such systems, which are held together by social altruism, have not yet been examined in distribution channel settings.

4. In the social sciences in general and the conflict literature in particular, there has been a considerable amount of controversy surrounding the distinction between conflict and competition. We believe that competition is distinguishable from conflict. Competition can be viewed as a form of opposition which is object-centered; conflict is opponent-centered behavior. Competition is indirect and impersonal; conflict is very direct and highly personal. In competition, a third party controls the goal or object; in conflict, the goal or object is controlled by the opponent. A swim meet is competition; a football game is conflict. For a discussion of the distinction between the two terms in a distribution channel context, see Stern (1971). For an excellent comprehensive review of the controversy, see Fink (1968).

REFERENCES

Alderson, W. (1957), *Marketing Behavior and Executive Action,* Homewood, IL: Irwin.

Aldrich, H.A. (1979), *Organizations and Environments,* Englewood Cliffs, NJ: Prentice-Hall, Inc.

Arndt, J. and T. Reve (1979), "Innovativeness in Vertical Marketing Systems," in *Proceedings of Fourth Macro Marketing Conference,* P. White & G. Fisk, eds., Boulder, CO: University of Colorado Press.

Arrow, K.J. (1974), *Limits of Organizations,* New York: John Wiley and Sons.

Baligh, H.H. and L.E. Richartz (1967), *Vertical Market Structures,* Boston: Allyn and Bacon.

Benson, J.K. (1975), "The Interorganizational Network as a Political Economy," *Administrative Science Quarterly,* 20 (June), 229-249.

Blois, K. (1972), "Vertical Quasi-Integration," *Journal of Industrial Economics,* 20 (July), 253-260.

Bonoma, T.V. (1976), "Conflict, Cooperation and Trust in Three Power Systems," *Behavioral Science,* 21 (November), 499-514.

Bucklin, L.P. (1966), *A Theory of Distribution Channel Structure,* Berkeley, CA: Institute of Business and Economic Research, University of California.

———, and J.M. Carman (1974), "Vertical Market Structure Theory and the Health Care Delivery System," in *Marketing Analysis of Societal Problems,* J.N. Sheth and P.L. Wright, eds., Urbana-Champaign, IL: Bureau of Economic and Business Research, 7-41.

Coser, L.A. (1956), *The Functions of Social Conflict,* Glencoe, IL: Free Press.

Cox, R., C. Goodman and T. Fichandler (1965), *Distribution in a High Level Economy,* Englewood Cliffs, NJ: Prentice-Hall, Inc.

El-Ansary, A. and L.W. Stern (1972), "Power Measurement in the Distribution Channel," *Journal of Marketing Research,* 9 (February), 47-52.

Emerson, R.M. (1962), "Power-Dependence Relations," *American Sociological Review,* 27 (February), 31-41.

———, (1972), "Exchange Theory, Part II: Exchange Relations and Network Structures," in *Sociological Theories in Progress,* J. Berger, M. Zelditch Jr., and A. Anderson, eds., Boston: Houghton Mifflin.

Etgar, M. (1976a), "The Effect of Administrative Control on Efficiency of Vertical Marketing Systems," *Journal of Marketing Research,* 13 (February), 12-24.

———, (1976b), "Channel Domination and Countervailing Power in Distribution Channels," *Journal of Marketing Research,* 13 (August), 254-262.

——— (1977), "Channel Environment and Channel Leadership," *Journal of Marketing Research,* 14 (February), 69-76.

——— (1978), "Differences in the Use of Manufacturer Power in Conventional and Contractual Channels," *Journal of Retailing,* 54 (Winter), 49-62.

Evan, W.M. (1965), "Toward a Theory of Inter-Organizational Relations," *Management Science,* 11 (August), B-217-230.

Fink, C.F. (1968), "Some Conceptual Difficulties in the Theory of Social Conflict," *Journal of Conflict Resolution,* 12 (December), 412-460.

Frazier, G.L. and J.R. Brown (1978), "Use of Power in the Interfirm Influence Process," in *Proceedings,* Eighth Annual Albert Haring Symposium, Indiana University, 6-30.

Frey, B.S. (1978), *Modern Political Economy,* Oxford, England: Martin Robertson.

Gattorna, J. (1978), "Channels of Distribution," *European Journal of Marketing,* 12, 7, 471-512.

Grønhaug, K. and T. Reve (1979), Economic Performance in Vertical Marketing Systems," *Proceedings of Fourth Macro Marketing Conference,* P. White and G. Fisk, eds., Boulder: University of Colorado Press.

Guetzkow, H. (1966), "Relations among Organizations," in *Studies in Organizations,* R.V. Bowers, ed., Athens, GA: University of Georgia Press, 13-44.

Gurr, T.R. (1970), *Why Men Rebel,* Princeton, NJ: Princeton University Press.

Hernes, G., editor (1978), *Forhandlingsøkonomi og Blandingsadministrasjon,* Bergen, Norway: Universitetsforlaget.

Hunt, S.D. and J.R. Nevin (1974), "Power in a Channel of Distribution: Sources and Consequences," *Journal of Marketing Research,* 11 (May), 186-193.

Jennergren, L.P. (1979), "Decentralization in Organizations," to appear in *Handbook of Organizational Design,* P.G. Nystrom and W.H. Starbuck, eds., Amsterdam: Elsevier.

Kaplan, M.A. (1957), "Balance of Power, Bipolar and Other Models of International Systems," *American Political Science Review,* 51 (September), 684-695.

Korpi, W. (1974), "Conflict and the Balance of Power," *Acta Sociologica,* 17, 2, 99-114.

Kriesberg, L. (1952), "The Retail Furrier: Concepts of Security and Success," *American Journal of Sociology,* 58 (March), 478-485.

——— (1955), "Occupational Control among Steel Distributors," *American Journal of Sociology,* 61 (November), 203-212.

Liebeler, W.J. (1976), "Integration and Competition," in *Vertical Integration in the U.S. Oil Industry,* E. Mitchell, ed., Washington DC: American Enterprise Institute for Public Policy Research, 5-34.

Lindblom, C.E. (1977), *Politics and Markets,* New York: Basic Books.

Lusch, R.F. (1976), "Sources of Power: Their Impact on Intrachannel Conflict," *Journal of Marketing Research,* 13 (November), 382-390.

McCammon, B.C. Jr. (1970), "Perspectives for Distribution Programming," in *Vertical Market Systems,* L.P. Bucklin, ed., Glenview, IL: Scott, Foresman, 32-51.

———, and A.D. Bates (1965), "The Emergence and Growth of Contractually Integrated Channels in the American Economy," in *Economic Growth, Competition, and World Markets,* P.D. Bennett, ed., Chicago: American Marketing Association, 496-515.

———, and R.W. Little (1965), "Marketing Channels: Analytical Systems and Approaches," in *Science in Marketing,* G. Schwartz, ed., New York: John Wiley and Sons, 321-384.

———, A.D. Bates and J.D. Guiltinan (1971), "Alternative Models for Programming Vertical Marketing Networks," in *New Essays in Marketing Theory,* G. Fisk, ed., Boston: Allyn and Bacon, 333-358.

McVey, P. (1960), "Are Channels of Distribution What the Textbooks Say?" *Journal of Marketing,* 24 (January), 61-65.

Palamountain, J.C. Jr. (1955), *The Politics of Distribution,* Cambridge, MA: Harvard University Press.

Pfeffer, J. and G.R. Salancik (1978), *The External Control of Organizations,* New York: Harper & Row.

Phillips, L. (1980), *The Study of Collective Behavior in Marketing: Methodological Issues In the Use of Key Informants,* unpublished doctoral dissertation, Evanston, IL: Northwestern University.

Porter, M. (1974), "Consumer Behavior, Retailer Power, and Market Performance in Consumer Goods Industries," *Review of Economics and Statistics,* 56 (November), 419-436.

Raven, B.H. and A.W. Kruglanski (1970), "Conflict and Power," in *The Structure of Conflict,* P. Swingle, ed., New York: Academic Press, 69-109.

Reve, T. and L.W. Stern (1979), "Interorganizational Relations in Marketing Channels," *Academy of Management Review,* 4 (July), 405-416.

Scherer, F.M. (1970), *Industrial Market Structure and Economic Performance,* Skokie, IL: Rand McNally.

Schmidt, S.M. and T.A. Kochan (1972), "Conflict: Toward Conceptual Clarity," *Administrative Science Quarterly,* 17 (September), 359-370.

Stern, L.W., editor (1969), *Distribution Channels: Behavioral Dimensions,* Boston: Houghton Mifflin.

——— (1971), "Antitrust Implications of a Sociological Interpretation of Competition, Conflict, and Cooperation in the Marketplace," *The Antitrust Bulletin,* 16 (Fall), 509-530.

———, and A.I. El-Ansary (1977), *Marketing Channels,* Englewood Cliffs, NJ: Prentice-Hall, Inc.

———, and R.H. Gorman (1969), "Conflict in Distribution Channels: An Exploration," in *Distribution Channels: Behavioral Dimensions,* L.W. Stern, ed., Boston: Houghton Mifflin, 156-175.

———, R.A. Schulz and J.R. Grabner (1973), "The Power Base-Conflict Relationship: Preliminary Findings," *Social Science Quarterly,* 54 (September), 412-419.

Sturdivant, F.D. (1966), "Determinants of Vertical Integration in Channel Systems," in *Science, Technology and Marketing,* R.M. Hass, ed., Chicago: American Marketing Association, 472-479.

Terreberry, S. (1968), "The Evolution of Organizational Environments," *Administrative Science Quarterly,* (March), 590-613.

Thomas, K. (1976), "Conflict and Conflict Management," in *Handbook of Industrial and Organizational Psychology,* M.D. Dunnette, ed., Chicago: Rand McNally, 889-935.

Thompson, J.D. (1967), *Organizations in Action,* New York: McGraw Hill.

Thorelli, H.B. (1965), "The Political Economy of the Firm: Basis for a New Theory of Competition?" *Schweizerische Zeitschrift fur Volkwirtschaft und Statistik,* 101, 3, 248-262.

Tivey, L. (1978), *The Politics of the Firm,* Oxford: Martin Robertson.

Van de Ven, A., D. Emmett and R. Koenig, Jr. (1974), "Framework for Interorganizational Analysis," *Organization and Administrative Sciences,* 5 (Spring), 113-129.

Wamsley, G. and M. Zald (1973), "The Political Economy of Public Organizations," *Public Administration Review,* 33 (January-February), 62-73.

———, and ——— (1976), *The Political Economy of Public Organizations,* Bloomington, IN: Indiana University Press.

Weik, J. (1972), "Discrepant Perceptions in Vertical Marketing Systems," in *1971 Combined Preceedings,* F. Allvine, ed., Chicago: American Marketing Association, 181-188.

Wilkinson, I. (1973), "Power in Distribution Channels," *Cranfield Research Papers in Marketing and Logistics,* Cranfield, England: Cranfield School of Management.

Williamson, O.E. (1975), *Markets and Hierarchies: Analysis and Antitrust Implications,* New York: Free Press.

Wittreich, W. (1962), "Misunderstanding the Retailer," *Harvard Business Review,* 40 (May-June), 147-155.

Yuchtman, E. and S. Seashore (1967), "A System Resources Approach to Organizational Effectiveness," *American Sociological Review,* 33 (December), 891-903.

Zald, M. (1970a), "Political Economy: A Framework for Comparative Analysis," in *Power in Organizations,* M. Zald, ed., Nashville: Vanderbilt University Press, 221-261.

——— (1970b), *Organizational Change: The Political Economy of the YMCA,* Chicago: University of Chicago Press.

33

Joseph P. Guiltinan

Risk-Aversive Pricing Policies: Problems and Alternatives

The marketing manager for a heavy-equipment manufacturing concern in northern Ohio recently suggested that before 1973 he spent no more than three days a year on pricing policy but that currently pricing dominates all marketing policy-making activities in his firm. This experience is not unusual. Decision makers are becoming increasingly aware that pricing policy changes must be made with consideration for possible major shifts in economic conditions such as the prices and availability of raw materials, aggregate demand, interest and exchange rates, and liquidity. Uncertainty regarding these economic forces leads to uncertain and fluctuating gross margins, creates difficulties in planning working capital needs, and impedes budgeting. Since price can influence cash flow and margins more quickly than other marketing variables, the development of policy regarding price levels, changes, and discounts has become of paramount concern in current marketing practice.

This article reviews some current pricing responses to economic uncertainties and identifies key problems associated with the implementation of these responses. In particular, responses that reflect risk-aversive, defensive perspectives are of primary concern. While it is often appropriate for managers to adopt policies that seek to minimize risk, this article contends that such responses may have unanticipated consequences that entail a good deal of risk. Alternative courses of action for developing pricing policies under economic uncertainty are also presented. The analysis is based on concepts, practices, and theories gleaned from marketing theory, general business periodicals, and a series of executive development pricing seminars in which the author has participated with senior pricing executives.

Reprinted from the *Journal of Marketing* (January 1976), pp. 10-15, published by the American Marketing Association.

Joseph Guiltinan is Professor of Marketing at the University of Kentucky and previously taught at the University of Massachusetts. He received his D.B.A. from Indiana University.

CURRENT PRICING RESPONSES

Most current pricing responses reported in the literature are concerned with reducing the risk of low margins, avoiding bottlenecks, and improving cash flows.[1] In general, these responses are of two types: cost based and selling related.

Cost-Based Pricing Responses

Many current pricing methods and related product decisions are primarily responses to production cost uncertainties and related pressures on margins.

Adoption of "delayed-quotation" pricing. In this approach, which is particularly widespread among manufacturers of custom-made products such as machine tools, the seller sets a final price only when the items have reached the stage of finished goods. This is due to a combination of long production lead times (often because of bottlenecks on key materials) and rapidly escalating prices (typically in metals and petro-chemicals). This approach (which includes the "price at time of delivery" variation) is not novel but has been practiced much more broadly the past couple of years.

Elimination of low-margin products. This policy has also received widespread attention by firms that are uncertain about future cost increases or their ability to pass such increases forward. In addition, the cost and unavailability of working capital have made it unprofitable to maintain inventories of low-margin items.

Adoption of "escalator" clauses. This policy is simply one in which price increases (frequently across-the-board increases on all items in a product line) are automatically implemented based on a previously stated formula. The objective is to alleviate the risks involved in cost increases. The bases for such escalations include simple factors such as increases in wholesale price indexes, industry-specific published indexes, listed price increases of raw material suppliers, or highly complex formulas that incorporate increased costs of labor, energy, and several material inputs. The effective use of such escalators depends on the willingness of customers to accept them, and on the firm's ability to change the formula over time as cost structures change and to measure variations in cost changes across products.

Selling-Related Pricing Responses

These responses focus on increasing margins by reducing customer incentives used by the sales force (particularly in industrial firms). While they reflect cost pressures, unlike cost-based responses they have a minimal impact on direct list prices. Rather, they reflect an attempt to redirect sales efforts to nonprice approaches.

Unbundling of services. In this response, a firm that has priced a major product (typically a large, complex piece of equipment) to include special services, peripheral equipment, or replacement parts shifts to a policy in which each element of the product-service mix is priced separately. Typically, the sum of the prices (after unbundling) will exceed the old, single price. Thus, unbundling represents the elimination of a form of product-line discount to buyers purchasing the full mix.

Reduce cash and quantity discounts. Because discounts represent direct reductions in the gross margins earned by sellers, there is a temptation to arbitrarily eliminate many cash and quantity discounts as a means of improving margins. Further, many firms have found that large customers (including many government agencies) often subtract the cash discount but still fail to pay invoices within the stipulated period. The incentive to maintain quantity discounts is also reduced for suppliers who experience shortages of key materials.

Elimination of price "shading." The concept of varying price policy, or "shading," is one in which reductions from list price are made as the result of negotiations between buyers and salesmen. The recent trend toward a "one-price" policy in many firms can be attributed to the desire to maintain gross margins (as was the case with discounts), to centralize control over pricing (by removing the sales force from this role), and to attempt to generate more sales effort in nonprice attributes of the product.

While price is generally a competitive tool for increasing demand for a firm (and often a tool for stimulating industry demand), risk-aversive policies generally do not explicitly consider competitive response and consumer demand as significant inputs to the pricing decision. This appears to result from the knowledge that similar pressures (such as the rising cost of materials) also usually plague competitors, from the expectation that competitors will adopt (or have adopted) similar policies (especially on discounts or escalators), or from limitations in the comparability of products and services among competitors.

PROBLEMS EXPERIENCED WITH CURRENT PRICING RESPONSES

For a variety of reasons, an individual enterprise may find that the foregoing responses are difficult to implement or that they lead to unintended consequences. Marketing theory and the experiences of many pricing executives are used in this section to illustrate such difficulties.

Distribution and Sales Force Problems

Distributors may react negatively to the elimination of discounts because in some cases this may eliminate part of their competitive advantage, because it typically violates traditional trade practices, and because it reduces possible bases for promoting the product to final buyers. Similarly, they will react negatively to any changes that influence the total effectiveness of a product line (such as the elimination of an important low-margin, sales-leading product). Consequently, the degree of reseller support may be influenced by such pricing policies.

It is also important to understand the nature of distributors' cost and profit structures before radically changing discount policies. For instance, one St. Louis manufacturer eliminated quantity discounts to improve margins and then learned that many of the firm's distributors relied almost exclusively on the discount for the profit they made on that company's products.

Many of the risk-aversive responses also lead to a serious alteration in the role of the company sales force, often diminishing the role of the salesman while giving him the task of smoothing over customer reactions to price increases and product shortages and backlogs. This role change is likely to lead to increased sales force dissatisfaction and turnover.

Product-Line Problems

Where arbitrary elimination of low-margin items or unbundling takes place, product-line considerations on both the production and demand sides become important. Low-margin items may significantly stimulate sales of complementary, high-margin items, especially where items are bundled. Accordingly, care must be taken to ascertain the competitiveness of each element of the mix when unbundling takes place. For instance, a small institutional services firm in Tennessee found that it was not equally competitive on all components of the product-service mix, and declining sales of part of the line more than offset the revenue gains from price changes.

When a price change significantly affects end prices, buyers' perceptions of the entire line's price/quality image may be influenced.[2] A western manufacturer of special fertilizer products recently introduced a third, middle-of-the-line product. However, pricing executives failed to price it high enough to avoid a perception of similarity in quality to the low-end product, which had just experienced a price increase. Thus, both products appealed to the same market and few new customers were obtained.

Where bottlenecks are a problem, the decision to concentrate on so-called high-margin items may backfire. To the extent that high-margin items require materials, labor, or equipment in short supply, production capacity will be under-utilized and total dollar margins may not be maximized.

Escalator Clauses and Cost-Forecasting Problems

Probably no pricing problems are as pervasive as those associated with escalators. Most firms can readily appreciate the problem of spiraling costs and, consequently, industrial buyers appear more willing to accept some sort of escalator provision today.

Problems related to escalators fall into categories typified by the following:

- A California aircraft supplier must bid now on products to be delivered in 1983.
- An Indiana automotive parts manufacturer has had a bid for a large order rejected until the company indicates what percentage of a cost increase it will absorb itself and what portion of its escalator clause is attributable to labor and each of various materials.
- A New England manufacturer in the electronics industry developed a cost escalator based heavily on the price of copper. When copper prices fell, his customers demanded sharp price decreases; yet other cost elements that were not incorporated into the escalator formula had recently increased significantly.

These considerations demonstrate the need for improved and realistic costing. This is true whether a firm is developing an escalator clause for direct use in a contract or for setting a fixed future price.

Problems Related to Demand Curve Assumptions

A fundamental problem with all cost-based pricing strategies is the implicit assumption that demand is inelastic. Such assumptions gain credence if recent price increases have not resulted in any major loss of sales. Even where demand curve estimates are developed, however, three factors must be considered.[3]

Cumulative price increase effects and confounding real income effects. The presence of either or both of these effects often results in the invalidation of historical price/quantity relationships.

Illustrative of this is the plight of a Texas manufacturer of metal home improvement products. Normally, sales in this industry are booming and demand is inelastic when new construction is down. As the recession began to take shape in mid-1974, however, this firm's home improvement sales began to slide when prices were raised to reflect steel and aluminum cost increases, even though new housing starts remained low.

This situation probably resulted from both of the effects suggested above. As price increases become more frequent, historical relationships become less applicable because the historical range of price/quantity observations is increasingly remote from current price levels. The firm may well have moved into a range where demand elasticity is higher.

Demand estimates may also be confounded when economic forces (such as recessions) result in a downward shift in the demand curve. Smaller quantities are demanded at all (or most) price levels as either the rate of use or number of users diminishes.

In both cases, the failure of historical relationships to hold reduces the usefulness of simple statistical demand curve models and of untempered executive judgments that rely on recent sales history. More complex forecasting models that incorporate economic conditions as well as price variables may reduce confounding effects. Where feasible, the use of experimentation or surveys may provide some information for updating judgments.

Poor sales force estimates of demand. Sales force estimates of the effect of price changes are considered inadequate by many pricing executives. The tendency to rely on price selling and the desire to be more competitive have generally made subjective sales force estimates of the effects of a price reduction very optimistic and their estimates of the effects of increases very pessimistic. The controller of an Ohio-based equipment manufacturer suggested that his sales force typically overestimates actual sales increases by about one-fourth of unit volume when queried about the effects of prospective price decreases. Consequently, sales force estimates may be ignored if not accompanied by supportive value analysis comparisons, data on customer revenue trends, or other specific customer purchasing constraints.

Limitations of the demand curve concept. Elasticity and demand curve estimates reflect the impact of price on total revenue only. While revenue may increase as a result of a price increase, reduced unit volume may result in sharply increased average unit costs when fixed costs are a major portion of total costs.

Problems with Cost Orientation in General

In the long run, perhaps the most serious problem facing firms that adopt cost-oriented approaches to pricing is the self-perpetuating nature of the price squeeze that often results—particularly in periods of reduced consumer and industrial demand. Automatic and continual escalation of prices merely to preserve target gross margins is a fundamental culprit in prolonging recessions. When such increases occur in the elastic zone of a demand curve, reductions in demand in response to these changes often lead to increased average unit costs. This, in turn, leads to increased prices by those firms that rely on target margins as a pricing device (even in the absence of further increases in labor, energy, and material costs).

The foregoing problems in demand curve estimation notwithstanding, pricing executives must consider the unit-sales implications of average-cost pricing. When the pricing objective is to maximize profit, then it is appropriate to use marginal analysis of the incremental costs and expected incremental revenue associated with either a price cut or the attempt to avoid a price increase.

In short, many firms are now realizing that pricing to maintain a given gross margin may not really be a low-risk strategy. In an economy where demand may be increasingly elastic and where fixed costs are very high for most industries, lower margins may be required to maintain adequate demand. Stated alternatively, it will generally prove counterproductive to rely solely on higher prices and margins to deal with problems of cost control and cost forecasting. Since risk-aversive policies may not achieve the objectives for which they were designed, perhaps more positive approaches are needed.

DEVELOPING SOME ALTERNATIVE RESPONSES

Given that many of the current pricing responses will not be appropriate for a given firm due to the problems outlined above, some alternative responses do exist that may be more consistent with the actual decision environment. Further, some guidelines are available to help pricing executives evaluate and implement alternative policies.

Developing Price Objectives

Price responses are always made with some objective in mind, at least implicitly. As suggested earlier, objectives such as improving margins, avoiding bottlenecks, and improving cash flow seem to be the dominant forces behind current price responses. However, such objectives may not be mutually consistent. Focusing on high-margin products may lead to increased bottlenecks due to the materials or labor required, or it may lead to reduced total cash flow as a result of reduced sales of items complementary to low-margin items. Accordingly, a clear statement of the objectives of pricing policy is a fundamental requirement for selecting alternatives. Also, the impact of short-term policies and objectives on long-term profit must be clarified. As Kotler suggests, the identification of weak products should consider potential sales growth and annual cash flow generated per dollar of asset tied up in the product.[4]

Positive Pricing Perspective

While most current price responses are risk-aversive, organizations that have clearly defined price objectives, that have carefully analyzed the pricing and cost environment, and that are organized to absorb and act on all appropriate information should be in a position to act positively and opportunistically in creating pricing policy. The following policies illustrate this posture.

- Balance pricing policy on a major product with policy on related items. For instance, by restricting large price increases to replacement parts, services, and complementary items, a West Coast firm was able to hold the line on price increases for the major item.
- Employ a varying price policy (where injurious price discrimination is not a problem) as a tool that permits the sales force to orient demand toward those products that the firm wishes to promote and to obtain a foothold in new accounts for the long run. Maintaining this policy may be especially effective in softening the blow of price increases or reduced cash discounts.
- Rather than reduce quantity discounts and promotional allowances, use them creatively to stimulate demand for products not requiring critical resources, or to partly offset price-level increases. Further, as costs change, frequent review of the quantity discount structure becomes imperative and may lead to the discovery of more marketable and more competitive quantity discount policies. (Interestingly, many firms are not even aware of competitors' quantity discount structures.)
- Where cash discounts are under review, be sure to consider both the marketing

and financial issues involved (including changes in short-term interest rates). A period of tight money and inflation may present opportunities to obtain new customers and build long-term goodwill. Many firms have countered the trend toward eliminating cash discounts by initiating or expanding them. One California manufacturer reported that the average age of accounts receivable was reduced by over 40 days with the initiation of a 1½% cash discount, thus dramatically reducing working capital binds. (Note that paying 1½% for getting payment 40 days earlier is tantamount to paying: $\frac{360 \text{ days/year}}{40 \text{ days}} \times 1\tfrac{1}{2}\% = 13.5\%$ annual interest for that money.)

- Where buyers fail to pay invoices on time, several firms have invoked penalty charges at 1% to 1½% per month with some success.
- To spread the financing costs of large-scale capital projects, a Pennsylvania construction firm began to write contracts that included progress payments – with the first payment made at the start of construction.
- Discounts may also serve as an alternative to escalator clauses. An Ohio manufacturer with a large product line has begun to print price lists that are expected to last six months. However, at the start of the period, all products are discounted to all buyers; as cost increases occur, discounts are reduced. This practice reduces the number of price increases and eliminates the problem of delays in buyer notification of changes.
- Cash or merchandise rebates (promotion allowances) may be useful for industrial manufacturers as well as for consumer products manufacturers. As in the case of across-the-board discounting, this avoids a complete overhaul of price lists (and related notification) for short-term pricing policies.
- Conduct periodic audits of the cost structures of all major products or (where joint costs are difficult to separate) major product groups before developing escalator clauses. Such audits would examine possible savings in labor, energy, or distribution costs that might offset cost increases in materials. This approach frequently makes escalators more palatable to buyers by demonstrating the seller's good faith in holding down controllable costs and by developing an up-to-date data base for constructing realistic escalator indexes. Several firms have uncovered previously undetected productivity improvements on some items (often due to learning curve effects) which enabled them to set more competitive prices on those products.
- Exploit the product life cycle.[5] As products go through growth, maturity, and decline, price levels and promotional policy change to meet consumer, competitive, and technological changes. Typically, one would expect practices such as discounts, shading, and product-service bundles to be fundamental aspects of marketing strategy in the maturity/saturation stages, where price level and technological parity tend to exist.
- Where demand conditions permit, increase the use of long-term contracts to guarantee transactions, in part to reduce costs, but also to guard against multiple ordering by buyers who are attempting to hedge against further inflation and who will likely cancel out at a later time. This is particularly important for products where material shortages and long production backlogs formerly existed.[6]
- Employ new sales force incentives to meet production, cash flow, and margin objectives, to reduce reliance on price

shading, and to stimulate more sales force concern with accurate demand estimation.

- Promote distributor cooperation by: expanding cooperative promotions on key items, emphasizing any product improvement associated with price increases, contrasting price increases with either industry averages or the Industrial Wholesale Price Index, and noting that distributors selling on commission or fixed percentage discount will increase their gross income.[7]

CONCLUSION

Each firm faces a unique set of cost, supply, customer demand, and competitive forces at a given point in time, and each must select its price objectives and policies accordingly. This article has suggested some considerations for making policy selection. Pricing executives should avoid adopting current practices used by other firms without considering the problems that may hinder their implementation or that may lead to unintended consequences. Pricing responses should be developed on the basis of clearly defined price objectives, incorporating research on the anticipated effects of price changes. Further, pricing policy under uncertainty need not consist solely of defensive, risk-aversive alternatives, but can be positive and opportunistic in perspective.

Price has long been one of the most ignored dimensions of marketing policy in both academia and industry.[8] The cost-oriented, risk-aversive trends that are so prominent in current business practice seem to bear this out. Firms are defensive about pricing, probably because its ramifications are not well understood. Improved knowledge of this aspect of marketing may be an unforeseen benefit of attempts to deal with the current problems.

NOTES

1. This section was developed based particularly on: Daniel Nimer, "Pricing Capital Goods," *Industrial Marketing,* March 1971, pp. 53–55; "Profitless Boom in Machine Tools," *Business Week,* July 6, 1974, pp. 52–54; "Pricing Strategy in an Inflation Economy," *Business Week,* April 6, 1974, pp. 43–49; and "The Squeeze on Product Mix," *Business Week,* January 5, 1974, pp. 50–55; as well as from discussions with pricing executives.
2. This is treated in detail in Kent B. Monroe, "Buyers' Subjective Perceptions of Price," *Journal of Marketing Research,* Vol. 10 (February 1973), pp. 70–80.
3. For a more extensive discussion of demand curve estimation problems and approaches, see Mark Alpert, "Demand Curve Estimation and Psychological Pricing," in *Managerial Analysis in Marketing,* Frederick D. Sturdivant et al. (Glenview, Ill.: Scott, Foresman & Co., 1970), Chap. 10.
4. Philip Kotler, "Marketing During Periods of Shortage," JOURNAL OF MARKETING, Vol. 38 (July 1974), pp. 20–29.
5. See Chester Wasson, *Product Management* (St. Charles, Ill.: Challenge Books, 1971), for a thorough treatment of pricing over the product life cycle.
6. "A Reducing Diet for Inventories," *Business Week,* August 3, 1974.
7. "Is There a 'Best Way' to Tell Distributors of Price Hike?" *Industrial Marketing,* June 1967, pp. 27–32.
8. See Alfred Oxenfeldt, "A Decision-Making Structure for Price Decisions," JOURNAL OF MARKETING, Vol. 37 (January 1973), pp. 48–49, for an excellent discussion of this problem.

34

Robert J. Lavidge
Gary A. Steiner

A Model for Predictive Measurements of Advertising Effectiveness

What are the functions of advertising? Obviously the ultimate function is to help product sales. But all advertising is not, should not, and cannot be designed to produce immediate purchases on the part of all who are exposed to it. Immediate sales results (even if measurable) are, at best, an incomplete criterion of advertising effectiveness.

In other words, the effects of much advertising are "long-term." This is sometimes taken to imply that all one can really do is wait and see – ultimately the campaign will or will not produce.

However, if something is to happen in the long run, something must be happening in the short run, something that will ultimately lead to eventual sales results. And this process must be measured in order to provide anything approaching a comprehensive evaluation of the effectiveness of the advertising.

Ultimate consumers normally do not switch from disinterested individuals to convinced purchasers in one instantaneous step. Rather, they approach the ultimate purchase through a process or series of steps in which the actual purchase is but the final threshold.

SEVEN STEPS

Advertising may be thought of as a force, which must move people up a series of steps:

1. Near the bottom of the steps stand potential purchasers who are completely *una-*

Reprinted from the *Journal of Marketing*, published by the American Marketing Association (October 1961), pp. 59–62.

Robert J. Lavidge is president of Elrick and Lavidge, Chicago-based market research and marketing consulting firm. A faculty member in the Northwestern University Evening Division, he received his B.A. degree from DePauw and his M.B.A. from the University of Chicago. He is a past president of the American Marketing Association. He is co-editor (with R. J. Holloway) of Marketing and Society: The Challenge.

Gary A. Steiner was, before his death, professor of business at the University of Chicago, from which he earned an M.A. degree in sociology and a Ph.D. in psychology. He also served as a consultant in applications of psychological techniques. He was co-author (with B. L. Berenson) of Human Behavior: An Inventory of Scientific Findings.

ware of the existence of the product or service in question.

2. Closer to purchasing, but still a long way from the cash register, are those who are merely *aware of its existence.*
3. Up a step are prospects who *know what the product has to offer.*
4. Still closer to purchasing are those who have favorable attitudes toward the product – those who *like the product.*
5. Those whose favorable attitudes have developed to the point of *preference over all other possibilities are up still another step.*
6. Even closer to purchasing are consumers who couple preference with a desire to buy and the *conviction* that the purchase would be wise.
7. Finally, of course, is the step which translates this attitude into actual *purchase.*

Research to evaluate the effectiveness of advertisements can be designed to provide measures of movement on such a flight of steps.

The various steps are not necessarily equidistant. In some instances the "distance" from awareness to preference may be very slight, while the distance to purchase is extremely large. In other cases, the reverse may be true. Furthermore, a potential purchaser sometimes may move up several steps simultaneously.

Consider the following hypotheses. The greater the psychological and/or economic commitment involved in the purchase of a particular product, the longer it will take to bring consumers up these steps, and the more important the individual steps will be. Contrariwise, the less serious the commitment, the more likely it is that some consumers will go almost "immediately" to the top of the steps.

An impulse purchase might be consummated with no previous awareness, knowledge, liking, or conviction with respect to the product. On the other hand, an industrial good or an important consumer product ordinarily will not be purchased in such a manner.

DIFFERENT OBJECTIVES

Products differ markedly in terms of the role of advertising as related to the various positions on the steps. A great deal of advertising is designed to move people up the final steps toward purchase. At an extreme is the "Buy Now" ad, designed to stimulate immediate overt action. Contrast this with industrial advertising, much of which is not intended to stimulate immediate purchase in and of itself. Instead, it is designed to help pave the way for the salesman by making the prospects aware of his company and products, thus giving them knowledge and favorable attitudes about the ways in which those products or services might be of value. This, of course, involves movement up the lower and intermediate steps.

Even within a particular product category, or with a specific product, different advertisements or campaigns may be aimed primarily at different steps in the purchase process – and rightly so. For example, advertising for new automobiles is likely to place considerable emphasis on the lower steps when new models are first brought out. The advertiser recognizes that his first job is to make the potential customer aware of the new product, and to give him knowledge and favorable attitudes about the product. As the year progresses, advertising emphasis tends to move up the steps. Finally, at the end of the "model year" much emphasis is placed on the final step – the attempt to stimulate immediate purchase among prospects who are assumed, by then, to have information about the car.

The simple model assumes that potential purchasers all "start from scratch." However, some may have developed negative attitudes about the product, which place them even further from purchasing the product than those completely unaware of it. The first job, then, is to get them off the negative steps – before they can move up the additional steps which lead to purchase.

THREE FUNCTIONS OF ADVERTISING

The six steps outlined, beginning with "aware," indicate three major functions of advertising. The first two, awareness and knowledge, relate to *information or ideas.* The second two steps, liking and preference, have to do with favorable *attitudes or feelings* toward the product. The final two steps, conviction and purchase, are to produce *action*–the acquisition of the product.

These three advertising functions are directly related to a classic psychological model which divides behavior into three components or dimensions:

1. The *cognitive* component–the intellectual, mental, or "rational" states.
2. The *affective* component–the "emotional" or "feeling" states.
3. The *conative* or *motivational* component–the "striving" states, relating to the tendency to treat objects as positive or negative goals.

This is more than a semantic issue, because the actions that need to be taken to stimulate or channel motivation may be quite different from those that produce knowledge. And these, in turn, may differ from actions designed to produce favorable attitudes toward something.

FUNCTIONS OF ADVERTISING RESEARCH

Among the first problems in any advertising evaluation program are to:

1. Determine what steps are most critical in a particular case, that is, what the steps leading to purchase are for most consumers.
2. Determine how many people are, at the moment, on which steps.
3. Determine which people on which steps it is most important to reach.

Advertising research can then be designed to evaluate the extent to which the advertising succeeds in moving the specified "target" audience(s) up the critical purchase steps.

Table 34-1 summarizes the stair-step model, and illustrates how several common advertising and research approaches may be organized according to their various "functions."

Over-all and Component Measurements

With regard to most any product there are an infinite number of additional "subflights" which can be helpful in moving a prospect up the main steps. For example, awareness, knowledge and development of favorable attitudes toward a specific product feature may be helpful in building a preference for the line of products. This leads to the concept of other steps, subdividing or "feeding" into the purchase steps, but concerned solely with more specific product features or attitudes.

Advertising effectiveness measurements may, then, be categorized into:

1. Over-all or "global" measurements, concerned with measuring the results–the consumers' positions and movement on the purchase steps.
2. Segment or component measurements, concerned with measuring the relative effectiveness of various means of moving people up the purchase steps–the consumers' positions on ancillary flights of steps, and the relative importance of these flights.

Measuring Movement on the Steps

Many common measurements of advertising effectiveness have been concerned with movement up either the first steps or the final step on the primary purchase flight. Examples include surveys to determine the extent of brand

TABLE 34-1 *Advertising and Advertising Research Related to the Model*

Related Behavioral Dimensions	Movement Toward Purchase	Examples of Types of Promotion or Advertising Relevant to Various Steps	Examples of Research Approaches Related to Steps of Greatest Applicability
	PURCHASE ↑		
CONATIVE –the realm of motives. Ads stimulate or direct desires		Point-of-purchase Retail store ads Deals "Last-chance" offers Price appeals Testimonials	Market or sales tests Split-run tests Intention to purchase Projective techniques
	CONVICTION ↑		
	PREFERENCE ↑		
AFFECTIVE –the realm of emotions. Ads change attitudes and feelings		Competitive ads Argumentative copy "Image" ads Status, glamour appeals	Rank order of preference for brands Rating scales Image measurements, including check lists and semantic differentials Projective techniques
	LIKING ↑		
	KNOWLEDGE ↑		
COGNITIVE –the realm of thoughts. Ads provide information and facts		Announcements Descriptive copy Classified ads Slogans Jingles Sky writing	Information questions Play-back analyses Brand awareness surveys
	AWARENESS	Teaser campaigns	Aided recall

awareness and information and measures of purchase and repeat purchase among "exposed" versus "unexposed" groups.

Self-administered instruments, such as adaptations of the "semantic differential" and adjective check lists, are particularly helpful in providing the desired measurements of movement up or down the middle steps. The semantic differential provides a means of scaling attitudes with regard to a number of different issues in a manner which facilitates gathering the information on an efficient quantitative basis. Adjective lists, used in various ways, serve the same general purpose.

Such devices can provide relatively spontaneous, rather than "considered," responses. They are also quickly administered and can contain enough elements to make recall of specific responses by the test participant difficult, especially if the order of items is changed. This helps in minimizing "consistency" biases in various comparative uses of such measurement tools.

Efficiency of these self-administered devices make it practical to obtain responses to large numbers of items. This facilitates measurement of elements or components differing only slightly, though importantly, from each other.

Carefully constructed adjective check lists, for example, have shown remarkable discrimination between terms differing only in subtle shades of meaning. One product may be seen as "rich," "plush," and "expensive," while another one is "plush," "gaudy," and "cheap."

Such instruments make it possible to secure simultaneous measurements of both *global* attitudes and *specific* image components. These can be correlated with each other and directly related to the content of the advertising messages tested.

Does the advertising change the thinking of the respondents with regard to specific product attributes, characteristics or features, including not only physical characteristics but also various image elements such as "status"? Are these changes commercially significant?

The measuring instruments mentioned are helpful in answering these questions. They provide a means for correlating changes in specific attitudes concerning image components with changes in global attitudes or position on the primary purchase steps.

Testing the Model

When groups of consumers are studied over time, do those who show more movement on the measured steps eventually purchase the product in greater proportions or quantities? Accumulation of data utilizing the stair-step model provides an opportunity to test the assumptions underlying the model by measuring this question.

THREE CONCEPTS

This approach to the measurement of advertising has evolved from three concepts:

1. Realistic measurements of advertising effectiveness must be related to an understanding of the functions of advertising. It is helpful to think in terms of a model where advertising is likened to a force which, if successful, moves people up a series of steps toward purchase.
2. Measurements of the effectiveness of the advertising should provide measurements of changes at all levels on these steps – not just at the levels of the development of product or feature awareness and the stimulation of actual purchase.
3. Changes in attitudes as to specific image components can be evaluated together with changes in over-all images, to determine the extent to which changes in the image components are related to movement on the primary purchase steps.

35

Russell L. Ackoff
James R. Emshoff

Advertising Research at Anheuser-Busch, Inc. (1963–68)*

The association with Anheuser-Busch, Inc. (A-B) that is described here began in 1959. Over the last fifteen years research has been carried out on almost every aspect of A-B's operations and planning. The company's view of this association has appeared in several articles.[1] *Business Week* and *Fortune*[2] have described aspects of this work and some of the theoretical output has also appeared.[3] This article, however, is the first case study to be published. It provides an account of a sequence of investigations involving advertising of the company's principal product, BUDWEISER beer.

BACKGROUND

A-B's original contact was made by E. H. Vogel, Jr., then manager of business planning. Work over the first few years was devoted to determining when new breweries would be required, where they should be located, and what size they should be. Facility plans were developed to cover a ten-year period. Capital requirements for these facilities were estimated and a financial model of the firm was developed and used to predict capital availability. The model showed that not quite enough capital would have been available to finance the building program without increasing the company's traditional debt to debt-equity ratio. Research then turned to ways of making more capital available when needed.

Production operations involving scheduling and allocation of demand to breweries already had been studied and modified to yield much of the potential savings. Marketing, which involved a major share of the company's expen-

*The authors acknowledge the major roles of Drs. Eli S. Marks and Maurice Sasieni in the work reported in this article.
"Advertising Research at Anheuser-Busch, Inc.," Russell L. Ackoff and James R. Emshoff. Reprinted from *Sloan Management Review* (Winter 1975), pp. 1–15, by permission of Sloan Management Review.
Russell Ackoff holds an endowed chair at the University of Pennsylvania. He has been a pioneer in the areas of operations research and corporate planning. His Ph.D. is from the University of Pennsylvania, and he has served on the faculty at Case Institute of Technology.
James Emshoff is director of the Bureau of Research at the University of Pennsylvania. He has worked for McKinsey and Company as well as his own consulting firm.

ditures, had not yet been analyzed. An initial examination into this area revealed that the largest category of marketing cost involved advertising. Therefore, in 1961 we first recommended research into it. The proposal was turned down because of the widespread satisfaction with the company's advertising. Responsible managers were unwilling to evaluate and modify a successful program. Research turned instead to distribution and inventories.

ADVERTISING EXPENDITURES

Just before mid 1961 August A. Busch, Jr., then president and chairman of the board, asked us if we would evaluate an advertising decision he was about to make. In that year BUDWEISER was budgeted to receive about $15,000,000 worth of advertising. Mr. Busch had been approached by the vice president of marketing with a request for an additional $1,200,000 to be spent on advertising in twelve of the 198 areas into which the company divided its national market. The vice president had defended his proposal on the basis of the projected increase in sales that he believed would result. Mr. Busch explained that he was confronted with such a proposal every year and that he always had accepted it. He intended to do the same again, but he asked, "Is there any way I can find out at the end of the year whether I got what I paid for?" We said we would think about it and make some suggestions.

The proposal we presented to Mr. Busch shortly thereafter consisted of allowing the Marketing Department to select any six of the twelve areas initially proposed and giving it $600,000 for additional advertising. The remaining six areas would not be touched and would be used as controls. This biased selection procedure was intended to overcome some of the opposition that the Marketing Department felt toward any effort to evaluate its proposal.

Earlier we had developed an equation for forecasting monthly sales in each market area. Our plan now was to measure the deviation of actual monthly sales from the forecast for each market area in the test. Using the statistical characteristics of the forecasts we estimated that we had a 95 percent chance of detecting a 4 percent increase in sales in the areas with additional advertising. Since the increase predicted by the Marketing Department was in excess of this amount, Mr. Busch authorized the test and it was initiated.

The test was conducted over the last six months of 1961 yielding 72 (12 x 6) observations. The analysis of these data failed to reveal a significant difference between the test and control areas. Nevertheless, the control areas did better on average than was forecast. Therefore, we assumed that all the sales above those forecasted were attributable to the increased advertising and evaluated the results accordingly. Even under this assumption the increased amount of advertising was *not* justified by the deliberately overestimated increase in sales attributed to it.

Encouraged by these results, Mr. Busch asked us to design research directed at determining what amount should be spent on advertising. However, he wanted to proceed with caution, because he believed that much of the success of BUDWEISER, which was leading the beer market with a share of 8.14 percent in 1962, was due to its quality and the effectiveness with which this was communicated through its advertising. When we suggested research involving experimentation with market areas he authorized use of fifteen such areas provided they did not include any of the company's major markets.

Constrained in this way we sought an experimental design that would maximize learning about advertising expenditures. Our design effort was guided by two methodological principles. First, we knew that the company advertised for only one reason: to *increase sales*. Therefore, we were determined to measure the effect of advertising on *sales* and not on more easily measured intervening variables such as recall of messages or attitudes toward the product. For this reason we decided to continue to use deviations of actual from forecast sales as the variable to be observed. This allowed us to cancel out much of the effect on sales due to factors other than advertising. Accordingly, efforts to improve forecasting of monthly market-area sales were continuous.

Secondly, we were committed to an attempt to *explain* the casual effect of advertising on consumer purchases and not merely to find statistical correlations between them. Our search of the marketing literature for such an explanation was futile; it only revealed correlations and regressions between advertising and sales. These usually showed that increases (or decreases) in the former were associated with increases (or decreases) in the latter. From such associations it was almost universally inferred, and incorrectly, that increases in advertising yield increases in sales almost without limit. We believed that what these analyses really showed was that most companies forecast next year's sales quite accurately and then set their advertising budgets as a fixed percentage of predicted sales. In other words, forecasts of increased sales produce increased advertising.

Our commitment to experimentation derived from a determination to find a causal connection between advertising and sales, not merely an association between them, and to develop an ability to manipulate advertising so as to produce desired effects on sales that could be observed.

Since we knew of no tested theory, we fabricated our own. Our hunch was that advertising could be considered to be a stimulus and sales a response to it. Much is known about the general nature of stimulus-response functions. They usually take the form shown in Figure 35-1. Therefore, we formulated the following hypotheses:

> A small amount of advertising has virtually no effect on sales but as the amount is increased it pushes the response through a *threshold* after which it produces an increasing effect. This effect decreases and flattens out once the respon-

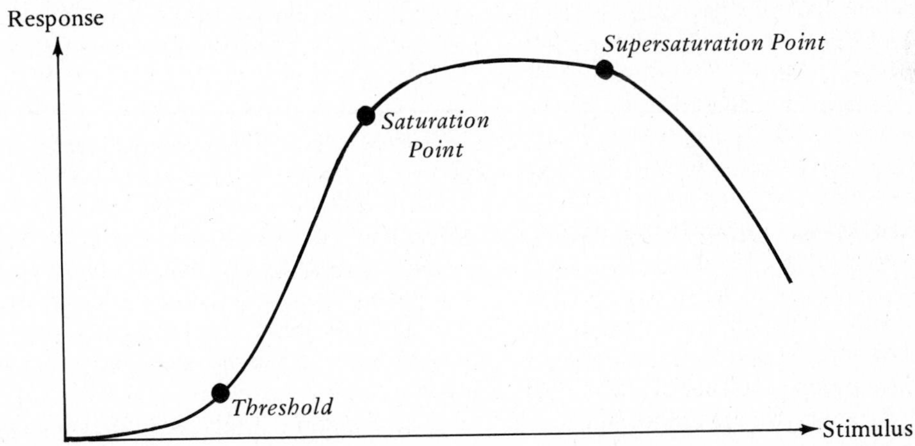

FIGURE 35-1 *A Typical Stimulus-Response Function*

dents are *saturated*; that is, they either turn off further exposure to the stimulus or are consuming up to their capabilities or capacities. Response to further increases in advertising remains relatively unchanged until the respondents reach *supersaturation,* a point beyond which they respond negatively.

In an earlier study conducted for the Lamp Division of the General Electric Company[4] we had found such a relationship between frequency of sales calls (stimulus) and purchases (response). In the sales-call context the idea of supersaturation is not as shocking as it is in advertising. Clearly, there is an amount of a salesman's presence that is intolerable to a buyer. Beyond this one would expect the buyer to try to get rid of the salesman by discontinuing his purchases. Similarly, we felt reasonably sure that, for example, if all television advertising were for only one product, the public would react negatively.

The First Experiment

A minimal experiment would have involved applying the same percentage change in advertising expenditure to each of the fifteen market areas allotted to us and comparing the results obtained from them with those obtained from an equal number of control areas. But we needed only nine areas to obtain the level of accuracy set as our target: to be able to detect a 2 percent difference in sales 95 percent of the time. The introduction of two different treatments, one involving an increase and the other a decrease in advertising expenditures, required eighteen test areas, three more than were available to us. However, even an experiment with two different treatments would yield only three points: the average effect of each treatment and that of the control group. The difficulty this presented derived from the fact that every configuration of three points except one, V-shaped, could be fitted to the relationship (Figure 35-1) that we wanted to test. Therefore, there was a very low probability that even a three-level experiment would disprove our hypothetical relationship; hence, it was a very poor test of the validity of this relationship.

For these reasons we decided to ask for three different treatments and a control group even though this would require twenty-seven markets plus nine under control. Four experimental points could disprove our theory as easily as it could confirm it and, therefore, would have provided a reasonable test of it.

We had nothing to go on but our intuition in selecting the experimental treatment levels: a 50 percent reduction, and 50 and 100 percent increases in budgeted levels of advertising. We wanted to make changes large enough to produce observable effects on sales, assuming such changes had any such effect, and large enough so that if there were no observable effects this fact could not be dismissed because the changes were believed to be too small. Two increases rather than decreases were selected to make the experiment more palatable to the Marketing Department.

When this four-level design was presented it was rejected because it involved the use of too many market areas. However, Mr. Busch agreed to our use of eighteen rather than fifteen areas provided that we change the reduction in advertising we had proposed from 50 to 25 percent. He felt that a 50 percent reduction might irreparably damage the areas so treated. This left us with a three-level experiment: −25%, 0%, and +50% changes from budget.

Although we were not completely happy with this outcome because it did not provide an adequate test of our theory, we were pleased that we had the opportunity to conduct even a limited experiment. We were reasonably sure that if it produced interesting results, restrictions on future experiments would be lifted.

A 3 x 3 x 3 factorially designed experiment

was prepared in which two other important marketing variables were explicitly controlled: *the amount spent on sales effort* (salesmen) and *the amount spent on point-of-sales displays and signs.* We also would have liked to control pricing but this was precluded. This design is illustrated in Figure 35-2.

Market areas were selected randomly from the "permissible list" and randomly assigned to the twenty-seven treatments. Use of the "permissible list" could obviously bias our results but again our hope was that the results would justify further experimentation and that it would not be so restricted.

The experiment was carried out over the calendar year 1962 thereby yielding twelve observations of each market area. We were able to reach a conclusion at the end of six months, but the experiment was continued to build up confidence in the results. The results, however, attracted little confidence; they were too much at variance with expectations within the company and its advertising agency. The three points shown in Figure 35-3 fell into the only configuration, V-shaped, that was inconsistent with our theory because the relationship being tested (Figure 35-1) had no V in it. In addition, we found no significant interaction between advertising, sales effort, and point-of-sales expenditures, a surprising but not an unacceptable result, and the results indicated that current levels of sales effort and point-of-sales expenditures were close to optimal. This last result was readily accepted.

No one found much difficulty in believing that a 50 percent increase in advertising produced a 7 percent increase in sales, but only Mr. Busch and Mr. Vogel were willing to consider seriously the possibility that a 25 percent reduction of advertising could produce a 14 percent increase in sales. Even they were not ready to act on this finding but they did want to analyze the situation further. Therefore, they asked us to design another experiment

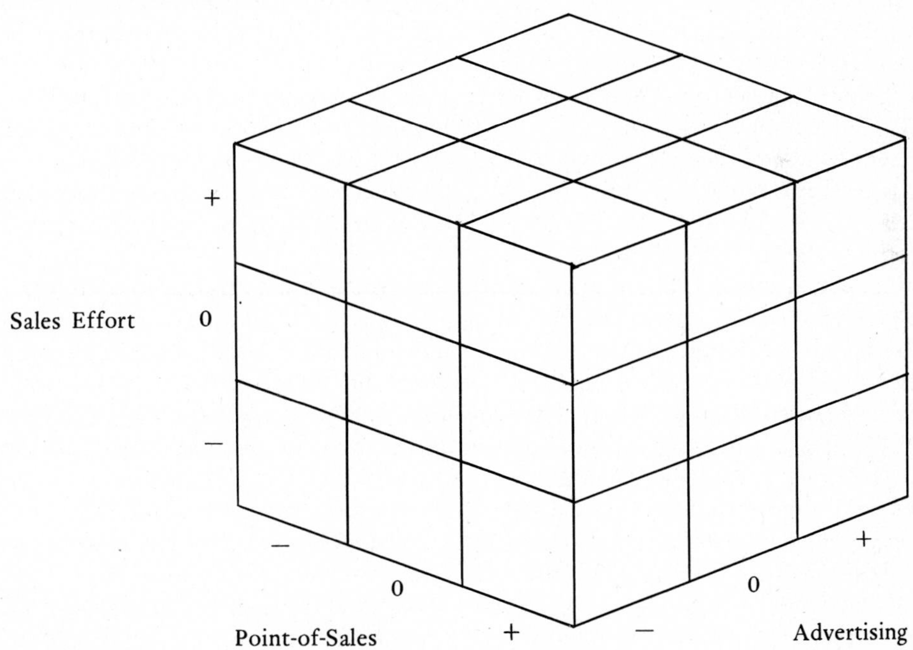

FIGURE 35-2 *The 3 x 3 x 3 Experiment*

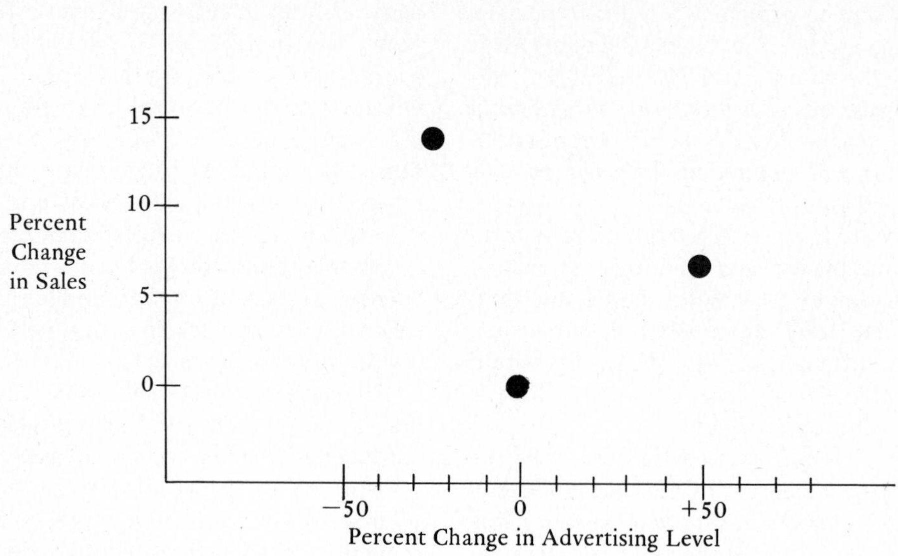

FIGURE 35-3 *Results of First Experiment (1962)*

that would check these results and that would be more convincing to others.

We had to revise our theory before designing the next experiment. On the surface it appeared necessary to reject the theory but we had grown very fond of it. Therefore, we sought a modification of the theory that would make it consistent with the experimental results.

It occurred to us that there might be two or more distinct consuming populations in each market area with a response curve like the one we had assumed but that these might be separated along the horizontal scale (see Figure 35-4). The aggregated response curve would then have a V in it. When this possibility was presented to Mr. Vogel, he thought it was quite reasonable and suggested that the markets might be segmented into three parts: heavy, moderate, and light beer drinkers. This made sense to us. One would expect heavy users of a product to be more sensitive to its advertising than moderate users, and moderate users more sensitive than light users. We looked for some way of testing this assumption and we found one.

It would have been very time-consuming and costly to determine how many beer drinkers of each type there were in each market area. We had neither the time nor the money required to do so. But we did know from previous studies that beer consumption correlated positively with discretionary income within the range of such income in which most beer drinkers fall. Therefore, we determined the average discretionary income in each market area that had been used in the previous experiment and compared it with the average deviations from forecasted sales in each area. There was a positive correlation between these deviations and average discretionary income, thereby lending some credence to the user-level segmentation assumption.

We revised our theory to incorporate three response functions for each market area. This meant that the aggregated response functions for markets as a whole could differ significantly because of different proportions of heavy, moderate, and light beer drinkers.

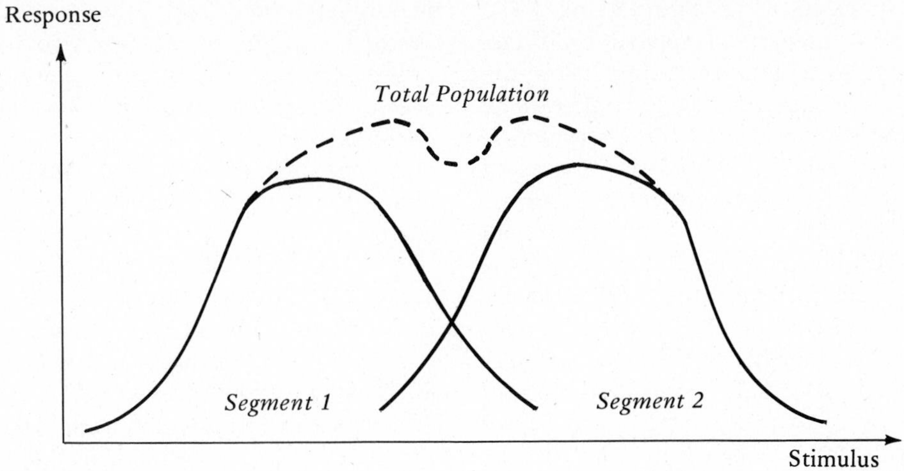

FIGURE 35-4 *Response Function of Segmented Population*

The Second Experiment

In order to test the revised theory we decided that we needed seven different advertising treatments. We wanted to repeat the earlier experiment and add treatments further out on both ends of the scale. Seven treatments were selected: −100% (no advertising), −50%, −25%, 0%, +50%, +100%, and +200%. Because of improvements in our forecasting methods only six areas were required for each treatment. This design was accepted with only slight modification: the number of test areas in the two extreme treatments was reduced.

The experiment was conducted over twelve months in 1963 and 1964. Again data were collected monthly. The results obtained confirmed the findings of the first experiment. When plotted the seven points fell on a curve such as is shown in Figure 35-5. There were

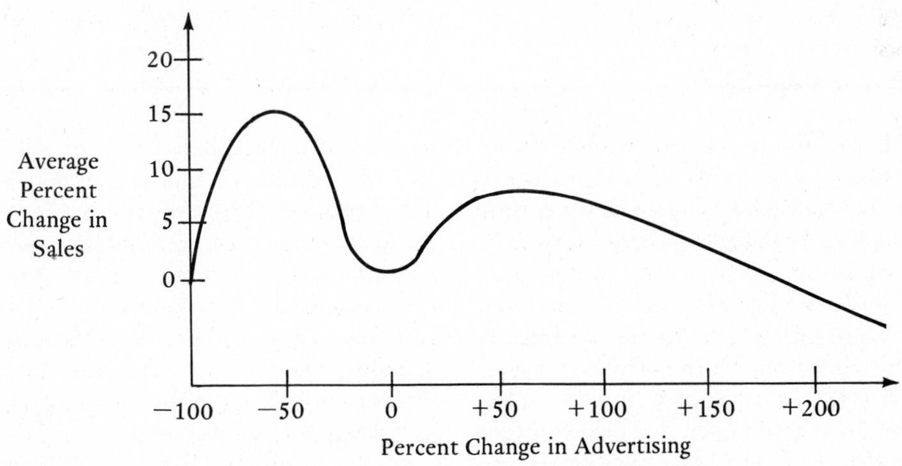

FIGURE 35-5 *Results of Second Advertising-Level Experiment (1963)*

two deviations from our expectations. First, only two, not three, peaks appeared. But this was not serious because the points out on the right were so far apart that there could well be a third hump concealed by the interpolation between the points. It was harder to explain the finding that the areas in which all advertising had been eliminated (−100%) survived the year with no significant difference in performance from the control areas (0%). Hardly anyone believed this result. Those who did attribute it to the long history, strength, and exposure of BUDWEISER in the marketplace. We suggested further tests of the effect of complete elimination of advertising.

Although a willingness to act on our findings had not yet developed, there was growing agreement on the desirability of continuing the research. The 1963–64 experiment was continued with particular attention given to the areas from which all advertising had been removed. The objective was to determine how long it would take before any deterioration of sales could be detected, at what rate it would take place, and how easily lost sales could subsequently be recaptured. We also initiated some research into the relative effectiveness of different media. While this research was going on, the first opportunity to apply the results already obtained presented itself.

Application of Results

In mid 1964 Mr. Busch wanted to make more cash available to meet some commitments he had made. He asked Mr. Vogel and us if this could be done. We jointly proposed that advertising be reduced by 15 percent in twenty-five of the smallest markets. The smallest markets were chosen in order to minimize any possible long-run harmful effects. The proposed change was capable of yielding more than the amount Mr. Busch asked for. We also pointed out that we could maintain very close watch over the areas affected and report immediately on any reduction of sales that might occur in them. We predicted, however, that the proposed decrease in advertising would produce about a 5 percent increase in sales. Mr. Busch decided to go ahead.

The predicted results were obtained by the end of the year. As a consequence, the number of reduction areas was increased to fifty and the amount of the reductions was increased to 25 percent. From then on more and more areas were similarly treated and the reductions were gradually increased until the advertising expenditure per barrel was $0.80 in contrast to $1.89 which it had been when the research was initiated. During this period (1962–68) sales of BUDWEISER increased from approximately 7.5 million to 14.5 million barrels and its market share increased from 8.14 to 12.94 percent.

TIMING OF ADVERTISING

Returning to the experiment involving complete deprivation of advertising, the areas thus deprived showed no response until more than a year and a half later. From then on a small decline was noted each month. This was allowed to continue only long enough to provide good estimates of the deterioration rate. Moves to correct these markets were then made. They were restored to their normal growth rate in about six months with only their normal amount of advertising.

These results led to a new line of speculation. Would it not be possible to *pulse* advertising, using an on-and-off pattern, and obtain the same effectiveness that is obtained by continuous advertising? We came to think of advertising as a motion picture which, of course, is really a sequence of motionless pictures. If sixteen still photographs are taken and projected per second, the appearance of motion is created because images are retained in the retina between exposures. We felt the same should be true of advertising.

Two types of pulsing were considered. In one, advertising expenditures in all media are on or off together. In the other, only one medium is used at any time but the media are alternated. We designed an experiment to test the first of these types of pulse. It involved four treatments: one control (I) and three pulsing patterns (II, III, and IV) shown in Table 35-1. In addition, the level of expenditure in each was varied as is shown in Table 35-2. The market areas used in this experiment were classified by median income and growth rates.

One of the pulsing patterns was found to be significantly better than the others and slightly better than normal advertising when accompanied by a high level of expenditure. Another pattern was found to be best when accompanied by a low level of expenditure. In addition, the pulsing patterns were found to interact significantly with median income level and the growth rate of the market area. Subsequent experimentation revealed no significant difference between time-pulsing and media-pulsing. Media-pulsing, however, was easier to administer.

These results were cautiously incorporated into small reductions of advertising expenditures that were made in series. It was only after one change was demonstrated to have the predicted effect that the next change was made. Regular monthly checks on the performance of each market area were initiated and continue to this day.

TABLE 35-1 *Pulsing Patterns*

	I	II	III	IV
Spring	X	X	O	X
Summer	X	O	X	X
Autumn	X	X	O	O
Winter	X	O	X	O

TABLE 35-2 *Percent of Local Budget Spent by Pulsing Pattern and Advertising Level*

Advertising Level	Pulsing Pattern I	II	III	IV
High	150%	100%	100%	100%
Low	100%	50%	50%	50%

MEDIA SELECTION

In the early experiments on advertising expenditures, the budgets for experimental areas were set by the research team but the way in which additional moneys were allocated or reductions were made was left entirely in the hands of the advertising agency. Five media were involved: billboards, magazines, newspapers, radio and television. We examined the relationship between the actual changes in media allocations and changes in sales. This preliminary analysis indicated no significant difference in effectiveness between magazines, newspapers, and radio, but it suggested that television was slightly superior and that billboards were substantially inferior.

An experiment was designed to test these tentative findings (see Table 35-3). Magazines were not included in this experiment because they could not be controlled within small areas. A distinction was made between *local* and *national* television. In each of twenty areas only one medium was used; in another twenty each medium was combined with national television. The results showed that national television was slightly superior to any local medium. Local television (with or without national television) and radio were more effective than newspapers or billboards. Billboards were the least effective.

To explain the poor showing of billboards, a number of observations were made to determine how much information could be conveyed by a billboard. We found that little more than the product name and a slogan could be

TABLE 35-3 *Media Experiment (1967–68): Number and Treatment of Market Areas*

	Local TV	Billboard	Radio	Newspaper
No National TV	5	5	5	5
National TV	5	5	5	5

communicated. This meant that billboards can do little more than remind one of the existence of an already familiar product; they cannot convey much, if any, new information about it. A second set of observations showed that the typical urban dweller in the United States saw but did not necessarily notice the word "BUDWEISER" on signs, displays, or beer containers almost ten times per day. He hardly needed additional reminding of its existence. On the basis of these findings virtually all billboard advertising was discontinued. The company had been spending about 20 percent of its advertising budget through this medium.

CONCLUSION

To summarize the results obtained by 1968, we note that volume had approximately doubled, market share had increased from 8.14 to 12.94 percent, and advertising expenditures were reduced from $1.89 to $0.80 per barrel, a 58 percent reduction. It would be foolish, of course, to claim that this improvement in performance was due entirely to changes in advertising. Other types of changes, some based on research and some not, were also made during this period. But one thing is clear: the changes induced by the research described here did not hurt Anheuser-Busch.

The strength of the opposition to the results of our early experiments is less surprising in retrospect than it was at the time. These results contradicted the strong beliefs of people who had good reason to believe they understood advertising and who had the success of the products involved to prove it. Furthermore, these people did not understand the logic of experimental design and the statistical analysis of the data yielded by experiments. They were convinced that sales were affected by a large number of complexly interacting and inherently qualitative variables and, therefore, that the effect of any one of these on sales could not be isolated or measured.

The greatest resistance came from those managers who had direct responsibility for the decisions to which the research was addressed and from the advertising agency people who were attached to the account. It was clear that the agency people felt that our research cast doubt on their competence and creativity. It also threatened the agency's income.

For these reasons it became apparent to us that three things had to be done if we were to gain acceptance, let alone support, of our efforts. First, we would have to bring those who had to deal with the research results to an understanding of the logic of experimental design and statistical analysis. Second, we would have to involve them actively in the design of the experiments and in the analysis and interpretation of their results. Finally, we would have to try to change the method of compensating the advertising agency so that its fee was not decreased as the efficiency of advertising was increased.

The process of education and involvement took time. It was carried out both informally and formally in sessions conducted specifically for this purpose. Managers at the highest levels were generally the first to approve of experimentation. They sometimes became impatient with their subordinates and tried to force early research results on them. Such pressure slowed acceptance at the lower levels. But in general, when top managers felt compelled to act, as Mr. Busch did on the first reduction of advertising expenditures, they worked hard to make the implementation itself experimental and to carry it out as gradually and nondisruptively as possible. In all, it took about three years (1962-65) for the educational efforts to begin to pay off.

These efforts were facilitated by two other important changes. First, we proposed that the basis for the agency's compensation be changed so that it would benefit financially when the company did. As long as the agency was paid a percentage of A-B's expenditures on advertising, it naturally resisted research that had the potential of reducing its earnings. Therefore, we suggested a scheme by which the agency's fee was increased if either sales increased with no increase in advertising or advertising expenditures decreased with no decrease in sales. The agency was persuaded to try this scheme for a year with assurances that it would receive no less in fees during the trial year than it had in the previous year. In the trial year advertising expenditures decreased but since sales increased the agency's compensation also increased. The scheme was continued for another year with repetition of this outcome and then became permanent. Because of it the agency became increasingly interested in research, strengthened its research department, and encouraged it to collaborate with us. This was done to our mutual benefit. By 1968 the difficulties with agency acceptance of research results were largely a thing of the past. The agency has since initiated such a compensation scheme with other clients.

Acceptance of research as an instrument of management was greatly facilitated by the establishment of two very competent in-house groups, one in marketing and the other in corporate planning. Leon Pritzker, who was the initial director of the group in marketing, had a major role in the later phases of the research reported here. August A. Busch, III, then executive vice president but now president, observed: "The University and company units work together very closely. . . ."[5] E. H. Vogel, Jr. continued: "Today we hardly make any decision of any consequence that does not involve our researchers in one way or another. This blending of research and management did not occur overnight. It developed slowly under careful guidance."[6]

Research results were built up slowly but accumulatively. The results of each piece of research were integrated with previous results where they were consistent. Where they were not, a more general explanation was sought, one that made integration possible, and then the integrating principle was thoroughly tested. No result was ever taken to be true for all time. As Mr. Vogel observed:

> We did not try to impose [research-based] recommendations as though we had suddenly gained possession of ultimate truth. We usually initiated the application of recommendations on a small scale with close controls imposed on them. As confidence in results developed, we extended applications.
>
> No matter how generally management accepted a research result it was never applied without a well-designed control system to tell us whether the recommendations worked as expected. We have learned as much from the feedback such control provided as we have from the research that produced the initial recommendations.
>
> More important, perhaps, is that we now design controls for evaluating decisions which management reaches without the benefit of research. This enables us to learn more rapidly and accurately from experience, and it has indoctrinated management with an experimental approach to decision making.[7]

NOTES

1. See Busch [2] and Vogel [6].
2. See "Computers Can't Solve Everything" [3], "Wharton Analyzes the Beer Drinker" [8] and "While Big Brewers Quaff, the Little Ones Thirst" [9].
3. See Ackoff and Emery [1], Curtis [4], and Rao [5].
4. See Waid, Clark and Ackoff [7].
5. See Busch [2].
6. See Vogel [6], p. 24.
7. See Vogel [6], pp. 24-25.

REFERENCES

1. Ackoff, R. L., and Emery, F. E. *On Purposeful Systems.* Chicago: Aldine-Atherton, 1972, Chapter 8.
2. Busch, A. A., III. "The Essentials of Corporate Growth." Address given to Charles Coolige Parlin Marketing Award Banquet, May 9, 1973.
3. "Computers Can't Solve Everything." *Fortune,* October 1969, p. 126 ff.
4. Curtis, K. P. *The Modeling of Consumer Purchase Behavior.* Unpublished Ph.D. dissertation, University of Pennsylvania, 1969.
5. Rao, A. G. *Quantitative Theories in Advertising.* New York: John Wiley & Sons, 1970.
6. Vogel, E. H., Jr. "Creative Marketing and Management Science." *Management Decision,* Spring 1969, pp. 21–25.
7. Waid, C.; Clark, D. F.; and Ackoff, R. L. "Allocation of Sales Effort in the Lamp Division of the General Electric Company." *Operations Research* 4 (1956): 629–647.
8. "Wharton Analyzes the Beer Drinker." *Business Week,* 24 March 1973, p. 44.
9. "While Big Brewers Quaff, the Little Ones Thirst." *Fortune.* November 1972, p. 103 ff.

Orville C. Walker, Jr.
Gilbert A. Churchill, Jr.
Neil M. Ford

36

Motivation and Performance in Industrial Selling: Present Knowledge and Needed Research

INTRODUCTION

In the words of one writer, sales management is like Topsy–it just grew [24, p. 130]. Each sales executive works out his own ideas about how to manage a salesforce from an assortment of "principles" he inherits from his predecessor, the customs of his industry, the expectations and demands of his superiors, and his own assumptions about what motivates salespeople and what leads to good sales performance.

Over the years, these executives have received relatively little information or guidance from marketing scholars. The structure and content of sales management texts have changed little since the field first was explored about 50 years ago. Few theories and even less empirical knowledge are available about most aspects of sales management. Though effective management of the salesforce is obviously crucial to the success of many organizations, academia has relegated the study of this field to "second-class" status. The authors attempt to rectify this situation by (1) reviewing the sparse literature on sales motivation and performance, (2) reviewing the general behavioral science literature on the motivation of employees, and (3) offering a set of propositions which should stimulate and provide directions for future research in sales management.

PRESENT VIEW OF SALES MOTIVATION AND PERFORMANCE

One particularly crucial aspect of sales management that has received little attention from marketing scholars is the motivation of

Reprinted from the *Journal of Marketing Research* (May 1977), pp. 156–168, published by the American Marketing Association.
Orville Walker is Professor of Marketing at the University of Minnesota and received his Ph.D. from the University of Wisconsin.
Gilbert Churchill is Donald Slichter Professor in Business Research at the University of Wisconsin and received his D.B.A. from Indiana University.
Neil Ford is Professor of Marketing at the University of Wisconsin and received his Ph.D. from the University of Illinois.

salesmen and the determinants of sales performance. In the marketing and sales management literature, the salesman's motivation to expend effort on the job and his resulting performance usually are viewed as functions of one or several independent variables considered separately. Most of this literature focuses on four sets of predictor variables: (1) the aptitude or ability of the salesman, (2) financial compensation and incentives, (3) psychological incentives, and (4) organizational and managerial factors.

Sales Aptitude

The limited empirical work investigating the effects of sales aptitude on performance is summarized in Ghiselli's [9] review of the predictive validity of various aptitude tests. He reports relatively high average validity coefficients between sales performance criteria and two types of aptitude tests: (1) tests of intellectual abilities (.31) and (2) tests of personality traits (.27) [9, p. 41]. Though the relationships between these kinds of aptitude tests and performance are stronger for salespeople than for persons in many other occupations, the two types of aptitude measures considered together as independent predictors still cannot explain more than 17% of the variance in sales performance.

Financial Compensation and Incentives

Much of the literature on motivation of salespeople concerns the design and administration of various compensation and incentive plans [12, 35, 36, 40]. Two basic assumptions pervade much of this work: (1) monetary rewards are the primary motivator of sales effort and (2) the pay package is the basic motivator whereas other financial incentives, such as bonuses and contests, operate only to induce effort over and above that produced by the basic plan in certain circumstances. Very little empirical support is offered for these assumptions, however, and it is drawn primarily from surveys of sales managers' opinions concerning the relative merits of various compensation and incentive plans [11].

Much of the empirical work involving workers in other occupational contexts is inconsistent with this traditional view of how to motivate salesmen. Many of these studies have found that money is not the primary motivator of job effort [1, 13, 18, 27].

It is possible, of course, that salesmen are systematically different in their motivations from workers in other occupations. As Smyth argues [36, p. 15]:

> . . . those individuals who are aggressive and relatively high in financial motivations eventually seek out such occupations as salesmen . . . the typical salesman is financially motivated far more strongly than the average employee in his company.

Though this argument may be plausible, the fact is that no research among salesmen themselves has been published to support, reject, or modify the conventional wisdom concerning how to motivate salesmen.

Psychological Motives and Incentives

Many marketing writers have recognized that psychological, nonmonetary incentives – such as recognition, opportunities for personal growth, and the like – are important in motivating salespeople. Many authors have identified a variety of psychological needs that salesmen may seek to satisfy on the job [2, p. 123–33; 4, 20]. Several case examples concerning firms that have instituted various kinds of recognition and job enlargement programs for their salesforces also have been published in *Sales Management* and other trade journals [33]. However, no empirical studies investigating the relative importance of psychological incentives to salesmen and their impact on sales performance have been published.

Organizational and Managerial Factors

Recently several researchers have examined the mediating effects of organizational and interpersonal factors on salesmen. This research suggests that variables such as selection policies, training procedures, supervisory policies, and other "organizational climate" variables affect the level of conflict and uncertainty salesmen experience [29, 38]. These organizational variables together with interpersonal variables such as conflict also have a major impact on salesmen's feelings of job satisfaction [5, 7, 25, 30]. Unfortunately there is little theoretical structure to relate these variables directly to job performance in industrial selling.

Evaluation of the Literature

This brief review reflects the piecemeal and largely nonempirical nature of much of the literature concerning the motivation and performance of field salesmen. Research on the salesman falls far short of the kind and volume of research that has been done with workers in many other occupations. Little attention has been given to (1) the identification of a reasonably exhaustive set of factors affecting sales performance, (2) the interactions among those factors, or (3) the mental processes through which these variables act to initiate, direct, and change the behavior of individual salesmen.

A FRAMEWORK FOR FUTURE RESEARCH

As a first step toward improving knowledge of the industrial salesman, the authors offer a multivariate model of sales motivation and performance. This model is based on, and attempts to integrate, present theories and empirical evidence concerning worker motivation and performance found in industrial psychology and other behavioral science disciplines. It identifies a set of individual, interpersonal, organizational, and environmental variables that may influence a salesman's performance, and it specifies the interrelationships and interactions among those variables.

One purpose for the development of this model, then, is simply to review and integrate concepts and findings from other disciplines that may improve understanding of sales motivation. More importantly, however, the model is used to generate a set of research hypotheses which specifically address questions of sales motivation. It is hoped that these hypotheses will stimulate and provide an initial framework for future research in the sales management field.

A secondary purpose of this model is to provide sales managers with an explicit, integrated conceptual framework to aid decisionmaking. Though the model has not been validated empirically, the authors hope that it will help sales executives organize their thinking about the wide range of variables that affect sales performance. Accordingly, some of the managerial implications of the model are explored throughout the following discussion.

THE MODEL

In 1964, Victor Vroom developed the first application of expectancy theory to organizational behavior [37]. Vroom's formulation is one of a class of similar theories that are based on the central idea that "the strength of a tendency to act in a certain way depends on the strength of an expectancy that the act will be followed by a given consequence (or outcome) and on the value or attractiveness of that consequence (or outcome) to the actor" [17, p. 45].

Vroom's original theory was concerned primarily with predicting the amount of effort a worker would expend on various tasks associated with his job – his motivation to work. Several theorists subsequently expanded the original theory in an attempt to predict not only the worker's motivation level, but also the level of job performance that would result [8, 28]. The model developed hereafter is a further extension and modification of these models, specifically adapted to an industrial selling context. The model is outlined in Figure 36-1.

Performance

The model hypothesizes that a salesman's job performance is a function of three basic factors: (1) his level of motivation, (2) his sales aptitude or ability, and (3) his perceptions about how his role should be performed. The relationships among these three factors are likely to be multiplicative. If a salesperson is deficient in any one factor, performance is likely to be low. For example, if a salesman has ability and accurately perceives how the job should be performed but lacks motivation, he is likely to perform at a low level. Thus, the first general hypothesis suggested by this model can be stated as

Proposition 1: Performance = F(motivation x aptitude x role perceptions).

The model indicates that each of the three determinants of performance is influenced by a variety of antecedent variables. These variables include personal characteristics of the salesperson (e.g., intelligence, personality, education, experience), characteristics of the company (e.g., type of product, compensation practices, supervisory style, training programs), and factors in the broader economic environment (e.g., demand conditions in the industry, availability of raw materials, unemployment rate). Obviously, it is possible for sales managers to control or influence some of these antecedent variables through organizational structure, supervision, and selection and training policies. Other variables, particularly the environmental factors, are beyond management's control. The model developed here concentrates primarily on suggesting the effects of the controllable vari-

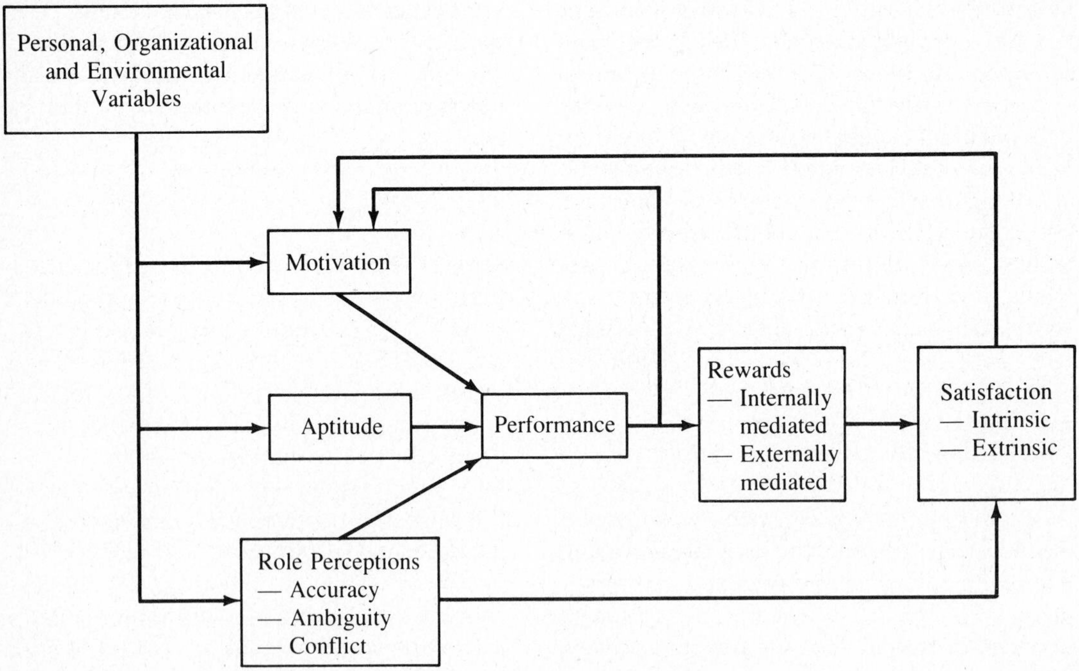

FIGURE 36-1 *The Model—Determinants of Salesperson's Performance*

ables on salesmen's motivation and performance. One area for further development of the model, therefore, would be the possible mediating effects of environmental factors on the relationships hypothesized hereafter.

Each of the three determinants of performance and some of the ways they are influenced by antecedent variables are examined in more detail in subsequent sections.

Rewards

The salesman's job performance affects the kinds and amounts of rewards he will receive. However, the relationship between performance and rewards is complex. One reason for this complexity is that there are several different dimensions of sales performance that a firm may or may not choose to evaluate and reward. A company might evaluate its salespeople on total sales volume, quota attainment, selling expenses, profitability of sales, new accounts generated, service provided to customers, performance of administrative duties, or some combination of such performance dimensions.

In addition to the multidimensional character of sales performance, there are a variety of rewards that a company might bestow for any given level of performance. The model distinguishes between two broad types of rewards. *Externally mediated rewards* are those controlled and bestowed by people other than the salesman, such as managers or customers. These rewards generally are related to lower-order human needs. They include such things as pay, financial incentives, security, recognition, and promotion. *Internally mediated rewards* are those which the salesman largely attains for himself and they relate to higher-order human needs. They include feelings of accomplishment, personal growth, career development, and self-worth.

As the model suggests, the salesman's perceptions of the kinds and amounts of rewards he will obtain in return for various types of job performance, together with the value he places on those rewards, strongly influence his motivation to perform.

Satisfaction

The rewards received by the salesman have a major impact on his satisfaction with his job and his work environment. Satisfaction is divided into two broad dimensions, intrinsic and extrinsic. Intrinsic satisfaction is related to the internally mediated rewards the salesman obtains from his job – satisfaction with the work itself and with the opportunities for personal growth and accomplishment. Extrinsic satisfaction is related to the externally mediated rewards bestowed upon the salesman – satisfaction with pay, company policies and support, supervision, fellow workers, chances for promotion, and customers.

The amount of satisfaction a salesman obtains from his job also is influenced by his role perceptions. As shown in a subsequent section, salesmen who experience considerable conflict or uncertainty on the job tend to be less satisfied than those who do not.

Finally, the salesman's level of job satisfaction is likely to have an impact on his motivation to perform. This relationship between satisfaction and motivation, however, is neither simple nor well understood. It is explored more fully in the discussion of the motivation component of the model.

THE ROLE PERCEPTIONS COMPONENT

The *role* attached to the position of salesman in any firm represents the set of activities or behaviors to be performed by any person occupying that position. This role is defined largely through the expectations, demands, and pressures communicated to the salesman by his role partners – persons both within and outside his firm who have a vested interest in how he performs his job, such as top management, his immediate supervisor, his customers, and members of his family. Thus, the salesman's *perceptions* of these role partners' expectations and demands strongly influence his definition of his role in the company and his behavior in performing his job.

The role perceptions component of the model is outlined in Figure 36-2. The major variables in this component are role accuracy, perceived role ambiguity, and perceived role conflict. All three variables are related to the salesman's perceptions of his role partners' expectations and demands.

The term *role accuracy* refers to the degree to which the salesman's perceptions of his role partners' demands – particularly those of his company superiors – are accurate. Does what the salesman thinks his superiors want him to do while performing his job correspond with their actual expectations and demands?

Perceived role conflict arises when the salesman believes that the role demands of two or more of his role partners are incompatible and he cannot possibly satisfy them all at the same time. A salesman suffers from perceptions of conflict, for example, when a customer demands a delivery schedule or credit terms that the salesman believes will be unacceptable to his company superiors.

Perceived role ambiguity occurs when the salesman feels he does not have the information necessary to perform his job adequately. He may be uncertain about what some or all of his role partners expect of him in certain situations, how he should go about satisfying those expectations, or how his performance will be evaluated and rewarded.

Consequences of Inaccuracy, Conflict, and Ambiguity

Psychological consequences. Research in other occupations suggests that perceptions of role conflict and ambiguity are psychologically uncomfortable and stress-producing [10, 14]. Therefore, the model hypothesizes that salesmen who experience high levels of conflict and ambiguity will suffer more mental anxiety or

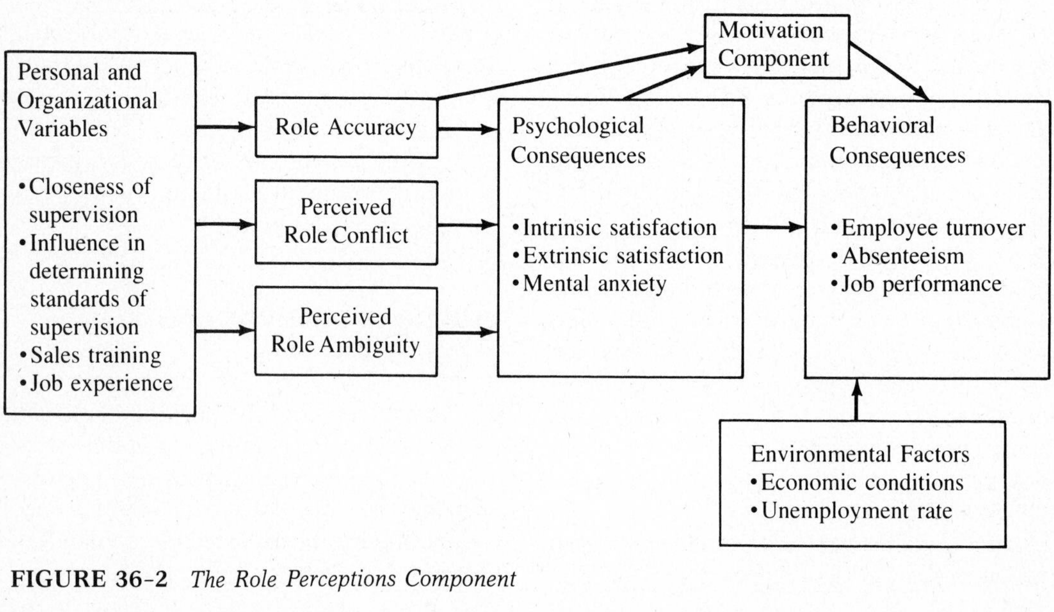

FIGURE 36–2 *The Role Perceptions Component*

job-related tension and will be less satisfied with their jobs.

Both perceived role ambiguity and role conflict are likely to have a negative effect on the salesman's satisfaction with the extrinsic aspects of his job. When a salesman is uncertain about how he should perform or how he will be evaluated, he is likely to be pessimistic about his chances for promotion, future pay raises, and other externally mediated rewards. Similarly, when he faces incompatible demands he may doubt his ability to satisfy the demands of those who control his external rewards.

Feelings of ambiguity are also likely to have a negative impact on a salesman's intrinsic satisfaction. It is difficult for a salesman to like his job and achieve feelings of personal accomplishment and growth when he is uncertain about how he is expected to do his job or how well he is doing it. The foregoing hypotheses are summarized in Table 36-1.

Evidence. Some recent research evidence supports these hypotheses concerning the impact of role conflict and ambiguity on the job satisfaction of industrial salesmen. In a study of 265 salesmen from 10 different firms in seven industries, the authors found a statistically significant negative correlation between the level of role ambiguity perceived by the salesmen and their level of intrinsic job satisfaction. Also, role ambiguity was found to be correlated negatively with several components of extrinsic job satisfaction: satisfaction with fellow workers, with company policies and support, with pay, and with customers. Similarly, significant negative relationships were found between the level of perceived role conflict and certain extrinsic satisfaction components: satisfaction with supervision, with company policies and support, with promotion opportunities, and with customers [5]. Overall, role conflict and ambiguity taken together explained 18% of the variation in total job satisfaction across salesmen and 13% of the variation in their mental anxiety scores [7].

TABLE 36-1 *Propositions Concerning the Consequences of Role Inaccuracy, Ambiguity, and Conflict*

Psychological Consequences	
Proposition 2:	The greater the role conflict perceived by a salesman: a. the greater his mental anxiety, b. the lower his overall level of job satisfaction.
Proposition 3:	The greater the role ambiguity experienced by a salesman: a. the greater his mental anxiety, b. the lower his overall level of job satisfaction.
Proposition 4:	The greater the role ambiguity experienced by a salesman, the lower his extrinsic job satisfaction.
Proposition 5:	The greater the role conflict experienced by a salesman, the lower his extrinsic job satisfaction.
Proposition 6:	The greater the role ambiguity experienced by a salesman, the lower his intrinsic job satisfaction.
Behavioral Consequences	
Proposition 7:	The higher the level of perceived role conflict within a salesforce, the higher the rate of employee turnover.
Proposition 8:	The higher the level of perceived role ambiguity within a salesforce, the higher the rate of employee turnover.

Behavioral consequences. Because the levels of role conflict and ambiguity perceived by salesmen can have a negative impact on their feelings of security and satisfaction with their jobs, these variables ultimately may affect the rates of employee turnover and absenteeism in the salesforce. Studies in other occupations have found a consistent negative relationship between job satisfaction and employee turnover, although this relationship is moderated somewhat by economic conditions and the availability of alternative jobs [31, p. 79–98; 34]. It is reasonable to expect a similar relationship in the industrial salesforce, as summarized in Table 36-1.

All three role perception variables – inaccuracy, ambiguity, and conflict – are also likely to have a negative impact on a salesman's job performance, both through their impact on his level of job satisfaction and because of their effect on his motivation to perform. A salesman's satisfaction with his current rewards may influence his motivation to attain more of these rewards. Also, inaccurate role perceptions may lead a salesman to misjudge the linkages between the effort he expends on the job, the level of performance he will achieve, and the rewards he is likely to attain as a result of that performance. These relationships between role perceptions, motivation, and ultimate job performance are examined in more detail in the discussion of the motivation component of the model.

Antecedents of Inaccuracy, Conflict, and Ambiguity

Several authors have pointed out that industrial salesmen are particularly vulnerable to role inaccuracy, ambiguity, and conflict because of the nature of their jobs. They must work at the boundary between two independent organizations. They must try to satisfy the divergent interests of both parties in an exchange relationship. They often face new and unusual situations in which there are no standard operating procedures for guidance. Consequently, salesmen are likely to perceive inaccurately what is expected of them, to feel uncertain about how to do their job, and to feel that they are caught in the middle between conflicting demands [3, 29].

Though much of the inaccuracy, ambiguity, and conflict experienced by salesmen may be inherent in their jobs, there probably are some personal and organizational variables that moderate their role perceptions. As a salesman gains experience on the job, for example, he is more likely to gain an accurate understanding of what is expected of him and of how he will be evaluated. Similarly, experience may teach him which role demands can safely be ignored or compromised, thus helping him reduce and cope with the conflicts he faces. Therefore, the longer the salesman's tenure in his position, the less role inaccuracy, ambiguity, and conflict he is likely to experience.

Because training is largely an attempt to compress the kind of learning that occurs with experience into a shorter time period, the kind and amount of training a salesman receives also may affect his role perceptions. However, the large variety of training methods used by different firms makes it difficult to state the relationship between sales training and role perception variables in a single proposition.

Most of the role conflicts salesmen experience are between the demands of the members of the firm on one side and those of customers and family members on the other; hence there is probably little that salesmanagers can do unilaterally to reduce such conflicts for the salesman. Inaccurate role perceptions and feelings of ambiguity, however, are likely to be influenced by the "supervisory style" of the salesman's superiors. When a salesman is supervised closely, for example, he is likely to learn more quickly what his superiors expect of him and how his performance is being evaluated. Under close supervision, behavior that is inconsistent with the superiors' expectations is more likely to be observed and brought to the salesman's attention than when supervision is relatively loose. Similarly, when salesmen are given the opportunity to provide input to management and to influence the standards used to guide and evaluate their performance, they are more likely to understand those standards accurately and fully. Thus, a close, participative supervisory style on the part of the sales manager can help to reduce the role inaccuracy and ambiguity experienced by the salesmen. The foregoing hypotheses are summarized in Table 36-2.

Evidence. Some of the foregoing propositions concerning the antecedents of role conflict and ambiguity have received empirical support from recent research. In a study involving 265 salesmen, the salesman's years of experience in his current position was correlated negatively with perceptions of both conflict and ambiguity at a statistically significant level. Also, both the closeness of supervision and the salesman's influence over supervisory standards were related negatively to perceptions of ambiguity, but had no significant effect on perceived conflict. Experience and the two supervisory variables taken together explained about 13% of the variance in perceived ambiguity across salesmen [38].

THE MOTIVATION COMPONENT

Motivation

The motivation component of the model is outlined in Figure 36-3. As the diagram suggests, *motivation* is viewed as the amount of effort the salesman desires to expend on each of the activities or tasks associated with his job, such as calling on potential new accounts, planning sales presentations, and filling out reports. The model assumes that expending effort on each of these activities will lead to some level of achievement on one or more dimensions of job performance, such as total sales volume, profitability of sales, new account sales, or quota attainment. It is assumed further that the salesman's level of performance on at least some of these dimensions will be evaluated by his superiors and will be rewarded with one or more of a variety of rewards, such as increased pay, recognition, or advancement.

According to the general tenets of expectancy theory, a salesman's motivation to expend effort on any task (i) will depend on two variables.

1. Expectancy (E_{ij}): the salesman's estimate of the probability that expending a given amount of effort on task (i) will lead to

TABLE 36-2 *Propositions Concerning the Antecedents of Role Inaccuracy, Ambiguity, and Conflict*

Proposition 9:	The longer the time a salesman has spent in his current position: a. the greater the accuracy of his role perceptions, b. the less the salesman's perceived role ambiguity, c. the less the salesman's perceived role conflict.
Proposition 10:	The more closely the salesman believes his performance is supervised: a. the greater the accuracy of the salesman's role perceptions, b. the less the salesman's perceived role ambiguity.
Proposition 11:	The greater the influence the salesman believes he has in determining the standards by which his performance is supervised and evaluated: a. the greater the accuracy of the salesman's role perceptions, b. the less the salesman's perceived role ambiguity.

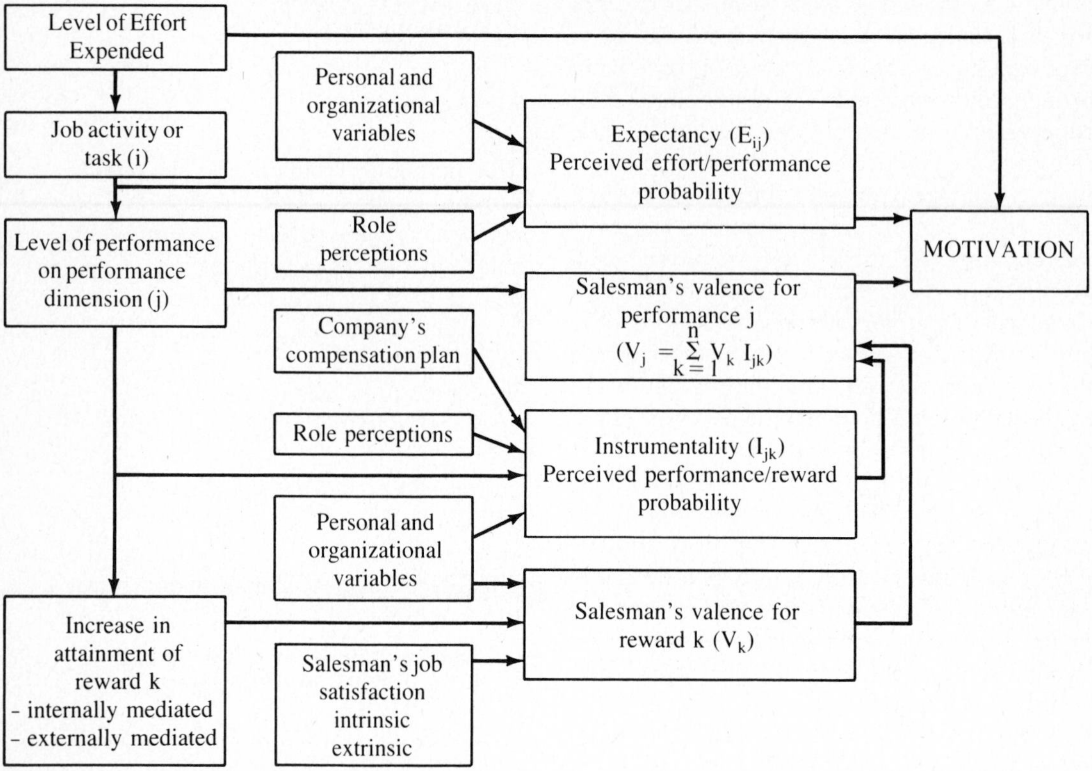

FIGURE 36-3 *The Motivation Component*

an improved level of performance on some performance dimension (j).

2. Valence for performance dimension (j) – (V_j): the salesman's perception of the desirability of attaining an improved level of performance on dimension (j).

Proposition 12: The salesman's motivation to expend effort on any task $(i) = (E_{ij} \times V_j)$.

The salesman's perceptions of both expectancies and the valences of various performance outcomes are influenced by several other variables.

Expectancies and Their Antecedents

Expectancies are the salesman's perceptions of the linkages between the effort he expends on various activities and the resulting level of performance he will achieve on various performance dimensions. The concept of expectancy can be illustrated by a statement such as: "If I increase my calls on potential new accounts by 10% (effort), then there is a 50% chance (expectancy) that my volume of new account sales will increase by 10% during the next six months (performance level)." From a managerial viewpoint, a salesman's expectancies can be evaluated on two dimensions, their magnitude and their accuracy.

Magnitude of expectancies. The magnitude of a salesman's expectancy estimates indicates the degree to which he believes that the effort he expends on job activities has an effect on his ultimate level of performance. In other words, these estimates reflect the salesman's perceptions of his ability to control or influence his own level of job performance.

Several individual and environmental characteristics are likely to affect these expectancies. Both Korman [15] and Lawler [16], for example, suggest that the worker's overall level of self-esteem and his perceived competence and ability at performing the necessary tasks will be related positively to the magnitude of his expectancy estimates. Though these propositions have not been tested empirically, they are intuitively appealing.

Another individual characteristic that may influence the size of a salesman's expectancies is his experience on the job. As a salesman gains experience he has the opportunity to improve both his skills and his confidence in his ability to perform his job successfully. The relationship between experience and the magnitude of expectancies, therefore, is hypothesized to be a positive one.

A salesman's perceptions of the linkages between effort and performance are also likely to be influenced by characteristics of the market environment in which he works. His perceptions of general economic conditions, the potential of his territory, the strength of the competition from other firms, and restrictions on product availability due to raw material shortages are all likely to affect the salesman's feelings concerning how much his sales performance can be improved by simply increasing his efforts. All the environmental factors that might be relevant are not identified here; but the general relationship between environmental conditions and expectancies can be summarized by saying that the greater the environmental constraints a salesman sees as restricting his performance, the lower his expectancy estimates will be.

Accuracy of expectancies. It is possible for a salesman to misjudge the true relationship between effort expended on a particular task and the resulting performance level achieved on some performance dimension. When this happens the salesman will misallocate his efforts. He will spend too much time and energy on activities that have relatively little impact on performance and not enough effort on activities with a greater impact.

Some of the salesman's perceptions of the relationship between effort and performance are learned as a result of his experiences on the job. As the salesman gains more experience, his expectancy estimates are likely to become more accurate.

A salesman's expectancies are influenced also by his perceptions of the role demands of his company superiors and his customers. When they communicate their role demands, these role partners are essentially telling the salesman that he should engage in certain activities in order to achieve a desired level of performance. If the salesman inaccurately perceives his role partners' demands, however, he may misjudge the relationships between effort and performance. Also, if the salesman feels his role partners' demands are ambiguous or conflicting, he may be uncertain about the linkages between effort and performance and his expectancy estimates are more likely to be inaccurate.

In most of the industrial psychology literature concerning work expectancies it is assumed that a worker's immediate superior is likely to perceive more accurately the linkages between effort and performance in the worker's job than the worker himself. Supervisors' expectancy estimates, in other words, are often used as the criteria for judging the accuracy of workers' expectancies.

Many industrial salesmen undoubtedly would argue with this assumption. Salesmen frequently complain that their superiors have an unrealistic view of conditions in the field and that they do not realize what is necessary to make a sale. In the absence of any empirical evidence, however, it is hypothesized that sales supervisors, by virtue of their experience, are likely to perceive accurately the linkages between sales effort and performance. Consequently, the more closely a sales manager supervises his salesmen and guides their efforts, the more likely it is that those salesmen will hold accurate expectancies.

All of the foregoing hypotheses concerning the variables that influence the magnitude and accuracy of salesmen's expectancies are summarized in Table 36-3.

Valence for Performance

As the model outlined in Figure 36-3 suggests, the valence or desirability in the salesman's mind of improved job performance on any dimension (*j*) is a function of two other variables.

1. *Instrumentality* (I_{jk}): the salesman's estimate of the probability that achieving an improved level of performance on performance dimension (*j*) will lead to increased attainment of a particular reward (*k*). Instrumentalities, in other words, are the salesman's perceptions of the linkages between performance and rewards.
2. *Valence for rewards* (V_k): the salesman's perception of the desirability of receiving increased amounts of each of the variety of rewards he might attain as a result of improved performance.

These two variables work to determine the valence of improved performance on dimension (*j*) as suggested in the following proposition.

Proposition 21: Valence for performance (*j*)

$$= \Sigma_{k=1}^{n} V_k \times I_{jk}.$$

Instrumentalities and Their Antecedents

Like expectancies, instrumentalities are probability estimates made by the salesman. An instrumentality is the salesman's estimate of the probability that a given improvement in performance on some performance dimension will

TABLE 36-3 *Propositions Concerning the Salesman's Expectancy Estimates*

Magnitude of expectancies	
Proposition 13:	The greater the salesman's feelings of self-esteem, the greater the average magnitude of his expectancy estimates.
Proposition 14:	The greater the salesman's perceived ability to carry out the activities associated with his job, the greater the average magnitude of his expectancy estimates.
Proposition 15:	The longer a salesman's tenure in his position, the greater the average magnitude of his expectancy estimates.
Proposition 16:	The greater the number of environmental constraints a salesman perceives as restricting his potential job performance, the lower the average magnitude of his expectancy estimates.
Accuracy of expectancies	
Proposition 17:	The longer a salesman's tenure in his position, the greater the accuracy of his expectancy estimates.
Proposition 18:	The greater the accuracy of a salesman's role perceptions, the greater the accuracy of his expectancy estimates.
Proposition 19:	The less the role ambiguity perceived by a salesman, the greater the accuracy of his expectancy estimates.
Proposition 20:	The lower the level of role conflict perceived by a salesman, the greater the accuracy of his expectancy estimates.
Proposition 21:	The more closely a salesman is supervised, the greater the accuracy of his expectancy estimates.

lead to his attainment of a specific increase in the amount of a particular reward. These probability estimates can be evaluated on two dimensions, their magnitude and their accuracy.

Magnitude of instrumentalities. One organizational variable that obviously has an impact on the magnitude of at least some of a salesman's instrumentality estimates is the compensation plan of his firm. A salesman who is compensated largely or entirely by commission is likely to perceive a greater probability of attaining more pay if he improves performance on those dimensions directly related to total sales volume (e.g., increase in total sales dollars, increased percentage of quota) than the salesman who is compensated by straight salary. In contrast, the salaried salesman is more likely to perceive a greater probability of receiving increased pay for improving his performance on dimensions not directly related to short-term sales volume (e.g., new account generation, reduction of selling expenses, performance of administrative duties) than the salesman on straight commission.

It must be noted, however, that the salesman may be rewarded with many things other than pay, such as promotion, recognition, and feelings of accomplishment. The salesman may value these other rewards more highly than an increase in pay. In any case, the company's compensation plan is unlikely to have any effect on the salesman's perceptions concerning the linkages between performance and these nonfinancial rewards. Therefore, a compensation plan by itself is inadequate for explaining difference in motivation across salesmen.

Several theorists in industrial psychology suggest that some personal characteristics of the salesman also may influence the magnitude of his instrumentality estimates. Both Rotter [32] and Lawler [16] argue that one psychological characteristic which influences instrumentality is the individual's perception of whether he has internal control over the events in his life or whether those events are determined by external forces beyond his control. Specifically, the greater the degree to which a salesman believes he has internal control over his life, the more likely he is to feel that an improvement in his performance will result in the attainment of more rewards.

Rotter's work also suggests that intelligence is related positively to feelings of internal control, although the relationship may not be a causal one [32]. Therefore, more intelligent salesmen may have larger average instrumentality estimates than less intelligent salesmen.

Accuracy of instrumentalities. The true linkages between performance on various dimensions and the resulting attainment of rewards in a firm are determined by management practices and policies concerning how sales performance is evaluated and what types and amounts of rewards are conferred for various levels of performance. Obviously, these policies and practices may be misperceived by the salesman. As a result, he may concentrate on improving his performance in areas that are relatively unimportant to management, and he ultimately may become disillusioned with his ability to attain desired rewards from his company.

The salesman's job experience and several organizational characteristics are likely to have an impact on the accuracy of the salesman's instrumentalities. The longer a salesman is on the job, for example, the more opportunities he has to learn how performance is evaluated and rewarded in his firm and the more accurate his instrumentality estimates are likely to be.

The supervisory style of his superiors also will help determine how accurately the salesman perceives the linkage between performance and rewards. The more closely he is supervised and the more influence he has in determining the standards by which he is evaluated and rewarded, the more likely his instrumentality perceptions are to be correct.

Finally, the level of role ambiguity perceived

by the salesman can influence his instrumentality perceptions. Many salesmen experience uncertainty about how their performance will be evaluated and rewarded. Therefore, those salesmen who perceive considerable role ambiguity are more likely to be uncertain about the linkage between performance and rewards, and to have inaccurate instrumentality estimates.

All of the foregoing hypotheses concerning the antecedents of both the magnitude and accuracy of salesmen's instrumentality estimates are summarized in Table 36-4.

Reward Valences and Their Antecedents

Satisfaction and valence. A salesman's perception of the desirability of attaining an increase in a particular reward depends to a large degree on how satisfied he is with the amount of that reward he currently is receiving. Several psychologists have theorized, however, that the nature of this relationship between satisfaction and the valence of rewards is different for externally and internally mediated rewards. Maslow's theory of a need hierarchy [21, 22], Herzberg's theory of motivation [13], and Alderfer's "existence, relatedness, and growth" theory [1] all suggest that lower-order, externally mediated rewards are valued most highly by workers who currently are dissatisfied with their attainment of those rewards. In other words, the more dissatisfied a salesman is with his current pay, job security, amount of recognition, and other such rewards related to his lower-order needs, the higher the valence he will attach to attaining increases in

TABLE 36-4 *Propositions Concerning the Salesman's Instrumentality Estimates*

Magnitude of Instrumentalities	
Proposition 22:	Salesmen who are compensated solely or partly by commission: a. will perceive a greater probability of receiving increased pay as a result of improved performance on dimensions directly related to short-term increases in sales volume than salaried salesmen, b. will perceive a smaller probability of receiving increased pay as a result of improved performance on dimensions not directly related to short-term increases in sales volume than salaried salesmen.
Proposition 23:	The type of compensation plan used by a firm is unrelated to the salesman's perceptions of the instrumentality of performance for attaining increases in nonfinancial rewards.
Proposition 24:	The greater the degree to which a salesman feels he has internal control over the events in his life, the greater the average magnitude of his instrumentality estimates.
Proposition 25:	The greater the salesman's intellectual ability, the greater the average magnitude of his instrumentality estimates.
Accuracy of Instrumentalities	
Proposition 26:	The longer a salesman's tenure in his position, the greater the accuracy of his instrumentality estimates.
Proposition 27:	The more closely the salesman is supervised, the greater the accuracy of his instrumentality estimates.
Proposition 28:	The greater the salesman's influence in determining the standards by which he is supervised and evaluated, the greater the accuracy of his instrumentality estimates.
Proposition 29:	The greater the role ambiguity perceived by the salesman, the more inaccurate his instrumentality estimates.

those rewards. In contrast, as the salesman becomes more satisfied with his attainment of externally mediated rewards, the value to him of further increases in those rewards will decline.

The theories of Maslow, Herzberg, and Alderfer further suggest that internally mediated rewards will not be valued highly by a salesman until he is relatively satisfied with his externally mediated rewards. In other words, the greater the salesman's satisfaction with his externally mediated rewards, the higher the valence of increased attainment of internally mediated rewards.

Perhaps the most controversial aspect of Maslow's and Alderfer's theories is the proposition that internally mediated rewards – such as feelings of self-fulfillment, personal growth, career development, and the like – have increasing marginal utility. The more satisfied a salesman is with the internally mediated rewards he is receiving from his job, the *higher* the value he will place on further increases in those rewards.

Several studies in industrial psychology have provided at least partial support for the foregoing hypotheses concerning the relationship between intrinsic and extrinsic satisfaction and the valence of internally and externally mediated rewards [1, 6, 19]. Some of this evidence is equivocal, however, and some of the propositions – particularly the idea that internally mediated rewards have increasing marginal utility – have not been tested adequately. Nevertheless, these propositions have received enough acceptance in industrial psychology to persuade the authors that they should be included in this model of sales motivation. They are summarized in Table 36-5.

Other personal and organizational antecedents of valence. A salesman's valence for various re-

TABLE 36-5 *Propositions Concerning the Salesman's Valence for Rewards*

Proposition 30:	The lower the salesman's satisfaction with externally mediated rewards, the higher the valence for increased amounts of those rewards.
Proposition 31:	The higher the salesman's satisfaction with externally mediated rewards, the higher the valence for increased amounts of internally mediated rewards.
Proposition 32:	The higher the salesman's satisfaction with internally mediated rewards, the higher the valence for increased amounts of those rewards.
Proposition 33:	The higher the salesman's current pay level: a. the lower his valence for externally mediated rewards, b. the higher his valence for internally mediated rewards.
Proposition 34:	The longer a salesman's tenure in his position: a. the lower his valence for externally mediated rewards, b. the higher his valence for internally mediated rewards.
Proposition 35:	The larger the number of family members a salesman must support: a. the higher his valence for externally mediated rewards, b. the lower his valence for internally mediated rewards.
Proposition 36:	The more closely a salesman is supervised: a. the lower his valence for externally mediated rewards, b. the higher his valence for internally mediated rewards.
Proposition 37:	The more influence the salesman feels he has in determining the standards by which he is supervised and evaluated: a. the lower his valence for externally mediated rewards, b. the higher his valence for internally mediated rewards.

wards is likely to be influenced by his personal characteristics and those of the company he works for. Many of these antecedent variables, however, may affect the salesman's valence largely because of their impact on his current satisfaction with his rewards. Some of the antecedent variables of workers' valence for pay have been identified empirically in the industrial psychology literature [18, p. 46–59]. Unfortunately, little empirical information is available concerning variables that might affect a salesman's valence for other kinds of rewards.

Research in other occupations does suggest that relatively highly paid workers tend to be more satisfied with their pay and therefore to have a lower valence for further increases in pay. Because pay is a major externally mediated reward, and because pay can be instrumental for attaining other external rewards such as feelings of security and recognition, it is reasonable to expect that salesmen who are relatively highly paid will have lower valences for externally mediated rewards than those receiving relatively low pay. Also, because highly paid salesmen are likely to be more satisfied with their externally mediated rewards, their valences for internally mediated rewards are likely to be higher.

Although it may not always be valid, the assumption often is made that the older, more experienced salesmen obtain higher levels of externally mediated rewards (e.g., higher pay, a better territory) than newer members of the salesforce. If this assumption is correct, more experienced salesmen should be more satisfied with their external rewards. Consequently, they also should have lower valences for externally mediated rewards and higher valences for internally mediated rewards than less experienced salesmen.

A salesman's satisfaction with his current level of externally mediated rewards is also likely to be influenced by the demands and responsibilities he must satisfy with those rewards. The salesman with a large family to support, for example, is less likely to be satisfied with any given level of external rewards than the unmarried salesman. Consequently, the larger the number of family members a salesman must support, the higher his valence for more externally mediated rewards and the lower his valence for internally mediated rewards.

Some research suggests that several organizational characteristics also have an impact on the salesman's satisfaction with the rewards he obtains from his job [5]. Therefore these organizational factors are also likely to affect his valence for rewards. Specifically, salesmen who are relatively closely supervised and who feel they have an influence in determining the standards by which they are supervised and evaluated are more satisfied with both their externally and internally mediated rewards. Such salesmen consequently are likely to have lower valences for external rewards and higher valences for internal rewards.

All of the foregoing hypotheses concerning the antecedents of a salesman's valence for rewards are summarized in Table 36-5.

THE APTITUDE COMPONENT

The overall model of sales performance outlined in Figure 36-1 treats the sales aptitude of an individual largely as a constraint on his *ability* to perform the sales job, given an adequate understanding of his role and motivation to perform. This view of aptitude has been taken by analysts who have attempted to predict sales performance within broad categories of selling jobs, such as retail clerking and "higher level" sales occupations, by measuring broad aspects of "aptitude" such as overall intellectual ability, personality traits, and occupational interests. Ghiselli's review suggests, however, that such broad measures of aptitude by themselves are not very useful for explaining variations in performance across salesmen [9, p. 41–3].

The foregoing discussion of the motivation component of the model suggests several things about sales aptitude that may make it a more relevant concept for understanding differences in sales performance. First, the authors have defined motivation as the desire to *expend effort on specific sales tasks* that, hopefully, will lead to improved performance on one or more dimensions and to increased rewards for the salesman. The linkage between the effort a salesman expends on any task (*i*) and the resulting level of performance achieved on performance dimensions (*j*) is moderated by that salesman's ability to carry out the task successfully. In other words, the relevant concept of sales ability or aptitude is very "task-specific." Therefore the appropriate definition of aptitude, and the appropriate measures of the construct, may vary greatly from industry to industry, firm to firm, and product line to product line, depending on what specific tasks must be performed and what dimensions of performance are considered important. The broad measures of aptitude that often are used may fail to capture the task-specific nature of the construct.

Finally, aptitude may affect performance in more ways than by simply moderating an individual's *ability* to do his job. It also may affect his motivation to perform. The authors have hypothesized that the salesman's *perceived* ability to perform a task and his general self-confidence have an effect on the magnitude of his expectancy estimates. Also, it is hypothesized that his intelligence and his perceived locus of control affect the magnitude of his instrumentality estimates. Thus, the salesman's intelligence and his perceptions of his own ability as a salesman may strongly influence his motivation to expend effort on various aspects of his job. These hypotheses suggest that objective measures of sales aptitude may be insufficient. Perhaps predictions can be improved by including measures of perceived aptitude as well.

DISCUSSION AND CONCLUSIONS

The authors believe the model presented here represents a conceptual advance in the field of sales management for several reasons. First, the model provides a conceptual framework which integrates many variables that historically have been considered independently in the sales management literature. It also introduces some new constructs that have been developed in other disciplines.

The model provides a richer conceptual rationale for some of the "conventional wisdom" that sales managers have developed over the years. The hypothesized impacts of "straight-salary" and "commission" compensation plans on the salesman's instrumentality estimates are good examples of this point. Several other managerial implications of the motivation component of the model are explored in more detail in [39].

Finally, the model focuses explicitly on the psychological mechanisms which work to motivate sales effort and performance. It approaches the question of sales motivation from the perspective of the salesman himself rather than relying on the perceptions and predictions of sales managers.

The Need for Empirical Support

Expectancy theories of motivation and their ability to predict the amount of effort expended on job tasks and/or the level of job performance have been tested empirically by several researchers in many nonselling occupations. Though the results of these studies have been generally positive, many of them are flawed by methodological shortcomings. (See [23] for a critical review of this empirical work.) Also, none of the present studies test a model that is as extensive as the one developed here. These studies generally do not incorporate measures of aptitude or role perceptions in their attempts to predict effort and performance.

The single study of expectancy theory in a selling context [26] had some success in predicting sales performance. However, this study also was somewhat limited in scope (data were collected from a single firm in the insurance industry) and in methodology (e.g., aggregate data were used to test an intra-individual model).

Realistically, then, the model presented here and all the specific hypotheses derived from it have yet to be tested empirically in a sales management context. Its ultimate contribution to sales management thought and practice will be determined only after much empirical research has been done. However, the stimulation of such research in sales management was the primary reason for development of this model in the first place.

REFERENCES

1. Alderfer, C. P. "An Empirical Test of a New Theory of Human Needs," *Organizational Behavior and Human Performance,* 4 (1969), 142–75.
2. Alexander, M. and E. Mazze. *Sales Management.* New York: Pitman Publishing Corp., 1965.
3. Belasco, J. A., "The Salesman's Role Revisited," *Journal of Marketing,* 30 (April 1966), 6–8.
4. Burton, W. L. "There's More to Motivating Salesmen than Money," in T. W. Meloan and J. M. Rathmell, eds., *Selling: Its Broader Dimensions.* New York: Macmillan and Co., Inc., 1960, 62–5.
5. Churchill, G. A., Jr., N. M. Ford, and O. C. Walker, Jr. "Organizational Climate and Job Satisfaction in the Salesforce," *Journal of Marketing Research,* 13 (November 1976).
6. Dachler, H. P. and C. L. Hulin, "A Reconsideration of the Relationship between Satisfaction and Judged Importance of Environmental and Job Characteristics," *Organizational Behavior and Human Performance,* 4 (1969), 252–66.
7. Ford, Neil M., Orville C. Walker, Jr., and Gilbert A. Churchill, Jr. "The Psychological Consequences of Role Conflict and Ambiguity in the Industrial Salesforce," in Kenneth L. Bernhardt, ed., *Marketing : 1776–1976 and Beyond.* Chicago: American Marketing Association, 1976, 403–8.
8. Galbraith, J. and L. L. Cummings. "An Empirical Investigation of the Motivational Determinants of Task Performance: Interactive Effects Between Instrumentality-Valence and Motivation-Ability," *Organizational Behavior and Human Performance,* 2 (1967), 237–57.
9. Ghiselli, E. E. *The Validity of Occupational Aptitude Tests.* New York: John Wiley and Sons, Inc., 1966.
10. Greene, C. N. and D. W. Organ. "An Evaluation of Causal Models Linking Received Role and Job Satisfaction," *Administrative Science Quarterly,* 18 (March 1973), 95–103.
11. Haring, A. and R. H. Meyers. "Special Incentives for Salesmen," *Journal of Marketing,* 18 (October 1953), 155–9.
12. ———, and M. L. Morris. *Contests, Prizes, Awards for Sales Motivation.* New York: Sales and Marketing Executives International, 1968.
13. Herzberg, F., B. Mausner, and B. Snyderman. *The Motivation to Work,* 2nd ed. New York: John Wiley and Sons, Inc., 1959.
14. Kahn, R. L., P. M. Wolfe, R. P. Quinn, J. D. Snoek, and R. A. Rosenthal. *Organizational Stress.* New York: John Wiley and Sons, Inc., 1964.
15. Korman, A. K. "Expectancies as Determinants of Performance," *Journal of Applied Psychology,* 55 (1971), 218–22.
16. Lawler, E. E., III. "Job Attitudes and Employee Motivation: Theory, Research, and Practice," *Personnel Psychology,* 23 (1970), 223–37.
17. ———. *Motivation in Work Organizations.* Monterey, California: Porter/Cole, Inc., 1973.
18. ———. *Pay and Organizational Effectiveness: A Psychological View.* New York: McGraw-Hill Book Co., Inc., 1971.
19. ——— and J. L. Suttle. "A Causal Correlation Test of the Need Hierarchy Concept," *Organizational Behavior and Human Performance,* 7 (1972), 265–87.
20. Leahy, J. I. "Total Motivation Equals Top Performance," *Sales Management,* (April 30, 1973), 12–13.
21. Maslow, A. H. "A Theory of Human Motivation," *Psychological Review,* 50 (1943), 370–96.
22. ———. *Motivation and Personality,* 2nd ed. New York: Harper and Row, Inc., 1970.
23. Mitchell, T. R. "Expectancy Models of Job Satisfaction, Occupational Preference and Effort: A Theoretical, Methodological and Empirical Appraisal," *Psychological Bulletin,* 81 (1974), 1053–77.
24. Newton, D. A. "Get the Most Out of Your Salesforce," *Harvard Business Review,* (September–October 1969).
25. ———. *Salesforce Performance and Turnover.* Cambridge, Massachusetts: Marketing Science Institute, 1973.
26. Oliver, R. L. "Expectancy Theory Predictions of Salesmen's Performance," *Journal of Marketing Research,* 11 (August 1974), 243–53.

27. Opsahl, R. L. and M. D. Dunnette, "The Role of Financial Compensation in Industrial Motivation," *Psychological Bulletin,* 66 (1966), 94–118.
28. Porter, L. W. and E. E. Lawler, III. *Managerial Attitudes and Performance.* Homewood, Illinois: Dorsey Press, 1968.
29. Pruden, H. O. "Interorganizational Conflict, Linkage and Exchange: A Study of Industrial Salesmen," *Academy of Management Journal,* 12 (September 1969), 339–50.
30. ——— and R. M. Reese. "Interorganizational Role-Set Relations and the Performance and Satisfaction of Industrial Salesmen," *Administrative Science Quarterly,* 17 (December 1972), 601–9.
31. Robinson, J. P., R. Athanasiou, and K. B. Head. *Measures of Occupational Attitudes and Occupational Characteristics.* Ann Arbor: University of Michigan Survey Research Center, 1969.
32. Rotter, J. B. "Generalized Expectancies for Internal Versus External Control of Reinforcement," *Psychological Monographs: General and Applied,* 80 (1966).
33. *Sales Management,* "Seduction Ain't Motivation," (September 1, 1970), 28–30.
34. Schwab, D. P. and L. L. Cummings. "Theories of Performance and Satisfaction: A Review," *Industrial Relations,* (October 1970), 408–30.
35. Smyth, R. C. "Financial Incentives for Salesmen," *Harvard Business Review,* (January–February 1968), 109–17.
36. ——— and M. J. Murphy. *Compensating and Motivating Salesmen.* New York: American Management Association, 1969.
37. Vroom, V. H. *Work and Motivation.* New York: John Wiley and Sons, Inc., 1964.
38. Walker, O. C., Jr., G. A. Churchill, Jr., and N. M. Ford. "Organizational Determinants of the Industrial Salesman's Role Conflict and Ambiguity," *Journal of Marketing,* 39 (January 1975), 32–9.
39. ———, ———, and ———. "Measuring and Improving Salesmen's Motivation," presented at American Marketing Association 59th Annual International Marketing Conference, Los Angeles, June 8, 1976.
40. Weeks, D. A. *Incentive Plans for Salesmen.* New York: The National Industrial Conference Board, 1970.

Index